PLAYFAIR
CRICKET ANNUAL 2001
54th edition
EDITED BY BILL FRINDALL
All statistics by the Editor unless otherwise stated

D1396325

EDITORIAL PREFACE

England have just won an incredible victory against all odds in Colombo and the spirits of all British cricket followers have soared to new levels – on the threshold of an Australian summer too. A close encounter for the Ashes after six one-sided series is for once a probability rather than a possibility, a notion fanned by India's astonishing victory in Calcutta (*see p 100*). Not since 1888 had England won a three-match rubber after losing the opening encounter and there have been only four other instances since. The force is with them.

Nasser Hussain has swiftly grown into a shrewd captain who, like Mike Brearley, is usually tactically ahead of the play and who now commands more affection and loyalty from his team than any England skipper since M.J.K.Smith. His partnership with coach Duncan Fletcher has gelled into the most effective in world cricket. Under their direction, backed by a dedicated and highly efficient support staff, the England team, no longer the victims of bizarre whims of selection, has gained in confidence and spirit. To have won consecutive series in Pakistan and Sri Lanka having lost five successive tosses and been condemned to the last use of wearing pitches tailor-made for the home spinners is an exceptional achievement. Not since 1979 had England won four successive series. There will be few empty seats on Test match grounds this summer, certainly not on the fifth day (should there be any) when free admission will be given to all youngsters under 16.

Regrettably the Sri Lanka series was blighted by more than 20 proven umpiring errors, a third of which were major howlers. The ICC is already addressing this problem and, committees willing, hopes to replace the existing independent list with an elite panel of the most competent and experienced umpires. They must also address the way technology has imposed itself on the game via the medium of television. SKY's coverage of England's winter tours has enlivened some deeply depressing months, particularly for those in rural areas. Riveting though the drama provided by special visual and audio effects has been, it is impossible not to feel sympathy for the poor umpire who has none of these aids available to him. One of three things must happen: the onfield umpire be given access to the replays preferably by a pocket receiver; or the replays are not shown publically until after the decision has been made and then only once in slow motion; or, the last resort, all decisions are made by the replay umpire. Perhaps a fourth alternative would be to abolish appeals but that would remove an essential element from the game.

Umpires have been woefully treated by players in recent years and many of the present problems could be removed by strong captaincy that adheres to the 'spirit of the game' so energetically promoted by Lord Colin Cowdrey, one of cricket's greatest ambassadors. A very thin demarcation separates gamesmanship from blatant cheating.

In the past year cricket has had to cope with its worst off-field crisis in the form of a match-fixing scandal which has already resulted in the termination of the playing careers of two national captains. One fears that many more unpleasant revelations are imminent, not only involving players. When I lived in north London I was often phoned by a Bombay bookmaker wanting to know the weather forecast for that day's play in The Oval Test. So were several other members of *Test Match Special* but he never even sent us a cake.

Last season saw the introduction of ECB contracts, a record seven Test matches and the first ten-match triangular limited-overs tournament in England. The contracts were obviously successful in the case of Darren Gough and Andrew Caddick. Their reduced workload enabled them to remain fit throughout the summer as they shared 64 wickets in those seven Tests. Whether such contracts are essential for batsmen and spinners remains to be seen. Their introduction has effectively removed the England team from county cricket. This has long been the case in Australia and South Africa but it inevitably devalues the County Championship, particularly when the ECB bans its contracted players from the decisive final fortnight of the new two-division format.

Two of our domestic competitions will have new sponsors this season, the County Championship (you can keep your own results chart on page 136) and the former Gillette Cup/NatWest Trophy. Their identities should be revealed around publication time. England's series against Pakistan and Australia will also unveil a new logo now that the obscurely named *npower* organisation has succeeded Cornhill after 23 seasons and 131 Tests. They have a very hard act to follow but what a season in which to start. Hopefully we will be blessed with a dry summer and some much improved pitches. The new sponsor's inaugural match will be the first to qualify for the ICC Test Match Championship (schedule on page 290). I hope that the points allocated will favour away wins.

The hex attributed to *Playfair*'s cover fortunately had no ill effect on Andrew Caddick's performances last season, particularly when he was despatching four West Indian batsmen in one over at Headingley. One wonders though if it was purely coincidental that Steve Waugh should be given out Handled the Ball on the day I stood the new cover on my desk.

Once again *Playfair* is greatly indebted to the county clubs' administrators, scorers and statisticians, to Alan Fordham (ECB), Clive Hitchcock (ICC), David Armstrong (MCCA) and to many overseas correspondents.

Sincere thanks are also due to Philip Bailey (ACS and CricInfo) who has again contributed the first-class and limited-overs career records, the latter now including all 'List A' matches, a category explained on page 166. Performances in these extra games now qualify for inclusion in the County Register. Also to Ric Finlay and David Fitzgerald who have made available their comprehensive Test Match and Internationals computer programmes. Marion Collin's task of updating the Women's Test section was eased by the ladies staging just one solitary Test match during the past year. Blackpool's scorer, Ronald Nuttall, has helped enormously by checking the 18-section County Register, while Wendy Wimbush, tireless Treasurer and Assistant Secretary of the Cricket Writers' Club, added the Test caps to the list of their Young Cricketers.

After 11 editions, Ian Marshall's workload at Hodder Headline has necessitated his delegating the onerous task of keeping me on schedule and it is Jo Roberts-Miller who has drawn the short straw. Her efficiency, cricket knowledge and good humour should ensure that the new partnership proves as enjoyable as the old.

Special thanks are due to Chris Leggett and his typesetting experts at Letterpart for meeting some tight schedules and introducing the latest technology, to proof-reader David Mitchell and to my wife, Debbie, for her invaluable secretarial assistance.

BILL FRINDALL
Urchfont
19 March 2001

THE DON REMEMBERED

A glance at the Test and first-class records which follow will confirm the astonishing talent of Sir Donald Bradman, AC, who has left us when within just eight years of yet another century. His average and ratio of innings per hundred suggest that he was twice as proficient as any other batsman who has played the game.

His career spanned a crucial period in Australia's development as a post-colonial nation and his prolific scoring feats, mostly achieved against the Mother Country, rapidly elevated him to near deity status.

Sir Leonard Hutton reckoned he had discovered the key to The Don's extraordinary batting skills when he visited the Australian dressing room in 1938. "He had very small feet," said Len profoundly before adding: "fast, nimble feet and perfect balance."

He was certainly ruthlessly acquisitive. In 1988 I had the rare honour of being invited into his elegant house in a leafy suburb of Adelaide. I suggested that if he had maintained his Test average of 99.94 and enjoyed the same number of innings as Sunil Gavaskar (then 198) he would have finished with the handy Test match tallies of 19,788 runs and 77 hundreds. "What makes you think I would only have maintained my average?" he asked. "If I had had the opportunity of playing in India, Pakistan and Sri Lanka I think I might have increased it."

My visit came hot on the heels of the Gatting/Shakoor Rana confrontation in Faisalabad and The Don's wise reactions to that fiasco are particularly relevant to England's recent experiences in Galle and Kandy: "An umpire's decision must be accepted, however incompetent he might be. If you don't accept his authority you have anarchy. The time to complain is off the field afterwards."

By 1988, computerised scoreboards at Sydney and Melbourne were already showing slow motion replays of stumpings and run outs. Bradman was convinced that umpires should be able to examine these replays before making their decision. "It is ridiculous that millions of viewers should have the benefit of this aid when umpires do not. But I would not support its use for lbws. There the umpire's unique positioning to exercise judgment should remain dominant."

Many players of the immediate post-war years condemned the use of batting helmets. The Don did not share their views. "If someone had produced a batting helmet during the Bodyline series I would certainly have worn it."

Bradman had an incredibly concise mind, ran a lucrative stock-broking business and would probably have been outstandingly successful at anything he had chosen to turn his hand to. His lonely vigils involving a golf ball, the base of a water tank and a stump used as a bat developed his tenacity of purpose as much as it did his hand-eye co-ordination and footwork. Golf became his passion in later life and he frequently achieved his goal of completing a round in fewer strokes than his age.

He was also a most able administrator dedicated to protecting cricket's traditions and integrity. It is no coincidence that the Adelaide Oval has retained its rural splendour and not been transformed into a concrete amphitheatre.

A master batsman and a shrewd captain, selector and administrator, The Don was as great an influence on cricket in the 20th century as W.G.Grace had been in its predecessor.

SIR DONALD BRADMAN IN TEST CRICKET
SERIES SUMMARY

Series	v	M	I	NO	HS	Runs	Avge	100	50
1928-29	E	4	8	1	123	468	66.85	2	2
1930	E	5	7	–	334	974	139.14	4	–
1930-31	WI	5	6	–	223	447	74.50	2	–
1931-32	SA	5	5	1	299*	806	201.50	4	–
1932-33	E	4	8	1	103*	396	56.57	1	3
1934	E	5	8	–	304	758	94.75	2	1
1936-37	E	5	9	–	270	810	90.00	3	1
1938	E	4	6	2	144	434	108.50	3	1
1946-47	E	5	8	1	234	680	97.14	2	3
1947-48	I	5	6	2	201	715	178.75	4	1
1948	E	5	9	2	173*	508	72.57	2	1
Totals		52	80	10	334	6996	99.94	29	13

TEST MATCH SUMMARY BY OPPONENTS

Opponents	M	I	NO	HS	Runs	Avge	100	50
England	37	63	7	334	5028	89.78	19	12
South Africa	5	5	1	299*	806	201.50	4	–
West Indies	5	6	–	223	447	74.50	2	–
India	5	6	2	201	715	178.75	4	1
Totals	52	80	10	334	6996	99.94	29	13

TEST MATCH SUMMARY BY VENUES

Venues	M	I	NO	HS	Runs	Avge	100	50
In Australia	33	50	6	299*	4322	98.22	18	10
In England	19	30	4	334	2674	102.84	11	3
Totals	52	80	10	334	6996	99.94	29	13

SIR DONALD BRADMAN IN ALL FIRST-CLASS MATCHES

Season	M	I	NO	HS	Runs	Avge	100	50
1927-28	5	10	1	134	416	46.22	2	1
1928-29	13	24	6	340*	1690	93.88	7	5
1929-30	11	16	2	452*	1586	113.28	5	4
1930	27	36	6	334	2960	98.66	10	5
1930-31	12	18	–	258	1422	79.00	5	4
1931-32	10	13	1	299*	1403	116.91	7	–
1932-33	11	21	2	238	1171	61.63	3	7
1933-34	7	11	2	253	1192	132.44	5	4
1934	22	27	3	304	2020	84.16	7	6
1935-36	8	9	–	369	1173	130.33	4	1
1936-37	12	19	1	270	1552	86.22	6	2
1937-38	12	18	2	246	1437	89.81	7	5
1938	20	26	5	278	2429	115.66	13	5
1938-39	7	7	1	225	919	153.16	6	–
1939-40	9	15	3	267	1475	122.91	5	4
1940-41	2	4	–	12	18	4.50	–	–
1945-46	2	3	1	112	232	116.00	1	2
1946-47	9	14	1	234	1032	79.38	4	4
1947-48	9	12	2	201	1296	129.60	8	1
1948	23	31	4	187	2428	89.92	11	8
1948-49	3	4	–	123	216	54.00	1	1
Totals	234	338	43	452*	28067	95.14	117	69

ENGLAND v PAKISTAN
SERIES RECORDS

1954 to 2000-01

HIGHEST INNINGS TOTALS

England	in England	558-6d	Nottingham	1954
	in Pakistan	546-8d	Faisalabad	1983-84
Pakistan	in England	708	The Oval	1987
	in Pakistan	569-9d	Hyderabad	1972-73

LOWEST INNINGS TOTALS

England	in England	130	The Oval	1954
	in Pakistan	130	Lahore	1987-88
Pakistan	in England	87	Lord's	1954
	in Pakistan	158	Karachi	2000-01

HIGHEST MATCH AGGREGATE	1274 for 25 wickets	Hyderabad	1972-73
	1274 for 37 wickets	Birmingham	1987
LOWEST MATCH AGGREGATE	509 for 28 wickets	Nottingham	1967

HIGHEST INDIVIDUAL INNINGS

England	in England	278	D.C.S.Compton	Nottingham	1954
	in Pakistan	205	E.R.Dexter	Karachi	1961-62
Pakistan	in England	274	Zaheer Abbas	Birmingham	1971
	in Pakistan	157	Mushtaq Mohammed	Hyderabad	1972-73

HIGHEST AGGREGATE OF RUNS IN A SERIES

England	in England	453	(av 90.60)	D.C.S.Compton	1954
	in Pakistan	449	(av 112.25)	D.I.Gower	1983-84
Pakistan	in England	488	(av 81.33)	Salim Malik	1992
	in Pakistan	407	(av 67.83)	Hanif Mohammed	1961-62

RECORD WICKET PARTNERSHIPS – ENGLAND

1st	198	G.Pullar (165)/R.W.Barber (86)	Dacca	1961-62
2nd	248	M.C.Cowdrey (182)/E.R.Dexter (172)	The Oval	1962
3rd	227	A.J.Stewart (190)/R.A.Smith (127)	Birmingham	1992
4th	188	E.R.Dexter (205)/P.H.Parfitt (111)	Karachi	1961-62
5th	192	D.C.S.Compton (278)/T.E.Bailey (36*)	Nottingham	1954
6th	166	G.P.Thorpe (118)/C.White (93)	Lahore	2000-01
7th	167	D.I.Gower (152)/V.J.Marks (83)	Faisalabad	1983-84
8th	99	P.H.Parfitt (119)/D.A.Allen (62)	Leeds	1962
9th	76	T.W.Graveney (153)/F.S.Trueman (29)	Lord's	1962
10th	79	R.W.Taylor (54)/R.G.D.Willis (28*)	Birmingham	1982

RECORD WICKET PARTNERSHIPS – PAKISTAN

1st	173	Mohsin Khan (104)/Shoaib Mohammed (80)	Lahore	1983-84
2nd	291	Zaheer Abbas (274)/Mushtaq Mohammed (100)	Birmingham	1971
3rd	180	Mudassar Nazar (114)/Haroon Rashid (122)	Lahore	1977-78
4th	322	Javed Miandad (153*)/Salim Malik (165)	Birmingham	1992
5th	197	Javed Burki (101)/Nasim-ul-Ghani (101)	Lord's	1962
6th	145	Mushtaq Mohammed (157)/Intikhab Alam (138)	Hyderabad	1972-73
7th	112	Asif Mujtaba (51)/Moin Khan (105)	Leeds	1996
8th	130	Hanif Mohammed (187*)/Asif Iqbal (76)	Lord's	1967
9th	190	Asif Iqbal (146)/Intikhab Alam (51)	The Oval	1967
10th	62	Sarfraz Nawaz (53)/Asif Masood (4*)	Leeds	1974

BEST INNINGS BOWLING ANALYSIS

England	in England	8- 34	I.T.Botham	Lord's	1978
	in Pakistan	7- 66	P.H.Edmonds	Karachi	1977-78
Pakistan	in England	7- 40	Imran Khan	Leeds	1987
	in Pakistan	9- 56	Abdul Qadir	Lahore	1987-88

BEST MATCH BOWLING ANALYSIS

England	in England	13- 71	D.L.Underwood	Lord's	1974
	in Pakistan	11- 83	N.G.B.Cook	Karachi	1983-84
Pakistan	in England	12- 99	Fazal Mahmood	The Oval	1954
	in Pakistan	13-101	Abdul Qadir	Lahore	1987-88

HIGHEST AGGREGATE OF WICKETS IN A SERIES

England	in England	22	(av 19.95)	F.S.Trueman	1962
	in Pakistan	17	(av 24.11)	A.F.Giles	2000-01
Pakistan	in England	22	(av 25.31)	Waqar Younis	1992
	in Pakistan	30	(av 14.56)	Abdul Qadir	1987-88

RESULTS SUMMARY

ENGLAND v PAKISTAN – IN ENGLAND

	Tests	Series			Lord's			Nottingham			Manchester			The Oval			Birmingham			Leeds		
		E	P	D	E	P	D	E	P	D	E	P	D	E	P	D	E	P	D	E	P	D
1954	4	1	1	2	–	–	1	1	–	–	–	–	1	–	1	–						
1962	5	4	–	1	1	–	–	–	–	1				1	–	–	1	–	–	1	–	–
1967	3	2	–	1	–	–	1	1	–	–				1	–	–						
1971	3	1	–	2	–	–	1										–	–	1	1	–	–
1974	3	–	–	3	–	–	1							–	–	1				–	–	1
1978	3	2	–	1	1	–	–										1	–	–	–	–	1
1982	3	2	1	–	–	1	–										1	–	–	1	–	–
1987	5	–	1	4	–	–	1				–	–	1	–	–	1	–	–	1	–	1	–
1992	5	1	2	2	–	1	–				–	–	1	–	1	–	–	–	1	1	–	–
1996	3	–	2	1	–	1	–							–	1	–				–	–	1
	37	13	7	17	2	3	5	2	–	1	–	–	3	2	3	2	3	–	3	4	1	3

ENGLAND v PAKISTAN – IN PAKISTAN

	Tests	Series			Lahore			Dacca			Karachi			Hyderabad			Faisalabad		
		E	P	D	E	P	D	E	P	D	E	P	D	E	P	D	E	P	D
1961-62	3	1	–	2	1	–	–	–	–	1	–	–	1						
1968-69	3	–	–	3	–	–	1	–	–	1	–	–	1						
1972-73	3	–	–	3	–	–	1				–	–	1	–	–	1			
1977-78	3	–	–	3	–	–	1				–	–	1	–	–	1			
1983-84	3	–	1	2	–	–	1				–	1	–				–	–	1
1987-88	3	–	1	2	–	1	–				–	–	1				–	–	1
2000-01	3	1	–	2	–	–	1				1	–	–				–	–	1
	21	2	2	17	1	1	5	–	–	2	1	1	5	–	–	2	–	–	3
Totals	58	15	9	34															

7

PAKISTAN REGISTER

Pakistan's touring team had not been selected at the time of going to press. Career statistics are to the start of their series in New Zealand (18 February). See page 16 for key to abbreviations, and pages 173 and 184 for full Limited-Overs International and Test Match records. Team abbreviations: ADBP – Agricultural Development Bank of Pakistan; KRL – Khan Research Laboratories; PIA – Pakistan International Airlines; PNSC – Pakistan National Shipping Corporation; WAPDA – Water and Power Development Authority.

ABDUR RAZZAQ (Furqan Model HS, Shahdara, Lahore), b Lahore 2 Dec 1979. 5'11". RHB, RFM. F-c debut (Lahore City) 1996-97. **Tests:** 12 (1999-00 to 2000-01); HS 100* v E (Faisalabad) 2000-01; BB 4-56 v SL (Rawalpindi) 1999-00. Hat-trick 1999-00. **LOI:** 69 (1996-97 to 2000-01); HS 75* (off 40 balls) v E (Karachi) 2000-01; BB 5-31 v SL (Sharjah) 1999-00. FC HS 117 KRL v Customs (Faisalabad) 1997-98. FC BB 7-51 Lahore City v Karachi Whites (Thatta) 1996-97 – on debut.

ARSHAD KHAN (Govt HS No. 2 and Govt C, Peshawar), b Peshawar 22 Mar 1971. 6'3". RHB, OB. F-c debut (Peshawar) 1988-89. **Tests:** 8 (1997-98 to 2000-01); HS 9*; BB 5-38 v SL (Dhaka) 1998-99. **LOI:** 48 (1992-93 to 2000-01); HS 20 v I (Jamshedpur) 1998-99; BB 3-22 v I (Jaipur) 1998-99. FC HS 57 Peshawar v Lahore (Lahore) 2000-01. FC BB 8-115 Peshawar v Faisalabad (Peshawar) 1994-95.

AZHAR MAHMOOD (F.G. No. 1 HS, Islamabad), b Multan 28 Feb 1975. 5'11". RHB, RFM. F-c debut (Islamabad) 1993-94. **Tests:** 19 (1997-98 to 2000-01); HS 136 v SA (Johannesburg) 1997-98; BB 4-53 v WI (Rawalpindi) 1997-98. Scored 128* and 50* v SA (Rawalpindi) 1997-98 on debut. **LOI:** 90 (1996-97 to 2000-01); HS 67 v I (Adelaide) 1999-00; BB 6-18 v WI (Sharjah) 1999-00. FC HS 136 (*see Tests*). FC BB 7-65 Islamabad v Faisalabad (Islamabad) 1996-97.

HUMAYUN FARHAT (Govt C, Lahore), b Lahore 24 Jan 1981. Elder brother of Imran Farhat; nephew of Shehzad Hussain (Railways). 5'7". RHB, WK. F-c debut (Lahore City) 1997-98. **Tests:** 0. **LOI:** 0. FC HS 188 Lahore Blues v Sargodha (Sargodha) 2000-01.

IJAZ AHMED (Islamia C, Sialkot), b Sialkot 20 Sep 1968. 5'9". RHB, LM. F-c debut 1983-84. **Tests:** 58 (1986-87 to 1999-00); HS 211 v SL (Dhaka) 1998-99; BB 1-9. **LOI:** 250 (1986-87 to 2000-01); HS 139* v I (Lahore) 1997-98; BB 2-31 v NZ (Sialkot) 1990-91. FC HS 211 (*see Tests*). FC BB 5-95 Habib Bank v PIA (Karachi) 1992-93.

IMRAN FARHAT, b Lahore 20 May 1982. Younger brother of Humayun Farhat; nephew of Shehzad Hussain (Railways). LHB, LB. F-c debut (Lahore City) 1998-99. **Tests:** 0. **LOI:** 0. FC HS 200 Lahore Blues v Bahawalpur (Lahore) 2000-01. FC BB 3-25 Lahore Blues v Lahore (Lahore) 2000-01.

IMRAN NAZIR, b Gujranwala 16 Dec 1981. RHB, LB. F-c debut (Lahore City) 1998-99. **Tests:** 5 (1998-99 to 2000-01); HS 131 v WI (Bridgetown) 1999-00. **LOI:** 29 (1998-99 to 2000-01); HS 105* v Z (St George's, Grenada) 1999-00. BB 1-3. FC HS 131 (*see Tests*).

INZAMAM-UL-HAQ (Govt C, Multan), b Multan 3 Mar 1970. Younger brother of Intizar-ul-Haq (Multan). 6'2". RHB, occ SLA. F-c debut (Multan) 1985-86. **Tests:** 70 (1992 to 2000-01); 200* v SL (Dhaka) 1998-99. **LOI:** 234 (1991-92 to 2000-01); HS 137* v NZ (Sharjah) 1993-94; BB 1-4. FC HS 201* United Bank v PNSC (Karachi) 1988-89. FC BB 5-80 Multan v Bahawalpur (Sahiwal) 1989-90.

MOHAMMAD SAMI, b Karachi 24 Feb 1981. RHB, RF. F-c debut (Karachi) 2000-01. FC HS 9. FC BB 6-72 Karachi v Lahore (Karachi) 2000-01.

MOIN KHAN (Govt C of Commerce, Karachi), b Rawalpindi 23 Sep 1971. Younger brother of Nadeem Khan (Karachi, PIA and Pakistan). 5'8". RHB, WK. F-c debut (Karachi) 1986-87. **Tests:** 61 (1990-91 to 2000-01 – 11 as captain); HS 117* v SL (Sialkot) 1995-96. **LOI:** 185 (1990-91 to 2000-01, 29 as captain); HS 69* v I (Toronto) 1998-99. FC HS 129 Karachi Whites v Karachi Blues (Karachi) 1989-90. FC BB 2-78 P v Northants (Northampton) 1996.

MUSHTAQ AHMED (Mahmoodia HS, Sahiwal), b Sahiwal 28 Jun 1970. 5'5". RHB, LBG. F-c debut (Multan) 1986-87. Somerset 1993-95, 1997-98; cap 1993. *Wisden* 1996. **Tests:** 49 (1989-90 to 2000-01); HS 59 v SA (Rawalpindi) 1997-98; BB 7-56 (10-171 match) v NZ (Christchurch) 1995-96. **LOI:** 143 (1988-89 to 2000-01); HS 34* v SA (Colombo) 2000-01; BB 5-36 v I (Toronto) 1996-97. FC HS 90 Somerset v Sussex (Taunton) 1993. FC BB 9-93 Multan v Peshawar (Sahiwal) 1990-91.

SAEED ANWAR (Kulsoom Bai Valika S and NED U, Karachi), b Karachi 6 Sep 1968. 5'8½". LHB, SLA. F-c debut (Karachi Blues) 1986-87. *Wisden* 1996. **Tests:** 52 (1990-91 to 2000-01, 7 as captain); HS 188* v I (Calcutta) 1998-99. **LOI:** 213 (1988-89 to 2000-01, 11 as captain); HS 194 (*LOI record*) v I (Madras) 1996-97; BB 2-9 v B (Dhaka) 1998-99. FC HS 221 Karachi Whites v Multan (Karachi) 1989-90. FC BB 3-83 ADBP v United Bank (Lahore) 1990-91.

SALIM ELAHI (Islamia HS, Lahore), b Sahiwal 20 Nov 1976. 5'11". Younger brother of Manzoor Elahi (Pakistan) and Zahoor Elahi (Pakistan). RHB, WK. F-c debut (Pakistanis v WA) 1995-96. **Tests:** 7 (1995-96 to 2000-01); HS 72 v E (Faisalabad) 2000-01. **LOI:** 22 (1995-96 to 2000-01); HS 102* v SL (Gujranwal) 2000-01 – on debut. FC HS 229 Pakistan A v Worcs (Worcester) 1997.

SAQLAIN MUSHTAQ – *see SURREY.*

SHAHID AFRIDI (Ibrahim Alibhai S and Islamia Science C, Karachi), b Kohat 1 Mar 1980. Younger brother of Tariq Afridi (Karachi). 5'11". RHB, LBG. F-c debut (Combined XI v England A) 1995-96. **Tests:** 11 (1998-99 to 2000-01); HS 141 v I (Madras) 1998-99; BB 5-52 v A (Karachi) 1998-99 – on debut. **LOI:** 120 (1997-98 to 2000-01); HS 109 v I (Toronto) 1998-99; BB 5-40 v E (Lahore) 2000-01. Scored a 37-ball hundred (*LOI record*) which included 11 sixes (*equalled record*) v SL (Nairobi) 1996-97 in his first LOI innings. FC HS 141 (*see Tests*). FC BB 6-101 Habib Bank v KRL (Rawalpindi) 1997-98.

SHOAIB AKHTAR (Elliott HS and Asghar Mal Govt C, Rawalpindi), b Rawalpindi 13 Jun 1975. 5'11½". RHB, RF. F-c debut (PIA) 1994-95. **Tests:** 15 (1997-98 to 2000-01); HS 26 v SL (Karachi) 1999-00; BB 5-43 v SA (Durban) 1997-98. **LOI:** 41 (1997-98 to 1999-00); HS 36 v A (Karachi) 1998-99; BB 4-37 v E (Sharjah) 1998-99. FC HS 26 (*see Tests*). FC BB 6-69 Rawalpindi B v Lahore City (Lahore) 1994-95.

WAQAR YOUNIS (Government C, Vehari), b Vehari 16 Nov 1969. Elder brother of Faisal Younis (Lahore City). 6'0". RHB, RF. F-c debut (Multan) 1987-88. Surrey 1990-91 and 1993; cap 1990. Glamorgan 1997-98; cap 1997. *Wisden* 1991. **Tests:** 68 (1989-90 to 2000-01; 1 as captain); HS 45 v SA (Rawalpindi) 1997-98; BB 7-76 v NZ (Faisalabad) 1990-91. **LOI:** 199 (1989-90 to 2000-01, 4 as captain); HS 37 v A (Sydney) 1999-00; BB 6-26 v SL (Sharjah) 1989-90. FC HS 55 P v Natal (Durban) 1994-95. FC BB 8-17 Gm v Sussex (Swansea) 1997. Hat-trick 1997.

WASIM AKRAM (Islamia C, Lahore), b Lahore 3 Jun 1966. 6'3". LHB, LF. F-c debut (BCCP XI v NZ) 1984-85. Lancashire 1988-98; cap 1989; captain 1998; benefit 1998. *Wisden* 1992. **Tests:** 100 (1984-85 to 2000-01, 25 as captain); HS 257* v Z (Sheikhupura) 1996-97; BB 7-119 v NZ (Wellington) 1993-94. Two hat-tricks (first by a captain and in successive Tests) 1998-99. **LOI:** 311 (1984-85 to 2000-01, 109 as captain); HS 86 v A (Melbourne) 1989-90; BB 5-15 v Z (Karachi) 1993-94. FC HS 257* (*see Tests*). FC BB 8-30 (13-147 match) Lancs v Somerset (Southport) 1994. Three hat-tricks.

YOUNIS KHAN, b Mardan 29 Nov 1977. RHB, LB. F-c debut (Peshawar) 1998-99. **Tests:** 9 (1999-00 to 2000-01); HS 116 v SL (Galle) 2000-01. **LOI:** 18 (1999-00 to 2000-01); HS 59 v SL (Colombo) 2000-01. FC HS 221 Peshawar v Lahore (Lahore) 2000-01. FC BB 1-0.

YOUSUF YOUHANA (Don Bosco HS and FC C, Lahore), b Lahore 27 Aug 1974. RHB. F-c debut (Bahawalpur) 1996-97. **Tests:** 27 (1997-98 to 2000-01); HS 124 v E (Lahore) 2000-01. **LOI:** 73 (1997-98 to 2000-01); HS 104* v WI (Toronto) 1999-00. FC HS 163* WAPDA v Habib Bank (Sheikhupura) 1997-98.

ENGLAND v AUSTRALIA
SERIES RECORDS
1876-77 to 1998-99

HIGHEST INNINGS TOTALS

England	in England	903-7d	The Oval	1938
	in Australia	636	Sydney	1928-29
Australia	in England	729-6d	Lord's	1930
	in Australia	659-8d	Sydney	1946-47

LOWEST INNINGS TOTALS

England	in England	52	The Oval	1948
	in Australia	45	Sydney	1886-87
Australia	in England	36	Birmingham	1902
	in Australia	42	Sydney	1887-88

HIGHEST MATCH AGGREGATE 1753 for 40 wickets Adelaide 1920-21
LOWEST MATCH AGGREGATE 291 for 40 wickets Lord's 1888

HIGHEST INDIVIDUAL INNINGS

England	in England	364	L.Hutton	The Oval	1938
	in Australia	287	R.E.Foster	Sydney	1903-04
Australia	in England	334	D.G.Bradman	Leeds	1930
	in Australia	307	R.M.Cowper	Melbourne	1965-66

HIGHEST AGGREGATE OF RUNS IN A SERIES

England	in England	732	(av 81.33)	D.I.Gower (6 Tests)	1985
	in Australia	905	(av 113.12)	W.R.Hammond	1928-29
Australia	in England	974	(av 139.14)	D.G.Bradman	1930
	in Australia	810	(av 90.00)	D.G.Bradman	1936-37

RECORD WICKET PARTNERSHIPS – ENGLAND

1st	323	J.B.Hobbs (178)/W.Rhodes (179)	Melbourne	1911-12
2nd	382	L.Hutton (364)/M.Leyland (187)	The Oval	1938
3rd	262	W.R.Hammond (177)/ D.R.Jardine (98)	Adelaide	1928-29
4th	288	N.Hussain (207)/G.P.Thorpe (138)	Birmingham	1997
5th	206	E.Paynter (216*)/D.C.S.Compton (102)	Nottingham	1938
6th	215	L.Hutton (364)/J.Hardstaff jr (169*)	The Oval	1938
	215	G.Boycott (107)/A.P.E.Knott (135)	Nottingham	1977
7th	143	F.E.Woolley (133*)/J.Vine (36)	Sydney	1911-12
8th	124	E.H.Hendren (169)/H.Larwood (70)	Brisbane	1928-29
9th	151	W.H.Scotton (90)/W.W.Read (117)	The Oval	1884
10th	130	R.E.Foster (287)/W.Rhodes (40*)	Sydney	1903-04

RECORD WICKET PARTNERSHIPS – AUSTRALIA

1st	329	G.R.Marsh (138)/M.A.Taylor (219)	Nottingham	1989
2nd	451	W.H.Ponsford (266)/D.G.Bradman (244)	The Oval	1934
3rd	276	D.G.Bradman (187)/A.L.Hassett (128)	Brisbane	1946-47
4th	388	W.H.Ponsford (181)/D.G.Bradman (304)	Leeds	1934
5th	405	S.G.Barnes (234)/D.G.Bradman (234)	Sydney	1946-47
6th	346	J.H.W.Fingleton (136)/D.G.Bradman (270)	Melbourne	1936-37
7th	165	C.Hill (188)/H.Trumble (46)	Melbourne	1897-98
8th	243	R.J.Hartigan (116)/C.Hill (160)	Adelaide	1907-08
9th	154	S.E.Gregory (201)/J.M.Blackham (74)	Sydney	1894-95
10th	127	J.M.Taylor (108)/A.A.Mailey (46*)	Sydney	1924-25

BEST INNINGS BOWLING ANALYSIS

England	in England	10-53	J.C.Laker	Manchester	1956
	in Australia	8-35	G.A.Lohmann	Sydney	1886-87
Australia	in England	8-31	F.Laver	Manchester	1909
	in Australia	9-121	A.A.Mailey	Melbourne	1920-21

BEST MATCH BOWLING ANALYSIS

England	in England	19-90	J.C.Laker	Manchester	1956
	in Australia	15-124	W.Rhodes	Melbourne	1903-04
Australia	in England	16-137	R.A.L.Massie	Lord's	1972
	in Australia	13-77	M.A.Noble	Melbourne	1901-02

HIGHEST AGGREGATE OF WICKETS IN A SERIES

England	in England	46	(av 9.60)	J.C.Laker	1956
	in Australia	38	(av 23.18)	M.W.Tate	1924-25
Australia	in England	42	(av 21.26)	T.M.Alderman (6 Tests)	1981
	in Australia	41	(av 12.85)	R.M.Hogg (6 Tests)	1978-79

RESULTS SUMMARY
ENGLAND v AUSTRALIA – IN ENGLAND

	Tests	Series			The Oval			Manchester			Lord's			Nottingham			Leeds			Birmingham			Sheffield		
		E	A	D	E	A	D	E	A	D	E	A	D	E	A	D	E	A	D	E	A	D	E	A	D
1880	1	1	–	–	1	–	–																		
1882	1	–	1	–	–	1	–																		
1884	3	1	–	2	–	–	1	–	–	1	1	–	–												
1886	3	3	–	–	1	–	–	1	–	–	1	–	–												
1888	3	2	1	–	1	–	–	1	–	–	–	1	–												
1890	2	2	–	–	1	–	–				1	–	–												
1893	3	1	–	2	1	–	–	–	–	1	–	–	1												
1896	3	2	1	–	1	–	–	–	1	–	1	–	–												
1899	5	–	1	4	–	–	1	–	–	1	–	1	–	–	–	1	–	–	1						
1902	5	1	2	2	1	–	–	–	1	–	–	–	1							–	–	1	–	1	–
1905	5	2	–	3	–	–	1	1	–	–	–	–	1	1	–	–	–	–	1						
1909	5	1	2	2	–	–	1	–	–	1	–	1	–				–	1	–	1	–	–			
1912	3	1	–	2	1	–	–	–	–	1	–	–	1												
1921	5	–	3	2	–	–	1	–	–	1	–	1	–	–	1	–	–	1	–						
1926	5	1	–	4	1	–	–	–	–	1	–	–	1	–	–	1	–	–	1						
1930	5	1	2	2	–	1	–	–	–	1	–	1	–	1	–	–	–	–	1						
1934	5	1	2	2	–	1	–	–	–	1	1	–	–	–	1	–	–	–	1						
1938	4	1	1	2	1	–	–				–	–	1	–	–	1	–	1	–						
1948	5	–	4	1	–	1	–	–	–	1	–	1	–	–	1	–	–	1	–						
1953	5	1	–	4	1	–	–	–	–	1	–	–	1	–	–	1	–	–	1						
1956	5	2	1	2	–	–	1	1	–	–	–	1	–	–	–	1	1	–	–						
1961	5	1	2	2	–	–	1	–	1	–	–	1	–				1	–	–	–	–	1			
1964	5	–	1	4	–	–	1	–	–	1	–	–	1	–	–	1	–	1	–						
1968	5	1	1	3	1	–	–	–	1	–	–	–	1				–	–	1	–	–	1			
1972	5	2	2	1	–	1	–	1	–	–	–	1	–	–	–	1	1	–	–						
1975	4	–	1	3	–	–	1				–	–	1				–	–	1	–	1	–			
1977	5	3	–	2	–	–	1	1	–	–	–	–	1	1	–	–	1	–	–						
1980	1	–	–	1							–	–	1												
1981	6	3	1	2	–	–	1	1	–	–	–	–	1	–	1	–	1	–	–	1	–	–			
1985	6	3	1	2	1	–	–	–	–	1	–	1	–	–	–	1	1	–	–	1	–	–			
1989	6	–	4	2	–	–	1	–	1	–	–	1	–	–	1	–	–	1	–	–	–	1			
1993	6	1	4	1	1	–	–	–	1	–	–	1	–	–	–	1	–	1	–	–	1	–			
1997	6	2	3	1	1	–	–	–	1	–	–	–	1	–	1	–	–	1	–	1	–	–			
	141	40	41	60	15	5	12	7	7	13	5	12	14	3	6	9	6	8	8	4	2	4	–	1	–

Tests	Series E	A	D	Melbourne E	A	D	Sydney E	A	D	Adelaide E	A	D	Brisbane E	A	D	Perth E	A	D
1876-77 2	1	1	–	1	1	–												
1878-79 1	–	1	–	–	1	–												
1881-82 4	–	2	2	–	–	2	–	2	–									
1882-83 4	2	2	–	1	1	–	1	1	–									
1884-85 5	3	2	–	2	–	–	–	2	–	1	–	–						
1886-87 2	2	–	–				2	–	–									
1887-88 1	1	–	–				1	–	–									
1891-92 3	1	2	–	–	1	–	–	1	–	1	–	–						
1894-95 5	3	2	–	2	–	–	1	1	–	–	1	–						
1897-98 5	1	4	–	–	2	–	1	1	–	–	1	–						
1901-02 5	1	4	–	–	2	–	1	1	–	–	1	–						
1903-04 5	3	2	–	1	1	–	2	–	–	–	1	–						
1907-08 5	1	4	–	1	1	–	–	2	–	–	1	–						
1911-12 5	4	1	–	2	–	–	1	1	–	1	–	–						
1920-21 5	–	5	–	–	2	–	–	2	–	–	1	–						
1924-25 5	1	4	–	1	1	–	–	2	–	–	1	–						
1928-29 5	4	1	–	1	1	–	1	–	–	1	–	–	1	–	–			
1932-33 5	4	1	–	–	1	–	2	–	–	1	–	–	1	–	–			
1936-37 5	2	3	–	–	2	–	1	–	–	–	1	–	1	–	–			
1946-47 5	–	3	2	–	–	1	–	2	–	–	–	1	–	1	–			
1950-51 5	1	4	–	1	1	–	–	1	–	–	1	–	–	1	–			
1954-55 5	3	1	1	1	–	–	1	–	1	1	–	–	–	1	–			
1958-59 5	–	4	1	–	2	–	–	–	1	–	1	–	–	1	–			
1962-63 5	1	1	3	1	–	–	–	1	1	–	–	1	–	–	1			
1965-66 5	1	1	3	–	–	2	1	–	–	–	1	–	–	–	1			
1970-71 6	2	–	4	–	–	1	2	–	–	–	–	1	–	–	1	–	–	1
1974-75 6	1	4	1	1	–	1	–	1	–	–	1	–	–	1	–	–	1	–
1976-77 1	–	1	–	–	1	–												
1978-79 6	5	1	–	–	1	–	2	–	–	1	–	–	1	–	–	1	–	–
1979-80 3	–	3	–	–	1	–	–	1	–							–	1	–
1982-83 5	1	2	2	1	–	–	–	–	1	–	1	–	–	1	–	–	–	1
1986-87 5	2	1	2	1	–	–	–	1	–	–	–	1	1	–	–	–	–	1
1987-88 1	–	–	1				–	–	1									
1990-91 5	–	3	2	–	1	–	–	–	1	–	–	1	–	1	–	–	1	–
1994-95 5	1	3	1	–	1	–	–	–	1	1	–	–	–	1	–	–	1	–
1998-99 5	1	3	1	1	–	–	–	1	–	–	1	–	–	–	1	–	1	–
155	**53**	**76**	**26**	**19**	**25**	**7**	**20**	**24**	**7**	**8**	**14**	**5**	**5**	**8**	**4**	**1**	**5**	**3**
Totals **296**	**93**	**117**	**86**															

Matches abandoned without a ball bowled (Manchester 1890 and 1938, Melbourne 1970-71) are excluded from these tables.

2000 RUNS

	Tests	I	NO	HS	Runs	Avge	100	50
D.G.Bradman (A)	37	63	7	334	5028	89.78	19	12
J.B.Hobbs (E)	41	71	4	187	3636	54.26	12	15
A.R.Border (A)	47	82	19	200*	3548	56.31	8	21
D.I.Gower (E)	42	77	4	215	3269	44.78	9	12
G.Boycott (E)	38	71	9	191	2945	47.50	7	14
W.R.Hammond (E)	33	58	3	251	2852	51.85	9	7
H.Sutcliffe (E)	27	46	5	194	2741	66.85	8	16
C.Hill (A)	41	76	1	188	2660	35.46	4	16
J.H.Edrich (E)	32	57	3	175	2644	48.96	7	13
G.A.Gooch (E)	42	79	0	196	2632	33.31	4	16
G.S.Chappell (A)	35	65	8	144	2619	45.94	9	12
S.R.Waugh (A)	37	60	16	177*	2574	58.50	7	12
M.A.Taylor (A)	33	61	2	219	2496	42.30	6	15

M.C.Cowdrey (E)	43	75	4	113	2433	34.26	5	11
L.Hutton (E)	27	49	6	364	2428	56.46	5	14
R.N.Harvey (A)	37	68	5	167	2416	38.34	6	12
V.T.Trumper (A)	40	74	5	185*	2263	32.79	6	9
D.C.Boon (A)	31	57	8	184	2237	45.65	7	8
W.M.Lawry (A)	29	51	5	166	2233	48.54	7	13
S.E.Gregory (A)	52	92	7	201	2193	25.80	4	8
W.W.Armstrong (A)	42	71	9	158	2172	35.03	4	6
I.M.Chappell (A)	30	56	4	192	2138	41.11	4	16
K.F.Barrington (E)	23	39	6	256	2111	63.96	5	13
A.R.Morris (A)	24	43	2	206	2080	50.73	8	8

D.G.Bradman holds the unique record of scoring 2000 runs in both countries in this series (2674 runs in England and 2354 in Australia); J.B.Hobbs is the only other batsman to score 2000 runs in either country (2493 runs in Australia).

100 WICKETS

	Tests	Balls	Runs	Wkts	Avge	Best	5wI	10wM
D.K.Lillee (A)	29	8516	3507	167	21.00	7- 89	11	4
I.T.Botham (E)	36	8479	4093	148	27.65	6- 78	9	2
H.Trumble (A)	31	7895	2945	141	20.88	8- 65	9	3
R.G.D.Willis (E)	35	7294	3346	128	26.14	8- 43	7	–
M.A.Noble (A)	39	6845	2860	115	24.86	7- 17	9	2
R.R.Lindwall (A)	29	6728	2559	114	22.44	7- 63	6	–
W.Rhodes (E)	41	5791	2616	109	24.00	8- 68	6	1
S.F.Barnes (E)	20	5749	2288	106	21.58	7- 60	12	1
C.V.Grimmett (A)	22	9224	3439	106	32.44	6- 37	11	2
D.L.Underwood (E)	29	8000	2770	105	26.38	7- 50	4	2
A.V.Bedser (E)	21	7065	2859	104	27.49	7- 44	7	2
G.Giffen (A)	31	6457	2791	103	27.09	7-117	7	1
W.J.O'Reilly (A)	19	7864	2587	102	25.36	7- 54	8	3
R.Peel (E)	20	5216	1715	101	16.98	7- 31	5	1
C.T.B.Turner (A)	17	5195	1670	101	16.53	7- 43	11	2
T.M.Alderman (A)	17	4717	2117	100	21.17	6- 47	11	1
J.R.Thomson (A)	21	4951	2418	100	24.18	6- 46	5	–

100 WICKET-KEEPING DISMISSALS

	Tests	Ct	St	Total
R.W.Marsh (A)	42	141	7	148
I.A.Healy (A)	33	123	12	135
A.P.E.Knott (E)	34	97	8	105

R.W.Marsh (141 catches) and W.A.S.Oldfield (31 stumpings) hold the respective individual records in Anglo-Australian Tests.

AUSTRALIA REGISTER

Australia's touring team had not been selected at the time of going to press. Career statistics are to the start of their series in India (27 February). See page 16 for key to abbreviations, and pages 173 and 184 for full Limited-Overs International and Test Match records.

BEVAN, Michael Gwyl – *see SUSSEX.*

BICHEL, Andrew John – *see WORCESTERSHIRE.*

FLEMING, Damien William (Heatherhill HS; Deakin U), b Perth, WA 24 Apr 1970. 6'0". RHB, RFM. Victoria 1989-90 to date. **Tests:** 19 (1994-95 to 1999-00). HS 71* v E (Brisbane) 1998-99; BB 5-30 v I (Adelaide) 1999-00; hat-trick v P (Rawalpindi) 1994-95 – one debut. **LOI:** 82 (1993-94 to 2000-01); HS 29 v SA (Durban) 1999-00; BB 5-36 v I (Bombay) 1995-96. FC HS 71* (*see Tests*). FC BB 7-90 Vic v S Aus (Adelaide) 1992-93.

GILCHRIST, Adam Craig (Kadina HS, Lismore), b Bellingen, NSW 14 Nov 1971. 6'0". LHB, WK. NSW 1992-93 to 1993-94. WA 1994-95 to date. **Tests:** 14 (1999-00 to 2000-01); HS 149* v P (Hobart) 1999-00. **LOI:** 108 (1996-97 to 2000-01); HS 154 v SL (Melbourne) 1998-99. FC HS 203* WA v S Aus (Perth) 1997-98.

GILLESPIE, Jason Neil (Cabra C), b Darlinghurst, NSW 19 Apr 1975. 6'5". RHB, RFM. S Australia 1994-95 to date. **Tests:** 18 (1996-97 to 2000-01); HS 41 v SL (Kandy) 1999-00; BB 7-37 v E (Leeds) 1997. Took 4 wickets in 6 balls v E (Perth) 1998-99. **LOI:** 21 (1996-97 to 2000-01); HS 26 v SA (Jo'burg) 1996-97; BB 4-26 v I (Colombo) 1999-00. FC HS 58 S Aus v WA (Perth) 1996-97. FC BB 7-34 A v Border (East London) 1996-97.

HARVEY, Ian Joseph – *see GLOUCESTERSHIRE.*

HAYDEN, Matthew Lawrence – *see NORTHAMPTONSHIRE.*

KASPROWICZ, Michael Scott (Brisbane State HS), b South Brisbane 10 Feb 1972. 6'4". RHB, RFM. Queensland 1989-90 to date. Essex 1994; cap 1994. Leicestershire 1999; cap 1999. **Tests:** 16 (1996-97 to 1999-00); HS 25 v I (Calcutta) 1997-98; BB 7-36 v E (Oval) 1997. **LOI:** 16 (1995-96 to 1998-99); HS 28* v E (Lord's) 1997; BB 3-50 v I (Cochin) 1997-98. FC HS 73 Leics v Hants (Southampton) 1999. FC BB 7-36 (*see Tests*).

LANGER, Justin Lee – *see MIDDLESEX.*

LEHMANN, Darren Scott – *see YORKSHIRE.*

MacGILL, Stuart Charles Glyndwr (Christ Church GS, Perth), b Mount Lawley, WA 25 Feb 1971. Grandson of C.W.T. (WA 1938-39), son of T.M.D. (WA 1968-69). 6'0". RHB, LBG. W Australia 1993-94. NSW 1996-97 to date. Somerset 1997 (unregistered). Devon 1997 to 1998 (NWT only). **Tests:** 16 (1997-98 to 2000-01); HS 43 v E (Melbourne) 1998-99; BB 7-50 (12-107 match) v E (Sydney) 1998-99. **LOI:** 3 (1999-00); HS 1 and BB 4-19 v P (Sydney) 1999-00 – on debut. FC HS 43 (*see Tests*). FC BB 7-29 A v WI Pres XI (Pointe-à-Pierre) 1998-99.

McGRATH, Glenn Donald – *see WORCESTERSHIRE.*

MARTYN, Damien Richard (Girrawheen HS), b Darwin 21 Oct 1971. 5'10". RHB, RMF, occ WK. W Australia 1990-91 to date. **Tests:** 11 (1992-93 to 2000-01); HS 89* v NZ (Hamilton) 1999-00. **LOI:** 70 (1992-93 to 2000-01); HS 144* Z (Perth) 2000-01; BB 2-21 v Z (Harare) 1999-00. FC HS 203* WA v Tas (Perth) 1995-96. FC BB 4-30 WA v Q (Brisbane) 1998-99 (Sheffield Shield Final).

MILLER, Colin Reid, b Footscray, Vic 6 Feb 1964. RHB, RMF/OB. Victoria 1985-86. S Australia 1988-89 to 1991-92. Tasmania 1992-93 to date. **Tests:** 17 (1998-99 to 2000-01); HS 43 v WI (St John's) 1998-99; BB 5-32 (10-113 match) v WI (Adelaide) 2000-01. **LOI:** 0. FC HS 60* (at No. 11) Tas v S Aus (Adelaide) 1998-99. FC BB 7-49 Tas v Vic (Melbourne) 1997-98.

PONTING, Ricky Thomas (Brooks HS), b Launceston 19 Dec 1974. 5'10". RHB, OB. Tasmania 1992-93 to date. **Tests:** 39 (1995-96 to 2000-01); HS 197 v P (Perth) 1999-00; BB 1-0. **LOI:** 114 (1994-95 to 2000-01); HS 145 v Z (Delhi) 1997-98; BB 1-12. FC HS 233 Tasmania v Q (Albion) 2000-01. FC BB 2-11 A v SL Board Pres XI (Colombo) 1999-00.

SLATER, Michael Jonathon (Wagga Wagga HS), b Wagga Wagga, NSW, Australia 21 Feb 1970. 5'9". RHB, RM. NSW 1991-92 to date. Derbyshire 1998-99; cap 1998. **Tests:** 67 (1993 to 2000-01); HS 219 v SL (Perth) 1995-96; BB 1-4. **LOI:** 42 (1993-94 to 1997); HS 73 v SA (Melbourne) 1993-94 – on debut. FC HS 221 A v Karachi City CA XI (Karachi) 1998-99. FC BB 1-4 (*see Tests*).

SYMONDS, Andrew (All Saints Anglican School, Mudgeeraba, Queensland), b Birmingham 9 Jun 1975. 6'1½". RHB, RMF/OB. Emigrated to Australia when 18 months old. Queensland 1994-95 to date. Gloucestershire 1995-96; cap 1996. Kent 1999; cap 1999. YC 1995. Surrendered England qualification by appearing for Australia A v WI 1996-97. **Tests:** 0. **LOI:** 36 (1998-99 to 2000-01); HS 68* v I (Galle) 1999-00; BB 4-11 v I (Sydney) 1999-00. FC HS 254* Gs v Glam (Abergavenny) 1995 (including record 16 sixes); hit record 20 sixes in match. FC BB 4-39 Q v WA (Perth) 1998-99.

WARNE, Shane Keith – *see HAMPSHIRE.*

WAUGH, Mark Edward (East Hills HS), b Canterbury, Sydney 2 Jun 1965. Younger twin of Steve. 6'1". RHB, OB. NSW 1985-86 to date. Essex 1988-90, 1992 and 1995; cap 1989; *Wisden* 1990. **Tests:** 108 (1990-91 to 2000-01); HS 153* v I (Bangalore) 1997-98; BB 5-40 v E (Adelaide) 1994-95. **LOI:** 230 (1988-89 to 2000-01); HS 173 v WI (Melbourne) 2000-01; BB 5-24 v WI (Melbourne) 1992-93. FC HS 229* NSW v WA (Perth) 1990-91, sharing world record 5th wkt stand of 464* with S.R.Waugh. FC BB 6-68 Aus XI v Board President's XI (Patiala) 1996-97.

WAUGH, Stephen Rodger (East Hills HS), b Canterbury, Sydney 2 Jun 1965. Elder twin of Mark. 5'11". RHB, RMF. NSW 1984-85 to date. Somerset 1987-88. Ireland 1998. *Wisden* 1988. **Tests:** 132 (1985-86 to 2000-01, 21 as captain); HS 200 v WI (Kingston) 1994-95; BB 5-28 v SA (Cape Town) 1993-94. Holds world record for most nineties in Tests (9). **LOI:** 306 (1985-86 to 2000-01, 87 as captain – HS 120* v SA (Leeds) 1999: BB 4-33 v SL (Sydney) 1987-88. FC HS 216* NSW v WA (Perth) 1990-91, sharing world record 5th wkt stand of 464* with M.E.Waugh. FC BB 6-51 NSW v Queensland (Sydney) 1988-89.

COUNTY
OVERSEAS REGISTRATIONS 2001

Derbyshire	M.J.Di Venuto
Durham	M.L.Love
Essex	S.G.Law
Glamorgan	J.P.Maher
Gloucestershire	I.J.Harvey
Hampshire	N.C.Johnson
Kent	D.J Cullinan
Lancashire	M.Muralitharan
Leicestershire	D.J.Marsh
Middlesex	S.P.Fleming
Northamptonshire	M.E.Hussey
Nottinghamshire	G.S.Blewett
Somerset	J.Cox
Surrey	Saqlain Mushtaq
Sussex	M.W.Goodwin
Warwickshire	V.C.Drakes
Worcestershire	A.J.Bichel
Yorkshire	D.S.Lehmann

THE FIRST-CLASS COUNTIES REGISTER, RECORDS AND 2000 AVERAGES

Career statistics are to 16 February 2001 and include all England's winter tours

ABBREVIATIONS – General

*	not out/unbroken partnership	LOI	Limited-Overs Internationals
b	born	Tests	Official Test Matches
BB	Best innings bowling analysis	Tours	Overseas tours involving first-class
Cap	Awarded 1st XI County Cap		appearances
HS	Highest Score	f-c	first-class
l-o	limited-overs		

Awards

BHC	Benson and Hedges Cup 'Gold' Award
NWT	NatWest Trophy/Gillette Cup 'Man of the Match' Award
Wisden 1999	One of *Wisden Cricketers' Almanack's* Five Cricketers of 1999
YC 2000	Cricket Writers' Club Young Cricketer of 2000

ECB Competitions

BHC	Benson & Hedges Cup
CC	PPP County Championship
NWT	NatWest Trophy
NL	National League (1999-2000)
SL	Sunday League (1969-98)

Overseas Competitions

BHS	Benson & Hedges Night Series (SA)
FAI	Federated Automobile Insce Cup (A)
MM	Mercantile Mutual Cup (A)
RSB	Red Stripe Bowl (WI)
SBC	Standard Bank Cup (SA)
SST	Shell/Sandals Trophy (WI)
WT	Wills Trophy (I)

Education

BHS	Boys' High School
C	College
CFE	College of Further Education
CHE	College of Higher Education
CS	Comprehensive School
GS	Grammar School
HS	High School
IHE	Institute of Higher Education
RGS	Royal Grammar School
S	School
SFC	Sixth Form College
SM	Secondary Modern School
SS	Secondary School
TC	Technical College
T(H)S	Technical (High) School
U	University
UMIST	University of Manchester Institute of Science and Technology
UWIC	University of Wales Institute, Cardiff

Playing Categories

LBG	Bowls right-arm leg-breaks and googlies
LF	Bowls left-arm fast
LFM	Bowls left-arm fast-medium
LHB	Bats left-handed
LM	Bowls left-arm medium pace
LMF	Bowls left-arm medium fast
OB	Bowls right-arm off-breaks
RF	Bowls right-arm fast
RFM	Bowls right-arm fast-medium
RHB	Bats right-handed
RM	Bowls right-arm medium pace
RMF	Bowls right-arm medium-fast
RSM	Bowls right-arm slow-medium
SLA	Bowls left-arm leg-breaks
SLC	Bowls left-arm 'Chinamen'
WK	Wicket-keeper

Teams (see also p 1**)

ACT	Australian Capital Territory
B	Bangladesh
CD	Central Districts
DHR	D.H.Robins' XI
EP	Eastern Province
GW	Griqualand West
K	Kenya
NSW	New South Wales
NT	Northern Transvaal
(O)FS	(Orange) Free State
PIA	Pakistan International Airlines
Q	Queensland
RW	Rest of the World XI
SAB	South African Breweries XI
SAU	South African Universities
WA	Western Australia
WP	Western Province

DERBYSHIRE

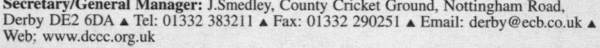

Formation of Present Club: 4 November 1870
Colours: Chocolate, Amber and Pale Blue
Badge: Rose and Crown
County Champions: (1) 1936
NatWest Trophy/Gillette Cup Winners: (1) 1981
Benson and Hedges Cup Winners: (1) 1993
National League (Div 1) Winners: (0); best – 8th (Div 2) 1999
Sunday League Winners: (1) 1990
Match Awards: NWT 45; BHC 69

Secretary/General Manager: J.Smedley, County Cricket Ground, Nottingham Road, Derby DE2 6DA ▲ Tel: 01332 383211 ▲ Fax: 01332 290251 ▲ Email: derby@ecb.co.uk ▲ Web: www.dccc.org.uk

Captain: D.G.Cork. **Vice-Captain:** T.A.Munton. **Overseas Player:** M.J.Di Venuto.
2001 Beneficiary: D.G.Cork. **Scorer:** J.M.Brown.

ALDRED, Paul (Lady Manner's S, Bakewell), b Chellaston 4 Feb 1969. 5'10". RHB, RM. Debut 1995; cap 1999. Cheshire 1994. HS 83 v Hants (Chesterfield) 1997. 50 wkts (1): 50 (1999). BB 7-101 (13-184 match) v Lancs (Derby) 1999. LO HS 39* v Surrey (Derby) 1999 (NL). LO BB 4-30 v Lincs (Lincoln) 1997 (NWT).

BAILEY, Robert John (Biddulph HS), b Biddulph, Staffs 28 Oct 1963. 6'3". RHB, OB. Northamptonshire 1982-99; cap 1985; benefit 1993; captain 1996-97. Derbyshire debut/cap 2000. Staffordshire 1980. YC 1984. **Tests:** 4 (1988 to 1989-90); HS 43 v WI (Oval) 1988. **LOI:** 4 (1984-85 to 1989-90); HS 43* v SL (Oval) 1988. Tours: SA 1991-92 (Nh); WI 1989-90; Z 1994-95 (Nh). 1000 runs (13); most – 1987 (1990). HS 224* Nh v Glam (Swansea) 1986. De HS 118 v Leics (Derby) 2000. BB 5-54 Nh v Notts (Northampton) 1993. De BB 1-7. Awards: NWT 7; BHC 9. LO HS 153* Nh v Pak A (Northampton) 1997. LO BB 5-45 v Durham (Chester-le-St) 2000 (BHC).

‡BOSSANO, Christopher Warwick Godfrey (Tasmania U), b East London, SA 11 Sep 1975. RHB, LB. British passport (English mother). Tasmania 2nd XI. Staff 2001 – awaiting f-c debut.

CORK, Dominic Gerald (St Joseph's C, Stoke-on-Trent), b Newcastle-under-Lyme, Staffs 7 Aug 1971. 6'2". RHB, RFM. Debut 1990; cap 1993; captain 1998 to date; benefit 2001. *Wisden* 1995. Staffordshire 1989-90. **Tests:** 31 (1995 to 2000); HS 59 v NZ (Auckland) 1996-97; BB 7-43 v WI (Lord's) 1995 – on debut (record England analysis by Test match debutant); hat-trick v WI (Manchester) 1995 – the first in Test history to occur in the opening over of a day's play. **LOI:** 25 (1992 to 1996-97); HS 31* v NZ (Napier) 1996-97; BB 3-27 v WI (Lord's) 1995. Tours: SA 1995-96 (Eng A), 1998-99; SA 1993-94 (Eng A), 1995-96; WI 1991-92 (Eng A); NZ 1996-97; I 1994-95 (Eng A); P 2000-01 (*part*). HS 200* v Durham (Derby) 2000. 50 wkts (5); most – 90 (1995). BB 9-43 (13-93 match) v Northants (Derby) 1995. Took 8-53 before lunch on his 20th birthday v Essex (Derby) 1991. 2 hat-tricks: 1994 and 1995 (*see Tests*). Awards: NWT 3; BHC 4. LO HS 93 v Derbys CB (Derby) 2000 (NWT). LO BB 6-21 v Glam (Chesterfield) 1997 (SL).

DEAN, Kevin James (Leek HS; Leek C), b Derby 16 Oct 1975. 6'5". LHB, LMF. Debut 1996. Cap 1998. HS 27* v SA (Derby) 1998. CC HS 25* v Essex (Derby) 1998. 50 wkts (1): 74 (1998). BB 8-52 v Kent (Canterbury) 2000. 2 hat-tricks (1998, 2000). Award: NWT 1. LO HS 16* v Glam (Cardiff) 1998 (SL). LO BB 5-32 v Glos (Derby) 1996 (SL).

Di VENUTO, Michael James (St Virgil's C; Hobart), b Hobart, Australia 12 Dec 1973. 6'0". LHB, RM/LB. Tasmania 1991-92 to date. Sussex 1999; cap 1999. Derbyshire debut/cap 2000. LOI (A): 9 (1996-97 to 1997-98); HS 89 v SA (Jo'burg) 1996-97.Tours: Z 1995-96 (Tas); Sc/Ire 1998 (Aus A). 1000 runs (1): 1067 (1999). HS 189 Tas v WA (Perth) 1997-98. CC HS 162 Sx v Glos (Hove) 1999. De HS 92* v Surrey (Derby) 2000. BB 1-0 (Tas). UK BB (Sx) 1-3. Award: NWT 1. LO HS 173* v Derbys CB (Derby) 2000 (NWT). LO BB (Tas) 1-10 (MM).

DOWMAN, Mathew Peter (St Hugh's CS; Grantham C), b Grantham, Lincs 10 May 1974. 5'10". LHB, RMF. Nottinghamshire 1994-99; cap 1998. Derbyshire debut/cap 2000. Scored 267 for England YC v WI YC (Hove) 1993 – record score in youth 'Tests'. 1000 runs (1): 1091 (1997). HS 149 Nt v Leics (Leicester) 1997. De HS 140 v Durham (Derby) 2000. BB 3-10 Nt v Pak A (Nottingham) 1997. CC BB 2-10 Nt v Kent (Canterbury) 1998. De BB 2-46 v Durham (Darlington) 2000. Award: BHC 1. LO HS 92 Nt v Northants (Nottingham) 1997 (BHC). LO BB 3-21 Nt v Worcs (Nottingham) 1996 (BHC).

‡**DUMELOW, Nathan** Robert Charles (Denstone C), b Derby 30 Apr 1981. RHB, OB. Joined staff 2001 – awaiting f-c debut. LO HS 32 Derbys CB v Wales (Dunstall) 1999 (NWT). LO BB 2-21 Derbys CB v Glos CB (Heanor) 2000 (NWT).

‡**ILLINGWORTH, Richard** Keith (Salts GS), b Bradford, Yorks 23 Aug 1963. 5'11". RHB, SLA. Worcestershire 1982-2000; cap 1986; benefit 1997. Natal 1988-89. **Tests**: 9 (1991 to 1995-96); HS 28 v SA (Pt Elizabeth) 1995-96; BB 4-96 v WI (Nottingham) 1995. Took wicket of P.V.Simmons with his first ball in Tests – v WI (Nottingham) 1991. **LOI**: 25 (1991 to 1995-96); HS 14 v P (Melbourne) 1991-92; BB 3-33 v Z (Albury) 1991-92. Tours: SA 1995-96; NZ 1991-92; P 1990-91 (Eng A); SL 1990-91 (Eng A); Z 1989-90 (Eng A), 1990-91 (Wo), 1993-94 (Wo), 1996-97 (Wo). HS 120* Wo v Warwks (Worcester) 1987 – as night-watchman. Scored 106 for England A v Z (Harare) 1989-90 – also as night-watchman. 50 wkts (5); most – 75 (1990). BB 7-50 Wo v OU (Oxford) 1985. CC BB 7-79 Wo v Hants (Southampton) 1997. LO HS 36* Wo v Kent (Worcester) 1990 (BHC). LO BB 5-24 Wo v Somerset (Worcester) 1983 (SL).

‡**KHAN, Wasim** Gulzar (Small Heath CS; Josiah Mason SFC, Erdington), b Birmingham 26 Feb 1971. 6'1". LHB, LB. Warwickshire 1995-97. Sussex 1998-2000. HS 181 Wa v Hants (Southampton) 1995. LO HS 33 Sx v Glam (Hove) 1998 (BHC) and 33 Sx v Warwks (Hove) 1998 (SL).

KHAN, Zubair Mahmood, b Birmingham 7 Feb 1983. LHB, RFM. Debut 2000. Awaiting CC debut. HS – and BB 1-32 v CU (Cambridge) 2000.

KRIKKEN, Karl Matthew (Rivington & Blackrod HS & SFC), b Bolton, Lancs 9 Apr 1969. Son of B.E. (Lancs and Worcs 1966-69). 5'9". RHB, WK. GW 1988-89. Derbyshire debut 1989; cap 1992. HS 104 v Lancs (Manchester) 1996. BB 1-54. LO HS 55 v Kent (Derby) 1996 (NWT).

LUNGLEY, Thomas (St John S, Houghton; SE Derbyshire C), b Derby 25 Jul 1979. LHB, RM. Debut 2000. Awaiting CC debut. HS – and BB 3-10 (6-41 match) v CU (Cambridge) 2000 – on debut. LO HS 15 (thrice in successive NL matches v Durham, Warwks and Essex 2000. LO BB 2-26 v Warwks (Derby) 2000 (NL).

‡**MARSH, Adrian** John (Abbotsholme S, Rocester), b Nottingham 4 Nov 1978. LHB, RM. Joined staff 2001 – awaiting f-c debut. Award: NWT 1. LO HS 53 Derbys CB v Glos CB (Heanor) 2000 (NWT).

MUNTON, Timothy Alan (Sarson HS; King Edward VII Upper S), b Melton Mowbray, Leics 30 Jul 1965. 6'6". RHB, RMF. Warwickshire 1985-99; cap 1989; captain 1997 (no appearances – back injury); benefit 1998. Derbyshire debut/cap 2000. *Wisden* 1994. **Tests**: 2 (1992); HS 25* v P (Manchester) 1992. BB 2-22 v P (Leeds) 1992. Tours: SA 1992-93 (Wa); WI 1991-92 (Eng A); P 1990-91 (Eng A), 1995-96 (Eng A – part); SL 1990-91 (Eng A); Z 1993-94 (Wa). HS 54* Wa v Worcs (Worcester) 1996. De HS 52 v Durham (Darlington) 2000. 50 wkts (6); most – 81 (1994). BB 8-89 (11-128 match) Wa v Middx (Birmingham) 1991. De BB 7-34 v Surrey (Derby) 2000. Hat-trick (Wa) 1999. Awards: NWT 2; BHC 1. LO HS 18 v Essex (Chelmsford) 2000 (NL). LO BB 5-23 Wa v Glos (Moreton-in-M) 1990 (SL).

‡PIERSON, Adrian Roger Kirshaw (Kent C, Canterbury; Hatfield Poly), b Enfield, Middx 21 Jul 1963. 6'4". RHB, OB. Warwickshire 1985-91. Leicestershire 1993-97; cap 1995. Somerset 1998-2000. Cambridgeshire 1992. MCC YC. Tour (Le): SA 1996-97. HS 108* Sm v Sussex (Hove) 1998. 50 wkts (1): 69 (1995). BB 8-42 Le v Warwks (Birmingham) 1994. Awards: NWT 1; BHC 1. LO HS 31* Sm v Northants (Northampton) 2000 (NL). LO BB 5-36 Le v Derbys (Leicester) 1995 (SL).

PYEMONT, James Patrick (Tonbridge S; Trinity Hall, Cambridge), b Eastbourne, Sussex 10 Apr 1978. Son of C.P. (Cambridge U 1967; cricket and hockey blue). 6'0". RHB, OB. Sussex 1997 – no CC appearances. Cambridge U 1998-99; blue 1998-99. Derbyshire debut 1999 (dismissed first ball in both innings – first instance by Derbyshire player). British U 2000. HS 124 CU v OU (Lord's) 2000. De HS 40 v Hants (Southampton) 2000. BB (CU) 1-26. LO HS 50 v Hants (Southampton) 2000 (NL).

SMITH, Trevor Mark (Friesland S, Sandiacre; Broxtowe C, Chilwell), b Derby 18 Jan 1977. 6'3". LHB, RFM. Debut 1997. HS 53* v Lancs (Derby) 2000. BB 6-32 v Essex (Derby) 1998. LO HS 12 v Notts (Nottingham) 2000 (NL). LO BB 4-38 v Somerset (Derby) 1999 (NL).

SPENDLOVE, Benjamin Lee (Trent C), b Belper 4 Nov 1978. 6'1". RHB, OB. Debut 1997. HS 63 v Warwks (Birmingham) 1999. LO HS 58 v Leics (Leicester) 1998 (NWT).

STUBBINGS, Stephen David (Frankston HS; Swinburne U), b Huddersfield, Yorks 31 Mar 1978. 6'3". LHB, OB. Debut 1997. HS 135* v Kent (Canterbury) 2000. LO HS 59 v Notts (Nottingham) 2000 (NL).

SUTTON, Luke David (Millfield S; Durham U), b Keynsham, Somerset 4 Oct 1976. 5'11". RHB, WK. Somerset 1997-98. Derbyshire debut 2000. HS 79 v Hants (Derby) 2000. LO HS 60 Brit U v Kent (Oxford) 1998 (BHC).

TITCHARD, Stephen Paul (Lymm County HS; Priestley C), b Warrington 17 Dec 1967. 6'3". RHB, RM. Lancashire 1990-98; cap 1995. Derbyshire debut 1999. HS 163 La v Essex (Chelmsford) 1996. De HS 141* v Kent (Canterbury) 2000. BB 1-11 (La twice). Award: NWT 1. LO HS 96 La v Essex (Chelmsford) 1994 (SL). LO BB (De) 1-19 (NL).

‡WELCH, Graeme (Hetton CS), b Durham City 21 Mar 1972. 5'11½". RHB, RM. Warwickshire 1994-2000; cap 1997. Tour: SA 1994-95 (Wa). HS 84* Wa v Notts (Birmingham) 1994. 50 wkts (1): 65 (1997). BB 6-115 (11-140 match) Wa v Lancs (Blackpool) 1997. Award: BHC 1. LO HS 71 Wa v Kent (Maidstone) 1999 (NL). LO BB 4-31 Wa v Kent (Birmingham) 1998 (NWT).

WHARTON, Lian James (Ecclesbourne S; Malkworth C), b Holbrook 21 Feb 1977. 5'9". LHB, SLA. Debut 2000. HS 7. CC HS 6*. BB 5-96 (9-179 match) v WI (Derby) 2000. CC BB 1-46. LO HS 7* (NL). LO BB 3-29 v Durham (Derby) 2000 (NL). Represented England at Indoor Cricket.

DECEASED/RELEASED/RETIRED
(Having made a first-class County appearance in 2000)

CASSAR, M.E. – *see NORTHAMPTONSHIRE.*

LACEY, Simon James (Aldercar CS; Ripley Mill Hill SFC), b Nottingham 9 Mar 1975. 5'11". RHB, OB. Derbyshire 1997-2000. HS 55* v Hants (Derby) 2000. BB 4-84 v Hants (Derby) 2000. LO HS 40 v Middx (Lord's) 2000 (NL). LO BB 3-38 v Notts (Nottingham) 1999 (NL).

SAXELBY, Mark (Nottingham HS), b Worksop, Notts 4 Jan 1969; d Queen's Medical Centre, Nottingham 12 Oct 2000. 6'3". LHB, RM. Younger brother of K. (Notts 1978-90). Nottinghamshire 1989-93. Durham 1994-95. Derbyshire 2000 (1 match). 1000 runs (1): 1102 (1994). HS 181 Du v Derbys (Chesterfield) 1994. De HS 17 v Lancs (Derby) 2000. BB 3-41 Nt v Derbys (Derby) 1991. Award: BHC 1. LO HS 100* Nt v Durham (Chester-le-St) 1993 (SL). LO BB 4-29 Nt v Leics (Leicester) 1991 (SL).

SHAH, Kasir Zamir, b Jhelum, Pakistan 15 Jun 1978. LHB, LMF. Derbyshire 2000. HS 38* v Kent (Derby) 2000. BB 2-24 v Lancs (Derby) 2000 – on debut. LO HS 20 v Essex (Chelmsford) 2000 (NL). LO BB 2-36 v Middx (Derby) 1999 (NL).

DERBYSHIRE 2000

RESULTS SUMMARY

	Place	Won	Lost	Tied	Drew	No Result
County Championship (1st Division)	9th	2	6		8	
All First-Class Matches		2	7		9	
NatWest Trophy	4th Round					
Benson & Hedges Cup	4th in North Group					
National League (2nd Division)	9th	2	13			1

COUNTY CHAMPIONSHIP AVERAGES

BATTING AND FIELDING

Cap		M	I	NO	HS	Runs	Avge	100	50	Ct/St
1993	D.G.Cork	10	11	2	200*	452	50.22	1	2	7
–	S.P.Titchard	9	16	2	141*	517	36.92	1	3	–
2000	R.J.Bailey	12	17	2	118	551	36.73	1	4	3
2000	M.J.Di Venuto	16	25	2	92*	725	32.95	–	6	12
–	S.D.Stubbings	16	29	4	135*	767	30.68	1	3	4
2000	M.P.Dowman	15	26	3	140	699	30.39	2	3	9
–	L.D.Sutton	8	13	1	79	355	29.58	–	2	14/1
–	K.Z.Shah	3	5	2	38*	88	29.33	–	–	–
–	S.J.Lacey	9	15	3	55*	240	20.00	–	1	–
1992	K.M.Krikken	10	13	–	51	221	17.00	–	1	18/2
–	T.M.Smith	9	12	2	53*	148	14.80	–	1	3
–	M.E.Cassar	12	17	–	47	234	13.76	–	–	1
2000	T.A.Munton	16	22	7	52	191	12.73	–	1	7
1999	P.Aldred	11	14	1	38	149	11.46	–	–	4
1998	K.J.Dean	11	15	3	22	49	4.08	–	–	1
–	L.J.Wharton	5	8	4	6*	8	2.00	–	–	1

Also batted: J.P.Pyemont (3 matches) 4, 40, 20; M.Saxelby (1) 17, 6.

BOWLING

	O	M	R	W	Avge	Best	5wI	10wM
K.J.Dean	223	45	754	38	19.84	8-52	3	–
M.E.Cassar	174.5	43	599	26	23.03	6-76	1	–
D.G.Cork	246.5	63	641	22	29.13	6-41	1	–
T.A.Munton	439.3	122	1093	35	31.22	7-34	–	–
S.J.Lacey	182.5	40	512	14	36.57	4-84	–	–
P.Aldred	203.3	44	624	17	36.70	4-97	–	–

Also bowled: R.J.Bailey 41-7-104-2; M.J.Di Venuto 8.3-3-19-0; M.P.Dowman 17-2-53-2; J.P.Pyemont 4-0-15-0; K.Z.Shah 28-4-97-2; T.M.Smith 143.3-23-543-9; S.P.Titchard 2-0-4-0; L.J.Wharton 86-17-248-3.

The First-Class Averages (pp 118-132) give the records of Derbyshire players in all first-class county matches (Derbyshire's other opponents being the West Indians and Cambridge University), with the exception of D.G.Cork, whose full county figures are as above, and;
  J.P.Pyemont 4-5-0-40-79-15.80-0-0-0ct. 8-0-35-0.

DERBYSHIRE RECORDS

FIRST-CLASS CRICKET

Highest Total	For 645		v	Hampshire	Derby	1898
	V 662		by	Yorkshire	Chesterfield	1898
Lowest Total	For 16		v	Notts	Nottingham	1879
	V 23		by	Hampshire	Burton upon T	1958
Highest Innings	For 274	G.A.Davidson	v	Lancashire	Manchester	1896
	V 343*	P.A.Perrin	for	Essex	Chesterfield	1904

Highest Partnership for each Wicket

1st	322	H.Storer/J.Bowden	v	Essex	Derby	1929
2nd	417	K.J.Barnett/T.A.Tweats	v	Yorkshire	Derby	1997
3rd	316*	A.S.Rollins/K.J.Barnett	v	Leics	Leicester	1997
4th	328	P.Vaulkhard/D.Smith	v	Notts	Nottingham	1946
5th	302*†	J.E.Morris/D.G.Cork	v	Glos	Cheltenham	1993
6th	212	G.M.Lee/T.S.Worthington	v	Essex	Chesterfield	1932
7th	258	M.P.Dowman/D.G.Cork	v	Durham	Derby	2000
8th	198	K.M.Krikken/D.G.Cork	v	Lancashire	Manchester	1996
9th	283	A.Warren/J.Chapman	v	Warwicks	Blackwell	1910
10th	132	A.Hill/M.Jean-Jacques	v	Yorkshire	Sheffield	1986

† 346 runs were added for this wicket in two separate partnerships

Best Bowling	For 10- 40	W.Bestwick	v	Glamorgan	Cardiff	1921
(Innings)	V 10- 45	R.L.Johnson	for	Middlesex	Derby	1994
Best Bowling	For 17-103	W.Mycroft	v	Hampshire	Southampton	1876
(Match)	V 16-101	G.Giffen	for	Australians	Derby	1886

Most Runs – Season	2165	D.B.Carr	(av 48.11)	1959
Most Runs – Career	23854	K.J.Barnett	(av 41.12)	1979-98
Most 100s – Season	8	P.N.Kirsten		1982
Most 100s – Career	53	K.J.Barnett		1979-98
Most Wkts – Season	168	T.B.Mitchell	(av 19.55)	1935
Most Wkts – Career	1670	H.L.Jackson	(av 17.11)	1947-63

LIMITED-OVERS CRICKET

Highest Total	NWT	365-3	v	Cornwall	Derby	1986
	BHC	366-4	v	Combined U	Oxford	1991
	NL	292-9	v	Worcs	Knypersley	1985
Lowest Total	NWT	79	v	Surrey	The Oval	1967
	BHC	98	v	Worcs	Derby	1994
	NL	61	v	Hampshire	Portsmouth	1990
Highest Innings	NWT	173* M.J.Di Venuto	v	Derbys CB	Derby	2000
	BHC	142 D.M.Jones	v	Minor C	Derby	1996
	NL	141* C.J.Adams	v	Kent	Chesterfield	1992
Best Bowling	NWT	8-21 M.A.Holding	v	Sussex	Hove	1988
	BHC	6-33 E.J.Barlow	v	Glos	Bristol	1978
	NL	6- 7 M.Hendrick	v	Notts	Nottingham	1972

DURHAM

Formation of Present Club: 10 May 1882
Colours: Navy Blue, Yellow and Maroon
Badge: Coat of Arms of the County of Durham
County Champions: (0) 8th 1999, 8th (Div 1) 2000
NatWest Trophy/Gillette Cup Winners: (0); best –
quarter-finalist 1992
Benson and Hedges Cup Winners: (0); best – quarter-finalist
1998, 2000
National League (Div 1) Winners: (0); best – 7th (Div 2) 2000
Sunday League Winners: (0); best – 7th 1993
Match Awards: NWT 20; BHC 15

Chief Executive: D.Harker, County Ground, Riverside, Chester-le-Street, Co Durham
DH3 3QR ▲ Tel: 0191 387 1717 ▲ Fax: 0191 387 1616 ▲ Email:
marketing@durham-ccc.org.uk ▲ Web: www.durham-ccc.org.uk

Captain: J.J.B.Lewis. **Vice-Captain:** No appointment. **Overseas Player:** M.L.Love.
2001 Beneficiary: S.J.E.Brown. **Scorer:** B.Hunt. ‡ New registration
*Durham initially awarded caps immediately their players joined the staff but revised this
policy in 1998 and now cap players on merit, past 'awards' having been nullified.*

BRIDGE, Graeme David (Southmoor S, Sunderland), b Sunderland 4 Sep 1980. 5'8".
RHB, SLA. Debut 1999. No f-c appearances 2000. HS 6. BB 1-60. LO HS 15 Durham CB
v Glos (Chester-le-St) 1999 (NWT). LO BB 1-27.

‡BRINKLEY, James Edward (Marist C, Canberra; Trinity C, Perth), b Helensburgh,
Scotland 13 Mar 1974. 6'3". RHB, RFM. Worcestershire 1993-94 (Z tour) to 1995.
Matabeleland 1994-95. Scotland 1998 to date. Essex (one SL appearance) 1998. Hereford-
shire 2000. **LOI** (Scot): 5 (1999); HS 23 v A (Worcester) 1999 – on debut; BB 1-29. Tour:
Z 1993-94 (Wo). HS 43* Scot v Ire (Ayr) 2000. CC HS (Wo) 5. BB 6-35 Matabeleland v
Mashonaland CD (Harare South) 1994-95. CC BB 6-98 Wo v Surrey (Oval) 1994 on UK
debut. LO HS 30* Scot v Yorks (Linlithgow) 1998 (BHC). LO BB 3-55 Scot v NZ (Kuala
Lumpur) 1998-99.

BROWN, Simon John Emmerson (Boldon CS), b Cleadon 29 Jun 1969. 6'3". RHB, LFM.
Northamptonshire 1987-90. Durham debut 1992; captain 1996 (part); cap 1998; benefit
2001. **Tests:** 1 (1996); HS 10* and BB 1-60 v P (Lord's) 1996. HS 69 v Leics (Durham)
1994. 50 wkts (7); most – 79 (1996). BB 7-51 v Lancs (Chester-le-St) 2000. Awards: NWT
1; BHC 1. LO HS 18 v Derbys (Derby) 1996 (SL). LO BB 6-30 v Northants (Chester-le-St)
1997 (BHC).

COLLINGWOOD, Paul David (Blackfyne CS; Derwentside C), b Shotley Bridge 26 May
1976. 5'11". RHB, RMF. Debut 1996 v Northants (Chester-le-St) taking wicket of D.J.Capel
with his first ball before scoring 91 and 16; cap 1998. HS 111 v Derbys (Darlington) 2000.
BB 3-7 v Glam (Cardiff) 1999. Award: BHC 1. LO HS 86 v Northants (Northampton) 1999
(NL) and 86 v Surrey (Oval) 2000 (NL). LO BB 4-31 v Yorks (Chester-le-St) 2000 (BHC).

DALEY, James Arthur (Hetton CS), b Sunderland 24 Sep 1973. 5'10". RHB, RM. Debut
1992; cap 1999. MCC YC. HS 159* v Hants (Portsmouth) 1994. BB 1-12. LO HS 105 v
Surrey (Oval) 2000 (NL).

DAVIES, Anthony Mark (Northfield CS, Billingham), b Stockton-on-Tees 4 Oct 1980. 6'2".
RHB, RM. Development-contracted Durham Academy player awaiting f-c debut. LO HS 0.
LO BB 3-15 v Derbys (Darlington) 2000 (NL).

GOUGH, Michael Andrew (English Martyrs CS; Hartlepool SFC), b Hartlepool 18 Dec
1979. 6'5". Son of M.P. (Durham 1974-77). RHB, OB. Debut 1998. Tours (Eng A): NZ
1999-00; B 1999-00. HS 123 v CU (Cambridge) 1998. CC HS 67 v Kent (Stockton) 1999.
BB 4-49 v Notts (Chester-le-St) 1999. LO HS 36 v Hants (Chester-le-St) 2000 (NL).

HARMISON, Stephen James (Ashington HS), b Ashington, Northumb 23 Oct 1978. 6'4". RHB, RF. Debut 1996; cap 1999. Northumberland 1996. Tours (Eng A): SA 1998-99; Z 1998-99. HS 36 v Kent (Canterbury) 1998. 50 wkts (2); most – 64 (1999). BB 5-70 v Glos (Chester-le-St) 1998. LO HS 8* (BHC). LO BB 3-45 v Middx (Chester-le-St) 2000 (NL).

HATCH, Nicholas Guy (Barnard Castle S; Hull U), b Darlington 21 Apr 1979. 6'7". RHB, RMF. Joined staff 1999 on summer contract – awaiting f-c debut.

HUNTER, Ian David (Fyndoune Community C, Sacriston; Durham New C), b Durham City 11 Sep 1979. 6'1". RHB, RMF. Debut 2000. HS 63 v Leics (Chester-le-St) 2000 – on debut. BB 4-73 v Yorks (Chester-le-St) 2000. LO HS 14* v Hants (Chester-le-St) 2000 (NL). LO BB 4-29 v Essex (Ilford) 2000 (NL).

KILLEEN, Neil (Greencroft CS; Derwentside C; Teesside U), b Shotley Bridge 17 Oct 1975. 6'2". RHB, RFM. Debut 1995; cap 1999. HS 48 v Somerset (Chester-le-St) 1995. 50 wkts (1): 58 (1999). BB 7-85 v Leics (Leicester) 1999. LO HS 32 v Middx (Lord's) 1996 (SL). LO BB 6-31 v Derbys (Derby) 2000 (NL).

‡**LAW, Danny** Richard (Steyning GS), b Lambeth, London 15 Jul 1975. 6'5". RHB, RFM. Sussex 1993-96; cap 1996. Essex 1997-2000. HS 115 Sx v Young A (Hove) 1995. CC HS 97 Sx v Glos (Bristol) 1996. BB 5-33 Sx v Durham (Hove) 1996. Hat-trick (Ex) 1998. LO HS 82 Ex v Durham (Chelmsford) 1997 (SL). LO BB 3-26 Ex v Leics (Leicester) 1999 (NL).

LEWIS, Jonathan James Benjamin (King Edward VI S, Chelmsford; Roehampton IHE), b Isleworth, Middx 21 May 1970. 5'9½". RHB, RSM. Essex 1990-96; cap 1994; scored 116* on debut v Surrey (Oval). Durham debut 1997; cap 1998; captain 2001. 1000 runs (2); most – 1252 (1997). HS 210* v OU (Oxford) 1997 – on Du debut. CC HS 160* v Derbys (Chester-le-St) 1997. BB 1-73. Award: BHC 1. LO HS 102 v Glos (Cheltenham) 1997.

‡**LOVE, Martin** Lloyd (Toowoomba GS; Queensland U), b Mundubbera, Queensland, Australia 30 Mar 1974. 6'1". RHB, RM. Queensland 1992-93 to date. Tour: E 1995 (Young A). 1000 (0+1): 1097 (1994-95). HS 228 Q v NSW (Brisbane) 1990-00. BB 1-5 (Q). LO HS 75 Q v WA (Perth) 1997-98 (MW).

‡**PATTISON, Ian** (Seaham CS), b Seaham 5 May 1982. RHB, RM. Development-contracted Durham Academy player – awaiting f-c debut. LO HS 48* and LO BB 1-25 Durham CB v Leics CB (Gateshead) 2000 (NWT).

PENG GILLENDER, Nicky (*registered as 'Nicky PENG BUTTHAT'*) (Newcastle upon Tyne RGS), b Newcastle upon Tyne, Northumb 18 Sep 1982. 6'2". RHB, OB. Debut 2000. HS 98 v Surrey (Chester-le-St) 2000 – on debut. LO HS 36 v Notts (Chester-le-St) 2000 (NL).

PHILLIPS, Nicholas Charles (Wm Parker S, Hastings), b Pembury, Kent 10 May 1974. 5'10½". RHB, OB. Sussex 1993-97. Durham debut 1998. HS 53 Sx v Young A (Hove) 1995. CC HS 52 Sx v Lancs (Lytham) 1995. Du HS 42 v Glos (Cheltenham) 1999. BB 6-97 (12-268 match) v Glam (Cardiff) 1999. Award: NWT 1. LO HS 38* Sx v Essex (Chelmsford) 1996 (SL). LO BB 4-13 v Derbys (Chester-le-St) 1999 (NL).

PRATT, Andrew (Willington Parkside CS; Durham New C), b Helmington Row, Crook 4 Mar 1975. Elder brother of G.J. 6'0". LHB, WK. Debut 1997. MCC YC. HS 38 v Somerset (Taunton) 2000. LO HS 26 v Sussex (Hove) 1999 (NL).

PRATT, Gary Joseph (Willington Parkside CS), b Bishop Auckland 22 Dec 1981. Younger brother of A. 5'11". LHB. Debut 2000. Development-contracted Durham Academy player. HS 23 v Kent (Chester-le-St) 2000.

SPEAK, Nicholas Jason (Parrs Wood HS, Manchester), b Manchester 21 Nov 1966. 6'0". RHB, LB. Lancashire 1986-87 to 1996; cap 1992. Durham debut 1997; cap 1998; captain 2000. Tours (La): WI 1986-87, 1995-96. 1000 runs (3); most – 1892 (1992). HS 232 La v Leics (Leicester) 1992. Du HS 124* v CU (Cambridge) 1997. BB 1-0. Awards: BHC 2. LO HS 102* La v Yorks (Leeds) 1992 (SL).

SPEIGHT, Martin Peter (Hurstpierpoint C; Durham U), b Walsall, Staffs 24 Oct 1967. 5'9". RHB, WK. Sussex 1986-96; cap 1991. Wellington 1989-90 to 1992-93. Durham debut 1997; cap 1998. 1000 runs (3); most – 1375 (1990). HS 184 Sx v Notts (Eastbourne) 1993. Du HS 97* v Hants (Southampton) 1998 and 97* v Glam (Cardiff) 1999. BB 1-2. Awards: BHC 2. LO HS 126 Sx v Somerset (Taunton) 1993 (SL).

SYMINGTON, Marc Joseph (St Michaels, Billingham; Stockton SFC), b Newcastle upon Tyne, Northumb 10 Jan 1980. 5'8". RHB, RM. Durham debut 1998. HS 36 v Yorks (Chester-le-St) 2000. BB 3-55 v Derbys (Derby) 1998. LO HS 16 v Derbys (Darlington) 2000 (NL). LO BB 1-15 (NL).

RELEASED/RETIRED

(Having made a first-class County appearance in 2000)

ALI, Syed Muazam (Chigwell S), b Whipps Cross, Essex 23 Oct 1979. 5'7". RHB, LB. Durham 2000. MCC YC. HS 18 v Somerset (Chester-le-St) 2000. LO HS 36 v Hants (Basingstoke) 2000 (NL).

BETTS, M.M. – *see WARWICKSHIRE.*

KATICH, Simon Mathew (Trinity C, WA; U of WA), b Middle Swan, Midland, W Australia 21 Aug 1975. 6'0". LHB. SLC. W Australia 1996-97 to date. Durham 2000; cap 2000. **LOI** (A): 1 (2000-01); dnb v Z (Melbourne) 2000-01. Tour (A): SL 1999-00. 1000 (1+1): most – 1632 (1998-99). HS 154* WA v Tasmania (Hobart) 1998-99. Du HS 137* v Leics (Chester-le-St) 2000. BB 1-4 (WA). Du BB 1-10. LO HS 116 WA v S Aus (Perth) 1999-00 (MM). LO BB 1-16 (WA).

WOOD, J. – *see LANCASHIRE.*

SCORING OF EXTRAS 2001

The confusing variations of penalties involved in scoring no-balls and wides in our international and county cricket remain unchanged from last season:

COMPETITION	NO-BALL PENALTY	WIDE PENALTY
Test Matches Limited-Overs Internationals	} 1 + other runs scored	1 + other runs scored
County Championship Second XI Championship	} 2 + other runs scored	2 + other runs scored
Tourist Matches (First-Class) Tourist Matches (Limited-Overs) Benson & Hedges Cup The Trophy AON Trophy	} 2 + other runs scored	1 + other runs scored
National League	} 2 + other runs scored + a free hit next ball	1 + other runs scored

DURHAM 2000

RESULTS SUMMARY

	Place	Won	Lost	Tied	Drew	No Result
County Championship (1st Division)	**8th**	2	9		5	
All First-Class Matches		2	9		5	
NatWest Trophy	4th Round					
Benson & Hedges Cup	Quarter-Finalist					
National League (2nd Division)	**7th**	5	11			

COUNTY CHAMPIONSHIP AVERAGES

BATTING AND FIELDING

Cap		M	I	NO	HS	Runs	Avge	100	50	Ct/St
2000	S.M.Katich	16	28	3	137*	1089	43.56	3	5	21
1998	N.J.Speak	14	24	5	89*	552	29.05	–	4	3
1998	P.D.Collingwood	16	27	–	111	681	25.22	1	4	19
1998	J.J.B.Lewis	16	28	2	115	645	24.80	1	4	8
–	A.Pratt	7	10	1	38	191	21.22	–	–	7
1998	M.P.Speight	11	18	1	55	354	20.82	–	1	29
–	I.D.Hunter	3	4	–	63	83	20.75	–	1	–
–	N.Peng	8	14	–	98	231	16.50	–	1	1
–	M.A.Gough	7	12	–	33	176	14.66	–	–	3
1999	J.A.Daley	10	17	–	50	247	14.52	–	1	4
1998	M.M.Betts	11	18	4	55	192	13.71	–	1	7
1998	J.Wood	10	15	–	44	181	12.06	–	–	2
1999	N.Killeen	10	15	1	38*	144	10.28	–	–	1
1998	S.J.E.Brown	14	21	12	19	82	9.11	–	–	2
1999	S.J.Harmison	11	15	3	33*	104	8.66	–	–	2
–	N.C.Phillips	5	9	–	29	76	8.44	–	–	3
–	S.M.Ali	4	5	–	18	25	5.00	–	–	1

Also batted: G.J.Pratt (2 matches) 5, 11, 23 (1 ct); M.J.Symington (1) 8*, 36.

BOWLING

	O	M	R	W	Avge	Best	5wI	10wM
M.M.Betts	354	91	832	44	18.90	7-30	1	1
S.J.E.Brown	442.2	110	1208	56	21.57	7-51	4	–
J.Wood	319.4	66	918	33	27.81	5-36	3	–
S.J.Harmison	304.1	69	822	26	31.61	4-74	–	–
N.Killeen	288.3	84	697	22	31.68	3-14	–	–
P.D.Collingwood	214.2	61	474	12	39.50	2-21	–	–

Also bowled: S.M.Ali 3-0-9-0; J.A.Daley 7-0-20-0; M.A.Gough 76.1-14-280-5; I.D.Hunter 69.3-12-228-6; S.M.Katich 117.4-14-342-5; N.C.Phillips 156.5-36-415-7; M.J.Symington 17-2-67-1.

Durham played no first-class fixtures outside the County Championship in 2000.

DURHAM RECORDS

FIRST-CLASS CRICKET

Highest Total	For 625-6d		v	Derbyshire	Chesterfield	1994
	V 810-4d		by	Warwicks	Birmingham	1994
Lowest Total	For 67		v	Middlesex	Lord's	1996
	V 73		by	Oxford U	Oxford	1994
Highest Innings	For 210*	J.J.B.Lewis	v	Oxford U	Oxford	1997
	V 501*	B.C.Lara	for	Warwicks	Birmingham	1994

Highest Partnership for each Wicket

1st	334*	S.Hutton/M.A.Roseberry	v	Oxford U	Oxford	1996
2nd	206	W.Larkins/D.M.Jones	v	Glamorgan	Cardiff	1992
3rd	205	G.Fowler/S.Hutton	v	Yorkshire	Leeds	1993
4th	204	J.J.B.Lewis/J.Boiling	v	Derbyshire	Chester-le-St[2]	1997
5th	185	P.W.G.Parker/J.A.Daley	v	Warwicks	Darlington	1993
6th	193	D.C.Boon/P.D.Collingwood	v	Warwicks	Birmingham	1998
7th	119	N.Killeen/M.P.Speight	v	Glamorgan	Cardiff	1999
8th	134	A.C.Cummins/D.A.Graveney	v	Warwicks	Birmingham	1994
9th	127	D.G.C.Ligertwood/S.J.E.Brown	v	Surrey	Stockton	1996
10th	103	M.M.Betts/D.M.Cox	v	Sussex	Hove	1996

Best Bowling	For 9- 64	M.M.Betts	v	Northants	Northampton	1997
(Innings)	V 8- 22	D.Follett	for	Middlesex	Lord's	1996
Best Bowling	For 14-177	A.Walker	v	Essex	Chelmsford	1995
(Match)	V 12- 68	J.N.B.Bovill	for	Hampshire	Stockton	1995

Most Runs – Season	1536	W.Larkins	(av 37.46)		1992
Most Runs – Career	5670	J.E.Morris	(av 32.77)		1994-99
Most 100s – Season	4	D.M.Jones			1992
	4	W.Larkins			1992
	4	J.E.Morris			1994
Most 100s – Career	14	J.E.Morris			1994-99
Most Wkts – Season	77	S.J.E.Brown	(av 25.87)		1996
Most Wkts – Career	502	S.J.E.Brown	(av 28.41)		1992-00

LIMITED-OVERS CRICKET

Highest Total	NWT	326-4	v	Herefords	Chester-le-St[2]	1995
	BHC	287-5	v	Leics	Leicester	1996
	NL	281-2	v	Derbyshire	Durham	1993
Lowest Total	NWT	82	v	Worcs	Chester-le-St[1]	1968
	BHC	162	v	Derbyshire	Chesterfield	1996
	NL	99	v	Warwicks	Birmingham	1996
Highest Innings	NWT	125	S.Hutton	v	Herefords	Chester-le-St[2]	1995
	BHC	145	J.E.Morris	v	Leics	Leicester	1996
	NL	131*	W.Larkins	v	Hampshire	Portsmouth	1994
Best Bowling	NWT	7-32	S.P.Davis	v	Lancashire	Chester-le-St[1]	1983
	BHC	6-30	S.J.E.Brown	v	Northants	Chester-le-St[2]	1997
	NL	6-31	N.Killeen	v	Derbyshire	Derby	2000

[1] Chester-le-Street CC (Ropery Lane)   [2] Riverside Ground

ESSEX

Formation of Present Club: 14 January 1876
Colours: Blue, Gold and Red
Badge: Three Seaxes above Scroll bearing 'Essex'
County Champions: (6) 1979, 1983, 1984, 1986, 1991, 1992
NatWest Trophy/Gillette Cup Winners: (2) 1985, 1997
Benson and Hedges Cup Winners: (2) 1979, 1998
National League (Div 1) Winners: (0); best – 9th 1999
Sunday League Winners: (3) 1981, 1984, 1985
Match Awards: NWT 48; BHC 84

Chief Executive: D.E.East, County Ground, New Writtle Street, Chelmsford CM2 0PG ▲
Tel: 01245 252420 ▲ Fax: 01245 254030 ▲ Email: administration.essex@ecb.co.uk ▲
Web: www.essexcricket.org.uk

Club Captain: N.Hussain. **Team Captain:** R.C.Irani. **Vice-Captain:** No appointment.
Overseas Player: S.G.Law.
2001 Beneficiary: P.M.Such. **Scorer:** D.J.Norris. ‡ New registration

ANDERSON, Ricaldo Sherman Glenroy (Alperton HS; Barnet C; North West London C),
b Hammersmith, London 22 Sep 1976. 5'10". RHB, RFM. Debut 1999. HS 67* v Sussex
(Chelmsford) 2000. 50 wkts (1): 50 (1999). DD 6-34 (11-111 match) v Northants (Ilford)
2000. LO HS 10 v K (Canterbury) 1999 (NL) and 10 v Warwks (Colchester) 1999 (NL). LO
BB 3-32 v Glos (Bristol) 1999 (NL).

BISHOP, Justin Edward (Bury St Edmunds County Upper S), b Bury St Edmunds, Suffolk
4 Jan 1982. 6'0". LHB, LMF. Debut 1999. Awaiting CC debut. No f-c appearances 2000. HS
17 and BB 2-89 v SL A (Chelmsford) 1999. LO HS 16* v Hants (Colchester) 2000 (NL).
LO BB 1-17 (Suffolk – NWT).

COWAN, Ashley Preston (Framlingham C), b Hitchin, Herts 7 May 1975. 6'4". RHB, RFM.
Debut 1995; cap 1997. Cambridgeshire 1993. Tour: WI 1997-98. HS 94 v Leics (Leicester)
1998. 50 wkts (1): 52 (1997). BB 6-47 v Glam (Cardiff) 1999. Hat-trick 1996. Award: BHC
1. LO HS 40* v Notts (Chelmsford) 1998 (SL). LO BB 5-28 v Middx (Lord's) 1998 (BHC).

‡DAVIES, Michael Kenton (Loughborough GS, Loughborough U), b Ashby-de-la-Zouch,
Leics 17 Jul 1976. 6'0". RHB, SLA. Northamptonshire 1997-2000. British U 1998. Tours
(Eng A): NZ 1999-00; B 1999-00. HS 32* Nh v Durham (Northampton) 1999. BB 6-49 Nh
v Hants (Northampton) 1999. LO HS 4 (Nh – NL). LO BB 3-11 Brit U v Somerset
(Taunton) 1998 (BHC).

FOSTER, James Savin (Forest S, Snaresbrook; Durham U), b Whipps Cross 15 Apr 1980.
6'0". RHB, WK. British U 2000. Essex debut 2000. Tour: WI 2000-01 (Eng A). HS 52 v
Glam (Southend) 2000. LO HS 22* v Glam (Southend) 2000 (NL).

GRAYSON, Adrian Paul (Bedale CS), b Ripon, Yorks 31 Mar 1971. 6'1". RHB, SLA.
Yorkshire 1990-95. Essex debut/cap 1996. **LOI:** 1 (2000-01); HS 0 v SA (Nairobi) 2000-01.
Tour: SA 1991-92 (Y). 1000 runs (3); most – 1083 (1999). HS 159* v Hants (Ilford) 1999.
BB 4-16 v Middx (Southend) 1999. LO HS 82* v Worcs (Chelmsford) 1997 (NWT). LO
BB 4-25 Y v Glam (Cardiff) 1994 (SL).

HUSSAIN, Nasser (Forest S, Snaresbrook; Durham U), b Madras, India 28 Mar 1968. Son of J. (Madras 1966-67); brother of M. (Worcs 1985). 5'11". RHB, LB. Debut 1987; cap 1989; captain 1999; club captain 2000 to date; benefit 1999. YC 1989. **ECB contract 2000. Tests:** 59 (1989-90 to 2000-01, 20 as captain); HS 207 v A (Birmingham) 1997. **LOI:** 50 (1989-90 to 2000-01, 18 as captain); HS 95 v B (Nairobi) 2000-01. Tours (C=captain): A 1998-99; SA 1999-00C; WI 1989-90, 1991-92 (Eng A), 1993-94, 1997-98; NZ 1996-97; P 1990-91 (Eng A), 1995-96C (Eng A), 2000-01C; SL 1990-91 (Eng A), 2000-01C; Z 1996-97. 1000 runs (5); most – 1854 (1995). HS 207 (*see Tests*). Ex HS 197 v Surrey (Oval) 1990. BB 1-38. Awards: NWT 3; BHC 3. LO HS 118 Comb U v Somerset (Taunton) 1989 (BHC).

HYAM, Barry James (Havering SFC), b Romford 9 Sep 1975. RHB, WK. Debut 1993; cap 1999. MCC YC. HS 53 v Glos (Bristol) 2000. LO HS 37 v Leics (Leicester) 1999 (NL).

ILOTT, Mark Christopher (Francis Combe S, Garston), b Watford, Herts 27 Aug 1970. 6'0½". LHB, LFM. Debut 1988; cap 1993. Hertfordshire 1987-88 (at 16, the youngest to represent that county). **Tests:** 5 (1993 to 1995-96); HS 15 v A (Oval) 1993; BB 3-48 v SA (Durban) 1995-96. Tours: A 1992-93 (Eng A); SA 1993-94 (Eng A), 1995-96; I 1994-95 (Eng A – part); SL 1990-91 (Eng A). HS 60 Eng A v Warwks (Birmingham) 1995. Ex HS 58 v Worcs (Worcester) 1996. 50 wkts (6); most – 78 (1995). BB 9-19 (14-105 match; inc hat-trick – all lbw) v Northants (Luton) 1995. Hat-trick 1995. Awards: BHC 2. LO HS 56* v Sussex (Hove) 1995 (SL). LO BB 5-21 v Scot (Forfar) 1993 (BHC).

IRANI, Ronald Charles (Smithills CS, Bolton), b Leigh, Lancs 26 Oct 1971. 6'3". RHB, RMF. Lancashire 1990-93. Essex debut/cap 1994; captain 2000 to date. **Tests:** 3 (1996 to 1999); HS 41 v I (Lord's) 1996; BB 1-22. **LOI:** 10 (1996 to 1996-97); HS 45* v P (Birmingham) 1996; BB 1-23. Tours: NZ 1996-97, 1999-00 (Eng A); P 1995-96 (Eng A); Z 1996-97; B 1999-00 (Eng A). 1000 runs (5); most – 1196 (2000). HS 168* v Glam (Cardiff) 2000. 50 wkts (1): 51 (1999). BB 5-19 Eng A v Comb XI (Karachi) 1995. Ex BB 5-27 v Notts (Chelmsford) 1996. Awards: NWT 3; BHC 2. LO HS 124 v Durham (Chelmsford) 1996 (NWT). LO BB 5-33 v Hants (Southampton) 1999 (NL).

JEFFERSON, William Ingleby (Beeston Hall S, Norfolk; Oundle S; Durham U), b Derby 25 Oct 1979. Son of R.I. (Cambridge U and Surrey 1961-66). 6'8". RHB, RMF. British U 2000. Essex debut 2000. Scored 50 and 65 in first two 1-o innings. HS 41 Brit U v Z (Cambridge) 2000 – on debut. Ex HS 4. LO HS 65 v Glam (Southend) 2000.

LAW, Stuart Grant (Craigslea State HS), b Herston, Brisbane, Australia 18 Oct 1968. 6'2". RHB, RM/LB. Queensland 1988-89 to date; captain 1994-95 to 1996-97. Essex debut/cap 1996. *Wisden* 1997. **Tests** (A): 1 (1995-96); HS 54* v SL (Perth) 1995-96. **LOI** (A): 54 (1994-95 to 1998-99); HS 110 v Z (Hobart) 1994-95; BB 2-22 v P (Sydney) 1996-97. Tours: E 1995 (Young A); Z 1991-92 (Aus B). 1000 runs (4+1); most – 1833 (1999). HS 263 v Somerset (Chelmsford) 1999. BB 5-39 Q v Tasmania (Brisbane) 1995-96. Ex BB 3-27 v Worcs (Chelmsford) 1997. Awards: NWT 4; BHC 1. LO HS 163 Young A v Surrey (Oval) 1995. LO BB 5-26 Q v SL (Cairns) 1995-96.

McGARRY, Andrew Charles (King Edward VI GS, Chelmsford; Southend C), b Basildon 8 Nov 1981. 6'5". RHB, RFM. Debut 1999. HS 1. BB 3-29 v Worcs (Chelmsford) 2000. LO HS 0* (NL). LO BB 2-20 v Surrey (Colchester) 2000 (NL).

MASON, Timothy James (Denstone C), b Leicester 12 Apr 1975. 5'8". RHB, OB. Leicestershire 1994-99. Essex debut 2000. HS 52* v Glam (Cardiff) 2000. BB 3-32 Le v Worcs (Worcester) 1999. Ex BB 3-38 v Glos (Colchester) 2000. LO HS 36 Le v Yorks (Leicester) 1997 (NWT). LO BB 4-12 Le v Essex (Leicester) 1998 (SL).

NAPIER, Graham Richard (The Gilberd S, Colchester), b Colchester 6 Jan 1980. 5'9½". RHB, RM. Debut 1997. HS 35* v Notts (Worksop) 1997. BB 2-25 v CU (Cambridge) 1997. CC BB 2-59 v Sussex (Chelmsford) 1998. Award: NWT 1. LO HS 79 Essex CB v Lancs CB (Chelmsford) 2000 (NWT). LO BB 3-22 v Derbys (Derby) 1998 (SL).

PETERS, Stephen David (Coopers Coborn & Co S), b Harold Wood 10 Dec 1978. 5'9". RHB, occ LB. Debut 1996 scoring 110 and 12* v CU (Cambridge). HS 110 (as above). CC HS 81 v Glam (Cardiff) 1999. BB 1-19 (not CC). Award: NWT 1. LO HS 73* v Glam (Southend) 2000 (NL).

PETTINI, Mark Lewis, Brighton, Sussex 7 Aug 1983. RHB. Staff 2000 – awaiting f-c debut.

PHILLIPS, Timothy James (Felsted S), b Cambridge 13 Mar 1981. 6'1". LHB, SLA. Debut 1999. No f-c appearances 2000. HS 16 and BB 4-42 v SL A (Chelmsford) 1999 – on debut. CC HS 7. CC BB 1-66. LO HS 0 and BB 2-56 v Hants (Southend) 1999 (NL).

PRICHARD, Paul John (Brentwood HS), b Billericay 7 Jan 1965. 5'10". RHB, RSM. Debut 1984; cap 1986; captain 1995-98; benefit 1996. Tour (Eng A): A 1992-93. 1000 runs (8); most – 1485 (1992). HS 245 v Leics (Chelmsford) 1990. BB 1-28. Awards: NWT 1; DIIC 4. LO HS 114 v Somerset (Chelmsford) 1997 (BHC).

ROBINSON, Darren David John (Tabor HS, Braintree; Chelmsford CFE), b Braintree 2 Mar 1973. 5'10½". RHB, RMF. Debut 1993; cap 1997. HS 200 v NZ (Chelmsford) 1999. CC HS 148 v Worcs (Chelmsford) 1997. Awards: BHC 2. LO HS 137* v Sussex (Hove) 1998 (BHC). LO BB 1-7 (SL).

SHARIF, Zoheb Khalid, b Leytonstone 22 Feb 1983. LHB, LB. Staff 2000 – awaiting f-c debut.

SUCH, Peter Mark (Harry Carlton CS, Ex Leake, Notts), b Helensburgh, Dunbartonshire 12 Jun 1964. 5'11". RHB, OB. Nottinghamshire 1982-86. Leicestershire 1987-89. Essex debut 1990; cap 1991; benefit 2001. Tests: 11 (1993 to 1999); HS 14* and BB 6-67 v A (Manchester) 1993 – on debut. Tours: A 1992-93 (Eng A), 1998-99; SA 1993-94 (Eng A). HS 54 v Worcs (Chelmsford) 1993 and 54 v Notts (Chelmsford) 1996. 50 wkts (6); most – 82 (1996). BB 8-93 (11-160 match) v Hants (Colchester) 1995. LO HS 19* v Notts (Ilford) 1994 (SL). LO BB 5-29 v Glam (Cardiff) 1997 (SL).

RELEASED/RETIRED
(Having made a first-class County appearance in 2000)

FLANAGAN, Ian Nicholas (Colne Community S), b Colchester 5 Jun 1980. 6'0". LHB, OB. Essex 1997-2000. HS 61 v Warwks (Birmingham) 1998. BB 1-50 (not CC).

LAW, D.R. – *see DURHAM.*

THOMPSON, David James Jonathan (Ernest Bevin S, Wandsworth; Westminster C), b Wandsworth, London 11 Mar 1976. 6'3". RHB, RFM. Surrey 1994 (one match). Lancashire staff 1995-96. Essex 1999-2000. HS 22 Sy v OU (Oval) 1994 and 22 v Northants (Northampton) 1999. BB 4-46 v Somerset (Chelmsford) 1999. LO HS 1* and LO BB 2-34 v Worcs (Worcester) 1999 (NL).

ESSEX 2000

RESULTS SUMMARY

	Place	Won	Lost	Tied	Drew	No Result
County Championship (2nd Division)	2nd	5	2		9	
All First-Class Matches		5	2		11	
NatWest Trophy	4th Round					
Benson & Hedges Cup	5th in South Group					
National League (2nd Division)	5th	7	7			2

COUNTY CHAMPIONSHIP AVERAGES

BATTING AND FIELDING

Cap		M	I	NO	HS	Runs	Avge	100	50	Ct/St
1996	S.G.Law	15	26	2	189	1352	56.33	5	6	18
1994	R.C.Irani	16	28	7	168*	1175	55.95	1	9	2
–	J.S.Foster	3	4	2	52	109	54.50	–	1	4
–	R.S.G.Anderson	7	7	3	67*	151	37.75	–	1	–
1997	D.D.J.Robinson	11	17	2	93*	519	34.60	–	4	5
1996	A.P.Grayson	15	28	2	144	772	29.69	1	5	10
–	S.D.Peters	15	26	6	77*	576	28.80	–	4	12
1986	P.J.Prichard	16	30	3	96	747	27.66	–	5	10
1997	A.P.Cowan	13	18	5	67	236	18.15	–	1	4
–	D.R.Law	13	20	2	68*	275	15.27	–	1	6
1993	M.C.Ilott	10	13	4	25	119	13.22	–	–	4
–	T.J.Mason	8	11	2	52*	108	12.00	–	1	4
1999	B.J.Hyam	13	21	–	53	219	10.42	–	1	45/6
–	I.N.Flanagan	3	6	–	21	61	10.16	–	–	7
1989	N.Hussain	3	5	–	24	41	8.20	–	–	5
1991	P.M.Such	10	11	2	14	44	4.88	–	–	2

Also batted: W.I.Jefferson (1 match) 1,4 (1 ct); A.C.McGarry (3) 1, 0*, 0*; G.R.Napier (1) 21, 5 (4 ct).

BOWLING

	O	M	R	W	Avge	Best	5wI	10wM
R.C.Irani	407.3	120	1008	42	24.00	5- 79	1	–
A.P.Cowan	392.5	96	1164	47	24.76	5- 54	2	–
M.C.Ilott	283.2	85	724	26	27.84	3- 37	–	–
P.M.Such	398.4	92	999	34	29.38	7-167	3	1
R.S.G.Anderson	198.4	47	647	19	34.05	6- 34	2	1
D.R.Law	261.4	40	968	28	34.57	5- 78	1	–
A.P.Grayson	176	38	441	10	44.10	3- 55	–	–
T.J.Mason	217.3	51	626	14	44.71	3- 38	–	–

Also bowled: S.G.Law 1-0-11-0; A.C.McGarry 57-10-227-6; G.R.Napier 8-2-28-0; D.D.J.Robinson 0.3-0-8-0.

The First-Class Averages (pp 118-132) give the records of Essex players in all first-class county matches (Essex's other opponents being the Zimbabweans and Cambridge University), with the exception of J.S.Foster and W.I.Jefferson, whose full county figures are as above, and:

N.Hussain 4-6-0-33-74-12.33-0-0-5. Did not bowl.

ESSEX RECORDS

FIRST-CLASS CRICKET

Highest Total	For 761-6d		v	Leics	Chelmsford	1990
	V 803-4d		by	Kent	Brentwood	1934
Lowest Total	For 30		v	Yorkshire	Leyton	1901
	V 14		by	Surrey	Chelmsford	1983
Highest Innings	For 343*	P.A.Perrin	v	Derbyshire	Chesterfield	1904
	V 332	W.H.Ashdown	for	Kent	Brentwood	1934

Highest Partnership for each Wicket

1st	316	G.A.Gooch/P.J.Prichard	v	Kent	Chelmsford	1994
2nd	403	G.A.Gooch/P.J.Prichard	v	Leics	Chelmsford	1990
3rd	347*	M.E.Waugh/N.Hussain	v	Lancashire	Ilford	1992
4th	314	Salim Malik/N.Hussain	v	Surrey	The Oval	1991
5th	316	N.Hussain/M.A.Garnham	v	Leics	Leicester	1991
6th	206	J.W.H.T.Douglas/J.O'Connor	v	Glos	Cheltenham	1923
	206	B.R.Knight/R.A.G.Luckin	v	Middlesex	Brentwood	1962
7th	261	J.W.H.T.Douglas/J.Freeman	v	Lancashire	Leyton	1914
8th	263	J.W.H.Vigor/R.M.Taylor	v	Warwicks	Southend	1946
9th	251	J.W.H.T.Douglas/S.N.Hare	v	Derbyshire	Leyton	1921
10th	218	F.H.Vigar/T.P.B.Smith	v	Derbyshire	Chesterfield	1947

Best Bowling	For 10- 32	H.Pickett	v	Leics	Leyton	1895
(Innings)	V 10- 40	E.G.Dennett	for	Glos	Bristol	1906
Best Bowling	For 17-119	W.Mead	v	Hampshire	Southampton	1895
(Match)	V 17- 56	C.W.L.Parker	for	Glos	Gloucester	1925

Most Runs – Season	2559	G.A.Gooch	(av 67.34)		1984
Most Runs – Career	30701	G.A.Gooch	(av 51.77)		1973-97
Most 100s – Season	9	J.O'Connor			1929, 1934
	9	D.J.Insole			1955
Most 100s – Career	94	G.A.Gooch			1973-97
Most Wkts – Season	172	T.P.B.Smith	(av 27.13)		1947
Most Wkts – Career	1610	T.P.B.Smith	(av 26.68)		1929-51

LIMITED-OVERS CRICKET

Highest Total	NWT	386-5		v	Wiltshire	Chelmsford	1988
	BHC	388-7		v	Scotland	Chelmsford	1992
	NL	310-5		v	Glamorgan	Southend	1983
Lowest Total	NWT	57		v	Lancashire	Lord's	1996
	BHC	61		v	Lancashire	Chelmsford	1992
	NL	69		v	Derbyshire	Chesterfield	1974
Highest Innings	NWT	144	G.A.Gooch	v	Hampshire	Chelmsford	1990
	BHC	198*	G.A.Gooch	v	Sussex	Hove	1982
	NL	176	G.A.Gooch	v	Glamorgan	Southend	1983
Best Bowling	NWT	5- 8	J.K.Lever	v	Middlesex	Westcliff	1972
		5- 8	G.A.Gooch	v	Cheshire	Chester	1995
	BHC	5-13	J.K.Lever	v	Middlesex	Lord's	1985
	NL	8-26	K.D.Boyce	v	Lancashire	Manchester	1971

GLAMORGAN

Formation of Present Club: 6 July 1888
Colours: Blue and Gold
Badge: Gold Daffodil
County Champions: (3) 1948, 1969, 1997
NatWest Trophy/Gillette Cup Winners: (0); best – finalists 1977
Benson and Hedges Cup Winners: (0); best – finalists 2000
National League (Div 1) Winners: (0); best – 4th (Div 2) 1999
Sunday League Winners: (1) 1993
Match Awards: NWT 43; BHC 56

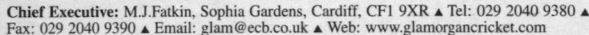

Chief Executive: M.J.Fatkin, Sophia Gardens, Cardiff, CF1 9XR ▲ Tel: 029 2040 9380 ▲ Fax: 029 2040 9390 ▲ Email: glam@ecb.co.uk ▲ Web: www.glamorgancricket.com

Captain: S.P.James. **Vice-Captain:** A.Dale. **Overseas Player:** J.P.Maher.
2001 Beneficiary: S.P.James. **Scorer:** B.T.Denning. ‡ New registration

CHERRY, Daniel David (Tonbridge S; U of Wales, Swansea), b Newport, Gwent 7 Feb 1980. 5'9". LHB, RM. Debut 1998. No appearances 2000. HS 11 v Derbys (Cardiff) 1998 – on debut.

COSKER, Dean Andrew (Millfield S), b Weymouth, Dorset 7 Jan 1978. 5'11". RHB, SLA. Debut 1996; cap 2000. Tours (Eng A): SA 1998-99, SL 1997-98; Z 1998-99, K 1997-98. HS 49 v Sussex (Cardiff) 1999. LO HS 27* v Somerset (Taunton) 1999 (NL). LO BB 3-18 v Warwks (Birmingham) 1998 (SL).

CROFT, Robert Damien Bale (St John Lloyd Catholic CS; W Glam IHE), b Morriston 25 May 1970. 5'10½". RHB, OB. Debut 1989; cap 1992; benefit 2000. **Tests:** 20 (1996 to 2000-01); HS 37* v SA (Manchester) 1998; BB 5-95 v NZ (Christchurch) 1996-97. **LOI:** 46 (1996 to 2000); HS 32 v SL (Perth) 1998-99; BB 3-51 v SA (Oval) 1998. Tours: A 1998-99; SA 1993-94 (Eng A), 1995-96 (Gm); WI 1991-92 (Eng A), 1997-98; NZ 1996-97; SL 2000-01; Z 1990-91 (Gm), 1994-95 (Gm), 1996-97. HS 143 v Somerset (Taunton) 1995. 50 wkts (5); most – 76 (1996). BB 8-66 (14-169 match) v Warwks (Swansea) 1992. Awards: NWT 1; BHC 2. LO HS 77 v Essex (Cardiff) 1998 (BHC). LO BB 6-20 v Worcs (Cardiff) 1994 (SL).

DALE, Adrian (Chepstow CS; Swansea U), b Germiston, SA 24 Oct 1968 (to UK at 6 mths). 5'11½". RHB, RM. Debut 1989; cap 1992. Tours (Gm): SA 1993-94 (Eng A), 1995-96; Z 1990-91, 1994-95. 1000 runs (3); most – 1472 (1993). HS 214* v Middx (Cardiff) 1993. BB 6-18 v Warwks (Cardiff) 1993. Awards: NWT 2; BHC 3. LO HS 110 v Lincs (Swansea) 1994 (NWT). LO BB 6-20 v Durham (Colwyn Bay) 1993 (SL).

DAVIES, Adam James (Bishop of Llandaff HS, Cardiff), b Cardiff 26 Oct 1980. Son of H.D. (Glamorgan 1955-60). 6'3½". RHB, RFM. Staff 1999 – awaiting f-c debut.

DAVIES, Andrew Philip (Dwr-y-Felin CS; Christ C, Brecon), b Neath 7 Nov 1976. 5'11". LHB, RMF. Debut 1995. Wales (MC). No appearances 2000. HS 34 v Essex (Chelmsford) 1998. BB 2-22 v Sussex (Hove) 1998. LO HS 18 v Essex (Chelmsford) 1998 (SL). LO BB 2-17 v Warwks (Birmingham) 1998 (SL).

EVANS, Alun Wyn (Fishguard SS; Neath Tertiary C), b Glanamman, Dyfed 20 Aug 1975. 5'8". RHB, RM. Debut 1996 v OU (Oxford), scoring 66* and 71*. MCC YC. HS 125 v CU (Cambridge) 1998. CC HS 88* v Durham (Cardiff) 1999. LO HS 108 v Derbys (Cardiff) 1999 (NL).

HARRISON, David Stuart (W Monmouth CS; Pontypool C), b Newport, Gwent 30 Jul 1981. Son of S.C. (Glamorgan 1971-76). 6'4". RHB, RM. Glamorgan debut 1999. HS 27 v Glos (Bristol) 2000. BB 1-15 (not CC). LO HS 5* (NL).

HUGHES, Jonathan (Coed-y-Land CS, Pontypridd), b Pontypridd 30 Jun 1981. 5'10". RHB, RM. Staff 1999 – awaiting f-c debut. MCC YC.

JAMES, Stephen Peter (Monmouth S; Swansea U; Hughes Hall, Cambridge), b Lydney, Glos 7 Sep 1967. 6'0". RHB. Debut 1985; cap 1992; captain 2001; benefit 2001. Cambridge U 1989-90; blue 1989-90. Mashonaland 1993-94 to date. **Tests:** 2 (1998); HS 36 v SL (Oval) 1998. Tours: SA 1995-96 (Gm); SL 1997-98; Z 1999-91 (Gm); K 1997-98. 1000 runs (8); most – 1775 (1997). HS 309* v Sussex (Colwyn Bay) 2000. Awards: NWT 3; BHC 2. LO HS 135 v Comb U (Cardiff) 1992 (BHC).

JONES, Simon Philip (Coedcae CS; Millfield S), b Swansea 25 Dec 1978. Son of I.J. (Glamorgan and England 1960-68). 6'3½". LHB, RF. Debut 1998. HS 19* v OU (Oxford) 1999. CC HS 13 v Sussex (Cardiff) 1999 and 13 v Sussex (Hove) 2000. BB 5-31 v Sussex (Cardiff) 1999. LO HS 12* and BB 1-39 v Notts (Nottingham) 1999 (NL).

MAYNARD, Matthew Peter (David Hughes S, Anglesey), b Oldham, Lancs 21 Mar 1966. 5'10½". RHB, RM. Debut 1985 v Yorks (Swansea), scoring 102 out of 117 in 87 min, reaching 100 with 3 sixes off successive balls; cap 1987; captain 1996-2000; benefit 1996. *Wisden* 1997. N Districts 1990-91 to 1991-92. Otago 1996-97 to 1997-98. YC 1988. **Tests:** 4 (1988 to 1993-94); HS 35 v WI (Kingston) 1993-94. LOI: 14 (1993-94 to 2000); HS 41 v P (Manchester) 1996. Tours: SA 1989-90 (Eng XI), 1995-96 (Gm – captain); WI 1993-94; Z 1994-95 (Gm). 1000 runs (11); most – 1803 (1991). HS 243 v Hants (Southampton) 1991. BB 3-21 v OU (Oxford) 1987. CC BB 1-3. Awards: NWT 4; BHC 9. LO HS 151* v Durham (Darlington) 1991 (NWT) and 151* v Middx (Lord's) 1996 (BHC). LO BB 1-13 (NL).

‡**MAHER, James** Patrick (St Augustine's C, Cairns), b Innisfail, Queensland, Australia 27 Feb 1974. LHB, RM. Queensland 1993-94 to date. **LOI**: 2 (1997-98); HS 13 v SA (Perth) 1997-98. HS 208* Q v S Aus (Adelaide) 1998-99. BB 3-11 Q v WA (Perth) 1995-96. LO HS 128 Q v ACT (Canberra) 1999-00.

NEWELL, Keith (Ifield Community C), b Crawley, Sussex 25 Mar 1972. Brother of M. (Sussex 1996-98). 6'0". RHB, RM. Sussex 1995-98. Matabeleland 1995-96. Glamorgan debut 1999. HS 135 Sx v WI (Hove) 1995. Gm HS 64 v OU (Oxford) 2000. CC HS 112 and BB 4-61 Sx v Kent (Horsham) 1997. Gm BB 2-15 v Worcs (Worcester) 1999. Award: NWT 1. LO HS 129 v Dorset (Bournemouth) 2000 (NWT). LO BB 5-33 Sx v Worcs (Worcester) 1998 (SL).

PARKIN, Owen Thomas (Bournemouth GS, Bath U), b Coventry, Warwks 24 Sep 1972. 6'2". RHB, RFM. Dorset 1992. Debut 1994. HS 24* v Essex (Chelmsford) 1998. BB 5-24 v Somerset (Cardiff) 1998. LO HS 8 (BHC). LO BB 5-28 v Sussex (Hove) 1996 (SL).

POWELL, Michael John (Crickhowell HS; Pontypool CFE), b Abergavenny 3 Feb 1977. 6'1". RHB, RSM. Debut 1997 scoring 200* v OU (Oxford); cap 2000. 1000 runs (1): 1060 (1999). HS 200* (*see above*). LO HS 164 v Notts (Colwyn Bay) 1999. BB 2-39 v OU (Oxford) 1999. CC BB – . LO HS 86 v Middx (Cardiff) 2000 (NL).

SHAW, Adrian David (Neath Tertiary C), b Neath 17 Feb 1972. 5'11". RHB, WK. Wales (MC) 1990-92. Debut 1994; cap 1999. HS 140 v OU (Oxford) 1999. CC HS 88* v Glos (Cardiff) 2000. LO HS 48 v Glos (Swansea) 1997 (SL).

THOMAS, Ian James (Bedwas CS; Bassaleg CS; UWIC), b Newport, Gwent 9 May 1979. 5'11". LHB, OB. Debut 2000. Wales MC. HS 82 v Essex (Southend) 2000 – on debut. LO HS 36 v Notts (Nottingham) 2000 (NL).

THOMAS, Stuart Darren (Graig CS, Llanelli; Neath Tertiary C), b Morriston 25 Jan 1975. 6'0". LHB, RFM. Debut v Derbys (Chesterfield) 1992, taking 5-80 when aged 17yr 217d; cap 1997. Tours (Eng A): SA 1995-96 (Gm), 1998-99; NZ 1999-00; Z 1994-95 (Gm), 1998-99. HS 78* v Glos (Abergavenny) 1995. 50 wkts (4); most – 71 (1998). BB 8-50 Eng A v Zim A (Harare) 1998-99 – record Eng A analysis. CC BB 5-24 v Sussex (Swansea) 1997. Award: BHC 1. LO HS 40 v Hants CB (Southampton) 1999 (NWT). LO BB 7-16 v Surrey (Swansea) 1998 (SL).

WALLACE, Mark Alexander (Crickhowell HS), b Abergavenny, Gwent 19 Nov 1981. 5'9". LHB, WK. Debut 1999. Eng U-19 to NZ 1998-99. HS 64* v Yorks (Leeds) 1999. LO HS 8* (NL).

WATKIN, Steven Llewellyn (Cymer Afan CS; S Glamorgan CHE), b Maesteg 15 Sep 1964. 6'3". RHB, RMF. Debut 1986; cap 1989. Benefit 1998. *Wisden* 1993. **Tests:** 3 (1991 to 1993); HS 13 and BB 4-65 v A (Oval) 1993. **LOI:** 4 (1993-94); HS 4; BB 4-49 v WI (Kingston) 1993-94. Tours: SA 1995-96 (Gm); WI 1991-92 (Eng A), 1993-94; P 1990-91 (Eng A); Z 1989-90 (Eng A), 1990-91 (Gm), 1994-95 (Gm). HS 51 v Glos (Cardiff) 2000. 50 wkts (9); most – 94 (1989). BB 8-59 v Warwks (Birmingham) 1988. Awards: NWT 1; BHC 2. LO HS 31* v Derbys (Checkley) 1991 (SL). LO BB 5-23 v Warwks (Birmingham) 1990 (SL).

WHARF, Alexander George (Buttershaw Upper S), b Bradford, Yorks 4 Jun 1975. 6'5". RHB, RMF. Yorkshire 1994-97. Nottinghamshire 1998-99. Glamorgan debut 2000, scoring 100* v OU (Oxford); cap 2000. HS 101* v Northants (Northampton) 2000. BB 5-68 v Sussex (Colwyn Bay) 2000. LO HS 38* Nt v Surrey (Nottingham) 1999 (NL). LO BB 4-29 Y v Notts (Leeds) 1996 (BHC).

RELEASED/RETIRED
(Having made a first-class County appearance in 2000)

ELLIOTT, Matthew Thomas Gray (Kyabram Secondary C; La Trobe U), b Chelsea, Victoria, Australia 28 Sep 1971. 6'3". LHB, LM/SLC. Victoria 1992-93 to date. Glamorgan 2000; cap 2000. *Wisden* 1997. **Tests** (A): 20 (1996-97 to 1998-99); HS 199 v E (Leeds) 1997. **LOI** (A): 1 (1997); HS 1 v E (Lord's) 1997. Tours (A): E 1995 (Young A), 1997; SA 1996-97; WI 1998-99. 1000 runs (2+4); most – 1233 (1995-96). HS 203 Vic v Tasmania (Melbourne) 1995-96. UK HS 199 (*see Tests*). Gm HS 177 v Sussex (Colwyn Bay) 2000. BB 1-3 (Vic). Award: NWT 1. LO HS 156 v Dorset (Bournemouth) 2000 (NWT).

LAW, Wayne Lincoln (Graig CS; Graig SFC, Llanelli), b Swansea 4 Sep 1978. 5'11". RHB, OB. Glamorgan 1997-2000. MCC YC. HS 131 v Lancs (Colwyn Bay) 1998. BB 2-29 v CU (Cambridge) 1998. CC BB 1-31. LO HS 24 v Leics (Pontypridd) 1998 (SL).

COUNTY CAPS AWARDED IN 2000

Derbyshire	R.J.Bailey, M.J.Di Venuto, M.P.Dowman, T.A.Munton
Durham	S.M.Katich
Essex	–
Glamorgan	D.A.Cosker, M.T.G.Elliott, M.J.Powell, A.G.Wharf
Gloucestershire	–
Hampshire	A.D.Mullally, S.K.Warne
Kent	R.Dravid, P.A.Nixon, M.J.Walker
Lancashire	G.Keedy
Leicestershire	J.M.Dakin, A.Kumble
Middlesex	D.C.Nash, O.A.Shah
Northamptonshire	J.F.Brown, D.M.Cousins
Nottinghamshire	U.Afzaal, D.J.Bicknell, A.J.Harris, D.J.Millns, J.E.Morris, P.R.Reiffel, R.D.Stemp
Somerset	–
Surrey	I.J.Ward
Sussex	R.S.C.Martin-Jenkins
Warwickshire	M.A.Wagh
Worcestershire	G.D.McGrath
Yorkshire	M.J.Hoggard, R.J.Sidebottom

GLAMORGAN 2000

RESULTS SUMMARY

	Place	Won	Lost	Tied	Drew	No Result
County Championship (2nd Division)	**3rd**	5	3		8	
All First-Class Matches		6	4		8	
NatWest Trophy	Quarter-Finalist					
Benson & Hedges Cup	Finalist					
National League (2nd Division)	**6th**	7	7	2		

COUNTY CHAMPIONSHIP AVERAGES

BATTING AND FIELDING

Cap		M	I	NO	HS	Runs	Avge	100	50	Ct/St
2000	M.T.G.Elliott	12	19	–	177	1042	54.84	4	4	17
–	I.J.Thomas	3	5	1	82	177	44.25	–	1	3
1999	A.D.Shaw	10	15	5	88*	423	42.30	–	3	24/3
1992	S.P.James	16	26	2	309*	1004	41.83	3	2	5
1992	A.Dale	16	25	3	81	805	36.59	–	5	7
1987	M.P.Maynard	14	21	1	119*	645	32.25	2	4	17/2
2000	M.J.Powell	16	25	–	128	784	31.36	2	4	9
–	O.T.Parkin	3	4	3	13*	30	30.00	–	–	–
–	M.A.Wallace	3	5	1	59*	116	29.00	–	1	10
1997	S.D.Thomas	16	19	6	52	318	24.46	–	1	2
1992	R.D.B.Croft	11	12	2	56	227	22.70	–	2	4
1989	S.L.Watkin	13	13	6	51	125	17.85	–	1	1
2000	A.G.Wharf	8	12	1	101*	184	16.72	1	–	4
–	K.Newell	11	18	1	38*	253	14.88	–	–	4
–	A.W.Evans	3	5	–	19	56	11.20	–	–	–
–	W.L.Law	6	8	1	27	74	10.57	–	–	3
2000	D.A.Cosker	10	13	3	14*	87	8.70	–	–	6

Also batted: D.S.Harrison (1 match) 0, 27; S.P.Jones (4) 0, 0, 13.

BOWLING

	O	M	R	W	Avge	Best	5wI	10wM
S.L.Watkin	389.4	108	1067	48	22.22	6- 26	2	–
A.G.Wharf	214.3	41	815	30	27.16	5- 68	1	–
A.Dale	236.4	54	629	23	27.34	5- 25	2	–
S.D.Thomas	468.4	88	1579	51	30.96	5- 43	2	–
D.A.Cosker	384.5	129	831	24	34.62	4- 82	–	–
R.D.B.Croft	454	109	1185	29	40.86	5-108	1	–

Also bowled: M.T.G.Elliott 20-5-43-0; D.S.Harrison 10-2-45-0; S.P.Jones 81-6-319-7; M.P.Maynard 15.3-5-32-0; K.Newell 40-17-82-3; O.T.Parkin 69-17-197-7.

The First-Class Averages (pp 118-132) give the records of Glamorgan players in all first-class county matches (Glamorgan's other opponents being the West Indians and Oxford University), with the exception of:
R.D.B.Croft 12-14-3-56-236-21.45-0-2-4ct. 510.1-136-1255-37-33.91-5/26-2-0.

GLAMORGAN RECORDS

FIRST-CLASS CRICKET

Highest Total	For 718-3d		v	Sussex	Colwyn Bay	2000
	V 712		by	Northants	Northampton	1998
Lowest Total	For 22		v	Lancashire	Liverpool	1924
	V 33		by	Leics	Ebbw Vale	1965
Highest Innings	For 309*	S.P.James	v	Sussex	Colwyn Bay	2000
	V 322*	M.B.Loye	for	Northants	Northampton	1998

Highest Partnership for each Wicket

1st	374	M.T.G.Elliott/S.P.James	v	Sussex	Colwyn Bay	2000
2nd	249	S.P.James/H.Morris	v	Oxford U	Oxford	1987
3rd	313	D.E.Davies/W.E.Jones	v	Essex	Brentwood	1948
4th	425*	A.Dale/I.V.A.Richards	v	Middlesex	Cardiff	1993
5th	264	M.Robinson/S.W.Montgomery	v	Hampshire	Bournemouth	1949
6th	230	W.E.Jones/B.L.Muncer	v	Worcs	Worcester	1953
7th	211	P.A.Cottey/O.D.Gibson	v	Leics	Swansea	1996
8th	202	D.Davies/J.J.Hills	v	Sussex	Eastbourne	1928
9th	203*	J.J.Hills/J.C.Clay	v	Worcs	Swansea	1929
10th	143	T.Davies/S.A.B.Daniels	v	Glos	Swansea	1982

Best Bowling	For	10- 51	J.Mercer	v	Worcs	Worcester	1936
(Innings)	V	10- 18	G.Geary	for	Leics	Pontypridd	1929
Best Bowling	For	17-212	J.C.Clay	v	Worcs	Swansea	1937
(Match)	V	16- 96	G.Geary	for	Leics	Pontypridd	1929

Most Runs – Season	2276	H.Morris	(av 55.51)		1990
Most Runs – Career	34056	A.Jones	(av 33.03)		1957-83
Most 100s – Season	10	H.Morris			1990
Most 100s – Career	52	A.Jones			1957-83
	52	H.Morris			1981-97
Most Wkts – Season	176	J.C.Clay	(av 17.34)		1937
Most Wkts – Career	2174	D.J.Shepherd	(av 20.95)		1950-72

LIMITED-OVERS CRICKET

Highest Total	NWT	373-7		v	Beds	Cardiff	1998
	BHC	318-3		v	Combined U	Cardiff	1995
	NL	294-4		v	Surrey	Pontypridd	1999
Lowest Total	NWT	76		v	Northants	Northampton	1968
	BHC	68		v	Lancashire	Manchester	1973
	NL	42		v	Derbyshire	Swansea	1979
Highest Innings	NWT	162*	I.V.A.Richards	v	Oxfordshire	Swansea	1993
	BHC	151*	M.P.Maynard	v	Middlesex	Lord's	1996
	NL	155*	J.H.Kallis	v	Surrey	Pontypridd	1999
Best Bowling	NWT	5-13	R.J.Shastri	v	Scotland	Edinburgh	1988
	BHC	6-20	S.D.Thomas	v	Combined U	Cardiff	1995
	NL	7-16	S.D.Thomas	v	Surrey	Swansea	1998

GLOUCESTERSHIRE

Formation of Present Club: 1871
Colours: Blue, Gold, Brown, Silver, Green and Red
Badge: Coat of Arms of the City and County of Bristol
County Champions (since 1890): (0); best – 2nd 1930, 1931, 1947, 1959, 1969, 1986
NatWest Trophy/Gillette Cup Winners: (3) 1973, 1999, 2000
Benson and Hedges Cup Winners: (3) 1977, 1999, 2000
National League (Div 1) Winners: (1) 2000
Sunday League Winners: (0); best – 2nd 1988
Match Awards: NWT 52; BHC 62

Chief Executive: tba, County Ground, Nevil Road, Bristol BS7 9EJ ▲ Tel: 0117 910 8000
▲ Fax: 0117 924 1193 ▲ Email: info@glosccc.co.uk ▲ Web: www.glosccc.co.uk

Captain: M.W.Alleyne. **Vice-Captain:** T.H.C.Hancock. **Overseas Player:** I.J.Harvey.
2001 Beneficiary: A.M.Smith. **Scorer:** K.T.Gerrish. ‡ New registration

ALLEYNE, Mark Wayne (Harrison C, Barbados; Cardinal Pole S, London E9; Haringey Cricket C), b Tottenham, London 23 May 1968. 5'10". RHB, RM. Debut 1986; cap 1990; captain 1997 to date; benefit 1999. *Wisden* 2000. **LOI:** 10 (1998-99 to 2000-01); HS 53 v SA (E London) 1999-00; BB 3-27 v SL (Sydney) 1998-99. Tours (Eng A) (C=captain): WI 2000-01C; NZ 1999-00C; SL 1986-87 (Gs), 1992-93 (Gs); B 1999-00C. 1000 runs (6); most – 1189 (1998). HS 256 v Northants (Northampton) 1990. 50 wkts (1): 54 (1996). BB 6-49 v Middx (Lord's) 2000. Awards: NWT 3; BHC 2. LO HS 134* v Leics (Bristol) 1992 (SL). LO BB 5-27 v Comb U (Bristol) 1988 (BHC).

AVERIS, James Maxwell Michael (Cathedral S, Bristol; Portsmouth U; St Cross C, Oxford), b Bristol 28 May 1974. 5'11". RHB, RMF. Oxford U 1997; blue 1997; rugby blue 1996-97. Gloucestershire debut 1997. HS 42 OU v Durham (Oxford) 1997 – on debut. Gs HS 25* v Glam (Cardiff) 2000. BB 5-98 OU v Hants (Oxford) 1997. Gs BB 3-42 v Derbys (Bristol) 1999. Award: BHC 1. LO HS 23* v Lancs (Manchester) 2000 (NL). LO BB 5-20 v Northants (Northampton) 2000 (NL.)

BALL, Martyn Charles John (King Edmund SS; Bath CFE), b Bristol 26 Apr 1970. 5'8". RHB, OB. Debut 1988; cap 1996. Tour (Gs): SL 1992-93. HS 71 v Notts (Bristol) 1993. BB 8-46 (14-169 match) v Somerset (Taunton) 1993. Award: NWT 1. LO HS 51 v SL A (Cheltenham) 1999. LO BB 5-42 v Yorks (Cheltenham) 1999 (NL).

BARNETT, Kim John (Leek HS), b Stoke-on-Trent, Staffs 17 Jul 1960. 6'1". RHB, RM/LB. Derbyshire 1979-98; cap 1982; captain 1983-95; benefit 1992. Boland 1982-83 to 1987-88. Staffordshire 1976. Gloucestershire debut/cap 1999. *Wisden* 1988. **Tests:** 4 (1988 to 1989); HS 80 v A (Leeds) 1989. **LOI:** 1 (1988); HS 84 v SL (Oval) 1988. Tours: SA 1989-90 (Eng XI); NZ 1979-80 (DHR); SL 1985-86 (Eng E). 1000 runs (15); most – 1734 (1984). HS 239* De v Leics (Leicester) 1988. Gs HS 125 v Kent (Canterbury) 1999. BB 6-28 De v Glam (Chesterfield) 1991. Gs BB 2-52 v Worcs (Cheltenham) 1999. Awards: NWT 6; BHC 11. LO HS 136 English XI v SA (Jo'burg) 1989-90. LO BB 6-24 De v Cumb (Kendal) 1984 (NWT).

BRESSINGTON, Alastair Nigel (Marling GS, Stroud; UWIC), b Downend, Bristol 28 Nov 1979. 6'1". LHB, RMF. Debut 2000. HS 2* and BB 4-36 v Glam (Bristol) 2000 – on debut. LO HS 54 Glos CB v Yorks CB (Cheltenham) 1999 (NWT). LO BB 3-21 Glos CB v Notts CB (Cheltenham) 2000 (NWT).

CAWDRON, Michael John (Cheltenham C), b Luton, Beds 7 Oct 1974. 6'2". LHB, RM. Staff 1994; debut 1999 – taking 15 wickets in first four innings. HS 42 and Gs BB 5-35 v Hants (Bristol) 1999 – on debut. BB 6-25 (10-74 match) FCC Select XI v NZ A (Milton Keynes) 2000. LO HS 50 v Essex (Cheltenham) 1995 (SL). LO BB 4-17 v Warwks (Cheltenham) 1999 (NL).

COTTERELL, Thomas Paul (King's S, Gloucester; U of Kent), b Hounslow, Middx 9 Mar 1977. 6'2". LHB, SLA. Debut 1999. HS 5*. BB 3-69 v Northants (Northampton) 1999 – on debut. LO HS – and LO BB 2-33 Glos CB v Notts CB (Cheltenham) 2000 (NWT).

CUNLIFFE, Robert John (Banbury S; Banbury TC), b Oxford 8 Nov 1973. 5'10". RHB, RM. Debut 1994. Oxfordshire 1991-94. HS 190* v OU (Bristol) 1995. CC HS 108 v Northants (Northampton) 1999. Awards: BHC 3. LO HS 137* v Surrey (Oval) 1996 (BHC).

FORDER, Damian Joseph (Marlwood S; City of Bristol C), b Bristol 11 Mar 1979. 6'3". RHB, LMF. Staff 2000 – awaiting f-c debut. LO HS (Glos CB) 3* (NWT).

GANNON, Benjamin Ward (Dragon S, Oxford; Abingdon S; Cheltenham & Gloucester CHE), b Oxford 5 Sep 1975. 6'3". RHB, RMF. Debut 1999. Herefordshire 1996. HS 28 v Essex (Colchester) 2000. BB 6-80 v Glam (Cardiff) 1999 – on debut. LO HS 2. LO BB 2-29 v SL A (Cheltenham) 1999.

HANCOCK, Timothy Harold Coulter (St Edward's S, Oxford; Henley C), b Reading, Berks 20 Apr 1972. 5'10". RHB, RM. Debut 1991; cap 1998. Oxfordshire 1990. Tour: SL 1992-93 (Gs). 1000 runs (1): 1227 (1998). HS 220* v Notts (Nottingham) 1998. BB 3-5 v Essex (Colchester) 1998. Awards: NWT 3. LO HS 110 v Northants (Bristol) 2000 (NWT). LO BB 6-58 v Scot (Bristol) 1997 (NWT).

HARDINGES, Mark Andrew (Malvern C; Bath U), b Gloucester 5 Feb 1978. 6'1". RHB, RMF. Debut 1999. British U 2000. HS 3 (Brit U). Gs HS 1. BB 2-16 v Essex (Bristol) 2000. LO HS 1 and LO BB 2-50 v SL A (Cheltenham) 1999.

HARVEY, Ian Joseph, b Wonthaggi, Victoria, Australia 10 Apr 1972. 5'10". RHB, RMF. Victoria 1993-94 to date. Gloucestershire debut/cap 1999. **LOI** (A): 27 (1997-98 to 2000-01); HS 47* v WI (Sydney) 2000-01; BB 4-28 v Z (Melbourne) 2000-01. Tour: NZ 1994-95 (Aus Academy). HS 136 Vic v S Aus (Melbourne) 1995-96. Gs HS 123 v Kent (Canterbury) 1999. BB 7-44 Vic v S Aus (Melbourne) 1996-97. Gs BB 6-19 (10-32 match) v Sussex (Hove) 2000. Awards: NWT 1; BHC 1. LO HS 88 v Sussex (Hove) 2000 (BHC). LO BB 5-19 v Northants (Bristol) 2000 (NL).

HEWSON, Dominic Robert (Cheltenham C), b Cheltenham 3 Oct 1974. 5'8". RHB, occ RM. Debut 1996. HS 87 v Hants (Southampton) 1996 (on CC debut). BB 1-7. LO HS 64 v SL A (Cheltenham) 1999.

LEWIS, Jonathan (Churchfields S, Swindon; Swindon C), b Aylesbury, Bucks 26 Aug 1975. 6'2". RHB, RMF. Debut 1995; cap 1998. Wiltshire 1993. Northamptonshire staff 1994. Tour: WI 2000-01 (Eng A). HS 62 v Worcs (Cheltenham) 1999. 50 wkts (3); most – 72 (2000). BB 8-95 v Z (Gloucester) 2000. CC BB 7-56 (10-92 match) v Notts (Bristol) 1999. Hat-trick 2000. Award: BHC 1. LO HS 33* v Somerset (Bristol) 1998 (BHC). LO BB 3-27 v Warwks (Birmingham) 1995 (SL) and 3-27 v Somerset (Taunton) 1996 (NWT).

POPE, Stephen Patrick (Cheltenham Bournside CS), b Cheltenham 25 Jan 1983. 5'8". RHB, WK. Awaiting f-c debut. LO HS (Glos CB) 0 (NWT).

RUSSELL, Robert Charles (*'Jack'*) (Archway CS), b Stroud 15 Aug 1963. 5'8½". LHB, WK, occ OB. Debut 1981 – youngest Glos wicket-keeper (17yr 307d), setting record for most match dismissals on f-c debut – 8 v SL (Bristol); cap 1985; benefit 1994; captain 1995. *Wisden* 1989. MBE 1996. **Tests:** 54 (1988 to 1997-98); HS 128* v A (Manchester) 1989; 11 ct v SA (Jo'burg) 1995-96 (Test record); 27 dis 1995-96 series v SA (Eng record). **LOI:** 40 (1987-88 to 1998-99); HS 50 v I (Nottingham) 1990. Tours: A 1990-91, 1992-93 (Eng A); SA 1995-96; WI 1989-90, 1993-94, 1997-98; NZ 1991-92, 1996-97; P 1987-88; SL 1986-87 (Gs). 1000 runs (1): 1049 (1997). HS 129* Eng XI v Boland (Paarl) 1995-96. Gs HS 124 v Notts (Nottingham) 1996. BB 1-4. Awards: NWT 1; BHC 3. LO HS 119* v Brit U (Bristol) 1998 (BHC).

SMITH, Andrew **Michael** (Queen Elizabeth GS, Wakefield; Exeter U), b Dewsbury, Yorks 1 Oct 1967. 5'9". RHB, LMF. Debut 1991; cap 1995; benefit 2001. **Tests:** 1 (1997); HS 4* v A (Leeds) 1997. Tour: P 1995-96 (Eng A – *part*). HS 61 v Yorks (Gloucester) 1998. 50 wkts (5); most – 83 (1997). BB 8-73 (10-118 match) v Middx (Lord's) 1996. Award: BHC 1. LO HS 26* v Kent (Moreton-in-M) 1996 (SL). LO BB 6-39 v Hants (Southampton) 1995 (BHC).

SNAPE, Jeremy Nicholas (Denstone C; Durham U), b Stoke-on-Trent, Staffs 27 Apr 1973. 5'8½". RHB, OB. Northamptonshire 1992-97. Combined U 1994. Gloucestershire debut/cap 1999. Tour: Z 1994-95 (Nh). HS 98* v Essex (Gloucester) 1999. BB 5-65 Nh v Durham (Northampton) 1995. Gs BB 3-67 v Glam (Cardiff) 1999. Awards: BHC 3. LO HS 78* Nh v SL (Northampton) 1998. LO BB 5-32 Nh v Leics (Northampton) 1997 (BHC).

‡**SUTCLIFF, Michael** David Richard (Wreake Community C), b Melton Mowbray, Leics 8 Nov 1975. LHB, WK. LO HS 5 (Le CB).

TAYLOR, Christopher Glyn (Colston's Collegiate S), b Southmead, Bristol 27 Sep 1976. 5'7". RHB, OB. Debut 2000, scoring 104 v Middx – first to score a hundred at Lord's in a Championship match on his first-class debut. HS 104 (*see Debut*). BB 3-126 v Northants (Cheltenham) 2000. LO HS 41 v Leics (Leicester) 2000 (NWT).

WILLIAMS, Richard Charles James (*'Reggie'*) (Millfield S), b Southmead, Bristol 8 Aug 1969. 5'8". LHB, WK. Debut 1990; cap 1996. Tour: SL 1992-93 (Gs). HS 90 v OU (Bristol) 1995. CC HS 55* v Derbys (Gloucester) 1991. LO HS 38 v Pak A (Cheltenham) 1997.

WINDOWS, Matthew Guy Newman (Clifton C; Durham U), b Bristol 5 Apr 1973. Son of A.R. (Glos and CU 1960-68). 5'7". RHB, LM. Debut 1992, cap 1998. Combined U 1995. Tours (Eng A): SA 1998-99; Z 1998-99. 1000 runs (2); most – 1173 (1998). HS 184 v Warwks (Cheltenham) 1996. BB 1-6 (Comb U). Gs BB – . LO HS 72 v Somerset (Bristol) 1994.

RELEASED/RETIRED
(Having made a first-class County appearance in 2000)

MOHAMMED, Imraan (St Patrick's HS, Karachi; Karachi GS; Joseph Chamberlain C, Birmingham; St Catharine's C, Cambridge); b Solihull, Warwicks 31 Dec 1976. Son of Sadiq (Karachi, PIA, Essex, Gloucestershire, Tasmania, United Bank and Pakistan 1959 60 to 1986); nephew of Hanif (Bahawalpur, Karachi, PIA and Pakistan 1951-52 to 1975-76), Mushtaq (Karachi, PIA, Northamptonshire and Pakistan 1956-57 and 1984), Raees (Karachi), Wazir (Karachi, Bahawalpur and Pakistan 1949-50 to 1963-64); cousin of Asif (PIA), Shahid (PIA) and Shoaib (Pakistan). 5'10". RHB, OB. Cambridge U 1997-99; blue 1998-99. British U 1999. (Pakistan) Customs 1999-00. Gloucestershire 2000. Cornwall 1998-99. HS 210* Customs v Gujranwala (Sialkot) 1999-00. UK HS 136 (and BB 1-13) CU v Yorks (Leeds) 1998. Gs HS 24 v Warwks (Cheltenham) 2000. Award: NWT 1. LO HS 53 Glos CB v Notts CB (Cheltenham) 2000 (NWT). LO BB 1-38 (Glos CB).

GLOUCESTERSHIRE 2000

RESULTS SUMMARY

	Place	Won	Lost	Tied	Drew	No Result
County Championship (2nd Division)	4th	6	4		6	
All First-Class Matches		6	5		7	
NatWest Trophy	Winners					
Benson & Hedges Cup	Winners					
National League (1st Division)	1st	9	6			1

COUNTY CHAMPIONSHIP AVERAGES

BATTING AND FIELDING

Cap		M	I	NO	HS	Runs	Avge	100	50	Ct/St
1999	K.J.Barnett	10	15	1	106	522	37.28	1	3	8
1998	M.G.N.Windows	16	26	3	107	790	34.34	1	6	3
1999	J.N.Snape	13	18	3	54*	491	32.73	–	3	7
1985	R.C.Russell	14	20	3	110*	522	30.70	1	2	39/3
1999	I.J.Harvey	10	14	1	79	395	30.38	–	4	10
–	C.G.Taylor	10	18	2	104	459	28.68	1	–	6
–	D.R.Hewson	10	19	1	67	410	22.77	–	3	5
1996	M.C.J.Ball	8	12	2	53	212	21.20	–	1	13
1990	M.W.Alleyne	15	23	–	126	409	17.78	1	–	13
–	I.Mohammed	3	4	–	24	67	16.75	–	–	1
1998	T.H.C.Hancock	13	21	1	46	322	16.10	–	–	7
–	M.J.Cawdron	3	5	–	27	74	14.80	–	–	1
1995	A.M.Smith	9	10	6	14	54	13.50	–	–	1
–	B.W.Gannon	7	8	3	28	64	12.80	–	–	3
–	R.J.Cunliffe	7	12	–	36	127	10.58	–	–	10
–	J.M.M.Averis	4	7	1	25*	60	10.00	–	–	1
1998	J.Lewis	14	20	2	38	156	8.66	–	–	3
–	T.P.Cotterell	6	8	3	5*	6	1.20	–	–	1

Also batted: A.N.Bressington (1 match) 2* (1 ct); M.A.Hardinges (1) 0, 0; R.C.J.Williams (cap 1996 – 2) 28*, 5, 43 (11 ct, 1 st).

BOWLING

	O	M	R	W	Avge	Best	5wI	10wM
I.J.Harvey	254.2	79	658	40	16.45	6-19	3	1
A.M.Smith	250.4	70	623	30	20.76	5-52	1	–
M.J.Cawdron	98.1	32	258	12	21.50	5-45	1	–
B.W.Gannon	164.5	31	589	27	21.81	5-58	1	–
J.Lewis	463.4	131	1285	56	22.94	6-47	3	–
M.W.Alleyne	241.5	68	665	24	27.70	6-49	1	–
M.C.J.Ball	218.1	55	540	15	36.00	3-31	–	–

Also bowled: J.M.M.Averis 118.2-29-388-5; A.N.Bressington 20-6-49-5; T.P.Cotterell 121-31-329-6; T.H.C.Hancock 65-20-143-8; M.A.Hardinges 23-9-36-3; J.N.Snape 77.3-20-202-6; C.G.Taylor 27.3-5-136-3.

The First-Class Averages (pp 118-132) give the records of Gloucestershire players in all first-class county matches (Gloucestershire's other opponents being the Zimbabweans and Oxford University), with the exception of M.A.Hardinges, whose full county figures are as above, and:

M.J.Cawdron 5-7-0-27-93.13.28-0-0-1ct. 159.1-49-460-15-30.66-6/45-1-0.
R.J.Cunliffe 8-13-0-74-201-15.46-0-1-10ct. Did not bowl.
J.Lewis 16-22-2-38-160-8.00-0-0-3ct. 526-152-1447-69-20.97-8/95-4-0.
J.N.Snape 14-19-3-69-560-35.00-0-4-8ct. 106.3-40-220-10-22.00-3/70.
C.G.Taylor 11-20-2-104-476-26.44-1-0-7ct. 27.3-5-136-3-45.33-3/136.
M.G.N.Windows 18-29-3-166-1028-39.53-2-6-4ct. Did not bowl.

GLOUCESTERSHIRE RECORDS

FIRST-CLASS CRICKET

Highest Total	For	653-6d	v	Glamorgan	Bristol	1928
	V	774-7d	by	Australians	Bristol	1948
Lowest Total	For	17	v	Australians	Cheltenham	1896
	V	12	by	Northants	Gloucester	1907
Highest Innings	For	318 *	W.G.Grace	v	Yorkshire	Cheltenham	1876
	V	296	A.O.Jones	for	Notts	Nottingham	1903

Highest Partnership for each Wicket

1st	395	D.M.Young/R.B.Nicholls	v	Oxford U	Oxford	1962
2nd	256	C.T.M.Pugh/T.W.Graveney	v	Derbyshire	Chesterfield	1960
3rd	336	W.R.Hammond/B.H.Lyon	v	Leics	Leicester	1933
4th	321	W.R.Hammond/W.L.Neale	v	Leics	Gloucester	1937
5th	261	W.G.Grace/W.O.Moberley	v	Yorkshire	Cheltenham	1876
6th	320	G.L.Jessop/J.H.Board	v	Sussex	Hove	1903
7th	248	W.G.Grace/E.L.Thomas	v	Sussex	Hove	1896
8th	239	W.R.Hammond/A.E.Wilson	v	Lancashire	Bristol	1938
9th	193	W.G.Grace/S.A.P.Kitcat	v	Sussex	Bristol	1896
10th	131	W.R.Gouldsworthy/J.G.Bessant	v	Somerset	Bristol	1923

Best Bowling	For	10-40	E.G.Dennett	v	Essex	Bristol	1906
(Innings)	V	10-66	A.A.Mailey	for	Australians	Cheltenham	1921
		10-66	K.Smales	for	Notts	Stroud	1956
Best Bowling	For	17-56	C.W.L.Parker	v	Essex	Gloucester	1925
(Match)	V	15-87	A.J.Conway	for	Worcs	Moreton-in-M	1914

Most Runs – Season	2860	W.R.Hammond	(av 69.75)		1933
Most Runs – Career	33664	W.R.Hammond	(av 57.05)		1920-51
Most 100s – Season	13	W.R.Hammond			1938
Most 100s – Career	113	W.R.Hammond			1920-51
Most Wkts – Season	222	T.W.J.Goddard	(av 16.80)		1937
	222	T.W.J.Goddard	(av 16.37)		1947
Most Wkts – Career	3170	C.W.L.Parker	(av 19.43)		1903-35

LIMITED-OVERS CRICKET

Highest Total	NWT	351-2		v	Scotland	Bristol	1997
	BHC	308-3		v	Ireland	Dublin	1996
	NL	284-4		v	Leics	Cheltenham	1996
Lowest Total	NWT	82		v	Notts	Bristol	1987
	BHC	62		v	Hampshire	Bristol	1975
	NL	49		v	Middlesex	Bristol	1978
Highest Innings	NWT	177	A.J.Wright	v	Scotland	Bristol	1997
	BHC	154*	M.J.Procter	v	Somerset	Taunton	1972
	NL	146*	S.Young	v	Yorkshire	Leeds	1997
Best Bowling	NWT	6-21	C.A.Walsh	v	Kent	Bristol	1990
		6-21	C.A.Walsh	v	Cheshire	Bristol	1992
	BHC	6-13	M.J.Procter	v	Hampshire	Southampton	1977
	NL	6-52	J.N.Shepherd	v	Kent	Bristol	1983

HAMPSHIRE

Formation of Present Club: 12 August 1863
Colours: Blue, Gold and White
Badge: Tudor Rose and Crown
County Champions: (2) 1961, 1973
NatWest Trophy/Gillette Cup Winners: (1) 1991
Benson and Hedges Cup Winners: (2) 1988, 1992
National League (Div 1) Winners: (0); best – 8th 1999
Sunday League Winners: (3) 1975, 1978, 1986
Match Awards: NWT 61; BHC 65

Chief Executive: A.F.Baker, The Hampshire Rose Bowl, Botley Road, West End, Southampton SO30 3XH ▲ Tel: 023 8047 2002 ▲ Fax: 023 8047 2122 ▲ Email: enquiries.hants@ecb.co.uk ▲ Web: www.hampshire.cricket.org

Captain: R.A.Smith. **Vice-Captain:** W.S.Kendall. **Overseas Player:** N.C.Johnson.
2001 Beneficiary: J.P.Stephenson. **Scorer:** V.H Isaacs. ‡ New registration

ADAMS, James Henry Kenneth (Sherborne S; University C, London), b Winchester 23 Sep 1980. 6'2". LHB, LM. Staff 2000 – awaiting f-c debut. Dorset 1998.

AYMES, Adrian Nigel (Bellemoor SM, Southampton), b Southampton 4 Jun 1964. 6'0". RHB, WK. Debut 1987; cap 1991; benefit 2000. HS 133 v Leics (Leicester) 1998. BB 2-135 v Northants (Southampton) 1998. Awards: NWT 1; BHC 1. LO HS 73* v Middx (Lord's) 1998 (NWT).

BRUNNSCHWEILER, Iain (King Edward VI S, Southampton), b Southampton 10 Dec 1979. 6'0". RHB, WK. Debut 2000 – awaiting CC debut. HS 19 v NZ A (Portsmouth) 2000 – on debut.

‡FRANCIS, John Daniel (King Edward VI S, Southampton), b Bromley, Kent 13 Nov 1980. Younger brother of S.R.G. LHB, SLA. Joined staff 2001 – awaiting f-c debut.

FRANCIS, Simon Richard George (Yardley Court, Tonbridge; King Edward VI S, Southampton; Durham U), b Bromley, Kent 15 Aug 1978. Elder brother of J.D. 6'2". RHB, RMF. Debut 1997. British U 1998-99. HS 30* and BB 4-95 v Surrey (Oval) 2000. LO HS 8* (twice – NL). LO BB 2-28 v Kent (Canterbury) 1999 (NL).

HAMBLIN, James Rupert Christopher (Charterhouse S; Bristol U), b Pembury, Kent 16 Aug 1978. Son of C.B. (Oxford U 1971-73). 6'0". RHB, RMF. Staff 1998 – awaiting f-c debut.

‡JOHNSON, Neil Clarkson (Howick HS, Natal; Port Elizabeth U), b Salisbury, Rhodesia 24 Jan 1970. 6'2". LHB, RFM. EP B 1989-90 to 1991-92. Natal 1992-93 to 1997-98. Leicestershire 1997; cap 1997. Matabeleland 1999-00. WP 2000-01. **Tests** (Z): 13 (1998-99 to 2000); HS 107 v P (Peshawar) 1998-99; BB 4-77 v WI (Kingston) 1999-00. **LOI** 48 (1998-99 to 2000); HS 132* v A (Lord's) 1999; BB 4-42 v K (Taunton) 1999. Tours (Z): E 2000; SA 1999-00; WI 1999-00; Z 1994-95 (SA A). HS 150 Leics v Lancs (Leicester) 1997. BB 5-79 Natal v Boland (Stellenbosch) 1993-94. LO HS 146* Natal v GW (Kimberley) 1996-97 (SBC). LO BB 4-19 Natal v K (Durban) 1996-97 (SBC).

KENDALL, William Salwey (Bradfield C; Keble C, Oxford), b Wimbledon, Surrey 18 Dec 1973. 5'10". RHB, RM. Oxford U 1994-96; blue 1995-96. Hampshire debut 1996; cap 1999. 1000 runs (1): most – 1186 (1999). HS 201 v Sussex (Southampton) 1995. BB 3-37 OU v Derbys (Oxford) 1995. H BB 2-46 v Notts (Southampton) 1996. LO HS 85* v Glam (Southampton) 2000 (NL).

KENWAY, Derek (St George's S, Southampton; Barton Peveril C, Eastleigh), b Fareham 12 Jun 1978. 5'11". RHB, RM, occ WK. Debut 1997. 1000 runs (1): 1055 (1999). HS 136 v Derbys (Derby) 2000. BB 1-5. LO HS 90 v Derbys (Southampton) 2000 (NL).

LANEY, Jason Scott (Pewsey Vale SS; St John's SFC, Marlborough; Leeds U), b Winchester 27 Apr 1973. 5'10". RHB, OB. Debut 1995; cap 1996. Matabeleland 1995-96. 1000 runs (1): 1163 (1996). HS 112 v OU (Oxford) 1996. CC HS 105 v Kent (Canterbury) 1996. BB 1-24. Award: NWT 1. LO HS 153 v Norfolk (Southampton) 1996 (NWT).

MASCARENHAS, Adrian Dimitri (Trinity C, Perth, Australia), b Hammersmith, London 30 Oct 1977. Resident in Australia 1979-96. RHB, RMF. Debut 1996, taking 6-88 v Glamorgan (Southampton); took 16 wickets in first two CC matches; cap 1998. Dorset 1996. HS 100 v Derbys (Derby) 2000. BB 6-88 (*see Debut*). Awards: NWT 3. LO HS 79 v Worcs (Southampton) 1999 (NL). LO BB 4-25 v Middx (Lord's) 2000 (NWT).

MORRIS, Alexander Corfield (Holgate S; Barnsley C), b Barnsley, Yorks 4 Oct 1976. Elder brother of Z.C. 6'3". LHB, RMF. Yorkshire 1995-97. Yorks 2nd XI debut when 16yr 332d. Hampshire debut 1998. Tour: Z 1995-96 (Y). HS 60 Y v Lancs (Manchester) 1996 (not CC) and 60 v Leics (Southampton) 2000. 50 wkts (1): 50 (1998). BB 5-52 (10-111 match) v Yorkshire (Southampton) 1999. LO HS 48* Y v Durham (Chester-le-St) 1996 (SL). LO BB 5-32 Y v Young A (Leeds) 1995.

MORRIS, Zachary Clegg (Holgate S, Barnsley), b Barnsley, Yorks 4 Sep 1978. Younger brother of A.C. 6'1". RHB, SLA. Debut 1998. No f-c appearances 2000. HS 10 v Glos (Southampton) 1998.

MULLALLY, Alan David (Cannington HS, Perth, Australia; Wembley TC), b Southend-on-Sea, Essex 12 Jul 1969. 6'5". RHB, LFM. W Australia 1987-88 to 1989-90. Victoria 1990 91. Hampshire 1988 (1 match), 2000 to date, cap 2000. Leicestershire 1990-99; cap 1993. **Tests:** 18 (1996 to 1999-00); HS 24 v P (Oval) 1996; BB 5-105 v A (Brisbane) 1998-99. **LOI:** 41 (1996 to 2000); HS 20 v Z (Harare) 1996-97; BB 4-18 v A (Brisbane) 1998-99. Tours: A 1998-99; SA 1999-00; NZ 1996-97; Z 1996-97. HS 75 Le v Middx (Leicester) 1996. H HS 12 v Surrey (Southampton) 2000. 50 wkts (4); most – 70 (1996). BB 9-93 (14-188 match) v Derbys (Derby) 2000. Award: NWT 1. LO HS 38 Le v Kent (Leicester) 1994 (SL). LO BB 6-38 Le v NZ (Leicester) 1990.

PRITTIPAUL, Lawrence Roland (St John's C, Southsea; Portsmouth C), b Portsmouth 19 Oct 1979. Cousin of S.Chanderpaul (Guyana and West Indies 1991-92 to date). 6'1". RHB, RM. Debut 2000. HS 152 v Derbys (Southampton) 2000. LO HS 61 v Notts (Southampton) 2000 (NL). LO BB 2-53 Hants CB v Suffolk (Bury St Edmunds) 1999 (NWT).

SEXTON, Andrew John (Corfe Hills S; Poole C), b Southampton 23 Jul 1979. 5'11". LHB, OB. Debut 2000. Dorset 1997-2000. HS 36 v Durham (Basingstoke) 2000 – on debut. LO HS 34 Dorset v Norfolk (Bournemouth) 2000 (NWT).

‡**SHAH, Irfan** Hussain (City of Westminster S), b Barking, Essex 20 Jun 1979. RHB, OB. MCC YC. Joined staff 2001 – awaiting f-c debut.

SMITH, Robin Arnold (Northlands BHS), b Durban, SA 13 Sep 1963. Brother of C.L. (Natal, Glam, Hants and England 1977-78 to 1992) and grandson of Dr V.L.Shearer (Natal). 5'11". RHB, LB. Natal 1980-81 to 1984-85. Hampshire debut 1982; cap 1985; benefit 1996; captain 1998 to date. *Wisden* 1989. **Tests:** 62 (1988 to 1995-96); HS 175 v WI (St John's) 1993-94. **LOI:** 71 (1988 to 1995-96); HS 167* v A (Birmingham) 1993 – Eng record. Tours. A 1990-91; SA 1995-96; WI 1993-94; 1993-94; NZ 1991-92; I/SL 1992-93. 1000 runs (11); most – 1577 (1989). HS 209* v Essex (Southend) 1987. BB 2-11 v Surrey (Southampton) 1985. Awards: NWT 9; BHC 5. LO HS 167* (*see LOI*). LO BB 2-13 v Berks (Southampton) 1985 (NWT).

STEPHENSON, John Patrick (Felsted S; Durham U), b Stebbing, Essex 14 Mar 1965. 6'1". RHB, RM. Essex 1985-94 (cap 1989). Hampshire debut/cap 1995; captain 1996-97; benefit 2001. Boland 1988-89. **Tests:** 1 (1989); HS 25 v A (Oval) 1989. Tours: WI 1991-92 (Eng A); Z 1989-90 (Eng A). 1000 runs (5); most – 1887 (1990). HS 202* Ex v Somerset (Bath) 1990. H HS 140 v OU (Oxford) 1997. BB 7-51 v Middx (Lord's) 1995. Awards: NWT 1; BHC 5. LO HS 142 Ex v Warwks (Birmingham) 1991 (BHC). LO BB 6-33 v Worcs (Southampton) 1997 (SL).

TREMLETT, Christopher Timothy (Thornden S, Chandler's Ford; Taunton's C; Southampton), b Southampton 2 Sep 1981. Son of T.M. (Hampshire 1976-91); grandson of M.F. (Somerset, CD and England 1947-60). 6'7". RHB, RMF. Debut 2000 – awaiting CC debut. HS 17 and BB 4-16 v NZ A (Portsmouth) 2000 – on debut. LO HS 30* v Glam (Southampton) 2000 (NL). LO BB 2-35 Hants CB v Hunts (Cove) 2000 (NWT).

UDAL, Shaun David (Cove CS), b Cove, Farnborough 18 Mar 1969. Grandson of G.F.U. (Middx 1932 and Leics 1946); great-great-grandson of J.S. (MCC 1871-75). 6'2". RHB, OB. Debut 1989; cap 1992. **LOI:** 10 (1994 to 1995); HS 11* v Z (Brosbane) 1994-95; BB 2-37 v A (Sydney) 1994-95. Tours: A 1994-95; P 1995-96 (Eng A). HS 117* v Warwks (Southampton) 1997. 50 wkts (5); most – 74 (1993). BB 8-50 v Sussex (Southampton) 1992. Awards: NWT 1; BHC 1. LO HS 78 v Surrey (Guildford) 1997 (SL). LO BB 5-43 v Surrey (Oval) 1998 (SL).

VAN DER GUCHT, Charles Graham (Radley C; Durham U), b Wimbledon, Surrey 14 Jan 1980. Grandson of P.I. (Gloucestershire 1932-33). 6'0". LHB, LM/SLA. Debut 2000 – awaiting CC debut. Award: NWT 1. HS 0* and BB 3-75 v Z (Southampton) 2000 – on debut. LO HS 3 and LO BB 3-35 Hants CB v Glam (Southampton) 1999 (NWT).

WHITE, Giles William (Millfield S; Loughborough U), b Barnstaple, Devon 23 Mar 1972. 6'0". RHB, LB. Somerset 1991 (one match). Combined U 1994. Hampshire debut 1994; cap 1998. Devon 1988-94. 1000 runs (1): 1211 (1998). HS 156 v SL (Southampton) 1998. CC HS 145 v Yorks (Portsmouth) 1997. BB 3-23 v Notts (Nottingham) 1999. LO HS 76 v Glam (Southampton) 1998 (SL). LO BB 1-45 (Devon – NWT).

RELEASED/RETIRED
(Having made a first-class County appearance in 2000)

HARTLEY, Peter John (Greenhead GS; Bradford C), b Keighley, Yorks 18 Apr 1960. 6'0". RHB, RMF. Warwickshire 1982. Yorkshire 1985-97; cap 1987; benefit 1996. Hampshire 1998-2000; cap 1998. Tours (Y): SA 1991-92; WI 1986-87; Z 1995-96. HS 127* Y v Lancs (Manchester) 1988. H HS 58 v Middx (Lord's) 1999. 50 wkts (7); most – 81 (1995). BB 9-41 (inc hat-trick, 4 wkts in 5 balls and 5 in 9; 11-68 match) Y v Derbys (Chesterfield) 1995. H BB 8-65 (11-117 match) v Yorks (Basingstoke) 1999. Hat-trick 1995. Awards: NWT 1; BHC 2. LO HS 83 Y v Ire (Leeds) 1997 (NWT). LO BB 5-20 v Sussex (Hove) 2000 (BHC).

RENSHAW, Simon John (Birkenhead S; Leeds U), b Bebington, Cheshire 6 Mar 1974. 6'3". RHB, RMF. Combined U 1995. Hampshire 1996-2000. Cheshire 1994-95. HS 56 v Surrey (Guildford) 1997. BB 5-110 v Derbys (Chesterfield) 1997. LO HS 27* v Lancs (Manchester) 1999 (NL). LO BB 6-25 v Surrey (Southampton) 1997 (BHC).

SAVIDENT, Lee (Guernsey GS; Guernsey CFE), b Guernsey 22 Oct 1976. 6'5". RHB, RM. Hampshire 1997-2000. HS 10* v Z (Southampton) 2000. BB 2-86 v Yorks (Portsmouth) 1997. LO HS 39 v Somerset (Taunton) 1998 (SL). LO BB 3-41 v Middx (Lord's) 1997 (SL).

WARNE, Shane Keith (Hampton HS; Mentone GS), b Upper Ferntree Gully, Melbourne, Australia 13 Sep 1969. 6'0". RHB, LBG. Victoria 1990-91 to date; captain 1997-98 to 1998-99. Hampshire 2000; cap 2000. *Wisden* 1993 (also one of *Five Cricketers of the Century*). Tests (A): 84 (1991-92 to 1999-00); HS 86 v I (Adelaide) 1999-00; BB 8-71 v E (Brisbane) 1994-95; hat-trick v E (Melbourne) 1994-95. **LOI** (A): 158 (1992-93 to 2000-01, 11 as captain); HS 55 v SA (Pt Elizabeth) 1993-94. BB 5-33 v WI (Sydney) 1996-97. Tours (A): E 1993, 1997; SA 1993-94, 1996-97; WI 1994-95, 1998-99; NZ 1992-93, 1999-00; I 1997-98, 2000-01; P 1994-95; SL 1992-93, 1999-00; Z 1991-92 (Aus B), 1999-00. HS 86 (*see Tests*). H HS 69 v Kent (Portsmouth) 2000. 50 wkts (3+1); most – 75 (1993). BB 8-71 (*see Tests*). H BB 6-34 v Kent (Canterbury) 2000. Award: BHC 1. LO HS 55 (*see LOI*). LO BB 5-33 (*see LOI*).

HAMPSHIRE 2000

RESULTS SUMMARY

	Place	Won	Lost	Tied	Drew	No Result
County Championship (1st Division)	7th	3	9		4	
All First-Class Matches		3	10		5	1
NatWest Trophy	Semi-Finalist					
Benson & Hedges Cup	Quarter-Finalist					
National League (2nd Division)	8th	5	11			

COUNTY CHAMPIONSHIP AVERAGES

BATTING AND FIELDING

Cap		M	I	NO	HS	Runs	Avge	100	50	Ct/St
–	L.R.Prittipaul	4	6	–	152	298	49.66	1	1	1
1999	W.S.Kendall	16	27	2	161	979	39.16	3	3	16
1998	G.W.White	16	28	4	96	742	30.91	–	5	13
–	D.A.Kenway	13	23	1	136	615	27.95	1	3	11/1
1991	A.N.Aymes	13	22	5	74*	398	23.41	–	3	32/6
2000	S.K.Warne	15	22	–	69	431	21.55	–	3	14
1998	A.D.Mascarenhas	15	22	1	100	448	21.33	1	2	3
1985	R.A.Smith	16	27	–	61	529	19.59	–	2	3
1996	J.S.Laney	12	21	1	81	364	18.20	–	2	11
1998	P.J.Hartley	9	11	5	23*	103	17.16	–	–	–
–	A.C.Morris	7	11	1	60	153	15.30	–	1	3
1992	S.D.Udal	11	19	3	35	230	14.37	–	–	7
–	S.J.Renshaw	3	6	1	26	57	11.40	–	–	–
–	A.J.Sexton	3	5	–	36	52	10.40	–	–	3
–	S.R.G.Francis	7	10	5	30*	43	8.60	–	–	1
1995	J.P.Stephenson	8	12	–	19	84	7.00	–	–	6
2000	A.D.Mullally	8	12	2	12	60	6.00	–	–	–

BOWLING

	O	M	R	W	Avge	Best	5wI	10wM
A.D.Mullally	343.5	105	832	49	16.97	9-93	5	1
S.K.Warne	639.4	183	1620	70	23.14	6-34	5	–
S.D.Udal	300.3	84	745	28	26.60	5-58	1	–
A.D.Mascarenhas	277.5	80	698	25	27.92	4-52	–	–
A.C.Morris	159.1	34	506	18	28.11	3-48	–	–
S.R.G.Francis	120.1	26	434	10	43.40	4-95	–	–
P.J.Hartley	204.2	33	697	15	46.46	3-91	–	–

Also bowled: A.N.Aymes 1-0-13-1; S.J.Renshaw 57.1-17-133-5; R.A.Smith 2-0-26-0; J.P.Stephenson 137-26-452 9; G.W.White 8.1-1-34-2.

The First-Class Averages (pp 118-132) give the records of Hampshire players in all first-class county matches (Hampshire's other opponents being the Zimbabweans, New Zealand A and Oxford University, the latter fixture being abandoned because of rain).

HAMPSHIRE RECORDS

FIRST-CLASS CRICKET

Highest Total	For 672-7d		v	Somerset	Taunton	1899
	V 742		by	Surrey	The Oval	1909
Lowest Total	For 15		v	Warwicks	Birmingham	1922
	V 23		by	Yorkshire	Middlesbrough	1965
Highest Innings	For 316	R.H.Moore	v	Warwicks	Bournemouth	1937
	V 303*	G.A.Hick	for	Worcs	Southampton	1997

Highest Partnership for each Wicket

1st	347	V.P.Terry/C.L.Smith	v	Warwicks	Birmingham	1987
2nd	321	G.Brown/E.I.M.Barrett	v	Glos	Southampton	1920
3rd	344	C.P.Mead/G.Brown	v	Yorkshire	Portsmouth	1927
4th	263	R.E.Marshall/D.A.Livingstone	v	Middlesex	Lord's	1970
5th	235	G.Hill/D.F.Walker	v	Sussex	Portsmouth	1937
6th	411	R.M.Poore/E.G.Wynyard	v	Somerset	Taunton	1899
7th	325	G.Brown/C.H.Abercrombie	v	Essex	Leyton	1913
8th	227	K.D.James/T.M.Tremlett	v	Somerset	Taunton	1985
9th	230	D.A.Livingstone/A.T.Castell	v	Surrey	Southampton	1962
10th	192	H.A.W.Bowell/W.H.Livsey	v	Worcs	Bournemouth	1921

Best Bowling	For 9- 25	R.M.H.Cottam	v	Lancashire	Manchester	1965
(Innings)	V 10- 46	W.Hickton	for	Lancashire	Manchester	1870
Best Bowling	For 16- 88	J.A.Newman	v	Somerset	Weston-s-Mare	1927
(Match)	V 17-119	W.Mead	for	Essex	Southampton	1895

Most Runs – Season	2854	C.P.Mead	(av 79.27)	1928
Most Runs – Career	48892	C.P.Mead	(av 48.84)	1905-36
Most 100s – Season	12	C.P.Mead		1928
Most 100s – Career	138	C.P.Mead		1905-36
Most Wkts – Season	190	A.S.Kennedy	(av 15.61)	1922
Most Wkts – Career	2669	D.Shackleton	(av 18.23)	1948-69

LIMITED-OVERS CRICKET

Highest Total	NWT	371-4	v	Glamorgan	Southampton	1975
	BHC	321-1	v	Minor C (S)	Amersham	1973
	NL	313-2	v	Sussex	Portsmouth	1993
Lowest Total	NWT	98	v	Lancashire	Manchester	1975
	BHC	50	v	Yorkshire	Leeds	1991
	NL	43	v	Essex	Basingstoke	1972
Highest Innings	NWT	177	C.G.Greenidge	v	Glamorgan	Southampton	1975
	BHC	173*	C.G.Greenidge	v	Minor C (S)	Amersham	1973
	NL	172	C.G.Greenidge	v	Surrey	Southampton	1987
Best Bowling	NWT	7-30	P.J.Sainsbury	v	Norfolk	Southampton	1965
	BHC	6-25	S.J.Renshaw	v	Surrey	Southampton	1997
	NL	6-20	T.E.Jesty	v	Glamorgan	Cardiff	1975

KENT

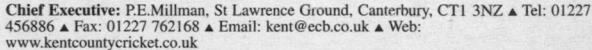

Formation of Present Club: 1 March 1859
Substantial Reorganisation: 6 December 1870
Colours: Maroon and White
Badge: White Horse on a Red Ground
County Champions: (6) 1906, 1909, 1910, 1913, 1970, 1978
Joint Champions: (1) 1977
NatWest Trophy/Gillette Cup Winners: (2) 1967, 1974
Benson and Hedges Cup Winners: (3) 1973, 1976, 1978
National League (Div 1) Winners: (0); best – 3rd 1999
Sunday League Winners: (4) 1972, 1973, 1976, 1995
Match Awards: NWT 50; BHC 92

Chief Executive: P.E.Millman, St Lawrence Ground, Canterbury, CT1 3NZ ▲ Tel: 01227 456886 ▲ Fax: 01227 762168 ▲ Email: kent@ecb.co.uk ▲ Web: www.kentcountycricket.co.uk

Captain: M.V.Fleming. **Vice-Captain:** No appointment. **Overseas Player:** D.J.Cullinan.
2001 Beneficiary: M.V.Fleming, **Scorer:** J.C.Foley. ‡ New registration

BANES, Matthew John (Tonbridge S; Durham U), b Pembury 10 Dec 1979. 5'9". RHB, OB. Debut 1999. British U 2000. HS 53 v NZ (Canterbury) 1999 – on debut. CC HS 5.

‡CULLINAN, Daryll John (Queens C, Queenstown; Stellenbosch U), b Kimberley, SA 4 Mar 1967. Brother of R.E. (Border and OFS 1984-85 to 1992-93). 5'10". RHB, OB. Border 1983-84 to 1984-85 and 1994-95 to 1995-96, making debut whilst at school. WP 1985-86/1990-91. Transvaal/Gauteng 1991-92 to 1993-94 and 1996-97 to date. At 16yr 304d remains youngest player to score f-c hundred in SA. Derbyshire 1995. **Tests** (SA): 65 (1992-93 to 2000-01); HS 275* (SA record) v NZ (Auckland) 1998-99; BB 1-10. **LOI** (SA): 138 (1992-93 to 2000-01); HS 124 v P (Nairobi) 1996-97; BB 2-30 v E (Manchester) 1998. Tours (SA): E 1994, 1998; A 1993-94, 1997-98; WI 2000-01; NZ 1994-95, 1998-99; I 1996-97, 1999-00; P 1997-98; SL 1993-94, 2000-01; Z 1995-96, 1999-00. 1000 runs (1): 1003 (1995). HS 337* Transvaal v N Transvaal (Jo'burg) 1993-94 (SA f-c record). UK HS 200* SA v Durham (Chester-le-St) 1998. BB 2-27 Border v Natal B (E London) 1983-84. Awards: NWT 1; BHC 1. LO HS 124 (*see LOI*). LO BB 2-30 (*see LOI*).

EALHAM, Mark Alan (Stour Valley SS, Chartham), b Willesborough, Ashford 27 Aug 1969. Son of A.G.E. (Kent 1966-82). 5'9". RHB, RMF. Debut 1989; cap 1992. **Tests:** 8 (1996 to 1998); HS 53* v A (Birmingham) 1997; BB 4-21 v I (Nottingham) 1996. **LOI:** 60 (1996 to 2000-01); HS 45 v WI (Bridgetown) 1997-98; BB 5-15 v Z (Kimberley) 1999-00 – Eng record. Tours: A 1996-97 (Eng A); SA 1999-00 (*part*); SL 1997-98; Z 1992-93 (K); K 1997-98. 1000 runs (1): 1055 (1997). HS 139 v Leics (Canterbury) 1997. BB 8-36 (10-74 match) v Warwks (Birmingham) 1996. Awards: NWT 2; BHC 6. LO HS 112 v Derbys (Maidstone) 1995 (off 44 balls – SL record). LO BB 6-53 v Hants (Basingstoke) 1993 (SL).

‡FERLEY, Robert Stephen (Sutton Valence S), b Norwich, Norfolk 4 Feb 1982. RHB, SLA. Staff 2001 – awaiting f-c debut.

FLEMING, Matthew Valentine (St Aubyns S, Rottingdean; Eton C), b Macclesfield, Cheshire 12 Dec 1964. 5'11½". RHB, RM. Debut 1989; cap 1990; captain 1999 to date; benefit 2001. **LOI:** 11 (1997-98 to 1998); HS 33 v WI (Sharjah) 1997-98; BB 4-45 v I (Sharjah) 1997-98 – on debut. Tour: Z 1992-93 (K). HS 138 v Essex (Canterbury) 1997 and 138 v Worcs (Worcester) 1999. BB 5-51 v Notts (Nottingham) 1997. Awards: NWT 2; BHC 7. LO HS 117* v Cheshire (Bowdon) 1999 (NWT). LO BB 5-27 v Hants (Canterbury) 1997 (BHC).

47

FULTON, David Paul (The Judd S; Kent U), b Lewisham 15 Nov 1971. 6'2". RHB, SLA, occ WK. Debut 1992; cap 1998. HS 207 v Yorks (Maidstone) 1998. BB 1-37. CC BB – . LO HS 69 v Glos (Tunbridge Wells) 2000 (NL).

GOLDING, James Matthew (Kent C, Canterbury; University C, Worcester), b Canterbury 19 Jul 1977. 6'4". RHB, RMF. Debut 1999. Awaiting CC debut. HS 18* and BB 1-38 v Z (Canterbury) 2000. Award: NWT 1. LO HS 47 Kent CB v Hants (Canterbury) 1999 (NWT). LO BB 3-20 v Middx (Canterbury) 2000 (BHC).

HOCKLEY, James Bernard (Kelsey Park S, Beckenham), b Beckenham 16 Apr 1979. 6'2". RHB, OB. Debut 1998. HS 74 v Z (Canterbury) 2000. CC HS 34 v Glos (Canterbury) 1999. BB 1-57. LO HS 64 v Worcs (Canterbury) 2000 (NL).

‡**JONES, Geraint** Owen (Harris Town HS, Toowoomba, Queensland, Australia), b Papua New Guinea 14 Jul 1976. RHB, WK. Staff 2001 – awaiting f-c debut.

KEY, Robert William Trevor (Colfe's S), b East Dulwich, London 12 May 1979. 6'1". RHB, RM/OB. His mother played for Kent Ladies. Debut 1998. Tours (Eng A): SA 1998-99; Z 1998-99. HS 125 v Somerset (Taunton) 1999. LO HS 76* v York (Canterbury) 1999 (NL).

KHAN, Amjad, b Copenhagen, Denmark 14 Oct 1980. RHB, RMF. Staff 2000 – awaiting f-c debut.

‡**LAZENBURY, Paul** Stuart (Malmesbury S), b Bath, Somerset 10 Aug 1978. 6'0". LHB, OB. Gloucestershire staff 1999 – no appearances. Kent staff 2001 – awaiting f-c debut. Herefordshire 2000, scoring 723 runs (avge 51.64) with 4 hundreds, including 118 in ECB 38-County Cup final win v Cheshire. LO HS (Glos CB) 3 (NWT).

McCAGUE, Martin John (Hedland Sr HS; Carine Tafe C), b Larne, N Ireland 24 May 1969. 6'5". RHB, RFM. W Australia 1990-91 to 1991-92. Kent debut 1991; cap 1992. **Tests**: 3 (1993 to 1994-95); HS 11 v A (Leeds) 1993; BB 4-121 v A (Nottingham) 1993. Tours: A 1994-95 (part); SA 1993-94 (Eng A). HS 72 v Yorks (Canterbury) 2000. 50 wkts (4); most – 76 (1996). BB 9-86 (15-147 match) v Derbys (Derby) 1994. Hat-trick 1996. Award: NWT 1. LO HS 56 v Leics (Canterbury) 2000 (NL). LO BB 5-26 v Middx (Canterbury) 1993 (NWT).

MASTERS, David Daniel (Fort Luton HS; Mid Kent CHE), b Chatham 22 Apr 1978. Son of K.D. (Kent 1981-85, Surrey 1986). 6'4". RHB, RMF. Debut 2000. HS 21 v Hants (Canterbury) 2000. BB 6-27 v Durham (Tunbridge Wells) 2000. LO HS 12* v Middx (Canterbury) 2000 (BHC). LO BB 2-10 v Northants (Canterbury) 2000 (NL).

NIXON, Paul Andrew (Ullswater HS, Penrith), b Carlisle, Cumberland 21 Oct 1970. 6'0". LHB, WK. Leicestershire 1989-99; cap 1994. Kent debut/cap 2000. Cumberland 1987. MCC YC. Tours: SA 1996-97 (Le); I 1994-95 (Eng A); P 2000-01; SL 2000-01 (no f-c). 1000 runs (1): 1046 (1994). HS 134* v Hants (Canterbury) 2000. Award: BHC 1. LO HS 101 Le v SL A (Galle) 1998-99.

PATEL, Minal Mahesh (Dartford GS; Erith TC), b Bombay, India 7 Jul 1970. 5'9". RHB, SLA. Debut 1989; cap 1994. **Tests**: 2 (1996); HS 27 and BB 1-101 v I (Nottingham) 1996. Tour: I 1994-95 (Eng A). HS 67 v Glos (Canterbury) 1999. 50 wkts (3); most – 90 (1994). BB 8-96 v Lancs (Canterbury) 1994. LO HS 18* v Glam (Canterbury) 1996 (BHC). LO BB 3-22 v Essex (Canterbury) 1999 (NL).

PHILLIPS, Ben James (Langley Park S and SFC, Beckenham), b Lewisham 30 Sep 1974. 6'6". RHB, RFM. Debut 1996. No f-c appearances 2000. HS 100* v Lancs (Manchester) 1997. BB 5-47 v Sussex (Horsham) 1997. Award: NWT 1. LO HS 29 v Glam (Cardiff) 1996 (SL). LO BB 4-25 v Northants (Canterbury) 2000 (NL).

SAGGERS, Martin John (Springwood HS; King's Lynn; Huddersfield U), b King's Lynn, Norfolk 23 May 1972. 6'2". RHB, RMF. Durham 1996-98. Norfolk 1995-96. Kent debut 1999. HS 24 v Derbys (Derby) 2000. 50 wkts (1): 57 (2000). BB 7-79 v Durham (Chester-le-St) 2000. Award: BHC 1. LO HS 34* Minor C v Leics (Jesmond) 1996 (BHC). LO BB 4-35 Du v Essex (Chelmsford) 1997 (SL).

SMITH, Edward Thomas (Tonbridge S; Peterhouse, Cambridge), b Pembury 19 Jul 1977. 6'2". RHB, RM. Cambridge U 1996-98, scoring 101 v Glam (Cambridge) on debut; blue 1996-97 (injured 1998). Kent debut 1996. British U 1998. 1000 runs (1): 1163 (1997). HS 190 CU v Leics (Cambridge) 1997. K HS 175 v Durham (Chester-le-St) 2000. LO HS 72* v Hants (Portsmouth) 1997 (SL).

TROTT, Benjamin James (Court Fields Community S, Wellington; Richard Huish C, Taunton; Plymouth U), b Wellington, Somerset 14 Mar 1975. 6'5". RHB, RMF. Somerset 1997-98. Kent debut 2000. Devon 2000. HS 1* and BB 3-74 Sm v Glam (Taunton) 1997. K HS 0*. K BB 2-44 v Hants (Portsmouth) 2000. LO HS – (SL). LO BB 1-29 (SL).

WALKER, Matthew Jonathan (King's S, Rochester), b Gravesend 2 Jan 1974. Grandson of Jack (Kent 1949). 5'8". LHB, RM. Debut 1992-93 (Z tour); UK debut 1994; cap 2000. Tour: Z 1992-93 (K). HS 275* v Somerset (Canterbury) 1996. BB 1-3 (FCC Select XI). K BB 1-4. Awards: BHC 2. LO HS 117 v Warwks (Canterbury) 1997 (BHC). LO BB 2-27 v Lancs (Manchester) 2000 (NL).

WELLS, Alan Peter (Tideway CS, Newhaven), b Newhaven, Sussex 2 Oct 1961. Younger brother of C.M. (Sussex, Derbyshire, Border and WP 1979-96). 6'0". RHB, RM. Sussex 1981-96; cap 1986; captain 1992-96; benefit 1996. Border 1981-82. Kent debut/cap 1997. **Tests:** 1 (1995); HS 3* v WI (Oval) 1995. **LOI:** 1 (1995); HS 15 v WI (Lord's) 1995. Tours (Eng A): SA 1989-90 (Eng XI), 1993-94; I 1994-95 (captain). 1000 runs (11); most – 1784 (1991). 253* Sx v Yorks (Middlesbrough) 1991. K HS 111 v Durham (Stockton) 1999. BB 3-67 Sx v Worcs (Worcester) 1987. Awards: NWT 3; BHC 1. LO HS 127 Sx v Hants (Portsmouth) 1993 (SL). LO BB (Sx) 1-0 (SL).

RELEASED/RETIRED
(Having made a first-class County appearance in 2000)

ADAMS, Kristian (Lindsey CS; Lindsey SFC), b Cleethorpes, Lincs 26 Nov 1976. 5'10". RHB, LMF. Debut 2000. Lincolnshire 1997. HS – and BB 2-58 v Surrey (Canterbury) 2000. Award: NWT 1. LO HS 6* (NL). LO BB 6-24 v Cumb (Carlisle) 2000 (NWT).

DRAVID, Rahul (St Joseph's HS; Bangalore U), b Indore, India 11 Jan 1973. 5'11½". RHB, OB, WK. Karnataka 1990-91 to date. Kent 2000; cap 2000. *Wisden* 1999. **Tests** (I): 40 (1996 to 2000-01); HS 200* v Z (Delhi) 2000-01. **LOI** (I): 139 (1995-96 to 2000-01, 1 as captain); HS 153 v NZ (Hyderabad) 1999-00; BB 2-43 v SA (Cochin) 1999-00. Tours (I): E 1996; A 1999-00; SA 1996-97; WI 1996-97; NZ 1998-99; SL 1997-98, 1998-99, Z 1998-99; B 2000-01. 1000 runs (1+2); most – 1264 (1997-98). HS 215 Karnataka v Uttar Pradesh (Bangalore) 1997-98. K HS 182 v Z (Canterbury) 2000. CC HS 137 v Hants (Portsmouth) 2000. BB 2-16 v Surrey (Oval) 2000. LO HS 153 (*see LOI*). LO BB 2-43 (*see LOI*).

SCOTT, Darren Anthony (Geoffrey Chaucer GS; Christ Church C, Canterbury), b Canterbury 26 Aug 1972. 6'2". LHB, OB. Kent 1998-2000. HS 17* v OU (Canterbury) 1998. CC HS 12* v Lancs (Manchester) 1999. BB 4-151 v NZ (Canterbury) 1999. CC BB 1-48. LO HS 27 v Northants (Northampton) 2000 (NL). LO BB 3-21 v Worcs (Canterbury) 2000 (NL).

KENT 2000

RESULTS SUMMARY

		Place	Won	Lost	Tied	Drew	No Result
County Championship	(1st Division)	**6th**	4	4		8	
All First-Class Matches			5	4		8	
NatWest Trophy		4th Round					
Benson & Hedges Cup		4th in South Group					
National League	(1st Division)	**5th**	7	7			2

COUNTY CHAMPIONSHIP AVERAGES

BATTING AND FIELDING

Cap		M	I	NO	HS	Runs	Avge	100	50	Ct/St
2000	R.Dravid	15	24	3	137	1039	49.47	1	8	13
2000	P.A.Nixon	16	23	7	134*	513	32.06	1	2	41/2
1990	M.V.Fleming	13	17	2	47	433	28.86	–	–	2
2000	M.J.Walker	14	23	3	61	490	24.50	–	1	12
–	E.T.Smith	10	17	–	175	411	24.17	1	–	5
1992	M.A.Ealham	11	14	1	83	293	22.53	–	2	3
–	R.W.T.Key	15	26	1	83	558	22.32	–	5	4
1998	D.P.Fulton	14	24	1	115	512	22.26	1	1	29
1994	M.M.Patel	12	15	1	60	258	18.42	–	1	11
1992	M.J.McCague	7	11	–	72	191	17.36	–	1	1
1997	A.P.Wells	11	18	2	60*	239	14.93	–	1	2
–	J.B.Hockley	4	4	–	33	37	9.25	–	–	2
–	M.J.Saggers	14	17	5	24	91	7.58	–	–	3
–	D.D.Masters	15	19	7	21	71	5.91	–	–	3

Also played: K.Adams (1) did not bat; D.A.Scott (2 matches) 2, 4*, 2* (1 ct); B.J.Trott (2) 0*, 0* (1 ct).

BOWLING

	O	M	R	W	Avge	Best	5wI	10wM
M.J.Saggers	425.2	98	1148	57	20.14	7-79	2	–
M.M.Patel	471.1	159	960	37	25.94	6-77	2	–
M.V.Fleming	267.1	68	743	28	26.53	4-77	–	–
D.D.Masters	400.2	93	1080	39	27.69	6-27	2	–
M.A.Ealham	271.5	67	703	24	29.29	5-35	1	–
M.J.McCague	129.4	20	412	14	29.42	5-52	1	–

Also bowled: K.Adams 22-4-58-2; R.Dravid 53.5-11-128-4; D.P.Fulton 17-5-45-0; J.B.Hockley 3-3-0-0; R.W.T.Key 9.4-1-34-0; P.A.Nixon 3-1-10-0; D.A.Scott 46-16-114-1; E.T.Smith 6-0-20-0; B.J.Trott 42-9-133-4; M.J.Walker 62-8-166-4.

The First-Class Averages (pp 118-132) give the records of Kent players in all first-class county matches (Kent's other opponents being the Zimbabweans), with the exception of M.J.Walker, whose full county figures are as above, M.J.Banes, whose only first-class appearance was for British Universities, and:

R.W.T.Key 16-27-1-83-562-21.61-0-5-4ct. 9.4-1-34-0.
P.A.Nixon 17-24-7-134*-567-33.35-1-3-43ct/2st. 3-1-10-0.
M.M.Patel 13-15-1-60-258-18.42-0-1-13ct. 527.3-183-1086-43-25.25-6/77-2-0.

KENT RECORDS

FIRST-CLASS CRICKET

Highest Total	For 803-4d		v	Essex	Brentwood	1934
	V 676		by	Australians	Canterbury	1921
Lowest Total	For 18		v	Sussex	Gravesend	1867
	V 16		by	Warwicks	Tonbridge	1913
Highest Innings	For 332	W.H.Ashdown	v	Essex	Brentwood	1934
	V 344	W.G.Grace	for	MCC	Canterbury	1876

Highest Partnership for each Wicket

1st	300	N.R.Taylor/M.R.Benson	v	Derbyshire	Canterbury	1991
2nd	366	S.G.Hinks/N.R.Taylor	v	Middlesex	Canterbury	1990
3rd	321*	A.Hearne/J.R.Mason	v	Notts	Nottingham	1899
4th	368	P.A.de Silva/G.R.Cowdrey	v	Derbyshire	Maidstone	1995
5th	277	F.E.Woolley/L.E.G.Ames	v	New Zealand	Canterbury	1931
6th	315	P.A.de Silva/M.A.Ealham	v	Notts	Nottingham	1995
7th	248	A.P.Day/E.Humphreys	v	Somerset	Taunton	1908
8th	157	A.L.Hilder/A.C.Wright	v	Essex	Gravesend	1924
9th	171	M.A.Ealham/P.A.Strang	v	Notts	Nottingham	1997
10th	235	F.E.Woolley/A.Fielder	v	Worcs	Stourbridge	1909

Best Bowling	For 10- 30	C.Blythe	v	Northants	Northampton	1907
(Innings)	V 10- 48	C.H.G.Bland	for	Sussex	Tonbridge	1899
Best Bowling	For 17- 48	C.Blythe	v	Northants	Northampton	1907
(Match)	V 17-106	T.W.J.Goddard	for	Glos	Bristol	1939

Most Runs – Season	2894	F.E.Woolley	(av 59.06)		1928
Most Runs – Career	47868	F.E.Woolley	(av 41.77)		1906-38
Most 100s – Season	10	F.E.Woolley			1928
	10	F.E.Woolley			1934
Most 100s – Career	122	F.E.Woolley			1906-38
Most Wkts – Season	262	A.P.Freeman	(av 14.74)		1933
Most Wkts – Career	3340	A.P.Freeman	(av 17.64)		1914-36

LIMITED-OVERS CRICKET

Highest Total	NWT	384-6		v	Berkshire	Finchampstead	1994
	BHC	338-6		v	Somerset	Maidstone	1996
	NL	327-6		v	Leics	Canterbury	1993
Lowest Total	NWT	60		v	Somerset	Taunton	1979
	BHC	73		v	Middlesex	Canterbury	1979
	NL	83		v	Middlesex	Lord's	1984
Highest Innings	NWT	136*	C.L.Hooper	v	Berkshire	Finchampstead	1994
	BHC	143	C.J.Tavaré	v	Somerset	Taunton	1985
	NL	145	C.L.Hooper	v	Leics	Leicester	1996
Best Bowling	NWT	8-31	D.L.Underwood	v	Scotland	Edinburgh	1987
	BHC	6-41	T.N.Wren	v	Somerset	Canterbury	1995
	NL	6- 9	R.A.Woolmer	v	Derbyshire	Chesterfield	1979

LANCASHIRE

Formation of Present Club: 12 January 1864
Colours: Red, Green and Blue
Badge: Red Rose
County Champions (since 1890): (7) 1897, 1904, 1926, 1927, 1928, 1930, 1934
Joint Champions: (1) 1950
NatWest Trophy/Gillette Cup Winners: (7) 1970, 1971, 1972, 1975, 1990, 1996, 1998
Benson and Hedges Cup Winners: (4) 1984, 1990, 1995, 1996
National League (Div 1) Winners: (1) 1999.
Sunday League Winners: (4) 1969, 1970, 1989, 1998
Match Awards: NWT 72; BHC 81

Chief Executive: J.Cumbes, Old Trafford, Manchester M16 0PX ▲ Tel: 0161 282 4000 ▲ Fax: 0161 282 4100 ▲ Email: cricket@lancs.co.uk ▲ Web: www.lccc.co.uk

Captain: J.P.Crawley. **Vice-Captain:** No appointment. **Overseas Player:** M.Muralitharan.
2001 Beneficiary: G.D.Lloyd. **Scorer:** A.West. ‡ New registration

‡ANDERSON, James Michael (St Theodore CS, Burnley), b Burnley 30 Jul 1982. RHB, RFM. Staff 2001 – awaiting f-c debut. LO HS 5* and LO BB 2-64 Lancs CB v Essex CB (Chelmsford) 2000 (NWT).

ATHERTON, Michael Andrew (Manchester GS; Downing C, Cambridge), b Failsworth, Manchester 23 Mar 1968. 5'11". RHB, LB. Cambridge U 1987-89; blue 1987-88-89; captain 1988-89. Lancashire debut 1987; cap 1989; benefit 1997. YC 1990. *Wisden* 1990. OBE 1997. **ECB contract 2000.** Tests: 108 (1989 to 2000-01, 52 as captain – England record); HS 185* v SA (Johannesburg) 1995-96; BB 1-20. **LOI:** 54 (1990 to 1998, 43 as captain); HS 127 v WI (Lord's) 1995. Tours (C=captain): A 1990-91, 1994-95C, 1998-99; SA 1995-96C, 1999-00; WI 1993-94C, 1995-96 (La), 1997-98C; NZ 1996-97C; I 1992-93; P 2000-01; SL 1992-93, 2000-01; Z 1989-90 (Eng A), 1996-97C. 1000 runs (7); most – 1924 (1990). Scored 1193 in season of f-c debut. HS 268* v Glam (Blackpool) 1999. BB 6-78 v Notts (Nottingham) 1990. Awards: NWT 4; BHC 4. LO HS 127 (*see LOI*). LO BB 4-42 Comb U v Somerset (Taunton) 1989 (BHC).

AUSTIN, Ian David (Haslingden HS), b Haslingden 30 May 1966. 5'10". LHB, RM. Debut 1987; cap 1990; benefit 2000. *Wisden* 1998. **LOI:** 9 (1998 to 1999); HS 11* v SL (Lord's) 1998; BB 2-25 v SL (Lord's) 1999. Tours (La): WI 1995-96; Z 1988-89. HS 115* v Derbys (Blackpool) 1992. BB 6-43 v SL A (Manchester) 1999. CC BB 5-23 (10-60 match) v Middx (Manchester) 1994. Awards: NWT 2; BHC 3. LO HS 97 v Sussex (Hove) 1997 (NWT). LO BB 5-56 v Derbys (Derby) 1991 (SL).

CHAPPLE, Glen (West Craven HS; Nelson & Colne C), b Skipton, Yorks 23 Jan 1974. 6'1". RHB, RFM. Debut 1992; cap 1994. Tours (Eng A): A 1996-97; WI 1995-96 (La); I 1994-95. HS 109* v Glam (Manchester) 1993 (100 off 27 balls in contrived circumstances). HS (authentic) 83 v Derbys (Derby) 1999. 50 wkts (2); most – 55 (1994). BB 6-42 v Durham (Chester-le-St) 2000. Awards: NWT 1; BHC 1. LO HS 43 v Worcs (Manchester) 1996 (SL). LO BB 6-18 v Essex (Lord's) 1996 (NWT).

CHILTON, Mark James (Manchester GS; Durham U), b Sheffield, Yorks 2 Oct 1976. 6'3". RHB, RM. Debut 1997. British U 1998. HS 106* v CU (Cambridge) 1999. CC HS 102 v Northants (Manchester) 1999. BB 1-1. CC BB – . Awards: BHC 2. LO HS 56 Brit U v Kent (Oxford) 1998 (BHC). LO BB 5-26 Brit U v Sussex (Cambridge) 1997 (BHC).

CRAWLEY, John Paul (Manchester GS; Trinity C, Cambridge), b Maldon, Essex 21 Sep 1971. Brother of M.A. (Oxford U, Lancs and Notts 1987-94) and P.M. (Cambridge U 1992). 6'1". RHB, RM, occ WK. Debut 1990; cap 1994; captain 1999 to date. Cambridge U 1991-93; blue 1991-92-93; captain 1992-93. YC 1994. **Tests:** 29 (1994 to 1998-99); HS 156* v SL (Oval) 1998. **LOI:** 13 (1994-95 to 1998-99); HS 73 v Z (Harare) 1996-97. Tours: A 1994-95, 1998-99; SA 1993-94 (Eng A), 1995-96; WI 1995-96 (La), 1997-98, 2000-01 (Eng A); NZ 1996-97; Z 1996-97. 1000 runs (7); most – 1851 (1998). HS 286 England A v E Province (Port Elizabeth) 1993-94. La HS 281* v Somerset (Southport) 1994. BB 1-90. Award: BHC 1. LO HS 114 v Notts (Manchester) 1995 (BHC).

‡**DRIVER, Ryan** Craig (Redruth Community C; Durham U), b Truro, Cornwall 30 Apr 1979. 6'3½". LHB, RM. Worcestershire 1998-2000. British U 1999. Cornwall 1996-97. HS 64 Wo v Sussex (Worcester) 2000. BB 1-13. Award: NWT 1. LO HS 61* Wo v Glos (Worcester) 2000 (NWT). LO BB 1-17 (Wo – NL).

FAIRBROTHER, Neil Harvey (Lymm GS), b Warrington 9 Sep 1963. 5'8". LHB, LM. Debut 1982; cap 1985; captain 1992-93; benefit 1995. Transvaal 1994-95. **Tests:** 10 (1987 to 1992-93); HS 83 v I (Madras) 1992-93. **LOI:** 75 (1986-87 to 1999); HS 113 v WI (Lord's) 1991. Tours: NZ 1987-88, 1991-92; I/SL 1992-93; P 1987-88, 1990-91 (Eng A); SL 1990-91 (Eng A). 1000 runs (10); most – 1740 (1990). HS 366 v Surrey (Oval) 1990 (ground record), including 311 in a day and 100 or more in each session. BB 2-91 v Notts (Manchester) 1987. Awards: NWT 6; BHC 10. LO HS 145 v H (Manchester) 1990 (BHC). LO BB 1-12 (BHC).

FLINTOFF, Andrew (Ribbleton Hall HS), b Preston 6 Dec 1977. 6'4". RHB, RM. Debut 1995; cap 1998. **ECB contract 2000. Tests:** 9 (1998 to 2000); HS 42 and BB 2-31 v SA (Pt Elizabeth) 1999-00. **LOI:** 20 (1998-99 to 2000-01); HS 84 v P (Karachi) 2000-01; BB 2-3 v P (Sharjah) 1998-99. Tours (Eng A): SA 1998-99, 1999-00 (Eng); SL 1997-98; Z 1998-99; K 1997-98. HS 160 v Yorks (Manchester) 1999. BB 5-24 v Hants (Southampton) 1999. Awards: NWT 1; BHC 1. LO HS 143 (off 66 balls) v Essex (Chelmsford) 1999 (NL). LO BB 4-22 Eng A v Zim A (Harare) 1998-99.

GREEN, Richard James (Bridgewater HS, Cheshire; Mid-Cheshire C), b Warrington 13 Mar 1976. 6'1". RHB, RM. Debut 1995. HS 51 v Essex (Manchester) 1997. BB 6-41 v Yorks (Manchester) 1996 (non-CC match). CC BB 4-21 v Yorks (Manchester) 1999. LO HS 14* v Worcs (Manchester) 1999 (NL). LO BB 3-18 v Yorks (Manchester) 1997 (SL).

HAYNES, Jamie Jonathan (St Edmunds C, Canberra; Canberra U), b Bristol 5 Jul 1974. 5'11". RHB, WK. Debut 1996. Represented Australian Capital Territory at cricket and Australian Rules football. HS 80 v SL A (Manchester) 1999. CC HS 18 v Kent (Manchester) 1997. LO HS 12 v Somerset (Manchester) 2000 (NL).

HEGG, Warren Kevin (Unsworth HS, Bury; Stand C, Whitefield), b Whitefield 23 Feb 1968. 5'8". RHB, WK. Debut 1986; cap 1989; benefit 1999. **Tests:** 2 (1998-99); HS 15 v A (Sydney) 1998-99. Tours: A 1996-97 (Eng A), 1998-99; WI 1986-87 (La), 1995-96 (La); SL 1990-91 (Eng A); Z 1988-89 (I.a). HS 134 v Leics (Manchester) 1996. Held 11 catches (equalling world f-c match record) v Derbys (Chesterfield) 1989. Award: BHC 1. LO HS 81 v Yorks (Manchester) 1996 (BHC).

‡**HOGG, Kyle** William, b Birmingham 2 Jul 1983. RHB, RFM. Staff 2001 – awaiting f c debut.

KEEDY, Gary (Garforth CS), b Wakefield, Yorks 27 Nov 1974. 6'0". LHB, SLA. Yorkshire 1994 (one match). Lancashire debut 1995; cap 2000. Tour: WI 1995-96 (La). HS 34 v Surrey (Manchester) 2000. BB 6-56 (10-155 match) v Durham (Manchester) 2000. LO HS 1 (NL). LO BB 5-30 v Sussex (Manchester) 2000 (NL).

LLOYD, Graham David (Hollins County HS), b Accrington 1 Jul 1969. Son of D. (Lancs and England 1965-83). 5'9". RHB, RM. Debut 1988; cap 1992; benefit 2001. **LOI:** 6 (1996 to 1998-99); HS 22 v A (Oval) 1997. Tours: A 1992-93 (Eng A); WI 1995-96 (La). 1000 runs (5); most – 1389 (1992). HS 241 v Essex (Chelmsford) 1996. BB 1-4. Awards: BHC 2. LO HS 134 v Durham (Manchester) 1997 (SL). LO BB 1-23 (NWT).

MARTIN, Peter James (Danum S, Doncaster), b Accrington 15 Nov 1968. 6'4". RHB, RFM. Debut 1989; cap 1994. **Tests:** 8 (1995 to 1997); HS 29 v WI (Lord's) 1995; BB 4-60 v SA (Durban) 1995-96. **LOI:** 20 (1995 to 1998-99); HS 6; BB 4-44 v WI (Oval) 1995 – on debut. Tour: SA 1995-96. HS 133 v Durham (Gateshead) 1992. 50 wkts (3); most – 58 (1997). BB 8-32 (13-79 match) v Middx (Uxbridge) 1997. Awards: NWT 2. LO HS 35* v Worcs (Manchester) 1996 (SL). LO BB 5-21 v Northants (Manchester) 1997 (SL).

MURALITHARAN, Muthiah (St Anthony's C, Kandy), b Kandy, Sri Lanka 17 Apr 1972. 5'5". RHB, OB. Central Province 1989-90 to date. Tamil Union 1991-92 to date. Lancashire 1999 (taking 7-44 and 7-73 v Warwks at Southport on debut); cap 1999. *Wisden* 1998. **Tests** (SL): 62 (1992-93 to 2000-01); HS 39 v I (Colombo) 1997-98; BB 9-65 (16-220 match) v E (Oval) 1998. **LOI** (SL): 159 (1993-94 to 2000-01); HS 18 v E (Lord's) 1998; BB 7-30 v I (Sharjah) 2000-01. Tours (SL): E 1991, 1998; A 1995-96; SA 1992-93 (SL U-24), 1994-95, 1997-98, 2000-01; WI 1996-97; NZ 1994-95, 1996-97; I 1993-94, 1997-98; P 1995-96, 1999-00; Z 1994-95, 1999-00. HS 39 (*see Tests*). La HS 10 v Derbys (Derby) 1999. 50 wkts (1+2); most – 66 (1996-97; 1999 – in 7 CC matches). BB 9-65 (*see Tests*). La BB 7-39 (11-61 match) v Derbys (Derby) 1999. LO HS 18 (*see LOI*). LO BB 5-23 (*see LOI*).

‡**ROBERTS, Timothy** William (Bishop's Stopford S, Kettering; Durham U), b Kettering, Northants 4 Mar 1978. Younger brother of A.R. (Northants 1987-98). RHB, OB. British U 1999. Bedfordshire 2000. Lancashire staff 2001. HS 49 Brit U v NZ (Oxford) 1999 – on debut.

SCHOFIELD, Christopher Paul (Wardle HS), b Birch Hill, Rochdale 6 Oct 1978. 6'2". LHB, LB. Debut 1998. **ECB contract 2000. Tests:** 2 (2000); HS 57 v Z (Nottingham) 2000. Tours (Eng A): WI 2000-01; NZ 1999-00; B 1999-00. HS 74 Eng A v CD (Palmerston N) 1999-00. La HS 70* v Kent (Manchester) 2000. BB 6-120 Eng A v Bangladesh (Chittagong) 1999-00. La BB 5-48 v CU (Cambridge) 2000. CC BB 5-66 v Durham (Manchester) 1999. LO HS 34 v Worcs (Worcester) 2000 (NL). LO BB 4-34 v Durham (Manchester) 2000 (BHC) and 4-34 v Essex (Manchester) 2000 (NWT).

SCUDERI, Joseph Charles, b Ingham, Queensland, Australia 24 Dec 1968. 5'11". RHB, RM. S Australia 1988-89 to 1997-98. Special ECB registration (holds Italian passport). Italy 1998-1999. Lancashire debut 2000. HS 125* S Aus v WA (Adelaide) 1991-92. La HS 51 v CU (Cambridge) 2000 – on UK debut. CC HS 46 and La BB 4-58 v Somerset (Taunton) 2000. BB 7-79 S Aus v NSW (Adelaide) 1991-92. LO HS 58 S Aus v Vic (Adelaide) 1989-90 (FAI). LO BB 3-36 S Aus v Vic (Melbourne) 1994-95 (MM).

SMETHURST, Michael Paul (Hulme GS, Oldham; Salford U), b Oldham 11 Oct 1976. 6'5". RHB, RM. Debut 1999. HS 66 v Surrey (Manchester) 2000. 50 wkts (1): 56 (2000). BB 7-37 v NZ A (Liverpool) 2000. CC BB 7-50 v Durham (Chester-le-St) 2000. Award: NWT 1. LO HS 10* v Leics (Manchester) 2000 (BHC). LO BB 4-46 v Hants (Southampton) 1999 (NWT).

WATKINSON, Michael (Rivington and Blackrod HS, Horwich), b Westhoughton 1 Aug 1961. 6'1". RHB, RMF/OB. Debut 1982; cap 1987; captain 1994-97; benefit 1996. Cheshire 1982. No f-c appearances 2000. **Tests:** 4 (1995 to 1995-96); HS 82* v WI (Nottingham) 1995; BB 3-64 v WI (Manchester) 1995 – on debut. **LOI:** 1 (1995-96); dnb v SA (Jo'burg) 1995-96. Tours: SA 1995-96; WI 1995-96 (La – captain). 1000 runs (1): 1016 (1993). HS 161 v Essex (Manchester) 1995. 50 wkts (7); most – 66 (1992). BB 8-30 (11-87 match) v Hants (Manchester) 1994 – completing match 'double' with 128 runs. Hat-trick 1992. Awards: NWT 3; BHC 3. LO HS 130 v Herts (Radlett) 1999 (NWT). LO BB 5-44 v Derbys (Chesterfield) 1996 (BHC).

‡**WOOD, John** (Crofton HS; Wakefield District C; Leeds Poly), b Crofton, Yorks 22 Jul 1970. 6'3". RHB, RFM. GW in Nissan Shield 1990-91. Durham 1992-2000; cap 1998. HS 63* Du v Notts (Chester-le-St) 1993. 50 wkts (1): 62 (1998). BB 7-58 Du v Yorks (Leeds) 1999. LO HS 28* Du v Leics (Leicester) 2000 (BHC) and 28* Du v Notts (Nottingham) 2000 (NL). LO BB 4-17 Du v Kent (Darlington) 1997 (SL).

YATES, Gary (Manchester GS), b Ashton-under-Lyne 20 Sep 1967. 6'0". RHB, OB. Debut 1990; cap 1994. HS 134* v Northants (Manchester) 1993. HS 6-64 v Kent (Manchester) 1999. LO HS 38 v Essex (Chelmsford) 1996 (SL). LO BB 4-34 v Warwks (Birmingham) 1994 (SL). **RELEASED/RETIRED** see p 69

54

LANCASHIRE 2000

RESULTS SUMMARY

	Place	Won	Lost	Tied	Drew	No Result
County Championship (1st Division)	**2nd**	7	1		8	
All First-Class Matches		8	1		9	
NatWest Trophy	Semi-Finalist					
Benson & Hedges Cup	Semi-Finalist					
National League (1st Division)	**8th**	6	8	1		1

COUNTY CHAMPIONSHIP AVERAGES

BATTING AND FIELDING

Cap		M	I	NO	HS	Runs	Avge	100	50	Ct/St
1985	N.H.Fairbrother	14	22	4	138	754	41.88	2	2	12
1998	A.Flintoff	9	13	–	119	490	37.69	1	3	10
1989	W.K.Hegg	16	22	5	128	631	37.11	1	4	36/5
1989	M.A.Atherton	10	15	1	113	505	36.07	1	4	10
1994	J.P.Crawley	13	20	1	139	669	35.21	3	–	4
–	S.C.Ganguly	13	19	–	99	644	33.89	–	6	10
–	C.P.Schofield	13	17	2	70*	399	26.60	–	3	6
1992	G.D.Lloyd	14	19	–	126	475	25.00	1	1	18
–	M.J.Chilton	9	12	1	46	270	24.54	–	–	9
–	J.C.Scuderi	7	10	1	46	198	22.00	–	–	–
	M.P.Smethurst	14	18	9	66	158	17.55	–	1	3
1994	P.J.Martin	8	10	2	40	120	15.00	–	–	2
1994	G.Chapple	15	18	1	41	218	12.82	–	–	4
2000	G.Keedy	12	15	3	34	144	12.00	–	–	1

Also batted: I.D.Austin (cap 1990 – 1 match) 0; R.J.Green (2) 0, 29*; P.C.McKeown (2) 30, 4; N.T.Wood (1) 27; G.Yates (cap 1994 – 3) 0, 3, 7 (3 ct).

BOWLING

	O	M	R	W	Avge	Best	5wI	10wM
A.Flintoff	92.2	30	199	14	14.21	4-18	–	–
P.J.Martin	203.2	65	417	28	14.89	7-67	3	–
J.C.Scuderi	96	25	251	11	22.81	4-58	–	–
M.P.Smethurst	324	69	1057	43	24.58	7-50	2	–
G.Chapple	398.5	89	1126	44	25.59	6-42	1	–
G.Keedy	445	132	950	36	26.38	6-56	1	1
C.P.Schofield	291.5	62	877	30	29.23	4-25	–	–

Also bowled: I.D.Austin 24-14-32-2; M.J.Chilton 1-0-3-0; J.P.Crawley 1-0-19-0; N.H.Fairbrother 6.2-2-11-1; S.C.Ganguly 83.4-11-311-4; R.J.Green 34-7-120-1; G.Yates 85.4-28-192-9.

The **First-Class Averages** (pp 118-132) give the records of Lancashire players in all first-class county matches (Lancashire's other opponents being New Zealand A and Cambridge University), with the exception of:

M.A.Atherton 11-17-1-113-532-33.25-1-4-11ct. Did not bowl.

A.Flintoff 10-14-1-119-570-43.84-1-4-11ct. 99.2-34-207-14-14.78-4/18.

C.P.Schofield 15-19-2-70*-461-27.11-0-3-6ct. 356-78-1029-39-26.38-5/48-1-0.

LANCASHIRE RECORDS

FIRST-CLASS CRICKET

Highest Total	For 863		v	Surrey	The Oval	1990
	V 707-9d		by	Surrey	The Oval	1990
Lowest Total	For 25		v	Derbyshire	Manchester	1871
	V 22		by	Glamorgan	Liverpool	1924
Highest Innings	For 424	A.C.MacLaren	v	Somerset	Taunton	1895
	V 315*	T.W.Hayward	for	Surrey	The Oval	1898

Highest Partnership for each Wicket

1st	368	A.C.MacLaren/R.H.Spooner	v	Glos	Liverpool	1903
2nd	371	F.B.Watson/G.E.Tyldesley	v	Surrey	Manchester	1928
3rd	364	M.A.Atherton/N.H.Fairbrother	v	Surrey	The Oval	1990 ·
4th	358	S.P.Titchard/G.D.Lloyd	v	Essex	Chelmsford	1996
5th	249	B.Wood/A.Kennedy	v	Warwicks	Birmingham	1975
6th	278	J.Iddon/H.R.W.Butterworth	v	Sussex	Manchester	1932
7th	248	G.D.Lloyd/I.D.Austin	v	Yorkshire	Leeds	1997
8th	158	J.Lyon/R.M.Ratcliffe	v	Warwicks	Manchester	1979
9th	142	L.O.S.Poidevin/A.Kermode	v	Sussex	Eastbourne	1907
10th	173	J.Briggs/R.Pilling	v	Surrey	Liverpool	1885

Best Bowling	For 10-46	W.Hickton	v	Hampshire	Manchester	1870
(Innings)	V 10-40	G.O.B.Allen	for	Middlesex	Lord's	1929
Best Bowling	For 17-91	H.Dean	v	Yorkshire	Liverpool	1913
(Match)	V 16-65	G.Giffen	for	Australians	Manchester	1886

Most Runs – Season	2633	J.T.Tyldesley	(av 56.02)		1901
Most Runs – Career	34222	G.E.Tyldesley	(av 45.20)		1909-36
Most 100s – Season	11	C.Hallows			1928
Most 100s – Career	90	G.E.Tyldesley			1909-36
Most Wkts – Season	198	E.A.McDonald	(av 18.55)		1925
Most Wkts – Career	1816	J.B.Statham	(av 15.12)		1950-68

LIMITED-OVERS CRICKET

Highest Total	NWT	381-3		v	Herts	Radlett	1999
	BHC	353-7		v	Notts	Manchester	1995
	NL	301-6		v	Essex	Chelmsford	1999
Lowest Total	NWT	59		v	Worcs	Worcester	1963
	BHC	82		v	Yorkshire	Bradford	1972
	NL	68		v	Yorkshire	Leeds	2000
Highest Innings	NWT	135*	A.Flintoff	v	Surrey	The Oval	2000
	BHC	136	G.Fowler	v	Sussex	Manchester	1991
	NL	143	A.Flintoff	v	Essex	Chelmsford	1999
Best Bowling	NWT	6-18	G.Chapple	v	Essex	Lord's	1996
	BHC	6-10	C.E.H.Croft	v	Scotland	Manchester	1982
	NL	6-25	G.Chapple	v	Yorkshire	Leeds	1998

LEICESTERSHIRE

Formation of Present Club: 25 March 1879
Colours: Dark Green and Scarlet
Badge: Gold Running Fox on Green Ground
County Champions: (3) 1975, 1996, 1998
NatWest Trophy/Gillette Cup Winners: (0); best – finalist 1992
Benson and Hedges Cup Winners: (3) 1972, 1975, 1985
National League (Div 1) Winners: (0); best – 4th 2000
Sunday League Champions: (2) 1974, 1977
Match Awards: NWT 43; BHC 73

Secretary/General Manager: J.J.Whitaker, County Ground, Grace Road, Leicester LE2 8AD ▲ Tel: 0116 283 2128 ▲ Fax: 0116 244 0363 ▲ Email: leics@ecb.co.uk ▲ Web: www.leicestershireccc.co.uk

Captain: V.J.Wells. **Vice-Captain:** B.F.Smith. **Overseas Player:** D.J.Marsh.
2001 Beneficiary: V.J.Wells. **Scorer:** G.A.York. ‡ New registration

ADSHEAD, Stephen John (Bridley Moor HS, Redditch), b Worcester 29 Jan 1980. 5'9". RHB, WK. Herefordshire 1999. Debut 2000 – awaiting CC debut. HS 0. LO HS 22 Herefords v Wilts (Brockhampton) 1999 (NWT).

BOSWELL, Scott Antony John (Pocklington S; Wolverhampton U), b Fulford, Yorks 11 Sep 1974. 6'5". RHB, RFM. British U 1996. Northamptonshire 1996-98. Leicestershire debut 1999. HS 35 Nh v Leics (Northampton) 1997. Le HS 20 and Le BB 3-39 v Hants (Southampton) 2000. BB 5-94 Nh v Worcs (Northampton) 1997. LO HS 14 Brit U v Essex (Chelmsford) 1996 (BHC). Lo BB 3-32 Le v SL B (Galle) 1998-99.

BURNS, Neil David (Moulsham HS, Chelmsford), b Chelmsford, Essex 19 Sep 1965. 5'10". LHB, WK, occ SLA. W Province B 1985-86. Essex 1986. Somerset 1987-93; cap 1987. Leicestershire debut 1994. Buckinghamshire 1995-99. HS 166 Sm v Glos (Taunton) 1990. Le HS 67* v Hants (Leicester) 2000. LO HS 58 Sm v Sussex (Hove) 1990 (SL).

CROWE, Carl Daniel (Lutterworth GS), b Leicester 25 Nov 1975. 6'0". RHB, OB. Debut 1995. HS 44* v Northants (Northampton) 2000. BB 4-55 v Hants (Southampton) 2000. LO HS 19 v SL A (Moratuwa) 1998-99. LO BB 1-26 (v Z).

DAKIN, Jonathan Michael (King Edward VII S, Johannesburg) b Hitchin, Herts 28 Feb 1973. 6'4". LHB, RM. Debut 1993; cap 2000. Tour (Le): SA 1996-97. HS 190 v Northants (Northampton) 1997. BB 4-27 v Worcester (Worcester) 1999. Award: BHC 1. LO HS 108* v Durham (Leicester) 1996 (BHC). LO BB 5-30 v Kent (Leicester) 1999 (NL).

DeFREITAS, Phillip Anthony Jason (Willesden HS, London), b Scotts Head, Dominica 18 Feb 1966. 6'0". RHB, RFM, UK resident since 1976. Leicestershire 1985-88; cap 1986. Lancashire 1989-93; cap 1989. Boland 1993-94 and 1995-96. Derbyshire 1994-99; cap 1994; captain 1997 (part). *Wisden* 1991. **Tests:** 44 (1986-87 to 1995-96), IIS 88 v A (Adelaide) 1994-95; BB 7-70 v SL (Lord's) 1991. **LOI:** 103 (1986-87 to 1997); HS 67 v SL (Faisalabad) 1995-96; BB 4-35 v A (Adelaide) 1986-87. Tours: A 1986-87, 1990-91, 1994-95, WI 1989-90; NZ 1987-88, 1991-92; P 1987-88; I 1992-93; Z 1988-89 (La) HS 123* v Lancs (Leicester) 2000. 50 wkts (12); most – 94 (1986). Took his 1000th f-c wicket 1999. BB 7-21 La v Middx (Lord's) 1989. Le BB 7-44 (13-86 match) v Essex (Southend) 1986. Hat-trick 1994. Awards: NWT 5; BHC 4. LO HS 75* La v Hants (Manchester) 1990 (BHC). LO BB 5-13 La v Cumb (Kendal) 1989 (NWT).

GRIFFITHS, Paul (Codsall HS, Wolverhampton; Cheltenham & Gloucester CHE, Gloucester), b Wolverhampton, Staffs 14 Sep 1975. 6'7". RHB, RMF. Debut 2000 – awaiting CC debut. HS – and BB 1-65 v WI (Leicester) 2000.

HABIB, Aftab (Millfield S; Taunton S), b Reading, Berkshire 7 Feb 1972. 5'11". Cousin of Zahid Sadiq (Surrey and Derbys 1988-90). RHB, RMF. Middlesex 1992 (one match). Leicestershire debut 1995; cap 1998. **Tests:** 2 (1999); HS 19 v NZ (Lord's) 1999. Tours (Eng A): WI 2000-01 (*part*); NZ 1999-00; B 1999-00. 1000 runs (2); most – 1055 (1999). HS 215 v Worcs (Leicester) 1996. Award: BHC 1. LO HS 111 v Durham (Chester-le-St) 1997 (BHC). LO BB 2-5 v Ire (Dublin) 1999.

MADDY, Darren Lee (Wreake Valley C), b Leicester 23 May 1974. 5'9". RHB, RM/OB. Debut 1994; cap 1996. **Tests:** 3 (1999 to 1999-00); HS 24 v SA (Durban) 1999-00. **LOI:** 8 (1998 to 1999-00); HS 53 v Z (Harare) 1999-00. Tours (Eng A): SA 1996-97 (Le), 1998-99, 1999-00 (Eng); SL 1997-98; Z 1998-99; K 1997-98. 1000 runs (2); most – 1060 (1999). HS 202 Eng A v Kenya (Nairobi) 1997-98. Le HS 162 v Durham (Darlington) 1998. BB 3-5 v Glos (Leicester) 1999. Awards: NWT 1; BHC 7 (inc 5 in 1998). LO HS 151 v Minor C (Leicester) 1998 (BHC). LO BB 4-16 v Somerset (Taunton) 2000 (NL).

‡**MALCOLM, Devon** Eugene (St Elizabeth THS; Richmond S, Sheffield; Derby CHE), b Kingston, Jamaica 22 Feb 1963. Qualified for England 1987. 6'2". RHB, RF. Derbyshire 1984-97; cap 1989; benefit 1997. Northamptonshire 1998-2000; cap 1999. *Wisden* 1994. **Tests:** 40 (1989 to 1997); HS 29 v A (Sydney) 1994-95; BB 9-57 v SA (Oval) 1994. **LOI:** 10 (1990 to 1993-94); HS 4; BB 3-40 v I (Gwalior) 1992-93. Tours: A 1990-91, 1994-95; SA 1995-96; WI 1989-90, 1991-92 (Eng A), 1993-94; I 1992-93; SL 1992-93. HS 51 De v Surrey (Derby) 1989. 50 wkts (7); most – 82 (1996). BB 9-57 (*see Tests*). CC BB 6-23 De v Lancs (Derby) 1997. Awards: NWT 1; BHC 1. LO HS 42 De v Surrey (Oval) 1996 (SL). LO BB 7-35 De v Northants (Derby) 1997 (NWT).

‡**MARSH, Daniel** James (), b Subiaco, Perth, Australia 14 Jun 1973. Son of R.W. (WA and Australia 1968-69 to 1983-84). RHB, SLA. S Australia 1993-94 to 1995-96. Tasmania 1996-97 to date. HS 157 Tas v I (Hobart) 1999-00. BB 7-57 Tas v NSW (Sydney) 1997-98. LO HS 78* Tas v S Aus (Adelaide) 1999-00 (MC). LO BB 3-47 Tas v ACT (Hobart) 1999-00 (MC).

‡**NEW, Thomas**, b Sutton in Ashfield, Notts 18 Jan 1985. LHB, WK. Summer contract 2001 – awaiting f-c debut.

ORMOND, James (St Thomas More S, Nuneaton), b Walsgrave, Coventry, Warwks 20 Aug 1977. 6'3". RHB, RFM. Debut 1995; cap 1999. Tours (Eng A): SL 1997-98; K 1997-98. HS 50* v Warwks (Leicester) 1999. 50 wkts (1): 52 (1999). BB 6-33 (9-62 match) v Somerset (Leicester) 1998. Award: BHC 1. LO HS 18 v Notts (Leicester) 1997 (SL). LO BB 4-12 v Middx (Leicester) 1998 (SL).

SMITH, Benjamin Francis (Kibworth HS), b Corby, Northants 3 Apr 1972. 5'9". RHB, RM. Debut 1990; cap 1995. Tour (Le): SA 1996-97. 1000 runs (2); most – 1243 (1996). HS 204 v Surrey (Oval) 1998. BB 1-5. Award: NWT 1. LO HS 115 v Somerset (Weston-s-M) 1995 (SL). LO BB 1-26.

STELLING, William Frederik (Michaelhouse; St Stithians; Cape Town U), b Johannesburg, SA 30 Jun 1969. Special ECB registration (Dutch passport). RHB, RFM. W Province 1991-92 to 1993-94. Boland 1994-95 to 1996-97. Leicestershire debut 2000. Holland 1995. Berkshire 1999. HS 53 WP B v Natal B (Pietermaritzburg) 1991-92 – off 88 balls on debut. Le HS – and BB 5-49 v Kent (Leicester) 2000 – on UK debut. Award: NWT 1. LO HS 76* Berks v Devon (Torquay) 1999 (NWT). LO BB 3-18 Berks v Warwks (Reading) 1999 (NWT).

STEVENS, Darren Ian (Hinkley C), b Leicester 30 Apr 1976. 5'11". RHB, RM. Debut 1997. HS 130 v Sussex (Arundel) 1999. BB 1-5. Award: NWT 1. LO HS 133 v Northumb (Jesmond) 2000 (NWT).

SUTCLIFFE, Iain John (Leeds GS; Queen's C, Oxford), b Leeds, Yorks 20 Dec 1974. 6'2". LHB, occ OB. Oxford U 1994-96; blue 1995-96; boxing blue 1993-94. Leicestershire debut 1995; cap 1997. Tour (Le): SA 1996-97. HS 167 v Middx (Leicester) 1998. BB 2-21 OU v CU (Lord's) 1996. CC BB 1-17. Awards: NWT 1; BHC 1. LO HS 105* v Notts (Nottingham) 1998 (BHC).

WARD, Trevor Robert (Hextable CS, nr Swanley), b Farningham, Kent 18 Jan 1968. 5'11". RHB, OB. Kent 1986-99; cap 1989; benefit 1999. Leicestershire debut 2000. Tour: Z 1992-93 (K). 1000 runs (6); most – 1648 (1992). HS 235* K v Middx (Canterbury) 1991. Le HS 39 v Lancs (Manchester) 2000. BB 2-10 K v Yorks (Canterbury) 1996. Awards: NWT 1; BHC 2. LO HS 131 K v Notts (Nottingham) 1993 (SL). LO BB 3-20 K v Glam (Canterbury) 1989 (SL).

WELLS, Vincent John (Sir William Nottidge S, Whitstable), b Dartford, Kent 6 Aug 1965. 6'0". RHB, RMF. Kent 1988-91. Leicestershire debut 1992; cap 1994; captain 2000 to date; benefit 2001. **LOI:** 9 (1998-99); HS 39 v A (Sydney) 1998-99; BB 3-30 v A (Sydney) 1998-99. Tour (Le): SA 1996-97. 1000 runs (2); most – 1331 (1996). HS 224 v Middx (Lord's) 1997. BB 5-18 v Notts (Worksop) 1998. Hat-trick 1994. Awards: NWT 3; BHC 1. LO HS 201 v Berks (Leicester) 1996 (NWT). LO BB 6-25 v Minor C (Leicester) 1998 (BHC).

‡**WHILEY, Matthew** Jeffrey Allen (Harry Carlton CS, Nottingham), b Clifton, Nottingham 6 May 1980. 6'5½". RHB, LMF. Nottinghamshire 1998-2000. HS 0*. BB 1-44. CC BB 1-66.

WRIGHT, Ashley Spencer (King Edward VII S, Melton Mowbray), b Grantham, Lincs 21 Oct 1980. 6'0". RHB, RM. Staff 1998 – awaiting f-c debut. Award: NWT 1. LO HS 112 Leics CB v Durham CB (Gateshead) 2000 (NWT).

RELEASED/RETIRED
(Having made a first-class County appearance in 2000)

KUMBLE, Anil (National HS; R.V. Engineering C, Bangalore), b Bangalore, India 17 Oct 1970. 6'1½". RHB, LB. Karnataka 1989-90 to date. Northamptonshire 1995 (cap 1995). Leicestershire 2000; cap 2000. *Wisden* 1995. **Tests** (I): 61 (1990 to 1999-00); HS 88 v SA (Calcutta) 1996-97; BB 10-74 (14-149 match) v P (Delhi) 1998-99 (second-best innings analysis in Test cricket). **LOI** (I): 208 (1989-90 to 2000-01); HS 26 v A (Perth) 1999-00; BB 6-12 v WI (Calcutta) 1993-94. Tours (I): E 1990, 1996; A 1999-00; SA 1992-93, 1996-97; WI 1996-97; NZ 1993-94, 1998-99; SL 1993-94, 1997-98, 1998-99; Z 1992-93, 1998-99. HS 154* Karnataka v Kerala (Bijapur) 1991-92. Le HS 56 and Le BB 6-44 (10-105 match) v Kent (Canterbury) 2000. 50 wkts (1+1) inc 100 (1): 105 (1995). BB 10-74 (*see Tests*). UK BB 7-82 Nh v Warwks (Birmingham) 1995. LO HS 30* Karnataka v Wills XI (Bangalore) 1994-95 (WT). LO BB 6-12 (*see LOI*).

LEWIS, Clairmonte Christopher (Willesden HS, London), b Georgetown, Guyana 14 Feb 1968. 6'2½". RHB, RFM. Leicestershire 1987-91, 1998-2000; cap 1990. Nottinghamshire 1992-94; cap 1992. Surrey 1996-97; cap 1996. **Tests:** 32 (1990 to 1996); HS 117 v I (Madras) 1992-93; BB 6-111 v WI (Birmingham) 1991. **LOI:** 53 (1989-90 to 1998); HS 33 v SA (Melbourne) 1991-92; BB 4-30 v SL (Ballarat) 1991-92. Tours: A 1990-91 (*part*), 1994-95 (*part*); WI 1989-90 (*part*), 1993-94; NZ 1991-92; I/SL 1992-93. HS 247 Nt v Durham (Chester-le-St) 1993. Le HS 189* v Essex (Chelmsford) 1990. 50 wkts (2); most – 56 (1990). BB 6-22 v OU (Oxford) 1988. CC BB 6-55 v Glam (Cardiff) 1990. Award: NWT 1. LO HS 116* v Kent (Canterbury) 1999 (NL). LO BB 5-19 v Staffs (Leicester) 1998 (NWT).

WILLIAMSON, Dominic (St Leonard's CS, Durham; Durham SFC), b Durham City 15 Nov 1975. 5'8". RHB, RM. Leicestershire 1996-2000. MCC YC. HS 47 v Surrey (Guildford) 2000. BB 3-19 v Glam (Leicester) 1997 – on CC debut. Le HS 39 v Worcs (Leicester) 1999 (NL). LO BB 5-32 v Sussex (Eastbourne) 1997 (SL).

LEICESTERSHIRE 2000

RESULTS SUMMARY

		Place	Won	Lost	Tied	Drew	No Result
County Championship (1st Division)		4th	4	3		9	
All First-Class Matches			4	3		10	
NatWest Trophy		4th Round					
Benson & Hedges Cup		5th in North Group					
National League (1st Division)		4th	7	6	2		1

COUNTY CHAMPIONSHIP AVERAGES

BATTING AND FIELDING

Cap		M	I	NO	HS	Runs	Avge	100	50	Ct/St
1998	A.Habib	16	22	1	172*	1038	49.42	2	8	8
–	D.Williamson	2	4	2	47	95	47.50	–	–	–
1986	P.A.J.DeFreitas	14	18	3	123*	677	45.13	1	4	1
2000	J.M.Dakin	8	11	1	135	447	44.70	1	3	2
1995	B.F.Smith	16	22	2	111*	610	30.50	2	1	9
1996	D.L.Maddy	16	23	–	102	581	26.40	1	4	16
–	N.D.Burns	16	21	4	67*	445	26.17	–	3	36/1
1994	V.J.Wells	14	18	–	98	465	25.83	–	3	8
–	D.I.Stevens	14	20	–	78	434	21.70	–	2	5
1997	I.J.Sutcliffe	11	15	–	53	283	18.86	–	2	10
–	C.D.Crowe	7	7	1	30	100	16.66	–	–	2
–	S.A.J.Boswell	5	7	3	20	63	15.75	–	–	–
–	T.R.Ward	7	10	1	39	110	12.22	–	–	8
1999	J.Ormond	12	15	7	30*	95	11.87	–	–	1
1990	C.C.Lewis	5	7	–	24	80	11.42	–	–	6
2000	A.Kumble	12	16	–	56	181	11.31	–	1	3

Also played: W.F.Stelling (1 match) did not bat.

BOWLING

	O	M	R	W	Avge	Best	5wI	10wM
A.Kumble	498.3	139	1133	45	25.17	6-44	2	1
J.Ormond	380.3	75	1116	44	25.36	6-50	3	–
V.J.Wells	211.3	46	616	23	26.78	4-54	–	–
C.D.Crowe	148.3	36	364	12	30.33	4-55	–	–
P.A.J.DeFreitas	459.2	122	1105	33	33.48	4-41	–	–
J.M.Dakin	186.4	36	551	12	45.91	2-20	–	–

Also bowled: S.A.J.Boswell 93.4-21-278-9; C.C.Lewis 98.1-12-302-7; D.L.Maddy 75-16-220-6; B.F.Smith 2-0-6-0; W.F.Stelling 25-8-49-5; D.I.Stevens 6-2-14-0; I.J.Sutcliffe 1.3-0-12-0; D.Williamson 33-4-113-2.

The First-Class Averages (pp 118-132) give the records of Leicestershire players in all first-class county matches (their other opponents being the West Indians).

LEICESTERSHIRE RECORDS

FIRST-CLASS CRICKET

Highest Total	For 701-4d		v	Worcs	Worcester	1906
	V 761-6d		by	Essex	Chelmsford	1990
Lowest Total	For 25		v	Kent	Leicester	1912
	V 24		by	Glamorgan	Leicester	1971
	24		by	Oxford U	Oxford	1985
Highest Innings	For 261	P.V.Simmons	v	Northants	Leicester	1994
	V 341	G.H.Hirst	for	Yorkshire	Leicester	1905

Highest Partnership for each Wicket

1st	390	B.Dudleston/J.F.Steele	v	Derbyshire	Leicester	1979
2nd	289*	J.C.Balderstone/D.I.Gower	v	Essex	Leicester	1981
3rd	316*	W.Watson/A.Wharton	v	Somerset	Taunton	1961
4th	290*	P.Willey/T.J.Boon	v	Warwicks	Leicester	1984
5th	322	B.F.Smith/P.V.Simmons	v	Notts	Worksop	1998
6th	284	P.V.Simmons/P.A.Nixon	v	Durham	Chester-le-St	1996
7th	219*	J.D.R.Benson/P.Whitticase	v	Hampshire	Bournemouth	1991
8th	172	P.A.Nixon/D.J.Millns	v	Lancashire	Manchester	1996
9th	160	W.W.Odell/R.T.Crawford	v	Worcs	Leicester	1902
10th	228	R.Illingworth/K.Higgs	v	Northants	Leicester	1977

Best Bowling	For 10- 18	G.Geary	v	Glamorgan	Pontypridd	1929
(Innings)	V 10- 32	H.Pickett	for	Essex	Leyton	1895
Best Bowling	For 16- 96	G.Geary	v	Glamorgan	Pontypridd	1929
(Match)	V 16-102	C.Blythe	for	Kent	Leicester	1909

Most Runs – Season	2446	L.G.Berry	(av 52.04)		1937
Most Runs – Career	30143	L.G.Berry	(av 30.32)		1924-51
Most 100s – Season	7	L.G.Berry			1937
	7	W.Watson			1959
	7	B.F.Davison			1982
Most 100s – Career	45	L.G.Berry			1924-51
Most Wkts – Season	170	J.E.Walsh	(av 18.96)		1948
Most Wkts – Career	2130	W.E.Astill	(av 23.19)		1906-39

LIMITED-OVERS CRICKET

Highest Total	NWT	406-5	v	Berkshire	Leicester	1996
	BHC	382-6	v	Minor C	Leicester	1998
	NL	344-4	v	Durham	Chester-le-St	1996
Lowest Total	NWT	56	v	Northants	Leicester	1964
	BHC	56	v	Minor C	Wellington	1982
	NL	36	v	Sussex	Leicester	1973
Highest Innings	NWT	201 V.J.Wells	v	Berkshire	Leicester	1996
	BHC	158* B.F.Davison	v	Warwicks	Coventry	1972
	NL	152 B.Dudleston	v	Lancashire	Manchester	1975
Best Bowling	NWT	6-20 K.Higgs	v	Staffs	Longton	1975
	BHC	6-25 V.J.Wells	v	Minor C	Leicester	1998
	NL	6-17 K.Higgs	v	Glamorgan	Leicester	1973

MIDDLESEX

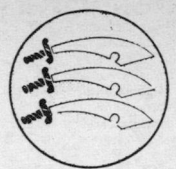

Formation of Present Club: 2 February 1864
Colours: Blue
Badge: Three Seaxes
County Champions (since 1890): (10) 1903, 1920, 1921, 1947, 1976, 1980, 1982, 1985, 1990, 1993
Joint Champions: (2) 1949, 1977
NatWest Trophy/Gillette Cup Winners: (4) 1977, 1980, 1984, 1988
Benson and Hedges Cup Winners: (2) 1983, 1986
National League (Div 1) Winners: (0); best – 4th (Div 2) 2000
Sunday League Winners: (1) 1992
Match Awards: NWT 58; BHC 60

Secretary: V.J.Codrington, Lord's Cricket Ground, London NW8 8QN ▲ Tel: 020 7289 1300 ▲ Fax: 020 7289 5831 ▲ Email: enquiries.middx@ecb.co.uk ▲ Web: www.middlesexccc.com

Captain: A.R.C.Fraser. **Vice-Captain:** no appointment. **Overseas Player:** S.P.Fleming. **2001 Beneficiary:** "Middlesex's Crusade for Kids Cricket". **Scorer:** M.J.Smith. ‡ New registration

ALLEYNE, David (Enfield GS; Hertford Regional C; City & Islington C), b York 17 Apr 1976. 5'11". RHB, WK. Staff 1999 – awaiting f-c debut. LO HS 58 v Notts (Nottingham) 2000 (NL).

BLOOMFIELD, Timothy Francis (Halliford S, Shepperton), b Ashford 31 May 1973. 6'2". RHB, RMF. Debut 1997. Berkshire 1996. HS 20* v Sussex (Hove) 1998. BB 5-36 v Glam (Cardiff) 1999. Award: NWT 1. LO HS 15 v Warwks (Lord's) 1998 (SL). LO BB 4-17 v Somerset (Southgate) 2000 (NWT).

BROWN, Michael James (Queen Elizabeth GS, Blackburn; Durham U), b Burnley, Lancs 9 Feb 1980. 6'0". RHB, OB. Debut 1999. No appearances 2000. HS 24* v CU (Cambridge) 1999 – on debut. CC HS 5.

BRYAN, Russell Barnaby (Shebbear C), b Maidstone, Kent 14 Feb 1981. 6'1". RHB, RMF. Staff 1999 – awaiting f-c debut. Devon 1999. LO HS – (Devon – NWT).

COOK, Simon James (Matthew Arnold S), b Oxford 15 Jan 1977. 6'4". RHB, RM. Debut 1999. HS 51 v Hants (Lord's) 1999. BB 4-13 v Essex (Lord's) 2000. LO HS 28* v Surrey (Lord's) 2000 (NL). LO BB 3-16 v Glam (Cardiff) 1999 (NL).

CREESE, Matthew Leonard (Goffs S; Durham U), b Enfield 13 Feb 1982. 6'2". LHB, SLA. Debut 1999 – awaiting CC debut. 2nd XI debut when aged 15y 188d. No appearances 2000.

HS 4 and BB 1-37 v CU (Cambridge) 1999 – on debut.

‡DALRYMPLE, James William Murray (Radley C), b Nairobi, Kenya 21 Jan 1981. RHB, OB. Staff 2000 – awaiting f-c debut. LO HS – and LO BB 1-37 v Glam (Cardiff) 2000 (NL).

‡FLEMING, Stephen Paul (Cashmere HS, Canterbury; Christchurch C), b Christchurch, New Zealand 1 Apr 1973. 6'3". LHB. Left-hand batsman. Canterbury 1991-92 to date. **Tests** (NZ): 57 (1993-94 to 2000-01, 33 as captain); HS 174* v SL (Colombo) 1997-98. **LOI** (NZ): 147 (1993-94 to 2000-01, 87 as captain); HS 116* v A (Melbourne) 1997-98; BB 1-8. Tours (NZ) (C=captain): E 1994, 1999C; A 1997-98C; SA 1993-94 (Cant), 1994-95, 2000-01C; WI 1995-96; I 1995-96, 1999-00C; P 1996-97; SL 1997-98C; Z 1997-98C, 2000-01C. HS 174* (*see Tests*). LO HS 116* (*see LOI*). LO BB 1-8 (*LOI*).

FRASER, Angus Robert Charles (Gayton HS, Harrow; Orange Hill HS, Edgware), b Billinge, Lancs 8 Aug 1965. Brother of A.G.J. (Middx and Essex 1986-92). 6'5". RHB, RMF. Debut 1984; cap 1988; benefit 1997; testimonial 2001. MBE 1999. *Wisden* 1995. **Tests:** 46 (1989 to 1998-99); HS 32 v SL (Oval) 1998; BB 8-53 (11-110 match) v WI (P-of-S) 1997-98 – record England innings analysis v WI. **LOI:** 42 (1989-90 to 1999); HS 38* v A (Melbourne) 1990-91; BB 4-22 v A (Melbourne) 1994-95. Tours: A 1990-91, 1994-95 (part), 1998-99; SA 1995-96; WI 1989-90, 1993-94, 1997-98. HS 92 v Surrey (Oval) 1990. 50 wkts (7); most – 92 (1989). BB 8-53 (*see Tests*). M BB 7-40 v Leics (Lord's) 1993. LO HS 38* (*see LOI*). LO BB 5-32 v Derbys (Lord's) 1995 (SL).

HEWITT, James Peter (Teddington S; Richmond C; City of Westminster C), b Southwark, London 26 Feb 1976. 6'2½". LHB, RMF. Debut 1996; cap 1998. No f-c appearances 2000. HS 75 v Essex (Chelmsford) 1997. 50 wkts (1): 60 (1997). BB 6-14 v Glam (Cardiff) 1997. Took wicket of R.I.Dawson (Glos) with first ball in f-c cricket. LO HS 32* v Glos (Bristol) 1997 (SL). LO BB 4-24 v Worcs (Uxbridge) 1998 (SL).

HUNT, Thomas Aaron *'Thos'* (Acton HS: St Clement Danes S), b Melbourne, Australia 19 Jan 1982. 6'2". Resident in UK since 1985 (English parents). LHB, RMF. Staff 1999 – awaiting f-c debut.

HUTTON, Benjamin Leonard (Radley C; Durham U), b Johannesburg, SA 29 Jan 1977. 6'2". Elder son of R.A. (Yorkshire, Transvaal & England 1962 to 1975-76); grandson of Sir Leonard (Yorkshire and England 1934-60). LHB, RMF. British U 1998-99. Middlesex debut 1999. HS 59 v Notts (Southgate) 1999. BB 2-9 v Glam (Southgate) 2000. LO HS 49 v Warwks (Lord's) 2000 (NL). LO BB 4-32 v Warwks (Birmingham) 2000 (NL).

JOYCE, Edmund Christopher (Presentation C, Bray; Trinity C, Dublin), b Dublin, Ireland 22 Sep 1978. 5'11". LHB, RM. Ireland 1997 to date. Middlesex debut 1999. HS 51 v Notts (Nottingham) 2000. LO HS 73 Ire v Warwks (Birmingham) 1998 (NWT).

‡**KEEGAN, Chad** Blake, b Sandton, near Johannesburg, SA 30 Jul 1979. RHB, RF. Staff 2001 – awaiting f-c debut.

LARAMAN, Aaron William (Enfield GS), b Enfield 10 Jan 1979. 6'5". RHB, RFM. Debut 1998 – awaiting CC debut. HS – . BB 4-33 v CU (Cambridge) 2000. LO HS 11* v Derbys (Derby) 2000 (NL). LO BB 6-42 v Glam (Cardiff) 2000 (NL).

MAUNDERS, John Kenneth (Ashford HS; Spelthorne C), b Ashford 4 Apr 1981. 5'10". LHB, RM. Debut 1999 (awaiting CC debut). Middx 2nd XI debut aged 16y 19d. No appearances 2000. HS 9.

NASH, David Charles (Sunbury Manor S; Malvern C), b Chertsey, Surrey 19 Jan 1978. 5'8". RHB, occ LB, WK. Debut 1997; cap 2000. Tour: SL 1997-98 (Eng A). HS 114 v Somerset (Lord's) 1998. BB 1-8. LO HS 43 v Surrey (Oval) 1999 (NL).

ROSEBERRY, Michael Anthony (Durham S), b Sunderland 28 Nov 1966. Elder brother of A. (Leics and Glam 1992-94). 6'1". RHB, RM. Middlesex 1986-94 and 1999 to date; cap 1990; benefit 2000. Durham 1995-98; captain 1995-96; cap 1998. Tour: A 1992-93 (Eng A). 1000 runs (4) inc 2000 (1): 2044 (1992). HS 185 v Leics (Lord's) 1993. BB 1-1. Awards: NWT 1; BHC 1. LO HS 121 Du v Herefords (Chester-le-St) 1995 (NWT). LO BB 1-22 (NWT).

SHAH, Owais Alam (Isleworth & Syon S), b Karachi, Pakistan 22 Oct 1978. 6'0". RHB, OB. Debut 1996; cap 2000. Tours (Eng A): A 1996-97; SL 1997-98. HS 140 v Yorks (Lord's) 1998. BB 3-33 v Glos (Bristl) 1999. LO HS 134 v Sussex (Arundel) 1999 (NL). LO BB 2-2 v Glam (Cardiff) 1998 (BHC).

STRAUSS, Andrew John (Radley C; Durham U), b Johannesburg, SA 2 Mar 1977. 5'11". LHB, LM. Debut 1998. Oxfordshire 1996. HS 111* v Northants (Lord's) 2000. LO HS 90 v Durham (Chester-le-St) 2000 (NL).

TUFNELL, Philip Clive Roderick (Highgate S), b Barnet, Herts 29 Apr 1966. 6'0". RHB, SLA. Debut 1986; cap 1990; benefit 1999. MCC YC. **Tests:** 41 (1990-91 to 1999-00); HS 22* v I (Madras) 1992-93; BB 7-47 (11-147 match) v NZ (Christchurch) 1991-92, took 11-93 v A (Oval) 1997. **LOI:** 20 (1990-91 to 1996-97); HS 5*; BB 4-22 v NZ (Christchurch) 1996-97. Tours: A 1990-91, 1994-95; SA 1999-00; WI 1993-94, 1997-98; NZ 1991-92, 1996-97; I/SL 1992-93, Z 1996-97. HS 67* v Worcs (Lord's) 1996. 50 wkts (8); most – 88 (1991). BB 8-29 v Glam (Cardiff) 1993. Award: NWT 1. LO HS 18 v Warwks (Lord's) 1991 (BHC). LO BB 5-28 v Leics (Lord's) 1993 (SL).

WEEKES, Paul Nicholas (Homerton House SS, Hackney), b Hackney, London 8 Jul 1969. 5'10". LHB, OB. Debut 1990; cap 1993. Tour: I 1994-95 (Eng A). MCC YC. 1000 runs (1): 1218 (1996). HS 171* v Somerset (Uxbridge) 1996. BB 8-39 v Glam (Lord's) 1996. Awards: NWT 2; BHC 3. LO HS 143* v Cornwall (St Austell) 1995 (NWT). LO BB 4-26 v Derbys (Derby) 2000 (NL).

WESTON, Robin Michael Swann (Durham S; Loughborough U), b Durham 7 Jun 1975. Brother of W.P.C. (*see WORCESTERSHIRE*). 5'10". RHB, LB. Durham 1995-97. Derbyshire 1998-99 (scored 72, 129*, 22, 124 and 156 in consecutive CC innings 1999). Middlesex debut 2000. Minor C debut 1991 when aged 15yr 355d (Durham record). HS 156 De v Somerset (Derby) 1999. M HS 39 v Northants (Lord's) 2000 – on Middx debut. BB 1-15 (De). LO HS 56 De v Leics (Leicester) 1998 (NWT) and 56 De v Notts (Nottingham) 1999 (NL).

RELEASED/RETIRED
(Having made a first-class County appearance in 2000)

BATT, Christopher James (Cox Green CS), b Taplow, Bucks 22 Sep 1976. 6'4". LHB, LMF. Sussex 1997 – no CC appearances. Middlesex 1998-2000. Berkshire 1997. MCC YC. HS 43 v Warwks (Lord's) 1998. BB 6-101 v Notts (Nottingham) 1998. LO HS 8* (NL). LO BB 3-26 v Yorks (Lord's) 1998 (SL).

DUTCH, K.P. – *see SOMERSET*.

JOHNSON, R.L. – *see SOMERSET*.

LANGER, Justin Lee (Aquinas C; U of WA), b Perth, Australia 21 Nov 1970. 5'8". LHB, RM. W Australia 1991-92 to date. Middlesex 1998-2000; cap 1998; captain 2000. *Wisden* 2000. **Tests** (A): 38 (1992-93 to 2000-01); HS 223 v I (Sydney) 1999-00. **LOI:** 8 (1993-94 to 1997); HS 36 v I (Sharjah) 1993-94. Tours (A): E 1995 (Young A), 1997; SA 1996-97; WI 1994-95, 1998-99; NZ 1992-93, 1999-00; I 2000-01; P 1994-95, 1998-99; SL 1999-00; Z 1999-00. 1000 runs (3+3); most – 1472 (2000). HS 274* WA v S Australia (Perth) 1996-97. M HS 241* v Kent (Lord's) 1999. BB 2-17 Aus A v SA A (Brisbane) 1997-98. M BB 1-10. Awards: NWT 2. LO HS 146 WA v S Aus (Perth) 1999-00 (MM). LO BB 3-51 v Surrey (Guildford) 1998 (SL). Expected to return in 2002.

RAMPRAKASH, M.R. – *see SURREY*.

MIDDLESEX 2000

RESULTS SUMMARY

	Place	Won	Lost	Tied	Drew	No Result
County Championship (2nd Division)	8th	2	6		8	
All First-Class Matches		2	6		9	
NatWest Trophy	Quarter-Finalist					
Benson & Hedges Cup	6th in South Group					
National League (2nd Division)	4th	8	5	1		2

COUNTY CHAMPIONSHIP AVERAGES

BATTING AND FIELDING

Cap		M	I	NO	HS	Runs	Avge	100	50	Ct/St
1990	M.R.Ramprakash	13	21	4	120*	1088	64.00	4	6	9
1998	J.L.Langer	16	27	3	213*	1472	61.33	5	7	25
–	A.J.Strauss	16	28	2	111*	862	33.15	1	3	6
–	E.C.Joyce	6	8	1	51	195	27.85	–	1	7
1990	M.A.Roseberry	10	19	2	87	410	24.11	–	2	3
2000	O.A.Shah	11	19	–	76	446	23.47	–	3	7
–	K.P.Dutch	4	7	–	91	160	22.85	–	2	4
1995	R.L.Johnson	15	23	3	69	414	20.70	–	2	13
2000	D.C.Nash	16	24	2	75*	445	20.22	–	1	32/4
1993	P.N.Weekes	7	12	–	39	239	19.91	–	–	7
–	R.M.S.Weston	5	9	–	39	138	15.33	–	–	2
–	S.J.Cook	6	10	–	43	145	14.50	–	–	2
1988	A.R.C.Fraser	15	22	6	30	227	14.18	–	–	4
–	B.L.Hutton	9	14	2	55	157	13.08	–	1	8
1990	P.C.R.Tufnell	16	21	9	19	100	8.33	–	–	4
–	T.F.Bloomfield	9	8	2	4*	16	2.66	–	–	1

Also batted: C.J.Batt (2 matches) 21, 0, 6 (1 ct).

BOWLING

	O	M	R	W	Avge	Best	5wI	10wM
K.P.Dutch	121.4	38	323	15	21.53	6-62	1	–
P.C.R.Tufnell	738.3	255	1500	65	23.07	6-48	3	–
A.R.C.Fraser	474.3	150	1111	48	23.14	6-64	1	–
S.J.Cook	115	36	281	10	28.10	4-13	–	–
R.L.Johnson	473	129	1429	50	28.58	6-71	2	–
T.F.Bloomfield	192.3	31	751	18	41.72	4-46	–	–

Also bowled: C.J.Batt 41-11-146-4; B.L.Hutton 56.2-14-200-5; E.C.Joyce 5-1-24-0;
J.L.Langer 6-1-35-1; M.R.Ramprakash 67-18-147-1; O.A.Shah 35-8-126-4; A.J.Strauss
1-0-13 0; P.N.Weekes 64.5-16-190-4.

The First-Class Averages (pp 118-132) give the records of Middlesex players in all
first-class county matches (Middlesex's other opponents being Cambridge University), with
the exception of M.R.Ramprakash whose full county figures are as above.

MIDDLESEX RECORDS

FIRST-CLASS CRICKET

Highest Total	For 642-3d		v	Hampshire	Southampton	1923
	V 665		by	W Indians	Lord's	1939
Lowest Total	For 20		v	MCC	Lord's	1864
	V 31		by	Glos	Bristol	1924
Highest Innings	For 331*	J.D.B.Robertson	v	Worcs	Worcester	1949
	V 316*	J.B.Hobbs	for	Surrey	Lord's	1926

Highest Partnership for each Wicket

1st	372	M.W.Gatting/J.L.Langer	v	Essex	Southgate	1998
2nd	380	F.A.Tarrant/J.W.Hearne	v	Lancashire	Lord's	1914
3rd	424*	W.J.Edrich/D.C.S.Compton	v	Somerset	Lord's	1948
4th	325	J.W.Hearne/E.H.Hendren	v	Hampshire	Lord's	1919
5th	338	R.S.Lucas/T.C.O'Brien	v	Sussex	Hove	1895
6th	270	J.D.Carr/P.N.Weekes	v	Glos	Lord's	1994
7th	271*	E.H.Hendren/F.T.Mann	v	Notts	Nottingham	1925
8th	182*	M.H.C.Doll/H.R.Murrell	v	Notts	Lord's	1913
9th	160*	E.H.Hendren/T.J.Durston	v	Essex	Leyton	1927
10th	230	R.W.Nicholls/W.Roche	v	Kent	Lord's	1899

Best Bowling	For	10- 40	G.O.B.Allen	v	Lancashire	Lord's	1929
(Innings)	V	9- 38	R.C.R-Glasgow†	for	Somerset	Lord's	1924
Best Bowling	For	16-114	G.Burton	v	Yorkshire	Sheffield	1888
(Match)		16-114	J.T.Hearne	v	Lancashire	Manchester	1898
	V	16-109	C.W.L.Parker	for	Glos	Cheltenham	1930

Most Runs – Season	2669	E.H.Hendren	(av 83.41)		1923
Most Runs – Career	40302	E.H.Hendren	(av 48.81)		1907-37
Most 100s – Season	13	D.C.S.Compton			1947
Most 100s – Career	119	E.H.Hendren			1907-37
Most Wkts – Season	158	F.J.Titmus	(av 14.63)		1955
Most Wkts – Career	2361	F.J.Titmus	(av 21.27)		1949-82

LIMITED-OVERS CRICKET

Highest Total	NWT	304-7		v	Surrey	The Oval	1995
		304-8		v	Cornwall	St Austell	1995
	BHC	325-5		v	Leics	Leicester	1992
	NL	290-6		v	Worcs	Lord's	1990
Lowest Total	NWT	41		v	Essex	Westcliff	1972
	BHC	73		v	Essex	Lord's	1985
	NL	23		v	Yorkshire	Leeds	1974
Highest Innings	NWT	158	G.D.Barlow	v	Lancashire	Lord's	1984
	BHC	143*	M.W.Gatting	v	Sussex	Hove	1985
	NL	147*	M.R.Ramprakash	v	Worcs	Lord's	1990
Best Bowling	NWT	6-15	W.W.Daniel	v	Sussex	Hove	1980
	BHC	7-12	W.W.Daniel	v	Minor C (E)	Ipswich	1978
	NL	6- 6	R.W.Hooker	v	Surrey	Lord's	1969

† R.C.Robertson-Glasgow

NORTHAMPTONSHIRE

Formation of Present Club: 31 July 1878
Colours: Maroon
Badge: Tudor Rose
County Champions: (0); best – 2nd 1912, 1957, 1965, 1976
NatWest Trophy/Gillette Cup Winners: (2) 1976, 1992
Benson and Hedges Cup Winners: (1) 1980
National League (Div 1) Winners: (0); best – 3rd 2000
Sunday League Winners: (0); best – 3rd 1991
Match Awards: NWT 54; BHC 56

Chief Executive: S.P.Coverdale, County Ground, Wantage Road, Northampton, NN1 4TJ ▲ Tel: 01604 514455 ▲ Fax: 01604 514488 ▲ Email: post@nccc.co.uk ▲ Web: www.nccc.co.uk

Captain: D.Ripley. **Vice-Captain:** A.L.Penberthy. **Overseas Player** M.E.Hussey.
2001 Beneficiary: None. **Scorer:** A.C.Kingston. ‡ New registration

BAILEY, Tobin Michael Barnaby (Bedford S; Loughborough U), b Kettering 28 Aug 1976. 5'10". RHB, WK. Debut 1996. British U 1998. Bedfordshire 1994-96. HS 96* v Worcs (Worcester) 2000. LO HS 52 Brit U v Glos (Bristol) 1997.

BLAIN, John Angus Rae (Penicuik HS; Jewel & Esk Valley C), b Edinburgh, Scotland 4 Jan 1979. 6'1". RHB, RMF. Scotland 1996-99. Northamptonshire debut 1997. **LOI** (Scot): 5 (1999); 9 v SA and BB 4-37 v B (Edinburgh) 1999. HS 31* v OU (Oxford) 2000. CC HS 0. BB 1-18. LO HS 10* Scot v Notts (Nottingham) 1996 (BHC). LO BB 5-24 v Derbys (Derby) 1997 (SL).

BROWN, Jason Fred (St Margaret Ward HS & SFC), b Newcastle-under-Lyme, Staffs 10 Oct 1974. 6'0". RHB, OB. Debut 1996; cap 2000. Staffordshire 1994-95. Tours: WI 2000-01 (*part*) (Eng A); SL 2000-01 (*no f-c*). HS 16* v Durham (Northampton) 1997. 50 wkts (1): 61 (2000). BB 7-78 (11-131 match) v Sussex (Northampton) 2000. LO HS 4 (NL). LO BB 4-26 v Leics (Northampton) 1997 (SL).

‡CASSAR, Matthew Edward (Sir Joseph Banks HS, Sydney), b Sydney, Australia 16 Oct 1972. Husband of Jane Cassar (*née* Smit; England 1991-92 to date). 6'0". RHB, RFM. Derbyshire 1994-2000. ECB qualified/CC debut 1997. HS 121 De v Sussex (Horsham) 1998. BB 6-76 De v Yorks (Derby) 2000. Award: NWT 1. LO HS 134 De v Northants (Northampton) 1998 (SL). LO BB 4-29 De v Hants (Southampton) 2000 (NL).

COOK, Jeffrey William (James Cook HS, Sydney), b Sydney, Australia 2 Feb 1972. 6'4". LHB, RM. Resident in UK since 1993 – ECB qualified. Debut 2000. NSW U-19. HS 137 v Glos (Cheltenham) 2000. Award: NWT 1. LO HS 130 Northants CB v Wilts (Northampton) 1999 (NWT).

COUSINS, Darren Mark (Netherhall CS; Impington Village C), b Cambridge 24 Sep 1971. 6'2". RHB, RMF. Essex 1993-98. Surrey (NL only) 1999. Northamptonshire debut/cap 2000. Cambridgeshire 1990, 1999. HS 29* v Glam (Northampton) 2000. 50 wkts (1): 67 (2000). BB 6-35 Ex v CU (Cambridge) 1994. CC BB 5-123 v Middx (Lord's) 2000. LO HS 18 v Yorks (Northampton) 2000 (NL). LO BB 3-18 Ex v Warwks (Birmingham) 1994 (SL).

DOBSON, Martyn Colin, b Scunthorpe, Lincs 28 May 1982. Brother of A.M. (Northants staff 1997-98). RHB, OB. Staff 1999 – awaiting f-c debut.

‡HUSSEY, Michael Edward, b Morley, WA, Australia 27 May 1975. LHB, RM. W Australia 1994-95 to date. Tour (Aus A): Sc/Ire 1998. HS 187 WA v Tas (Perth) 1998-99. BB 2-21 WA v Q (Perth) 1998-99. LO HS 100* and LO BB 3-52 WA v Vic (Melbourne) 1999-00 (MM).

INNES, Kevin John (Weston Favell Upper S), b Wellingborough 24 Sep 1975. 5'10". RHB, RM. 2nd XI debut 1990 (aged 14yr 8m – Northamptonshire record). Debut 1994. HS 63 and BB 4-61 v Lancs (Northampton) 1996. LO HS 55 v Worcs (Worcester) 2000 (NL). LO BB 4-36 v Kent (Northampton) 2000 (NL).

LOYE, Malachy Bernhard (Moulton S), b Northampton 27 Sep 1972. 6'2". RHB, OB. Debut 1991; cap 1994. Tours (Eng A): SA 1993-94, 1998-99; Z 1994-95 (Nh), 1998-99. 1000 runs (2); most – 1198 (1998). HS 322* v Glam (Northampton) 1998 – record Northants score. Award: BHC 1. LO HS 122 v Somerset (Luton) 1993 (SL).

PANESAR, Mudhsuden Singh '*Monty*' (Bedford Modern S), b Luton, Beds 25 Apr 1982. RHB, SLA. Bedfordshire 1998-99. Debut 2000 – awaiting f-c debut.

PENBERTHY, Anthony Leonard (Camborne CS), b Troon, Cornwall 1 Sep 1969. 6'1". LHB, RM. Debut 1989; cap 1994. Cornwall 1987-89. Tours (Nh): SA 1991-92; Z 1994-95. HS 128 v Warwks (Northampton) 1998. BB 5-37 v Glam (Swansea) 1993. Took wicket of M.A.Taylor (A) with his first ball in f-c cricket. Award: NWT 1. LO HS 81* v Surrey (Northampton) 1997 (SL). LO BB 5-29 v Glos (Bristol) 2000 (NL).

POWELL, Mark John (Campion S, Bugbrooke; Loughborough U), b Northampton 4 Nov 1980. 5'11". RHB, OB. Debut 2000. HS 1 (twice).

RIPLEY, David (Royds SS, Leeds), b Leeds, Yorks 13 Sep 1966. 5'9". RHB, WK. Debut 1984; cap 1987; benefit 1997; captain 2001. Tours (Nh): SA 1991-92; Z 1994-95. HS 209 v Glam (Northampton) 1998. BB 2-89 v Essex (Ilford) 1987. Award: BHC 1. LO HS 52* v Surrey (Northampton) 1993 (SL).

ROLLINS, Adrian Stewart (Little Ilford CS), b Barking, Essex 8 Feb 1972. Brother of R.J. (Essex 1992-99). 6'5". RHB, occ WK, occ RM. Derbyshire 1993-99; cap 1995. Northamptonshire debut 2000. 1000 runs (3); most – 1142 (1997). HS 210 De v Hants (Chesterfield) 1997. Nh HS 100 v Middx (Lord's) 2000. BB 1-19 (De). LO HS 126* De v Surrey (Derby) 1995 (SL).

SALES, David John Grimwood (Caterham S; Cumnor House S), b Carshalton, Surrey 3 Dec 1977. 6'0". RHB, RM. Debut 1996 v Worcs (Kidderminster) scoring 0 and 210* – record Championship score on f-c debut; youngest (18yr 237d) to score 200 in a Championship match; cap 1999. Tours (Eng A): NZ 1999-00; SL 1997-98; K 1997-98; B 1999-00. 1000 runs (1): 1291 (1999). HS 303* v Essex (Northampton) 1999 – youngest Englishman (21y 240d) to score a f-c 300. BB 4-25 v SL A (Northampton) 1999. CC BB 2-7 v Yorks (Scarborough) 1999. Award: BHC 1. LO HS 91* v SL (Northampton) 1998. Sustained severe knee injury prior to start of England A tour of WI 2000-01.

STRONG, Michael Richard (Brighton C; Brunel UC), b Cuckfield, Sussex 28 Jun 1974. 6'1". LHB, RMF. Sussex 1998-99. Northamptonshire debut 2000. HS 35* Sx v Leics (Arundel) 1999. Nh HS 27* v Glam (Northampton) 2000. BB 4-46 v OU (Oxford) 2000 – on Northants debut. CC BB 4-50 v Glam (Cardiff) 2000. Award: NWT 1. LO HS 21 v Glos (Bristol) 2000 (NWT). LO BB 5-39 v Z (Northampton) 2000.

SWANN, Alec James (Risade S; Sponne S, Towcester), b Northampton 26 Oct 1976. Son of R. (Northumberland 1969-72; Bedfordshire 1988-95); elder brother of G.P. 6'1". RHB, RM/OB. Debut 1996. Bedfordshire 1994. HS 154 v Notts (Northampton) 1999. BB 2-30 v Glos (Northampton) 1999 (NWT).

SWANN, Graeme Peter (Sponne SS, Towcester), b Northampton 24 Mar 1979. Son of R. (Northumberland 1969-72; Bedfordshire 1988-95); younger brother of A.J. 6'0". RHB, OB. Debut 1998; cap 1999. Bedfordshire 1996. **LOI:** 1 (1999-00); dnb v SA (Bloemfontein) 1999-00. Tours (Eng A): SA 1998-99, 1999-00 (Eng); WI 2000-01 (*part*); Z 1998-99. HS 130* v SL A (Northampton) 1999. CC HS 111 v Leics (Leicester) 1998. 50 wkts (1): 57 (1999). BB 6-41 (11-126 match) v Leics (Northampton) 1999. LO HS 63 v Glam (Northampton) 1999 (NL). LO BB 5-35 v Durham (Chester-le-St) 1999 (NL).

TAYLOR, Jonathan Paul (Pingle S, Swadlincote), b Ashby-de-la-Zouch, Leics 8 Aug 1964. 6'2". LHB, LFM. Derbyshire 1984-86. Northamptonshire debut 1991; cap 1992; benefit 2000. Staffordshire 1989-90. **Tests:** 2 (1992-93 to 1994); HS 17* v I (Calcutta) 1992-93. BB 1-18. **LOI:** 1 (1992-93); HS 1 v SL (Moratuwa) 1992-93. Tours: SA 1993-94 (Eng A – part); I 1992-93; Z 1994-95 (Nh). HS 86 v Durham (Northampton) 1995. 50 wkts (6); most – 69 (1993). BB 7-23 v Hants (Bournemouth) 1992. Award: BHC 1. LO HS 24 v Worcs (Northampton) 1993 (SL). LO BB 5-45 v Notts (Northampton) 1996 (BHC).

WARREN, Russell John (Kingsthorpe Upper S), b Northampton 10 Sep 1971. 6'1". RHB, OB. Debut 1992; cap 1995. HS 201* v Glam (Northampton) 1996. Award: NWT 1. LO HS 100* v Ire (Northampton) 1994 (NWT).

‡WEEKES, Lesroy Charlesworth (Montserrat SS), b Montserrat, WI 19 Jul 1971. 6'2". RHB, RFM. Leeward Is 1993-94 to 1996-97. Yorkshire 1994, 2000 (two matches as an unregistered player). HS 46 Leeward Is v Guyana (Blairmont, Berbice) 1993-94. BB 6-56 and UK HS 10 (twice) 2000. LO HS 8 (Y – NWT) 1997. LO BB 4-33 Leeward Is v Guyana (Georgetown) 1994-95 (SST).

WHITE, Robert Allan (Stowe S; Durham U), b Chelmsford, Essex 15 Oct 1979. 5'11". RHB, LB. Debut 2000 – awaiting CC debut. HS 20 v OU (Oxford) 2000 – on debut.

RELEASED/RETIRED
(Having made a first-class County appearance in 2000)

DAVIES, M.K. – *see ESSEX.*

HAYDEN, Matthew Lawrence (Marist C, Ashgrove; Queensland U of Tech), b Kingaroy, Queensland, Australia 29 Oct 1971. 6'2". LHB, RM Queensland 1991-92 to date. Hampshire 1997; cap 1997. Northamptonshire 1999-2000; cap 1999; captain 1999-2000. **Tests** (A): 13 (1993-94 to 2000-01); HS 125 v WI (Adelaide) 1996-97. **LOI** (A): 19 (1993 to 1999-00); HS 67 v NZ (Sharjah) 1993-94. Tours (A): E 1993, 1995 (Young A); Sc/Ire 1998 (Aus A); SA 1993-94, 1996-97; NZ 1999-00; I 2000-01; SL 1999-00. 1000 runs (3+3); most – 1446 (1997). HS 235* H v Warwks (Southampton) 1997. Nh HS 170 v Notts (Northampton) 1999. BB 3-10 v Worcs (Northampton) 1999. Awards: NWT 2; BHC 1. LO HS 152* Q v Vic (Melbourne) 1998-99 (MM). LO BB 2-38 H v Leics (Southampton) 1997 (SL).

LOGAN, R.J. – *see NOTTINGHAMSHIRE.*

MALCOLM. D.E – *see LEICESTERSHIRE.*

LANCASHIRE – RELEASED/RETIRED (continued from p 54)
(Having made a first-class County appearance in 2000)

GANGULY, Sourav Chandidas (St Xavier's Collegiate S), b Calcutta, India 8 Jul 1972. Brother of Snchasish C. Ganguly (Bengal 1986-87 to 1996-97). 5'11". LHB, RM. Bengal 1989-90 to date. Lancashire 2000. **Tests** (I): 38 (1996 to 2000-01, 3 as captain); HS 173 v SL (Bombay) 1997-98; BB 3-28 v A (Calcutta) 1997-98. **LOI** (I): 158 (1991-92 to 2000-01, 29 as captain); HS 183 v SL (Taunton) 1999; BB 5-16 v P (Toronto) 1997-98. Tours (I) (C=captain). E 1996; A 1991 92, 1999 00; SA 1996-97; WI 1996-97; NZ 1998-99; SL 1997-98, 1998 99, Z 1998-99; B 2000 01C. HS 200* Bengal v Tripura (Calcutta) 1993-94 and 200* Bengal v Bihar (Calcutta) 1994-95. La HS 99 v Somerset (Taunton) 2000. BB 6 87 Bengal v Delhi (Delhi) 1997-98. La BB 2-39 v Derbys (Derby) 2000. Awards: NWT 2; BHC 1. LO HS 183 (*see LOI*). LO BB 5-16 (*see LOI*).

McKEOWN, Patrick Christopher (Merchant Taylors S; Rossall S), b Liverpool 1 Jun 1976. 6'3". RHB, OB. Lancashire 1996-2000. HS 75 v CU (Cambridge) 1999. CC HS 64 v Warwks (Birmingham) 1996. LO HS 69 v Northants (Northampton) 1996 (SL).

WOOD, Nathan Theodore (Wm Hulme's GS), b Thornhill Edge, Yorks 4 Oct 1974. Son of B. (Yorks, Lancs, Derbys and England 1964-83). 5'8". LHB, OB. Lancashire 1996-2000. HS 155 v Surrey (Oval) 1997. LO HS 23 v Sussex (Hove) 1998 (SL).

NORTHAMPTONSHIRE 2000

RESULTS SUMMARY

	Place	Won	Lost	Tied	Drew	No Result
County Championship (2nd Division)	1st	7	4		5	
All First-Class Matches		7	5		5	
NatWest Trophy	Quarter-Finalist					
Benson & Hedges Cup	4th in Mid/West/Wales Group					
National League (1st Division)	3rd	9	7			

COUNTY CHAMPIONSHIP AVERAGES

BATTING AND FIELDING

Cap		M	I	NO	HS	Runs	Avge	100	50	Ct/St
1999	M.L.Hayden	15	22	–	164	1270	57.72	4	6	21
1994	A.L.Penberthy	15	21	2	116	785	41.31	1	5	10
1995	R.J.Warren	8	11	1	151	384	38.40	1	2	1
–	T.M.B.Bailey	3	5	1	96*	149	37.25	–	1	8/1
1999	D.J.G.Sales	13	20	–	276	713	35.65	1	5	9
–	J.W.Cook	10	15	1	137	465	33.21	2	1	4
1987	D.Ripley	13	18	3	56	475	31.66	–	3	38/4
1994	M.B.Loye	12	18	1	93	504	29.64	–	3	1
–	A.S.Rollins	16	24	–	100	636	26.50	1	4	19
1999	G.P.Swann	15	22	–	72	524	23.81	–	2	7
2000	D.M.Cousins	16	23	7	29*	210	13.12	–	–	3
–	M.R.Strong	3	5	1	27*	48	12.00	–	–	1
–	M.K.Davies	4	6	–	25	65	10.83	–	–	2
1992	J.P.Taylor	7	10	1	27	96	10.66	–	–	3
–	R.J.Logan	6	8	1	24	51	7.28	–	–	1
2000	J.F.Brown	9	13	4	11	29	3.22	–	–	3
1999	D.E.Malcolm	7	10	1	8	24	2.66	–	–	–

Also batted: K.J.Innes (1 match) 5, 25; M.J.Powell (1) 1, 1; A.J.Swann (2) 61*, 19, 13 (1 ct).

BOWLING

	O	M	R	W	Avge	Best	5wI	10wM
D.M.Cousins	510.4	142	1318	67	19.67	5-123	1	–
J.F.Brown	485	138	1149	57	20.15	7- 78	4	2
A.L.Penberthy	131	30	358	16	22.37	5- 54	1	–
J.P.Taylor	212.3	50	540	24	22.50	6- 27	1	1
D.E.Malcolm	184.1	46	541	19	28.47	5- 45	1	–
G.P.Swann	445.3	89	1293	41	31.53	6-118	2	–
R.J.Logan	133.1	33	453	11	41.18	5- 61	1	–

Also bowled: J.W.Cook 1-0-7-0; M.K.Davies 109-37-273-8; M.L.Hayden 15-2-56-1; K.J.Innes 4.3-0-28-1; M.R.Strong 57.2-7-192-6; A.J.Swann 28-13-42-3.

The First-Class Averages (pp 118-132) give the records of Northamptonshire players in all first-class county matches (Northamptonshire's other opponents being Oxford University).

NORTHAMPTONSHIRE RECORDS

FIRST-CLASS CRICKET

Highest Total	For	781-7d		v	Notts	Northampton	1995
	V	670-9d		by	Sussex	Hove	1921
Lowest Total	For	12		v	Glos	Gloucester	1907
	V	33		by	Lancashire	Northampton	1977
Highest Innings	For	322	M.B.Loye	v	Glamorgan	Northampton	1998
	V	333	K.S.Duleepsinhji	for	Sussex	Hove	1930

Highest Partnership for each Wicket

1st	372	R.R.Montgomerie/M.B.Loye	v	Yorkshire	Northampton	1996
2nd	344	G.Cook/R.J.Boyd-Moss	v	Lancashire	Northampton	1986
3rd	393	A.Fordham/A.J.Lamb	v	Yorkshire	Leeds	1990
4th	370	R.T.Virgin/P.Willey	v	Somerset	Northampton	1976
5th	401	M.B.Loye/D.Ripley	v	Glamorgan	Northampton	1998
6th	376	R.Subba Row/A.Lightfoot	v	Surrey	The Oval	1958
7th	293	D.J.G.Sales/D.Ripley	v	Essex	Northampton	1999
8th	164	D.Ripley/N.G.B Cook	v	Lancashire	Manchester	1987
9th	156	R.Subba Row/S.Starkie	v	Lancashire	Northampton	1955
10th	148	B.W.Bellamy/J.V.Murdin	v	Glamorgan	Northampton	1925

Best Bowling	For	10-127	V.W.C.Jupp	v	Kent	Tunbridge W	1932
(Innings)	V	10- 30	C.Blythe	for	Kent	Northampton	1907
Best Bowling	For	15- 31	G.E.Tribe	v	Yorkshire	Northampton	1958
(Match)	V	17- 48	C.Blythe	for	Kent	Northampton	1907

Most Runs – Season	2198	D.Brookes	(av 51.11)		1952
Most Runs – Career	28980	D.Brookes	(av 36.13)		1934-59
Most 100s – Season	8	R.A.Haywood			1921
Most 100s – Career	67	D.Brookes			1934-59
Most Wkts – Season	175	G.E.Tribe	(av 18.70)		1955
Most Wkts – Career	1097	E.W.Clark	(av 21.31)		1922-47

LIMITED-OVERS CRICKET

Highest Total	NWT	360-2		v	Staffs	Northampton	1990
	BHC	304-6		v	Scotland	Northampton	1995
	NL	306-2		v	Surrey	Guildford	1985
Lowest Total	NWT	62		v	Leics	Leicester	1974
	BHC	85		v	Sussex	Northampton	1978
	NL	41		v	Middlesex	Northampton	1972
Highest Innings	NWT	145	R.J.Bailey	v	Staffs	Stone	1991
	BHC	134	R.J.Bailey	v	Glos	Northampton	1987
	NL	172*	W.Larkins	v	Warwicks	Luton	1983
Best Bowling	NWT	7-37	N.A.Mallender	v	Worcs	Northampton	1984
	BHC	5-14	F.A.Rose	v	Minor C	Luton	1998
	NL	7-39	A.Hodgson	v	Somerset	Northampton	1976

NOTTINGHAMSHIRE

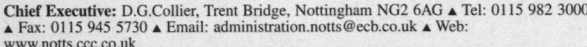

Formation of Present Club: March/April 1841
Substantial Reorganisation: 11 December 1866
Colours: Green and Gold
Badge: Badge of City of Nottingham
County Champions (since 1890): (4) 1907, 1929, 1981, 1987
NatWest Trophy/Gillette Cup Winners: (1) 1987
Benson and Hedges Cup Winners: (1) 1989
National League (Div 1) Winners: (0); best – 2nd (Div 2) 2000
Sunday League Winners: (1) 1991
Match Awards: NWT 42; BHC 68

Chief Executive: D.G.Collier, Trent Bridge, Nottingham NG2 6AG ▲ Tel: 0115 982 3000 ▲ Fax: 0115 945 5730 ▲ Email: administration.notts@ecb.co.uk ▲ Web: www.notts.ccc.co.uk

Captain: J.E.R.Gallian. **Vice-Captain:** No appointment. **Overseas Player:** G.S.Blewett.
2001 Beneficiary: None. **Scorer:** G.Stringfellow. ‡ New registration

AFZAAL, Usman (Manvers Pierrepont CS; S Notts C), b Rawalpindi, Pakistan 9 Jun 1977. 6'0". LHB, SLA. Debut 1995; cap 2000. Tours: SA 1996-97 (Nt); WI 2000-01 (Eng A). 1000 runs (1): 1018 (2000). HS 151* v Worcs (Nottingham) 2000. BB 4-101 v Glos (Nottingham) 1998. LO HS 95* v Hants (Southampton) 2000 (NL). LO BB 2-25 v Yorks (Cleethorpes) 1995 (SL).

BICKNELL, Darren John (Robert Haining SS; Guildford TC), b Guildford, Surrey 24 Jun 1967. Elder brother of M.P. 6'4". LHB, SLA. Surrey 1987-99; cap 1990; benefit 1999. Nottinghamshire debut/cap 2000. Tours (Eng A): WI 1991-92; P 1990-91; SL 1990-91; Z 1989-90. 1000 runs (6); most – 1888 (1991). HS 235* Sy v Notts (Nottingham) 1994. Nt HS 180* v Warwks (Birmingham) 2000 – sharing unbroken 1st wkt stand of 406 with G.E.Welton. BB 3-7 Sy v Sussex (Guildford) 1996. Awards: NWT 1; BHC 4. LO HS 135* Sy v Yorks (Oval) 1989 (NWT). LO BB 1-11 (Sy – SL).

‡BLEWETT, Gregory Scott (Prince Alfred C), b Adelaide, Australia 28 Oct 1971. Son of R.W. (South Australia 1975-76 to 1978-79). 6'0". RHB, RM. South Australia 1991-92 to date. Yorkshire 1999; cap 1999. **Tests** (A): 46 (1994-95 to 1999-00); HS 214 v SA (Johannesburg) 1996-97; scored 102* v E (Adelaide) on debut; first to score hundreds in his first 3 Ashes Tests; BB 2-9 v WI (St John's) 1998-99. **LOI** (A): 32 (1994-95 to 1998-99); HS 57* v WI (Melbourne) 1996-97; BB 2-6 v SL (Adelaide) 1998-99. Tours (A): E 1997; SA 1996-97; WI 1994-95, 1998-99; NZ 1999-00; I 1997-98; SL 1999-00; Z 1999-00. 1000 runs (0+3); most – 1187 (1998-99). HS 268 S Aus v Vic (Melbourne) 1993-94. CC HS 190 Y v Northants (Scarborough) 1999. BB 5-29 Aus XI v WI (Hobart) 1996-97. CC BB 2-16 Y v Durham (Leeds) 1999. LO HS 113 Aus A v E (Sydney) 1994-95. LO BB 4-18 Y v Lancs (Manchester) 1999 (NWT).

‡CLOUGH, Gareth David (Pudsey Grangefield S), b Leeds, Yorks 23 May 1978. 6'0". RHB, RM. Yorkshire 1998. Nottinghamshire staff 2001. HS 33 Y v Glam (Cardiff) 1998 – on debut.

FRANKS, Paul John (Southwell Minster CS), b Mansfield 3 Feb 1979. 6'2". LHB, RMF. Debut 1996; cap 1999. YC 2000. **LOI:** 1 (2000); HS 4 v WI (Nottingham) 2000. Tours (Eng A): SA 1998-99; WI 2000-01; NZ 1999-00; B 1999-00. HS 66* v Kent (Canterbury) 1998. 50 wkts (2); most – 63 (1999). BB 7-56 v Middx (Lord's) 2000. Hat-trick 1997. Award: NWT 1. LO HS 40 v Glam (Nottingham) 1999 (NL). LO BB 6-27 v Durham (Chester-le-St) 2000 (NL).

GALLIAN, Jason Edward Riche (Pittwater House S, Sydney; Keble C, Oxford), b Manly, Sydney, Australia 25 Jun 1971. Qualified for England 1994. 6'0". RHB, RM. Lancashire 1990-97, taking wicket of D.A.Hagan (OU) with his first ball; cap 1994. Oxford U 1992-93; blue 1992-93; captain 1993. Nottinghamshire debut/cap 1998; captain 1998 (part) to date. Captained Australia YC v England YC 1989-90, scoring 158* in 1st 'Test'. **Tests:** 3 (1995 to 1995-96); HS 28 v SA (Pt Elizabeth) 1995-96. Tours: A 1996-97 (Eng A); S 1995-96 (La); SA 1995-96 (part); I 1994-95 (Eng A); P 1995-96 (Eng A). 1000 runs (2); most – 1156 (1996). HS 312 La v Derbys (Manchester) 1996 (record score at Old Trafford). Nt HS 150 v Glam (Nottingham) 2000. BB 6-115 La v Surrey (Southport) 1996. Nt BB 2-28 v Warwks (Nottingham) 1999. Awards: NWT 2; BHC 2. LO HS 134 La v Notts (Manchester) 1995 (BHC). LO BB 5-15 La v Minor C (Leek) 1995 (BHC).

HARRIS, Andrew James (Hadfield CS; Glossopdale Community C), b Ashton-under-Lyne, Lancs 26 Jun 1973. 6'1". RHB, RM. Derbyshire 1994-99; cap 1996. Nottinghamshire debut/cap 2000. Tour: A 1996-97 (Eng A). HS 39 v Worcs (Nottingham) 2000 – on Notts debut. 50 wkts (1): 72 (1996). BB 6-40 (12-88 match) De v Middx (Derby) 1996. Nt BB 6-110 v Sussex (Nottingham) 2000. Award: NWT 1. LO HS 11* De v Kent (Derby) 1996 (NWT). LO BB 5-35 v Hants (Nottingham) 2000 (NL).

HEWISON, Christopher Jon (Whickham CS and SFC), b Gateshead, Co Durham 6 Oct 1979. 6'1". RHB, RMF. Debut 2000. HS 24 v Glam (Nottingham) 2000 – on debut. LO HS 19 Durham CB v Staffs (Gateshead) 1999 (NWT).

JOHNSON, Paul (Grove CS, Balderton), b Newark 24 Apr 1965 5'7". RHB, RM. Debut 1982; cap 1986; benefit 1995; captain 1996-98. Tours: SA 1996-97 (Nt); WI 1991-92 (Eng A). 1000 runs (9); most – 1518 (1990). HS 187 v Lancs (Manchester) 1993. BB 1-9. CC BB 1-14. Awards: NWT 2; BHC 3. LO HS 167* v Kent (Nottingham) 1993 (SL).

‡**LOGAN, Richard** James (Wolverhampton GS), b Stone, Staffs 28 Jan 1980. 6'1". RHB, RMF. Northamptonshire 1999-2000. HS 24 Nh v Essex (Ilford) 2000. BB 5-61 Nh v Middx (Northampton) 2000. LO HS 17 Nh v Worcs (Worcester) 2000 (NL). LO BB 3-52 Nh v Glam (Northampton) 2000 (BHC).

LUCAS, David Scott (Djanogoly CTC, Nottingham), b Nottingham 19 Aug 1978. 6'2". RHB, LMF. Debut 1999. HS 46* v Middx (Nottingham) 2000. BB 5-104 v Essex (Nottingham) 1999. LO HS 19* v Sussex (Hove) 1999 (NL). LO BB 4-27 v Derbys (Derby) 2000 (NL).

‡**MALIK, Muhammad Nadeem,** (Wilford Meadows CS), b Nottingham 6 Oct 1982. RHB, RMF. Staff 2001. 2nd XI debut 1999 when aged 16y 337d. LO HS 1* (Notts CB – NWT).

MILLNS, David James (Garibaldi CS), b Clipstone, Notts 27 Feb 1965. 6'3". LHB, RF. Nottinghamshire 1988-89, 2000 to date; cap 2000. Leicestershire 1990-99; cap 1991; benefit 1999. Boland 1996-97. Tours: A 1992-93 (Eng A); SA 1996-97 (Le). HS 121 Le v Northants (Northampton) 1997. Nt HS 50* v Northants (Northampton) 2000. 50 wkts (4); most – 76 (1994). BB 9-37 (12-91 match) Le v Derbys (Derby) 1991. Nt BB 5-58 v Northants (Nottingham) 2000. Awards: NWT 1; BHC 1. LO HS 39* Le v Warwks (Birmingham) 1996 (BHC). LO BB 4-26 Le v Durham (Stockton) 1995 (BHC).

MORRIS, John Edward (Shavington CS; Dane Bank CFE), b Crewe, Cheshire 1 Apr 1964. 5'10". RHB, RM Derbyshire 1982-93; cap 1986. GW 1988-89 and 1993-94. Durham 1994-99; cap 1998; benefit 1999. Nottinghamshire debut/cap 2000. **Tests:** 3 (1990); HS 32 v I (Oval) 1990. **LOI:** 8 (1990-91). HS 63* v NZ (Adelaide) 1990-91. Tour: A 1990-91. 1000 runs (11); most – 1739 (1986). HS 229 De v Glos (Cheltenham) 1993. Nt HS 115 v Sussex (Hove) 2000. BB 1-6 (De). Nt BB 1-26. Awards: NWT 2; BHC 2. LO HS 145 Du v Leics (Leicester) 1996 (BHC). LO BB 1-44 (GW – NS).

NOON, Wayne Michael (Caistor S), b Grimsby, Lincs 5 Feb 1971. 5'9". RHB, WK. Northamptonshire 1989-93. Nottinghamshire debut 1994; cap 1995. Canterbury 1994-95. Worcs 2nd XI debut when aged 15yr 199d. Tours: SA 1991-92 (Nh), 1996-97 (Nt). HS 83 v Northants (Northampton) 1997. LO HS 46 v Warwks (Birmingham) 1998 (BHC).

‡**PIETERSEN, Kevin** Peter (Maritzburg C; Natal U), b Pietermaritzburg, SA 27 Jun 1980. British passport (English mother). RHB, OB. Natal/KwaZulu-Natal 1997-98 to date. HS 61* and BB 4-141 KZ-Natal v E (Durban) 1999-00. LO HS 11 and BB 2-43 KZN v Boland (Paarl) 1999-00 (SBC).

RANDALL, Stephen John (W Bridgford S), b Nottingham 9 Jun 1980. 5'10". RHB, OB. Debut 1999. HS 20 v Glam (Colwyn Bay) 1999. BB 1-109. LO HS 1 (Notts CB – NWT).

READ, Christopher Mark Wells (Torquay GS; Bath U), b Paignton, Devon 10 Aug 1978. 5'8". RHB, WK. Gloucestershire (L-O) 1997. Nottinghamshire debut 1998; cap 1999. Devon 1995-97. **Tests:** 3 (1999); HS 37 v NZ (Lord's) 1999. **LOI:** 9 (1999-00); HS 26* v SA (Cape Town) 1999-00. Tours (Eng A): SA 1998-99, 1999-00 (Eng); WI 2000-01; SL 1997-98; Z 1998-99; K 1997-98. HS 160 v Warwks (Nottingham) 1999. LO HS 62 v Somerset (Nottingham) 1999 (NL).

‡**SMITH, Gregory** James (Pretoria BHS; Pretoria Technikon), b Pretoria, SA 30 Oct 1971. British passport. RHB, LF. N Transvaal/Northerns 1993-94 to date. Natal v A: E 1996. HS 68 NT v WP (Pretoria) 1995-96. BB 6-35 Northerns v WP (Pretoria) 1997-98. LO HS 9 (SBC) LO BB 5-11 (SBC) NT v GW (Kimberley) 1995-96.

STEMP, Richard David (Britannia HS, Rowley Regis), b Erdington, Birmingham 11 Dec 1967. 6'0". RHB, SLA. Worcestershire 1990-92. Yorkshire 1993-98; cap 1996. Nottinghamshire debut 1999; cap 2000. Tours (Eng A): SA 1992-93 (Y); I 1994-95; P 1995-96. HS 65 Y v Durham (Chester-le-St) 1996. Nt HS 18 v Sussex (Hove) 1999. BB 6-37 Y v Durham (Durham) 1994. Nt BB 5-123 v Worcs (Worcester) 2000. Award: BHC 1. LO HS 29* v Somerset (Nottingham) 1999 (NL). LO BB 4-25 Y v Glos (Bristol) 1996 (SL).

TOLLEY, Christopher Mark (King Edward VI C, Stourbridge; Loughborough U), b Kidderminster, Worcs 30 Dec 1967. 5'9". RHB, LMF. Worcestershire 1989-95; cap 1993. Nottinghamshire debut 1996; cap 1997; Cricket Development Officer – Elite Squad 2000 to date – available for l-o matches. Tours (Wo): SA 1996-97 (Nt); Z 1990-91, 1993-94. HS 84 Wo v Derbys (Derby) 1994. Nt HS 78 v Glos (Nottingham) 1998. BB 7-45 v Worcs (Kidderminster) 1998. Hat-trick 1997. Awards: NWT 1; BHC 1. LO HS 77 v Somerset (Nottingham) 1998 (NWT) and 77 Comb U v Lancs (Cambridge) 1990 (BHC). LO BB 5-16 v Hants (Southampton) 1996 (SL).

WELTON, Guy Edward (Healing CS; Grimsby C), b Grimsby, Lincs 4 May 1978. 6'1". RHB, OB. Debut 1997. MCC YC. HS 200* v Warwks (Birmingham) 2000 – sharing unbroken 1st wkt stand of 406 with D.J.Bicknell. LO HS 104* v Durham (Nottingham) 1999 (NL).

RELEASED/RETIRED
(Having made a first-class County appearance in 2000)

BOWEN, Mark Nicholas (Sacred Heart, Redcar; St Mary's C; Tees-Side Poly), b Redcar, Yorks 6 Dec 1967. 6'2". RHB, RM. Northamptonshire 1991-92/1994. Nottinghamshire 1996-2000; cap 1997. Tours: SA 1991-92 (Nh), 1996-97 (Nt). HS 32 v Northants (Northampton) 1997 and 32 v Durham (Nottingham) 1998. BB 7-73 v Somerset (Taunton) 1998. LO HS 31 v Hants (Southampton) 2000 (NL). LO BB 4-29 v Warwks (Nottingham) 1997 (SL). Retired – now employed at Sellafield Nuclear Power Plant, Cumbria.

REIFFEL, Paul Ronald (Jordanville TS), b Box Hill, Victoria, Australia 19 Apr 1966. 6'2". RHB, RFM. Victoria 1987-88 to date. Nottinghamshire 2000; cap 2000. **Tests:** 35 (1991-92 to 1997-98); HS 79* v SA (Melbourne) 1997-98; BB 6-71 v E (Birmingham) 1993. **LOI** (A): 92 (1991-92 to 1999); HS 58 v SA (Pt Elizabeth) 1993-94; BB 4-13 v SA (Sydney) 1993-94. Tours (A): E 1993, 1997; SA 1993-94, 1996-97; WI 1994-95, I 1996-97; NZ 1992-93, Z 1991-92 (Aus B). 50 wkts (0+2): 59 (1999-00). HS 86 and BB 6-57 V v Tasmania (Melbourne) 1990-91. Nt HS 74 v Sussex (Nottingham) 2000. Nt BB 5-62 v Warwks (Nottingham) 2000. UK BB 6-71 (*see Tests*). LO HS 58 (*see LOI*). LO BB 4-13 (*see LOI*).

WHILEY, M.J.A. – *see LEICESTERSHIRE*.

NOTTINGHAMSHIRE 2000

RESULTS SUMMARY

	Place	Won	Lost	Tied	Drew	No Result
County Championship (2nd Division)	7th	2	4		10	
All First-Class Matches		2	4		10	1
NatWest Trophy	3rd Round					
Benson & Hedges Cup	6th in North Group					
National League (2nd Division)	2nd	11	4			1

COUNTY CHAMPIONSHIP AVERAGES

BATTING AND FIELDING

Cap		M	I	NO	HS	Runs	Avge	100	50	Ct/St
2000	P.R.Reiffel	7	8	4	74	275	68.75	–	3	–
2000	U.Afzaal	16	26	3	151*	1018	44.26	3	4	9
1998	J.E.R.Gallian	16	26	3	150	796	34.60	3	–	23
2000	D.J.Bicknell	16	28	3	180*	858	34.32	2	2	3
–	G.E.Welton	13	23	2	200*	674	32.09	1	3	8
2000	J.E.Morris	13	20	–	115	601	30.05	1	3	7
1997	C.M.Tolley	6	9	1	60	223	27.87	–	2	2
2000	D.J.Millns	8	11	4	50*	195	27.85	–	1	2
1999	P.J.Franks	13	18	1	60	447	26.29	–	3	5
–	D.S.Lucas	10	12	5	46*	184	26.28	–	–	3
1999	C.M.W.Read	16	23	3	56*	479	23.95	–	3	40
1986	P.Johnson	12	19	2	100	353	20.76	1	–	9
2000	A.J.Harris	11	14	4	39	153	15.30	–	–	4
1997	M.N.Bowen	4	6	–	24	83	13.83	–	–	2
2000	R.D.Stemp	11	11	5	11	45	7.50	–	–	7

Also played (1 match each): C.J.Hewison 24, 6 (5 ct); W.M.Noon (cap 1995) 0, 7 (1ct); S.J.Randall did not bat; M.J.A.Whiley 0, 0, (1 ct).

BOWLING

	O	M	R	W	Avge	Best	5wI	10wM
P.R.Reiffel	233.3	60	586	21	27.90	5- 62	1	–
R.D.Stemp	398.2	140	946	33	28.66	5-123	1	–
D.J.Millns	226.1	42	880	30	29.33	5- 58	1	–
P.J.Franks	393.4	81	1247	42	29.69	7- 56	2	–
A.J.Harris	384.3	62	1358	44	30.86	6-110	4	–
D.S.Lucas	271.5	57	888	27	32.88	4- 61	–	–

Also bowled: U.Afzaal 149.2-46-379-9; D.J.Bicknell 1-1-0-0; M.N.Bowen 68-14-208-4; J.E.R.Gallian 92-24-278-5; J.E.Morris 2.4-0-26-1; S.J.Randall 22-2-109-1; C.M.Tolley 52-22-107-4; G.E.Welton 1-0-1-0; M.J.A.Whiley 13.3-2-76-0.

The First-Class Averages (pp 118-132) give the records of Nottinghamshire players in all first-class county matches (Nottinghamshire's other opponents being Cambridge University, the fixture being abandoned because of rain).

NOTTINGHAMSHIRE RECORDS

FIRST-CLASS CRICKET

Highest Total	For 739-7d		v	Leics	Nottingham	1903
	V 781-7d		by	Northants	Northampton	1995
Lowest Total	For 13		v	Yorkshire	Nottingham	1901
	V 16		by	Derbyshire	Nottingham	1879
	16		by	Surrey	The Oval	1880
Highest Innings	For 312*	W.W.Keeton	v	Middlesex	The Oval	1939
	V 345	C.G.Macartney	for	Australians	Nottingham	1921

Highest Partnership for each Wicket

1st	406*	D.J.Bicknell/G.E.Welton	v	Warwicks	Birmingham	2000
2nd	398	A.Shrewsbury/W.Gunn	v	Sussex	Nottingham	1890
3rd	369	W.Gunn/J.R.Gunn	v	Leics	Nottingham	1903
4th	361	A.O.Jones/J.R.Gunn	v	Essex	Leyton	1905
5th	266	A.Shrewsbury/W.Gunn	v	Sussex	Hove	1884
6th	303*	F.H.Winrow/P.F.Harvey	v	Derbyshire	Nottingham	1947
7th	301	C.C.Lewis/B.N.French	v	Durham	Chester-le-St	1993
8th	220	G.F.H.Heane/R.Winrow	v	Somerset	Nottingham	1935
9th	170	J.C.Adams/K.P.Evans	v	Somerset	Taunton	1994
10th	152	E.B.Alletson/W.Riley	v	Sussex	Hove	1911
	152	U.Afzaal/A.J.Harris	v	Worcs	Nottingham	2000

Best Bowling	For 10-66	K.Smales	v	Glos	Stroud	1956
(Innings)	V 10-10	H.Verity	for	Yorkshire	Leeds	1932
Best Bowling	For 17-89	F.C.Matthews	v	Northants	Nottingham	1923
(Match)	V 17-89	W.G.Grace	for	Glos	Cheltenham	1877

Most Runs – Season	2620	W.W.Whysall	(av 53.46)		1929
Most Runs – Career	31592	G.Gunn	(av 35.69)		1902-32
Most 100s – Season	9	W.W.Whysall			1928
	9	M.J.Harris			1971
	9	B.C.Broad			1990
Most 100s – Career	65	J.Hardstaff jr			1930-55
Most Wkts – Season	181	B.Dooland	(av 14.96)		1954
Most Wkts – Career	1653	T.G.Wass	(av 20.34)		1896-1920

LIMITED-OVERS CRICKET

Highest Total	NWT	344-6		v	Northumb	Jesmond	1994
	BHC	296-6		v	Kent	Nottingham	1989
	NL	329-6		v	Derbyshire	Nottingham	1993
Lowest Total	NWT	123		v	Yorkshire	Scarborough	1969
	BHC	74		v	Leics	Leicester	1987
	NL	66		v	Yorkshire	Bradford	1969
Highest Innings	NWT	149*	D.W.Randall	v	Devon	Torquay	1988
	BHC	130*	C.E.B.Rice	v	Scotland	Glasgow	1982
	NL	167*	P.Johnson	v	Kent	Nottingham	1993
Best Bowling	NWT	6-10	K.P.Evans	v	Northumb	Jesmond	1994
	BHC	6-22	M.K.Bore	v	Leics	Leicester	1980
		6-22	C.E.B.Rice	v	Northants	Northampton	1981
	NL	6-12	R.J.Hadlee	v	Lancashire	Nottingham	1980

SOMERSET

Formation of Present Club: 18 August 1875
Colours: Black, White and Maroon
Badge: Somerset Dragon
County Champions: (0); best – 3rd 1892, 1958, 1963, 1966, 1981
NatWest Trophy/Gillette Cup Winners: (2) 1979, 1983
Benson and Hedges Cup Winners: (2) 1981, 1982
National League (Div 1) Winners: (0); best – 6th 2000
Sunday League Winners: (1) 1979
Match Awards: NWT 55; BHC 66

Chief Executive: P.W.Anderson, The County Ground, Taunton TA1 1JT ▲ Tel: 01823 272946 ▲ Fax: 01823 332395 ▲ Email: somerset@ecb.co.uk ▲ Web: None.

Captain/Overseas Player: J.Cox. **Vice-Captain:** M.E.Trescothick.
2001 Beneficiary: Somerset CCC Museum and the Tony Coles Charitable Trust for the Development of Youth Cricket. **Scorer:** G.A.Stickley. ‡ New registration

BLACKWELL, Ian David (Brookfield Community S), b Chesterfield, Derbys 10 Jun 1978. 6'1". LHB, SLA. Derbyshire 1997-99. Somerset debut 2000, HS 109 v Leics (Taunton) 2000. Sm 5-115 De v Surrey (Oval) 1998. Sm BB 4-18 v OU (Taunton) 2000 – on Somerset debut. LO HS 97 De v Glam (Derby) 1999 (NL). LO BB 4-36 v Worcs (Worcester) 2000 (NL).

BOWLER, Peter Duncan (Educated at Canberra, Australia), b Plymouth, Devon 30 Jul 1963. 6'1" RHB, OB, occ WK. Leicestershire 1986 – first to score hundred on f-c debut for Leics (100* and 62 v Hants). Tasmania 1986-87. Derbyshire 1988-94; cap 1989; scored 155* v CU (Cambridge) on debut – first instance of hundreds on debut for two counties. Somerset debut/cap 1995; captain 1997-98; benefit 2000. 1000 runs (9) inc 2000 (1): 2044 (1992). HS 241* De v Hants (Portsmouth) 1992. Sm HS 207 v Surrey (Taunton) 1996. BB 3-25 v Northants (Taunton) 1998. Awards: BHC 4. LO HS 138* De v Somerset (Derby) 1993 (SL). LO BB 3-31 De v Glos (Cheltenham) 1991 (SL).

BULBECK, Matthew Paul Leonard (Taunton S; Richard Huish C), b Taunton 8 Nov 1979. 6'3½". LHB, LMF. Debut 1998. HS 76* v Durham (Chester-le-St) 1999. 50 wkts (1): 51 (1999). BB 5-45 (10-108 match) v Northants (Northampton) 1999. LO HS 5 (NL). LO BB 4-40 v Notts (Nottingham) 1999 (NL).

BURNS, Michael (Walney CS), b Barrow-in-Furness, Lancs 6 Jun 1969. 6'0". RHB, RM, WK. Cumberland 1988-90. Warwickshire 1992-96. Somerset debut 1997; cap 1999. HS 160 v OU (Taunton) 2000 – earliest hundred on f-c matches (Apr 7). CC HS 109 v Leics (Taunton) 1999. BB 3-11 v Lancs (Taunton) 2000. Award: BHC 1. LO HS 115* v Middx (Taunton) 1997 (SL). LO BB 4-39 v Glos (Taunton) 1997 (SL).

CADDICK, Andrew Richard (Papanui HS), b Christchurch, NZ 21 Nov 1968. Son of English emigrants – qualified for England 1992. 6'5". RHB, RFM. Debut 1991; cap 1992; benefit 1999. Represented NZ in 1987-88 Youth World Cup. **ECB contract 2000.** *Wisden* 2000. **Tests:** 43 (1993 to 2000-01); HS 48 v SA (Jo'burg) 1999-00; BB 7-46 v SA (Durban) 1999-00. **LOI:** 29 (1993 to 2000-01); HS 21* v Z (Harare) 1999-00; BB 4-19 v SA (Jo'burg) 1999-00. **Tours:** A 1992-93 (Eng A); SA 1999-00; WI 1993-94, 1997-98; NZ 1996-97; P 2000-01; SL 2000-01; Z 1996-97. HS 92 v Worcs (Worcester) 1995. 50 wkts (8) inc 100 (1): 105 (1998). BB 9-32 (12-120 match) v Lancs (Taunton) 1993. Awards: NWT 2. LO HS 39 v Hants (Taunton) 1996 (SL). LO BB 6-30 v Glos (Taunton) 1992 (NWT).

COX, Jamie (Wynyard HS; Deakin U), b Burnie, Tasmania, Australia 15 Oct 1969. 6'0". RHB, OB. Tasmania 1987-88 to date; vice-captain 1996-97 to date. Somerset debut/cap 1999; captain 1999 to date. Tours: Z 1991-92 (Aus B), 1995-96 (Tas). 1000 runs (1+1); most – 1617 (1999). HS 245 Tas v NSW (Hobart) 1999-00. Sm HS 216 v Hants (Southampton) 1999. BB 3-46 v Middx (Taunton) 1999. Awards: NWT 2. LO HS 114 v Surrey (Taunton) 1999 (NWT). LO BB 3-28 v Durham (Taunton) 1999 (NL).

‡DUTCH, Keith Philip (Nower Hill HS; Weald C), b Harrow, Middlesex 21 Mar 1973. 5'10". RHB, OB. Middlesex 1993-2000. MCC YC. HS 91 and BB 6-62 M v Essex (Chelmsford) 2000. LO HS 58 M v Kent (Lord's) 1997 (SL). LO BB 5-35 M v Somerset (Taunton) 1999 (NL).

GAZZARD, Carl Matthew (Mounts Bay CS, Penzance; Richard Huish C), b Penzance, Cornwall 15 Apr 1982. 6'0". RHB, WK. Cornwall 1998-2000. Staff 2000 – awaiting f-c debut. LO HS 16 Cornwall v Cumb (Kendal) 1999 (NWT).

GROVE, Jamie Oliver (Bury St Edmunds County Upper S), b Bury St Edmunds, Suffolk 3 Jul 1979. 6'1". RHB, RMF. Essex 1998-99. Somerset debut 2000. HS 33 Ex v Surrey (Chelmsford) 1998. Sm HS 17 v WI (Taunton) 2000. BB 5-90 v Leics (Leicester) 2000 – on Somerset debut. LO HS 0 (v Z).

HOLLOWAY, Piran Christopher Laity (Millfield S; Taunton S; Loughborough U), b Helston, Cornwall 1 Oct 1970. 5'8". LHB, WK. Warwickshire 1988-93. Somerset debut 1994; cap 1997. Awards: NWT 1; BHC 1. HS 168 v Middx (Uxbridge) 1996. LO HS 117 v Glos (Taunton) 1997 (SL).

‡HUNKIN, Christopher Andrew (Richard Huish C), b St Austell, Cornwall 14 Dec 1980.RHB, RM. Staff 2001. Awaiting f-c debut. LO HS 10* and LO BB 1-25 Somerset CB v Staffs (Walsall) 2000 (NWT).

‡JOHNSON, Richard Leonard (Sunbury Manor S; S Pelthorne C), b Chertsey, Surrey 29 Dec 1974. 6'2". RHB, RMF. Middlesex 1992-2000; cap 1995. Tour: I 1994-95 (Eng A – part). HS 69 M v Essex (Chelmsford) 2000. 50 wkts (3); most – 50 (1997, 1998, 2000). BB 10-45 M v Derbys (Derby) 1994 (second youngest to take all ten wickets in any f-c match). Award: NWT 1. LO HS 45* M v Durham (Southgate) 1998 (NWT). LO BB 5-50 M v Kent (Lord's) 1997 (NWT).

JONES, Ian (Fyndoune Community C, Sacriston), b Edmonton, Middx 11 Mar 1977. 6'4". RHB, RFM. Debut 1999. No appearances 2000. HS 35 v Durham (Chester-le-St) 1999. BB 3-81 v NZ (Taunton) 1999. CC BB 2-102 v Kent (Taunton) 1999. LO HS 5* (NL). LO BB 1-53 (NL).

JONES, Philip Steffan (Stradey CS, Llanelli; Neath TC; Loughborough U; Homerton C, Cambridge), b Llanelli, Wales 9 Feb 1974. 6'2". RHB, RMF. Cambridge U 1997; blue 1997. Somerset debut 1997. Wales MC 1992-96. HS 105 v NZ (Taunton) 1999. CC HS 56* v Yorks (Scarborough) 2000. BB 6-67 CU v OU (Lord's) 1997. Sm BB 5-41 v Surrey (Taunton) 2000. LO HS 27 v Northants (Northampton) 2000 (NL). LO BB 5-23 v Warwks (Taunton) 1998 (SL).

KERR, Jason Ian Douglas (Withins HS; Bolton C), b Bolton, Lancs 7 Apr 1974. 6'2". RHB, RMF. Debut 1993. HS 80 v WI (Taunton) 1995. CC HS 68* v Derbys (Taunton) 1996. BB 7-23 v Leics (Taunton) 1999. Hat-trick 2000. LO HS 56 v Middx (Southgate) 1999 (NL). LO BB 4-28 v Hants (Basingstoke) 1997 (SL).

LATHWELL, Mark Nicholas (Braunton S, Devon), b Bletchley, Bucks 26 Dec 1971. 5'8". RHB, RM. Debut 1991; cap 1992. YC 1993. MCC YC. **Tests:** 2 (1993); HS 33 v A (Nottingham) 1993. Tours (Eng A): A 1992-93; SA 1993-94. 1000 runs (5); most – 1230 (1994). HS 206 v Surrey (Bath) 1994. BB 2-21 v Sussex (Hove) 1994. Awards: NWT 1; BHC 2. LO HS 121 v Middx (Lord's) 1996 (BHC). LO BB 1-23 (NWT).

PARSONS, Keith Alan (The Castle S, Taunton; Richard Huish C), b Taunton 2 May 1973. Identical twin brother of K.J. (Somerset staff 1992-94). 6'1". RHB, RM. Debut 1992; cap 1999. HS 193* v WI (Taunton) 2000. CC HS 108* v Yorks (Taunton) 2000. BB 5-13 v Lancs (Taunton) 2000. LO HS 69 v Leics (Taunton) 2000 (NL). LO BB 4-43 v Surrey (Taunton) 1999 (NWT).

ROSE, Graham David (Northumberland Park S, Tottenham), b Tottenham, London 12 Apr 1964. 6'4". RHB, RM. Middlesex 1985-86. Somerset debut 1987; cap 1988; benefit 1997. 1000 runs (1): 1000 (1990). HS 191 v Sussex (Taunton) 1997. 50 wkts (5); most – 63 (1997). BB 7-47 (13-88 match) v Notts (Taunton) 1996. Awards: BHC 4. LO HS 148 v Glam (Neath) 1990 (SL). LO BB 4-16 v SL (Taunton) 1990.

‡SUPPIAH, Arul, b Kuala Lumpur, Malaysia 30 Aug 1983. RHB, SLA. Staff 2001. Awaiting f-c debut.

TREGO, Peter David (Wyvern S, W-s-M), b Weston-super-Mare 12 Jun 1981. RHB, RM. Somerset debut 2000. 2nd XI debut 1997 when aged 16y 20d. HS 62 v Yorks (Taunton) 2000. BB 4-84 v Yorks (Scarborough) 2000. LO HS 14 v Yorks (Taunton) 2000 (NL). LO BB 2-30 v Salop (Telford) 2000 (NWT).

TRESCOTHICK, Marcus Edward (Sir Bernard Lovell S), b Keynsham 25 Dec 1975. 6'2". LHB, RM. Debut 1993; cap 1999. **Tests**: 9 (2000 to 2000-01); HS 122 v SL (Galle) 2000-01; BB 1-34. **LOI**: 12 (2000 to 2000-01); HS 87* v WI (Chester-le-St) 2000; BB 2-7 v Z (Manchester) 2000. Tours: NZ 1999-00 (Eng A); P 2000-01; SL 2000-01. D 1999 00 (Eng A). HS 190 v Middx (Taunton) 1999. BB 4-36 (inc hat-trick) v Young A (Taunton) 1995. CC BB 4-82 v Yorks (Leeds) 1998. Hat-trick 1995. Award: NWT 1. LO HS 122 v Ire (Erlington) 1995 (BHC). LO BB 4-50 v Northants (Northampton) 2000 (NL).

TUCKER, Joseph Peter (Colston Collegiate S; Richard Huish C), b Bath 14 Sep 1979. 6'3". RHB, RMF. Debut 2000 – awaiting CC debut. 2nd XI debut 1995 when aged 15y 257d. HS 14 and BB 1-28 (dismissing B.C.Lara with his 2nd ball) v WI (Taunton) 2000 on debut.

TURNER, Robert Julian (Millfield S; Magdalene C, Cambridge), b Malvern, Worcs 25 Nov 1967. 6'1½". RHB, WK. Brother of S.J. (Somerset 1984-85). Cambridge U 1988-91; blue 1988-89-90-91; captain 1991. Somerset debut 1991; cap 1994. Tours (Eng A): NZ 1999-00; B 1999-00. 1000 runs (2); most – 1217 (1999). HS 144 v Kent (Taunton) 1997. Award: BHC 1. LO HS 70 v Glam (Cardiff) 1996 (BHC).

‡WEBLEY, Thomas (King's C, Taunton), b Bristol 2 Mar 1983. RHB, SLA. Staff 2001. Awaiting f-c debut. 2nd XI debut 1999 when aged 16y 49d.

‡WOOD, Matthew James (Exmouth Community C), b Exeter, Devon 30 Sep 1980. RHB, OB. Staff 2001. Awaiting f-c debut. 2nd XI debut 1997 when aged 16y 345d. Devon 1998-2000. LO HS 43 Devon v Surrey (Exmouth) 2000 (NWT).

RELEASED/RETIRED
(Having made a first-class County appearance in 2000)

JARVIS, Paul William (Bydales CS, Marske), b Redcar, Yorks 29 Jun 1965. 5'10". RHB, RFM. Yorkshire 1981-93; cap 1986; youngest Yorkshire debutant at 16yr 75d. Sussex 1994-98; cap 1994. Somerset 1999-2000. **Tests**: 9 (1987-88 to 1992-93); HS 29* and BB 4-107 v WI (Lord's) 1988. **LOI**: 16 (1987-88 to 1993); HS 16* v SL (Colombo) 1992-93; BB 5-35 v I (Bangalore) 1992-93. Tours: SA 1989-90 (Eng XI), WI 1986 87 (Y); NZ 1987-88; I/SL 1992-93; P 1987-88. HS 80 Y v Northants (Scarborough) 1992. Sm HS 20 v Sussex (Taunton) 1999. 50 wkts (4); most – 81 (1987). BB 7-55 Y v Surrey (Leeds) 1986. Sm BB 4-21 v OU (Taunton) 2000. Hat-trick 1985 (Y). Award: BHC 1. LO HS 63 Sx v Kent (Canterbury) 1997 (BHC). LO BB 6-27 Y v Somerset (Taunton) 1989 (SL).

PIERSON. A.R.K. – see DERBYSHIRE.

SOMERSET 2000

	Place	Won	Lost	Tied	Drew	No Result
County Championship (1st Division)	**5th**	2	4		10	
All First-Class Matches		4	4		10	
NatWest Trophy	4th Round					
Benson & Hedges Cup	6th in Mid/West/Wales Group					
National League (1st Division)	**6th**	7	8			1

COUNTY CHAMPIONSHIP AVERAGES

BATTING AND FIELDING

Cap		M	I	NO	HS	Runs	Avge	100	50	Ct/St
1995	P.D.Bowler	16	23	4	139*	1090	57.36	4	4	7
1999	M.E.Trescothick	8	12	1	105	470	42.72	1	2	8
1988	G.D.Rose	14	18	5	124	510	39.23	2	1	4
1999	J.Cox	15	23	1	171	835	37.95	2	3	5
1999	K.A.Parsons	14	20	1	108*	550	28.94	1	1	14
1999	M.Burns	13	17	–	108	482	28.35	1	3	2
–	J.I.D.Kerr	3	4	1	34	84	28.00	–	–	–
–	I.D.Blackwell	16	21	2	109	518	27.26	1	2	5
1997	P.C.L.Holloway	12	18	1	113	376	22.11	1	1	9
–	A.R.K.Pierson	5	7	3	18	77	19.25	–	–	3
–	P.D.Trego	6	8	1	62	134	19.14	–	1	3
1994	R.J.Turner	16	22	–	75	410	18.63	–	2	33
1992	A.R.Caddick	3	4	1	21*	52	17.33	–	–	1
1992	M.N.Lathwell	8	12	–	47	199	16.58	–	–	4
–	P.S.Jones	15	16	4	56*	122	10.16	–	1	4
–	J.O.Grove	9	9	5	12*	39	9.75	–	–	4

Also batted: M.P.L.Bulbeck 3*, 3 (2 matches); P.W.Jarvis (1) 1 (1 ct).

BOWLING

	O	M	R	W	Avge	Best	5wI	10wM
A.R.Caddick	114	32	294	25	11.76	7-64	3	2
M.Burns	119.2	29	354	13	27.23	3-11	–	–
P.S.Jones	403.4	88	1294	40	32.35	5-41	1	–
G.D.Rose	317.3	76	886	27	32.81	5-74	1	–
P.D.Trego	146.1	28	556	16	34.75	4-84	–	–
K.A.Parsons	139.4	38	398	10	39.80	5-13	1	–
J.O.Grove	158.3	24	610	15	40.66	5-90	1	–
I.D.Blackwell	364.3	109	912	16	57.00	3-72	–	–

Also bowled: M.P.L.Bulbeck 16-4-55-2; J.Cox 14-3-35-0; P.C.L.Holloway 2-0-4-0; P.W.Jarvis 23.2-3-103-3; J.I.D.Kerr 38-4-190-4; A.R.K.Pierson 103-25-244-6; M.E.Trescothick 53-10-182-2.

The First-Class Averages (pp 118-132) give the records of Somerset players in all first-class county matches (Somerset's other opponents being the West Indians and Oxford University), with the exception of A.R.Caddick, whose full county figures are as above, and:
    M.E.Trescothick 9-14-1-105-548-42.15-1-3-8ct. 61-13-205-3-68.33-1/18.

SOMERSET RECORDS

FIRST-CLASS CRICKET

Highest Total	For 675-9d		v	Hampshire	Bath	1924
	V 811		by	Surrey	The Oval	1899
Lowest Total	For 25		v	Glos	Bristol	1947
	V 22		by	Glos	Bristol	1920
Highest Innings	For 322	I.V.A.Richards	v	Warwicks	Taunton	1985
	V 424	A.C.MacLaren	for	Lancashire	Taunton	1895

Highest Partnership for each Wicket

1st	346	H.T.Hewett/L.C.H.Palairet	v	Yorkshire	Taunton	1892
2nd	290	J.C.W.MacBryan/M.D.Lyon	v	Derbyshire	Burton upon T	1924
3rd	319	P.M.Roebuck/M.D.Crowe	v	Leics	Taunton	1984
4th	310	P.W.Denning/I.T.Botham	v	Glos	Taunton	1980
5th	235	J.C.White/C.C.C.Case	v	Glos	Taunton	1927
6th	265	W.E.Alley/K.E.Palmer	v	Northants	Northampton	1961
7th	279	R.J.Harden/G.D.Rose	v	Sussex	Taunton	1997
8th	172	I.V.A.Richards/I.T.Botham	v	Leics	Leicester	1983
	172	A.R.K.Pierson/P.S.Jones	v	N Zealanders	Taunton	1999
9th	183	C.H.M.Greetham/H.W.Stephenson	v	Leics	Weston-s-Mare	1963
	183	C.J.Tavaré/N.A.Mallender	v	Sussex	Hove	1990
10th	143	J.J.Bridges/A.H.D.Gibbs	v	Essex	Weston-s-Mare	1919

Best Bowling	For 10- 49	E.J.Tyler	v	Surrey	Taunton	1895
(Innings)	V 10- 35	A.Drake	for	Yorkshire	Weston-s-Mare	1914
Best Bowling	For 16- 83	J.C.White	v	Worcs	Bath	1919
(Match)	V 17-137	W.Brearley	for	Lancashire	Manchester	1905

Most Runs – Season	2761	W.E.Alley	(av 58.74)	1961
Most Runs – Career	21142	H.Gimblett	(av 36.96)	1935-54
Most 100s – Season	11	S.J.Cook		1991
Most 100s – Career	49	H.Gimblett		1935-54
Most Wkts – Season	169	A.W.Wellard	(av 19.24)	1938
Most Wkts – Career	2166	J.C.White	(av 18.02)	1909-37

LIMITED-OVERS CRICKET

Highest Total	NWT	413-4	v	Devon	Torquay	1990
	BHC	349-7	v	Ireland	Taunton	1997
	NL	360-3	v	Glamorgan	Neath	1990
Lowest Total	NWT	58	v	Middlesex	Southgate	2000
	BHC	98	v	Middlesex	Lord's	1982
	NL	58	v	Essex	Chelmsford	1977
Highest Innings	NWT	162*	C.J.Tavaré	v	Devon	Torquay	1990
	BHC	177	S.J.Cook	v	Sussex	Hove	1990
	NL	175*	I.T.Botham	v	Northants	Wellingborough	1986
Best Bowling	NWT	7-15	R.P.Lefebvre	v	Devon	Torquay	1990
	BHC	7-24	Mushtaq Ahmed	v	Ireland	Taunton	1997
	NL	6-24	I.V.A Richards	v	Lancashire	Manchester	1983

SURREY

Formation of Present Club: 22 August 1845
Colours: Chocolate
Badge: Prince of Wales' Feathers
County Champions (since 1890): (17) 1890, 1891, 1892, 1894, 1895, 1899, 1914, 1952, 1953, 1954, 1955, 1956, 1957, 1958, 1971, 1999, 2000
Joint Champions: (1) 1950
NatWest Trophy/Gillette Cup Winners: (1) 1982
Benson and Hedges Cup Winners: (2) 1974, 1997
National League (Div 1) Winners: (0); best – 1st (Div 2) 2000
Sunday League Winners: (1) 1996
Match Awards: NWT 51; BHC 69

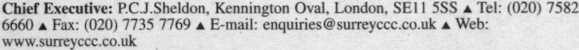

Chief Executive: P.C.J.Sheldon, Kennington Oval, London, SE11 5SS ▲ Tel: (020) 7582 6660 ▲ Fax: (020) 7735 7769 ▲ E-mail: enquiries@surreyccc.co.uk ▲ Web: www.surreyccc.co.uk

Captain: A.J.Hollioake. **Vice-Captain:** No appointment. **Overseas Player:** Saqlain Mushtaq. **2001 Beneficiary:** Surrey Community Trust. **Scorer:** K.R.Booth. ‡ New registration

AMIN, Rupesh Mahesh (Riddlesdown HS; John Ruskin C; Croydon C), b Clapham, London 20 Aug 1977. 6'0". RHB, SLA. Debut 1997. HS 12 v Leics (Oval) 1998. BB 4-87 v Somerset (Oval) 1999. LO HS – (SL). LO BB 2-43 v Lancs (Oval) 1997 (SL).

BATTY, Gareth Jon (Bingley GS), b Bradford, Yorks 13 Oct 1977. Younger brother of J.D. (Yorkshire and Somerset 1989-96). 5'11". RHB, OB. Yorkshire 1997. Surrey (L-O matches) 1998. Awaiting CC debut. No f-c appearances 2000. HS 25* and BB 2-45 v SL A (Oval) 1999. LO HS 37 v Derbys (Oval) 1998 (SL). LO BB 2-42 Surrey CB v Salop (Shifnal) 2000 (NWT).

BATTY, Jonathan Neil (Wheatley Park S, Oxon; Repton S; Durham U; Keble C, Oxford), b Chesterfield, Derbys 18 Apr 1974. 5'10". RHB, WK. Minor C 1994. Comb U 1995. Oxford U 1996; blue 1996. Surrey debut 1997. Oxfordshire 1993-96. HS 100* v Somerset (Oval) 2000. BB 1-21. LO HS 40 v Derbys (Oval) 1998 (SL).

BICKNELL, Martin Paul (Robert Haining SS), b Guildford 14 Jan 1969. Younger brother of D.J. (*see NOTTINGHAMSHIRE*). 6'3". RHB, RFM. Debut 1986; cap 1989; benefit 1997. *Wisden* 2000. **Tests:** 2 (1993); HS 14 and BB 3-99 v A (Birmingham) 1993. **LOI:** 7 (1990-91); HS 31* v A (Perth) 1990-91; BB 3-55 v NZ (Christchurch) 1990-91. Tours: A 1990-91; SA 1993-94 (Eng A); Z 1989-90 (Eng A). HS 88 v Hants (Southampton) 1992. 50 wkts (9); most – 71 (1992, 1999). BB 9-45 v CU (Oval) 1988. CC BB 9-47 (16-119 match) v Leics (Guildford) 2000. Awards: BHC 3. LO HS 66* v Northants (Oval) 1991 (NWT). LO BB 7-30 v Glam (Oval) 1999 (NL).

BISHOP, Ian Emlyn (Castle S; Somerset C of Art & Tech), b Taunton, Somerset 26 Aug 1977. 6'1". RHB, RMF. Somerset 1996. Surrey debut 1999. HS 12 v Durham (Chester-le-St) 2000. BB 2-45 v Derbys (Derby) 1999. Award: BHC 1. LO HS 15* v Middx (Lord's) 1999 (NL). LO BB 4-34 v Durham (Oval) 1999 (NL).

BROWN, Alistair Duncan (Caterham S), b Beckenham, Kent 11 Feb 1970. 5'10". RHB, occ LB. Debut 1992; cap 1994. **LOI:** 13 (1996 to 1998-99); HS 118 v I (Manchester) 1996. 1000 runs (5); most – 1382 (1993). HS 295* v Leics (Oakham) 2000 – record score (all levels) in Rutland. BB 1-56. Awards: BHC 2. LO HS 203 v Hants (Guildford) 1997 (SL). LO BB 3-39 v Notts (Nottingham) 2000 (NL).

BUTCHER, Gary Paul (Trinity S; Riddlesdown S; Heath Clark C), b Clapham, London 11 Mar 1975. Son of A.R. (Surrey, Glam and England 1972-92); brother of M.A. 5'9". RHB, RM. Glamorgan 1994-98. Surrey debut 1999. Tours (Gm): SA 1995-96; Z 1994-95. HS 101* Gm v OU (Oxford) 1997. CC HS 89 Gm v Northants (Northampton) 1996. Sy HS 70 v Warwks (Birmingham) 1999. BB 7-77 Gm v Glos (Bristol) 1996. Sy BB 5-18 v Derbys (Oval) 2000 – including 4 wickets in 4 balls. Hat-trick (4 in 4) 2000. LO HS 48 Gm v Beds (Cardiff) 1997 (NWT). LO BB 4-32 Gm v Glos (Bristol) 1996 (SL).

BUTCHER, Mark Alan (Trinity S; Archbishop Tenison's S, Croydon), b Croydon 23 Aug 1972. Son of A.R. (Surrey, Glamorgan and England 1972-92); brother of G.P. 5'11". LHB, RM/OB. Debut 1992; cap 1996. **Tests:** 27 (1997 to 1999-00, 1 as captain); HS 116 v SA (Leeds) 1998 and 116 v A (Brisbane) 1998-99; BB 2-32 v SA (Durban) 1999-00. Tours: A 1996-97 (Eng A), 1998-99; SA 1999-00; WI 1997-98. 1000 runs (5); most – 1604 (1996). HS 259 v Leics (Leicester) 1999. BB 5-86 v Lancs (Manchester) 2000. Awards: NWT 2; BHC 1. LO HS 91 v Somerset (Oval) 1996 (NWT). LO BB 3-23 v Sussex (Oval) 1992 (SL).

CARBERRY, Michael Alexander (St John Rigby C), b Croydon 29 Sep 1980. 6'0". LHB, OB. Awaiting f-c debut. LO HS 19 Surrey CB v Norfolk (Guildford) 1999 (NWT).

‡GIDDINS, Edward Simon Hunter (Eastbourne C), b Eastbourne, Sussex 20 Jul 1971. 6'4½". RHB, RFM. Sussex 1991-96; cap 1994. Warwickshire 1998-2000; cap 1998. MCC YC. Tests: 4 (1999 to 2000); HS 7 and BB 5-15 v Z (Lord's) 2000. Tour: P 1995-96 (Eng A). HS 34 Sx v Essex (Hove) 1995. Wa HS 18 v Kent (Maidstone) 1999. 50 wkts (4); most – 84 (1998). BB 6-47 Sx v Yorks (Eastbourne) 1996. Wa BB 6-79 (11-164 match) v Glos (Bristol) 1998. Award: BHC 1. LO HS 13 Sx v Essex (Hove) 1994 (NWT). LO BB 5-21 Wa v Leics (Leicester) 1999 (BHC).

GREENIDGE, Carl Gary (Lodge S and St Michael S, Barbados; Heathcote S, Chingford; W Hatch HS; City of Westminster C), b Basingstoke, Hants 20 Apr 1978. Son of C.G. (Hampshire, Barbados and West Indies 1970-92). 5'10". RHB, RMF. MCC YC. Debut 1999. HS 14 v SLA (Oval) 1999. CC HS 6. BB 5-60 (8-124 match) v Yorks (Oval) 1999 – on CC debut. LO HS 3* (NL). LO BB 2-43 v Glam (Oval) 2000 (NL).

HOLLIOAKE, Adam John (St Joseph's C, Sydney; St Patrick's C, Ballarat; St George's C, Weybridge; Surrey Tutorial C), b Melbourne, Australia 5 Sep 1971. Brother of B.C. 5'11". RHB, RMF. Debut 1993, scoring 13 and 123 v Derbys (Ilkeston); cap 1995; captain 1997 to date. Qualified for England 1992. **Tests:** 4 (1997 to 1997-98); HS 45 and BB 2-31 v A (Nottingham) 1997 – on debut. **LOI:** 35 (1996 to 1999, 14 as captain); HS 83* v SA (Dhaka) 1998-99; BB 4-23 v P (Birmingham) 1996 – on debut. Tours: A 1996-97 (Eng A – captain); WI 1997-98. 1000 runs (2); most – 1522 (1996). HS 182 v Middx (Lord's) 1997. BB 5-62 v Glam (Swansea) 1998. Awards: NWT 1; BHC 1. LO HS 111 v Glam (Oval) 2000 (NL). LO BB 5-29 v Durham (Chester-le-St) 2000 (NL).

HOLLIOAKE, Benjamin Caine (Millfield S), b Melbourne, Australia 11 Nov 1977. Brother of A.J. 6'2". RHB, RFM. Debut 1996; cap 1999. YC 1997. **Tests:** 2 (1997 to 1998); HS 28 v A (Nottingham) 1997 on debut; BB 2-105 v SL (Oval) 1998. **LOI:** 7 (1997 to 1998-99); HS 63 v A (Lord's) 1997 – on debut; BB 2-43 v WI (P-o-S) 1997-98. Tours: A 1998-99; SL (Eng A) 1997-98. HS 163 Eng A v SL A (Moratuwa) 1997-98. Sy 76 v Middx (Lord's) 1997. BB 5-51 v Glam (Oval) 1999. Awards: BHC 2. LO HS 98 v Kent (Lord's) 1997 (BHC). LO BB 5-10 v Derbys (Oval) 1996 (SL).

MURTAGH, Timothy James (John Fisher S; St Mary's C), b Lambeth 2 Aug 1981. Nephew of A.J.Murtagh (Hants and E Province 1973-73). 6'0". RHB, RMF. British U 2000. Surrey contract 2000 – awaiting county debut. HS 12* and BB 1-6 Brit U v Z (Cambridge) 2000. LO HS 0 (NL). LO BB 1-50 (NL).

PATTERSON, Mark William (Belfast Royal Academy; Ulster U), b Belfast, N Ireland 2 Feb 1974. Elder brother of A.D. (Ireland 1996). 6'1". RHB, RFM. Debut 1996, taking 6-80 v SA A (Oval). No f-c appearances 2000. HS 4 and BB 6-80 (*see above*). CC HS 0 and BB 3-25 v Notts (Oval) 1999. LO HS (Ire) 9 (BHC). LO BB 3-48 Ire v Somerset (Eglinton) 1995 (BHC).

PORTER, Joseph James (St John's, Leatherhead; Oxford Brookes U), b Hammersmith 5 May 1980. 5'11". LHB, SLA. Oxford U 2000. British U 2000. Surrey contract 2000 – awaiting county debut. HS 93 Brit U v Z (Cambridge) 2000.

‡RAMPRAKASH, Mark Ravin (Gayton HS; Harrow Weald SFC), b Bushey, Herts 5 Sep 1969. 5'9". RHB, RM. Middlesex 1987-2000; cap 1990; captain 1997-99. YC 1991. **ECB contract 2000. Tests:** 42 (1991 to 2000); HS 154 v WI (Bridgetown) 1997-98; BB 1-2. **LOI:** 13 (1991 to 1997-98); HS 51 v WI (P-o-S) 1997-98. Tours A 1994-95 (part), 1998-99; SA 1995-96; WI 1991-92 (Eng A), 1993-94, 1997-98; NZ 1991-92; I 1994-95 (Eng A); P 1990-91 (Eng A); SL 1990-91 (Eng A). 1000 runs (10) inc 2000 (1): 2258 (1995). HS 235 M v Yorks (Leeds) 1995. BB 3-32 M v Glam (Lord's) 1998. Awards: NWT 2; BHC 3. LO HS 147* M v Worcs (Lord's) 1990 (SL). LO BB 5-38 M v Leics (Lord's) 1993 (SL).

RATCLIFFE, Jason David (Sharman's Cross SS; Solihull SFC), b Solihull, Warwks 19 Jun 1969. Son of D.P. Warwickshire 1988-94. Surrey debut 1995; cap 1998. Tours (Wa): SA 1991-92, 1992-93; Z 1993-94. HS 135 v Worcs (Worcester) 1997. BB 6-48 v SL A (Oval) 1999. BB 3-28 v Kent (Tunbridge W) 1999. Awards: NWT 2. LO HS 105 Wa v Yorks (Leeds) 1993 (NWT). LO BB 3-15 v Sussex (Hove) 2000 (BHC).

SALISBURY, Ian David Kenneth (Moulton CS), b Northampton 21 Jan 1970. 5'11". RHB, LBG. Sussex 1989-96; cap 1991. Surrey debut 1997; cap 1998. MCC YC. YC 1992. *Wisden* 1992. **Tests:** 15 (1992 to 2000-01); HS 50 v P (Manchester) 1992; BB 4-163 v WI (Georgetown) 1993-94. **LOI:** 4 (1992-93 to 1993-94); HS 5; BB 3-41 v WI (P-o-S) 1993-94. Tours: WI 1991-92 (Eng A), 1993-94; I 1992-93; 1994-95 (Eng A); P 1990-91 (Eng A), 1995-96 (Eng A), 2000-01; SL 1990-91 (Eng A). HS 100* v Somerset (Oval) 1999. 50 wkts (6); most – 87 (1992). BB 8-60 (12-91 match) v Somerset (Oval) 2000. Awards: NWT 1; BHC 2. LO HS 48* Sx v Glam (Swansea) 1995 (SL). LO BB 5-30 Sx v Leics (Leicester) 1992 (SL).

SAMPSON, Philip James (Pretoria BHS, SA), b Manchester 6 Sep 1980. 6'1". RHB, RFM. Staff 2000 – awaiting f-c debut. Buckinghamshire 1999. LO HS 4* (Surrey CB – NWT).

SAQLAIN MUSHTAQ (Govt Muslim League HS, M.A.O. College, Lahore), b Lahore, Pakistan 29 Dec 1976. Brother of Sibtain Mushtaq (Lahore 1988-89). 5'11". RHB, OB. Islamabad 1994-95. PIA 1994-95 to date. Surrey debut 1997; cap 1998. *Wisden* 1999. **Tests** (P): 31 (1995-96 to 2000-01); HS 79 v Z (Sheikhupura) 1996-97; BB 8-164 v E (Lahore) 2000-01. **LOI** (P): 129 (1995-96 to 2000-01); HS 37* v A (Brisbane) 1999-00; BB 5-20 v E (Rawalpindi) 2000-01, 2 hat-tricks. Tours (P): E 1996; A 1995-96, 1996-97, 1999-00; SA 1997-98; WI 1999-00; NZ 2000-01; I 1998-99, SL 1996-97; Z 1997-98; B 1998-99. HS 79 (*see Tests*). Sy HS 66 v Leics (Oakham) 2000. 50 wkts (3+1); most – 66 (2000). BB 8-65 (11-107 match) v Derbys (Oval) 1998. Took 7-11 v Derbys (Oval) 2000. Hat-tricks 1997 and 1999. Awards: NWT 2. LO HS 37* (*see LOI*). LO BB 5-29 (*see LOI*).

‡SCOTT, Ben James Matthew, b Isleworth, Middx 4 Aug 1981. RHB, WK. Staff 2001 – awaiting f-c debut. LO HS 11 Middx CB v Cumb (Southgate) 1999 (NWT).

SHAHID, Nadeem (Ipswich S), b Karachi, Pakistan 23 Apr 1969. 6'0". RHB, LB. Essex 1989-94. Surrey debut 1995; cap 1998. Suffolk 1988. 1000 runs (1): 1003 (1990). HS 139 v Yorks (Oval) 1995. BB 3-91 Ex v Surrey (Oval) 1992. Sy BB 3-93 v SA A (Oval) 1996. LO HS 109* v Notts (Nottingham) 2000 (NL). LO BB 3-30 v Bucks (Oval) 1998 (NWT).

STEWART, Alec James (Tiffin S), b Merton 8 Apr 1963. Son of M.J. (Surrey and England 1954-72). 5'11". RHB, WK. Debut 1981; cap 1985; captain 1992-97; benefit 1994. *Wisden* 1992. MBE 1998. **ECB contract 2000. Tests:** 108 (1989-90 to 2000-01, 14 as captain); HS 190 v P (Birmingham) 1992. **LOI:** 137 – Eng record (1989-90 to 2000-01, 34 as captain); HS 116 v I (Sharjah) 1997-98. Tours (C=captain): A 1990-91, 1994-95, 1998-99C; SA 1995-96, 1999-00; WI 1989-90, 1993-94, 1997-98; NZ 1991-92, 1996-97; I 1992-93; P 2000-01; SL 1992-93C, 2000-01; Z 1996-97. 1000 runs (8); most – 1665 (1986). HS 271* v Yorks (Oval) 1997. BB 1-7. Held 11 catches (equalling world f-c match record) v Leics (Leicester) 1989. Awards: NWT 5; BHC 6. LO HS 167* v Somerset (Oval) 1994 (BHC).

THORPE, Graham Paul (Weydon CS; Farnham SFC), b Farnham 1 Aug 1969. 5'11". LHB, RM. Debut 1988; cap 1991; benefit 2000. *Wisden* 1997. **Tests:** 66 (1993 to 2000-01); HS 138 v A (Birmingham) 1997; scored 114* v A (Nottingham) 1993 on debut. **LOI:** 65 (1993 to 2000-01); HS 89 v Z (Brisbane) 1994-95 and 89 v H (Peshawar) 1995-96; BB 2-15 v I (Manchester) 1996. Tours: A 1992-93 (Eng A), 1994-95, 1998-99 (*part*); SA 1995-96; WI 1991-92 (Eng A), 1993-94, 1997-98; NZ 1996-97; P 1990-91 (Eng A), 2000-01; SL 1990-91 (Eng A), 2000-01; Z 1989-90 (Eng A), 1996-97. 1000 runs (8); most – 1895 (1992). HS 223* Eng XI v S Aus (Adelaide) 1998-99. Sy HS 222 v Glam (Oval) 1997. BB 4-40 v A (Oval) 1993. CC BB 2-14 v Derbys (Oval) 1996. Awards: NWT 3; BHC 1. LO HS 145* v Lancs (Oval) 1994 (NWT). LO BB 3-21 v Somerset (Oval) 1991 (SL).

TUDOR, Alex Jeremy (St Mark's S, Hammersmith; City of Westminster C), b West Brompton, London 23 Oct 1977. 6'5". RHB, RF. Debut 1995; cap 1999. YC 1999. **Tests:** 3 (1998-99 to 1999); HS 99* v NZ (Birmingham) 1999 – record score by an England 'night-watchman'; BB 4-89 v A (Perth) 1998-99 – on debut. Tours: A 1998-99; SA 1999-00; WI 2000-01 (Eng A). HS 99* v Hants (Oval) 2000. BB 7-48 v Lancs (Oval) 2000. LO HS 29* v Essex (Oval) 1995 (SL). LO BB 4-26 v Hants (Oval) 2000 (NL).

WARD, Ian James (Millfield S), b Plymouth, Devon 30 Sep 1972. 5'8½". LHB, RM. Surrey 1992, 1996 to date; cap 2000. Tours (Eng A): WI 2000-01; NZ 1999-00; B 1999-00. 1000 runs (1): 1018 (1999). HS 158* v Kent (Canterbury) 2000. LO HS 91 v Middx (Guildford) 1998 (SL).

YOUNG CRICKETER OF THE YEAR

This annual award, made by The Cricket Writers' Club (founded 1946), is currently restricted to players qualified for England, Andrew Symonds meeting that requirement at the time of his award, and under the age of 23 on 1 May. In 1986 their ballot resulted in a dead heat. To 1 May 2001 their selections have gained a tally of 1,716 England caps (shown in brackets).

1950	R.Tattersall (16)	1976	G.Miller (34)
1951	P.B.H.May (66)	1977	I.T.Botham (102)
1952	F.S.Trueman (67)	1978	D.I.Gower (117)
1953	M.C.Cowdrey (114)	1979	P.W.G.Parker (1)
1954	P.J.Loader (13)	1980	G.R.Dilley (41)
1955	K.F.Barrington (82)	1981	M.W.Gatting (79)
1956	B.Taylor	1982	N.G.Cowans (19)
1957	M.J.Stewart (8)	1983	N.A.Foster (29)
1958	A.C.D.Ingleby-Mackenzie	1984	R.J.Bailey (4)
1959	G.Pullar (28)	1985	D.V.Lawrence (5)
1960	D.A.Allen (39)	1986	A.A.Metcalfe
1961	P.H.Parfitt (37)		J.J.Whitaker (1)
1962	P.J.Sharpe (12)	1987	R.J.Blakey (2)
1963	G.Boycott (108)	1988	M.P.Maynard (4)
1964	J.M.Brearley (39)	1989	N.Hussain (59)
1965	A.P.E.Knott (95)	1990	M.A.Atherton (108)
1966	D.L.Underwood (86)	1991	M.R.Ramprakash (42)
1967	A.W.Greig (58)	1992	I.D.K.Salisbury (15)
1968	R.M.H.Cottam (4)	1993	M.N.Lathwell (2)
1969	A.Ward (5)	1994	J.P.Crawley (29)
1970	C.M.Old (46)	1995	A.Symonds
1971	J.Whitehouse	1996	C.E.W.Silverwood (5)
1972	D.R.Owen-Thomas	1997	B.C.Hollioake (2)
1973	M.Hendrick (30)	1998	A.Flintoff (9)
1974	P.H.Edmonds (51)	1999	A.J.Tudor (3)
1975	A.Kennedy	2000	P.J.Franks

SURREY 2000

RESULTS SUMMARY

	Place	Won	Lost	Tied	Drew	No Result
County Championship (1st Division)	**1st**	9	2		5	
All First-Class Matches		9	2		5	
NatWest Trophy	Quarter-Finalist					
Benson & Hedges Cup	Semi-Finalist					
National League (2nd Division)	**1st**	11	3			2

COUNTY CHAMPIONSHIP AVERAGES

BATTING AND FIELDING

Cap		M	I	NO	HS	Runs	Avge	100	50	Ct/St
1994	A.D.Brown	16	23	5	295*	935	51.94	2	4	16
1996	M.A.Butcher	16	25	4	191	891	42.42	2	3	13
2000	I.J.Ward	16	25	3	158*	894	40.63	3	3	4
–	G.P.Butcher	4	4	1	66	110	36.66	–	1	–
1998	N.Shahid	9	12	–	80	434	36.16	–	3	13
1989	M.P.Bicknell	15	18	2	79*	500	31.25	–	4	5
1995	A.J.Hollioake	16	23	–	80	689	29.95	–	3	27
1999	A.J.Tudor	14	16	6	64*	283	28.30	–	1	5
1985	A.J.Stewart	3	4	–	42	108	27.00	–	–	7
1998	I.D.K.Salisbury	16	19	6	57*	313	24.07	–	2	6
1991	G.P.Thorpe	8	12	–	115	280	23.33	1	1	6
–	J.N.Batty	13	16	2	100*	276	19.71	1	–	29/7
1998	Saqlain Mushtaq	12	14	2	66	217	18.08	–	2	8
1999	B.C.Hollioake	10	14	1	29	142	10.92	–	–	8
1998	J.D.Ratcliffe	2	4	–	26	28	7.00	–	–	2

Also batted: R.M.Amin (1 match) 3 (1 ct); I.E.Bishop (2) 0, 12, 2; C.G.Greenidge (3) 3, 6.

BOWLING

	O	M	R	W	Avge	Best	5wI	10wM
Saqlain Mushtaq	451.2	127	1016	66	15.39	7-11	6	2
M.P.Bicknell	413.2	115	1052	60	17.53	9-47	3	1
I.D.K.Salisbury	380.3	101	984	52	18.92	8-60	3	2
A.J.Tudor	304.3	71	1071	47	22.78	7-48	3	
B.C.Hollioake	117.5	25	407	11	37.00	4-41		

Also bowled: R.M.Amin 21-4-67-0; J.N.Batty 6-0-21-1; I.E.Bishop 29-8-98-2; A.D.Brown 28-9-70-1; G.P.Butcher 21.3-4-65-5; M.A.Butcher 27-7-86-5; C.G.Greenidge 35-13-106-1; A.J.Hollioake 42.2-12-119-3; J.D.Ratcliffe 9.5-2-46-1; N.Shahid 1-0-6-0; I.J.Ward 5-2-10-0.

Surrey played no first-class fixtures outside the County Championship in 2000. The Ffirst-Class Averages (pp 118-132) give the records of Surrey players in all first-class county matches, with the exception of A.J.Stewart and G.P.Thorpe, whose full county figures are as above, and J.J.Porter and T.J.Murtagh, whose only first-class appearances were in University matches.

SURREY RECORDS

FIRST-CLASS CRICKET

Highest Total	For 811		v	Somerset	The Oval	1899
	V 863		by	Lancashire	The Oval	1990
Lowest Total	For 14		v	Essex	Chelmsford	1983
	V 16		by	MCC	Lord's	1872
Highest Innings	For 357*	R.Abel	v	Somerset	The Oval	1899
	V 366	N.H.Fairbrother	for	Lancashire	The Oval	1990

Highest Partnership for each Wicket

1st	428	J.B.Hobbs/A.Sandham	v	Oxford U	The Oval	1926
2nd	371	J.B.Hobbs/E.G.Hayes	v	Hampshire	The Oval	1909
3rd	413	D.J.Bicknell/D.M.Ward	v	Kent	Canterbury	1990
4th	448	R.Abel/T.W.Hayward	v	Yorkshire	The Oval	1899
5th	308	J.N.Crawford/F.C.Holland	v	Somerset	The Oval	1908
6th	298	A.Sandham/H.S.Harrison	v	Sussex	The Oval	1913
7th	262	C.J.Richards/K.T.Medlycott	v	Kent	The Oval	1987
8th	205	I.A.Greig/M.P.Bicknell	v	Lancashire	The Oval	1990
9th	168	E.R.T.Holmes/E.W.J.Brooks	v	Hampshire	The Oval	1936
10th	173	A.Ducat/A.Sandham	v	Essex	Leyton	1921

Best Bowling	For 10-43	T.Rushby	v	Somerset	Taunton	1921
(Innings)	V 10-28	W.P.Howell	for	Australians	The Oval	1899
Best Bowling	For 16-83	G.A.R.Lock	v	Kent	Blackheath	1956
(Match)	V 15-57	W.P.Howell	for	Australians	The Oval	1899

Most Runs – Season	3246	T.W.Hayward	(av 72.13)		1906
Most Runs – Career	43554	J.B.Hobbs	(av 49.72)		1905-34
Most 100s – Season	13	T.W.Hayward			1906
	13	J.B.Hobbs			1925
Most 100s – Career	144	J.B.Hobbs			1905-34
Most Wkts – Season	252	T.Richardson	(av 13.94)		1895
Most Wkts – Career	1775	T.Richardson	(av 17.87)		1892-1904

LIMITED-OVERS CRICKET

Highest Total	NWT	350		v	Worcs	The Oval	1994
	BHC	333-6		v	Hampshire	The Oval	1996
	NL	375-4		v	Yorkshire	Scarborough	1994
Lowest Total	NWT	74		v	Kent	The Oval	1967
	BHC	89		v	Notts	Nottingham	1984
	NL	64		v	Worcs	Worcester	1978
Highest Innings	NWT	146	G.S.Clinton	v	Kent	Canterbury	1985
	BHC	167*	A.J.Stewart	v	Somerset	The Oval	1994
	NL	203	A.D.Brown	v	Hampshire	Guildford	1997
Best Bowling	NWT	7-33	R.D.Jackman	v	Yorkshire	Harrogate	1970
	BHC	5-15	S.G.Kenlock	v	Ireland	The Oval	1995
	NL	7-30	M.P.Bicknell	v	Glamorgan	The Oval	1999

SUSSEX

Formation of Present Club: 1 March 1839
Substantial Reorganisation: August 1857
Colours: Dark Blue, Light Blue and Gold
Badge: County Arms of Six Martlets
County Champions: (0); best – 2nd 1902, 1903, 1932, 1933, 1934, 1953, 1981
NatWest Trophy/Gillette Cup Winners: (4) 1963, 1964, 1978, 1986
Benson and Hedges Cup Winners: (0); best – semi-finalists 1982, 1999
National League (Div 1) Winners: (0); best – 9th 2000
Sunday League Winners: (1) 1982
Match Awards: NWT 56; BHC 57

Chief Executive: D.R.Gilbert, County Ground, Eaton Road, Hove BN3 3AN ▲ Tel: 01273 827100 ▲ Fax: 01273 771549 ▲ Email: fran@sccc.demon.co.uk ▲ Web: www.sussexcricket.co.uk

Captain: C.J.Adams. **Vice-Captain:** R.J.Kirtley. **Overseas Player:** M.W.Goodwin.
2001 Beneficiary: None. **Scorer:** L.V.Chandler. ‡ New registration

ADAMS, Christopher John (Repton S), b Whitwell, Derbyshire 6 May 1970. 6'0". RHB, RM/OB. Derbyshire 1988-97; cap 1992. Sussex debut/cap 1998; captain 1998 to date. **Tests:** 5 (1999-00); HS 31 v SA (Cape Town) 1999-00; BB 1-42. **LOI:** 5 (1998 to 1999-00); HS 42 v SA (Cape Town) 1999-00. Tour: SA 1999-00. 1000 runs (4); most – 1742 (1998). HS 239 De v Hants (Southampton) 1996. Sx HS 170 v Middx (Hove) 1998. BB 4-29 De v Lancs (Derby) 1991. Sx BB 3-37 v Glos (Hove) 1999. Awards: NWT 2; BHC 5. LO HS 163 v Middx (Arundel) 1999 (NL). LO BB 5-16 v Middx (Hove) 1998 (SL).

‡AMBROSE, Timothy R., b Newcastle, NSW, Australia 1 Dec 1982. ECB qualified. RHB, WK. Staff 2001 – awaiting f-c debut.

CARPENTER, James Robert (Birkenhead S), b Birkenhead, Cheshire 20 Oct 1975. 6'1½". LHB, SLA. MCC YC. Debut 1997. HS 65 v Notts (Nottingham) 1998. BB 1-50. LO HS 64* v Notts (Cleethorpes) 1999 (NL).

CLAPP, Dominic Adrian (Lancing C; Worthing SFC), b Southport, Lancs 25 May 1980. 6'0". RHB, RM. Staff 2000 – awaiting f-c debut. 2nd XI debut 1997 when aged 16y 347d. LO HS 10 Sussex CB v Berks (Hastings) 2000 (NWT). LO BB 3-46 Sussex CB v Herefords (Colwall) 2000 (NWT).

COTTEY, Phillip Anthony (Bishopston CS, Swansea), b Swansea, Glamorgan 2 Jun 1966. 5'4". RHB, OB. Glamorgan 1986-98; cap 1992. Sussex debut/cap 1999. E Transvaal 1991-92. Tours (Gm): SA 1995-96; Z 1990-91, 1994-95. 1000 runs (7); most – 1543 (1996). HS 203 and BB 4-49 Gm v Leics (Swansea) 1996. Sx HS 154 v Essex (Chelmsford) 2000. Sx BB – . LO HS 96 Gm v Sussex (Hove) 1998 (BHC). LO BB 4-56 Gm v Essex (Chelmsford) 1996 (SL).

‡DAVIS, Mark Jeffrey Gronow (Woodbridge HS; Grey HS; Pretoria U), b Port Elizabeth, SA 10 Oct 1971. ECB qualified. RHB, OB. N Transvaal/Northerns 1990-91 to date. MCC 1999 and 2000. HS 71 NT v OFS (Bloemfontein) 1995-96. BB 8-37 (12-84 match) NT B v W Transvaal (Potchefstroom) 1994-95. LO HS 35 NT v EP (Verwoerdburg) 1994-95 (BHS). LO BB 4-35 Northerns v EP (Pt Elizabeth) 1997-98 (SBC).

‡**GOODWIN, Murray** William (Newton Moore HS, Bunbury, WA), b Salisbury, Rhodesia 11 Dec 1972. Younger brother of D.G. (Zimbabwe 1986-97 to 1989-90). 5'9". Emigrated to Australia in Nov 1986. Gained Zimbabwean citizenship in Sept 1997. RHB, LB. Western Australia 1994-95 to 1996-97, 2000-01. Mashonaland 1997-98 to 1998-99. Holland 1997. **Tests** (Z): 19 (1997-98 to 2000); HS 166* v P (Bulawayo) 1997-98. **LOI** (Z): 71 (1997-98 to 2000); HS 112* v WI (Chester-le-St) 2000; BB 1-12. Tours (Z): E 2000, SA 1999-00; WI 1999-00; NZ 1997-98; P 1998-99; SL 1997-98. HS 194 Z v Glos (Gloucester) 2000. BB 2-23 Z v Lahore City (Lahore) 1998-99. LO HS 115 Mashonaland A v Matabeleland (Bulawayo) 1997-98. LO BB 1-9 Mashonaland v Eng A (Harare) 1998-99.

HAVELL, Paul Matthew (Warden Park S; Haywards Heath C), b Melbourne, Australia 4 Jul 1980. 6'3". LHB, RFM. Staff 2000 – awaiting f-c debut.

HOUSE, William John (Sevenoaks S; Gonville & Caius C, Cambridge), b Sheffield, Yorks 16 Mar 1976. 5'11". LHB, RM. Cambridge U 1996-98, scoring 136 v Derbys on debut; blue 1996-97-98. Kent 1997-99. British U 1998. HS 136 (*see above*). CC HS 35 v Warwks (Hove) 2000. BB 1-34 (twice – CU, Sx). Awards: BHC 2. LO HS 93 Brit U v Surrey (Oval) 1997 (BHC). LO BB 5-58 Brit U v Glos (Bristol) 1998 (BHC).

KIRTLEY, Robert James (Clifton C), b Eastbourne 10 Jan 1975. 6'0". RHB, RFM. Debut 1995; cap 1998. Mashonaland 1996-97. Tours (Eng A): NZ 1999-00; B 1999-00. HS 59 v Durham (Eastbourne) 1998. 50 wkts (3); most – 65 (1999). BB 7-21 v Hants (Southampton) 1999. Took 5-53 (7-88 match) for Mashonaland v Eng XI (Harare) 1996-97. Award: NWT 1. LO HS 17* v Somerset (Hove) 1999 (NL). LO BB 5-39 v Salop (Hove) 1997 (NWT).

LEWRY, Jason David (Durrington HS, Worthing), b Worthing 2 Apr 1971. 6'2". LHB, LFM. Debut 1994; cap 1996. Tour: Z 1998-99 (Eng A). HS 39 v Warwks (Hove) 2000. 50 wkts (3); most – 62 (1998). BB 7-38 (10-113 match) v Derbys (Derby) 1999. Hat-trick 1998. LO HS 14* v Ire (Hove) 1995 (BHC). LO BB 4-29 v Somerset (Bath) 1995 (SL).

MARTIN-JENKINS, Robin Simon Christopher (Radley C; Durham U), b Guildford, Surrey 28 Oct 1975. Son of C.D.A. (*Times* Chief Cricket Correspondent/BBC Commentator). 6'5". RHB, RFM. Debut 1995; cap 2000. British U 1996. HS 86 v Essex (Arundel) 2000. BB 7-54 v Glam (Hove) 1998. Award: BHC 1. LO HS 45 v Hants (Hove) 2000 (BHC). LO BB 4-57 v Glos (Bristol) 1997 (BHC).

MONTGOMERIE, Richard Robert (Rugby S; Worcester C, Oxford), b Rugby, Warwks 3 Jul 1971. 5'10½". RHB, OB. Oxford U 1991-94; blue 1991-92-93-94; captain 1994; half blues for rackets and real tennis. Northamptonshire 1991-98; cap 1995. Sussex debut/cap 1999. Tour: Z 1994-95 (Nh). 1000 runs (2); most – 1178 (1996). HS 192 Nh v Kent (Canterbury) 1995. Sx HS 133 v Notts (Hove) 2000. LO HS 129* v Z (Hastings) 2000.

‡**PRIOR, Matthew** James (Brighton C), b Johannesburg, SA, 24 Feb 82. RHB, WK. Staff 2001 – awaiting f-c debut. LO HS 3 (Sx CB – NWT).

RASHID, Umer Bin Abdul (Ealing Green HS, Ealing Tertiary C, Southbank U), b Southampton, Hants 6 Feb 1976. 6'3". LHB, SLA. Middlesex 1996-98. Sussex debut 1999. HS 110 v Glam (Colwyn Bay) 2000. BB 5-103 v Notts (Northampton) 2000. LO HS 82 Brit U v Hants (Oxford) 1997. LO BB 5-24 v Glam (Swansea) 1999 (NL.).

ROBINSON, Mark Andrew (Hull GS), b Hull, Yorkshire 23 Nov 1966. 6'3". RHB, RFM. Northamptonshire 1987-90; cap 1990. Canterbury 1988-89. Yorkshire 1991-95; cap 1992. Sussex debut/cap 1997. Tours (Y): SA 1991-92, 1992-93. Failed to score in 12 successive f-c innings 1990 – world record. HS 27 v Lancs (Manchester) 1997. 50 wkts (1): 50 (1992). BB 9-37 (12-124 match) Y v Northants (Harrogate) 1993. Sx BB 6-78 v Northants (Hove) 1997 on Sussex debut. Award: BHC 1. LO HS 15* v Lancs (Manchester) 2000 (NL). LO BB 4-23 Y v Northants (Leeds) 1993 (SL) and 4-23 v Leics (Leicester) 2000 (NL).

TAYLOR, Billy Victor (Bitterne Park S, Southampton), b Southampton, Hants 11 Jan 1977. Brother of J.L. (Wiltshire 1998 to date). 6'3". LHB, RMF. Debut 1999. Wiltshire 1996-98. HS 14 v Derbys (Derby) 1999 – on debut. BB 3-27 v Worcs (Worcester) 2000. Award: NWT 1. LO HS 21* v Notts (Cleethorpes) 1999 (NL). LO BB 4-26 v Middx CB (Southgate) 2000 (NWT).

WILTON, Nicholas James (Beacon Community C and SFC; City of Westminster C), b Pembury, Kent 23 Sep 1978. 5'11". RHB, WK. Debut 1998. MCC YC. HS 55 v Leics (Arundel) 1999. LO HS 17 v SL A (Hove) 1999.

YARDY, Michael Howard (William Parker S, Hastings), b Pembury, Kent 27 Nov 1980. 6'0". LHB, LM. Debut 2000. HS 25 v NZ A (Hove) 2000. CC HS 14 v Glos (Hove) 2000. LO HS 15 and BB 1-46 Sussex CB v Herefords (Colwall) 2000 (NWT).

ZUIDERENT Bastiaan ('*Bas*') (Erasmiaans Gymnasium, Rotterdam; Amsterdam U), b Utrecht, Holland 2 Mar 1977. 6'3". RHB, OB. Holland 1994 to date. **LOI** (H): 5 (1995-96 World Cup); HS 54 v E (Peshawar) 1995-96. Awaiting f-c debut. LO HS 99 Holland v Worcs (Worcester) 1997 (NWT).

RELEASED/RETIRED
(Having made a first-class County appearance in 2000)

BATES, Justin Jonathan (Hurstpierpoint C), b Farnborough, Hants 9 Apr 1976. 5'11". RHB, OB. Sussex 1997-2000. HS 57 v Hants (Southampton) 1999. BB 5-67 (9-136 match) v Northants (Northampton) 1998. LO HS 25* v SL A (Hove) 1999. LO BB 2-42 v Northants (Northampton) 1998 (SL).

BEVAN, Michael Gwyl (Western Creek HS, Canberra), b Belconnen, ACT, Australia 8 May 1970. 5'11½". LHB, SLC. S Australia 1989-90. NSW 1990-91 to date. Yorkshire 1995-96; cap 1995. Sussex 1998, 2000 (returns 2002); cap 1998. **Tests** (A): 18 (1994-95 to 1997-98); HS 91 v P (Lahore) 1994-95; BB 6-82 (10-113 match) v WI (Adelaide) 1996-97. **LOI** (A): 154 (1993-94 to 2000-01); HS 108* v E (Oval) 1997; BB 3-36 v P (Melbourne) 1996-97. Tours (A): E 1997; SA 1996-97; I 1996-97; P 1994-95; Z 1991-92 (Aus B). 1000 runs (3); most – 1598 (1995). HS 203* NSW v WA (Sydney) 1993-94. UK HS 174 v Notts (Hove) 2000. BB 6-82 (*see Tests*). UK BB 3-36 Y v Warwks (Leeds) 1996 and 3-36 v Kent (Tunbridge W) 1998. Awards: NWT 2; BHC 6. LO HS 157* v Essex (Chelmsford) 2000 (BHC).LO BB 5-29 v Sussex (Eastbourne) 1996 (SL). Expected to return in 2002.

HUMPHRIES, Shaun (The Weald, Billingshurst; Kingston C, London), b Horsham 11 Jan 1973. 5'9". RHB, WK. Sussex 1993-2000. HS 66 v Kent (Tunbridge W) 1998. LO HS 16 v Glam (Hove) 1998 (BHC).

KHAN, W.G. – *see DERBYSHIRE.*

PATTERSON, Andrew David, b Belfast, N Ireland 4 Sep 1975, RHB, WK. Ireland 1996 to date. Sussex 2000. HS 31 Ire v Scot (Dublin) 1997. Sx HS 8 (thrice). LO HS 50 Ire v Somerset (Taunton) 1997 (BHC).

PEIRCE, Michael Toby Edward (Ardingly C; Durham U), b Maidenhead, Berks 14 Jun 1973. 5'10". LHB, SLA. Combined U 1994. Sussex 1995-2000. HS 123 v Glam (Cardiff) 1999. BB 1-16. LO HS 44 Comb U v Middx (Lord's) 1995 (BHC).

SUSSEX 2000

RESULTS SUMMARY

	Place	Won	Lost	Tied	Drew	No Result
County Championship (2nd Division)	9th	3	6		7	
All First-Class Matches		3	7		7	
NatWest Trophy	4th Round					
Benson & Hedges Cup	Quarter-Finalist					
National League (1st Division)	9th	5	8	1		2

COUNTY CHAMPIONSHIP AVERAGES

BATTING AND FIELDING

Cap		M	I	NO	HS	Runs	Avge	100	50	Ct/St
1998	M.G.Bevan	12	18	3	174	1124	74.93	5	1	2
1998	C.J.Adams	16	26	3	156	913	39.69	1	7	15
–	U.B.A.Rashid	14	20	3	110	560	32.94	1	4	6
1999	P.A.Cottey	16	23	–	154	740	32.17	2	2	8
1999	R.R.Montgomerie	16	28	2	133	769	29.57	2	3	17
2000	R.S.C.Martin-Jenkins	14	21	1	86	465	23.25	–	2	3
	W.G.Khan	2	4	–	74	85	21.25	–	1	–
–	M.T.E.Peirce	13	22	1	86	401	19.09	–	2	3
–	N.J.Wilton	8	11	2	46	150	16.66	–	–	19
–	W.J.House	5	8	1	35	90	12.85	–	–	3
1996	J.D.Lewry	16	22	4	39	149	8.27	–	–	5
–	J.J.Bates	3	4	–	17	33	8.25	–	–	5
1998	R.J.Kirtley	16	22	4	26*	146	8.11	–	–	5
–	M.H.Yardy	3	6	1	14	39	7.80	–	–	–
1997	M.A.Robinson	9	11	8	8*	19	6.33	–	–	3
–	B.V.Taylor	5	6	4	6	9	4.50	–	–	–
–	A.D.Patterson	7	9	–	8	37	4.11	–	–	15

Also batted: S.Humphries (1 match) 4, 18 (3ct, 1st).

BOWLING

	O	M	R	W	Avge	Best	5wI	10wM
R.J.Kirtley	521.4	138	1559	63	24.74	6- 41	4	–
J.D.Lewry	494.4	122	1507	51	29.54	6- 66	3	–
M.A.Robinson	228	77	537	16	33.56	3- 88	–	–
R.S.C.Martin-Jenkins	335.1	71	1135	32	35.46	5- 94	1	–
U.B.A.Rashid	297.5	73	892	23	38.78	5-103	1	–

Also bowled: C.J.Adams 27-3-110-2; J.J.Bates 79-14-254-3; M.G.Bevan 103.4-11-400-5; P.A.Cottey 1-1-0-0; W.J.House 17-2-62-1; W.G.Khan 7-0-22 0; M.T.E.Peirce 11-3-37-1; B.V.Taylor 118-28-405-6; M.H.Yardy 5-0-17-0.

The First-Class Averages (pp 118-132) give the records of Sussex players in all first-class county matches (Sussex's other opponents being New Zealand A), with the exception of A.D.Patterson, whose full county figures are as above.

SUSSEX RECORDS

FIRST-CLASS CRICKET

Highest Total	For 705-8d		v	Surrey	Hastings	1902
	V 726		by	Notts	Nottingham	1895
Lowest Total	For 19		v	Surrey	Godalming	1830
	19		v	Notts	Hove	1873
	V 18		by	Kent	Gravesend	1867
Highest Innings	For 333	K.S.Duleepsinhji	v	Northants	Hove	1930
	V 322	E.Paynter	for	Lancashire	Hove	1937

Highest Partnership for each Wicket

1st	490	E.H.Bowley/J.G.Langridge	v	Middlesex	Hove	1933
2nd	385	E.H.Bowley/M.W.Tate	v	Northants	Hove	1921
3rd	298	K.S.Ranjitsinhji/E.H.Killick	v	Lancashire	Hove	1901
4th	326*	J.Langridge/G.Cox	v	Yorkshire	Leeds	1949
5th	297	J.H.Parks/H.W.Parks	v	Hampshire	Portsmouth	1937
6th	255	K.S.Duleepsinhji/M.W.Tate	v	Northants	Hove	1930
7th	344	K.S.Ranjitsinhji/W.Newham	v	Essex	Leyton	1902
8th	229*	C.L.A.Smith/G.Brann	v	Kent	Hove	1902
9th	178	H.W.Parks/A.F.Wensley	v	Derbyshire	Horsham	1930
10th	156	G.R.Cox/H.R.Butt	v	Cambridge U	Cambridge	1908

Best Bowling	For 10- 48	C.H.G.Bland	v	Kent	Tonbridge	1899
(Innings)	V 9- 11	A.P.Freeman	for	Kent	Hove	1922
Best Bowling	For 17-106	G.R.Cox	v	Warwicks	Horsham	1926
(Match)	V 17- 67	A.P.Freeman	for	Kent	Hove	1922

Most Runs – Season	2850	J.G.Langridge	(av 64.77)		1949
Most Runs – Career	34152	J.G.Langridge	(av 37.69)		1928-55
Most 100s – Season	12	J.G.Langridge			1949
Most 100s – Career	76	J.G.Langridge			1928-55
Most Wkts – Season	198	M.W.Tate	(av 13.47)		1925
Most Wkts – Career	2211	M.W.Tate	(av 17.41)		1912-37

LIMITED-OVERS CRICKET

Highest Total	NWT	384-9	v	Ireland	Belfast	1996
	BHC	316-3	v	Essex	Chelmsford	2000
	NL	312-8	v	Hampshire	Portsmouth	1993
Lowest Total	NWT	49	v	Derbyshire	Chesterfield	1969
	BHC	61	v	Middlesex	Hove	1978
	NL	59	v	Glamorgan	Hove	1996
Highest Innings	NWT	158	R.K.Rao	v	Derbyshire	Derby	1997
	BHC	157*	M.G.Bevan	v	Essex	Chelmsford	2000
	NL	163	C.J.Adams	v	Middlesex	Arundel	1999
Best Bowling	NWT	6- 9	A.I.C.Dodemaide	v	Ireland	Downpatrick	1990
	BHC	5- 8	Imran Khan	v	Northants	Northampton	1978
	NL	7-41	A.N.Jones	v	Notts	Nottingham	1986

WARWICKSHIRE

Formation of Present Club: 8 April 1882
Substantial Reorganisation: 19 January 1884
Colours: Dark Blue, Gold and Silver
Badge: Bear and Ragged Staff
County Champions: (5) 1911, 1951, 1972, 1994, 1995
NatWest Trophy/Gillette Cup Winners: (5) 1966, 1968, 1989, 1993, 1995
Benson and Hedges Cup Winners: (1) 1994
National League (Div 1) Winners: (0); best – 7th 1999
Sunday League Winners: (3) 1980, 1994, 1997
Match Awards: NWT 69; BHC 61

Chief Executive: D.L.Amiss MBE, County Ground, Edgbaston, Birmingham, B5 7QU ▲ Tel: 0121 446 4422 ▲ Fax: 0121 446 4544 ▲ Email: info@warwk.co.org ▲ Web: www.thebears.co.uk

Captain: M.J.Powell. **Vice-Captain:** D.L.Hemp. **Overseas Player:** V.C.Drakes.
2001 Beneficiary: K.J.Piper. **Scorer:** D.E.Wainwright. ‡ New registration

BELL, Ian Ronald (Princethorpe C), b Walsgrave-on-Sowe 11 Apr 1982. 5'9". Debut 1999. No appearances 2000. Tour (Eng A): WI 2000-01 *(part)*. HS 0. LO HS 10 Warwks CB v Berks (Reading) 1999 (NWT).

‡BETTS, Melvyn Morris (Fyndoune CS, Sacriston), b Sacriston, Co Durham 26 Mar 1975. 5'10". RHB, RFM. Durham 1993-2000; cap 1998. Tour: Z 1998-99. HS 57* Du v Sussex (Hove) 1996. BB 9-64 (Durham record; 13-143 match) v Northants (Northampton) 1997. LO HS 21 Du v Hants (Chester-le-St) 1997 (SL). LO BB 4-34 Du v Berks (Finchampstead) 2000 (NWT).

BROWN, Douglas Robert (Alloa Academy; W London IHE), b Stirling, Scotland 29 Oct 1969. 6'2". RHB, RFM. Scotland 1989. Warwickshire debut 1991-92 (SA tour); cap 1995. Wellington 1995-96. **LOI:** 9 (1997-98); HS 21 v WI (Bridgetown) 1997-98; BB 2-28 v WI (Sharjah) 1997-98. Tours (Wa): SA 1991-92, 1994-95; SL 1997-98 (Eng A). HS 203 v Sussex (Hove) 2000. 50 wkts (2); most – 81 (1997). BB 8-89 (11-154 match) F-C Counties XI v Pak A (Chelmsford) 1997. Wa BB 7-66 v Durham (Chester-le-St) 1999. Award: BHC 1. LO HS 78* v Notts (Nottingham) 1995 (SL). LO BB 5-31 v Worcs (Worcester) 1997 (BHC).

‡CARTER, Neil Miller, b Cape Town, SA 25 Jan 1975. LHB, LMF. ECB qualified – British passport. Boland 1999-00 to date. HS 37 Boland v EP (Pt Elizabeth) 1999-00. BB 3-48 Boland v Gauteng (Paarl) 1999-00. LO HS 7* (Boland – SBC). LO BB 4-31 Boland v Easterns (Benoni) 1999-00 (SBC).

DAGNALL, Charles Edward (Bridgewater H3, Wornley; UMIST), b Bury, Lancs 10 Jul 1976. 6'3". RHB, RMF. Debut 1999. Cumberland 1997-98. HS 6*. BB 4-20 v OU (Oxford) 1999 – on debut CC BB 2-57 v Essex (Chelmsford) 2000. LO HS 4 (NWT). LO BB 4-34 v Derbys (Birmingham) 2000 (NL).

‡DRAKES, Vasbert Conneil (St Lucy SS), b St James, Barbados 5 Aug 1969. 6'2". RHB, RFM. Barbados 1991-92 to 1997-98. Sussex 1996-97; cap 1996. Border 1996-97 to date. Nottinghamshire 1999; cap 1999. **LOI** (WI): 5 (1994-95); HS 16 v A (P-o-S) 1994-95; BB 1-36. Tour (WI): E 1995. HS 180* Barbados v Leeward Is (Anguilla) 1994-95. UK HS 145* Sx v Essex (Chelmsford) 1996. 50 wkts (2+2); most – 80 (1999). BB 8-59 Border v Natal (Durban) 1996-97. UK BB 6-39 (12-110 match) Nt v Warwks (Nottingham) 1999. LO HS 104 Border v Boland (Paarl) 1996-97 (SBC). LO BB 5-19 v Ire (Hove) 1996 (BHC). Took 4 wkts in 4 balls v Derbys (Nottingham) 1999 (NL).

FRANKLIN, Gavin David (Malvern C; Durham U), b Wolverhampton, Staffs 9 Jan 1978. RHB, OB. British U 2000. Staffordshire 1997. Contracted since 1998 – awaiting county debut. HS 12 Brit U v Z (Cambridge) 2000.

FROST, Tony (James Brinkley HS; Stoke-on-Trent C), b Stoke-on-Trent, Staffs 17 Nov 1975. 5'11". RHB, WK. Debut 1997; cap 1999. HS 111* v OU (Oxford) 1998. CC HS 66 v Sussex (Birmingham) 1999. LO HS 22* v Kent (Birmingham) 1999.

GILES, Ashley Fraser (George Abbot S, Guildford), b Chertsey, Surrey 19 Mar 1973. 6'3". RHB, SLA. Debut 1993; cap 1996. Tour: A 1996-97 (Eng A). **Tests:** 7 (1998 to 2000-01): HS 37* v P (Lahore) 2000-01; BB 5-75 v P (Faisalabad) 2000-01. **LOI:** 8 (1997 to 2000-01); HS 11 v P (Rawalpindi) 2000-01; BB 2-37 v SA (Oval) 1998. Tours: P 2000-01; SL 1997-98 (Eng A), 2000-01; K 1997-98 (Eng A). HS 128* v Sussex (Hove) 2000. 50 wkts (2); most – 64 (1996). BB 8-90 (12-135 match) v Northants (Northampton) 2000. Awards: NWT 2; BHC 1. LO HS 107 v Derbys (Birmingham) 2000 (NWT). LO BB 5-21 v Norfolk (Birmingham) 1997 (NWT).

HEMP, David Lloyd (Olchfa CS; Millfield S; W Glamorgan C), b Bermuda 8 Nov 1970. UK resident since 1976. 6'0". LHB, RM. Glamorgan 1991-96; cap 1994. Warwickshire debut/cap 1997. Wales (MC) 1992-94. Tours: SA 1995-96 (Gm); I 1994-95 (Eng A); Z 1994-95 (Gm). 1000 runs (3); most – 1452 (1994). HS 157 Gm v Glos (Abergavenny) 1995. Wa HS 144 v Worcs (Birmingham) 1999. BB 3-23 Gm v SA A (Cardiff) 1996. CC BB 2-29 v Glos (Birmingham) 2000. Awards: NWT 4; BHC 2. LO HS 121 Gm v Comb U (Cardiff) 1995 (BHC). LO BB 4-32 v Minor C (Lakenham) 1998 (BHC).

KNIGHT, Nicholas Verity (Felsted S; Loughborough U), b Watford, Herts 28 Nov 1969. 6'0". LHB, occ RM. Essex 1991-94; cap 1994. Warwickshire debut 1994-95 (SA tour); cap 1995. **Tests:** 16 (1995 to 2000); HS 113 v P (Leeds) 1996. **LOI:** 53 (1996 to 1999-00); HS 125* v P (Nottingham) 1996. Tours: SA 1994-95 (Wa), 1999-00 (part); NZ 1996-97; I 1994-95 (Eng A); SL 1997-98 (Eng A – captain); P 1995-96 (Eng A); Z 1996-97; K 1997-98 (Eng A – captain). 1000 runs (2); most – 1196 (1996). HS 233 v Glam (Birmingham) 2000. BB 1-61. Awards: NWT 4; BHC 2. LO HS 151 v Somerset (Birmingham) 1995 (NWT). LO BB 1-14 (SL).

OSTLER, Dominic Piers (Princethorpe C; Solihull TC), b Solihull 15 Jul 1970. 6'3". RHB, occ RM. Debut 1990; cap 1991; benefit 1999. Tours: SA 1992-93 (Wa); P 1995-96 (Eng A). 1000 runs (5); most – 1284 (1991). HS 208 v Surrey (Birmingham) 1995. BB 1-46. Awards: NWT 2; BHC 1. LO HS 104 and LO BB 1-4 v Norfolk (Lakenham) 1993 (NWT).

PENNEY, Trevor Lionel (Prince Edward S, Salisbury), b Salisbury, Rhodesia 12 Jun 1968. 6'0". RHB, RM. Qualified for England 1992. Boland 1991-92. Warwickshire debut 1991-92 (SA tour); UK debut v CU (Cambridge) 1992, scoring 102*; cap 1994. Mashonaland 1993-94 to date. Tours (Wa): SA 1991-92, 1992-93, 1994-95; Z 1993-94. 1000 runs (2); most – 1295 (1996). HS 151 v Middx (Lord's) 1992. BB 3-18 Mashonaland v Mashonaland U-24 (Harare) 1993-94. Wa BB 1-40 (Z tour). CC BB – . Awards: NWT 2. LO HS 90 v Cornwall (St Austell) 1996 (NWT). LO BB 1-8 (NWT).

PIPER, Keith John (Haringey Cricket C), b Leicester 18 Dec 1969. 5'6". RHB, WK. Warwickshire debut 1989; cap 1992; benefit 2001. Tours (Wa): SA 1991-92, 1992-93, 1994-95; I 1994-95 (Eng A); P 1995-96 (Eng A); Z 1993-94. HS 116* v Durham (Birmingham) 1994. BB 1-57. LO HS 38* v Leics (Birmingham) 1999 (NL).

POWELL, Michael James (Lawrence Sheriff S, Rugby), b Bolton, Lancs 5 Apr 1975. 5'11". RHB, RM. Debut 1996; cap 1999; captain 2001. Tour (Eng A): WI 2000-01. 1000 runs (1): 1046 (2000). HS 145 v Northants (Northampton) 2000. BB 2-16 v OU (Oxford) 1998. CC BB 1-0. LO HS 51 v Yorks (Leeds) 1999 (NL). LO BB 2-13 v Hants (Southampton) 2000 (NL).

RICHARDSON, Alan (Alleyne's HS; Stafford CFE; Durham U), b Newcastle-under-Lyme, Staffs 6 May 1975. 6'2". RHB, RMF. Derbyshire 1995 (one match). Warwickshire debut 1999. Staffordshire 1996-98. HS 17* v Northants (Northampton) 2000. BB 8-51 (10-107 match) v Glos (Birmingham) 1999. LO HS 11* v Leics (Birmingham) 1999 (NL). LO BB 2-16 v Essex (Colchester) 1999 (NL).

SHEIKH, Mohammad Avez (Broadway S), b Birmingham 2 Jul 1973. 6'0". LHB, RM. Debut 1997. HS 58* v Northants (Northampton) 2000. BB 2-14 v Middx (Birmingham) 1997. LO HS 36 v Hants (Southampton) 2000 (NL). LO BB 3-28 v Glam (Birmingham) 1998 (SL).

SIERRA, Ryan Edward, b Pietersburg, SA 8 Sep 1980. ECB qualified – British passport. LHB, LM. Staff 2000 – awaiting f-c debut.

SMITH, Neil Michael Knight (Warwick S), b Birmingham 27 Jul 1967. Son of M.J.K. (Leics, Warwks and England 1951-75). 6'0". RHB, OB. Debut 1987; cap 1993; captain 1999-2000. MCC YC. **LOI:** 7 (1995-96 to 1996); HS 31 v H (Peshawar) 1995-96; BB 3-29 v UAE (Peshawar) 1995-96. Tours (Wa): SA 1991-92, 1994-95; Z 1993-94. 1000 runs (1): 1002 (1998). HS 161 v Yorks (Leeds) 1989. BB 7-42 v Lancs (Birmingham) 1994. Awards: NWT 1; BHC 2. LO HS 125 v Kent (Canterbury) 1997 (BHC). LO BB 6-33 v Sussex (Birmingham) 1995 (SL).

WAGH, Mark Anant (King Edward's S, Birmingham; Keble C, Oxford), b Birmingham 20 Oct 1976. 6'2". RHB, OB. Oxford U 1996-98; blue 1996-97-98; captain 1997. Warwickshire debut 1997; cap 2000. British U 1998. Mashonaland A 1998-99. 1000 runs (1): 1156 (1997). HS 216* v OU (Oxford) 1999. CC HS 137 v Essex (Chelmsford) 2000. BB 4-11 v Middx (Lord's) 1998. LO HS 31 v Derbys (Birmingham) 2000 (NL). LO BB 1-39 (Brit U – BHC).

WARREN, Nick Alexander (Solihull SFC), b Moseley, Birmingham 26 Jun 1982. 5'11". RHB, RMF. Staff 2000 – awaiting f-c debut. 2nd XI debut 1998 when aged 16y 76d.

RELEASED/RETIRED
(Having made a first-class County appearance in 2000)

ALTREE, Darren Anthony (Ashlawn S, Rugby), b Rugby 30 Sep 1974. 5'11". RHB, LMF. Warwickshire 1996-2000. HS 4. BB 3-41 v P (Birmingham) 1996. CC BB 2-108 v Hants (Southampton) 1997. LO HS 6 (Warwks CB – NWT).

DONALD, Allan Anthony (Grey College HS), b Bloemfontein, SA 20 Oct 1966. 6'2". RHB, RF. OFS/FS 1985-86 to date. Warwickshire 1987-93, 1995, 1997, 1999-2000; cap 1989; benefit 1999. *Wisden* 1991. **Tests** (SA): 65 (1991-92 to 2000-01); HS 34 v WI (Pt Elizabeth) 1998-99; BB 8-71 (11-113 match) v Z (Harare) 1995-96. **LOI** (SA): 131 (1991-92 to 2000-01); HS 12 v SL (Nottingham) 1998; BB 6-23 v K (Nairobi) 1996-97. Tours (SA): E 1994, 1998; A 1993-94, 1997-98; WI 1991-92, 2000-01; NZ 1994-95, 1998-99; I 1996-97, 1999-00; P 1997-98; SL 1993-94; Z 1995-96, 1999-00. HS 55* SA v Tasmania (Devonport) 1997-98. Wa HS 44 v Essex (Ilford) 1995. 50 wkts (5): most – 89 (1995). BB 8-37 OFS v Transvaal (Johannesburg) 1986-87. Wa BB 7-37 v Durham (Birmingham) 1992. Awards: NWT 4. LO HS 23* v Leics (Leicester) 1989 (BHC). LO BB 6-15 v Yorks (Birmingham) 1995 (SL).

GIDDINS, E.S.H. – *see SURREY.*

SINGH, A. – *see WORCESTERSHIRE.*

WELCH, G. – *see DERBYSHIRE.*

WARWICKSHIRE 2000

RESULTS SUMMARY

	Place	Won	Lost	Tied	Drew	No Result
County Championship (2nd Division)	6th	2	3		11	
All First-Class Matches		2	3		12	
NatWest Trophy	Finalist					
Benson & Hedges Cup	3rd in Mid/West/Wales Group					
National League (2nd Division)	3rd	10	5		1	

COUNTY CHAMPIONSHIP AVERAGES

BATTING AND FIELDING

Cap		M	I	NO	HS	Runs	Avge	100	50	Ct/St
1995	N.V.Knight	5	7	–	233	472	67.42	1	1	4
1991	D.P.Ostler	15	23	2	145	1021	48.61	2	6	19
2000	M.A.Wagh	9	16	3	137	592	45.53	2	3	4
1999	M.J.Powell	16	25	2	145	1006	43.73	2	8	9
1996	A.F.Giles	12	14	3	128*	444	40.36	1	1	4
1995	D.R.Brown	15	21	5	203	618	38.62	1	2	11
1997	D.L.Hemp	16	23	2	129	738	35.14	1	4	9
1994	T.L.Penney	12	17	3	85	469	33.50	–	2	8
1993	N.M.K.Smith	16	19	2	87	436	25.64	–	4	8
–	A.Singh	5	7	–	79	156	22.28	–	1	1
–	A.Richardson	13	9	7	17*	43	21.50	–	–	3
1992	K.J.Piper	16	18	3	69	260	17.33	–	1	28/3
1997	G.Welch	7	8	1	55	116	16.57	–	1	1
1989	A.A.Donald	7	9	2	18	69	9.85	–	–	3
1998	E.S.H.Giddins	8	6	1	14	15	3.00	–	–	1

Also batted: D.A.Altree (1 match) 4; C.E.Dagnall (2) 5*, 6*; M.A.Sheikh (1) 58*.

BOWLING

	O	M	R	W	Avge	Best	5wI	10wM
A.F.Giles	526.4	163	1200	52	23.07	8-90	5	2
A.A.Donald	201.3	56	530	18	29.44	4-59	–	–
N.M.K.Smith	310.4	70	875	28	31.25	5-66	1	–
E.S.H.Giddins	234.5	78	642	20	32.10	4-70	–	–
D.R.Brown	268.2	49	917	24	38.20	5-87	1	–
A.Richardson	368.2	96	1040	27	38.51	4-69	–	–

Also bowled: D.A.Altree 20.1-1-77-0; C.E.Dagnall 54.4-16-181-5; D.L.Hemp 20-3-80-2; D.P.Ostler 5-0-46-1; M.J.Powell 24-6-80-2; M.A.Sheikh 23-7-68-1; A.Singh 6.5-0-66-0; M.A.Wagh 25-9-55-0; G.Welch 156-32-564-3.

The First-Class Averages (pp 118-132) give the records of Warwickshire's players in all first-class county matches (Warwickshire's other opponents being Oxford University), with the exception of G.D.Franklin, whose only first-class appearance was for British Universities, and:

E.S.H.Giddins 9-6-1-14-15-3.00-0-0-1ct. 237.5-78-652-21-31.04-4/70.
N.V.Knight 6-8-0-233-474-59.25-1-1-4ct. Did not bowl.

WARWICKSHIRE RECORDS

FIRST-CLASS CRICKET

Highest Total	For 810-4d			v	Durham	Birmingham	1994
	V 887			by	Yorkshire	Birmingham	1896
Lowest Total	For 16			v	Kent	Tonbridge	1913
	V 15			by	Hampshire	Birmingham	1922
Highest Innings	For 501*	B.C.Lara		v	Durham	Birmingham	1994
	V 322	I.V.A.Richards		for	Somerset	Taunton	1985

Highest Partnership for each Wicket

1st	377*	N.F.Horner/K.Ibadulla	v	Surrey	The Oval	1960
2nd	465*	J.A.Jameson/R.B.Kanhai	v	Glos	Birmingham	1974
3rd	327	S.P.Kinneir/W.G.Quaife	v	Lancashire	Birmingham	1901
4th	470	A.I.Kallicharran/G.W.Humpage	v	Lancashire	Southport	1982
5th	322*	B.C.Lara/K.J.Piper	v	Durham	Birmingham	1994
6th	220	H.E.Dollery/J.Buckingham	v	Derbyshire	Derby	1938
7th	289	D.Brown/A.F.Giles	v	Sussex	Hove	2000
8th	228	A.J.W.Croom/R.E.S.Wyatt	v	Worcs	Dudley	1925
9th	154	G.W.Stephens/A.J.W.Croom	v	Derbyshire	Birmingham	1925
10th	141	A.F.Giles/T.A.Munton	v	Worcs	Worcester	1996

Best Bowling	For	10-41	J.D.Bannister	v	Comb Servs	Birmingham	1959
(Innings)	V	10-36	H.Verity	for	Yorkshire	Leeds	1931
Best Bowling	For	15-76	S.Hargreave	v	Surrey	The Oval	1903
(Match)	V	17-92	A.P.Freeman	for	Kent	Folkestone	1932

Most Runs – Season	2417	M.J.K.Smith	(av 60.42)		1959
Most Runs – Career	35146	D.L.Amiss	(av 41.64)		1960-87
Most 100s – Season	9	A.I.Kallicharran			1984
	9	B.C.Lara			1994
Most 100s – Career	78	D.L.Amiss			1960-87
Most Wkts – Season	180	W.E.Hollies	(av 15.13)		1946
Most Wkts – Career	2201	W.E.Hollies	(av 20.45)		1932-57

LIMITED-OVERS CRICKET

Highest Total	NWT	392-5		v	Oxfordshire	Birmingham	1984
	BHC	369-8		v	Minor C	Jesmond	1996
	NL	301-6		v	Essex	Colchester	1982
Lowest Total	NWT	98		v	Leics	Leicester	1998
	BHC	94		v	Glos	Bristol	2000
	NL	65		v	Kent	Maidstone	1979
Highest Innings	NWT	206	A.I.Kallicharran	v	Oxfordshire	Birmingham	1984
	BHC	137*	T.A.Lloyd	v	Lancashire	Birmingham	1985
	NL	134	N.V.Knight	v	Hampshire	Birmingham	1996
Best Bowling	NWT	6-32	K.Ibadulla	v	Hampshire	Birmingham	1965
		6-32	A.I.Kallicharran	v	Oxfordshire	Birmingham	1984
	BHC	7-32	R.G.D.Willis	v	Yorkshire	Birmingham	1981
	NL	6-15	A.A.Donald	v	Yorkshire	Birmingham	1995

WORCESTERSHIRE

Formation of Present Club: 11 March 1865
Colours: Dark Green and Black
Badge: Shield Argent a Fess between three Pears Sable
County Championships: (5) 1964, 1965, 1974, 1988, 1989
NatWest Trophy/Gillette Cup Winners: (1) 1994
Benson and Hedges Cup Winners: (1) 1991
National League (Div 1) Winners: (0); best – 2nd 1999
Sunday League Winners: (3) 1971, 1987, 1988
Match Awards: NWT 45; BHC 68

Secretary: Revd M.D.Vockins OBE (*retires June 2001 to be succeeded by M.Newton as Chief Executive*), County Ground, New Road, Worcester, WR2 4QQ ▲ Tel: 01905 748474 ▲ Fax: 01905 748005 ▲ Email: admin@wccc.co.uk ▲ Web: www.wccc.co.uk

Captain: G.A.Hick (tbc). **Vice-Captain:** S.J.Rhodes (tbc). **Overseas Player:** A.J.Bichel.
2001 Beneficiary: Worcestershire CCC. **Scorer:** S.S.Hale. ‡ New registration

ALI, Kabir (Moseley CS and SFC), b Moseley, Birmingham 24 Nov 1980. 6'0". RHB, RMF. Debut 1999. HS 50* v Notts (Worcester) 2000. BB 4-114 v Essex (Kidderminster) 2000. Award: BHC 1. LO HS 11 v NZ A (Worcester) 2000. LO BB 4-29 v Glam (Worcester) 2000 (BHC).

ALI, Kadeer (Handsworth GS), b Moseley, Birmingham 7 Mar 1983. 6'1". RHB, LB. Debut 2000. HS 8. LO HS 24 Worcs CB v Kent CB (Maidstone) 1999 (NWT).

‡BICHEL, Andrew John (Laidley HS; Ipswich C, Queensland), b Laidley, Queensland 27 Aug 1970. RHB, RFM. 5'11". Queensland 1992-93 to date. **Tests:** 5 (1996-97 to 2000-01); HS 18 v WI (Perth) 1996-97; BB 5-60 v WI (Melbourne) 2000-01. **LOI:** 17 (1996-97 to 1997-98); HS 27* v SA (Perth) 1997-98; BB 3-17 v P (Hobart) 1996-97. Tours (A): E 1997; Scot 1998 (Aus A); SA 1996-97; WI 1998-99. HS 110 (off 110 balls) Q v Vic (Brisbane) 1997-98. 50 wkts (0+1): 60 (1999-00). BB 6-45 Q v Tas (Hobart) 1999-00. LO HS 42* Q v P (Brisbane) 1996-97. LO BB 4-45 Q v S Aus (Brisbane) 1995-96 (MM).

‡BOULTON, Nicholas Ross (King's C, Taunton), b Johannesburg, SA 22 Mar 1979. 6'1½". LHB, RM. Somerset 1997 (one match – no CC appearances). HS 14 Sm v Pak A (Taunton) 1997.

CATTERALL, Duncan Neil (Queen Elizabeth's GS, Blackburn; Loughborough U), b Preston, Lancs 19 Sep 1978. 5'11". RHB, RMF. Debut 1998. HS 60 v Essex (Chelmsford) 1999 and 60 v Middx (Worcester) 1999 – in successive innings. BB 4-50 v WI (Worcester) 2000. CC BB 2-16 v Essex (Chelmsford) 1999. LO HS 21* v NZ A (Worcester) 2000. LO BB 2-35 v Yorks (Worcester) 1999 (NL).

HICK, Graeme Ashley (Prince Edward HS, Salisbury), b Salisbury, Rhodesia 23 May 1966. 6'3". RHB, OB. Zimbabwe 1983-84 to 1985-86. Worcestershire debut 1984; cap 1986; benefit 1999; captain 2000. N Districts 1987-88 to 1988-89. Queensland 1990-91. *Wisden* 1986. **ECB contract 2000. Tests:** 65 (1991 to 2000-01); HS 178 v I (Bombay) 1992-93; BB 4-126 v NZ (Wellington) 1991-92. **LOI:** 117 (1991 to 2000-01); HS 126* v SL (Adelaide) 1998-99; BB 5-33 v Z (Harare) 1999-00. Tours: E 1985 (Z); A 1994-95, 1998-99 (*part*); SA 1995-96, 1999-00 (*part*); WI 1993-94; NZ 1991-92; I 1992-93; P 2000-01; SL 1983-84 (Z), 1992-93, 2000-01; Z 1990-91 (Wo), 1996-97 (Wo). 1000 runs (15+1) inc 2000 (3); most – 2713 (1988); youngest to score 2000 (1986). Scored 1019 runs before June 1988, including a record 410 runs in April. Fewest innings for 10,000 runs in county cricket (179). Youngest (24) to score 50 f-c hundreds. Second-youngest (32) to score 100 f-c hundreds. Scored 645 runs without being dismissed (UK record) in 1990. HS 405* (Worcs record and then second highest in UK f-c matches) v Somerset (Taunton) 1988. BB 5-18 v Leics (Worcester) 1995. Awards: NWT 4; BHC 11. LO HS 172* v Devon (Worcester) 1987 (NWT). LO BB 5-19 E v Pak A (Lahore) 1998-99.

LAMPITT, Stuart Richard (Kingswinford S; Dudley TC), b Wolverhampton, Staffs 29 Jul 1966. 5'11". RHB, RMF. Debut 1985; cap 1989; benefit 2000. Tours (Wo): Z 1990-91, 1993-94, 1996-97. HS 122 v Middx (Lord's) 1994. 50 wkts (7); most – 64 (1994). BB 7-45 v Warwks (Worcester) 2000. Awards: NWT 1; BHC 4. LO HS 54 v Scot (Edinburgh) 1998 (NWT). LO BB 6-26 v Derbys (Derby) 1994 (BHC).

LEATHERDALE, David Anthony (Pudsey Grangefield S), b Bradford, Yorks 26 Nov 1967. 5'10½". RHB, RM. Debut 1988; cap 1994. Tours (Wo): Z 1993-94, 1996-97. 1000 runs (1): 1001 (1998). HS 157 v Somerset (Worcester) 1991. BB 5-20 v Glos (Worcester) 1998. LO HS 70* v Yorks (Worcester) 1999 (NL). LO BB 5-10 v A (Worcester) 1997.

LIPTROT, Christopher George (The Deanery HS), b Wigan, Lancs 13 Feb 1980. 6'2". LHB, RFM. Debut 1999. HS 61 v Warwks (Birmingham) 1999. BB 6-44 v Warwks (Worcester) 2000. LO HS 15* and LO BB 3-44 v Kent (Canterbury) 2000 (NL).

PATEL, Depesh Balvant (Moseley Park GS; Bilston Community C), b Wolverhampton, Staffs 23 Sep 1981. 6'3". RHB, RMF. Awaiting f-c debut. LO HS 19* and LO BB 1-36 Worcs CB v Kent CB (Maidstone) 1999 (NWT).

PIPE, David James (Queensbury S, Bradford), b Bradford, Yorks 16 Dec 1977. 5'11". RHB, WK. Debut 1998. HS 54 v Warwks (Worcester) 2000 – on CC debut. LO HS 56 Worcs CB v Kent CB (Kidderminster) 2000 (NWT).

POLLARD, Paul Raymond (Gedling CS), b Carlton, Nottingham 24 Sep 1968. 5'11". LHB, RM. Nottinghamshire 1987-98; cap 1992. Worcestershire debut 1999. Tour (N): SA 1996-97. 1000 runs (3); most – 1463 (1993). HS 180 Nt v Derbys (Nottingham) 1993. Wo HS 123* v Essex (Kidderminster) 2000. BB 2-79 Nt v Glos (Bristol) 1993. LO HS 132* Nt v Somerset (Nottingham) 1995 (SL).

RAWNSLEY, Matthew James (Shenley Court CS, Birmingham), b Birmingham 8 Jun 1976. 6'2". RHB, SLA. Debut 1996. HS 26 v Essex (Chelmsford) 1997. BB 6-44 (11-116 match) v OU (Oxford) 1998. CC BB 5-125 v Middx (Southgate) 2000. LO HS 9 (v NZ A). LO BB 5-26 v Kent (Tunbridge W) 1999 (NL).

RHODES, Steven John (Lapage Middle S; Carlton-Bolling S, Bradford), b Bradford, Yorks 17 Jun 1964. Son of W.E. (Notts 1961-64). 5'7". RHB, WK. Yorkshire 1981-84. Worcestershire debut 1985; cap 1986; benefit 1996. *Wisden* 1994. **Tests:** 11 (1994 to 1994-95); HS 65* v SA (Leeds) 1994. **LOI:** 9 (1989 to 1994-95); HS 56 v SA (Manchester) 1994. Tours: A 1994-95; SA 1993-94 (Eng A); WI 1991-92 (Eng A); SL 1985-86 (Eng B), 1990-91 (Eng A); Z 1989-90 (Eng A), 1990-91 (Wo), 1993-94 (Wo), 1996-97 (Wo – captain). 1000 runs (2); most – 1018 (1995). HS 122* v Young A (Worcester) 1995. CC HS 116* v Warwks (Worcester) 1992. Awards: NWT 1; BHC 2. LO HS 105 v Lancs (Manchester) 1991 (RAC).

SHERIYAR, Alamgir (George Dixon S; Joseph Chamberlain SFC; Oxford Poly), b Birmingham 15 Nov 1973. 6'1". RHB, LFM. Leicestershire 1994-95. Worcestershire debut 1996; cap 1997. Tours (Eng A): NZ 1999-00; B 1999-00. HS 21 v Notts (Nottingham) 1997 and 21 v Pak A (Worcester) 1997. 50 wkts (2); most – 92 (1999). BB 7-130 (10-172 match) v Hants (Southampton) 1999. Hat-tricks (2): 1994 (Le), 1999. LO HS 19 v Derbys (Chesterfield) 1996 (SL). LO BB 4-18 v Yorks (Leeds) 1997 (SL).

‡SINGH, Anurag (King Edward's, Birmingham; Gonville & Caius C, Cambridge), b Kanpur, India 9 Sep 1975. 5'11½". RHB, OB. Warwickshire 1995-2000. Cambridge U 1996-98; blue 1996-97-98; captain 1997-98. British U 1998 (captain). HS 157 CU v Sussex (Hove) 1996. CC HS 79 Wa v Worcs (Worcester) 2000. Award: BHC 1. LO HS 123 Brit U v Somerset (Taunton) 1996 (BHC).

SOLANKI, Vikram Singh (Regis S, Wolverhampton), b Udaipur, India 1 Apr 1976. 6'0". RHB, OB. Debut 1995; cap 1998. Tours (Eng A): SA 1999-00 (Eng – *part*); WI 2000-01; NZ 1999-00; Z 1996-97 (Wo), 1998-99; B 1999-00. **LOI:** 8 (1999-00). HS 185 Eng A v Bangladesh (Chittagong) 1999-00. Wo HS 171 v Glos (Cheltenham) 1999. BB 5-69 v Middx (Lord's) 1996. LO HS 120* v Derbys (Derby) 1998 (SL). LO BB 2-40 Eng A v Zim Academy (Harare) 1998-99.

SPIRING, Karl Reuben (Monmouth S; Durham U), b Southport, Lancs 13 Nov 1974. 5'11". RHB, OB. Debut 1994; cap 1997. 1000 runs (1): 1084 (1996). HS 150 v Essex (Chelmsford) 1997. LO HS 71 v Sussex (Hove) 2000 (NL).

WESTON, William Philip Christopher (Durham S), b Durham 16 Jun 1973. Son of M.P. (Durham; England RFU); brother of R.M.S. (*see MIDDLESEX*). 6'3". LHB, LM. Debut 1991; cap 1995. Tours (Wo): Z 1993-94, 1996-97. 1000 runs (3); most – 1389 (1996). HS 205 v Northants (Northampton) 1997. BB 2-39 v P (Worcester) 1992. CC BB – . LO HS 125 v Warwks (Birmingham) 1999 (NL). LO BB 1-2 (SL).

WILSON, Elliott James (Felsted S; Durham U), b St Pancras, London 3 Nov 1976. 6'3". RHB, RM. Debut 1998. British U 1999. Cambridgeshire 1996. HS 116 v Middx (Worcester) 1999. LO HS 62 v Warwks (Worcester) 1999 (NL).

RELEASED/RETIRED
(Having made a first-class County appearance in 2000)

DRIVER, R.C. – *see* LANCASHIRE.

ILLINGWORTH, R.K. – *see* DERBYSHIRE.

McGRATH, Glenn Donald (Narromine HS), b Dubbo, NSW, Australia 9 Feb 1970. 6'6". RHB, RF. New South Wales 1992-93 to date. Worcestershire 2000; cap 2000. *Wisden* 1997. **Tests** (A): 67 (1993-94 to 2000-01); HS 39 v WI (P-o-S) 1998-99; BB 8-38 v E (Lord's) 1997. **LOI** (A): 130 (1993-94 to 2000-01); HS 11 v NZ (Auckland) 1999-00; BB 5-14 v WI (Manchester) 1999. Tours (A): E 1997; SA 1993-94, 1996-97; WI 1994-95, 1998-99; NZ 1999-00; I 1996-97, 2000-01; P 1994-95, 1998-99; SL 1999-00; Z 1999-00. HS 55 v Notts (Worcester) 2000. 50 wkts (1+1); most – 80 (2000). BB 8-38 (*see Tests*). Wo BB 8-41 (12-116 match) v Northants (Worcester) 2000. LO HS 11 (*see LOI*). LO BB 5-14 (*see LOI*).

STOP PRESS

INDIA ENDS AUSTRALIA'S RECORD RUN

**Calcutta (11-15 March): Australia 445 and 212;
India 171 and (following on) 657-7 dec.**

A capacity Eden Gardens crowd estimated at 90,000 saw India gain their most famous victory when they beat Australia by 171 runs with 6.3 overs to spare. They became only the third team to win a Test after following on, Australia having been the victim of similar instances by England at Sydney in 1894-95 (by 10 runs) and at Leeds in 1981 (by 18 runs). This defeat ended Australia's unprecedented unbroken sequence of 16 wins. Since October 1999 they had beaten India (4), New Zealand (3), Pakistan (3), West Indies (5) and Zimbabwe (1), with 11 of those victories being gained at home.

India's *volte-face* began with a national record fifth-wicket partnership of 376 between V.V.S.Laxman (281) and Rahul Dravid (180). Laxman's score was the highest for India (surpassing Sunil Gavaskar's 236 not out) and the record for all Tests in India (previously Rohan Kanhai's 256 for West Indies). They became the 12th pair to bat throughout an uninterrupted day's play when they added 335 on the fourth day.

India's total of 657-7 declared was their second-highest and only New Zealand (671-4 v Sri Lanka in 1990-91) had amassed a higher tally in their second innings.

Earlier, Punjabi off-spinner Harbhajan Singh had taken India's first Test hat-trick. That feat and his match figures of 13 wickets for 196 prompted his employers, Indian Airlines, to promote him to Assistant Manager (Commercial) and award him and his family a free holiday anywhere on its network.

WORCESTERSHIRE 2000

RESULTS SUMMARY

		Place	Won	Lost	Tied	Drew	No Result
County Championship (2nd Division)		5th	5	5		6	
All First-Class Matches			5	5		8	
NatWest Trophy		3rd Round					
Benson & Hedges Cup		5th in Mid/West/Wales Group					
National League (1st Division)		7th	6	8			2

COUNTY CHAMPIONSHIP AVERAGES

BATTING AND FIELDING

Cap		M	I	NO	HS	Runs	Avge	100	50	Ct/St
1998	V.S.Solanki	14	25	2	161*	1062	46.17	2	7	17
1986	G.A.Hick	8	14	2	122	521	43.41	2	2	8
1994	D.A.Leatherdale	16	28	4	132*	953	39.70	2	7	9
1997	K.R.Spiring	3	4	1	38	96	32.00	–	–	–
1986	S.J.Rhodes	16	26	6	103	583	29.15	1	1	49/1
	P.R.Pollard	12	21	1	123*	560	28.00	1	4	3
–	E.J.Wilson	15	28	1	104*	647	23.96	2	2	9
	D.J.Pipe	3	5	–	54	107	21.40	–	1	–
–	R.C.Driver	9	17	2	64	283	18.86	–	1	2
	Kabir Ali	9	14	3	50*	201	18.27	–	1	5
1995	W.P.C.Weston	9	18	2	58*	264	16.50	–	2	1
1989	S.R.Lampitt	16	25	7	56*	290	16.11	–	1	10
1986	R.K.Illingworth	8	11	2	44*	140	15.55	–	–	3
2000	G.D.McGrath	13	15	3	55	112	9.33	–	1	3
1997	A.Sheriyar	10	11	3	17	69	8.62	–	–	–
–	M.J.Rawnsley	9	13	–	18	102	7.84	–	–	5
–	Kadeer Ali	3	6	–	8	10	1.66	–	–	1

Also batted: C.G.Liptrot (3 matches) 1, 0 (2 ct).

BOWLING

	O	M	R	W	Avge	Best	5wI	10wM
G.D.McGrath	404.4	125	1047	76	13.77	8- 41	6	3
S.R.Lampitt	361.5	91	1050	50	21.00	7- 45	2	–
D.A.Leatherdale	137	28	473	16	29.56	3- 17	–	–
A.Sheriyar	254	50	1010	27	37.40	4- 51	–	–
Kabir Ali	180	34	661	17	38.88	4-114	–	–

Also bowled: R.C.Driver 11.2-2-44-2; G.A.Hick 45-6-135-1; R.K.Illingworth 157.5-45-382-9; C.G.Liptrot 67-10-281-7; P.R.Pollard 0.1-0-4-0; M.J.Rawnsley 204-55-573-9; V.S.Solanki 62.3-7-202-6;

The First-Class Averages (pp 118-132) give the records of Worcestershire's players in all first-class county matches (Worcestershire's other opponents being the West Indians and Cambridge University), with the exception of G.A.Hick, whose full county figures are as above.

WORCESTERSHIRE RECORDS

FIRST-CLASS CRICKET

Highest Total	For	670-7d	v	Somerset	Worcester	1995
	V	701-4d	by	Leics	Worcester	1906
Lowest Total	For	24	v	Yorkshire	Huddersfield	1903
	V	30	by	Hampshire	Worcester	1903
Highest Innings	For	405*	G.A.Hick	v	Somerset	Taunton	1988
	V	331*	J.D.B.Robertson	for	Middlesex	1949

Highest Partnership for each Wicket

1st	309	F.L.Bowley/H.K.Foster	v	Derbyshire	Derby	1901
2nd	300	W.P.C.Weston/G.A.Hick	v	Indians	Worcester	1996
3rd	438*	G.A.Hick/T.M.Moody	v	Hampshire	Southampton	1997
4th	281	J.A.Ormrod/Younis Ahmed	v	Notts	Nottingham	1979
5th	393	E.G.Arnold/W.B.Burns	v	Warwicks	Birmingham	1909
6th	265	G.A.Hick/S.J.Rhodes	v	Somerset	Taunton	1988
7th	205	G.A.Hick/P.J.Newport	v	Yorkshire	Worcester	1988
8th	184	S.J.Rhodes/S.R.Lampitt	v	Derbyshire	Kidderminster	1991
9th	181	J.A.Cuffe/R.D.Burrows	v	Glos	Worcester	1907
10th	119	W.B.Burns/G.A.Wilson	v	Somerset	Worcester	1906

Best Bowling	For	9- 23	C.F.Root	v	Lancashire	Worcester	1931
(Innings)	V	10- 51	J.Mercer	for	Glamorgan	Worcester	1936
Best Bowling	For	15- 87	A.J.Conway	v	Glos	Moreton-in-M	1914
(Match)	V	17-212	J.C.Clay	for	Glamorgan	Swansea	1937

Most Runs – Season	2654	H.H.I.Gibbons	(av 52.03)		1934
Most Runs – Career	34490	D.Kenyon	(av 34.18)		1946-67
Most 100s – Season	10	G.M.Turner			1970
	10	G.A.Hick			1988
Most 100s – Career	81	G.A.Hick			1984-00
Most Wkts – Season	207	C.F.Root	(av 17.52)		1925
Most Wkts – Career	2143	R.T.D.Perks	(av 23.73)		1930-55

LIMITED-OVERS CRICKET

Highest Total	NWT	404-3		v	Devon	Worcester	1987
	BHC	314-5		v	Lancashire	Manchester	1980
	NL	307-4		v	Derbyshire	Worcester	1975
Lowest Total	NWT	98		v	Durham	Chester-le-St	1968
	BHC	81		v	Leics	Worcester	1983
	NL	86		v	Yorkshire	Leeds	1969
Highest Innings	NWT	180*	T.M.Moody	v	Surrey	The Oval	1994
	BHC	143*	G.M.Turner	v	Warwicks	Birmingham	1976
	NL	160	T.M.Moody	v	Kent	Worcester	1991
Best Bowling	NWT	7-19	N.V.Radford	v	Beds	Bedford	1991
	BHC	6- 8	N.Gifford	v	Minor C (S)	High Wycombe	1979
	NL	6-26	A.P.Pridgeon	v	Surrey	Worcester	1978

YORKSHIRE

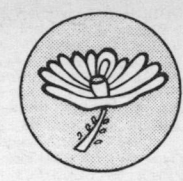

Formation of Present Club: 8 January 1863
Substantial Reorganisation: 10 December 1891
Colours: Dark Blue, Light Blue and Gold
Badge: White Rose
County Championships (since 1890): (29) 1893, 1896, 1898, 1900, 1901, 1902, 1905, 1908, 1912, 1919, 1922, 1923, 1924, 1925, 1931, 1932, 1933, 1935, 1937, 1938, 1939, 1946, 1959, 1960, 1962, 1963, 1966, 1967, 1968.
Joint Champions: (1) 1949
NatWest Trophy/Gillette Cup Winners: (2) 1965, 1969
Benson and Hedges Cup Winners: (1) 1987
National League (Div 1) Winners: (0); best – 2nd 2000
Sunday League Winners: (1) 1983
Match Awards: NWT 38; BHC 74

Chief Executive: C.D.Hassell, Headingley Cricket Ground, Leeds, LS6 3BU ▲ Tel: 0113 278 7394 ▲ Fax: 0113 278 4099 ▲ Email: cricket@yorkshire-ccc.org.uk ▲ Web: www.yorkshireccc.org.uk

Captain: D.Byas. **Vice-Captain/Overseas Player:** D.S.Lehmann.
2001 Beneficiary: D.Gough. **Scorer:** J.T.Potter. ‡ New registration

‡**BAKER, Thomas** Michael (Whitcliffe Mount S; Huddersfield TC), b Dewsbury 6 Jul 1981. RHB, RFM. Staff 2001 – awaiting f-c debut.

BLAKEY, Richard John (Rastrick GS), b Huddersfield 15 Jan 1967. 5'9". RHB, WK. Debut 1985; cap 1987; benefit 1998. YC 1987. **Tests:** 2 (1992-93); HS 6. **LOI:** 3 (1992 to 1992-93); HS 25 v P (Lord's) 1992 – on debut. Tours: SA 1991-92 (Y); WI 1986-87 (Y); I 1992-93; P 1990-91 (Eng A); SL 1990-91 (Eng A); Z 1989-90 (Eng A), 1995-96 (Y). 1000 runs (5); most – 1361 (1987). HS 221 Eng A v Z (Bulawayo) 1989-90. Y HS 204* v Glos (Leeds) 1987. BB 1-68. Awards: BHC 2. LO HS 130* v Kent (Scarborough) 1991 (SL).

BYAS, David (Scarborough C), b Kilham 26 Aug 1963. 6'4". LHB, RM. Debut 1986; cap 1991; captain 1996 to date. Tours (Y): SA 1991-92, 1992-93; Z 1995-96. 1000 runs (5); most – 1913 (1995). HS 213 v Worcs (Scarborough) 1995. BB 3-55 v Derbys (Chesterfield) 1990. Awards: BHC 3. LO HS 116* v Surrey (Oval) 1996 (BIIC). LO BB 3-19 v Notts (Leeds) 1989 (SL).

CRAVEN, Victor John (Harrogate GS), b Harrogate 31 Jul 1980. 6'0". LHB, RM. Debut 2000. HS 58 v Derbys (Derby) 2000. LO HS 28 v Worcs (Leeds) 2000 (NL).

DAWSON, Richard Kevin James (Batley GS; Exeter U), b Doncaster 4 Aug 1980. 6'3". RHB, OB. British U 2000. Yorkshire contract 1999 to date – awaiting county debut, Devon 1999-2000. HS 1 and BB 1-115 Brit U v Z (Cambridge) 2000 – on debut. LO HS 7 and LO BB 2-32 Devon v Worcs (Exmouth) 1999 (NWT).

ELSTUB, Christopher John (Whitcliffe Mount S and SFC; Leeds Metropolitan U), b Dewsbury 3 Feb 1981. 5'11". RHB, RMF. Debut 2000. HS 4* and CC BD 2-40 v Lancs (Leeds) 2000. BB 3-37 v WI (Leeds) 2000. LO HS – (NL).

FELLOWS, Gary Matthew (N Halifax GS), b Halifax 30 Jul 1978. 5'9". RHB, RM. Matabeleland 1996-97. Yorkshire debut 1998. HS 50 Matabeleland v Mashonaland (Bulawayo) 1996-97. Y HS 46 v Lancs (Leeds) 2000. BB 2-27 v Surrey (Scarborough) 2000. LO HS 65 v Leics (Leeds) 2000 (NL). LO BB 1-16 (NL).

FISHER, Ian Douglas (Beckfoot GS, Bingley; Thomas Danby C, Leeds), b Bradford 31 Mar 1976. 5'10½". LHB, SLA. Debut 1995-96 (Y tour). UK debut 1996. Tour: Z 1995-96 (Y). HS 68* v Somerset (Taunton) 2000. BB 5-35 v Mashonaland Inv XI (Harare) 1995-96 – on debut. CC BB 5-73 v Essex (Chelmsford) 1999. LO HS 20 and LO BB 3-20 v Somerset (Scarborough) 2000 (NL).

103

GOUGH, Darren (Priory CS, Lundwood), b Barnsley 18 Sep 1970. 5'11". RHB, RF. Debut 1989; cap 1993; benefit 2001. *Wisden* 1998. **ECB contract 2000. Tests:** 49 (1994 to 2000-01); HS 65 v NZ (Manchester) 1994 – on debut; BB 6-42 v SA (Leeds) 1998; hat-trick v A (Sydney) 1998-99 – first for E v A since 1899. **LOI:** 86 (1994 to 2000-01); HS 45 v A (Melbourne) 1998-99; BB 5-44 v Z (Sydney) 1994-95 and 5-44 v A (Lord's) 1997. Took wickets with his sixth balls in both Tests and LOIs. Tours: A 1994-95, 1998-99; SA 1991-92 (Y), 1992-93 (Y), 1993-94 (Eng A), 1995-96, 1999-00; NZ 1996-97; P 2000-01; SL 2000-01; Z 1996-97. HS 121 v Warwks (Leeds) 1996. 50 wkts (5); most – 67 (1996). BB 7-28 (10-80 match) v Lancs (Leeds) 1995 (not CC). CC BB 7-42 (10-96 match) v Somerset (Taunton) 1993. 2 hat-tricks (1995, 1998-99); took 4 wkts in 5 balls v Kent (Leeds) 1995. Awards: NWT 2; BHC 1. LO HS 72* v Leics (Leicester) 1991 (SL). LO BB 7-27 v Ire (Leeds) 1997 (NWT).

GUY, Simon Mark (Wickersley CS), b Rotherham 17 Nov 1978. 5'7". RHB, WK. Debut 2000. HS 42 v Somerset (Taunton) 2000.

HAMILTON, Gavin Mark (Hurstmere SS, Kent), b Broxburn, Scotland 16 Sep 1974. 6'1". LHB, RFM. Scotland 1993-94. Yorkshire debut 1994; cap 1998. **Tests:** 1 (1999-00); HS 0 v SA (Jo'burg) 1999-00. **LOI** (Scot): 5 (1999); HS 76 and BB 2-36 v P (Chester-le-St) 1999. Tours: SA 1999-00; Z 1995-96 (Y). HS 125 v Hants (Leeds) 1998. 50 wkts (1): 59 (1998). BB 7-50 (11-72 match) v Surrey (Leeds) 1998. Match double (79, 70; 5-69, 5-43) v Glam (Cardiff) 1998 – first instance for Yorks since 1964 (R.Illingworth). Award: BHC 1. LO HS 76 (*see LOI*). LO BB 5-16 v Hants (Leeds) 1998 (SL).

HOGGARD, Matthew James (Grangefield S, Pudsey), b Leeds 31 Dec 1976. 6'2". RHB, RFM. Debut 1996; cap 2000. Free State 1998-99 to 1999-00. **Tests:** 1 (2000); HS 12* v WI (Lord's) 2000. Tours: P 2000-01; SL 2000-01. HS 21* FS v Gauteng (Jo'burg) 1999-00. Y HS 21 v Somerset (Taunton) 1999. 50 wkts (1): 50 (2000). BB 5-47 v Derbys (Derby) 1999. LO HS 2* (thrice). LO BB 5-28 v Leics (Leicester) 2000 (NL).

HUTCHISON, Paul Michael (Crawshaw HS, Pudsey), b Leeds 9 Jun 1977. 6'3". LHB, LFM. Debut 1995-96 (Y tour); cap 1998. The Rest 1996. Tours (Eng A): SI 1997-98; Z 1995-96 (Y); K 1997-98. HS 30 v Essex (Scarborough) 1998. 50 wkts (1): 59 (1998). BB 7-31 v Sussex (Hove) 1998. Award: NWT 1. LO HS 4* (NWT/BHC). LO BB 4-34 v Glos (Gloucester) 1998 (SL).

LAMBERT, Greg Andrew (Tadcaster GS), b Stoke-on-Trent, Staffs 4 Jan 1980. 6'8". RHB, RMF. Debut 2000. HS 3* and BB 2-62 v Kent (Canterbury) 2000. LO HS 0 and LO BB 2-22 Yorks CB v Bucks (Sheffield) 1999 (NWT).

LEHMANN, Darren Scott (Gawler HS), b Gawler, South Australia 5 Feb 1970. 5'10. LHB, SLA. South Australia 1987-88 to 1989-90, 1993-94 to date; captain 1998-99. Victoria 1990-91 to 1992-93. Yorkshire 1997-98, 2000; cap 1997. *Wisden* 2000. **Tests** (A): 5 (1997-98 to 1998-99); HS 98 v P (Rawalpindi) 1998-99; BB 1-6. **LOI** (A): 66 (1996-97 to 2000-01); HS 110* v WI (St George's, Grenada) 1998-99; BB 2-4 v I (Colombo) 1999-00. Tours (A): E 1991 (Vic); I 1997-98; P 1998-99. 1000 runs (2+5); most – 1575 (1997). HS 255 S Aus v Queensland (Adelaide) 1996-97. Y HS 200 v Worcs (Worcester) 1998. BB 4-22 v Kent (Maidstone) 1998. Awards: BHC 2. LO HS 142* S Aus v Tas (Adelaide) 1994-95 (MM). LO BB 3-14 A v SA (Kuala Lumpur) 1998.

LUMB, Michael John (St Stithians C, Jo'burg), b Johannesburg, SA 12 Feb 1980. Son of R.G. (Yorkshire 1970-84); nephew of A.J.S.Smith (SAU and Natal 1971-72 to 1983-84). 6'0". LHB, RM. Debut 2000 – no CC appearances (ECB qualified 2001). HS 66* v Z (Leeds) 2000 – on debut.

McGRATH, Anthony (Yorkshire Martyrs Collegiate S), b Bradford 6 Oct 1975. 6'2". RHB, OB. Debut 1995; cap 1999. Tours (Eng A): A 1996-97; P 1995-96; Z 1995-96 (Y). HS 142* v Middx (Leeds) 1999. BB 3-18 v Surrey (Oval) 1999. Awards: NWT 1; BHC 1. LO HS 109* v Minor C (Leeds) 1997 (BHC). LO BB 2-10 v Scot (Leeds) 1996 (BHC).

MIDDLEBROOK, James Daniel (Pudsey Crawshaw S), b Leeds 13 May 1977. 6'1". RHB, OB. Debut 1998. HS 45 v Derbys (Derby) 2000. BB 6-82 (10-170 match) v Hants (Southampton) 2000 – including 4 wkts in 5 balls. LO HS 15* v Sussex (Scarborough) 2000 (NL). LO BB 3-16 v Glos (Leeds) 2000 (NL).

RAMSDEN, Gary (Castle Hall S; New C, Huddersfield), b Dewsbury 2 Mar 1983. 5'11". RHB, RMF. Debut 2000. HS 0* and BB 1-32 v Derbys (Derby) 2000 – on debut. LO HS – and LO BB 2-26 v Glos (Leeds) 2000 (NL).

RICHARDSON, Scott Andrew (Manchester GS), b Oldham, Lancs 5 Sep 1977. RHB. Debut 2000 – awaiting f-c debut. HS 11 v WI (Leeds) 2000 – on debut.

SIDEBOTTOM, Ryan Jay (King James's GS, Almondbury), b Huddersfield 15 Jan 1978. Son of A. (Yorks, OFS and England 1973-91). 6'3". LHB, LFM. Debut 1997; cap 2000. Tour (Eng A): WI 2000-01. HS 54 v Glam (Cardiff) 1998. BB 6-16 (11-43 match) v Kent (Leeds) 2000. LO HS 24* v Hants (Basingstoke) 1999 (NL). LO BB 6-40 v Glam (Cardiff) 1998 (SL).

SILVERWOOD, Christopher Eric Wilfred (Garforth CS), b Pontefract 5 Mar 1975. 6'1". RHB, RFM. Debut 1993; cap 1996. YC 1996. **Tests:** 5 (1996-97 to 1999-00); HS 7*; BB 5-91 v SA (Cape Town) 1999. **LOI:** 6 (1996-97 to 1997); HS 12 v NZ (Auckland) 1996-97; BB 2-27 v Z (Bulawayo) 1996-97 – on debut. Tours: SA 1999-00 (part); WI 1997-98, 2000-01 (Eng A); NZ 1996-97; Z 1995-96 (Y), 1996-97. HS 58 v Lancs (Manchester) 1997. 50 wkts (2); most – 59 (1999). BB 7-93 (12-148 match) v Kent (Leeds) 1997. Awards: BHC 2. LO HS 38* Eng A v NZ Academy (Lincoln) 1999-00. LO BB 5-28 v Scot (Leeds) 1996 (BHC).

STEAD, Roger Alexander (Hipperholme & Lightcliffe HS; Durham U), b Dewsbury 18 Apr 1980. RHB. Staff 2000 – awaiting f-c debut.

‡**TAYLOR, Christopher** Robert (Benton Park HS), b Leeds 21 Feb 1981. RHB. Staff 2001 – awaiting f-c debut.

VAUGHAN, Michael Paul (Silverdale CS, Sheffield), b Manchester, Lancs 29 Oct 1974. 6'2". RHB, OB. Debut 1993; cap 1995. **ECB contract 2000. Tests:** 9 (1999-00 to 2000-01); HS 76 v WI (Leeds) 2000. Tours (C=captain): A 1996-97 (Eng A); SA 1998-99C (Eng A), 1999-00; I 1994-95 (Eng A); P 2000-01; SL 2000-01; Z 1995-96 (Y), 1998-99C (Eng A). 1000 runs (4); most – 1244 (1995). HS 183 v Glam (Cardiff) 1996. BB 4-39 v OU (Oxford) 1994. CC BB 4-62 v Surrey (Middlesbrough) 1996. Awards: NWT 2; BHC 1. LO HS 88 v Warwks (Birmingham) 1997 (BHC). LO BB 4-27 v Glos (Bristol) 2000 (NL).

WHITE, Craig (Flora Hill HS, Bendigo, Australia; Bendigo HS), b Morley 16 Dec 1969. 6'0". RHB, RFM. Debut 1990; cap 1993. Victoria 1990-91 (2 matches). **ECB contract 2000. Tests:** 18 (1994 to 2000-01); HS 93 v P (Lahore) 2000-01; BB 5-32 v WI (Oval) 2000. **LOI:** 34 (1994-95 to 2000-01); HS 38 v NZ (Napier) 1996-97; BB 5-21 v Z (Bulawayo) 1999-00. Tours: A 1994-95, 1996-97 (Eng A); SA 1991-92 (Y), 1992-93 (Y); NZ 1996-97; P 1995-96 (Eng A), 2000-01; SL 2000-01; Z 1996-97 (part). HS 181 v Lancs (Leeds) 1996. BB 8-55 v Glos (Gloucester) 1998 – inc hat-trick. Hat-trick 1998. Awards: NWT 2; BHC 3. LO HS 148 v Leics (Leicester) 1997 (SL). LO BB 5-21 (see LOI).

WIDDUP, Simon (Ridgewood CS; Danum SFC), b Doncaster 10 Nov 1977. 6'0". RHB, OB. Debut 2000. HS 44 and BB 1-22 v Somerset (Scarborough) 2000. LO HS 38 v Somerset (Taunton) 2000 (NL).

WOOD, Matthew James (Shelley HS & SFC), b Huddersfield 6 Apr 1977. 5'9". RHB, OB. Debut 1997. 1000 runs (1): 1080 (1998). HS 200* v Warwks (Leeds) 1998. LO HS 65* v Essex (Scarborough) 1998 (SL).

RELEASED/RETIRED
(Having made a first-class County appearance in 2000)

HARDEN, Richard John (King's C, Taunton), b Bridgwater, Somerset 16 Aug 1965. 5'11". RHB, SLA. Somerset 1985-98; cap 1989; benefit 1996. Yorkshire 1999-2000. C Districts 1987-88. 1000 runs (7); most – 1460 (1990). HS 187 Sm v Notts (Taunton) 1992. Y HS 69 v Leics (Leicester) 1999. BB 2-7 CD v Canterbury (Blenheim) 1987-88. CC BB 2-24 Sm v Hants (Taunton) 1986. Award: NWT 1. LO HS 108* Sm v Scot (Taunton) 1992 (NWT).

INGLIS, John William (Ripon GS; St Aiden's S, Harrogate), b Ripon 19 Oct 1979. 6'1". RHB, RM. Yorkshire 2000 (no CC appearances). HS 2 (twice).

WEEKES, L.C. – see NORTHAMPTONSHIRE.

YORKSHIRE 2000

RESULTS SUMMARY

	Place	Won	Lost	Tied	Drew	No Result
County Championship (1st Division)	3rd	7	2		7	
All First-Class Matches		7	4		7	
NatWest Trophy	4th Round					
Benson & Hedges Cup	Quarter-Finalist					
National League (1st Division)	2nd	9	7			

COUNTY CHAMPIONSHIP AVERAGES

BATTING AND FIELDING

Cap		M	I	NO	HS	Runs	Avge	100	50	Ct/St
1997	D.S.Lehmann	16	23	1	136	1477	67.13	4	9	8
1995	M.P.Vaughan	9	15	1	155*	697	49.78	2	3	2
1998	G.M.Hamilton	12	14	2	125	375	31.25	1	2	6
1999	A.McGrath	10	14	1	133	375	28.84	1	1	8
–	I.D.Fisher	5	8	2	68*	167	27.83	–	1	1
–	V.J.Craven	6	7	1	58	164	27.33	–	1	6
1991	D.Byas	15	22	1	84	523	24.90	–	2	22
–	G.M.Fellows	13	18	4	46	305	21.78	–	–	7
–	M.J.Wood	10	15	3	100*	224	18.66	1	–	5
–	S.Widdup	8	12	1	44	195	17.72	–	–	6
1987	R.J.Blakey	11	16	1	56	262	17.46	–	1	38/2
1996	C.E.W.Silverwood	9	11	1	48	173	17.30	–	–	1
–	J.D.Middlebrook	9	11	–	45	184	16.72	–	–	3
–	S.M.Guy	5	7	1	42	97	16.16	–	–	17/2
2000	M.J.Hoggard	14	15	3	20*	80	6.66	–	–	2
2000	R.J.Sidebottom	6	7	2	6*	15	3.00	–	–	2
1998	P.M.Hutchison	5	5	2	3*	3	1.00	–	–	2

Also batted: C.J.Elstub (3 matches) 4*, 2* (1 ct); D.Gough (3 – cap 1993) 23, 5 (1 ct); R.J.Harden (1 – cap 1999) 0; G.A.Lambert (2) 1, 3*, 2* (1 ct); G.Ramsden (1) 0*; C.White (3 – cap 1993) 17, 11, 10.

BOWLING

	O	M	R	W	Avge	Best	5wI	10wM
R.J.Sidebottom	134.2	46	300	24	12.50	6-16	4	1
D.Gough	100.5	22	245	16	15.31	6-63	1	–
C.White	76	18	194	12	16.16	3-12	–	–
J.D.Middlebrook	237.5	58	650	27	24.07	6-82	1	1
G.M.Hamilton	286	68	820	33	24.84	4-34	–	–
P.M.Hutchison	100.4	22	350	14	25.00	3-62	–	–
M.J.Hoggard	456.4	121	1216	46	26.43	5-50	2	–
C.E.W.Silverwood	292.3	80	762	26	29.30	4-60	–	–
I.D.Fisher	187.1	43	541	15	36.06	3-40	–	–

Also bowled: D.Byas 0.1-0-0-0; V.J.Craven 8-1-15-0; C.J.Elstub 50-10-138-5; G.M.Fellows 121-28-361-7; S.M.Guy 4-1-8-0; G.A.Lambert 46-7-133-4; D.S.Lehmann 112-18-310-8; G.Ramsden 12-1-68-1; M.P.Vaughan 51.5-12-127-6; S.Widdup 2.3-0-22-1.

The First-Class Averages (pp 118-132) give the records of Yorkshire players in all first-class county matches (Yorkshire's other opponents being the Zimbabweans and the West Indians), with the exception of D.Gough, M.P.Vaughan and C.White, whose full county figures are as above, R.K.J.Dawson, whose only first-class appearance was for British Universities, and: M.J.Hoggard 15-17-3-20*-91-6.50-0-0-2ct. 488.4-131-1274-50-25.48-5/50-2-0.

YORKSHIRE RECORDS

FIRST-CLASS CRICKET

Highest Total	For 887		v	Warwicks	Birmingham	1896
	V 681-7d		by	Leics	Bradford	1996
Lowest Total	For 23		v	Hampshire	Middlesbrough	1965
	V 13		by	Notts	Nottingham	1901
Highest Innings	For 341	G.H.Hirst	v	Leics	Leicester	1905
	V 318*	W.G.Grace	for	Glos	Cheltenham	1876

Highest Partnership for each Wicket

1st	555	P.Holmes/H.Sutcliffe	v	Essex	Leyton	1932
2nd	346	W.Barber/M.Leyland	v	Middlesex	Sheffield	1932
3rd	323*	H.Sutcliffe/M.Leyland	v	Glamorgan	Huddersfield	1928
4th	312	D.Denton/G.H.Hirst	v	Hampshire	Southampton	1914
5th	340	E.Wainwright/G.H.Hirst	v	Surrey	The Oval	1899
6th	276	M.Leyland/E.Robinson	v	Glamorgan	Swansea	1926
7th	254	W.Rhodes/D.C.F.Burton	v	Hampshire	Dewsbury	1919
8th	292	R.Peel/Lord Hawke	v	Warwicks	Birmingham	1896
9th	192	G.H.Hirst/S.Haigh	v	Surrey	Bradford	1898
10th	149	G.Boycott/G.B.Stevenson	v	Warwicks	Birmingham	1982

Best Bowling	For	10-10	H.Verity	v	Notts	Leeds	1932
(Innings)	V	10-37	C.V.Grimmett	for	Australians	Sheffield	1930
Best Bowling	For	17-91	H.Verity	v	Essex	Leyton	1933
(Match)	V	17-91	H.Dean	for	Lancashire	Liverpool	1913

Most Runs – Season	2883	H.Sutcliffe	(av 80.08)		1932
Most Runs – Career	38561	H.Sutcliffe	(av 50.20)		1919-45
Most 100s – Season	12	H.Sutcliffe			1932
Most 100s – Career	112	H.Sutcliffe			1919-45
Most Wkts – Season	240	W.Rhodes	(av 12.72)		1900
Most Wkts – Career	3608	W.Rhodes	(av 16.00)		1898-1930

LIMITED-OVERS CRICKET

Highest Total	NWT	345-5		v	Notts	Leeds	1996
	BHC	317-5		v	Scotland	Leeds	1986
	NL	318-7		v	Leics	Leicester	1993
Lowest Total	NWT	76		v	Surrey	Harrogate	1970
	BHC	88		v	Worcs	Leeds	1995
	NL	56		v	Warwicks	Birmingham	1995
Highest Innings	NWT	146	G.Boycott	v	Surrey	Lord's	1965
	BHC	142	G.Boycott	v	Worcs	Worcester	1980
	NL	148	C.White	v	Leics	Leicester	1997
Best Bowling	NWT	7-27	D.Gough	v	Ireland	Leeds	1997
	BHC	6-27	A.G.Nicholson	v	Minor C (N)	Middlesbrough	1972
	NL	7-15	R.A.Hutton	v	Worcs	Leeds	1969

FIRST-CLASS UMPIRES 2001

† New Appointment

BENSON, Mark Richard (Sutton Valence S), b Shoreham, Sussex 6 Jul 1958. LHB, OB. Kent 1980-95; cap 1981; captain 1991-96 (did not play in 1996); benefit 1991. **Tests:** 1 (1986); HS 30 v I (Birmingham) 1986. **LOI:** 1 (1986; HS 24). 1000 runs (11); most – 1725 (1987). HS 257 v Hants (Southampton) 1991. BB 2-55 v Surrey (Dartford) 1986. F-c career: 292 matches; 18387 runs @ 40.23, 48 hundreds; 5 wickets @ 98.60; 140 ct. Appointed 2000.

BURGESS, Graham Iefvion (Millfield S), b Glastonbury, Somerset 5 May 1943. RHB, RM. Somerset 1966-79; cap 1968; testimonial 1977. HS 129 v Glos (Taunton) 1973. BB 7-43 (13-75 match) v OU (Oxford) 1975. F-c career: 252 matches; 7129 runs @ 18.90, 2 hundreds; 474 wickets @ 28.57. Appointed 1991.

CLARKSON, Anthony (Harrogate GS), b Killinghall, Harrogate, Yorks 5 Sep 1939. RHB, OB. Yorkshire 1963. Somerset 1966-71; cap 1968. Devon. 1000 runs (2); most – 1246 (1970). HS 131 Sm v Northants (Northampton) 1969. BB 3-51 Sm v Essex (Yeovil) 1967. F-c career: 110 matches; 4458 runs @ 25.18, 2 hundreds; 13 wickets @ 28.23. Appointed 1996.

CONSTANT, David John, b Bradford-on-Avon, Wilts 9 Nov 1941. LHB, SLA. Kent 1961-63. Leicestershire 1965-68. HS 80 Le v Glos (Bristol) 1966. F-c career: 61 matches; 1517 runs @ 19.20; 1 wicket @ 36.00. Appointed 1969. Umpired 36 Tests (1971 to 1988) and 32 LOI (1972 to 2000). Represented Gloucestershire at bowls 1984-86.

COWLEY, Nigel Geoffrey (Dutchy Manor SS, Mere), b Shaftesbury, Dorset 1 Mar 1953. RHB, OB. Dorset 1972. Hampshire 1974-89; cap 1978; benefit 1988. Glamorgan 1990. 1000 runs (1): 1042 (1984). HS 109* H v Somerset (Taunton) 1977. BB 6-48 H v Leics (Southampton) 1982. F-c career: 271 matches; 7309 runs @ 23.35, 2 hundreds; 437 wickets @ 34.04. Appointed 2000.

DUDLESTON, Barry (Stockport S), b Bebington, Cheshire 16 Jul 1945. RHB, SLA. Leicestershire 1966-80; cap 1969; benefit 1980. Gloucestershire 1981-83. Rhodesia 1976-77 to 1979-80. 1000 runs (8); most – 1374 (1970). HS 202 Le v Derbys (Leicester) 1979. BB 4-6 Le v Surrey (Leicester) 1972. F-c career: 295 matches; 14747 runs @ 32.48, 32 hundreds; 47 wickets @ 29.04. Appointed 1984. Umpired 2 Tests (1991 to 1992) and 3 LOI (1992 to 2000).

†**EVANS, Jeffery** Howard, b Llanelli, Carms 7 Aug 1954. Appointed 2001.

HAMPSHIRE, John Harry (Oakwood THS, Rotherham), b Thurnscoe, Yorks 10 Feb 1941. RHB, LB. Son of J. (Yorks 1937); brother of A.W. (Yorks 1975). Yorkshire 1961-81; cap 1963; benefit 1976; captain 1979-80. Leicestershire 1980-81 (tour). Derbyshire 1982-84; cap 1982. Tasmania 1967-68 to 1978-79. **Tests:** 8 (1969 to 1975); 403 runs @ 26.86, HS 107 v WI (Lord's) 1969 on debut (only England player to score hundred at Lord's on Test debut). Tours: A 1970-71; SA 1972-73 (DHR), 1974-75 (DHR); WI 1964-65 (Cav); NZ 1970-71; P 1967-68 (Cwlth XI); SL 1969-70; Z 1980-81 (Le XI). 1000 runs (15); most – 1596 (1978). HS 183* Y v Sussex (Hove) 1971. BB 7-52 Y v Glam (Cardiff) 1963. F-c career: 577 matches; 28059 runs @ 34.55, 43 hundreds; 30 wickets @ 54.56; 445 ct. Appointed 1985. Umpired 16 Tests (1989 to 2000-01) and 14 LOI (1989 to 2000), including one Sharjah tournament. **Appointed to International Panel 1999.**

HARRIS, Michael John ('*Pasty*') (Gerrans S, nr Truro), b St Just-in-Roseland, Cornwall 25 May 1944. RHB, LB, WK. Middlesex 1964-68; cap 1967. Nottinghamshire 1969-82; cap 1970; benefit 1977. Eastern Province 1971-72. Wellington 1975-76. 1000 runs (11); most – 2238 (1971). Scored 9 hundreds in 1971 to equal Notts record. HS 201* Nt v Glam (Nottingham) 1973. BB 4-16 Nt v Warwks (Nottingham) 1969. F-c career: 344 matches; 19,196 runs @ 36.70, 41 hundreds; 79 wickets @ 43.78; 302 dismissals (288 ct, 14 st). Appointed 1998.

HOLDER, John Wakefield (Combermere S), b St George, Barbados 19 Mar 1945. RHB, RFM. Hampshire 1968-72. Hat-trick 1972. HS 33 v Sussex (Hove) 1971. BB 7-79 v Glos (Gloucester) 1972. F-c career: 47 matches; 374 runs @ 10.68; 139 wickets @ 24.56. Appointed 1983. Umpired 10 Tests (1988 to 1991) and 17 LOI (1988 to 2000) including 1989-90 Nehru Cup and one Sharjah tournament.

HOLDER, Vanburn Alonza (Richmond SM), b Deans Village, St Michael, Barbados 8 Oct 1945. RHB, RFM. Barbados 1966-67 to 1977-78. Worcestershire 1968-80; cap 1970; benefit 1979. Shropshire 1981. **Tests** (WI): 40 (1969 to 1978-79); 682 runs @ 14.20, HS 42 v NZ (P-o-S) 1971-72; 109 wkts @ 33.27, BB 6-28 v A (P-o-S) 1977-78. **LOI** (WI): 12. Tours (WI): E 1969, 1973, 1976; A 1975-76; I 1974-75, 1978-79; P 1973-74 (RW), 1974-75; SL 1974-75, 1978-79. HS 122 Barbados v Trinidad (Bridgetown) 1973-74. BB 7-40 Wo v Glam (Cardiff) 1974. F-c career: 311 matches; 3559 runs @ 13.03, 1 hundred; 947 wickets @ 24.48. Appointed 1992.

JESTY, Trevor Edward (Privet County SS, Gosport), b Gosport, Hants 2 Jun 1948. RHB, RM. Hampshire 1966-84; cap 1971; benefit 1982. Surrey 1985-87; cap 1985; captain 1985. Lancashire 1987-88 to 1991; cap 1989. Border 1973-74. GW 1974-75 to 1980-81. Canterbury 1979-80. *Wisden* 1982. **LOI**: 10. Tours: WI 1987-88 (La), 1982-83 (Int); Z 1988-89 (La). 1000 runs (10); most – 1645 (1982). HS 248 H v CU (Cambridge) 1984. Scored 122* La v OU (Oxford) 1991 in his final f-c innings. 50 wkts (2); most – 52 (1981). BB 7-75 H v Worcs (Southampton) 1976. F-c career: 490 matches; 21916 runs @ 32.71, 35 hundreds; 585 wickets @ 27.47. Appointed 1994.

JONES, Allan Arthur (St John's C, Horsham), b Horley, Surrey 9 Dec 1947. RHB, RFM. Sussex 1966-69. Somerset 1970-75; cap 1972. Middlesex 1976-79; cap 1976. Glamorgan 1980-81. Northern Transvaal 1972-73. Orange Free State 1976-77. HS 33 M v Kent (Canterbury) 1978. BB 9-51 Sm v Sussex (Hove) 1972. F-c career: 214 matches; 799 runs @ 5.39; 549 wickets @ 28.07. Appointed 1985. Umpired 1 LOI (1996).

JULIAN, Raymond (Wigston SM), b Cosby, Leics 23 Aug 1936. RHB, WK. Leicestershire 1953-71; cap 1961. HS 51 v Worcs (Worcester) 1962. F-c career: 192 matches; 2581 runs @ 9.73; 421 dismissals (382 ct, 39 st). Appointed 1972. Umpired 5 LOI (1996 to 2000).

KITCHEN, Mervyn John (Backwell SM, Nailsea), b Nailsea, Somerset 1 Aug 1940. LHB, RM. Somerset 1960-79; cap 1966, testimonial 1973. Tour: Rhodesia 1972-73 (Int W). 1000 runs (7); most – 1730 (1968). HS 189 v Pakistanis (Taunton) 1967. BB 1-4. F-c career: 354 matches; 15230 runs @ 26.25, 17 hundreds; 2 wickets @ 54.50. Appointed 1982. Umpired 20 Tests (1990 to 2000) and 27 LOI (1983 to 2000), including tournaments in Sharjah (1) and Nairobi (1). International Panel 1995-99.

LEADBEATER, Barrie (Harehills SS), b Harehills, Leeds, Yorks 14 Aug 1943. RHB, RM. Yorkshire 1966-79; cap 1969; joint benefit with G.A.Cope 1980. Tour: WI 1969-70 (DN). HS 140* v Hants (Portsmouth) 1976. F-c career: 147 matches; 5373 runs @ 25.34, 1 hundred; 1 wicket @ 5.00. Appointed 1981. Umpired 5 LOI (1983 to 2000).

LLOYDS, Jeremy William (Blundells S), b Penang, Malaya 17 Nov 1954. LHB, OB. Somerset 1979-84; cap 1982. Gloucestershire 1985-91; cap 1985. Orange Free State 1983-84 to 1987-88. Tour (Glos): SL 1986-87. 1000 runs (3); most – 1295 (1986). HS 132* Sm v Northants (Northampton) 1982. BB 7-88 Sm v Essex (Chelmsford) 1982. F-c career: 267 matches; 10,679 runs @ 31.04, 10 hundreds; 333 wickets @ 38.86; 229 ct. Appointed 1998. Umpired 1 LOI (2000).

MALLENDER, Neil Alan (Beverley GS), b Kirk Sandall, Yorks 13 Aug 1961. RHB, RFM. Northamptonshire 1980-86 and 1995-96; cap 1984. Somerset 1987-94; cap 1987; benefit 1994. Otago 1983-84 to 1992-93; captain 1990-91 to 1992-93. **Tests**: 2 (1992); 8 runs @ 2.66, HS 4; 10 wkts @ 21.50, BB 5-50 v P (Leeds) 1992 – on debut. Tour: Z 1994-95 (Nh). HS 100* Otago v CD (Palmerston N) 1991-92. UK HS 87* Sm v Sussex (Hove) 1990. 50 wkts (6); most – 56 (1983). BB 7-27 Otago v Auckland (Auckland) 1984-85. UK BB 7-41 Nh v Derbys (Northampton) 1987. F-c career: 345 matches; 4,709 runs @ 17.18, 1 hundred; 937 wickets @ 26.31; 111 ct. Appointed 1999.

PALMER, Kenneth Ernest (Southbroom SM, Devizes), b Winchester, Hants 22 Apr 1937. RHB, RFM. Brother of R. (*below*) and father of G.V. (Somerset 1982-88). Somerset 1955-69; cap 1958; testimonial 1968. Tours: WI 1963-64 (Cav); P 1963-64 (Cwlth XI). **Tests**: 1 (1964-65; while coaching in South Africa); 10 runs @ 10.00, HS 10 (1961). 100 wickets (4); most – 139 (1963). HS 125* v Northants (Northampton) 1961. BB 9-57 v Notts (Nottingham) 1963. F-c career: 314 matches; 7761 runs @ 20.64, 2 hundreds; 866 wickets @ 21.34. Appointed 1972. Umpired 22 Tests (1978 to 1994) and 22 LOI (1977 to 2000). International Panel 1994.

PALMER, Roy (Southbroom SM, Devizes), b Devizes, Wilts 12 Jul 1942. RHB, RFM. Brother of K.E. (*see above*). Somerset 1965-70. HS 84 v Leics (Taunton) 1967. BB 6-45 v Middx (Lord's) 1967. F-c career: 74 matches; 1037 runs @ 13.29; 172 wickets @ 31.62. Appointed 1980. Umpired 2 Tests (1992 to 1993) and 8 LOI (1983 to 1995).

SHARP, George (Elwick Road SS, Hartlepool), b West Hartlepool, Co Durham 12 Mar 1950. RHB, WK, occ LM. Northamptonshire 1968-85; cap 1973; benefit 1982. HS 98 v Yorks (Northampton) 1983. BB 1-47. F-c career: 306 matches; 6254 runs @ 19.85; 1 wicket @ 70.00; 655 dismissals (565 ct, 90 st). Appointed 1992. Umpired 13 Tests (1996 to 2000-01) and 24 LOI (1995-96 to 2000-01), including tournaments in Nairobi (1), Sharjah (2) and Singapore (1). **Appointed to International Panel 1996.**

SHEPHERD, David Robert (Barnstaple GS; St Luke's C, Exeter), b Bideford, Devon 27 Dec 1940. RHB, RM. Gloucestershire 1965-79; cap 1969; joint benefit with J.Davey 1978. Scored 108 on debut (v OU). Devon 1959-64. 1000 runs (2); most – 1079 (1970). HS 153 v Middx (Bristol) 1968. F-c career: 282 matches; 10672 runs @ 24.47, 12 hundreds; 2 wickets @ 53.00. Appointed 1981. Umpired 55 Tests (1985 to 2000-01) and 96 LOI (1983 to 2000-01), including 1987-88, 1991-92, 1995-96 and 1999 World Cups (2 finals), and tournaments in Sri Lanka (1), Dhaka (2), Sharjah (6), Toronto (1) and Nairobi (1). **Appointed to International Panel 1994.**

STEELE, John Frederick (Endon SS), b Brown Edge, Staffs 23 Jul 1946. RHB, SLA. Brother of D.S. (Northants, Derbys and England 1963-84). Leicestershire 1970-83; cap 1971; benefit 1983. Glamorgan 1984-86; cap 1984. Natal 1973-74 to 1977-78. Staffordshire 1965-69. Tour: SA 1974-75 (DHR). 1000 runs (6); most – 1347 (1972). HS 195 Le v Derbys (Leicester) 1971. BB 7-29 Natal B v GW (Umzinto) 1973-74, and Le v Glos (Leicester) 1980. F-c career: 379 matches; 15054 runs @ 28.95, 21 hundreds; 584 wickets @ 27.04; 413 ct. Appointed 1997.

WHITE, Robert Arthur (Chiswick GS), b Fulham, London 6 Oct 1936. LHB, OB. Middlesex 1958-65 (cap 1963). Nottinghamshire 1966-80; cap 1966; benefit 1974. 1000 runs (1): 1355 (1963). HS 116* Nt v Surrey (Oval) 1967. BB 7-41 Nt v Derbys (Ilkeston) 1971. F-c career: 413 matches; 12452 runs @ 23.18, 5 hundreds; 693 wickets @ 30.50. Appointed 1983.

WHITEHEAD, Alan Geoffrey Thomas, b Butleigh, Somerset 28 Oct 1940. LHB, SLA. Somerset 1957-61. HS 15 v Hants (Southampton) 1959 and v Leics (Leicester) 1960. BB 6-74 v Sussex (Eastbourne) 1959. F-c career: 38 matches; 137 runs @ 5.70; 67 wickets @ 34.41. Appointed 1970. Umpired 5 Tests (1982 to 1987) and 13 LOI (1979 to 1996).

WILLEY, Peter (Seaham SS), b Sedgefield, Co Durham 6 Dec 1949. RHB, OB. Northamptonshire 1966-83; cap 1971; benefit 1981. Leicestershire 1984-91; cap 1984; captain 1987. E Province 1982-83 to 1984-85. Northumberland 1992. **Tests:** 26 (1976 to 1986); 1184 runs @ 26.90, HS 102* v WI (St John's) 1980-81; 7 wkts @ 65.14, BB 2-73 v WI (Lord's) 1980. **LOI:** 26. Tours: A 1979-80; SA 1972-73 (DHR), 1981-82 (SAB); WI 1980-81, 1985-86; I 1979-80; SL 1977-78 (DHR). 1000 runs (10); most – 1783 (1982). HS 227 Nh v Somerset (Northampton) 1976. 50 wkts (3); most – 52 (1979). BB 7-37 Nh v OU (Oxford) 1975. F-c career: 559 matches; 24361 runs @ 30.56, 44 hundreds; 756 wickets @ 30.95. Appointed 1993. Umpired 22 Tests (1995-96 to 2000-01) and 21 LOI (1996 to 2000-01), including 1999 World Cup and tournaments in Dhaka and Nairobi. **Appointed to International Panel 1996.**

RESERVE FIRST-CLASS LIST: P.Adams, N.L.Bainton, †M.Dixon, †I.J.Gould, C.S.Kelly, N.J.Llong, K.J.Lyons, K.Shuttleworth.

CURRENT INTERNATIONAL PANEL: J.H.Hampshire, G.Sharp, D.R.Shepherd, P.Willey (England); D.B.Hair, D.J.Harper (Australia); A.V.Jayaprakesh, S.Venkataraghavan (India); D.B.Cowie, R.S.Dunne (New Zealand); Mian Aslam, Riazuddin (Pakistan); R.E.Koertzen, D.L.Orchard (South Africa); P.T.Manuel (Sri Lanka); S.A.Bucknor, E.A.Nicholls (West Indies); I.D.Robinson, R.B.Tiffin (Zimbabwe).

Test Match and LOI statistics to 19 March 2001. See page 16 for key to abbreviations.

TOURING TEAM REGISTER 2000

WEST INDIES

Full Names	Birthdate	Birthplace	Team	Type	F-C Debut
ADAMS, James Clive	9. 1.68	Port Maria	Jamaica	LHB/SLA/WK	1984-85
AMBROSE, Curtly Elconn Lynwall	21. 9.63	Swetes, Antigua	Leeward Is	LHB/RF	1985-86
CAMPBELL, Sherwin Legay	1.11.70	Belleplaine	Barbados	RHB/RM	1990-91
CHANDERPAUL, Shivnarine	18. 8.74	Unity	Guyana	LHB/LB	1991-92
COLLYMORE, Corey Delano	21.12.77	Boscobelle	Barbados	RHB/RMF	1998-99
GAYLE, Christopher Henry	21. 9.79	Kingston	Jamaica	LHB/OB	1998-99
GRIFFITH, Adrian Frank Gordon	19.11.71	Holders Hill	Barbados	LHB/RM	1991-92
HINDS, Wavell Wayne	7. 9.76	Kingston	Jamaica	LHB/RM	1995-96
JACOBS, Ridley Detamore	26.11.67	Swetes, Antigua	Leeward Is	LHB/WK	1991-92
KING, Reon Dane	6.10.74	Geod Fortin	Guyana	RHB/RFM	1995-96
LARA, Brian Charles	2. 5.69	Cantaro	Trinidad	LHB/LBG	1987-88
McLEAN, Nixon Alexei McNamara	20. 7.73	St Vincent	Windward Is	LHB/RF	1992-93
NAGAMOOTOO, Mahendra Vereen	9.10.75	Whim	Guyana	LHB/LBG	1994-95
PHILLIP, Wayne	25.11.77	Dominica	Windward Is	LHB/WK	1998-99
ROSE, Franklyn Albert	1. 2.72	St Ann's Bay	Jamaica	RHB/RF	1992-93
SARWAN, Ramnaresh Ronnie	23. 6.80	Wakenaam Is	Guyana	RHB/LB	1994-95
WALSH, Courtney Andrew	30.10.62	Kingston	Jamaica	RHB/RF	1981-82

ZIMBABWE

Full Names	Birthdate	Birthplace	Team	Type	F-C Debut
BRENT, Gary Bazil	13. 1.76	Sinoia	Mashonaland	RHB/RMF	1994-95
CAMPBELL, Alistair Douglas Ross	23. 9.72	Salisbury	Mashonaland	LHB/OB	1990-91
CARLISLE, Stuart Vance	10. 5.72	Salisbury	Mashonaland	RHB/RM	1993-94
FLOWER, Andrew	28. 4.68	Cape Town, SA	Mashonaland	LHB/OB/WK	1986-87
FLOWER, Grant William	20.12.70	Salisbury	Mashonaland	RHB/SLA	1989-90
GOODWIN, Murray William	11.12.72	Salisbury	Mashonaland	RHB/LB	1994-95
GRIPPER, Trevor Raymond	28.12.75	Salisbury	Matabeleland	RHB/OB	1996-97
JOHNSON, Neil Clarkson	24. 1.70	Salisbury	Matabeleland	LHB/RMF	1989-90
MBANGWA, Mpumelelo	26. 6.76	Plumtree	Mashonaland	RHB/RFM	1995-96
MURPHY, Brian Andrew	1.12.76	Salisbury	Mashonaland	RHB/LBG	1995-96
NKALA, Mluleki Luke	1. 4.81	Bulawayo	Matabeleland	RHB/RFM	1999-00
OLONGA, Henry Khaaba	3. 7.76	Lusaka	Matabeleland	RHB/RFM	1993-94
STRANG, Bryan Colin	9. 6.72	Bulawayo	Mashonaland	RHB/LMF	1994-95
STRANG, Paul Andrew	28. 7.70	Bulawayo	Mashonaland	RHB/LBG	1992-93
STREAK, Heath Hilton	6. 3.74	Bulawayo	Matabeleland	RHB/RFM	1992-93
TAIBU, Tatenda	14. 5.83	Salisbury	Mashonaland	RHB/WK	1999-00
VILJOEN, Dirk Peter	11. 3.77	Salisbury	Mashonaland	LHB/SLA	1994-95
WHITTALL, Guy James	5. 9.72	Chipinga	Matabeleland	RHB/RM	1990-91
WISHART, Craig Brian	9. 1.74	Salisbury	Mashonaland	RHB/RM	1992-93

NEW ZEALAND A

Full Names	Birthdate	Birthplace	Team	Type	F-C Debut
CANNING, Tamahau Karangatukituki	7. 4.77	Adelaide, Aust	Auckland	RHB/RFM	1998-99
CROY, Martyn Gilbert	23. 1.74	Hamilton	Otago	RHB/WK	1994-95
ENGLEFIELD, Jarrod Ian	18.12.79	Blenheim	Canterbury	RHB	1998-99
HAMILTON, Lance John	5. 4.73	Papakura	C Districts	RHB/LFM	1996-97
MARSHALL, James Andrew Hamilton	15. 2.79	Warkworth	N Districts	RHB/RM	1998-99
MARTIN, Bruce Philip	25. 4.80	Whangarei	N Districts	RHB/SLA	1999-00

111

Full Names	Birthdate	Birthplace	Team	Type	F-C Debut
MARTIN, Christopher Stewart	10.12.74	Christchurch	Canterbury	RHB/OB	1997-98
ORAM, Jacob David Philip	28. 7.78	Palmerston N	C Districts	LHB/RM	1997-98
PAPPS, Michael Hugh William	2. 7.79	Christchurch	Canterbury	RHB/WK	1998-99
REDMOND, Aaron James	23. 9.79	Perth, Aust	Canterbury	RHB/LB	1999-00
RICHARDSON, Mark Hunter	11. 6.71	Hastings	Otago	LHB/LM	1989-90
STYRIS, Scott Bernard	10. 7.75	Brisbane, Aust	N Districts	RHB/RMF	1994-95
SULZBERGER, Glen Paul	14. 3.73	Kaponga	C Districts	LHB/OB	1995-96
TUFFEY, Daryl Raymond	11. 6.78	Milton	N Districts	RHB/RFM	1996-97
WALKER, Brooke Graeme Keith	25. 3.77	Auckland	Auckland	RHB/LB	1997-98

IRELAND REGISTER 2000

Full Names	Birthdate	Birthplace	Bat/Bowl	F-C Debut
DUNLOP, Angus Richard	17. 3.67	Dublin	RHB/OB	1990
DWYER, Matthew Damian	22. 2.59	Dublin	LHB/SLA	1998
GILLESPIE, Mark Anthony	26. 8.69	Derry	RHB/LBG	2000
HAIRE, Ryan Samuel	1. 5.81	Dundonald, Belfast	LHB	2000
JOYCE, Augustine	10. 8.74	Dublin	RHB/WK	2000
McCALLAN, William Kyle	27. 8.75	Carrickfergus	RHB/OB	1996
McCOUBREY, Adrian George Agustus Mathew	3. 4.80	Ballymena	RHB/RFM	1999
MOONEY, Paul John Kevin	15.10.76	Dublin	RHB/RM	1998
NEELY, Gary Jason	28.11.74	Londonderry	RHB/RMF	2000
PATTERSON, Andrew David	4. 9.75	Belfast	RHB/WK	1996
SHIELDS, Ian Peter	21.10.79	Comber	RHB/WK	1999

SCOTLAND REGISTER 2000

Full Names	Birthdate	Birthplace	Bat/Bowl	F-C Debut
ASIM BUTT	24.10.67	Lahore, Pakistan	RHB/LMF	1983-84
BRINKLEY, James Edward	13. 3.74	Helensburgh	RHB/RFM	1993
LOCKHART, Douglas Ross	19. 1.76	Glasgow	RHB	1996
MAIDEN, Gregor Ian	22. 7.79	Glasgow	RHB/OB	1999
PARSONS, Robert Andrew	26. 7.75	Irvine	LHB/LM	1999
PATTERSON, Bruce Mathew Winston	29. 1.65	Ayr	RHB	1988
SALMOND, George	1.12.69	Dundee	RHB	1991
SMITH, Colin John Ogilvie	27. 9.72	Aberdeen	RHB/WK	1999
TENNANT, Andrew McBlain	17. 2.66	Ayr	RHB/SLA	1996
WILLIAMSON, John Greig	20.12.68	Glasgow	RHB/RM	1994
WRIGHT, Craig McIntyre	28. 4.74	Paisley	RHB/RFM	1997

MCC REGISTER 2000

Full Names	Birthdate	Birthplace	Team	Type	F-C Debut
ASIF MUJTABA, Mohammad	4.11.67	Karachi, Pakistan	Karachi/PIA	LHB/SLA	1984-85
CALLAGHAN, David John	1. 2.65	Queenstown, SA	E Province	RHB/RM	1983-84
DAVIS, Mark Jeffrey Gronow	10.10.71	Port Elizabeth, SA	Northerns	RHB/OB	1990-91
DEAN, Steven John	16.11.60	Cosford	Staffordshire	RHB	1994
DE BRUYN, Zander	5. 7.75	Johannesburg, SA	Gauteng	RHB/RFM	1995-96
GOOCH, Graham Alan	23. 7.53	Leytonstone	Ex Essex/Eng	RHB/RM	1973
KRUIS, Gideon Jacobus	9. 5.74	Pretoria, SA	Griqualand W	RHB/RFM	1993-94
PRYKE, David John	26.11.70	Welkom, SA	North West	RHB/RFM	1990-91
ROBINSON, Jonathan David	3. 8.66	Epsom	Ex Surrey	LHB/RM	1988
TOWNSEND, Christopher James	1.12.72	Wokingham	Ex OU	RHB/WK	1992
WRIGGLESWORTH, Ian Alastair	29.11.67	Sale, Australia	Victoria	LHB/RM	1993-94

FIRST-CLASS COUNTIES SELECT XI

(Excluding players listed in the County Register)

Full Names	Birthdate	Birthplace	Team	Bat/Bowl	F-C Debut
JOSEPH, Robert Hartman	20.1.82	Antigua	Kent 2nd XI	RHB/RF	2000

UNIVERSITY REGISTER 2000

CAMBRIDGE
(‡ Blue 2000)

Full Names	Birthdate	Birthplace	College	Bat/Bowl	F-C Debut
‡BIRKS, Malcolm James	29. 7.75	Keighley	Jesus	RHB/WK	1995
BLOCK, Stuart Anthony Allen	6. 1.79	Hereford	Downing	LHB/SLC	2000
‡COLLINS, Benjamin James	4.11.77	London	Girton	RHB	1998
‡DANSON, Andrew Richard	25.10.78	Sheffield	Jesus	RHB/RM	1999
‡HOWITT, Richard William John	17. 8.77	Grantham	Homerton	LHB/RMF	2000
‡HUGHES, Quentin John	17.10.74	Durham City	St Edmund's	LHB/OB	1997
‡HUGHES, Toby Roger	15. 2.79	Stourport-on-Severn	Homerton	RHB/RMF	2000
‡LEWIS, Simon James Ward	9.10.78	Bolton	Jesus	RHB	1998
LOWE, Jonathan Paul	13.11.77	Pontefract	Girton	RHB/RM	1998
‡PIMLOTT, Charles Robert	25. 2.79	Stockport	Downing	RHB/RFM	1999
PIPER, James William Stewart	9. 6.76	Sheffield	Pembroke	LHB/LB	2000
‡PYEMONT, James Patrick	10. 4.78	Eastbourne	Trinity Hall	RHB/OB	1997
ROSS, Jonathan Stuart	5. 4.79	Epsom	Emmanuel	RHB/LM	1999
‡SAYERS, Christopher Allan	19.12.78	Harrow	Trinity Hall	RHB/RMF	1999
‡SHEIKH, Samir Majid	16.10.78	London	St John's	RHB/RMF	1999

OXFORD
(‡ Blue 2000)

Full Names	Birthdate	Birthplace	College	Bat/Bowl	F-C Debut
BONES, Andrew Stephen	18. 2.78	Crewe	(Brookes U)	RHB/WK/OB	2000
BROOKER, Jonathan Anthony Dyson	20.12.80	Solihull	Westminster	RHB/LB	2000
‡BYRNE, Byron Walter	15. 2.72	Sydney	Magdalen	RHB/OB	1997
CARROLL, Richard William Stanley	30. 9.77	Singapore	Mansfield	RHB/LB	2000
‡CLAUGHTON, John Andrew	28.10.78	Southampton	Keble	RHB/RM	1998
‡GARLAND, Ross	26. 6.74	Durban, SA	Brasenose	RHB/RM	1998
GOFTON, Alan Frederick	4.10.79	Chesterfield	Wadham	RHB/RM	1999
‡HICKS, Thomas Charles	28. 8.79	Farnborough, Kent	St Catherine's	RHB/OB	1999
JANMOHAMMED, Abeed Mahmud Tajdin	10.12.78	Mombasa, Kenya	(Brookes U)	RHB/RM	2000
‡KIIAN, Salman Haider	4. 6.71	Rawalpindi	Wadham	RHB/RM	1998
‡MATHER, David Peter	20.11.75	Bebington	Green	LHB/LM	1995
‡MILLAR, Neil	3. 2.81	London	Christ Church	RHB/RM	2000
PORTER, Joseph James	5. 5.80	London	(Brookes U)	LHB/SLA	2000
‡REDMAYNE, James Richard Studdert	16. 7.79	London	Trinity	RHB	2000
SAWAL, Mohammed Ali	29.10.79	Multan, Pakistan	(Brookes U)	RHB/RFM	2000
‡SMALLEY, Richard George	20. 3.79	Newcastle-u-Tyne	Keble	LHB/WK	1999
‡VONWILLER, Benjamin Michael	16. 3.74	Sydney, Australia	Trinity	RHB/RMF	2000
WARREN, Charles Christopher Morel	11. 3.79	Portadown	Worcester	RHB	2000
‡WEENINK, Scott William	1. 1.73	Christchurch, NZ	Wolfson	RHB/OB	2000

BRITISH UNIVERSITIES
(Excluding players listed either above or in the County Register)

Full Names	Birthdate	Birthplace	University	Bat/Bowl	F-C Debut
TOURNIER, Mark Andrew	3.5.71	Melbourne, Aust	Loughborough	RHB/RFM	2000

THE 2000 FIRST-CLASS SEASON
STATISTICAL HIGHLIGHTS

NOTES ON THE 2000 SEASON

Commencing on 7 April, the earliest date on which a first-class match has been played in the British Isles, and continuing until 16 September, it was the longest British first-class season (163 days).

M.Burns, 160 for Somerset v Oxford Universities at Taunton, scored the earliest first-class hundred in Britain (off 96 balls on 7 April), shortly before P.D.Bowler (Somerset) and J.P.Crawley (Lancashire) completed hundreds on the same day.

The County Championship was split into two divisions for the first time, based on the final positions in the 1999 table.

Oxford University joined forces with Oxford Brookes University to form 'Oxford Universities', although players from the latter establishment were ineligible for the final University Match at Lord's.

Two matches were abandoned without a ball being bowled, both on 11-13 April: Nottinghamshire v Cambridge University at Nottingham and Oxford Universities v Hampshire at Oxford.

For the first time since 1966 a complete day of Championship cricket was rained off (26 April).

HIGHEST INNINGS TOTALS († County record)

718-3d†	Glamorgan v Sussex	Colwyn Bay
585	Northamptonshire v Nottinghamshire	Northampton
574-5d	Lancashire v Leicestershire	Leicester
568-9d	Warwickshire v Northamptonshire	Northampton
568	Zimbabweans v Gloucestershire	Gloucester
565	Somerset v Lancashire	Taunton
551-6d	Warwickshire v Glamorgan	Birmingham
548-7d	Warwickshire v Sussex	Hove
548	Surrey v Somerset	The Oval
543	Northamptonshire v Gloucestershire	Cheltenham
541-6d	Gloucestershire v Oxford U	Bristol
522	Hampshire v Derbyshire	Southampton
519	Northamptonshire v Worcestershire	Northampton
508-5d	Yorkshire v Derbyshire	Leeds
507-9d	Glamorgan v Essex	Southend
505-9d	Essex v Nottinghamshire	Nottingham
505	Surrey v Leicestershire	Oakham

LOWEST INNINGS TOTALS († One man absent hurt)

54	West Indies v England (2nd Test)	Lord's
61	West Indies v England (4th Test)	Leeds
65	Sussex v Northamptonshire	Eastbourne
68	Zimbabweans v Yorkshire	Leeds
71	Sussex v Gloucestershire	Hove
74†	Oxford U v Somerset	Taunton
81	Durham v Kent	Tunbridge Wells
82	Kent v Yorkshire	Leeds
83	Zimbabwe v England (1st Test)	Lord's
83	Durham v Hampshire	Basingstoke
84	Cambridge U v Derbyshire	Cambridge
85	Surrey v Durham	Chester-le-St
85	Gloucestershire v Essex	Bristol
87	Leicestershire v Surrey	Guildford
87	Gloucestershire v Worcestershire	Worcester

92	Durham v Lancashire	Chester-le-St
93†	Durham v Hampshire	Basingstoke
93	Durham v Leicestershire	Leicester
94†	Yorkshire v West Indians	Leeds
95	Hampshire v Lancashire	Liverpool
97	West Indians v Glamorgan	Cardiff
97	Derbyshire v Surrey	The Oval
98	Worcestershire v Gloucestershire	Worcester

LARGEST MARGIN OF VICTORY

| 524 runs | Zimbabweans beat Gloucestershire | Gloucester |
| 404 runs | Somerset beat Oxford U | Taunton |

ELEVEN BOWLERS IN AN INNINGS

| Kent v Derbyshire (293-0d) | Canterbury |

FIRST TO INDIVIDUAL TARGETS

1000 RUNS	M.G.Bevan	Sussex	31 July
2000 RUNS	–		
100 WICKETS	–		

TRIPLE HUNDRED († County record)

| S.P.James | 309*† | Glamorgan v Sussex | Colwyn Bay |

DOUBLE HUNDREDS († County record)

A.D.Brown	295*	Surrey v Leicestershire	Oakham
D.Brown	203	Warwickshire v Sussex	Hove
D.G.Cork	200*	Derbyshire v Durham	Derby
S.P.James	309*†	Glamorgan v Sussex	Colwyn Bay
N.V.Knight	233	Warwickshire v Glamorgan	Birmingham
J.L.Langer	213*	Middlesex v Glamorgan	Cardiff
M.H.Richardson	212*	New Zealand A v Sussex	Hove
D.J.G.Sales	276	Northamptonshire v Nottinghamshire	Northampton
G.E.Welton	200*	Nottinghamshire v Warwickshire	Birmingham

HUNDREDS IN THREE CONSECUTIVE INNINGS

M.G.Bevan (Sussex) 151* v Essex (Arundel), 166 and 174 v Nottinghamshire (Hove)

HUNDRED IN EACH INNINGS OF A MATCH

| M.G.Bevan | 166 | 174 | Sussex v Nottinghamshire | Hove |
| M.R.Ramprakash | 110* | 112 | Middlesex v Sussex | Southgate |

FASTEST HUNDRED (WALTER LAWRENCE TROPHY)

| D.S.Lehmann | 89 balls | Yorkshire v Kent | Canterbury |

HUNDRED BEFORE LUNCH

| | | Day | | |
| G.D.Lloyd | 17*-126* | 2 | Lancashire v Somerset | Manchester |

HUNDRED ON FIRST-CLASS DEBUT

| C.G.Taylor | 104 | Gloucestershire v Middlesex | Lord's |

First to score a hundred on County Championship debut at Lord's

HUNDRED ON FIRST-CLASS DEBUT IN BRITAIN

| W.W.Hinds | 105* | West Indians v Glamorgan | Cardiff |

CARRYING BAT THROUGH COMPLETED INNINGS († One man absent)

G.W.White	(2)	78*	Hampshire (126) v Somerset	Southampton
		80*	Hampshire (136) v Kent	Portsmouth
E.J.Wilson		104*	Worcestershire (182) v Middlesex	Worcester

NOTABLE PARTNERSHIPS († *County record*)

First Wicket
406*†	D.J.Bicknell/G.E.Welton	Nottinghamshire v Warwickshire	Birmingham
374†	M.T.G.Elliott/S.P.James	Glamorgan v Sussex	Colwyn Bay
359	M.A.Butcher/I.J.Ward	Surrey v Durham	The Oval
293*	S.D.Stubbings/S.P.Titchard	Derbyshire v Kent	Canterbury

Second Wicket
306	M.J.Powell/D.P.Ostler	Warwickshire v Northamptonshire	Northampton
292	R.R.Montgomerie/M.G.Bevan	Sussex v Nottinghamshire (*1st inns*)	Hove
265	R.R.Montgomerie/M.G.Bevan	Sussex v Nottinghamshire (*2nd inns*)	Hove

Third Wicket
276	S.L.Campbell/B.C.Lara	West Indians v Zimbabweans	Arundel

Fourth Wicket
305	P.D.Bowler/M.Burns	Somerset v Oxford U	Taunton

Fifth Wicket
275	A.Habib/J.M.Dakin	Leicestershire v Somerset	Leicester

Sixth Wicket
232	C.J.Adams/U.B.A.Rashid	Sussex v Glamorgan	Colwyn Bay

Seventh Wicket
289†	D.Brown/A.F.Giles	Warwickshire v Sussex	Hove
258†	M.P.Dowman/D.G.Cork	Derbyshire v Durham	Derby

Tenth Wicket
152†	U.Afzaal/A.J.Harris	Nottinghamshire v Worcestershire	Nottingham
141	A.D.Brown/Saqlain Mushtaq	Surrey v Leicestershire	Oakham
134	A.F.Gofton/S.H.Khan	Oxford U v Northamptonshire	Oxford
125	P.A.Nixon/D.D.Masters	Kent v Hampshire	Canterbury
116	M.P.Bicknell/Saqlain Mushtaq	Surrey v Lancashire	Manchester
103	Kabir Ali/G.D.McGrath	Worcestershire v Nottinghamshire	Worcester

EIGHT OR MORE WICKETS IN AN INNINGS

M.J.Bicknell		9-47	Surrey v Leicestershire	Guildford
K.J.Dean		8-52	Derbyshire v Kent	Canterbury
A.F.Giles		8-90	Warwickshire v Northamptonshire	Northampton
J.Lewis		8-95	Gloucestershire v Zimbabweans	Gloucester
G.D.McGrath	(2)	8-86	Worcestershire v Nottinghamshire	Nottingham
		8-41	Worcestershire v Northamptonshire	Worcester
A.D.Mullally		9-93	Hampshire v Derbyshire	Derby
I.D.K.Salisbury		8-60	Surrey v Somerset	The Oval

TEN OR MORE WICKETS IN A MATCH

R.S.G.Anderson		11-111	Essex v Northamptonshire	Ilford
M.M.Betts		10- 88	Durham v Derbyshire	Darlington
M.J.Bicknell		16-119	Surrey v Leicestershire	Guildford
J.F.Brown	(2)	11-178	Northamptonshire v Warwickshire	Birmingham
		11-131	Northamptonshire v Sussex	Northampton
A.R.Caddick	(2)	12-126	Somerset v Hampshire	Southampton
		10- 97	Somerset v Kent	Bath
M.J.Cawdron		10- 74	FCC Select XI v New Zealand A	Milton Keynes
A.F.Giles	(2)	12-135	Warwickshire v Northamptonshire	Northampton
		11-196	Warwickshire v Northamptonshire	Birmingham
I.J.Harvey		10- 32	Gloucestershire v Sussex	Hove
G.Keedy		10-155	Lancashire v Durham	Manchester
A.Kumble		10-105	Leicestershire v Kent	Canterbury

G.D.McGrath	(3)	10-143	Worcestershire v Nottinghamshire	Nottingham
		10- 69	Worcestershire v Gloucestershire	Worcester
		12-116	Worcestershire v Northamptonshire	Worcester
M.Mbangwa		10- 53	Northamptonshire v Derbyshire	Northampton
J.D.Middlebrook		10-170	Yorkshire v Hampshire	Southampton
A.D.Mullally		14-188	Hampshire v Derbyshire	Derby
I.D.K.Salisbury	(2)	12- 91	Surrey v Somerset	The Oval
		11-154	Surrey v Durham	The Oval
Saqlain Mushtaq	(2)	10-135	Surrey v Hampshire	Southampton
		11-104	Surrey v Yorkshire	The Oval
R.J.Sidebottom		11- 43	Yorkshire v Kent	Leeds
P.M.Such		12-218	Essex v Middlesex	Chelmsford
J.P.Taylor		10- 69	Northamptonshire v Sussex	Eastbourne
C.A.Walsh		10-117	West Indies v England (2nd Test)	Lord's

OUTSTANDING INNINGS ANALYSIS

| Saqlain Mushtaq | 7-11 | Surrey v Derbyshire | The Oval |

FOUR WICKETS WITH CONSECUTIVE BALLS

| G.P.Butcher | Surrey v Derbyshire | The Oval |

FOUR WICKETS WITH FIVE BALLS

| J.D.Middlebrook | Yorkshire v Hampshire | Southampton |

HAT-TRICKS

G.P.Butcher	Surrey v Derbyshire	The Oval
K.J.Dean	Derbyshire v Leicestershire	Leicester
J.I.D.Kerr	Somerset v West Indians	Taunton
J.Lewis	Gloucestershire v Nottinghamshire	Nottingham

WICKET WITH FIRST BALL IN FIRST-CLASS CRICKET

| C.T.Tremlett | Hampshire v New Zealand A | Portsmouth |

SIX OR MORE WICKET-KEEPING DISMISSALS IN AN INNINGS

| S.J.Rhodes | 6ct | Worcestershire v Nottinghamshire | Nottingham |

NINE OR MORE WICKET-KEEPING DISMISSALS IN A MATCH

| S.J.Rhodes | 9ct | Worcestershire v Gloucestershire | Worcester |

NO BYES CONCEDED IN TOTAL OF 500 OR MORE

| 565 | W.K.Hegg | Lancashire v Somerset | Taunton |
| 507-9d | J.S.Foster | Essex v Glamorgan | Southend |

FIVE CATCHES IN AN INNINGS IN THE FIELD

| K.P.Dutch | Middlesex v Cambridge U | Cambridge |

SIXTY EXTRAS IN AN INNINGS

	B	LB	W	NB			
76	27	15	34	–	Warwickshire (568-9d) v Northamptonshire	Northampton
76	5	11	8	52	Essex (462) v Worcestershire	Kidderminster
68	15	16	12	25	Yorkshire (399) v Hampshire	Leeds
64	1	15	2	46	Somerset (411-7d) v Leicestershire	Taunton
63	19	16	18	10	Nottinghamshire (368) v Warwickshire	Nottingham
61	1	26	4	30	Middlesex (412) v Nottinghamshire	Nottingham

Under ECB regulations (Test matches excluded), two extras were scored for each no-ball, in addition to any runs scored off that ball, and two extras were also scored for each wide. There were a further 16 instances of 50-59 extras in an innings.

2000 FIRST-CLASS AVERAGES

These averages involve the 480 cricketers who appeared in the 182 first-class matches played by 29 teams in the British Isles during the 2000 season.

'Cap' denotes the season in which the player was awarded a 1st XI cap by the county he represented in 2000.

Team abbreviations: BU – British Universities; CU – Cambridge University; De – Derbyshire; Du – Durham; E – England; Ex – Essex; FCC – First-Class Counties Select XI; Gm – Glamorgan; Gs – Gloucestershire; H – Hampshire; Ire – Ireland; K – Kent; La – Lancashire; Le – Leicestershire; M – Middlesex; MCC – Marylebone Cricket Club; Nh – Northamptonshire; Nt – Nottinghamshire; NZA – New Zealand A; OU – Oxford University; Sc – Scotland; Sm – Somerset; Sy – Surrey; Sx – Sussex; Wa – Warwickshire; WI – West Indies/Indians; Wo – Worcestershire; Y – Yorkshire; Z – Zimbabwe(ans).

† Left-handed batsman.

BATTING AND FIELDING

	Cap	M	I	NO	HS	Runs	Avge	100	50	Ct/St
Adams, C.J.(Sx)	1998	16	26	3	156	913	39.69	1	7	15
†Adams, J.C.(WI)	–	10	17	–	98	313	18.41	–	2	6
Adams, K.(K)	–	1	–	–	–	–	–	–	–	–
Adshead, S.J.(Le)	–	1	1	–	0	0	0.00	–	–	–/1
†Afzaal, U.(Nt)	2000	16	26	3	151*	1018	44.26	3	4	9
Aldred, P.(De)	1999	11	14	1	38	149	11.46	–	–	4
Ali, Kabir (Wo)	–	10	15	3	50*	213	17.75	–	1	5
Ali, Kadeer (Wo)	–	4	7	–	8	13	1.85	–	–	1
Ali, S.M.(Du)	–	4	5	–	18	25	5.00	–	–	1
Alleyne, M.W.(Gs)	1990	16	24	–	126	410	17.08	1	–	14
Altree, D.A.(Wa)	–	1	1	–	4	4	4.00	–	–	–
†Ambrose, C.E.L.(WI)	–	6	10	2	36*	117	14.62	–	–	1
Amin, R.M.(Sy)	–	1	1	–	3	3	3.00	–	–	1
Anderson, R.S.G.(Ex)	–	9	8	3	67*	170	34.00	–	1	–
†Asif Mujtaba (MCC)	–	1	2	–	76	82	41.00	–	1	2
Asim Butt (Sc)	–	1	1	–	10	10	10.00	–	–	–
Atherton, M.A.(La/E)	1989	18	29	1	136	1068	38.14	3	6	15
†Austin, I.D.(La)	1990	1	1	–	0	0	0.00	–	–	–
Averis, J.M.M.(Gs)	–	5	7	1	25*	60	10.00	–	–	1
Aymes, A.N.(H)	1991	13	22	5	74*	398	23.41	–	3	32/6
Bailey, R.J.(De)	2000	13	19	4	118	728	48.53	2	5	4
Bailey, T.M.B.(Nh)	–	4	7	2	96*	200	40.00	–	1	8/1
Ball, M.C.J.(Gs)	1996	9	14	2	53	244	20.33	–	1	13
Banes, M.J.(BU)	–	1	1	–	51	51	51.00	–	1	–
Barnett, K.J.(Gs)	1999	11	16	2	118*	640	45.71	2	3	8
Bates, J.J.(Sx)	–	4	6	–	17	54	9.00	–	–	5
†Batt, C.J.(M)	–	2	3	–	21	27	9.00	–	–	–
Batty, J.N.(Sy)	–	13	16	2	100*	276	19.71	1	–	29/7
Betts, M.M.(Du)	1998	11	18	4	55	192	13.71	–	1	7
†Bevan, M.G.(Sx)	1998	12	18	3	174	1124	74.93	5	1	2
Bicknell, D.J.(Nt)	2000	16	28	3	180*	858	34.32	2	2	3
Bicknell, M.P.(Sy)	1989	15	18	2	79*	500	31.25	–	4	5
Birks, M.J.(CU)	–	6	7	–	32	107	15.28	–	–	8/2
Bishop, I.E.(Sy)	–	2	3	–	12	14	4.66	–	–	–
†Blackwell, I.D.(Sm)	–	18	23	2	109	582	27.71	1	2	6
Blain, J.A.R.(Nh)	–	1	1	1	31*	31	–	–	–	1
Blakey, R.J.(Y)	1987	12	18	1	56	264	15.52	–	1	41/2
†Block, S.A.A.(CU)	–	2	4	–	23	31	7.75	–	–	–
Bloomfield, T.F.(M)	–	10	8	2	4*	16	2.66	–	–	1
Bones, A.S.(OU)	–	4	7	–	7	24	3.42	–	–	–

	Cap	M	I	NO	HS	Runs	Avge	100	50	Ct/St
Boswell, S.A.J.(Le)	–	5	7	3	20	63	15.75	–	–	–
Bowen, M.N.(Nt)	1997	4	6	–	24	83	13.83	–	–	2
Bowler, P.D.(Sm)	1995	18	26	5	157*	1305	62.14	5	4	8
Brent, G.B.(Z)	–	2	2	1	21*	21	21.00	–	–	1
†Bressington, A.N.(Gs)	–	1	1	1	2*	2	–	–	–	1
Brinkley, J.E.(Sc)	–	1	1	1	43*	43	–	–	–	3
Brooker, J.A.D.(OU)	–	1	–	–	–	–	–	–	–	1
Brown, A.D.(Sy)	1994	16	23	5	295*	935	51.94	2	4	16
Brown, D.R.(Wa)	1995	16	22	6	203	622	38.87	1	2	11
Brown, J.F.(Nh)	2000	10	14	5	11	30	3.33	–	–	3
Brown, S.J.E.(Du)	1998	14	21	12	19	82	9.11	–	–	2
Brunnschweiler, I.(H)	–	1	2	–	19	22	11.00	–	–	4
†Bulbeck, M.P.L.(Sm)	–	3	2	1	3*	6	6.00	–	–	–
Burns, M.(Sm)	1999	15	20	1	160	775	40.78	2	5	3
†Burns, N.D.(Le)	–	16	21	4	67*	445	26.17	–	3	36/1
Butcher, G.P.(Sy)	–	4	4	1	66	110	36.66	–	1	–
†Butcher, M.A.(Sy)	1996	16	25	4	191	891	42.42	2	3	13
*Byas, D.(Y)	1991	17	26	2	84	596	24.83	–	2	22
Byrne, B.W.(OU)	–	2	2	–	34	64	32.00	–	–	1
Caddick, A.R.(Sm/E)	1992	10	15	2	21*	141	10.84	–	–	3
Callaghan, D.J.(MCC)	–	1	2	–	54	54	27.00	–	1	4
†Campbell, A.D.R.(Z)	–	8	10	2	150*	292	36.50	1	1	11
Campbell, S.L.(WI)	–	12	20	–	146	629	31.45	1	4	13
Canning, T.K.(NZA)	–	2	3	–	3	5	1.66	–	–	1
Carlisle, S.V.(Z)	–	6	7	–	65	112	16.00	–	1	6
†Carpenter, J.R.(Sx)	–	1	2	–	8	8	4.00	–	–	–
Carroll, R.W.S.(OU)	–	1	1	1	0*	–	–	–	–	–
Cassar, M.E.(De)	–	14	20	2	77*	341	18.94	–	1	1
Catterall, D.N.(Wo)	–	1	1	–	25	25	25.00	–	–	1
†Cawdron, M.J.(Gs/FCC)	–	6	8	–	32	125	15.62	–	–	1
†Chanderpaul, S.(WI)	–	5	9	3	161*	418	69.66	2	1	3
Chapple, G.(La)	1994	16	19	1	41	218	12.11	–	–	4
Chilton, M.J.(La)	–	10	14	1	46	286	22.00	–	–	10
Claughton, J.A.(OU)	–	3	5	1	19*	45	11.25	–	–	–
Collingwood, P.D.(Du)	1998	16	27	–	111	681	25.22	1	4	19
Collins, B.J.(CU)	–	4	4	–	6	11	2.75	–	–	–
Collymore, C.D.(WI)	–	6	9	3	14	29	4.83	–	–	1
†Cook, J.W.(Nh)	–	11	17	1	137	502	31.37	2	1	4
Cook, S.J.(M)	–	7	10	–	43	145	14.50	–	–	2
Cork, D.G.(De/E)	1993	14	17	4	200*	542	41.69	1	2	10
Cosker, D.A.(Gm)	2000	12	15	4	14*	88	8.00	–	–	9
†Cotterell, T.P.(Gs)	–	8	10	4	5*	7	1.16	–	–	2
Cottey, P.A.(Sx)	1999	16	23	–	154	740	32.17	2	2	8
Cousins, D.M.(Nh)	2000	16	23	7	29*	210	13.12	–	–	3
Cowan, A.P.(Ex)	1997	14	20	6	67	245	17.50	–	1	4
Cox, J.(Sm)	1999	17	26	1	171	983	39.32	3	3	6
†Craven, V.J.(Y)	–	8	11	1	58	251	25.10	–	2	6
Crawley, J.P.(La)	1994	15	22	1	156	951	45.28	5	–	6
Croft, R.D.B.(Gm)	1992	14	17	4	56	282	21.69	–	2	4
Crowe, C.D.(Le)	–	8	8	2	30	103	17.16	–	–	4
Croy, M.G.(NZA)	–	5	8	3	28	88	17.60	–	–	14/3
Cunliffe, R.J.(Gs/FCC)	–	9	14	–	74	229	16.35	–	1	10
Dagnall, C.E.(Wa)	–	2	2	–	6*	11	–	–	–	2
†Dakin, J.M.(Le)	2000	9	12	1	135	458	41.63	1	3	2
Dale, A.(Gm)	1992	17	27	3	81	837	34.87	–	5	8
Daley, J.A.(Du)	1999	10	17	–	50	247	14.52	–	1	4
Danson, A.R.(CU)	–	6	9	2	117*	211	30.14	1	–	4

	Cap	M	I	NO	HS	Runs	Avge	100	50	Ct/St
Davies, M.K.(Nh)	–	5	8	–	25	79	9.87	–	–	2
Davis, M.J.G.(MCC)	–	1	2	–	19	28	14.00	–	–	1
Dawson, R.K.J.(BU)	–	1	1	–	1	1	1.00	–	–	–
†Dean, K.J.(De)	1998	12	15	3	22	49	4.08	–	–	–
Dean, S.J.(MCC)	–	1	1	–	12	12	12.00	–	–	–
De Bruyn, Z.(MCC)	–	1	2	–	9	14	7.00	–	–	–
DeFreitas, P.A.J.(Le)	1986	14	18	3	123*	677	45.13	1	4	1
†Di Venuto, M.J.(De)	2000	16	25	3	92*	725	32.95	–	6	12
Donald, A.A.(Wa)	1989	8	9	2	18	69	9.85	–	–	3
†Dowman, M.P.(De)	2000	17	29	3	140	833	32.03	2	4	11
Dravid, R.(K)	2000	16	25	3	182	1221	55.50	2	8	15
†Driver, R.C.(Wo)	–	11	20	4	64	372	23.25	–	1	2
Dunlop, A.R.(Ire)	–	1	2	–	150	160	80.00	1	–	–
Dutch, K.P.(M)	–	5	7	–	91	160	22.85	–	2	9
†Dwyer, M.D.(Ire)	–	1	2	1	4*	6	6.00	–	–	–
Ealham, M.A.(K)	1992	11	14	1	83	293	22.53	–	2	3
†Elliott, M.T.G.(Gm)	2000	13	21	–	177	1076	51.23	4	4	19
Elstub, C.J.(Y)	–	4	4	3	4*	6	6.00	–	–	1
Englefield, J.I.(NZA)	–	6	11	1	90	248	24.80	–	1	3
Evans, A.W.(Gm)	–	4	6	–	58	114	19.00	–	1	–
†Fairbrother, N.H.(La)	1985	15	23	5	138	823	45.72	2	3	16
Fellows, G.M.(Y)	–	14	20	4	46	341	21.31	–	–	8
†Fisher, I.D.(Y)	–	6	10	2	68*	181	22.62	–	1	1
†Flanagan, I.N.(Ex)	–	4	8	–	23	89	11.12	–	–	7
Fleming, M.V.(K)	1990	14	18	2	47	471	29.43	–	–	4
Flintoff, A.(La/E)	1998	13	19	1	119	631	35.05	1	4	12
†Flower, A.(Z)	–	7	10	1	116*	300	33.33	1	–	16/1
Flower, G.W.(Z)	–	7	13	2	76*	180	16.36	–	1	10
Foster, J.S.(BU/Ex)	–	4	5	2	52	125	41.66	–	1	6
Francis, S.R.G.(H)	–	9	13	7	30*	64	10.66	–	–	1
Franklin, G.D.(BU)	–	1	1	–	12	12	12.00	–	–	–
†Franks, P.J.(Nt)	1999	13	18	1	60	447	26.29	–	3	5
Fraser, A.R.C.(M)	1988	15	22	6	30	227	14.18	–	–	4
†Frost, T.(Wa)	1999	1	–	–	–	–	–	–	–	–
Fulton, D.P.(K)	1998	14	24	1	115	512	22.26	1	1	29
Gallian, J.E.R.(Nt)	1998	16	26	3	150	796	34.60	3	–	23
†Ganguly, S.C.(La)	–	14	21	–	99	671	31.95	–	6	10
Gannon, B.W.(Gs)	–	8	10	4	28	74	12.33	–	–	3
Garland, R.(OU)	–	4	6	1	15	27	5.40	–	–	1
†Gayle, C.H.(WI)	–	8	14	1	128	392	30.15	1	2	5
Giddins, E.S.H.(Wa/E)	1998	12	11	3	14	25	3.12	–	–	1
Giles, A.F.(Wa)	–	13	14	3	128*	444	40.36	1	1	4
†Gillespie, M.A.(Ire)	–	1	2	–	34	56	28.00	–	–	–
Gofton, A.F.(OU)	–	6	7	1	47*	117	19.50	–	–	–
Golding, J.M.(K)	–	1	1	1	18*	18	–	–	–	–
Gooch, G.A.(MCC)	–	1	2	–	5	5	2.50	–	–	–
Goodwin, M.W.(Z)	–	8	12	2	194	651	65.10	3	1	3
Gough, D.(Y)	1993	10	13	3	23*	131	13.10	–	–	3
Gough, M.A.(Du)	–	7	12	–	33	176	14.66	–	–	3
†Grayson, A.P.(Ex)	1996	17	31	2	144	807	27.82	1	5	10
Green, R.J.(La)	–	3	3	1	29*	29	14.50	–	–	2
Greenidge, C.G.(Sy)	–	3	2	–	6	9	4.50	–	–	–
†Griffith, A.F.G.(WI)	–	11	21	1	130	486	24.30	1	2	5
Griffiths, P.(Le)	–	1	–	–	–	–	–	–	–	–
Gripper, T.R.(Z)	–	6	11	2	66*	258	28.66	–	2	5
Grove, J.O.(Sm)	–	10	10	5	17	56	11.20	–	–	–
Guy, S.M.(Y)	–	6	9	2	42	136	19.42	–	–	21/2

120

	Cap	M	I	NO	HS	Runs	Avge	100	50	Ct/St
Habib, A.(Le)	1998	17	23	1	172*	1038	47.18	2	8	8
†Haire, R.S.(Ire)	–	1	2	–	0	0	0.00	–	–	–
†Hamilton, G.M.(Y)	1998	13	16	2	125	402	28.71	1	2	7
Hamilton, L.J.(NZA)	–	3	4	2	4	8	4.00	–	–	2
Hancock, T.H.C.(Gs)	1998	15	22	1	85	407	19.38	–	1	7
Harden, R.J.(Y)	1999	2	3	–	1	1	0.33	–	–	–
Hardinges, M.A.(Gs/BU)	–	2	3	–	3	3	1.00	–	–	–
Harmison, S.J.(Du)	1999	11	15	3	33*	104	8.66	–	–	2
Harris, A.J.(Nt)	2000	11	14	4	39	153	15.30	–	–	4
Harrison, D.S.(Gm)	–	1	2	–	27	27	13.50	–	–	–
Hartley, P.J.(H)	1998	9	11	5	23*	103	17.16	–	–	–
Harvey, I.J.(Gs)	1999	10	14	1	79	395	30.38	–	4	10
†Hayden, M.L.(Nh)	1999	15	22	–	164	1270	57.72	4	6	21
Haynes, J.J.(La)	–	1	2	2	27*	34	–	–	–	1
Hegg, W.K.(La)	1989	17	23	5	128	639	35.50	1	4	39/6
†Hemp, D.L.(Wa)	1997	17	24	2	129	834	37.90	1	5	9
Hewison, C.J.(Nt)	–	1	2	–	24	30	15.00	–	–	5
Hewson, D.R.(Gs)	–	11	21	1	67	448	22.40	–	3	5
Hick, G.A.(Wo/E)	1986	14	24	2	122	773	35.13	3	3	16
Hicks, T.C.(OU)	–	6	6	1	10	20	4.00	–	–	5
†Hinds, W.W.(WI)	–	11	19	1	150	669	37.16	3	3	11
Hockley, J.B.(K)	–	5	5	–	74	111	22.20	–	1	2
Hoggard, M.J.(Y/E)	2000	16	18	4	20*	103	7.35	–	–	3
Hollioake, A.J.(Sy)	1995	16	23	–	80	689	29.95	–	3	27
Hollioake, B.C.(Sy)	1999	10	14	1	29	142	10.92	–	–	8
†Holloway, P.C.L.(Sm)	1997	13	20	1	113	377	19.84	1	1	9
†House, W.J.(Sx)	–	6	10	1	35	112	12.44	–	–	3
†Howitt, R.W.J.(CU)	–	6	10	2	118*	274	34.25	1	1	–
†Hughes, Q.J.(CU)	–	6	10	3	119	237	33.85	1	1	–
Hughes, T.R.(CU)	–	6	3	2	13*	14	14.00	–	–	1
Humphries, S.(Sx)	–	2	4	1	18	41	13.66	–	–	4/1
Hunter, I.D.(Du)	–	3	4	–	63	83	20.75	–	1	–
Hussain, N.(Ex/E)	1989	10	16	1	33	166	11.06	–	–	7
†Hutchison, P.M.(Y)	1998	7	8	2	3*	3	0.50	–	–	3
Hutton, B.L.(M)	–	10	15	2	55	188	14.46	–	1	8
Hyam, B.J.(Ex)	1999	15	24	–	53	256	10.66	–	1	49/6
Illingworth, R.K.(Wo)	1986	10	12	2	44*	154	15.40	–	–	2
†Ilott, M.C.(Ex)	1993	10	13	4	25	119	13.22	–	–	4
Inglis, J.W.(Y)	–	1	2	–	2	4	2.00	–	–	–
Innes, K.J.(Nh)	–	2	4	1	32*	66	22.00	–	–	–
Irani, R.C.(Ex)	1994	17	29	7	168*	1196	54.36	1	9	2
†Jacobs, R.D.(WI)	–	8	14	2	78	281	23.41	–	1	23/2
James, S.P.(Gm)	1992	17	28	2	309*	1070	41.15	3	2	5
Janmohamed, A.M.T.(OU)	–	3	4	1	6	16	5.33	–	–	–
Jarvis, P.W.(Sm)	–	2	1	–	1	1	1.00	–	–	2
Jefferson, W.I.(BU/Ex)	–	2	3	–	41	46	15.33	–	–	1
†Johnson, N.C.(Z)	–	7	8	–	83	266	33.25	–	3	6
Johnson, P.(Nt)	1986	12	19	2	100	353	20.76	1	–	9
Johnson, R.L.(M)	1995	15	23	3	69	414	20.70	–	2	13
Jones, P.S.(Sm)	–	15	16	4	56*	122	10.16	–	1	4
†Jones, S.P.(Gm)	–	5	3	–	13	13	4.33	–	–	–
Joseph, R.H.(FCC)	–	1	1	1	0*	0	–	–	–	–
Joyce, A.(Ire)	–	1	2	–	29	31	15.50	–	–	–
†Joyce, E.C.(M)	–	6	8	1	51	195	27.85	–	1	7
†Katich, S.M.(Du)	2000	16	28	3	137*	1089	43.56	3	5	21
†Keedy, G.(La)	2000	13	15	3	34	144	12.00	–	–	2
Kendall, W.S.(H)	1999	18	31	3	161	1156	41.28	3	5	17

121

	Cap	M	I	NO	HS	Runs	Avge	100	50	Ct/St
Kenway, D.A.(H)	–	15	27	1	136	685	26.34	1	3	13/1
Kerr, J.I.D.(Sm)	–	4	5	1	34	116	29.00	–	–	–
Key, R.W.T.(K/FCC)	–	17	29	1	83	584	20.85	–	5	4
Khan, S.H.(OU)	–	5	5	1	87	143	35.75	–	1	2
†Khan, W.G.(Sx)	–	3	6	–	74	143	23.83	–	1	–
†Khan, Z.M.(De)	–	1	–	–	–	–	–	–	–	–
Killeen, N.(Du)	1999	10	15	1	38*	144	10.28	–	–	1
King, R.D.(WI)	–	9	12	4	21	62	7.75	–	–	–
Kirtley, R.J.(Sx)	1998	16	22	4	26*	146	8.11	–	–	5
†Knight, N.V.(Wa/E)	1995	10	15	–	233	593	39.53	1	1	7
Krikken, K.M.(De)	1992	10	13	–	51	221	17.00	–	1	18/2
Kruis, G.J.(MCC)	–	1	2	–	25	49	24.50	–	–	–
Kumble, A.(Le)	2000	12	16	–	56	181	11.31	–	1	3
Lacey, S.J.(De)	–	11	17	4	55*	242	18.61	–	1	1
Lambert, G.A.(Y)	–	2	3	2	3*	6	6.00	–	–	1
Lampitt, S.R.(Wo)	1989	18	27	8	56*	331	17.42	–	1	12
Laney, J.S.(H)	1996	14	25	1	81	489	20.37	–	2	12
†Langer, J.L.(M)	1998	16	27	3	213*	1472	61.33	5	7	25
†Lara, B.C.(WI)	–	10	18	–	176	519	28.83	2	1	15
Laraman, A.W.(M)	–	1	–	–	–	–	–	–	–	1
Lathwell, M.N.(Sm)	1992	9	14	1	54*	257	19.76	–	1	4
Law, D.R.(Ex)	1996	15	23	3	68*	360	18.00	–	2	6
Law, S.G.(Ex)	1996	16	27	2	189	1385	55.40	5	6	19
Law, W.L.(Gm)	–	8	11	1	85	161	16.10	–	1	4
Leatherdale, D.A.(Wo)	1994	17	30	5	132*	975	39.00	2	7	9
†Lehmann, D.S.(Y)	1997	16	23	1	136	1477	67.13	4	9	8
Lewis, C.C.(Le)	1990	5	7	–	24	80	11.42	–	–	6
Lewis, J.(Gs/FCC)	1998	17	23	2	38	169	8.04	–	–	4
Lewis, J.J.B.(Du)	1998	16	28	2	115	645	24.80	1	4	8
Lewis, S.J.W.(CU)	–	6	10	1	26	98	10.88	–	–	2
†Lewry, J.D.(Sx)	1996	17	24	5	39	149	7.84	–	–	5
†Liptrot, C.G.(Wo)	–	4	3	1	1	1	0.50	–	–	5
Lloyd, G.D.(La)	1992	16	22	1	126	608	28.95	1	2	20
Lockhart, D.R.(Sc)	–	1	1	–	0	0	0.00	–	–	2
Logan, R.J.(Nh)	–	6	8	1	24	51	7.28	–	–	1
Lowe, J.P.(CU)	–	3	3	1	6*	7	3.50	–	–	–
Loye, M.B.(Nh)	1994	12	18	1	93	504	29.64	–	3	1
Lucas, D.S.(Nt)	–	10	12	5	46*	184	26.28	–	–	3
†Lumb, M.J.(Y)	–	1	2	1	66*	68	68.00	–	1	–
†Lungley, T.(De)	–	1	–	–	–	–	–	–	–	–
McCague, M.J.(K)	1992	7	11	–	72	191	17.36	–	1	2
McCallan, W.K.(Ire)	–	2	–	17	17	8.50	–	–	–		
McCoubrey, A.G.A.M.(Ire)	–	1	1	–	0	0	0.00	–	–	–
McGarry, A.C.(Ex)	–	3	3	2	1	1	1.00	–	–	–
McGrath, A.(Y)	1999	10	14	1	133	375	28.84	1	1	8
McGrath, G.D.(Wo)	2000	14	15	3	55	112	9.33	–	1	2
McKeown, P.C.(La)	–	3	4	–	33	69	17.25	–	–	1
†McLean, N.A.M.(WI)	–	9	17	2	29	122	8.13	–	–	–
Maddy, D.L.(Le)	1996	17	25	1	102	630	26.25	1	4	16
Maiden, G.I.(Sc)	–	1	1	–	7	7	7.00	–	–	–
Malcolm, D.E.(Nh)	1999	7	10	1	8	24	2.66	–	–	–
Marshall, J.A.H.(NZA)	–	5	9	–	69	133	14.77	–	1	11
Martin, B.P.(NZA)	–	4	4	–	29	55	13.75	–	–	2
Martin, C.S.(NZA)	–	4	4	1	6*	8	2.66	–	–	2
Martin, P.J.(La)	1994	9	11	3	40	134	16.75	–	–	2
Martin-Jenkins, R.S.C.(Sx)	2000	15	23	1	86	499	22.68	–	2	4
Mascarenhas, A.D.(H)	1998	16	24	1	100	473	20.56	1	2	3

	Cap	M	I	NO	HS	Runs	Avge	100	50	Ct/St
Mason, T.J.(Ex)	–	10	14	2	52*	140	11.66	–	1	4
Masters, D.D.(K)	–	16	20	7	21	71	5.46	–	–	4
†Mather, D.P.(OU)	–	2	2	–	13	18	9.00	–	–	–
Maynard, M.P.(Gm)	1987	15	22	1	119*	716	34.09	2	5	17/2
Mbangwa, M.(Z)	–	8	8	5	9*	30	10.00	–	–	–
Middlebrook, J.D.(Y)	–	11	15	–	45	201	13.40	–	–	5
Millar, N.(OU)	–	2	1	–	0	0	0.00	–	–	1
†Millns, D.J.(Nt)	2000	8	11	4	50*	195	27.85	–	1	2
Mohammed, I.(Gs)	–	4	6	–	24	71	11.83	–	–	1
Montgomerie, R.R.(Sx)	1999	17	30	2	133	899	32.10	2	4	17
Mooney, P.J.K.(Ire)	–	1	2	–	9	11	5.50	–	–	–
†Morris, A.C.(H)	–	8	12	1	60	154	14.00	–	1	4
Morris, J.E.(Nt)	2000	13	20	–	115	601	30.05	1	3	7
Mullally, A.D.(H)	2000	8	12	2	12	60	6.00	–	–	–
Munton, T.A.(De)	2000	16	22	7	52	191	12.73	–	1	7
Murphy, B.A.(Z)	–	2	3	1	14	14	7.00	–	–	3
†Murtagh, T.J.(BU)	–	1	1	1	12*	12	–	–	–	–
†Nagamootoo, M.V.(WI)	–	9	16	2	100	381	27.21	1	–	2
Napier, G.R.(Ex)	–	1	2	–	21	26	13.00	–	–	4
Nash, D.C.(M)	2000	17	24	2	75*	445	20.22	–	1	32/4
Neely, G.J.(Ire)	–	1	1	–	0	0	0.00	–	–	–
Newell, K.(Gm)	–	13	21	1	61	356	17.80	–	1	5
†Nixon, P.A.(K/FCC)	2000	18	25	7	134*	578	32.11	1	3	46/2
Nkala, M.(Z)	–	4	6	1	40	92	18.40	–	–	1
Noon, W.M.(Nt)	1995	1	2	–	7	7	3.50	–	–	1
Olonga, H.K.(Z)	–	2	1	–	45	45	45.00	–	–	1
†Oram, J.D.P.(NZA)	–	4	7	–	27	93	13.28	–	–	1
Ormond, J.(Le)	1999	12	15	7	30*	95	11.87	–	–	1
Ostler, D.P.(Wa)	1991	16	24	2	145	1096	49.81	2	7	19
Papps, M.H.W.(NZA)	–	5	10	2	63	220	27.50	–	1	2/1
Parkin, O.T.(Gm)	–	5	6	3	13*	30	10.00	–	–	–
Parsons, K.A.(Sm)	1999	15	22	2	193*	745	37.25	2	1	17
†Parsons, R.A.(Sc)	–	1	2	1	27*	47	47.00	–	–	–
Patel, M.M.(K/FCC)	1994	14	16	1	60	269	17.93	–	1	13
Patterson, A.D.(Sx/Ire)	–	8	11	1	20*	67	6.70	–	–	17
Patterson, B.M.W.(Sc)	–	1	2	–	31	55	27.50	–	–	1
†Peirce, M T.E.(Sx)	–	14	24	1	86	446	19.39	–	2	3
†Penberthy, A.L.(Nh)	1994	15	21	2	116	785	41.31	1	5	10
Peng, N.(Du)	–	8	14	–	98	231	16.50	–	1	1
Penney, T.L.(Wa)	1994	13	18	4	100*	569	40.64	1	2	8
Peters, S.D.(Ex)	–	16	28	6	77*	602	27.36	–	4	12
†Phillip, W.(WI)	–	6	11	3	67*	155	19.37	–	1	22/1
Phillips, N.C.(Du)	–	5	9	–	29	76	8.44	–	–	3
Pierson, A.R.K (Sm)	–	6	9	3	48	126	21.00	–	–	3
Pimlott, C.R.(CU/BU)	–	5	3	1	31*	31	15.50	–	–	3
Pipe, D.J.(Wo)	–	3	5	–	54	107	21.40	–	1	–
†Piper, J W.S.(CU)	–	1	1	–	19	19	19.00	–	–	–
Piper, K.J.(Wa)	1992	16	18	3	69	260	17.33	–	1	28/3
†Pollard, P.R.(Wo)	–	14	24	1	123*	652	28.34	1	5	3
†Porter, J.J.(OU/BU)	–	6	10	–	93	297	29.70	–	4	–
Powell, M.J.(Gm)	2000	18	28	–	128	843	30.10	2	4	11
Powell, M.J.(Nh)	–	1	2	–	1	2	1.00	–	–	–
Powell, M.J.(Wa)	1999	17	26	2	145	1046	43.58	2	8	10
†Pratt, A.(Du)	–	7	10	1	38	191	21.22	–	–	7
†Pratt, G.J.(Du)	–	2	3	–	23	39	13.00	–	–	1
Prichard, P.J.(Ex)	1986	17	31	3	96	775	27.67	–	5	10
Prittipaul, L.R.(H)	–	4	6	–	152	298	49.66	1	1	1

123

	Cap	M	I	NO	HS	Runs	Avge	100	50	Ct/St
Pryke, D.J.(MCC)	–	1	2	1	5*	7	7.00	–	–	–
Pyemont, J.P.(CU/BU/De)	–	11	15	1	124	313	22.35	1	–	5
Ramprakash, M.R.(M/E)	1990	17	28	4	120*	1183	49.29	4	7	15
Ramsden, G.(Y)	–	1	1	1	0*	0	–	–	–	–
Randall, S.J.(Nt)	–	1	–	–				–	–	–
†Rashid, U.B.A.(Sx)	–	15	22	3	110	585	30.78	1	4	6
Ratcliffe, J.D.(Sy)	1998	2	4	–	26	28	7.00	–	–	2
Rawnsley, M.J.(Wo)	–	9	13	–	18	102	7.84	–	–	5
Read, C.M.W.(Nt)	1999	16	23	3	56*	479	23.95	–	3	40
Redmayne, J.R.S.(OU)	–	4	6	1	68	139	27.80	–	1	–
Redmond, A.J.(NZA)	–	3	5	–	92	142	28.40	–	1	4
Reiffel, P.R.(Nt)	2000	7	8	4	74	275	68.75	–	3	–
Renshaw, S.J.(H)	–	4	7	1	26	69	11.50	–	–	1
Rhodes, S.J.(Wo)	1986	18	28	6	103	591	26.86	1	1	54/1
Richardson, A.(Wa)	–	13	9	7	17*	43	21.50	–	–	3
†Richardson, M.H.(NZA)	–	6	11	2	212*	642	71.33	1	4	1
Richardson, S.A.(Y)	–	1	2	–	11	14	7.00	–	–	–
Ripley, D.(Nh)	1987	13	18	3	56	475	31.66	–	3	38/4
Robinson, D.D.J.(Ex)	1997	12	19	3	93*	561	35.06	–	4	5
†Robinson, J.D.(MCC)	–	1	2	–	35	45	22.50	–	–	–
Robinson, M.A.(Sx)	1997	9	11	8	8*	19	6.33	–	–	3
Rollins, A.S.(Nh)	–	16	24	–	100	636	26.50	1	4	19
Rose, F.A.(WI)	–	8	11	1	48	162	16.20	–	–	–
Rose, G.D.(Sm)	1988	15	18	5	124	510	39.23	2	1	4
Roseberry, M.A.(M)	1990	11	20	3	139*	549	32.29	1	2	3
Ross, J.S.(CU)	–	2	2	–	2	2	1.00	–	–	–
†Russell, R.C.(Gs)	1985	16	23	3	110*	593	29.65	1	2	50/4
Saggers, M.J.(K)	–	14	17	5	24	91	7.58	–	–	3
Sales, D.J.G.(Nh)	1999	13	20	2	276	713	35.65	1	5	9
Salisbury, I.D.K.(Sy)	1998	16	19	6	57*	313	24.07	–	2	6
Salmond, G.(Sc)	–	1	2	–	36	36	18.00	–	–	–
Saqlain Mushtaq (Sy)	1998	12	14	2	66	217	18.08	–	2	8
Sarwan, R.R.(WI)	–	9	16	2	59*	423	30.21	–	3	2
Savident, L.(H)	–	1	2	1	10*	17	17.00	–	–	1
Sawal, M.A.(OU)	–	1	2	1	2*	2	2.00	–	–	–
†Saxelby, M.(De)	–	1	2	–	17	23	11.50	–	–	–
Sayers, C.A.(CU)	–	6	8	2	46	71	11.83	–	–	4
†Schofield, C.P.(La/E)	–	17	22	2	70*	528	26.40	–	4	6
†Scott, D.A.(K)	–	3	3	2	4*	8	8.00	–	–	2
Scuderi, J.C.(La)	–	9	13	2	51	261	23.72	–	1	–
†Sexton, A.J.(H)	–	4	7	–	36	71	10.14	–	–	3
†Shah, K.Z.(De)	–	4	6	2	38*	102	25.50	–	–	–
Shah, O.A.(M)	2000	12	20	–	76	489	24.45	–	3	7
Shahid, N.(Sy)	1998	9	12	–	80	434	36.16	–	3	13
Shaw, A.D.(Gm)	1999	12	18	5	88*	462	35.53	–	3	29/4
†Sheikh, M.A.(Wa)	–	1	1	1	58*	58	–	–	1	–
Sheikh, S.M.(CU)	–	2	2	1	17	17	17.00	–	–	–
Sheriyar, A.(Wo)	1997	11	11	3	17	69	8.62	–	–	–
Shields, I.P.(Ire)	–	1	2	–	31	38	19.00	–	–	–
†Sidebottom, R.J.(Y)	2000	6	7	2	6*	15	3.00	–	–	2
Silverwood, C.E.W.(Y)	1996	9	11	1	48	173	17.30	–	–	1
Singh, A.(Wa)	–	5	7	–	79	156	22.28	–	1	1
†Smalley, R.G.(OU)	–	6	10	1	83	272	30.22	–	1	6/4
Smethurst, M.P.(La)	–	16	19	10	66	161	17.88	–	1	3
Smith, A.M.(Gs)	1995	9	10	6	14	54	13.50	–	–	1
Smith, B.F.(Le)	1995	17	23	2	111*	686	32.66	2	4	10
Smith, C.J.O.(Sc)	–	1	2	–	24	31	15.50	–	–	2

124

	Cap	M	I	NO	HS	Runs	Avge	100	50	Ct/St
Smith, E.T.(K)	–	11	18	–	175	415	23.05	1	–	7
Smith, N.M.K.(Wa)	1993	17	20	2	87	464	25.77	–	4	8
Smith, R.A.(H)	1985	17	29	–	61	595	20.51	–	3	3
†Smith, T.M.(De)	–	10	13	2	53*	152	13.81	–	1	4
Snape, J.N.(Gs/FCC)	1999	15	20	3	69	598	35.17	–	4	8
Solanki, V.S.(Wo)	1998	16	28	2	161*	1138	43.76	2	8	23
Speak, N.J.(Du)	1998	14	24	5	89*	552	29.05	–	4	3
Speight, M.P.(Du)	1998	11	18	1	55	354	20.82	–	1	29
Spendlove, B.L.(De)	–	1	1	–	0	0	0.00	–	–	2
Spiring, K.R.(Wo)	1997	3	4	1	38	96	32.00	–	–	1
Stelling, W.F.(Le)	–	1	–	–	–	–	–	–	–	–
Stemp, R.D.(Nt)	2000	11	11	5	11	45	7.50	–	–	7
Stephenson, J.P.(H)	1995	10	15	–	19	96	6.40	–	–	7
Stevens, D.I.(Le)	–	15	22	–	78	457	20.77	–	2	6
Stewart, A.J.(Sy/E)	1985	10	15	1	124*	451	32.21	2	–	24/1
Strang, B.C.(Z)	–	6	7	3	73	134	33.50	–	1	2
Strang, P.A.(Z)	–	3	2	–	36	48	24.00	–	–	1
†Strauss, A.J.(M)	–	17	28	2	111*	862	33.15	1	3	6
Streak, H.H.(Z)	–	5	5	1	71*	109	27.25	–	1	2
†Strong, M.R.(Nh)	–	4	7	2	27*	72	14.40	–	–	1
†Stubbings, S.D.(De)	–	18	32	4	135*	889	31.75	1	4	4
Styris, S.B.(NZA)	–	5	9	1	72	247	30.87	–	1	4
Such, P.M.(Ex)	1991	12	13	4	14	53	5.88	–	–	3
†Sulzberger, G.P.(NZA)	–	6	11	–	60	248	22.54	–	1	8
†Sutcliffe, I.J.(Le)	1997	12	17	1	53	319	19.93	–	2	11
Sutton, L.D.(De)	–	10	16	1	79	407	27.13	–	2	20/1
Swann, A.J.(Nh)	–	3	5	1	108	201	50.25	1	1	1
Swann, G.P.(Nh)	1999	16	24	–	72	597	24.87	–	3	8
Symington, M.J.(Du)	–	1	2	1	36	44	44.00	–	–	–
Taibu, T.(Z)	–	3	5	1	36	53	13.25	–	–	7
†Taylor, B.V.(Sx)	–	5	6	4	6	9	4.50	–	–	–
Taylor, C.G.(Gs/FCC)	–	12	22	3	104	492	25.89	1	–	8
†Taylor, J.P.(Nh)	1992	7	10	1	27	96	10.66	–	–	3
Tennant, A.M.(Sc)	–	1	1	–	5	5	5.00	–	–	–
†Thomas, I.J.(Gm)	–	3	5	1	82	177	44.25	–	1	3
†Thomas, S.D.(Gm)	1997	17	20	7	52	336	25.84	–	1	2
Thompson, D.J.(Ex)	–	2	1	–	15	15	15.00	–	–	–
†Thorpe, G.P.(Sy/E)	1991	11	16	–	115	376	23.50	1	1	9
Titchard, S.P.(De)	–	11	19	2	141*	530	31.17	1	3	–
Tolley, C.M.(Nt)	1997	6	9	1	60	223	27.87	–	2	2
Tournier, M.A.(BU)	–	1	–	–	–	–	–	–	–	–
Townsend, C.J.(MCC)	–	1	2	1	15*	18	18.00	–	–	1
Trego, P.D.(Sm)	–	7	8	1	62	134	19.14	–	1	3
Tremlett, C.T.(H)	–	1	2	–	17	33	16.50	–	–	–
†Trescothick, M.E.(Sm/E)	1999	12	19	2	105	738	43.41	1	5	11
Trott, B.J.(K)	–	2	2	2	0*	0	–	–	–	1
Tucker, J.P.(Sm)	–	1	1	–	14	14	14.00	–	–	1
Tudor, A.J.(Sy)	1999	14	16	6	64*	283	28.30	–	1	5
Tuffey, D.R.(NZA)	–	4	6	2	51	90	22.50	–	1	1
Tufnell, P.C.R.(M)	1990	16	21	9	19	100	8.33	–	–	4
Turner, R.J.(Sm)	1994	18	26	2	75	492	20.50	–	2	39
Udal, S.D.(H)	1992	12	21	3	85	346	19.22	–	1	8
†Van der Gucht, C.G.(H)	–	1	1	1	0*	0	–	–	–	–
Vaughan, M.P.(Y/E)	1995	13	21	1	155*	866	43.30	2	4	2
†Viljoen, D.P.(Z)	–	5	6	1	72*	155	31.00	–	1	3
Vonwiller, B.M.(OU)	–	2	2	1	1*	1	1.00	–	–	2
Wagh, M.A.(Wa)	2000	9	16	3	137	592	45.53	2	3	4

	Cap	M	I	NO	HS	Runs	Avge	100	50	Ct/St
Walker, B.G.K.(NZA)	–	4	5	1	22*	48	12.00	–	–	1
†Walker, M.J.(K/FCC)	2000	15	25	4	61	536	25.52	–	1	12
†Wallace, M.A.(Gm)	–	3	5	1	59*	116	29.00	–	1	10
Walsh, C.A.(WI)	–	6	9	3	7	26	4.33	–	–	–
†Ward, I.J.(Sy)	2000	16	25	3	158*	894	40.63	3	3	4
Ward, T.R.(Le)	–	7	10	1	39	110	12.22	–	–	8
Warne, S.K.(H)	2000	15	22	2	69	431	21.55	–	3	14
Warren, C.C.M.(OU)	–	3	5	1	21	41	10.25	–	–	1
Warren, R.J.(Nh)	1995	13	13	1	151	417	34.75	1	2	3
Watkin, S.L.(Gm)	1989	13	13	6	51	125	17.85	–	1	1
Weekes, L.C.(Y)	–	1	2	–	10	20	10.00	–	–	–
†Weekes, P.N.(M)	1993	8	13	1	39	244	20.33	–	–	8
Weenink, S.W.(OU)	–	6	9	2	72*	124	17.71	–	1	4
Welch, G.(Wa)	1997	7	8	1	55	116	16.57	–	1	1
Wells, A.P.(K)	1997	12	19	2	60*	297	17.47	–	2	3
Wells, V.J.(Le)	1994	15	19	–	98	549	28.89	–	4	8
Welton, G.E.(Nt)	–	13	23	2	200*	674	32.09	1	3	8
Weston, R.M.S.(M)	–	6	10	1	39	170	18.88	–	–	3
†Weston, W.P.C.(Wo)	1995	10	19	2	58*	269	15.82	–	2	1
Wharf, A.G.(Gm)	2000	10	15	2	101*	285	21.92	2	–	5
†Wharton, L.J.(De)	–	7	9	4	7	15	3.00	–	–	2
Whiley, M.J.A.(Nt)	–	1	2	–	0	0	0.00	–	–	2
White, C.(Y/E)	1993	7	9	1	27	100	12.50	–	–	1
White, G.W.(H)	1998	18	32	4	96	797	28.46	–	5	14
White, R.A.(Nh)	–	1	2	–	20	31	15.50	–	–	2
Whittall, G.J.(Z)	–	7	11	1	89	304	30.40	–	2	2
Widdup, S.(Y)	–	9	14	1	44	201	15.46	–	–	6
†Williams, R.C.J.(Gs)	1996	2	3	1	43	76	38.00	–	–	11/1
Williamson, D.(Le)	–	3	5	3	47	116	58.00	–	–	–
Williamson, J.G.(Sc)	–	1	2	–	41	48	24.00	–	–	1
Wilson, E.J.(Wo)	–	17	31	2	104*	779	26.86	2	4	9
Wilton, N.J.(Sx)	–	8	11	2	46	150	16.66	–	–	19
Windows, M.G.N.(Gs/FCC)	1998	19	31	0	166	1042	37.21	2	6	5
Wishart, C.B.(Z)	–	3	5	–	116	198	39.60	1	–	–
Wood, J.(Du)	1998	10	15	–	44	181	12.06	–	–	2
Wood, M.J.(Y)	–	11	17	3	100*	256	18.28	1	–	5
†Wood, N.T.(La)	–	1	1	–	27	27	27.00	–	–	–
†Wrigglesworth, I.A.(MCC)	–	1	2	–	85	94	47.00	–	1	2
Wright, C.M.(Sc)	–	1	2	1	40	55	55.00	–	–	–
†Yardy, M.H.(Sx)	–	4	8	1	25	64	9.14	–	–	3
Yates, G.(La)	1994	3	3	–	7	10	3.33	–	–	3

BOWLING

See BATTING and FIELDING section for details of caps and teams

	Cat	O	M	R	W	Avge	Best	5wI	10wM
Adams, C.J.	RM/OB	27	3	110	2	55.00	1- 17	–	–
Adams, J.C.	SLA	90	26	212	5	42.40	2- 5	–	–
Adams, K.	LMF	22	4	58	2	29.00	2- 58	–	–
Afzaal, U.	SLA	149.2	46	379	9	42.11	3- 26	–	–
Aldred, P.	RM	203.3	44	624	17	36.70	4- 97	–	–
Ali, Kabir	RMF	219	41	811	20	40.55	4-114	–	–
Ali, U.	LB	3	0	9	0			–	–
Alleyne, M.W.	RM	254.5	72	684	25	27.36	6- 49	1	–
Altree, D.A.	LMF	20.1	1	77	0			–	–
Ambrose, C.E.L.	RFM	207.1	65	403	18	22.38	4- 30	–	–
Amin, R.M.	SLA	21	4	67	0			–	–

	Cat	O	M	R	W	Avge	Best	5wI	10wM
Anderson, R.S.G.	RMF	234.4	56	729	24	30.37	6- 34	3	1
Asif Mujtaba	SLA	38.4	16	67	5	13.40	3- 48	–	–
Asim Butt	LMF	42.2	14	88	6	14.66	3- 25	–	–
Austin, I.D.	RM	24	14	32	2	16.00	2- 23	–	–
Averis, J.M.M.	RMF	145	36	466	7	66.57	2- 40	–	–
Aymes, A.N.	(WK)	1	0	13	1	13.00	1- 13	–	–
Bailey, R.J.	OB	46	10	109	2	54.50	1- 7	–	–
Ball, M.C.J.	OB	243.1	58	658	15	43.86	3- 31	–	–
Bates, J.J.	OB	126	35	374	5	74.80	2- 85	–	–
Batt, C.J.	LMF	41	11	146	4	36.50	2- 49	–	–
Batty, J.N.	(WK)	6	0	21	1	21.00	1- 21	–	–
Bevan, M.M.	SLC	103.4	11	400	5	80.00	3- 74	–	–
Betts, M.M.	RFM	354	91	832	44	18.90	7- 30	1	1
Bicknell, D.J.	SLA	1	1	0	0				
Bicknell, M.P.	RFM	413.2	115	1052	60	17.53	9- 47	3	1
Bishop, I.E.	RMF	29	8	98	2	49.00	1- 24	–	–
Blackwell, I.D.	SLA	411.3	123	1010	23	43.91	4- 18	–	–
Blain, J.A.R.	RMF	22	3	74	1	74.00	1- 37	–	–
Bloomfield, T.F.	RMF	222.3	35	834	23	36.26	4- 46	–	–
Boswell, S.A.J.	RFM	93.4	21	278	9	30.88	3- 39	–	–
Bowen, M.N	RM	68	14	208	4	52.00	2- 47	–	–
Brent, G.B.	RM	36.3	14	97	2	48.50	2- 71	–	–
Bressington, A.N.	RFM	20	6	49	5	9.80	4- 36	–	–
Brinkley, J.E.	RFM	33.5	13	71	4	17.75	3- 31	–	–
Brooker, J.A.D.	LB	6	0	38	0				
Brown, A.D.	LB	28	9	70	1	70.00	1- 56	–	–
Brown, D.R.	RFM	268.2	49	917	24	38.20	5- 87	1	–
Brown, J.F.	OB	517.5	142	1258	61	20.62	7- 78	4	2
Brown, S.J.E.	LFM	442.2	110	1208	56	21.57	7- 51	4	–
Bulbeck, M.P.L.	LMF	37	9	109	7	15.57	3- 23	–	–
Burns, M.	RM	132.2	33	387	14	27.64	3- 11	–	–
Butcher, G.P.	RM	21.3	4	65	5	13.00	5- 18	1	–
Butcher, M.A.	RM	27	7	86	5	17.20	5- 86	1	–
Byas, D.	RM	4.2	0	8	0				
Caddick, A.R.	RFM	329.4	98	848	55	15.41	7- 64	5	2
Callaghan, D.J.	RM	10	6	19	1	19.00	1- 19	–	–
Campbell, A.D.R.	LB	5	2	8	0				
Campbell, S.L.	RM	17	5	50	0				
Canning, T.K.	RFM	31	6	102	3	34.00	2- 19	–	–
Carroll, R.W.S.	LB	7	0	52	0				
Cassar, M.E.	RFM	212.2	54	702	30	23.40	6- 76	1	–
Catterall, D.N.	RMF	25.2	5	92	6	15.33	4- 50	–	–
Cawdron, M.J.	RMF	199.5	64	534	25	21.36	6- 25	2	1
Chapple, G.	RFM	431.5	101	1175	49	23.97	6- 42	1	–
Chilton, M.J.	RM	5	1	20	0				
Collingwood, P.D.	RMF	214.2	61	474	12	39.50	2- 21	–	–
Collymore, C.D.	RMF	126.4	40	369	15	24.60	3- 18	–	–
Cook, J.W.	RM	1	0	7	0				
Cook, S.J.	RM	137	41	335	11	30.45	4- 13	–	–
Cork, D.G.	RFM	356.4	94	886	42	21.09	6- 41	1	–
Cosker, D.A.	SLA	429.5	141	944	29	32.55	4- 82	–	–
Cotterell, T.P.	SLA	202	48	582	8	72.75	2- 69	–	–
Cottey, P.A.	OB	1	1	0	0				
Cousins, D.M.	RMF	510.4	142	1318	67	19.67	5-123	1	–
Cowan, A.P.	RFM	398.5	98	1175	47	25.00	5- 54	2	–
Cox, J.	OB	14	3	35	0				
Craven, V.J.	RM	8	1	15	0				

127

	Cat	O	M	R	W	Avge	Best	5wI	10wM
Crawley, J.P.	RM	1	0	19	0			–	–
Croft, R.D.B.	OB	586.1	153	1432	40	35.80	5- 26	2	–
Crowe, C.D.	OB	185.3	50	453	15	30.20	4- 55	–	–
Dagnall, C.E.	RM	54.4	16	181	5	36.20	2- 57	–	–
Dakin, J.M.	RM	211.4	39	641	14	45.78	2- 20	–	–
Dale, A.	RMF	240.4	54	645	23	28.04	5- 25	2	–
Daley, J.A.	RM	7	0	20	0			–	–
Danson, A.R.	RM	76	21	218	5	43.60	3- 20	–	–
Davies, M.K.	SLA	133	45	339	9	37.66	3- 25	–	–
Davis, M.J.G.	OB	31	16	44	1	44.00	1- 39	–	–
Dawson, R.K.J.	OB	34	7	115	1	115.00	1-115	–	–
Dean, K.J.	LMF	246	57	785	44	17.84	8- 52	4	–
De Bruyn, Z.	RFM	18	3	75	0			–	–
DeFreitas, P.A.J.	RFM	459.2	122	1105	33	33.48	4- 41	–	–
Di Venuto, M.J.	RM/LB	8.3	3	19	0			–	–
Donald, A.A.	RF	205.3	60	530	20	26.50	4- 59	–	–
Dowman, M.P.	RMF	53	11	155	4	38.75	2- 46	–	–
Dravid, R.	OB	53.5	11	128	4	32.00	2- 16	–	–
Driver, R.C.	RM	11.2	2	44	2	22.00	1- 13	–	–
Dutch, K.P.	OB	143.4	45	366	17	21.52	6- 62	1	–
Dwyer, M.D.	SLA	30	7	64	5	12.80	3- 39	–	–
Ealham, M.A.	RMF	271.5	67	703	24	29.29	5- 35	1	–
Elliott, M.T.G.	LM/SLC	20	5	43	0			–	–
Elstub, C.J.	RMF	70.1	13	175	8	21.87	3- 37	–	–
Fairbrother, N.H.	LM	6.2	2	11	1	11.00	1- 5	–	–
Fellows, G.M.	RM	139	32	403	9	44.77	2- 27	–	–
Fisher, I.D.	SLA	211.1	48	588	16	36.75	3- 40	–	–
Fleming, M.V.	RM	278.1	72	753	28	26.89	4- 77	–	–
Flintoff, A.	RFM	135.2	49	290	15	19.33	4- 18	–	–
Flower, G.W.	SLA	41	10	93	1	93.00	1- 62	–	–
Francis, S.R.G.	RMF	170.2	37	602	15	40.13	4- 95	–	–
Franklin, G.D.	OB	10	0	78	0			–	–
Franks, P.J.	RMF	393.4	81	1247	42	29.69	7- 56	2	–
Fraser, A.R.C.	RMF	474.3	150	1111	48	23.14	6- 64	1	–
Fulton, D.P.	SLA	17	5	45	0			–	–
Gallian, J.E.R.	RM	92	24	278	5	55.60	2- 42	–	–
Ganguly, S.C.	RM	83.4	11	311	4	77.75	2- 39	–	–
Gannon, B.W.	RMF	201.5	38	732	29	25.24	5- 58	1	–
Garland, R.	RM	68.3	8	325	7	46.42	2- 73	–	–
Gayle, C.H.	OB	61	8	188	5	37.60	4- 86	–	–
Giddins, E.S.H.	RFM	285.5	92	813	29	28.03	5- 15	1	–
Giles, A.F.	SLA	526.4	163	1200	52	23.07	8- 90	5	2
Gillespie, M.A.	LBG	24.2	5	75	4	18.75	2- 34	–	–
Gofton, A.F.	RM	88.2	7	386	1	386.00	1- 61	–	–
Golding, J.M.	RMF	17	7	38	1	38.00	1- 38	–	–
Goodwin, M.W.	RM/LB	4	1	19	0			–	–
Gough, D.	RF	324.1	62	949	50	18.98	6- 63	2	–
Gough, M.A.	OB	76.1	14	280	5	56.00	4-106	–	–
Grayson, A.P.	SLA	178	39	443	10	44.30	3- 55	–	–
Green, R.J.	RM	48	9	175	1	175.00	1- 68	–	–
Greenidge, C.G.	RFM	35	13	106	1	106.00	1- 35	–	–
Griffith, A.F.G.	RM	1	0	7	0			–	–
Griffiths, P.	RMF	21	3	65	1	65.00	1- 65	–	–
Gripper, T.R.	OB	7	1	36	0			–	–
Grove, J.O.	RMF	192.5	27	733	21	34.90	5- 90	1	–
Guy, S.M.	(WK)	4	1	8	0			–	–
Hamilton, G.M.	RFM	313.4	80	866	40	21.65	5- 22	1	–

128

	Cat	O	M	R	W	Avge	Best	5wI	10wM
Hamilton, L.J.	LFM	94	22	287	14	20.50	5- 55	1	–
Hancock, T.H.C.	RM	83	23	209	8	26.12	3- 24	–	–
Hardinges, M.A.	RMF	50	17	99	3	33.00	2- 16	–	–
Harmison, S.J.	RF	304.1	69	822	26	31.61	4- 74	–	–
Harris, A.J.	RM	384.3	62	1358	44	30.86	6-110	4	–
Harrison, D.S.	RFM	10	2	45	0				
Hartley, P.J.	RMF	204.2	33	697	15	46.46	3- 91	–	–
Harvey, I.J.	RM	254.2	79	658	40	16.45	6- 19	3	1
Hayden, M.L.	RM	15	2	56	1	56.00	1- 8	–	–
Hemp, D.L.	RM	20	3	80	2	40.00	2- 29	–	–
Hewson, D.R.	RM	5	1	30	0				
Hick, G.A.	OB	45	6	135	1	135.00	1- 13	–	–
Hicks, T.C.	OB	147	29	570	14	40.71	5- 54	1	–
Hinds, W.W.	RM	23.5	5	62	3	20.66	3- 32	–	–
Hockley, J.B.	OB	3	3	0	0				
Hoggard, M.J.	RFM	501.4	134	1323	50	26.46	5- 50	2	–
Hollioake, A.J.	RMF	42.2	12	119	3	39.66	1- 8	–	–
Hollioake, B.C.	RFM	117.5	25	407	11	37.00	4- 41	–	–
Holloway, P.C.L.	RM	2	0	4	0				
House, W.J.	RM	33	7	104	1	104.00	1- 34	–	–
Howitt, R.W.J.	RMF	60	8	254	4	63.50	2- 54	–	–
Hughes, Q.J.	OB	20	2	97	1	97.00	1- 90	–	–
Hughes, T.R.	RMF	121	30	408	9	45.33	3- 55	–	–
Hunter, I.D.	RMF	69.3	12	228	6	38.00	4- 73	–	–
Hutchison, P.M.	LFM	129.3	32	420	16	26.25	3- 42	–	–
Hutton, B.L.	RMF	66.2	17	217	5	43.40	2- 9	–	–
Illingworth, R.K.	SLA	221.5	72	483	13	37.15	3- 34	–	–
Ilott, M.C.	LFM	283.2	85	724	26	27.84	3- 37	–	–
Innes, K.J.	RM	22.1	4	82	6	13.66	3- 23	–	–
Irani, R.C.	RMF	407.3	120	1008	42	24.00	5- 79	1	–
Janmohamed, A.M.T.	RM	6	0	29	0				
Jarvis, P.W.	RFM	37.3	7	141	7	20.14	4- 21	–	–
Johnson, N.C.	RFM	158.5	44	500	13	38.46	4- 28	–	–
Johnson, R.L.	RMF	473	129	1429	50	28.58	6- 71	2	–
Jones, P.S.	RMF	403.4	88	1294	40	32.35	5- 41	1	–
Jones, S.P.	RF	104	12	374	10	37.40	4- 47	–	–
Joseph, R.H.	RFM	25	8	56	1	56.00	1- 23	–	–
Joyce, E.C.	RM	5	1	24	0				
Katich, S.M.	SLC	117.4	14	342	5	68.40	1- 10	–	–
Keedy, G.	SLA	478	142	1005	37	27.16	6- 56	1	1
Kendall, W.S.	RM	1	0	1	0				
Kerr, J.I.D.	RMF	62	13	248	9	27.55	4- 18	–	–
Key, R.W.T.	RM/OB	9.4	1	34	0				
Khan, S.H.	RM	135	25	417	6	69.50	2- 34	–	–
Khan, W.G.	LB	10	0	31	0				
Khan, Z.M.	RFM	20	5	45	1	45.00	1- 32	–	–
Killeen, N.	RFM	288.3	84	697	22	31.68	3- 14	–	–
King, R.D.	RF	195.1	45	618	25	24.72	3- 28	–	–
Kirtley, R.J.	RFM	521.4	138	1559	63	24.74	6- 41	4	–
Kruis, G.J.	RFM	52	13	149	7	21.28	5-100	1	–
Kumble, A.	LBG	498.3	139	1133	45	25.17	6- 44	2	1
Lacey, S.J.	OB	241.5	68	626	16	39.12	4- 84	–	–
Lambert, G.A.	RMF	46	7	133	4	33.25	2- 62	–	–
Lampitt, S.R.	RMF	412.5	108	1173	56	20.94	7- 45	2	–
Langer, J.L.	RM	6	1	35	1	35.00	1- 29	–	–
Laraman, A.W.	RFM	21	4	55	4	13.75	4- 33	–	–
Law, D.R.	RFM	291.4	50	1042	30	34.73	5- 78	1	–

	Cat	O	M	R	W	Avge	Best	5wI	10wM
Law, S.G.	RM/LB	1	0	11	0			–	–
Leatherdale, D.A.	RM	154	34	508	19	26.73	3- 17	–	–
Lehmann, D.S.	SLA	112	18	310	8	38.75	2- 9	–	–
Lewis, C.C.	RFM	98.1	12	302	7	43.14	2- 33	–	–
Lewis, J.	RMF	562.3	169	1506	72	20.91	8- 95	4	–
Lewry, J.D.	LFM	524.4	137	1569	53	29.60	6- 66	3	–
Liptrot, C.G.	RFM	78	11	324	7	46.28	6- 44	1	–
Logan, R.J.	RMF	133.1	33	453	11	41.18	5- 61	1	–
Lowe, J.P.	RM	79	30	181	1	181.00	1- 21	–	–
Lucas, D.S.	LFM	271.5	57	888	27	32.88	4- 61	–	–
Lungley, T.	RMF	23.2	11	41	6	6.83	3- 10	–	–
McCague, M.J.	RFM	129.4	20	412	14	29.42	5- 52	1	–
McCallan, W.K.	OB	34	6	93	1	93.00	1- 54	–	–
McCoubrey, A.G.A.M.	RFM	18	2	59	1	59.00	1- 43	–	–
McGarry, A.C.	RFM	57	10	227	6	37.83	3- 29	–	–
McGrath, G.D.	RFM	415.4	132	1057	80	13.21	8- 41	6	3
McLean, N.A.M.	RFM	271.3	68	803	35	22.94	5- 30	2	–
Maddy, D.L.	RM/OB	85	17	277	7	39.57	2- 10	–	–
Maiden, G.I.	OB	26	4	78	3	26.00	2- 50	–	–
Malcolm, D.E.	RF	184.1	46	541	19	28.47	5- 45	1	–
Martin, B.P.	SLA	133	35	378	10	37.80	3- 43	–	–
Martin, C.S.	RFM	118	38	321	5	64.20	2- 28	–	–
Martin, P.J.	RFM	236.2	83	464	30	15.46	7- 67	3	–
Martin-Jenkins, R.S.C.	RFM	360.1	75	1202	33	36.42	5- 94	1	–
Mascarenhas, A.D.	RMF	313.5	88	796	28	28.42	4- 52	–	–
Mason, T.J.	OB	239.3	55	710	14	50.71	3- 38	–	–
Masters, D.D.	RMF	435.2	104	1161	48	24.18	6- 27	3	–
Mather, D.P.	LM	54.2	11	202	3	67.33	2- 73	–	–
Maynard, M.P.	RM	15.3	5	32	0			–	–
Mbangwa, M.	RMF	211.5	86	428	30	14.26	6- 14	2	1
Middlebrook, J.D.	OB	281.1	68	771	31	24.87	6- 82	1	1
Millar, N.	RM	3	0	17	0			–	–
Millns, D.J.	RF	226.1	42	880	30	29.33	5- 58	1	–
Mooney, P.J.K.	RM	6	0	26	1	26.00	1- 26	–	–
Morris, A.C.	RMF	183.1	43	562	18	31.22	3- 48	–	–
Morris, J.E.	RM	2.4	0	26	1	26.00	1- 26	–	–
Mullally, A.D.	LFM	343.5	105	832	49	16.97	9- 93	5	1
Munton, T.A.	RMF	439.1	122	1093	35	31.22	7- 34	2	–
Murphy, B.A.	LB	49.2	13	112	3	37.33	1- 19	–	–
Murtagh, T.J.	RFM	2	0	6	1	6.00	1- 6	–	–
Nagamootoo, M.V.	LB	328.4	93	801	21	38.14	4- 12	–	–
Napier, G.R.	RM	8	2	28	0			–	–
Neely, G.J.	RMF	8.2	1	29	2	14.50	2- 29	–	–
Newell, K.	RM	51	23	100	5	20.00	2- 18	–	–
Nixon, P.A.	(WK)	3	1	10	0			–	–
Nkala, M.	RFM	91	19	308	9	34.22	3- 82	–	–
Olonga, H.K.	RFM	47.3	9	164	2	82.00	2- 73	–	–
Oram, J.D.P.	RM	52	12	123	2	61.50	1- 26	–	–
Ormond, J.	RFM	380.3	75	1116	44	25.36	6- 50	3	–
Ostler, D.P.	RM	5	0	46	1	46.00	1- 46	–	–
Parkin, O.T.	RFM	108	30	291	17	17.11	4- 14	–	–
Parsons, K.A.	RM	150.4	41	443	11	40.27	5- 13	1	–
Patel, M.M.	SLA	570.3	202	1157	46	25.15	6- 77	2	–
Peirce, M.T.E.	SLA	11	3	37	1	37.00	1- 37	–	–
Penberthy, A.L.	RM	131	30	358	16	22.37	5- 54	1	–
Phillips, N.C.	OB	156.5	36	415	7	59.28	3- 53	–	–
Pierson, A.R.K.	OB	129	37	313	7	44.71	3- 41	–	–

	Cat	O	M	R	W	Avge	Best	5wI	10wM
Pimlott, C.R.	RFM	93	31	303	12	25.25	3- 42	–	–
Piper, J.W.S.	LB	7	1	30	2	15.00	2- 30	–	–
Pollard, P.R.	RM	0.1	0	4	0				
Porter, J.J.	SLA	6	0	50	0				
Powell, M.J.(Wa)	RM	24	6	80	2	40.00	1- 0	–	–
Pryke, D.J.	RFM	10	0	32	3	10.66	3- 32	–	–
Pyemont, J.P.	OB	54.1	18	141	1	141.00	1- 26	–	–
Ramprakash, M.R.	RM	68	18	148	1	148.00	1- 11	–	–
Ramsden, G.	RMF	12	1	68	1	68.00	1- 32	–	–
Randall, S.J.	OB	22	2	109	1	109.00	1-109	–	–
Rashid, U.B.A.	SLA	343.5	84	994	23	43.21	5-103	1	–
Ratcliffe, J.D.	RM	9.5	2	46	1	46.00	1- 21	–	–
Rawnsley, M.J.	SLA	204	55	573	9	63.66	5-125	1	–
Redmond, J.	LB	7	1	32	0				
Reiffel, P.R.	RFM	233.3	60	586	21	27.90	5- 62	1	–
Renshaw, S.J.	RMF	82.1	22	219	7	31.28	3- 23	–	–
Richardson, A.	RMF	368.2	96	1040	27	38.51	4- 69	–	–
Robinson, D.D.J.	RMF	0.3	0	8	0				
Robinson, M.A.	RFM	228	77	537	16	33.56	3- 88	–	–
Rose, F.A.	RF	153	32	527	17	31.00	4- 63	–	–
Rose, G.D.	RM	332.3	79	908	29	31.31	5- 74	1	–
Ross, J.S.	LMF	39	11	108	1	108.00	1- 46	–	–
Saggers, M.J.	RMF	425.2	98	1148	57	20.14	7- 79	2	–
Salisbury, I.D.K.	LBG	380.3	101	984	52	18.92	8- 60	3	2
Saqlain Mushtaq	OB	451.2	127	1016	66	15.39	7- 11	6	2
Sarwan, R.R.	LB	6	5	1	1	1.00	1- 0	–	–
Savident, L.	RM	8	0	39	0				
Sawal, M.A.	RMF	28	9	96	2	48.00	2- 96	–	–
Schofield, C.P.	LB	374	80	1102	39	28.25	5- 48	1	–
Scott, D.A.	OB	57	18	157	4	39.25	2- 40	–	–
Scuderi, J.C.	RMF	120	28	333	14	23.78	4- 58	–	–
Shah, K.Z.	LMF	56	8	260	4	65.00	2- 24	–	–
Shah, O.A.	OB	35	8	126	4	31.50	1- 11	–	–
Shahid, N.	LB	1	0	6	0				
Sheikh, M.A.	RM	23	7	68	1	68.00	1- 36	–	–
Sheikh, S.M.	RMF	22	3	99	0				
Sheriyar, A.	LFM	278.2	59	1048	28	37.42	4- 51	–	–
Sidebottom, R.J.	LFM	134.2	46	300	24	12.50	6- 16	4	1
Silverwood, C.E.W.	RFM	292.3	80	762	26	29.30	4- 60	–	–
Singh, A.	OB	6.5	0	66	0				
Smethurst, M.P.	RM	378.1	90	1161	56	20.73	7- 37	3	–
Smith, A.M.	LMF	250.4	70	623	30	20.76	5- 52	1	–
Smith, B.F.	RM	3	1	6	0				
Smith, E.T.	RM	6	0	20	0				
Smith, N.M.K.	OB	310.4	70	875	28	31.25	5- 66	1	–
Smith, R.A.	LB	2	0	26	0				
Smith, T.M.	RFM	149	24	571	9	63.44	3- 51	–	–
Snape, J.N.	OB	113.3	44	239	10	23.90	3- 70	–	–
Solanki, V.S.	OB	82.3	9	270	9	30.00	3- 80	–	–
Stelling, W.F.	RFM	25	8	49	5	9.80	5- 49	1	–
Stemp, R.D.	SLA	398.2	140	946	33	28.66	5-123	1	–
Stephenson, J.P.	RM	172.1	33	566	13	43.53	4- 68	–	–
Stevens, D.I.	RM	6	2	14	0				
Strang, B.C.	LM	187.3	59	452	18	25.11	5- 68	1	–
Strang, P.A.	LBG	67	17	184	5	36.80	1- 11	–	–
Strauss, A.J.	LM	1	0	13	0				
Streak, H.H.	RFM	156.1	50	346	18	19.22	6- 87	2	–

	Cat	O	M	R	W	Avge	Best	5wI	10wM
Strong, M.R.	RMF	84.2	15	269	12	22.41	4- 46	–	–
Styris, S.B.	RMF	115.4	28	325	12	27.08	3- 45	–	–
Such, P.M.	OB	422.4	101	1055	36	29.30	7-167	3	1
Sulzberger, G.P.	OB	189.3	60	458	28	16.35	5- 55	1	–
Sutcliffe, I.J.	OB	1.3	0	12	0				
Swann, A.J.	RM/OB	28	13	42	3	14.00	2- 30	–	–
Swann, G.P.	OB	467.3	92	1366	41	33.31	6-118	2	–
Symington, M.J.	RM	17	2	67	1	67.00	1- 61	–	–
Taylor, B.V.	RMF	118	28	405	6	67.50	3- 27	–	–
Taylor, C.G.	OB	27.3	5	136	3	45.33	3-126	–	–
Taylor, J.P.	LFM	212.3	50	540	24	22.50	6- 27	1	1
Tennant, A.M.	SLA	34	17	65	4	16.25	3- 20	–	–
Thomas, S.D.	RFM	488	93	1612	56	28.78	5- 43	2	–
Thompson, D.J.	RFM	36.3	12	106	2	53.00	2- 76	–	–
Titchard, S.P.	RM	5	2	5	0				
Tolley, C.M.	LMF	52	22	107	4	26.75	3- 22	–	–
Tournier, M.A.	RFM	34	6	117	3	39.00	3-117	–	–
Trego, P.D.	RM	165.1	34	603	18	33.50	4- 84	–	–
Tremlett, C.T.	RMF	37	14	91	6	15.16	4- 16	–	–
Trescothick, M.E.	RM	62	13	207	3	69.00	1- 18	–	–
Trott, B.J.	RFM	42	9	133	4	33.25	2- 44	–	–
Tucker, J.P.	RMF	11	3	47	1	47.00	1- 28	–	–
Tudor, A.J.	RF	304.3	71	1071	47	22.78	7- 48	3	–
Tuffey, D.R.	RFM	116	23	373	16	23.31	5- 74	1	–
Tufnell, P.C.R.	SLA	738.3	255	1500	65	23.07	6- 48	3	–
Udal, S.D.	OB	350.3	104	818	30	27.26	5- 58	1	–
Van der Gucht, C.G.	SLA	22	7	75	3	25.00	3- 75	–	–
Vaughan, M.P.	OB	59.5	15	152	6	25.33	2- 32	–	–
Viljoen, D.P.	SLA	66	17	228	5	45.60	2- 33	–	–
Vonwiller, B.M.	RMF	30	4	137	3	45.66	2- 59	–	–
Wagh, M.A.	OB	25	9	55	0				
Walker, B.G.K.	LB	97.2	34	222	8	27.75	4- 32	–	–
Walker, M.J.	RM	74	12	187	6	31.16	1- 3	–	–
Walsh, C.A.	RFM	242.2	106	457	40	11.42	6- 74	3	1
Ward, I.J.	RM	5	2	10	0				
Warne, S.K.	LBG	639.4	183	1620	70	23.14	6- 34	5	–
Watkin, S.L.	RMF	389.4	108	1067	48	22.22	6- 26	2	–
Weekes, L.C.	RFM	23	10	56	6	9.33	6- 56	1	–
Weekes, P.N.	OB	86.3	20	242	7	34.57	2- 32	–	–
Weenink, S.W	OB	127	13	480	6	80.00	3-121	–	–
Welch, G.	RM	156	32	564	3	188.00	1- 56	–	–
Wells, V.J.	RMF	222.3	48	648	23	28.17	4- 54	–	–
Welton, G.E.	OB	1	0	1	0				
Wharf, A.G.	RMF	256.3	51	940	37	25.40	5- 68	1	–
Wharton, L.J.	SLA	164	42	464	12	38.66	5- 96	1	–
Whiley, M.J.A.	LMF	13.3	2	76	0				
White, C.	RFM	157.3	32	430	25	17.20	5- 32	2	–
White, G.W.	LB	13.1	1	58	2	29.00	2- 2	–	–
Whittall, G.J.	RMF	106	31	290	16	18.12	3- 14	–	–
Widdup, S.	OB	2.3	0	22	1	22.00	1- 22	–	–
Williamson, D.	RM	51	7	178	5	35.60	3- 65	–	–
Williamson, J.G.	RM	9	1	26	0				
Wood, J.	RFM	319.4	66	918	33	27.81	5- 36	3	–
Wrigglesworth, I.A.	RM	24	8	80	1	80.00	1- 31	–	–
Wright, C.M.	RFM	12	2	31	0				
Yardy, M.H.	LM	29	7	84	0				
Yates, G.	OB	85.4	28	192	9	21.33	4- 91	–	–

132

COUNTY CHAMPIONSHIP 2000
PPP HEALTHCARE FINAL TABLES

DIVISION 1

		P	W	L	D	Bonus Points Bat	Bonus Points Bowl	Total Points
1	SURREY (1)	16	9	2	5	44	41	213
2	Lancashire (2)	16	7	1	8	35	42	193
3	Yorkshire (6)	16	7	2	7	36	48	188†
4	Leicestershire (3)	16	4	3	9	42	39	165
5	Somerset (4)	16	2	4	10	41	40	145
6	Kent (5)	16	4	4	8	18	42	140
7	Hampshire (7)	16	3	9	4	20	48	112†
8	Durham (8)	16	2	9	5	27	41	112
9	Derbyshire (9)	16	2	6	8	19	44	111†

DIVISION 2

		P	W	L	D	Bonus Points Bat	Bonus Points Bowl	Total Points
1	NORTHAMPTONSHIRE (13)	16	7	4	5	39	45	188
2	Essex (12)	16	5	2	9	28	41	165
3	Glamorgan (14)	16	5	3	8	27	41	160
4	Gloucestershire (18)	16	6	4	6	20	42	158
5	Worcestershire (15)	16	5	5	6	25	42	151
6	Warwickshire (10)	16	2	3	11	47	35	150
7	Nottinghamshire (17)	16	2	4	10	41	43	148
8	Middlesex (16)	16	2	6	8	36	46	138
9	Sussex (11)	16	3	6	7	31	39	134

1999 (single Division) final positions are shown in brackets. † Includes deduction of 8 pitch penalty points.

SCORING OF POINTS 2000

(a) For a win, 12 points, plus any points scored in the first innings.

(b) In a tie, each side to score six points, plus any points scored in the first innings.

(c) In a drawn match, each side to score four points, plus any points scored in the first innings (see also paragraph (f) below).

(d) If the scores are equal in a drawn match, the side batting in the fourth innings to score six points plus any points scored in the first innings, and the opposing side to score four points plus any points scored in the first innings.

(e) **First Innings Points** (awarded only for performances **in the first 130 overs** of each first innings and retained whatever the result of the match)
  - A maximum of five batting points to be available as under:-
    200 to 249 runs – 1 point; 250 to 299 runs – 2 points; 300 to 349 runs – 3 points; 350 to 399 runs – 4 points; 400 runs or over – 5 points.
  - A maximum of three bowling points to be available as under:-
    3 to 5 wickets taken – 1 point; 6 to 8 wickets taken – 2 points; 9 to 10 wickets taken – 3 points.

(f) If play starts when less than eight hours playing time remains (in which event a one innings match shall be played as provided for in First Class Playing Condition 18), no first innings points shall be scored. The side winning on the one innings to score 12 points. In a tie, each side to score six points. In a drawn match, each side to score four points. If the scores are equal in a drawn match, the side batting in the second innings to score six points and the opposing side to score four points.

(g) If a match is abandoned without a ball being bowled, each side to score four points.

(h) The side which has the highest aggregate of points gained at the end of the season shall be the Champion County of their respective Division. Should any sides in the Championship table be equal on points, the following tie-breakers will be applied in the order stated: most wins, least losses, team achieving most points in contests between teams level on points, most wickets taken, most runs scored. At the end of the season, the top three teams from the Second Division will be promoted and the bottom three teams from the First Division will be relegated.

COUNTY CHAMPIONS

The English County Championship was not officially constituted until December 1889. Prior to that date there was no generally accepted method of awarding the title; although the 'least matches lost' method existed, it was not consistently applied. Rules governing playing qualifications were not agreed until 1873, and the first unofficial points system was not introduced until 1888.

Research has produced a list of champions dating back to 1826, but at least seven different versions exist for the period from 1864 to 1889 (see *The Wisden Book of Cricket Records*). Only from 1890 can any authorised list of county champions commence.

That first official Championship was contested between eight counties: Gloucestershire, Kent, Lancashire, Middlesex, Nottinghamshire, Surrey, Sussex and Yorkshire. The remaining counties were admitted in the following seasons: 1891 – Somerset, 1895 – Derbyshire, Essex, Hampshire, Leicestershire and Warwickshire, 1899 – Worcestershire, 1905 – Northamptonshire, 1921 – Glamorgan, and 1992 – Durham.

The Championship pennant was introduced by the 1951 champions, Warwickshire, and the Lord's Taverners' Trophy was first presented in 1973. The first sponsors, Schweppes (1977 to 1983), were succeeded by Britannic Assurance (1984 to 1998) and by PPP Healthcare (1999-2000).

1890 Surrey	1929 Nottinghamshire	1968 Yorkshire
1891 Surrey	1930 Lancashire	1969 Glamorgan
1892 Surrey	1931 Yorkshire	1970 Kent
1893 Yorkshire	1932 Yorkshire	1971 Surrey
1894 Surrey	1933 Yorkshire	1972 Warwickshire
1895 Surrey	1934 Lancashire	1973 Hampshire
1896 Yorkshire	1935 Yorkshire	1974 Worcestershire
1897 Lancashire	1936 Derbyshire	1975 Leicestershire
1898 Yorkshire	1937 Yorkshire	1976 Middlesex
1899 Surrey	1938 Yorkshire	1977 { Kent
1900 Yorkshire	1939 Yorkshire	{ Middlesex
1901 Yorkshire	1946 Yorkshire	1978 Kent
1902 Yorkshire	1947 Middlesex	1979 Essex
1903 Middlesex	1948 Glamorgan	1980 Middlesex
1904 Lancashire	1949 { Middlesex	1981 Nottinghamshire
1905 Yorkshire	{ Yorkshire	1982 Middlesex
1906 Kent	1950 { Lancashire	1983 Essex
1907 Nottinghamshire	{ Surrey	1984 Essex
1908 Yorkshire	1951 Warwickshire	1985 Middlesex
1909 Kent	1952 Surrey	1986 Essex
1910 Kent	1953 Surrey	1987 Nottinghamshire
1911 Warwickshire	1954 Surrey	1988 Worcestershire
1912 Yorkshire	1955 Surrey	1989 Worcestershire
1913 Kent	1956 Surrey	1990 Middlesex
1914 Surrey	1957 Surrey	1991 Essex
1919 Yorkshire	1958 Surrey	1992 Essex
1920 Middlesex	1959 Yorkshire	1993 Middlesex
1921 Middlesex	1960 Yorkshire	1994 Warwickshire
1922 Yorkshire	1961 Hampshire	1995 Warwickshire
1923 Yorkshire	1962 Yorkshire	1996 Leicestershire
1924 Yorkshire	1963 Yorkshire	1997 Glamorgan
1925 Yorkshire	1964 Worcestershire	1998 Leicestershire
1926 Lancashire	1965 Worcestershire	1999 Surrey
1927 Lancashire	1966 Yorkshire	2000 Surrey
1928 Lancashire	1967 Yorkshire	

COUNTY CHAMPIONSHIP RESULTS 2000

DIVISION 1

	DERBYS	DURHAM	HANTS	KENT	LANCS	LEICS	SOM'T	SURREY	YORKS
DERBYS	–	Derby De 232	Derby Drawn	Derby K 8w	Derby Drawn	Derby Drawn	Derby Drawn	Derby De 7w	Derby Drawn
DURHAM	Darl'ton Du 1/79	–	C-le-St H 6w	C-le-St Drawn	C-le-St La 141	C-le-St Drawn	C-le-St Drawn	C-le-St Du 231	C-le-St Y 6w
HANTS	So'ton H 1/3	Basing H 1/164	–	Ports K 6w	So'ton Drawn	So'ton Le 61	So'ton Sm 9w	So'ton Sy 120	So'ton Y 72
KENT	Cant Drawn	Tun W K 190	Cant K 15	–	Cant Drawn	Cant Drawn	Maid Drawn	Cant Drawn	Cant Y 32
LANCS	Man Drawn	Man La 6w	L'pool La 1/35	Man La 154	–	Man La 1/25	Man La 1/109	Man Drawn	Man La 9w
LEICS	Leics Le 10w	Leics Le 217	Leics Drawn	Leics Drawn	Leics Drawn	–	Leics Le 6w	Oakham Sy 1/178	Leics Drawn
SOM'T	Taunton Drawn	Taunton Drawn	Taunton Drawn	Bath Sm 2w	Taunton Drawn	Taunton Drawn	–	Taunton Drawn	Taunton Drawn
SURREY	Oval Sy 1/45	Oval Sy 1/68	Oval Sy 2	Oval Drawn	Oval Sy 272	Guild Sy 10w	Oval Sy 1/213	–	Oval Sy 203
YORKS	Leeds Y 1/79	Leeds Drawn	Leeds Y 1/100	Leeds Y 6w	Leeds Drawn	Leeds Drawn	Scar Y 1/6	Scar Drawn	–

DIVISION 2

	ESSEX	GLAM	GLOS	MIDDX	N'HANTS	NOTTS	SUSSEX	WARWKS	WORCS
ESSEX	–	S'end Drawn	Col Gs 104	Chelms M 237	Ilford E 5w	Chelms Drawn	Chelms Drawn	Chelms E 6w	Chelms E 4w
GLAM	Cardiff Drawn	–	Cardiff Drawn	Cardiff Drawn	Cardiff Gm 5w	Cardiff Drawn	Col Bay Gm 1/60	Cardiff Drawn	Cardiff Gm 81
GLOS	Bristol E 109	Bristol Gs 10w	–	Bristol Gs 7w	Chelt Nh 1/99	Bristol Gs 3w	Bristol Drawn	Chelt Drawn	Bristol Drawn
MIDDX	Lord's Drawn	S'gate Gm 2w	Lord's Gs 85	–	Lord's Drawn	Lord's Nt 169	S'gate Sx 7w	Lord's Drawn	S'gate Drawn
N'HANTS	No'ton Drawn	No'ton Gm 144	No'ton Nh 1/74	No'ton Drawn	–	No'ton Nh 1/124	No'ton Nh 1/17	No'ton Wa 1/53	No'ton Nh 1/72
NOTTS	N'ham Drawn	N'ham Nt 7w	N'ham Drawn	N'ham M 10w	N'ham Drawn	–	N'ham Drawn	N'ham Drawn	N'ham Wo 106
SUSSEX	Arundel Drawn	Hove Sx 1/18	Hove Gs 1/18	Horsham Drawn	E'brne Nh 162	Hove Drawn	–	Hove Wa 1/47	Hove Wo 7w
WARWKS	B'ham Drawn	B'ham Drawn	B'ham Drawn	B'ham Drawn	B'ham Nh 54	B'ham Drawn	B'ham Drawn	–	B'ham Drawn
WORCS	Kidd E 10w	Worcs Drawn	Worcs Wo 52	Worcs Wo 7w	Worcs Drawn	Worcs Drawn	Worcs Sx 8w	Worcs Wo 9w	–

COUNTY CHAMPIONSHIP RESULTS 2001

KEEP YOUR OWN RECORD (see page 135)

DIVISION 1

	ESSEX	GLAM	KENT	LANCS	LEICS	N'HANTS	SOM'T	SURREY	YORKS
ESSEX	–	Chelms	S'end	Col	Chelms	Chelms	Chelms	Ilford	Chelms
GLAM	Cardiff	–	Swansea	Col Bay	Cardiff	Cardiff	Cardiff	Cardiff	Swansea
KENT	Tun W	Maid	–	Cant	Cant	Cant	Cant	Cant	Cant
LANCS	Man	Man	Man	–	Man	Man	Man	Man	Man
LEICS	Leics	Leics	Leics	Leics	–	Leics	Leics	Leics	Leics
N'HANTS	No'ton	No'ton	No'ton	No'ton	No'ton	–	No'ton	No'ton	No'ton
SOM'T	Taunton	Taunton	Taunton	Taunton	Taunton	Taunton	–	Taunton	Bath
SURREY	Oval	Oval	Oval	Oval	Oval	Guild	Oval	–	Oval
YORKS	Scar	Scar	Leeds	Leeds	Leeds	Leeds	Leeds	Leeds	–

DIVISION 2

	DERBYS	DURHAM	GLOS	HANTS	MIDDX	NOTTS	SUSSEX	WARWKS	WORCS
DERBYS	–	Derby	Derby	Derby	Derby	Derby	Derby	Derby	Derby
DURHAM	C-le-St	–	C-le-St	C-le-St	C-le-St	C-le-St	C-le-St	C-le-St	C-le-St
GLOS	Bristol	Glos	–	Chelt	Bristol	Bristol	Chelt	Bristol	Bristol
HANTS	So'ton	So'ton	So'ton	–	So'ton	So'ton	So'ton	So'ton	So'ton
MIDDX	S'gate	Lord's	Lord's	S'gate	–	Lord's	Lord's	Lord's	Lord's
NOTTS	N'ham	N'ham	N'ham	N'ham	N'ham	–	N'ham	N'ham	N'ham
SUSSEX	Arundel	Hove	Hove	Hove	Hove	Hove	–	Hove	Horsham
WARWKS	B'ham	B'ham	B'ham	B'ham	B'ham	B'ham	B'ham	–	B'ham
WORCS	Worcs	Kidd	Worcs	Worcs	Worcs	Worcs	Worcs	Worcs	–

NATWEST TRIANGULAR SERIES 2000

Bristol 6 July (floodlit)

Toss: West Indies. ZIMBABWE beat **West Indies** by six wickets. West Indies 232-7 (50 overs) (W.W.Hinds 51, B.C.Lara 60). Zimbabwe 233-4 (45) (N.C.Johnson 95*).

The Oval 8 July

Toss: England. ZIMBABWE beat **England** by five wickets. England 207 (50) (M.E.Trescothick 79, G.A.Hick 50). Zimbabwe 210-5 (48.2) (A.D.R.Campbell 80, A.Flower 61).

Lord's 9 July

Toss: West Indies. England v West Indies – no result (rain). England 158-8 (43.5).

Canterbury 11 July

Toss: West Indies. ZIMBABWE beat **West Indies** by 70 runs. Zimbabwe 256-4 (50) (N.C.Johnson 51, G.J.Whittall 83, A.D.R.Campbell 77*). West Indies 186-8 (50) (N.A.M.McLean 50*).

Manchester 13 July (floodlit)

Toss: Zimbabwe. ENGLAND beat **Zimbabwe** by eight wickets. Zimbabwe 114 (38.4). England 115-2 (20.3).

Chester-le-Street 15 July

Toss: England. ENGLAND beat **West Indies** by ten wickets. West Indies 169-8 (50) (B.C.Lara 54). England 171-0 (35.2) (M.E.Trescothick 87*, A.J.Stewart 74*).

Chester-le-Street 16 July

Toss: West Indies. ZIMBABWE beat **West Indies** by six wickets. West Indies 287-5 (50) (S.L.Campbell 105, B.C.Lara 87). Zimbabwe 290-4 (49.1) (M.W.Goodwin 112*, G.W.Flower 96*).

Birmingham 18 July (floodlit)

Toss: England. ENGLAND beat **Zimbabwe** by 52 runs. England 262-8 (50) (A.J.Stewart 101). Zimbabwe 210-9 (50) (N.C.Johnson 52, A.D.R.Campbell 60).

Nottingham 20 July

Toss: England. WEST INDIES beat **England** by 3 runs. West Indies 195-9 (50). England 192 (49.5) (A.J.Stewart 100*).

	Played	Won	Lost	No Result	Points
Zimbabwe	6	4	2	–	8
England	6	3	2	1	7
West Indies	6	1	4	1	3

Final – Lord's 22 July

Toss: England. ENGLAND beat **Zimbabwe** by six wickets. Zimbabwe 169-7 (50) (G.W.Flower 53*). England 170-4 (45.2) (A.J.Stewart 97).

THE NATWEST TROPHY 2000 RESULTS CHART

THIRD ROUND 21 June	FOURTH ROUND 5, 6 July	QUARTER-FINALS 25, 26 July	SEMI-FINALS 12, 13, 14 August	FINAL 26, 27 August
Worcestershire†*	GLOUCESTERSHIRE			
GLOUCESTERSHIRE		GLOUCESTERSHIRE†		
Northumberland†	Leicestershire†		GLOUCESTERSHIRE†	
LEICESTERSHIRE				GLOUCESTERSHIRE (£53,000)
Durham CB†	NORTHAMPTONSHIRE†			
NORTHAMPTONSHIRE		Northamptonshire (£11,500)		
Yorkshire CB†	Yorkshire		Lancashire (£16,500)	
YORKSHIRE		LANCASHIRE		
Lincolnshire†	LANCASHIRE†			
LANCASHIRE				
Wales†	Essex			
ESSEX		Surrey† (£11,500)		
Devon†	SURREY†			
SURREY				
Middlesex CB†	Sussex			
SUSSEX				
Nottinghamshire	MIDDLESEX†			
MIDDLESEX†		Middlesex† (£11,500)		
Shropshire†	Somerset		Hampshire (£16,500)	
SOMERSET		HAMPSHIRE		
Kent CB†	HAMPSHIRE			
HAMPSHIRE				
Berkshire†	Durham†			
DURHAM				
Cumberland†	Kent†			
KENT		Glamorgan (£11,500)		
Dorset†	GLAMORGAN			
GLAMORGAN		WARWICKSHIRE†		
Derbyshire CB†	Derbyshire		WARWICKSHIRE†	
DERBYSHIRE				Warwickshire (£27,000)
Essex CB†	WARWICKSHIRE†			
WARWICKSHIRE†				

† Home team. Winning teams are in capitals. Prize-money shown in brackets. * Match replayed 4 July (Worcestershire fielded ineligible player).

138

NATWEST TROPHY
PRINCIPAL RECORDS 1963-2000
(Including The Gillette Cup)

Highest Total		413-4	Somerset v Devon	Torquay	1990
Highest Total in a Final		322-5	Warwicks v Sussex	Lord's	1993
Highest Total by a Minor Team		323-7	Herts v Leics Board	Radlett	1999
Highest Total Batting Second		350	Surrey v Worcs	The Oval	1994
Highest Total to Win Batting Second		329-5	Sussex v Derbyshire	Derby	1997
Lowest Total		39	Ireland v Sussex	Hove	1985
Lowest Total in a Final		57	Essex v Lancashire	Lord's	1996
Lowest Total to Win Batting First		98	Worcs v Durham	Chester-le-St	1968

Highest Score	206	A.I.Kallicharran	Warwicks v Oxon	Birmingham	1984
HS (Minor Team)	138	A.A.Metcalfe	Cumberland v Cornwall	Kendal	1999
Fastest Hundred	36 balls	G.D.Rose	Somerset v Devon	Torquay	1990
Most Hundreds	8	R.A.Smith	Hampshire		1985-99
Most Runs	2,547	(av 48.99)	G.A.Gooch	Essex	1973-96

Highest Partnership for each Wicket

1st	311	A.J.Wright/N.J.Trainor	Glos v Scotland	Bristol	1997
2nd	286	I.S.Anderson/A.Hill	Derbys v Cornwall	Derby	1986
3rd	309*	T.S.Curtis/T.M.Moody	Worcs v Surrey	The Oval	1994
4th	234*	D.Lloyd/C.H.Lloyd	Lancashire v Glos	Manchester	1978
5th	166	M.A.Lynch/G.R.J.Roope	Surrey v Durham	The Oval	1982
6th	226	N.J.Llong/M.V.Fleming	Kent v Cheshire	Bowdon	1999
7th	160*	C.J.Richards/I.R.Payne	Surrey v Lincs	Sleaford	1983
8th	112	A.L.Penberthy/J.E.Emburey	Northants v Lancs	Manchester	1996
9th	87	M.A.Nash/A.E.Cordle	Glamorgan v Lincs	Swansea	1974
10th	81	S.Turner/R.E.East	Essex v Yorkshire	Leeds	1982

Best Bowling	8-21	M.A.Holding	Derbys v Sussex	Hove	1988
	8-31	D.L.Underwood	Kent v Scotland	Edinburgh	1987
Most Wickets	87	(av 14.24)	A.A.Donald	Warwicks	1987-2000

Most Wicket-Keeping Dismissals in an Innings

7	(7ct)	A.J.Stewart	Surrey v Glamorgan	Swansea	1994
Most Appearances	67	M.W.Gatting	Middlesex		1975-98

Most Match Wins 79 – Lancashire   **Most Cup/Trophy Wins 7 – Lancashire**

GILLETTE CUP WINNERS

1963	Sussex	1969	Yorkshire	1975	Lancashire
1964	Sussex	1970	Lancashire	1976	Northamptonshire
1965	Yorkshire	1971	Lancashire	1977	Middlesex
1966	Warwickshire	1972	Lancashire	1978	Sussex
1967	Kent	1973	Gloucestershire	1979	Somerset
1968	Warwickshire	1974	Kent	1980	Middlesex

NATWEST TROPHY WINNERS

1981	Derbyshire	1988	Middlesex	1995	Warwickshire
1982	Surrey	1989	Warwickshire	1996	Lancashire
1983	Somerset	1990	Lancashire	1997	Essex
1984	Middlesex	1991	Hampshire	1998	Lancashire
1985	Essex	1992	Northamptonshire	1999	Gloucestershire
1986	Sussex	1993	Warwickshire	2000	Gloucestershire
1987	Nottinghamshire	1994	Worcestershire		

BENSON AND HEDGES CUP

RESULTS CHART 2000

QUARTER-FINALS *9 May*	SEMI-FINALS *27, 28, 29 May*	FINAL *10 June*

GLAMORGAN†
Hampshire (£10,500) } GLAMORGAN†
Yorkshire† (£10,500) }   } Glamorgan
SURREY }   (£26,000)
Durham (£10,500) } Surrey (£15,500)
LANCASHIRE† } Lancashire (£15,500)
GLOUCESTERSHIRE }   } GLOUCESTERSHIRE
Sussex† (£10,500) } GLOUCESTERSHIRE†   (£52,000)

† Home team. Winning teams are in capitals. Prize-money in brackets.

PRINCIPAL RECORDS 1972-2000

Highest Total		388-7		Essex v Scotland	Chelmsford	1992
Highest Total Batting Second		318-5		Lancashire v Leics	Manchester	1995
Lowest Total		50		Hampshire v Yorks	Leeds	1991
Highest Score	198*		G.A.Gooch	Essex v Sussex	Hove	1982
Hundreds	320					1972-2000
Fastest Hundred	62 min		M.A.Nash	Glamorgan v Hants	Swansea	1976

Highest Partnership for each Wicket

1st	252	V.P.Terry/C.L.Smith	Hants v Combined U	Southampton	1990
2nd	285*	C.G.Greenidge/D.R.Turner	Hants v Minor C (S)	Amersham	1973
3rd	271	C.J.Adams/M.G.Bevan	Sussex v Essex	Chelmsford	2000
4th	184*	D.Lloyd/B.W.Reidy	Lancashire v Derbys	Chesterfield	1980
5th	160	A.J.Lamb/D.J.Capel	Northants v Leics	Northampton	1986
6th	167*	M.G.Bevan/R.J.Blakey	Yorkshire v Lancs	Manchester	1996
7th	149*	J.D.Love/C.M.Old	Yorks v Scotland	Bradford	1981
8th	109	R.E.East/N.Smith	Essex v Northants	Chelmsford	1977
9th	83	P.G.Newman/M.A.Holding	Derbyshire v Notts	Nottingham	1985
10th	80*	D.L.Bairstow/M.Johnson	Yorkshire v Derbys	Derby	1981

Best Bowling

	7-12	W.W.Daniel	Middx v Minor C (E)	Ipswich	1978
	7-22	J.R.Thomson	Middx v Hampshire	Lord's	1981
	7-24	Mushtaq Ahmed	Somerset v Ireland	Taunton	1997
	7-32	R.G.D.Willis	Warwicks v Yorks	Birmingham	1981

Five Wickets in an Innings	159				1972-2000
Four Wickets in Four Balls		S.M.Pollock	Warwicks v Leics	Birmingham	1996

Most Wicket-Keeping Dismissals in an Innings

8 (8ct)	D.J.S.Taylor	Somerset v Combined U	Taunton	1982

Most Catches in an Innings

5	V.J.Marks	Combined U v Kent	Oxford	1976

Most Match Awards	22	G.A.Gooch	Essex	1973-97

BENSON AND HEDGES CUP WINNERS

1972	Leicestershire	1982	Somerset	1992	Hampshire
1973	Kent	1983	Middlesex	1993	Derbyshire
1974	Surrey	1984	Lancashire	1994	Warwickshire
1975	Leicestershire	1985	Leicestershire	1995	Lancashire
1976	Kent	1986	Middlesex	1996	Lancashire
1977	Gloucestershire	1987	Yorkshire	1997	Surrey
1978	Kent	1988	Hampshire	1998	Essex
1979	Essex	1989	Nottinghamshire	1999	Gloucestershire
1980	Northamptonshire	1990	Lancashire	2000	Gloucestershire
1981	Somerset	1991	Worcestershire		

NORWICH UNION NATIONAL LEAGUE 2000

FIRST DIVISION

		P	W	L	T	NR	Pts	NRR
1	GLOUCESTERSHIRE	16	9	6	–	1	38	+1.258
2	Yorkshire	16	9	7	–	–	36	+5.975
3	Northamptonshire	16	9	7	–	–	36	–3.983
4	Leicestershire	16	7	6	2	1	34	–0.458
5	Kent	16	7	7	–	2	32	+6.177
6	Somerset	16	7	8	–	1	30	–0.594
7	Worcestershire	16	6	8	–	2	28	–4.236
8	Lancashire	16	6	8	1	1	28	–5.829
9	Sussex	16	5	8	1	2	26	+0.345

SECOND DIVISION

		P	W	L	T	NR	Pts	NRR
1	SURREY	16	11	3	–	2	48	+11.93
2	Nottinghamshire	16	11	4	–	1	46	–2.177
3	Warwickshire	16	10	5	1	–	42	+7.098
4	Middlesex	16	8	5	1	2	38	–0.260
5	Essex	16	7	7	–	2	32	+0.359
6	Glamorgan	16	7	7	2	–	32	–2.184
7	Durham	16	5	11	–	–	20	+0.327
8	Hampshire	16	5	11	–	–	20	–5.780
9	Derbyshire	16	2	13	–	1	10	–8.999

Win = 4 points. Tie (T)/No Result (NR) = 2 points. Positions of counties finishing equal on points are decided by most wins or, if equal, by higher net run-rate (NRR – overall run-rate in all matches, i.e. total runs scored × 100 divided by balls received, minus the run-rate of its opponents in those same matches). Horizontal rules segregate the counties relegated and promoted for the 2001 competition.

SUNDAY LEAGUE CHAMPIONS

1969	Lancashire	1979	Somerset	1989	Lancashire
1970	Lancashire	1980	Warwickshire	1990	Derbyshire
1971	Worcestershire	1981	Essex	1991	Nottinghamshire
1972	Kent	1982	Sussex	1992	Middlesex
1973	Kent	1983	Yorkshire	1993	Glamorgan
1974	Leicestershire	1984	Essex	1994	Warwickshire
1975	Hampshire	1985	Essex	1995	Kent
1976	Kent	1986	Hampshire	1996	Surrey
1977	Leicestershire	1987	Worcestershire	1997	Warwickshire
1978	Hampshire	1988	Worcestershire	1998	Lancashire

NATIONAL LEAGUE CHAMPIONS

1999	Lancashire	2000	Gloucestershire

SUNDAY LEAGUE 1969-98

PRINCIPAL RECORDS

Highest Total		375-4	Surrey v Yorkshire	Scarborough	1994
Highest Total Batting Second		317-6	Surrey v Notts	The Oval	1993
Lowest Total		23	Middlesex v Yorks	Leeds	1974

Highest Score	203	A.D.Brown	Surrey v Hampshire	Guildford	1997
Fastest Hundred	44 balls	M.A.Ealham	Kent v Derbyshire	Maidstone	1995

Highest Partnership for each Wicket

1st	239	G.A.Gooch/B.R.Hardie	Essex v Notts	Nottingham	1985
2nd	273	G.A.Gooch/K.S.McEwan	Essex v Notts	Nottingham	1983
3rd	223	S.J.Cook/G.D.Rose	Somerset v Glam	Neath	1990
4th	219	C.G.Greenidge/C.L.Smith	Hampshire v Surrey	Southampton	1987
5th	190	R.J.Blakey/M.J.Foster	Yorkshire v Leics	Leicester	1993
6th	137	M.P.Speight/I.D.K.Salisbury	Sussex v Surrey	Guildford	1996
7th	132	K.R.Brown/N.F.Williams	Middx v Somerset	Lord's	1988
8th	110*	C.L.Cairns/B.N.French	Notts v Surrey	The Oval	1993
9th	105	D.G.Moir/R.W.Taylor	Derbyshire v Kent	Derby	1984
10th	82	G.Chapple/P.J.Martin	Lancashire v Worcs	Manchester	1996

Best Bowling	8-26	K.D.Boyce	Essex v Lancashire	Manchester	1971
	7-15	R.A.Hutton	Yorkshire v Worcs	Leeds	1969
	7-16	S.D.Thomas	Glamorgan v Surrey	Swansea	1998
	7-39	A.Hodgson	Northants v Somerset	Northampton	1976
	7-41	A.N.Jones	Sussex v Notts	Nottingham	1986

Four Wkts in Four Balls	A.Ward	Derbyshire v Sussex	Derby	1970

Most Wicket-Keeping Dismissals in an Innings

7	(6ct, 1st)	R.W.Taylor	Derbyshire v Lancs	Manchester	1975

Most Catches in an Innings

5		J.M.Rice	Hampshire v Warwicks	Southampton	1978

NATIONAL LEAGUE 1999-2000

PRINCIPAL RECORDS

Highest Total		301-6	Lancashire v Essex	Chelmsford	1999
Highest Total Batting Second		298	Essex v Lancashire	Chelmsford	1999
Lowest Total		44	Glamorgan v Surrey	The Oval	1999

Highest Score	163	C.J.Adams	Sussex v Middlesex	Arundel	1999
Fastest Hundred	50 balls	A.Flintoff	Lancashire v Essex	Chelmsford	1999

Record Partnership (Where superior to Sunday League)

5th	220*	C.C.Lewis/P.A.Nixon	Leics v Kent	Canterbury	1999

Best Bowling	7-30	M.P.Bicknell	Surrey v Glamorgan	The Oval	1999
Four Wkts in Four Balls		V.C.Drakes	Notts v Derbys	Nottingham	1999

MINOR COUNTIES CHAMPIONSHIP

FINAL TABLE 2000

	P	W	L	D	NR	Bonus Points Bat	Bonus Points Bowl	Total Points
EASTERN DIVISION								
CUMBERLAND	9	5	–	2	2	8	14	112
Lincolnshire	9	3	–	4	2	10	22	90
Suffolk	9	2	3	4	–	15	21	73‡
Northumberland	9	2	2	3	2	3	18	63
Bedfordshire	9	1	2	5	1	23	19	63
Buckinghamshire	9	2	3	4	–	11	19	62
Cambridgeshire	9	1	1	6	1	12	24	57
Norfolk	9	1	3	3	2	7	21	54
Staffordshire	9	–	–	7	2	10	22	42
Hertfordshire	9	–	3	4	2	12	16	36†
WESTERN DIVISION								
DORSET	9	6	–	2	1	22	19	140†
Oxfordshire	9	5	2	2	–	19	25	124
Shropshire	9	4	2	3	–	17	20	106‡
Herefordshire	9	3	3	2	1	18	24	95
Devon	9	2	3	2	2	21	25	88
Wiltshire	9	3	3	2	1	8	19	80
Berkshire	9	2	1	4	2	19	16	77
Cornwall	9	2	4	2	1	9	28	74
Cheshire	9	–	5	3	1	10	21	41‡
Wales	9	–	4	4	1	4	13	27‡

† Includes deduction of 2 points for slow over rate. ‡ Includes 5 points gained in lost one-day match.

CHAMPIONSHIP FINAL

At Bournemouth Sports Club on 10, 11, 12 September: **DORSET beat Cumberland by five wickets.** Cumberland 282-5 (70 overs; D.J.Pearson 108*, J.M.Lewis 60, S.T.Knox 59) and 152 (59.3 overs; T.J.Sharpe 4-19). Dorset 242-9 (70 overs; D.J.Cowley 75, M.Swarbrick 52) and 196-5 (68.3 overs; D.J.Cowley 63, N.J.Thurgood 62).

ECB 38 COUNTY CUP

At Lord's on 30 August: **HEREFORDSHIRE beat Cheshire by 42 runs.** Herefordshire 291-6 (50 overs; P.S.Lazenbury 118, C.W.Boroughs 94). Cheshire 249-9 (50 overs; P.R.J.Bryson 73; K.E.Cooper 5-29).

MINOR COUNTIES RECORDS

Highest Total	621		Surrey II v Devon	The Oval	1928
Lowest Total	14		Cheshire v Staffs	Stoke	1909
Highest Score	282	E.Garnett	Berkshire v Wiltshire	Reading	1908
Most Runs – Season	1212	A.F.Brazier	Surrey II		1949
Record Partnership					
2nd 388*	T.H.Clark and A.F.Brazier		Surrey II v Sussex II	The Oval	1949
Best Bowling – Innings	10- 11	S.Turner	Cambs v Cumberland	Penrith	1987
– Match	18-100	N.W.Harding	Kent II v Wiltshire	Swindon	1937
Most Wickets – Season	119	S.F.Barnes	Staffordshire		1906

MINOR COUNTIES CHAMPIONS

1895	Norfolk Durham Worcestershire	1929	Oxfordshire	1968	Yorkshire II
1896	Worcestershire	1930	Durham	1969	Buckinghamshire
1897	Worcestershire	1931	Leicestershire II	1970	Bedfordshire
1898	Worcestershire	1932	Buckinghamshire	1971	Yorkshire II
		1933	*Undecided*	1972	Bedfordshire
1899	Northamptonshire Buckinghamshire	1934	Lancashire II	1973	Shropshire
		1935	Middlesex II	1974	Oxfordshire
	Glamorgan	1936	Hertfordshire	1975	Hertfordshire
1900	Durham	1937	Lancashire II	1976	Durham
	Northamptonshire	1938	Buckinghamshire	1977	Suffolk
1901	Durham	1939	Surrey II	1978	Devon
1902	Wiltshire	1946	Suffolk	1979	Suffolk
1903	Northamptonshire	1947	Yorkshire II	1980	Durham
1904	Northamptonshire	1948	Lancashire II	1981	Durham
1905	Norfolk	1949	Lancashire II	1982	Oxfordshire
1906	Staffordshire	1950	Surrey II	1983	Hertfordshire
1907	Lancashire II	1951	Kent II	1984	Durham
1908	Staffordshire	1952	Buckinghamshire	1985	Cheshire
1909	Wiltshire	1953	Berkshire	1986	Cumberland
1910	Norfolk	1954	Surrey II	1987	Buckinghamshire
1911	Staffordshire	1955	Surrey II	1988	Cheshire
1912	*In abeyance*	1956	Kent II	1989	Oxfordshire
1913	Norfolk	1957	Yorkshire II	1990	Hertfordshire
1920	Staffordshire	1958	Yorkshire II	1991	Staffordshire
1921	Staffordshire	1959	Warwickshire II	1992	Staffordshire
1922	Buckinghamshire	1960	Lancashire II	1993	Staffordshire
1923	Buckinghamshire	1961	Somerset II	1994	Devon
1924	Berkshire	1962	Warwickshire II	1995	Devon
1925	Buckinghamshire	1963	Cambridgeshire	1996	Devon
1926	Durham	1964	Lancashire II	1997	Devon
1927	Staffordshire	1965	Somerset II	1998	Staffordshire
1928	Berkshire	1966	Lincolnshire	1999	Cumberland
		1967	Cheshire	2000	Dorset

LEADING BATTING AVERAGES 2000

(Qualification: 8 completed innings [or 500 runs] average 30.00)

		I	NO	HS	Runs	Avge
S.A.Kellett	Cambridgeshire	12	3	127*	572	63.55
N.A.Folland	Devon	15	5	110	607	60.70
A.A.Metcalfe	Cumberland	11	4	105*	418	59.71
N.T.Gadsby	Cambridgeshire	13	3	133*	561	56.10
D.J.Cowley	Dorset	15	4	103*	615	55.90
D.M.Ward	Hertfordshire	16	1	202*	835	55.66
J.R.Wood	Berkshire	15	3	100	620	51.66
T.C.Z.Lamb	Dorset	12	3	116	465	51.66
P.S.Lazenbury	Herefordshire	16	2	134	723	51.64
P.D.Atkins	Buckinghamshire	15	4	102*	521	47.36
M.Swarbrick	Dorset	17	1	114	740	46.25
T.W.Roberts	Bedfordshire	8	–	139	365	45.62
L.Potter	Staffordshire	13	1	146*	546	45.50
A.R.Roberts	Bedfordshire	15	2	140	557	42.84
J.M.Lewis	Cumberland	12	4	128*	342	42.75
P.J.Caley	Suffolk	15	7	50*	341	42.62
R.J.Sillence	Wiltshire	13	1	150	500	41.66
S.T.Knox	Cumberland	12	2	158*	397	39.70
R.J.Williams	Oxfordshire	14	5	61*	340	37.77
K.Pearson	Herefordshire	13	4	76	336	37.33
R.I.Dawson	Devon	15	–	151	550	36.66

144

		I	*NO*	*HS*	*Runs*	*Avge*
H.V.Patel	Herefordshire	13	3	91*	363	36.30
L.H.Nurse	Berkshire	11	1	108	361	36.10
R.J.Bates	Wiltshire	13	3	67	358	35.80
J.C.Harrison	Lincolnshire	11	2	74	322	35.77
G.E.Loveday	Berkshire	16	1	98	536	35.73
B.W.W.Platt	Shropshire	11	2	104*	320	35.55
I.Dawood	Herefordshire	16	2	142*	497	35.50
O.J.Clayson	Bedfordshire	16	3	74*	455	35.00
C.A.Haupt	Oxfordshire	17	3	121*	484	34.57
G.R.Treagus	Dorset	16	–	85	550	34.37
C.Amos	Norfolk	11	3	102*	275	34.37
C.S.Knightley	Oxfordshire	14	5	94*	302	33.55
D.J.M.Mercer	Bedfordshire	14	3	98*	368	33.45
S.V.Laudat	Oxfordshire	15	1	118	468	33.42
N.F.Williams	Cornwall	12	3	67	300	33.33
S.A.Seymour	Berkshire	12	2	79	331	33.10
N.W.Round	Herefordshire	15	5	98*	324	32.40
R.J.Rollins	Cambridgeshire	9	1	56	257	32.12
G.F.Archer	Staffordshire	15	–	113	476	31.73
G.T.J.Townsend	Devon	11	1	81	317	31.70
A.J.Trott	Bedfordshire	11	3	63	253	31.62
M.Catley	Suffolk	13	–	110	403	31.00
S.P.Naylor	Buckinghamshire	13	3	74*	309	30.90
R.J.Rowe	Wiltshire	14	1	65*	392	30.15

LEADING BOWLING AVERAGES 2000
(Qualification: 20 wickets, average 30.00)

		O	*M*	*R*	*W*	*Avge*
R.N.Dalton	Bedfordshire	88.5	22	234	22	10.63
S.Oakes	Lincolnshire	127	37	279	24	11.62
K.A.Arnold	Oxfordshire	348.1	98	838	62	13.51
D.J.Pipes	Lincolnshire	142.3	48	348	24	14.50
M.A.Sharp	Cumberland	194.5	67	422	29	14.55
K.P.Evans	Shropshire	235.4	68	530	34	15.58
S.P.Naylor	Buckinghamshire	88.4	13	328	21	15.61
A.M.Shimmons	Shropshire	159.5	34	487	29	16.79
E.J.Wilson	Lincolnshire	138.5	34	372	22	16.90
D.B.Pennett	Cumberland	178.2	46	543	32	16.96
C.Brown	Cheshire	125.5	19	448	26	17.23
J.M.Hands	Cornwall	157.5	27	553	32	17.28
R.W.Pineo	Suffolk	173	43	544	31	17.54
S.C.Goldsmith	Norfolk	158.3	46	387	22	17.59
V.J.Pike	Dorset	334.1	87	1045	57	18.33
G.M.Kirk	Suffolk	149.4	41	451	24	18.79
P.G.Newman	Norfolk	163.5	50	443	23	19.26
J.W.Shaw	Herefordshire	159	31	555	28	19.82
T.J.Sharpe	Dorset	147.5	33	476	24	19.83
A.Akhtar	Cambridgeshire	288.3	92	735	37	19.86
A.J.Procter	Devon	205	43	676	34	19.88
J.E.Emburey	Berkshire	277.5	57	739	36	21.08
C.R.Gibbens	Wiltshire	120.2	22	427	20	21.35
R.J.Bates	Wiltshire	174.1	35	632	29	21.79
J.N.B.Bovill	Buckinghamshire	174.2	37	526	24	21.91
G.Angus	Northumberland	165	31	505	23	21.95
S.V.Laudat	Oxfordshire	139.2	26	463	20	23.15
C.C.Finegan	Cheshire	134.2	24	492	21	23.42
G.Bulpitt	Staffordshire	221	60	586	25	23.44
N.A.Fusedale	Berkshire	273.3	70	848	36	23.55
S.F.Stanway	Buckinghamshire	248	74	605	25	24.20
R.J.Sillence	Wiltshire	126.5	18	538	22	24.45
A.R.Clarke	Norfolk	212.2	51	738	27	27.33

SECOND XI CHAMPIONSHIP 2000
FINAL TABLE

	P	W	L	D	Bonus Points Bat	Bonus Points Bowl	Total Points	Avge
1 MIDDLESEX (1)	13	6	1	6	43	39	178	13.69
2 Kent (5)	14	7	3	4	33	44	177	12.64
3 Warwickshire (10)	14	6	2	6	36	42	174	12.43
4 Nottinghamshire (11)	16	7	3	6	36	50	194	12.13
5 Yorkshire (14)	15	5	2	8	37	42	†173	11.53
6 Sussex (3)	12	5	4	3	22	37	131	10.92
7 Lancashire (4)	15	5	4	6	30	43	157	10.47
8 Surrey (9)	14	4	3	7	33	37	146	10.43
9 Gloucestershire (15)	14	4	1	9	21	33	138	9.86
10 Essex (12)	14	4	5	5	28	40	136	9.71
11 Hampshire (7)	14	4	7	3	25	44	129	9.21
12 Durham (8)	13	3	4	6	18	40	118	9.08
13 Glamorgan (17)	14	3	5	6	29	36	125	8.93
14 Northamptonshire (13)	16	3	4	9	21	48	141	8.81
15 Leicestershire (16)	12	2	6	4	29	33	102	8.50
16 Somerset (18)	13	2	6	5	30	35	109	8.38
17 Worcestershire (6)	14	2	7	5	30	37	111	7.93
18 Derbyshire (2)	15	3	8	4	21	39	112	7.47

Win = 16 points. † Includes 2 extra draw points in match where scores were level.
1999 final positions are shown in brackets.

ECB SECOND XI AWARDS 2000

Players of the Month:
C.G.Taylor (Gloucestershire); A.Pratt (Durham);
J.J.Bates (Sussex); M.J.Powell (Northamptonshire)

Player of the Season
R.M.S.Weston (Middlesex)

SECOND XI CHAMPIONS

1959 Gloucestershire	1973 Essex	1987 Kent/Yorkshire
1960 Northamptonshire	1974 Middlesex	1988 Surrey
1961 Kent	1975 Surrey	1989 Middlesex
1962 Worcestershire	1976 Kent	1990 Sussex
1963 Worcestershire	1977 Yorkshire	1991 Yorkshire
1964 Lancashire	1978 Sussex	1992 Surrey
1965 Glamorgan	1979 Warwickshire	1993 Middlesex
1966 Surrey	1980 Glamorgan	1994 Somerset
1967 Hampshire	1981 Hampshire	1995 Hampshire
1968 Surrey	1982 Worcestershire	1996 Warwickshire
1969 Kent	1983 Leicestershire	1997 Lancashire
1970 Kent	1984 Yorkshire	1998 Northamptonshire
1971 Hampshire	1985 Nottinghamshire	1999 Middlesex
1972 Nottinghamshire	1986 Lancashire	2000 Middlesex

FIRST-CLASS CAREER RECORDS

Compiled by Philip Bailey

The following career records are for all players who appeared in first-class or limited-overs cricket during the 2000 season and are complete to the end of that season. Some players who did not appear in 2000 but may do so in 2001 are also included.

BATTING AND FIELDING

'1000' denotes instances of scoring 1000 runs in a season. Where these have been achieved outside the British Isles they are shown after a plus sign.

	M	I	NO	HS	Runs	Avge	100	50	1000	Ct/St
Adams, C.J.	216	353	27	239	11850	36.34	27	58	4	251
Adams, J.C.	178	299	49	208*	10172	40.68	23	50	–	154
Adams, K.	1	–	–	–	–	–	–	–	–	–
Adshead, S.J.	1	1	–	0	0	0.00	–	–	–	–/1
Afzaal, U.	80	139	13	151*	3692	29.30	6	21	1	35
Aldred, P.	50	65	10	83	646	11.74	–	1	–	27
Ali, Kabir	11	16	3	50*	224	17.23	–	1	–	5
Ali, Kadeer	4	7	–	8	13	1.85	–	–	–	1
Ali, S.M.	4	5	–	18	25	5.00	–	–	–	1
Alleyne, M.W.	277	455	41	256	12869	31.08	18	64	6	229/2
Altree, D.A.	6	8	3	4	6	1.20	–	–	–	1
Ambrose, C.E.L.	239	317	70	78	3448	13.95	–	4	–	88
Amin, R.M.	11	14	7	12	34	4.85	–	–	–	4
Anderson, R.S.G.	24	28	5	67*	317	13.78	–	1	–	5
Asif Mujtaba	237	368	72	240	14947	50.49	40	80	1+3	217
Asim Butt	26	34	9	44	381	15.24	–	–	–	12
Atherton, M.A.	315	545	45	268*	20598	41.19	52	101	7	244
Austin, I.D.	124	172	37	115*	3778	27.98	2	20	–	35
Averis, J.M.M.	19	29	8	42	382	18.19	–	–	–	3
Aymes, A.N.	194	288	72	133	6714	31.08	7	34	–	457/41
Bailey, R.J.	360	603	88	224*	21329	41.41	46	109	13	264
Bailey, T.M.B.	13	15	3	96*	281	23.41	–	1	–	19/2
Ball, M.C.J.	142	221	39	71	3400	18.68	–	9	–	168
Banes, M.J.	3	5	–	53	111	22.20	–	2	–	1
Barnett, K.J.	457	744	71	239*	26923	40.00	57	145	15	273
Bates, J.J.	21	32	2	57	411	13.70	–	1	–	17
Batt, C.J.	12	17	2	43	177	11.80	–	–	–	3
Batty, G.J.	2	4	1	25*	54	18.00	–	–	–	–
Batty, J.N.	59	74	14	100*	1402	23.36	1	5	–	135/23
Bell, I.R.	1	1	–	0	0	0.00	–	–	–	2
Betts, M.M.	68	105	23	57*	957	11.67	–	2	–	21
Bevan, M.G.	180	301	54	203*	13796	55.85	47	62	3	101
Bichel, A.J.	57	74	7	110	1184	17.67	1	4	–	28
Bicknell, D.J.	227	397	38	235*	14058	39.15	34	62	6	81
Bicknell, M.P.	228	271	65	88	4344	21.08	–	18	–	78
Birks, M.J.	22	22	4	32	220	12.22	–	–	–	24/5
Bishop, I.E.	7	10	4	12	25	4.16	–	–	–	4
Bishop, J.E.	2	1	–	17	17	17.00	–	–	–	–
Blackwell, I.D.	43	62	4	109	1234	21.27	1	6	–	18
Blain, J.A.R.	4	2	1	31*	31	31.00	–	–	–	3
Blakey, R.J.	304	485	72	221	12760	30.89	11	75	5	668/50
Blewett, G.S.	154	271	18	268	11154	44.08	27	56	0+3	115
Block, S.A.A.	2	4	–	23	31	7.75	–	–	–	–

147

	M	I	NO	HS	Runs	Avge	100	50	1000	Ct/St
Bloomfield, T.F.	33	38	18	20*	137	6.85	–	–	–	4
Bones, A.S.	4	7	–	7	24	3.42	–	–	–	–
Boswell, S.A.J.	20	27	9	35	229	12.72	–	–	–	4
Bowen, M.N.	67	92	26	32	817	12.37	–	–	–	17
Bowler, P.D.	265	453	48	241*	16463	40.64	40	82	9	174/1
Brent, G.B.	26	33	5	55	453	16.17	–	1	–	12
Bressington, A.N.	1	1	1	2*	2	–	–	–	–	1
Bridge, G.D.	1	2	–	6	11	5.50	–	–	–	1
Brinkley, J.E.	19	22	5	43*	189	11.11	–	–	–	8
Brooker, J.A.D.	1	–	–	–	–	–	–	–	–	1
Brown, A.D.	141	221	24	295*	8726	44.29	24	35	5	159/1
Brown, D.R.	114	174	22	203	4145	27.26	2	22	–	68
Brown, J.F.	26	35	15	16*	81	4.05	–	–	–	7
Brown, M.J.	2	3	2	24*	48	48.00	–	–	–	2
Brown, S.J.E.	154	216	70	69	1732	11.86	–	2	–	41
Brunnschweiler, I.	1	2	–	19	22	11.00	–	–	–	4
Bulbeck, M.P.L.	26	28	15	76*	412	31.69	–	1	–	3
Burns, M.	78	119	5	160	3290	28.85	4	21	–	79/7
Burns, N.D.	172	255	56	166	5794	29.11	5	29	–	352/33
Butcher, G.P.	49	70	11	101*	1666	28.23	1	11	–	18
Butcher, M.A.	152	263	21	259	8992	37.15	16	52	5	145
Byas, D.	252	425	37	213	13545	34.90	24	77	5	313
Byrne, B.W.	27	45	6	94	1048	26.87	–	3	–	8
Caddick, A.R.	163	217	40	92	2763	15.61	–	5	–	57
Callaghan, D.J.	126	206	25	171	6798	37.55	16	34	–	98
Campbell, A.D.R.	99	171	22	196	4849	32.54	7	26	–	100
Campbell, S.L.	135	239	15	208	8393	37.46	20	43	2	132
Canning, T.K.	10	15	1	59	236	16.85	–	2	–	4
Carlisle, S.V.	40	65	4	147	1964	32.19	3	11	–	33
Carpenter, J.R.	13	24	–	65	383	15.95	–	2	–	5
Carroll, R.W.S.	1	1	1	0*	0	–	–	–	–	–
Carter, N.M.	2	4	–	37	60	15.00	–	–	–	1
Cassar, M.E.	55	87	11	121	1803	23.72	1	9	–	14
Catterall, D.N.	4	5	–	60	157	31.40	–	2	–	1
Cawdron, M.J.	12	17	2	42	251	16.73	–	–	–	2
Chanderpaul, S.	109	178	31	303*	7377	50.18	19	38	1	68
Chapple, G.	117	157	44	109*	2288	20.24	1	6	–	37
Cherry, D.D.	1	1	–	11	11	11.00	–	–	–	–
Chilton, M.J.	32	51	4	106*	1280	27.23	2	4	–	31
Claughton, J.A.	15	26	6	85	503	25.15	–	3	–	4
Clough, G.D.	1	2	–	33	34	17.00	–	–	–	1
Collingwood, P.D.	71	121	7	111	2986	26.19	4	16	–	77
Collins, B.J.	14	20	2	46	231	12.83	–	–	–	9
Collymore, C.D.	14	21	8	14	87	6.69	–	–	–	4
Cook, J.W.	11	17	1	137	502	31.37	2	1	–	4
Cook, S.J.	17	26	3	51	382	16.60	–	1	–	5
Cork, D.G.	187	277	41	200*	5963	25.26	4	34	–	127
Cosker, D.A.	72	81	23	49	577	9.94	–	–	–	45
Cotterell, T.P.	9	11	4	5*	7	1.00	–	–	–	2
Cottey, P.A.	236	381	50	203	12139	36.67	24	65	7	161
Cousins, D.M.	31	48	12	29*	369	10.25	–	–	–	8
Cowan, A.P.	75	110	23	94	1513	17.39	–	5	–	34
Cox, J.	159	280	17	245	11476	43.63	35	47	1+1	67
Craven, V.J.	8	11	1	58	251	25.10	–	2	–	6
Crawley, J.P.	215	349	32	286	15259	48.13	37	83	7	155
Creese, M.L.	1	1	–	4	4	4.00	–	–	–	–

148

	M	I	NO	HS	Runs	Avge	100	50	1000	Ct/St
Croft, R.D.B.	234	339	67	143	6704	24.64	2	29	–	116
Crowe, C.D.	19	23	5	44*	336	18.66	–	–	–	10
Croy, M.G.	49	77	9	104	1166	17.14	1	2	–	133/11
Cullinan, D.J.	203	347	50	337*	13126	44.19	35	62	1	189
Cunliffe, R.J.	57	95	5	190*	2280	25.33	3	10	–	47
Dagnall, C.E.	3	3	2	6*	11	11.00	–	–	–	–
Dakin, J.M.	42	60	6	190	1746	32.33	5	9	–	15
Dale, A.	198	326	27	214*	9803	32.78	17	49	3	76
Daley, J.A.	82	142	11	159*	3714	28.35	3	18	–	42
Danson, A.R.	12	19	6	117*	364	28.00	1	–	–	6
Davies, A.P.	9	9	2	34	79	11.28	–	–	–	1
Davies, M.K.	31	44	13	32*	316	10.19	–	–	–	8
Davis, M.J.G.	70	111	17	71	1514	16.10	–	4	–	46
Dawson, R.K.J.	1	1	–	1	1	1.00	–	–	–	–
Dean, K.J.	48	58	23	27*	330	9.42	–	–	–	5
Dean, S.J.	2	3	–	39	85	28.33	–	–	–	1
De Bruyn, Z.	23	43	7	126*	1047	29.08	1	6	–	8
DeFreitas, P.A.J.	314	444	42	123*	9177	22.82	8	46	–	110
Di Venuto, M.J.	110	188	9	189	7207	40.26	13	47	1	87
Donald, A.A.	290	334	124	55*	2507	11.93	–	1	–	108
Dowman, M.P.	79	138	10	149	3783	29.55	8	16	1	46
Drakes, V.C.	108	176	20	180*	3457	22.16	4	14	–	36
Dravid, R.	136	221	30	215	10453	54.72	28	56	1+2	140/1
Driver, R.C.	15	27	4	64	480	20.86	–	1	–	3
Dunlop, A.R.	8	15	1	150	603	43.07	2	4	–	3
Dutch, K.P.	27	35	2	91	497	15.06	–	3	–	22
Dwyer, M.D.	2	4	2	4*	7	3.50	–	–	–	–
Ealham, M.A.	149	240	38	139	6336	31.36	5	42	1	56
Elliott, M.T.G.	114	208	16	203	9712	50.58	33	40	2+4	130
Elstub, C.J.	4	4	3	4*	6	6.00	–	–	–	1
Englefield, J.I.	18	33	3	90	1013	33.76	–	10	–	14
Evans, A.W.	36	60	7	125	1449	27.33	1	6	–	23
Fairbrother, N.H.	342	542	75	366	19267	41.25	42	103	10	264
Fellows, G.M.	20	31	5	50	502	19.30	–	1	–	9
Fisher, I.D.	23	31	8	68*	517	22.47	–	2	–	1
Flanagan, I.N.	18	32	1	61	580	18.70	–	3	–	19
Fleming, M.V.	197	317	37	138	8602	30.72	10	41	–	77
Fleming, S.P.	110	182	17	174*	6750	40.90	12	41	–	142
Flintoff, A.	65	100	9	160	3255	35.76	6	18	–	82
Flower, A.	100	165	32	201	6544	49.20	20	32	–	205/16
Flower, G.W.	102	181	15	243*	6612	39.83	14	37	–	97
Foster, J.S.	4	5	2	52	125	41.66	–	1	–	6
Francis, S.R.G.	16	22	10	30*	91	7.58	–	–	–	1
Franklin, G.D.	1	1	–	12	12	12.00	–	–	–	–
Franks, P.J.	63	94	15	66*	1574	19.92	–	7	–	24
Fraser, A.R.C.	275	330	82	92	2749	11.08	–	2	–	50
Frost, T.	30	43	5	111*	895	23.55	1	3	–	72/3
Fulton, D.P.	107	190	12	207	5293	29.73	7	27	–	158
Gallian, J.E.R.	140	244	22	312	8101	36.49	18	36	2	112
Ganguly, S.C.	122	194	25	200*	7789	46.08	15	49	–	91
Gannon, B.W.	19	22	8	28	144	10.28	–	–	–	7
Garland, R.	12	15	5	56*	185	18.50	–	1	–	2
Gayle, C.H.	30	54	8	168	1430	31.08	3	6	–	27
Giddins, E.S.H.	125	150	61	34	465	5.22	–	–	–	19
Giles, A.F.	93	124	28	128*	2890	30.10	3	13	–	36
Gillespie, M.A.	1	2	–	34	56	28.00	–	–	–	–

149

	M	I	NO	HS	Runs	Avge	100	50	1000	Ct/St
Gofton, A.F.	11	15	2	47*	232	17.84	–	–	–	–
Golding, J.M.	2	3	2	18*	21	21.00	–	–	–	–
Gooch, G.A.	581	990	75	333	44846	49.01	128	217	20+1	555
Goodwin, M.W.	48	83	8	194	3484	46.45	8	19	–	37
Gough, D.	175	236	41	121	3070	15.74	1	11	–	40
Gough, M.A.	33	57	1	123	1302	23.25	1	7	–	35
Grayson, A.P.	142	232	20	159*	6318	29.80	8	36	3	102
Green, R.J.	31	32	12	51	324	16.20	–	1	–	7
Greenidge, C.G.	5	5	–	14	29	5.80	–	–	–	3
Griffith, A.F.G.	71	128	8	186	3628	30.23	7	18	–	51
Griffiths, P.	1	–	–	–	–	–	–	–	–	–
Gripper, T.R.	20	37	2	86	908	25.94	–	8	–	16
Grove, J.O.	18	22	7	33	161	10.73	–	–	–	–
Guy, S.M.	6	9	2	42	136	19.42	–	–	–	21/2
Habib, A.	87	125	19	215	4738	44.69	12	21	2	37
Haire, R.S.	1	2	–	0	0	0.00	–	–	–	–
Hamilton, G.M.	70	94	20	125	2116	28.59	1	14	–	26
Hamilton, L.J.	18	25	7	23	79	4.38	–	–	–	7
Hancock, T.H.C.	144	251	16	220*	6507	27.68	6	39	1	88
Harden, R.J.	253	417	63	187	13336	37.67	28	70	7	189
Hardinges, M.A.	3	4	–	3	4	1.00	–	–	–	–
Harmison, S.J.	46	67	18	36	443	9.04	–	–	–	9
Harris, A.J.	57	79	22	39	545	9.56	–	–	–	20
Harrison, D.S.	3	4	–	27	56	14.00	–	–	–	–
Hartley, P.J.	232	283	66	127*	4321	19.91	2	14	–	68
Harvey, I.J.	74	125	9	136	3359	28.95	4	21	–	55
Hayden, M.L.	171	296	31	235*	13870	52.33	44	60	3+3	150
Haynes, J.J.	6	9	3	80	215	35.83	–	1	–	21/2
Hegg, W.K.	275	401	77	134	8742	26.98	5	44	–	663/76
Hemp, D.L.	144	243	19	157	7478	33.38	13	42	3	95
Hewett, J.P.	56	76	11	75	1194	18.36	–	3	–	22
Hewison, C.J.	1	2	–	24	30	15.00	–	–	–	5
Hewson, D.R.	37	69	5	87	1356	21.18	–	9	–	17
Hick, G.A.	397	653	62	405*	32082	54.28	111	122	15+1	491
Hicks, T.C.	13	16	2	54	198	14.14	–	1	–	9
Hinds, W.W.	49	86	4	165	2661	32.45	8	12	–	24
Hockley, J.B.	7	8	–	74	175	21.87	–	1	–	2
Hoggard, M.J.	42	54	17	21*	258	6.97	–	–	–	9
Hollioake, A.J.	126	192	16	182	6780	38.52	13	38	2	115
Hollioake, B.C.	63	95	6	163	2208	24.80	2	10	–	50
Holloway, P.C.L.	107	179	27	168	4791	31.51	9	24	–	79/1
House, W.J.	34	53	8	136	1363	30.28	2	8	–	20
Howitt, R.W.J.	6	10	2	118*	274	34.25	1	1	–	–
Hughes, Q.J.	28	42	8	119	1086	31.94	2	5	–	7
Hughes, T.R.	6	3	2	13*	14	14.00	–	–	–	1
Humphries, S.	31	47	5	66	555	13.21	–	2	–	56/3
Hunter, I.D.	3	4	–	63	83	20.75	–	1	–	–
Hussain, N.	270	435	43	207	16664	42.51	43	81	5	308
Hussey, M.E.	61	110	7	187	4777	46.37	12	22	–	38
Hutchison, P.M.	41	42	22	30	178	8.90	–	–	–	9
Hutton, B.L.	19	31	2	59	529	18.24	–	3	–	13
Hyam, B.J.	54	86	9	53	1231	15.98	–	2	–	148/10
Illingworth, R.K.	371	427	121	120*	6902	22.55	4	20	–	161
Ilott, M.C.	176	228	48	60	2599	14.43	–	4	–	44
Inglis, J.W.	1	2	–	2	4	2.00	–	–	–	–
Innes, K.J.	17	25	5	63	436	21.80	–	1	–	9

150

	M	I	NO	HS	Runs	Avge	100	50	1000	Ct/St
Irani, R.C.	144	237	30	168*	7682	37.11	14	43	5	60
Jacobs, R.D.	81	129	27	119*	3585	35.14	6	20	–	250/22
James, S.P.	221	385	29	309*	14196	39.87	42	51	8	160
Janmohamed, A.M.T.	3	4	1	6	16	5.33	–	–	–	–
Jarvis, P.W.	215	268	67	80	3373	16.78	–	10	–	67
Jefferson, W.I.	2	3	–	41	46	15.33	–	–	–	1
Johnson, N.C.	99	151	18	150	4181	31.43	6	27	–	105
Johnson, P.	344	575	55	187	19188	36.90	38	112	9	222/1
Johnson, R.L.	92	130	14	69	1748	15.06	–	3	–	42
Jones, I.	3	4	1	35	78	26.00	–	–	–	–
Jones, P.S.	38	48	13	105	576	16.45	1	1	–	11
Jones, S.P.	18	19	6	19*	92	7.07	–	–	–	3
Joseph, R.H.	1	1	1	0*	0	–	–	–	–	–
Joyce, A.	1	2	–	29	31	15.50	–	–	–	2
Joyce, E.C.	9	13	1	51	286	23.83	–	1	–	9
Katich, S.M.	45	81	13	154*	3125	45.95	8	16	1+1	48
Keedy, G.	65	74	41	34	363	11.00	–	–	–	15
Kendall, W.S.	89	142	19	201	4850	39.43	9	243	3	82
Kenway, D.A.	38	65	8	136	1880	32.98	2	11	1	28/1
Kerr, J.I.D.	50	71	11	80	1227	20.45	–	5	–	15
Key, R.W.T	52	90	3	125	2084	23.95	3	11	–	37
Khan, S.H.	15	13	1	87	259	21.58	–	1	–	4
Khan, W.G.	57	101	8	181	2834	30.47	5	17	–	36
Khan, Z.M.	1	–	–	–	–	–	–	–	–	–
Killeen, N.	41	61	12	48	623	12.71	–	–	–	12
King, R.D.	44	62	17	30	240	5.33	–	–	–	4
Kirtley, R.J.	77	107	32	59	773	10.30	–	1	–	21
Knight, N.V.	153	255	25	233	9265	40.28	22	45	2	213
Krikken, K.M.	190	280	54	104	5106	22.59	1	22	–	466/30
Kruis, G.J.	39	58	14	57*	588	13.36	–	1	–	14
Kumble, A.	155	203	45	154*	4012	24.76	6	15	–	76
Lacey, S.J.	26	36	10	55*	553	21.26	–	2	–	8/1
Lambert, G.A.	2	3	2	3*	6	6.00	–	–	–	1
Lampitt, S.R.	226	298	69	122	5444	23.77	1	20	–	144
Laney, J.S.	76	135	4	112	3988	30.44	5	23	1	67
Langer, J.L.	177	311	35	274*	14668	53.14	46	56	3+3	159
Lara, B.C.	184	306	8	501*	14664	49.20	40	65	3+1	234
Laraman, A.W.	2	–	–	–	–	–	–	–	–	1
Lathwell, M.N.	143	251	10	206	8025	33.29	12	49	5	96
Law, D.R.	80	124	5	115	2332	19.59	1	11	–	42
Law, S.G.	210	352	36	263	15465	48.93	48	72	4+1	235
Law, W.L.	23	35	4	131	883	28.48	1	5	–	11
Leatherdale, D.A.	179	289	34	157	8446	33.12	12	46	1	138
Lehmann, D.S.	169	288	18	255	14829	54.92	48	69	2+5	94
Lewis, C.C.	189	275	34	247	7406	30.73	9	34	–	154
Lewis, J.	77	115	17	62	1140	11.63	–	2	–	17
Lewis, J.J.B.	123	217	21	210*	6624	33.79	10	41	2	84
Lewis, S.J.W.	11	18	1	26	171	10.05	–	–	–	5
Lewry, J.D.	74	108	23	39	763	8.97	–	–	–	10
Liptrot, C.G.	15	19	7	61	143	11.91	–	1	–	5
Lloyd, G.D.	193	306	27	241	10811	38.74	24	59	5	133
Lockhart, D.R.	12	20	1	77*	377	19.84	–	1	–	11
Logan, R.J.	8	10	1	24	52	5.77	–	–	–	2
Love, M.L.	80	138	8	228	5373	41.33	14	20	0+1	97
Lowe, J.P.	11	9	4	7*	20	4.00	–	–	–	1
Loye, M.B.	126	200	18	322*	6578	36.14	14	30	2	64

151

	M	I	NO	HS	Runs	Avge	100	50	1000	Ct/St
Lucas, D.S.	16	19	8	46*	242	22.00	–	–	–	3
Lumb, M.J.	1	2	1	66*	68	68.00	–	1	–	–
Lungley, T.	1	–	–	–	–	–	–	–	–	–
McCague, M.J.	133	185	45	72	2320	16.57	–	6	–	75
McCallan, W.K.	6	12	–	65	273	22.75	–	2	–	2
McCoubrey, A.G.A.M.	2	2	1	1*	1	1.00	–	–	–	–
McGarry, A.C.	4	4	3	1	1	1.00	–	–	–	–
McGrath, A.	93	158	10	142*	4300	29.05	7	19	–	57
McGrath, G.D.	114	120	38	55	518	6.31	–	1	–	32
McKeown, P.C.	19	27	1	75	679	26.11	–	3	–	14
McLean, N.A.M.	84	130	20	70	1612	14.65	–	2	–	20
Maddy, D.L.	121	189	10	202	5757	32.16	13	25	2	119
Maher, J.P.	80	141	19	208*	4347	35.63	6	24	–	77
Maiden, G.I.	3	3	1	23*	32	16.00	–	–	–	1
Malcolm, D.E.	268	319	98	51	1694	7.66	–	1	–	40
Marsh, D.J.	48	77	14	157	2350	37.30	5	10	–	42
Marshall, J.A.H.	25	44	2	122	1262	30.04	1	9	–	34
Martin, B.P.	11	14	5	29	151	16.77	–	–	–	9
Martin, C.S.	21	29	10	13	69	3.63	–	–	–	6
Martin, P.J.	171	199	51	133	2824	19.08	1	5	–	41
Martin-Jenkins, R.S.C.	44	69	6	86	1412	22.41	–	7	–	11
Mascarenhas, A.D.	55	79	6	100	1657	22.69	1	10	–	18
Mason, T.J.	17	20	3	52*	226	13.29	–	1	–	8
Masters, D.D.	16	20	7	21	71	5.46	–	–	–	4
Mather, D.P.	32	21	8	13	74	5.69	–	–	–	6
Mauders, J.K.	1	2	–	9	13	6.50	–	–	–	1
Maynard, M.P.	337	549	56	243	20897	42.38	47	114	11	326/7
Mbangwa, M.	45	56	21	21	177	5.05	–	–	–	11
Middlebrook, J.D.	19	27	2	45	340	13.60	–	–	–	12
Millar, N.	2	1	–	0	0	0.00	–	–	–	1
Millns, D.J.	170	201	62	121	3075	22.12	3	8	–	75
Mohammed, I.	25	35	4	210*	1193	38.48	3	4	–	3
Montgomerie, R.R.	130	227	22	192	6804	33.19	13	37	2	120
Mooney, P.J.K.	5	10	3	20*	94	13.42	–	–	–	3
Morris, A.C.	42	57	10	60	866	18.42	–	4	–	22
Morris, J.E.	354	596	33	229	20899	37.12	50	100	11	153
Morris, Z.C.	2	4	–	10	11	2.75	–	–	–	–
Mullally, A.D.	185	209	52	75	1374	8.75	–	2	–	36
Munton, T.A.	243	259	97	54*	1682	10.38	–	3	–	80
Murphy, B.A.	12	16	5	41	124	11.27	–	–	–	9
Murtagh, T.J.	1	1	1	12*	12	–	–	–	–	–
Nagamootoo, M.V.	48	78	7	100	1300	18.30	1	4	–	31
Napier, G.R.	6	8	2	35*	107	17.83	–	–	–	6
Nash, D.C.	56	81	12	114	1898	27.50	2	7	–	96/9
Neely, G.J.	1	1	–	0	0	0.00	–	–	–	–
Newell, K.	65	112	12	135	2634	26.34	4	10	–	20
Nixon, P.A.	200	283	62	134*	6888	31.16	12	26	1	515/42
Nkala, M.L.	6	7	1	40	120	20.00	–	–	–	1
Noon, W.M.	89	140	22	83	2474	20.96	–	12	–	187/20
Olonga, H.K.	43	62	17	45	431	9.57	–	–	–	23
Oram, J.D.P.	20	30	3	155	888	32.88	1	5	–	16
Ormond, J.	50	53	12	50*	486	11.85	–	1	–	10
Ostler, D.P.	176	291	23	208	9178	34.24	12	59	5	210
Papps, M.H.W.	11	22	3	84	530	27.89	–	4	–	9/1
Parkin, O.T.	36	43	20	24*	203	8.82	–	–	–	9
Parsons, K.A.	87	140	14	193*	3450	27.38	4	19	–	77

	M	I	NO	HS	Runs	Avge	100	50	1000	Ct/St
Parsons, R.A.	2	4	1	27*	55	18.33	–	–	–	2
Patel, M.M.	127	175	35	67	2117	15.12	–	6	–	70
Patterson, A.D.	10	15	1	31	155	11.07	–	–	–	18
Patterson, B.M.W.	10	18	1	114	831	48.88	3	4	–	11
Patterson, M.W.	2	3	–	4	6	2.00	–	–	–	–
Peirce, M.T.E.	69	122	2	123	2928	24.40	2	17	–	30
Penberthy, A.L.	148	218	25	128	5268	27.29	5	30	–	88
Peng, N.	8	14	–	98	231	16.50	–	1	–	1
Penney, T.L.	155	245	45	151	7953	39.76	15	36	2	90/2
Peters, S.D.	47	76	12	110	1737	27.14	2	9	–	40
Phillip, W.	18	29	6	67*	288	12.52	–	1	–	48/3
Phillips, B.J.	27	39	4	100*	584	16.68	1	2	–	8
Phillips, N.C.	47	69	12	53	858	15.05	–	3	–	25
Phillips, T.J.	3	4	–	16	27	6.75	–	–	–	1
Pierson, A.R.K.	179	222	69	108*	2641	17.26	1	5	–	86
Pietersen, K.P.	10	13	2	61*	253	23.00	–	2	–	10
Pimlott, C.R.	11	8	5	31*	72	24.00	–	–	–	3
Pipe, D.J.	5	7	–	54	128	18.28	–	1	–	2/1
Piper, J.W.S.	1	1	–	19	19	19.00	–	–	–	–
Piper, K.J.	172	239	37	116*	3892	19.26	2	11	–	437/31
Pollard, P.R.	182	320	23	180	9376	31.56	14	48	3	153
Porter, J.J.	6	10	–	93	297	29.70	–	4	–	–
Powell, M.J. (Gm)	55	89	10	200*	3029	38.34	6	14	1	27
Powell, M.J. (Nh)	1	2	–	1	2	1.00	–	–	–	–
Powell, M.J. (Wa)	44	71	3	145	2253	33.13	5	12	1	32
Pratt, A.	10	13	1	38	231	19.25	–	–	–	11
Pratt, G.J.	2	3	–	23	39	13.00	–	–	–	1
Prichard, P.J.	323	529	49	245	16633	34.65	31	97	8	201
Prittipaul, L.R.	4	6	–	152	298	49.66	1	1	–	1
Pryke, D.J.	32	30	11	48	290	15.26	–	–	–	16
Pyemont, J.P.	29	42	3	124	838	21.48	1	4	–	16
Ramprakash, M.R.	287	473	62	235	19048	46.34	51	97	10	170
Ramsden, G.	1	1	1	0*	0	–	–	–	–	–
Randall, S.J.	4	5	1	20	30	7.50	–	–	–	3
Rashid, U.B.A.	27	42	6	110	1054	29.27	1	7	–	11
Ratcliffe, J.D.	135	242	13	135	6545	28.58	5	38	–	68
Rawnsley, M.J.	27	32	3	26	292	10.06	–	–	–	14
Read, C.M.W.	60	89	13	160	1777	23.38	1	6	–	163/6
Redmayne, J.R.S.	4	6	1	68	139	27.80	–	1	–	–
Redmond, A.J.	10	18	2	92	505	31.56	–	4	–	10
Reiffel, P.R.	152	185	54	86	3231	24.66	–	15	–	71
Renshaw, S.J.	39	48	20	56	459	16.39	–	1	–	14
Rhodes, S.J.	382	541	142	122*	13019	32.62	11	65	2	969/113
Richardson, A.	20	18	10	17*	56	7.00	–	–	–	4
Richardson, M.H.	75	130	21	212*	4141	37.99	9	16	–	34
Richardson, S.A.	1	2	–	11	14	7.00	–	–	–	–
Ripley, D.	292	385	98	209	8212	28.61	9	32	–	633/82
Robinson, D.D.J.	89	155	7	200	4128	27.89	7	19	–	76
Robinson, J.D.	33	53	10	79	1020	23.72	–	5	–	12
Robinson, M.A.	214	242	104	27	548	3.97	–	–	–	40
Rollins, A.S.	117	211	18	210	6657	34.49	12	37	3	100/1
Rose, F.A.	78	106	17	96	1196	13.43	–	2	–	18
Rose, G.D.	245	339	63	191	8628	31.26	11	41	1	116
Roseberry, M.A.	225	384	41	185	11530	33.61	21	56	4	156
Ross, J.S.	4	5	1	2*	4	1.00	–	–	–	–
Russell, R.C.	425	632	132	129*	15031	30.06	8	79	1	1077/120

153

	M	I	NO	HS	Runs	Avge	100	50	1000	Ct/St
Saggers, M.J.	26	35	10	24	219	8.76	–	–	–	6
Sales, D.J.G.	74	115	10	303*	3711	35.34	8	15	1	53
Salisbury, I.D.K.	226	290	60	100*	4315	18.76	1	16	–	150
Salmond, G.	12	21	2	181	888	46.73	2	3	–	8
Saqlain Mushtaq	100	142	39	79	1535	14.90	–	6	–	45
Sarwan, R.R.	48	83	9	111	2230	30.13	3	14	–	29
Savident, L.	4	6	2	10*	32	8.00	–	–	–	2
Sawal, M.A.	1	2	1	2*	2	2.00	–	–	–	–
Saxelby, M.J.	61	106	7	181	2916	29.45	2	17	1	18
Sayers, C.A.	10	12	5	46	80	11.42	–	–	–	5
Schofield, C.P.	35	47	8	74	974	24.97	–	7	–	17
Scott, D.A.	8	10	8	17*	46	23.00	–	–	–	3
Scuderi, J.C.	70	113	16	125*	2928	30.18	3	14	–	24
Sexton, A.J.	4	7	–	36	71	10.14	–	–	–	3
Shah, K.Z.	4	6	2	38*	102	25.50	–	–	–	–
Shah, O.A.	63	105	8	140	2951	30.42	6	14	–	42
Shahid, N.	121	191	25	139	5348	32.21	7	29	1	117
Shaw, A.D.	71	96	15	140	1730	21.35	1	8	–	169/14
Sheikh, M.A.	5	7	2	58*	157	31.40	–	1	–	–
Sheikh, S.M.	6	4	2	17	26	13.00	–	–	–	1
Sheriyar, A.	93	95	33	21	505	8.14	–	–	–	15
Shields, I.P.	2	4	–	31	54	13.50	–	–	–	2
Sidebottom, R.J.	24	32	10	54	247	11.22	–	1	–	11
Silverwood, C.E.W.	97	128	28	58	1519	15.19	–	4	–	21
Singh, A.	43	67	3	157	1829	28.57	4	7	–	15
Smalley, R.G.	7	10	1	83	272	30.22	–	1	–	6/4
Smethurst, M.P.	21	23	10	66	166	12.76	–	1	–	4
Smith, A.M.	133	176	48	61	1590	12.42	–	4	–	25
Smith, B.F.	160	237	32	204	7553	36.84	16	32	2	74
Smith, C.J.O.	3	5	–	57	100	20.00	–	1	–	9/1
Smith, E.T.	61	103	6	190	3507	36.15	6	17	1	18
Smith, G.J.	58	72	27	68	580	12.88	–	2	–	9
Smith, N.M.K.	177	252	32	161	6054	27.51	4	31	1	62
Smith, R.A.	385	651	83	209*	24203	42.61	56	122	11	214
Smith, T.M.	26	32	9	53*	298	12.95	–	1	–	7
Snape, J.N.	71	105	20	98*	2255	26.52	–	14	–	50
Solanki, V.S.	101	170	12	185	5799	36.70	9	34	2	119
Speak, N.J.	174	303	33	232	9597	35.54	15	56	3	108
Speight, M.P.	185	308	28	184	8921	31.86	13	47	3	289/5
Spendlove, B.L.	20	36	2	63	656	19.29	–	2	–	10
Spiring, K.R.	45	78	10	150	2237	32.89	4	13	1	22
Stelling, W.F.	18	28	2	53	475	18.26	–	1	–	8
Stemp, R.D.	160	189	63	65	1544	12.25	–	2	–	67
Stephenson, J.P.	278	468	44	202*	13719	32.35	24	71	5	173
Stevens, D.I.	29	46	–	130	1057	22.97	1	5	–	19
Stewart, A.J.	395	654	70	271*	23357	39.99	46	129	8	581/21
Strang, B.C.	59	88	16	73	1073	14.90	–	4	–	20
Strang, P.A.	90	133	27	106*	3028	28.56	2	16	–	82
Strauss, A.J.	29	51	3	111*	1496	31.16	1	8	–	12
Streak, H.H.	87	126	22	131	2358	22.67	2	11	–	32
Strong, M.R.	6	10	4	35*	125	20.83	–	–	–	2
Stubbings, S.D.	24	44	4	135*	1129	28.22	1	4	–	7
Styris, S.B.	35	59	9	100*	1285	25.70	1	5	–	21
Such, P.M.	291	307	116	54	1528	8.00	–	2	–	112
Sulzberger, G.P.	37	61	4	159	1793	31.45	5	6	–	22
Sutcliffe, I.J.	88	132	12	167	3643	30.35	5	19	–	49

	M	I	NO	HS	Runs	Avge	100	50	1000	Ct/St
Sutton, L.D.	13	22	4	79	448	24.88	–	2	–	30/1
Swann, A.J.	31	48	2	154	1286	27.95	4	5	–	19
Swann, G.P.	55	79	7	130*	2061	28.62	2	9	–	36
Symington, M.J.	3	3	2	36	52	52.00	–	–	–	1
Taibu, T.	4	6	2	36	64	16.00	–	–	–	8
Taylor, B.V.	6	8	4	14	23	5.75	–	–	–	1
Taylor, C.G.	12	22	3	104	492	25.89	1	–	–	8
Taylor, J.P.	171	196	62	86	1980	14.77	–	8	–	58
Tennant, A.M.	3	3	–	5	5	1.66	–	–	–	1
Thomas, I.J.	4	6	2	82	186	46.50	–	1	–	5
Thomas, S.D.	112	150	34	78*	2223	19.16	–	9	–	38
Thompson, D.J.J.	11	13	–	22	109	8.38	–	–	–	1
Thorpe, G.P.	261	435	61	223*	16487	44.08	36	92	8	217
Titchard, S.P.	104	181	14	163	5227	31.29	6	30	–	54
Tolley, C.M.	106	148	31	84	2666	22.78	–	13	–	42
Tournier, M.A.	1	–	–	–	–	–	–	–	–	–
Townsend, C.J.	23	23	10	27	159	12.23	–	–	–	35/5
Trego, P.D.	7	8	1	62	134	19.14	–	1	–	3
Tremlett, C.T.	1	2	–	17	33	16.50	–	–	–	–
Trescothick, M.E.	104	173	7	190	5147	31.00	7	29	–	114
Trott, B.J.	5	4	3	1*	1	1.00	–	–	–	2
Tucker, J.P.	1	1	–	14	14	14.00	–	–	–	1
Tudor, A.J.	57	72	22	99*	1048	20.96	–	3	–	13
Tuffey, D.R.	26	31	10	89*	309	14.71	–	2	–	10
Tufnell, P.C.R.	285	314	120	67*	1925	9.92	–	1	–	103
Turner, R.J.	176	270	48	144	6803	30.64	8	35	2	446/39
Udal, S.D.	167	240	44	117*	4363	22.26	1	18	–	78
Van der Gucht, C.G.	1	1	1	0*	0	–	–	–	–	–
Vaughan, M.P.	144	255	13	183	8372	34.59	18	38	4	59
Viljoen, D.P.	28	43	4	173*	1071	27.46	1	5	–	17
Vonwiller, B.M.	2	2	1	1*	1	1.00	–	–	–	2
Wagh, M.A.	66	106	11	216*	3294	34.67	9	12	1	31
Walker, B.G.K.	30	41	7	107*	736	21.64	1	1	–	8
Walker, M.J.	70	117	12	275*	2845	27.09	3	11	–	47
Wallace, M.A.	6	9	2	64*	214	30.57	–	2	–	22
Walsh, C.A.	414	532	151	66	4473	11.74	–	8	–	116
Ward, I.J.	56	93	9	158*	2849	33.91	4	21	1	35
Ward, T.R.	213	365	20	235*	12007	34.80	24	70	6	205
Warne, S.K.	166	221	30	86	3170	16.59	–	9	–	123
Warren, C.C.M.	3	5	1	21	41	10.25	–	–	–	1
Warren, R.J.	88	142	17	201*	4095	32.76	5	23	–	97/3
Watkin, S.L.	251	280	102	51	1849	10.38	–	1	–	66
Watkinson, M.	308	459	49	161	10939	26.88	11	50	–	156
Weekes, I.C.	23	34	5	46	473	16.31	–	–	–	17
Weekes, P.N.	143	224	25	171*	6400	32.16	10	29	1	131
Weenink, S.W.	12	19	2	72*	224	13.17	–	1	–	7
Welch, G.	78	109	18	84*	1895	20.82	–	8	–	30
Wells, A.P.	376	628	81	253*	21099	38.57	46	101	11	227
Wells, V.J.	160	246	18	224	7708	33.80	14	39	2	106
Welton, G.E.	33	60	3	200*	1436	25.19	1	6	–	16
Weston, R.M.S.	41	72	3	156	1726	25.01	3	6	–	28
Weston, W.P.C.	144	253	25	205	7685	33.70	15	37	3	71
Wharf, A.G.	38	56	7	101*	849	17.32	2	3	–	21
Wharton, L.J.	7	9	4	7	15	3.00	–	–	–	2
Whiley, M.J.A.	3	4	1	0*	0	0.00	–	–	–	1
White, C.	169	259	36	181	6678	29.94	8	33	–	116

155

	M	I	NO	HS	Runs	Avge	100	50	1000	Ct/St
White, G.W.	103	177	15	156	5222	32.23	7	29	1	84
White, R.A.	1	2	–	20	31	15.50	–	–	–	2
Whittall, G.J.	83	144	13	203*	3948	30.13	8	19	–	51
Widdup, S.	9	14	1	44	201	15.46	–	–	–	6
Williams, R.C.J.	39	50	9	90	788	19.21	–	5	–	108/16
Williamson, D.	9	13	4	47	273	30.33	–	–	–	5
Williamson, J.G.	6	8	–	55	187	23.37	–	1	–	1
Wilson, E.J.	31	58	4	116	1416	26.22	3	7	–	18
Wilton, N.J.	16	25	4	55	352	16.76	–	1	–	37/2
Windows, M.G.N.	96	171	12	184	5456	34.31	10	29	2	61
Wishart, C.B.	70	122	9	144	2854	25.25	5	14	–	45
Wood, J.	88	132	20	63*	1335	11.91	–	2	–	23
Wood, M.J.	49	83	9	200*	1987	26.85	5	7	1	33
Wood, N.T.	30	45	5	155	1179	29.47	1	5	–	5
Wrigglesworth, I.A.	6	12	–	85	353	29.41	–	3	–	7
Wright, C.M.	4	6	2	40	86	21.50	–	–	–	2
Yardy, M.H.	4	8	1	25	64	9.14	–	–	–	–
Yates, G.	79	103	35	134*	1707	25.10	3	4	–	36

BOWLING

'50wS' denotes instances of taking 50 or more wickets in a season. Where these have been achieved outside the British Isles they are shown after a plus sign.

	Runs	Wkts	Avge	Best	5wI	10wM	50wS
Adams, C.J.	1719	31	55.45	4- 29	–	–	–
Adams, J.C.	3540	93	38.06	5- 17	1	–	–
Adams, K.	58	2	29.00	2- 58	–	–	–
Afzaal, U.	2406	44	54.68	4-101	–	–	–
Aldred, P.	3609	114	31.65	7-101	5	1	1
Ali, Kabir	869	23	37.78	4-114	–	–	–
Ali, S.M.	9	0					
Alleyne, M.W.	10753	334	32.19	6- 49	7	–	1
Altree, D.A.	497	8	62.12	3- 41	–	–	–
Ambrose, C.E.L.	19048	941	20.24	8- 45	50	8	5+2
Amin, R.M.	781	20	39.05	4- 87	–	–	–
Anderson, R.S.G.	2002	74	27.05	6- 34	5	1	1
Asif Mujtaba	6924	310	22.33	6- 17	18	4	0+2
Asim Butt	1302	51	25.52	5- 53	1	–	–
Atherton, M.A.	4733	108	43.82	6- 78	3	–	–
Austin, I.D.	7954	262	30.35	6- 43	6	1	–
Averis, J.M.M.	1958	33	59.33	5- 98	1	–	–
Aymes, A.N.	331	4	82.75	2-135	–	–	–
Bailey, R.J.	4899	114	42.97	5- 54	2	–	–
Ball, M.C.J.	9891	257	38.48	8- 46	8	1	–
Barnett, K.J.	6999	186	37.62	6- 28	3	–	–
Bates, J.J.	1528	49	31.18	5- 67	4	–	–
Batt, C.J.	1092	37	29.51	6-101	2	–	–
Batty, G.J.	128	4	32.00	2- 45	–	–	–
Batty, J.N.	61	1	61.00	1- 21	–	–	–
Betts, M.M.	6248	225	27.76	9- 64	10	2	–
Bevan, M.G.	4875	110	44.31	6- 82	1	1	–
Bichel, A.J.	5612	239	23.48	6- 45	13	2	0+1
Bicknell, D.J.	789	23	34.30	3- 7	–	–	–
Bicknell, M.P.	20143	826	24.38	9- 45	32	3	9
Bishop, I.E.	376	7	53.71	2- 45	–	–	–
Bishop, J.E.	180	3	60.00	2- 89	–	–	–

156

	Runs	Wkts	Avge	Best	5wI	10wM	50wS
Blackwell, I.D.	2356	51	46.19	5-115	1	–	–
Blain, J.A.R.	282	3	94.00	1- 18	–	–	–
Blakey, R.J.	68	1	68.00	1- 68	–	–	–
Blewett, G.S.	4141	100	41.41	5- 29	1	–	–
Bloomfield, T.F.	2759	91	30.31	5- 36	4	–	–
Boswell, S.A.J.	1504	36	41.77	5- 94	1	–	–
Bowen, M.N.	5925	183	32.37	7- 73	7	1	–
Bowler, P.D.	2009	33	60.87	3- 25	–	–	–
Brent, G.B.	1655	59	28.05	6- 84	1	–	–
Bressington, A.N.	49	5	9.80	4- 36	–	–	–
Bridge, G.D.	110	1	110.00	1- 60	–	–	–
Brinkley, J.E.	1453	51	28.49	6- 35	2	–	–
Brooker, J.A.D.	38	0					
Brown, A.D.	328	1	328.00	1- 56	–	–	–
Brown, D.R.	8052	307	26.22	8- 89	12	3	2
Brown, J.F.	2763	116	23.81	7- 78	8	3	1
Brown, S.J.E.	15402	534	28.84	7- 51	35	2	7
Bulbeck, M.P.L.	2174	90	24.15	5- 45	3	1	1
Burns, M.	1091	26	41.96	3- 11	–	–	–
Burns, N.D.	8	0					
Butcher, G.P.	2252	61	36.91	7- 77	2	–	–
Butcher, M.A.	3480	104	33.46	5- 86	1	–	–
Byas, D.	727	12	60.58	3- 55	–	–	–
Byrne, B.W.	1352	19	71.15	3- 66	–	–	–
Caddick, A.R.	17397	718	24.22	9- 32	49	13	8
Callaghan, D.J.	3078	102	30.17	4- 17	–	–	–
Campbell, A.D.R.	840	19	44.21	4- 82	–	–	–
Campbell, S.L.	129	1	129.00	1- 38	–	–	–
Canning, T.K.	745	37	20.13	5- 47	2	–	–
Carlisle, S.V.	0	0					
Carpenter, J.R.	81	1	81.00	1- 50	–	–	–
Carroll, R.W.S.	52	0					
Carter, N.M.	111	7	15.85	3- 48	–	–	–
Cassar, M.E.	2287	75	30.49	6- 76	2	–	–
Catterall, D.N.	308	11	28.00	4- 50	–	–	–
Cawdron, M.J.	800	41	19.51	6- 25	5	1	–
Chanderpaul, S.	2155	51	42.25	4- 48	–	–	–
Chapple, G.	9551	331	28.85	6- 42	11	–	2
Chilton, M.J.	153	2	76.50	1- 1	–	–	–
Clough, G.D.	11	0					
Collingwood, P.D.	1678	42	39.95	3- 7	–	–	–
Collymore, C.D.	1079	49	22.02	4- 39	–	–	–
Cook, I.W.	7	0					
Cook, S.J.	1289	38	33.92	4- 13	–	–	–
Cork, D.G.	15676	594	26.39	9- 43	20	2	5
Cosker, D.A.	5801	170	34.12	6-140	2	–	–
Cotterell, T.P.	663	11	60.27	3- 69	–	–	–
Cottey, P.A.	862	16	53.87	4- 49	–	–	–
Cousins, D.M.	2456	94	26.12	6- 35	2	–	1
Cowan, A.P.	6412	206	31.12	6- 47	7	–	1
Cox, J.	319	4	79.75	3- 46	–	–	–
Craven, V.J.	15	0					
Crawley, J.P.	199	1	199.00	1- 90	–	–	–
Creese, M.L.	98	1	98.00	1- 37	–	–	–
Croft, R.D.B.	23002	635	36.22	8- 66	28	4	5
Crowe, C.D.	1006	32	31.43	4- 55	–	–	–

	Runs	Wkts	Avge	Best	5wI	10wM	50wS
Cullinan, D.J.	289	5	57.80	2- 27	–	–	–
Dagnall, C.E.	269	11	24.45	4- 20	–	–	–
Dakin, J.M.	2323	58	40.05	4- 27	–	–	–
Dale, A.	7204	201	35.84	6- 18	4	–	–
Daley, J.A.	81	1	81.00	1- 12	–	–	–
Danson, A.R.	384	8	48.00	3- 20	–	–	–
Davies, A.P.	603	16	37.68	2- 22	–	–	–
Davies, M.K.	2425	93	26.07	6- 49	5	–	–
Davis, M.J.G.	4731	141	33.55	8- 37	3	1	–
Dawson, R.K.J.	115	1	115.00	1-115	–	–	–
Dean, K.J.	3837	174	22.05	8- 52	9	1	1
De Bruyn, Z.	729	19	38.36	6-120	1	–	–
DeFreitas, P.A.J.	29368	1060	27.70	7- 21	54	5	12
Di Venuto, M.J.	247	4	61.75	1- 0	–	–	–
Donald, A.A.	25394	1136	22.35	8- 37	65	9	5
Dowman, M.P.	1118	25	44.72	3- 10	–	–	–
Drakes, V.C.	10336	425	24.32	8- 59	21	3	2+2
Dravid, R.	240	4	60.00	2- 16	–	–	–
Driver, R.C.	44	2	22.00	1- 13	–	–	–
Dunlop, A.R.	143	2	71.50	1- 8	–	–	–
Dutch, K.P.	1191	38	31.34	6- 62	1	–	–
Dwyer, M.D.	148	10	14.80	4- 57	–	–	–
Ealham, M.A.	9592	334	28.71	8- 36	14	1	–
Elliott, M.T.G.	562	9	62.44	1- 3	–	–	–
Elstub, C.J.	175	8	21.87	3- 37	–	–	–
Englefield, J.I.	4	0					
Evans, A.W.	3	0					
Fairbrother, N.H.	453	6	75.50	2- 91	–	–	–
Fellows, G.M.	467	10	46.70	2- 27	–	–	–
Fisher, I.D.	1352	42	32.19	5- 35	2	–	–
Flanagan, I.N.	51	1	51.00	1- 50	–	–	–
Fleming, M.V.	9213	262	35.16	5- 51	2	–	–
Fleming, S.P.	110	0					
Flintoff, A.	1676	52	32.23	5- 24	1	–	–
Flower, A.	163	4	40.75	1- 1	–	–	–
Flower, G.W.	2853	83	34.37	7- 31	2	–	–
Francis, S.R.G.	1232	25	49.28	4- 95	–	–	–
Franklin, G.D.	78	0					
Franks, P.J.	5812	211	27.54	7- 56	8	–	2
Fraser, A.R.C.	22883	847	27.01	8- 53	35	5	7
Frost, T.	6	0					
Fulton, D.P.	110	1	110.00	1- 37	–	–	–
Gallian, J.E.R.	3825	94	40.69	6-115	1	–	–
Ganguly, S.C.	3691	96	38.44	6- 87	2	–	–
Gannon, B.W.	1724	62	27.80	6- 80	3	–	–
Garland, R.	777	15	51.80	2- 64	–	–	–
Gayle, C.H.	900	20	45.00	4- 86	–	–	–
Giddins, E.S.H.	11388	413	27.57	6- 47	21	2	4
Giles, A.F.	7155	279	25.64	8- 90	13	2	2
Gillespie, M.A.	75	4	18.75	2- 34	–	–	–
Gofton, A.F.	688	10	68.80	3- 41	–	–	–
Golding, J.M.	112	2	56.00	1- 38	–	–	–
Gooch, G.A.	8457	246	34.37	7- 14	3	–	–
Goodwin, M.W.	297	7	42.42	2- 23	–	–	–
Gough, D.	16682	630	26.47	7- 28	25	3	5
Gough, M.A.	660	11	60.00	4- 49	–	–	–

	Runs	Wkts	Avge	Best	5wI	10wM	50wS
Grayson, A.P.	4640	110	42.18	4-16	–	–	–
Green, R.J.	2297	55	41.76	6-41	1	–	–
Greenidge, C.G.	337	12	28.08	5-60	1	–	–
Griffith, A.F.G.	36	0					
Griffiths, P.	65	1	65.00	1-65	–	–	–
Gripper, T.R.	301	5	60.20	2-42	–	–	–
Grove, J.O.	1384	35	39.54	5-90	1	–	–
Guy, S.M.	8	0					
Habib, A.	52	0					
Hamilton, G.M.	5330	212	25.14	7-50	8	2	1
Hamilton, L.J.	1661	74	22.44	5-43	3	–	–
Hancock, T.H.C.	1558	43	36.23	3- 5	–	–	–
Harden, R.J.	1023	20	51.15	2- 7	–	–	–
Hardinges, M.A.	159	4	39.75	2-16	–	–	–
Harmison, S.J.	4491	148	30.34	5-70	2	–	2
Harris, A.J.	5893	181	32.55	6-40	8	1	1
Harrison, D.S.	109	1	109.00	1-15	–	–	–
Hartley, P.J.	20635	683	30.21	9-41	23	3	7
Harvey, I.J.	5559	192	28.95	7-44	8	1	–
Hayden, M.L.	548	16	34.25	3-10	–	–	–
Hegg, W.K.	7	0					
Hemp, D.L.	741	17	43.58	3-23	–	–	–
Hewitt, J.P.	4470	160	27.93	6-14	5	–	–
Hewson, D.R.	37	1	37.00	1- 7	–	–	–
Hick, G.A.	9789	223	43.89	5-18	5	1	–
Hicks, T.C.	1242	24	51.75	5-54	1	–	–
Hinds, W.W.	139	5	27.80	3-32	–	–	–
Hockley, J.B.	57	1	57.00	1-57	–	–	–
Hoggard, M.J.	3542	145	24.42	5-47	5	–	1
Hollioake, A.J.	3994	100	39.94	5-62	1	–	–
Hollioake, B.C.	3685	117	31.49	5-51	1	–	–
Holloway, P.C.L.	50	0					
House, W.J.	964	4	241.00	1-34	–	–	–
Howitt, R.W.J.	254	4	63.50	2-54	–	–	–
Hughes, Q.J.	323	5	64.60	2-73	–	–	–
Hughes, T.R.	408	9	45.33	3-55	–	–	–
Hunter, I.D.	228	6	38.00	4-73	–	–	–
Hussain, N.	322	2	161.00	1-38	–	–	–
Hussey, M.E.	107	3	35.66	2-21	–	–	–
Hutchison, P.M.	3338	148	22.55	7-31	7	1	1
Hutton, B.L.	485	8	60.62	2- 9	–	–	–
Hyam, B.J.	8	0					
Illingworth, R.K.	25897	821	31.54	7-50	27	6	5
Ilott, M.C.	15977	590	27.07	9-19	26	3	6
Innes, K.J.	786	29	27.10	4-61	–	–	–
Irani, R.C.	8131	269	30.22	5-19	5	–	1
James, S.P.	3	0					
Janmohamed, A.M.T.	29	0					
Jarvis, P.W	18914	654	28.92	7-55	22	3	4
Johnson, N.C.	5066	162	31.27	5-79	2	–	–
Johnson, P.	605	6	100.83	1- 9	–	–	–
Johnson, R.L.	7712	275	28.04	10-45	7	2	3
Jones, I.	341	6	56.83	3-81	–	–	–
Jones, P.S.	3123	88	35.48	6-67	2	–	–
Jones, S.P.	1495	36	41.52	5-31	1	–	–
Joseph, R.H.	56	1	56.00	1-23	–	–	–

	Runs	Wkts	Avge	Best	5wI	10wM	50wS
Joyce, E.C.	102	0					
Katich, S.M.	610	8	76.25	1- 4	–	–	–
Keedy, G.	5982	170	35.18	6- 56	4	2	–
Kendall, W.S.	417	10	41.70	3- 37	–	–	–
Kenway, D.A.	76	2	38.00	1- 5	–	–	–
Kerr, J.I.D.	3913	104	37.62	7- 23	2	–	–
Key, R.W.T.	35	0					
Khan, S.H.	1323	17	77.82	3- 70	–	–	–
Khan, W.G.	62	0					
Khan, Z.M.	45	1	45.00	1- 32	–	–	–
Killeen, N.	3616	128	28.25	7- 85	6	–	1
King, R.D.	3605	154	23.40	7- 82	8	1	–
Kirtley, R.J.	7088	275	25.77	7- 21	15	1	3
Knight, N.V.	191	1	191.00	1- 61	–	–	–
Krikken, K.M.	94	1	94.00	1- 54	–	–	–
Kruis, G.J.	3559	114	31.21	7- 58	4	–	–
Kumble, A.	16855	712	23.67	10- 74	49	13	1+1
Lacey, S.J.	1429	30	47.63	4- 84	–	–	–
Lambert, G.A.	133	4	33.25	2- 62	–	–	–
Lampitt, S.R.	16555	577	28.69	7- 45	19	–	7
Laney, J.S.	224	2	112.00	1- 24	–	–	–
Langer, J.L.	191	5	38.20	2- 17	–	–	–
Lara, B.C.	411	4	102.75	1- 1	–	–	–
Laraman, A.W.	55	4	13.75	4- 33	–	–	–
Lathwell, M.N.	684	13	52.61	2- 21	–	–	–
Law, D.R.	5214	152	34.30	5- 33	5	–	–
Law, S.G.	3781	80	47.26	5- 39	1	–	–
Law, W.L.	89	3	29.66	2- 29	–	–	–
Leatherdale, D.A.	2854	95	30.04	5- 20	2	–	–
Lehmann, D.S.	1557	33	47.18	4- 42	–	–	–
Lewis, C.C.	16225	543	29.88	6- 22	20	3	2
Lewis, J.	6853	264	25.95	8- 95	12	1	3
Lewis, J.J.B.	121	1	121.00	1- 73	–	–	–
Lewry, J.D.	6941	271	25.61	7- 38	17	2	3
Liptrot, C.G.	989	27	36.62	6- 44	2	–	–
Lloyd, G.D.	440	2	220.00	1- 4	–	–	–
Logan, R.J.	631	19	33.21	5- 61	1	–	–
Love, M.L.	5	1	5.00	1- 5	–	–	–
Lowe, J.P.	654	8	81.75	2- 42	–	–	–
Loye, M.B.	43	0					
Lucas, D.S.	1282	42	30.52	5-104	1	–	–
Lungley, T.	41	6	6.83	3- 10	–	–	–
McCague, M.J.	12293	454	27.07	9- 86	25	2	4
McCallan, W.K.	492	9	54.66	3- 63	–	–	–
McCoubrey, A.G.A.M.	137	5	27.40	3- 38	–	–	–
McGarry, A.C.	376	10	37.60	3- 29	–	–	–
McGrath, A.	528	15	35.20	3- 18	–	–	–
McGrath, G.D.	10797	514	21.00	8- 38	29	6	1+1
McLean, N.A.M.	7518	269	27.94	7- 28	8	–	1
Maddy, D.L.	1085	27	40.18	3- 5	–	–	–
Maher, J.P.	412	10	41.20	3- 11	–	–	–
Maiden, G.I.	139	6	23.16	2- 11	–	–	–
Malcolm, D.E.	27845	912	30.53	9- 57	37	7	7
Marsh, D.J.	3844	93	41.33	7- 57	1	–	–
Marshall, J.A.H.	45	0					
Martin, B.P.	1034	47	22.00	7- 33	5	2	–

	Runs	Wkts	Avge	Best	5wI	10wM	50wS
Martin, C.S.	1915	64	29.92	5- 44	1	–	–
Martin, P.J.	12968	469	27.65	8- 32	14	1	3
Martin-Jenkins, R.S.C.	3066	103	29.76	7- 54	2	–	–
Mascarenhas, A.D.	3378	99	34.12	6- 88	2	–	–
Mason, T.J.	1154	24	48.08	3- 32	–	–	–
Masters, D.D.	1161	48	24.18	6- 27	3	–	–
Mather, D.P.	2681	61	43.95	6- 74	1	1	–
Maynard, M.P.	861	6	143.50	3- 21	–	–	–
Mbangwa, M.	2667	99	26.93	6- 14	2	1	–
Middlebrook, J.D.	1193	44	27.11	6- 82	1	1	–
Millar, N.	17	0					
Millns, D.J.	15042	552	27.25	9- 37	23	4	4
Mohammed, I.	196	3	65.33	1- 13	–	–	–
Montgomerie, R.R.	72	0					
Mooney, P.J.K.	265	10	26.50	4- 12	–	–	–
Morris, A.C.	2579	105	24.56	5- 52	3	1	1
Morris, J.E.	939	8	117.37	1- 6	–	–	–
Morris, Z.C.	99	0					
Mullally, A.D.	16238	563	28.84	9- 93	23	4	4
Munton, T.A.	18406	718	25.63	8- 89	34	6	6
Murphy, B.A.	841	24	35.04	4- 71	–	–	–
Murtagh, T.J.	6	1	6.00	1- 6	–	–	–
Nagamootoo, M.V.	4627	169	27.37	7- 76	3	1	–
Napier, G.R.	185	5	37.00	2- 25	–	–	–
Nash, D.C.	19	1	19.00	1- 8	–	–	–
Neely, G.J.	29	2	14.50	2- 29	–	–	–
Newell, K.	975	24	40.62	4- 61	–	–	–
Nixon, P.A.	14	0					
Nkala, M.L.	366	12	30.50	3- 35	–	–	–
Noon, W.M.	34	0					
Olonga, H.K.	3672	113	32.49	5- 70	2	–	–
Oram, J.D.P.	665	29	22.93	5- 30	1	–	–
Ormond, J.	4310	176	24.48	6- 33	11	–	1
Ostler, D.P.	249	1	249.00	1- 46	–	–	–
Parkin, O.T.	2569	96	26.76	5- 24	2	–	–
Parsons, K.A.	2529	62	40.79	5- 13	2	–	–
Parsons, R.A.	10	0					
Patel, M.M.	12050	394	30.58	8- 96	21	8	3
Patterson, M.W.	163	10	16.30	6- 80	1	–	–
Peirce, M.T.E.	272	3	90.66	1- 16	–	–	–
Penberthy, A.L.	7145	189	37.80	5- 37	4	–	–
Penney, T.L.	184	6	30.66	3- 18	–	–	–
Peters, S.D.	19	1	19.00	1- 19	–	–	–
Phillips, B.J.	1914	65	29.44	5- 47	2	–	–
Phillips, N.C.	3951	80	49.38	6- 97	3	1	–
Phillips, T.J.	278	8	34.75	4- 42	–	–	–
Pierson, A.R.K.	13759	363	37.90	8- 42	14	–	1
Pietersen, K.P.	762	23	33.13	4-141	–	–	–
Pimlott, C.R.	586	17	34.47	3- 10	–	–	–
Piper, J.W.S.	30	2	15.00	2- 30	–	–	–
Piper, K.J.	57	1	57.00	1- 57	–	–	–
Pollard, P.R.	272	4	68.00	2- 79	–	–	–
Porter, J.J.	50	0					
Powell, M.J. (Gm)	111	2	55.50	2- 39	–	–	–
Powell, M.J. (Wa)	200	5	40.00	2- 16	–	–	–
Prichard, P.J.	497	2	248.50	1- 28	–	–	–

	Runs	Wkts	Avge	Best	5wI	10wM	50wS
Pryke, D.J.	1872	100	18.72	6- 27	5	1	–
Pyemont, J.P.	161	1	161.00	1- 26	–	–	–
Ramprakash, M.R.	1926	32	60.18	3- 32	–	–	–
Ramsden, G.	68	1	68.00	1- 32	–	–	–
Randall, S.J.	346	1	346.00	1-109	–	–	–
Rashid, U.B.A.	1675	38	44.07	5-103	1	–	–
Ratcliffe, J.D.	897	26	34.50	6- 48	1	–	–
Rawnsley, M.J.	1798	45	39.95	6- 44	3	1	–
Redmond, A.J.	594	12	49.50	4- 72	–	–	–
Reiffel, P.R.	13288	505	26.31	6- 57	16	2	0+2
Renshaw, S.J.	3580	93	38.49	5-110	1	–	–
Rhodes, S.J.	30	0					
Richardson, A.	1639	53	30.92	8- 51	1	1	–
Richardson, M.H.	1697	37	45.86	5- 77	1	–	–
Ripley, D.	103	2	51.50	2- 89	–	–	–
Robinson, D.D.J.	45	0					
Robinson, J.D.	1152	28	41.14	3- 22	–	–	–
Robinson, M.A.	16586	523	31.71	9- 37	10	2	1
Rollins, A.S.	122	1	122.00	1- 19	–	–	–
Rose, F.A.	6626	259	25.58	7- 39	13	2	1+1
Rose, G.D.	17713	601	29.47	7- 47	15	1	5
Roseberry, M.A.	406	4	101.50	1- 1	–	–	–
Ross, J.S.	237	1	237.00	1- 46	–	–	–
Russell, R.C.	68	1	68.00	1- 4	–	–	–
Saggers, M.J.	2109	96	21.96	7- 79	4	–	1
Sales, D.J.G.	163	9	18.11	4- 25	–	–	–
Salisbury, I.D.K.	20542	658	31.21	8- 60	33	6	6
Saqlain Mushtaq	9738	471	20.67	8- 65	40	12	3+1
Sarwan, R.R.	210	5	42.00	1- 0	–	–	–
Savident, L.	286	4	71.50	2- 86	–	–	–
Sawal, M.A.	96	2	48.00	2- 96	–	–	–
Saxelby, M.	903	11	82.09	3- 41	–	–	–
Sayers, C.A.	357	2	178.50	2- 21	–	–	–
Schofield, C.P.	2960	101	29.30	6-120	4	–	–
Scott, D.A.	613	13	47.15	4-151	–	–	–
Scuderi, J.C.	5755	170	33.85	7- 79	8	1	–
Shah, K.Z.	260	4	65.00	2- 24	–	–	–
Shah, O.A.	574	17	33.76	3- 33	–	–	–
Shahid, N.	1999	43	46.48	3- 91	–	–	–
Shaw, A.D.	7	0					
Sheikh, M.A.	187	7	26.71	2- 14	–	–	–
Sheikh, S.M.	437	12	36.41	4- 25	–	–	–
Sheriyar, A.	9175	305	30.08	7-130	13	3	2
Sidebottom, R.J.	1550	60	25.83	6- 16	4	1	–
Silverwood, C.E.W.	8502	312	27.25	7- 93	15	1	2
Singh, A.	111	0					
Smethurst, M.P.	1538	69	22.28	7- 37	3	–	1
Smith, A.M.	11147	454	24.55	8- 73	20	5	5
Smith, B.F.	221	2	110.50	1- 5	–	–	–
Smith, E.T.	45	0					
Smith, G.J.	4827	171	28.22	6- 35	5	–	–
Smith, N.M.K.	12336	333	37.04	7- 42	17	–	–
Smith, R.A.	993	14	70.92	2- 11	–	–	–
Smith, T.M.	1752	62	28.25	6- 32	5	1	–
Snape, J.N.	3974	87	45.67	5- 65	1	–	–
Solanki, V.S.	2887	69	41.84	5- 69	3	1	–

	Runs	Wkts	Avge	Best	5wI	10wM	50wS
Speak, N.J.	191	2	95.50	1- 0	–	–	–
Speight, M.P.	32	2	16.00	1- 2	–	–	–
Spiring, K.R.	10	0					
Stelling, W.F.	1029	33	31.18	5- 49	1	–	–
Stemp, R.D.	12788	368	34.75	6- 37	14	1	–
Stephenson, J.P.	11193	328	34.12	7- 51	10	–	–
Stevens, D.I.	25	1	25.00	1- 5	–	–	–
Stewart, A.J.	423	3	141.00	1- 7	–	–	–
Strang, B.C.	5226	208	25.12	7- 20	12	1	–
Strang, P.A.	8781	276	31.81	7- 75	16	2	1
Strauss, A.J.	13	0					
Streak, H.H.	6911	263	26.27	7- 69	8	–	1
Strong, M.R.	434	12	36.16	4- 46	–	–	–
Stubbings, S.D.	41	0					
Styris, S.B.	2622	87	30.13	6- 32	5	–	–
Such, P.M.	24574	825	29.78	8- 93	47	9	6
Sulzberger, G.P.	1434	51	28.11	5- 55	1	–	–
Sutcliffe, I.J.	212	5	42.40	2- 21	–	–	–
Swann, A.J.	196	4	49.00	2- 30	–	–	–
Swann, G.P.	4421	142	31.13	6- 41	6	1	1
Symington, M.J.	215	7	30.71	3- 55	–	–	–
Taylor, B.V.	513	8	64.12	3- 27	–	–	–
Taylor, C.G.	136	3	45.33	3-126	–	–	–
Taylor, J.P.	15273	530	28.81	7- 23	18	4	6
Tennant, A.M.	252	9	28.00	3- 20	–	–	–
Thomas, S.D.	10562	363	29.09	8- 50	15	–	4
Thompson, D.J.J.	914	29	31.51	4- 46	–	–	–
Thorpe, G.P.	1290	25	51.60	4- 40	–	–	–
Titchard, S.P.	195	4	48.75	1- 11	–	–	–
Tolley, C.M.	6623	189	35.04	7- 45	5	–	–
Tournier, M.A.	117	3	39.00	3-117	–	–	–
Trego, P.D.	603	18	33.50	4- 84	–	–	–
Tremlett, C.T.	91	6	15.16	4- 16	–	–	–
Trescothick, M.E.	1330	31	42.90	4- 36	–	–	–
Trott, B.J.	317	11	28.81	3- 74	–	–	–
Tucker, J.P.	47	1	47.00	1- 28	–	–	–
Tudor, A.J.	4427	170	26.04	7- 48	9	–	–
Tuffey, D.R.	2273	82	27.71	5- 44	3	–	–
Tufnell, P.C.R.	27915	952	29.32	8- 29	46	5	8
Turner, R.J.	29	0					
Udal, S.D.	15637	452	34.59	8- 50	24	4	5
Van der Gucht, C.G.	75	3	25.00	3- 75	–	–	–
Vaughan, M.P.	4443	94	47.26	4- 39	–	–	–
Viljoen, D.P.	928	32	29.00	6- 73	1	–	–
Vonwiller, B.M.	137	3	45.66	2- 59	–	–	–
Wagh, M.A.	1726	30	57.53	4- 11	–	–	–
Walker, B.G.K.	2020	63	32.06	8-107	2	–	–
Walker, M.J.	321	6	53.50	1- 3	–	–	–
Walsh, C.A.	37995	1755	21.64	9- 72	103	20	10·1
Ward, I.J.	102	0					
Ward, T.R.	647	8	80.87	2- 10	–	–	–
Warne, S.K.	18127	683	26.54	8- 71	31	4	3+1
Watkin, S.L.	23791	859	27.69	8- 59	30	4	9
Watkinson, M.	24960	739	33.77	8- 30	27	3	7
Weekes, L.C.	1764	66	26.72	6- 56	2	–	–
Weekes, P.N.	6739	163	41.34	8- 39	3	–	–

	Runs	Wkts	Avge	Best	5wI	10wM	50wS
Weenink, S.W.	641	10	64.10	4- 69	–	–	–
Welch, G.	6236	184	33.89	6-115	4	1	1
Wells, A.P.	820	10	82.00	3- 67	–	–	–
Wells, V.J.	6486	243	26.69	5- 18	3	–	–
Welton, G.E.	1	0					
Weston, R.M.S.	104	2	52.00	1- 15	–	–	–
Weston, W.P.C.	599	4	149.75	2- 39	–	–	–
Wharf, A.G.	2943	88	33.44	5- 68	1	–	–
Wharton, L.J.	464	12	38.66	5- 96	1	–	–
Whiley, M.J.A.	244	2	122.00	1- 44	–	–	–
White, C.	7781	296	26.28	8- 55	9	–	–
White, G.W.	456	9	50.66	3- 23	–	–	–
Whittall, G.J.	4232	125	33.85	6- 34	2	–	–
Widdup, S.	22	1	22.00	1- 22	–	–	–
Williamson, D.	529	14	37.78	3- 19	–	–	–
Williamson, J.G.	383	5	76.60	2- 51	–	–	–
Windows, M.G.N.	111	2	55.50	1- 6	–	–	–
Wishart, C.B.	769	25	30.76	5- 24	1	–	–
Wood, J.	8519	260	32.76	7- 58	11	–	1
Wood, M.J.	16	0					
Wood, N.T.	154	0					
Wrigglesworth, I.A.	432	9	48.00	3- 72	–	–	–
Wright, C.M.	278	8	34.75	3- 24	–	–	–
Yardy, M.H.	84	0					
Yates, G.	6861	180	38.11	6- 64	5	–	–

STOP PRESS
TROPHY FIXTURES 2001

Although the new sponsors of the former NatWest Trophy have yet to be revealed, venues for the opening round of this season's competition have just been released. See page 301 for the schedule of the later rounds and page 193 for the Second Round venues.

Round 1 – Tuesday 1 May (*reserve 2 May*)

1	Chippenham	Wiltshire	v	Derbyshire CB
2	Challow & Childrey	Oxfordshire	v	Huntingdonshire CB
3	Shrewsbury	Shropshire	v	Devon
4	Sleaford	Lincolnshire	v	Suffolk
5	North Perrott	Somerset CB	v	Wales
6	The Mote, Maidstone	Kent CB	v	Hampshire CB
7	Southgate	Middlesex CB	v	Northumberland
8	Wardown Park, Luton	Bedfordshire	v	Nottinghamshire CB
9	Porthill Park, Newcastle-u-Lyme	Staffordshire	v	Worcestershire CB
10	Nelson	Lancashire CB	v	Yorkshire CB

LEADING CURRENT PLAYERS

The leading career batting/bowling averages and wicket-keeping/fielding aggregates among players currently registered for first-class county cricket. All figures are to the end of the 2000 English season.

BATTING

(Qualification: 100 innings)

	Runs	Avge
D.S.Lehmann	14829	54.92
G.A.Hick	32082	54.28
S.G.Law	15465	48.93
J.P.Crawley	15259	48.13
M.E.Hussey	4777	46.37
M.R.Ramprakash	19048	46.34
A.Habib	4738	44.69
A.D.Brown	8726	44.29
D.J.Cullinan	13126	44.19
G.S.Blewett	11154	44.08
G.P.Thorpe	16487	44.08
J.Cox	11476	43.63
R.A.Smith	24203	42.61
N.Hussain	16664	42.51
M.P.Maynard	20897	42.38
R.J.Bailey	21329	41.41
M.L.Love	5373	41.33
N.H.Fairbrother	19267	41.25
M.A.Atherton	20598	41.19
S.P.Fleming	6750	40.90
P.D.Bowler	16463	40.64
N.V.Knight	9265	40.28
M.J.Di Venuto	7207	40.26
K.J.Barnett	26923	40.00
A.J.Stewart	23357	39.99
S.P.James	14196	39.87
T.L.Penney	7953	39.76
W.S.Kendall	4850	39.43
D.J.Bicknell	14058	39.15
G.D.Lloyd	10811	38.74
A.P.Wells	21099	38.57
A.J.Hollioake	6780	38.52
M.A.Butcher	8992	37.15
J.E.Morris	20899	37.12
R.C.Irani	7862	37.11

BOWLING

(Qualification: 100 wickets)

	Wkts	Avge
Saqlain Mushtaq	471	20.67
K.J.Dean	174	22.05
P.M.Hutchison	148	22.55
A.J.Bichel	239	23.48
J.F.Brown	116	23.81
A.R.Caddick	718	24.22
V.C.Drakes	425	24.32
M.P.Bicknell	826	24.38
M.J.Hoggard	145	24.42
J.Ormond	176	24.48
A.M.Smith	454	24.55
A.C.Morris	105	24.56
G.M.Hamilton	212	25.14
J.D.Lewry	271	25.61
T.A.Munton	718	25.63
A.F.Giles	279	25.64
R.J.Kirtley	275	25.77
J.Lewis	264	25.95
A.J.Tudor	170	26.04
D.R.Brown	307	26.22
C.White	296	26.28
D.G.Cork	594	26.39
D.Gough	630	26.47
V.J.Wells	243	26.69
A.R.C.Fraser	847	27.01
M.C.Ilott	590	27.07
M.J.McCague	454	27.07
D.J.Millns	552	27.25
C.E.W.Silverwood	312	27.25
P.J.Franks	211	27.54
E.S.H.Giddins	413	27.57
P.J.Martin	469	27.65
S.L.Watkin	859	27.69
P.A.J.DeFreitas	1060	27.70
J.P.Hewett	160	27.93

WICKET-KEEPING

	Total	Ct	St
R.C.Russell	1197	1077	120
S.J.Rhodes	1082	969	113
W.K.Hegg	739	663	76
R.J.Blakey	718	668	50
D.Ripley	715	633	82
A.J.Stewart	602	581	21
P.A.Nixon	557	515	42
A.N.Aymes	498	457	41

FIELDING

	Ct
G.A.Hick	491
M.P.Maynard	326
D.Byas	313
N.Hussain	308
K.J.Barnett	273
R.J.Bailey	264
N.H.Fairbrother	264
C.J.Adams	251

LIMITED-OVERS CAREER RECORDS

Compiled by Philip Bailey

The following career records, to the end of the 2000 season, are for all players currently registered with first-class counties. These records are restricted to performances in limited-overs matches of 'List A' status as defined by the Association of Cricket Statisticians and Historians. The following matches qualify for List A status and are included in the figures that follow:

Limited-Overs Internationals
Other international matches (e.g. Commonwealth Games, 'A' team internationals)
Premier domestic limited-overs tournaments in Test status countries
Official tourist matches against the main first-class teams

The following matches do NOT qualify for inclusion:

World Cup warm-up games
Tourist matches against first-class teams outside the major domestic competitions
(e.g. Universities, Minor Counties, etc.)
Festival and pre-season friendly games

	M	Runs	Avge	HS	100	50	Wkts	Avge	Best	Ct/St
Adams, C.J.	242	7633	39.34	163	15	49	28	35.64	5-16	121
Adshead, S.J.	3	41	20.50	22	–	–	–	–	–	3/3
Afzaal, U.	40	869	33.42	95*	–	7	12	32.08	2-25	14
Aldred, P.	71	290	12.08	39*	–	–	77	30.14	4-30	10
Ali, Kabir	17	32	6.40	11	–	–	23	23.43	4-29	5
Ali, Kadeer	3	58	19.33	24	–	–	–	–	–	–
Alleyne, D.	14	200	14.28	58	–	1	–	–	–	14/6
Alleyne, M.W.	340	6801	28.33	134*	5	27	314	29.90	5-27	138/1
Amin, R.M.	2	–	–	–	–	–	2	21.50	2-43	1
Anderson, J.M.	2	5	–	5*	–	–	3	32.66	2-64	–
Anderson, R.S.G.	14	29	4.14	10	–	–	8	61.75	3-32	–
Atherton, M.A.	273	9035	36.87	127	14	56	24	29.62	4-42	98
Austin, I.D.	308	2269	18.44	97	–	4	354	27.90	5-56	53
Averis, J.M.M.	44	91	7.58	23*	–	–	67	22.41	5-20	4
Aymes, A.N.	216	2167	23.30	73*	–	6	–	–	–	211/51
Bailey, R.J.	376	11473	39.15	153*	10	74	65	35.64	5-45	107
Bailey, T.M.B.	19	116	12.88	52	–	1	–	–	–	17/10
Ball, M.C.J.	180	1120	12.72	51	–	1	151	35.99	5-42	72
Barnett, K.J.	479	14312	35.51	136	14	86	105	25.30	6-24	165
Batty, G.J.	11	140	17.50	37	–	–	6	62.83	2-42	6
Batty, J.N.	48	338	13.00	40	–	–	–	–	–	37/8
Bell, I.R.	1	10	10.00	10	–	–	–	–	–	–
Betts, M.M.	71	303	10.10	21	–	–	83	30.59	4-34	12
Bichel, A.J.	58	321	16.05	42*	–	–	69	32.01	4-45	19
Bicknell, D.J.	186	5958	37.94	135*	8	40	3	27.33	1-11	43
Bicknell, M.P.	271	1222	16.73	66*	–	2	356	24.89	7-30	65
Bishop, I.E.	14	24	24.00	15*	–	–	14	28.21	4-34	1
Bishop, J.E.	4	18	9.00	16*	–	–	2	35.00	1-17	–
Blackwell, I.D.	52	872	21.26	97	–	4	39	30.41	4-36	18
Blain, J.A.R.	16	30	6.00	10*	–	–	26	26.34	5-24	3
Blakey, R.J.	308	6680	32.27	130*	3	35	–	–	–	288/42
Blewett, G.S.	103	2832	32.18	113	2	18	72	32.87	4-18	35
Bloomfield, T.F.	30	38	9.50	15	–	–	28	33.28	4-17	5
Boswell, S.A.J.	24	34	5.66	14	–	–	21	40.61	3-32	1
Bowler, P.D.	277	7881	31.65	138*	5	61	13	40.84	3-31	104/2
Bressington, A.N.	3	98	49.00	54	–	1	5	17.20	3-21	2

L-O	M	Runs	Avge	HS	100	50	Wkts	Avge	Best	Ct/St
Bridge, G.D.	4	24	24.00	15	–	–	2	75.00	1-27	2
Brinkley, J.E.	26	132	9.42	30*	–	–	23	35.47	3-55	3
Brown, A.D.	238	6695	30.71	203	11	27	8	31.50	3-39	72
Brown, D.R.	171	2521	20.83	78*	–	12	172	28.06	5-31	42
Brown, J.F.	18	11	3.66	4	–	–	23	27.73	4-26	5
Brown, S.J.E.	112	217	6.57	18	–	–	132	30.60	6-30	23
Bryan, R.B.	1	–	–	–	–	–	0	–	–	–
Bulbeck, M.P.L.	9	8	2.66	5	–	–	5	49.00	4-40	2
Burns, M.	129	2679	24.80	115*	1	17	37	26.59	4-39	58/12
Burns, N.D.	180	1894	17.86	58	–	5	–	–	–	193/34
Butcher, G.P.	59	622	17.27	48	–	–	24	47.33	4-32	6
Butcher, M.A.	131	2464	27.07	91	–	11	49	44.14	3-23	46
Byas, D.	287	7276	30.06	116*	5	41	25	26.36	3-19	116
Caddick, A.R.	169	509	10.18	39	–	–	225	24.40	6-30	30
Carberry, M.A.	2	23	11.50	19	–	–	–	–	–	–
Carpenter, J.R.	47	726	25.03	64*	–	5	0	–	–	25
Carter, N.M.	7	11	3.66	7*	–	–	9	25.66	4-31	–
Cassar, M.E.	54	1409	29.97	134	4	6	33	29.18	4-29	14
Catterall, D.N.	12	49	12.25	21*	–	–	5	64.40	2-35	2
Cawdron, M.J.	43	254	15.87	50	–	1	42	30.28	4-17	5
Chapple, G.	140	337	9.62	43	–	–	157	29.48	6-18	31
Chilton, M.J.	34	696	22.45	56	–	3	23	23.47	5-26	8
Clapp, D.A.	2	14	7.00	10	–	–	3	15.33	3-46	–
Collingwood, P.D.	95	2085	25.74	86	–	13	45	32.26	4-31	43
Cook, J.W.	19	421	23.38	130	1	–	0	–	–	8
Cook, S.J.	33	227	10.80	28*	–	–	40	26.02	3-16	6
Cork, D.G.	175	2408	20.75	93	–	13	223	27.99	6-21	70
Cosker, D.A.	61	199	9.04	27*	–	–	70	29.10	3-18	15
Cotterell, T.P.	1	–	–	–	–	–	2	16.50	2-33	–
Cottey, P.A.	237	4297	25.27	96	–	25	19	35.36	4-56	79
Cousins, D.M.	68	117	6.15	18	–	–	86	26.09	3-18	8
Cowan, A.P.	93	545	12.67	40*	–	–	108	29.47	5-28	33
Cox, J.	91	2793	31.73	114	3	20	3	27.33	3-28	26
Craven, V.J.	6	78	13.00	28	–	–	–	–	–	6
Crawley, J.P.	185	4949	29.81	114	3	30	0	–	–	50/4
Croft, R.D.B.	256	3172	21.43	77	–	13	258	32.22	6-20	63
Crowe, C.D.	7	56	28.00	19	–	–	2	53.50	1-26	–
Cullinan, D.J.	277	7580	32.67	124	7	45	6	43.16	2-30	137
Cunliffe, R.J.	68	1656	29.57	137*	3	10	–	–	–	17
Dagnall, C.E.	6	5	2.50	4	–	–	13	13.76	4-34	1
Dakin, J.M.	119	1533	17.22	108*	1	1	99	28.41	5-30	25
Dale, A.	235	5342	28.87	110	2	26	203	31.38	6-22	53
Daley, J.A.	58	1323	29.40	105	1	8	0	–	–	11
Dalrymple, J.W.M.	1	–	–	–	–	–	1	37.00	1-37	–
Davies, A.M.	5	0	0.00	0	–	–	7	17.71	3-15	1
Davies, A.P.	10	27	6.75	12	–	–	12	23.41	2-17	1
Davies, M.K.	10	8	4.00	4	–	–	8	42.87	3-11	–
Davis, M.J.G.	66	238	11.33	35	–	–	58	38.27	4-35	17
Dawson, R.K.J.	3	14	4.66	7	–	–	4	22.00	2-32	1
Dean, K.J.	67	131	14.55	16*	–	–	81	27.77	5-32	13
DeFreitas, P.A.J.	414	4320	18.46	75*	–	11	478	27.71	5-13	89
Di Venuto, M.J.	108	3263	35.08	173*	2	19	5	25.20	1-10	38
Dowman, M.P.	103	1846	20.51	92	–	8	41	33.82	3-21	26
Drakes, V.C.	128	1278	16.59	104	1	1	171	24.66	5-19	23
Driver, R.C.	13	196	16.33	61*	–	2	1	42.00	1-17	1

167

L-O	M	Runs	Avge	HS	100	50	Wkts	Avge	Best	Ct/St
Dumelow, N.R.C.	2	56	28.00	32	–	–	2	31.50	2-21	–
Dutch, K.P.	79	916	18.32	58	–	2	86	24.25	5-35	23
Ealham, M.A.	276	4347	24.98	112	1	19	303	27.95	6-53	66
Elstub, C.J.	2	–	–	–	–	–	0	–	–	–
Evans, A.W.	40	658	21.93	108	1	3	–	–	–	12
Fairbrother, N.H.	473	14173	42.81	145	8	104	3	58.66	1-17	177
Fellows, G.M.	41	543	19.39	65	–	2	2	82.50	1-16	9
Fisher, I.D.	26	68	8.50	20	–	–	28	22.21	3-20	6
Fleming, M.V.	273	5118	24.02	117*	3	21	331	25.55	5-27	71
Fleming, S.P.	198	5735	34.54	116*	6	38	1	28.00	1- 8	93
Flintoff, A.	98	2262	27.92	143	3	13	63	22.06	4-22	35
Forder, D.J.	2	4	–	3*	–	–	0	–	–	1
Foster, J.S.	6	81	27.00	22*	–	–	–	–	–	6/1
Francis, S.R.G.	12	25	8.33	8*	–	–	6	49.00	2-28	2
Franks, P.J.	71	566	17.68	40	–	–	105	22.68	6-27	11
Fraser, A.R.C.	319	824	11.60	38*	–	–	365	27.11	5-32	55
Frost, T.	27	104	11.55	22*	–	–	–	–	–	22/4
Fulton, D.P.	31	361	11.64	69	–	1	0	–	–	13
Gallian, J.E.R.	144	4193	32.50	134	7	23	52	32.75	5-15	50
Gannon, B.W.	2	3	3.00	2	–	–	3	23.66	2-29	–
Gazzard, C.M.	1	16	16.00	16	–	–	–	–	–	2
Giddins, E.S.H.	140	70	2.41	13	–	–	164	28.65	5-21	22
Giles, A.F.	130	1414	20.49	107	1	3	173	21.38	5-21	42
Golding, J.M.	8	59	11.80	47	–	–	5	49.60	3-20	4
Goodwin, M.W.	98	2518	27.97	115	3	14	7	39.71	1- 9	29
Gough, D.	252	1399	12.71	72*	–	1	370	22.93	7-27	47
Gough, M.A.	15	228	17.53	36	–	–	0	–	–	3
Grayson, A.P.	181	2382	19.20	82*	–	8	160	32.62	4-25	49
Green, R.J.	27	44	11.00	14*	–	–	32	30.68	3-18	3
Greenidge, C.G.	13	5	–	3*	–	–	5	86.40	2-43	4
Grove, J.O.	1	0	0.00	0	–	–	0	–	–	–
Habib, A.	101	1995	26.95	111	1	9	2	4.50	2- 5	36
Hamilton, G.M.	93	979	22.76	76	–	3	112	24.60	5-16	13
Hancock, T.H.C.	168	3209	21.53	110	1	15	47	24.00	6-58	56
Hardinges, M.A.	1	1	1.00	1	–	–	2	25.00	2-50	–
Harmison, S.J.	27	25	4.16	8*	–	–	25	38.00	3-45	3
Harris, A.J.	75	104	7.42	11*	–	–	96	28.55	5-35	18
Harrison, D.S.	3	11	5.50	5*	–	–	0	–	–	1
Harvey, I.J.	110	1979	23.01	88	–	9	175	20.45	5-19	28
Haynes, J.J.	3	12	12.00	12	–	–	–	–	–	3/1
Headley, D.W.	166	352	12.57	29*	–	–	204	27.16	6-42	29
Hegg, W.K.	319	2457	21.00	81	–	3	–	–	–	359/45
Hemp, D.L.	146	3034	25.49	121	4	15	8	20.87	4-32	54
Hewison, C.J.	2	19	9.50	19	–	–	–	–	–	1
Hewitt, J.P.	70	302	11.61	32*	–	–	62	32.85	4-24	21
Hewson, D.R.	23	365	21.47	64	–	1	–	–	–	5
Hick, G.A.	492	17394	43.05	172*	31	115	207	29.78	5-19	224
Hockley, J.B.	13	285	28.50	64	–	1	–	–	–	5
Hoggard, M.J.	45	19	1.90	2*	–	–	74	18.27	5-28	3
Hollioake, A.J.	212	4324	28.07	111	1	22	259	24.49	5-29	63
Hollioake, B.C.	102	1670	20.61	98	–	7	107	28.33	5-10	36
Holloway, P.C.L.	115	2534	29.81	117	2	17	–	–	–	52/8
House, W.J.	54	942	22.42	93	–	3	21	26.23	5-58	10
Hunkin, C.A.	1	10	–	10*	–	–	1	25.00	1-25	–
Hunter, I.D.	20	39	4.87	14*	–	–	22	27.13	4-29	2

168

L-O	M	Runs	Avge	HS	100	50	Wkts	Avge	Best	Ct/St
Hussain, N.	286	7865	34.80	118	6	55	–	–	–	135
Hussey, M.E.	26	730	31.73	100*	1	5	5	27.60	3-52	16
Hutchison, P.M.	32	18	4.50	4*	–	–	38	21.34	4-34	4
Hutton, B.L.	20	191	17.36	49	–	–	10	29.70	4-32	10
Hyam, B.J.	38	273	12.40	37	–	–	–	–	–	31/4
Illingworth, R.K.	368	1333	14.03	36*	–	–	397	26.97	5-24	89
Ilott, M.C.	181	792	12.18	56*	–	2	229	25.91	5-21	30
Innes, K.J.	44	377	22.17	55	–	1	42	29.35	4-36	12
Irani, R.C.	182	3945	27.97	124	2	23	213	25.35	5-33	40
James, S.P.	206	6304	35.21	135	7	44	–	–	–	55
Jefferson, W.I.	3	117	39.00	65	–	2	–	–	–	1
Johnson, N.C.	129	3997	38.06	146*	9	22	95	31.57	4-19	59
Johnson, P.	346	9369	32.53	167*	13	53	0	–	–	107
Johnson, R.L.	116	741	11.76	45*	–	–	126	32.74	5-50	14
Jones, I.	1	5	–	5*	–	–	1	53.00	1-53	–
Jones, P.S.	61	148	9.86	27	–	–	87	25.51	5-23	13
Jones, S.P.	3	12	–	12*	–	–	1	116.00	1-39	–
Joyce, E.C.	14	402	40.20	73	–	1	–	–	–	3
Katich, S.M.	45	1365	35.00	116	1	11	3	39.33	1-16	21
Keedy, G.	12	1	1.00	1	–	–	11	33.09	5-30	1
Kendall, W.S.	75	1275	21.98	85*	–	4	0	–	–	29
Kenway, D.A.	39	890	25.42	90	–	6	–	–	–	18/5
Kerr, J.I.D.	76	449	12.47	56	–	1	85	29.15	4-28	12
Key, R.W.T.	35	885	30.51	76*	–	8	–	–	–	4
Khan, A.	2	2	1.00	–	–	–	3	31.00	2-38	–
Killeen, N.	98	368	8.97	32	–	–	125	27.40	6-31	17
Kirtley, R.J.	80	166	11.85	17*	–	–	124	21.98	5-39	20
Knight, N.V.	245	7340	36.33	151	13	38	2	44.50	1-14	102
Krikken, K.M.	175	1423	18.48	55	–	1	–	–	–	175/31
Lambert, G.A.	1	0	0.00	0	–	–	2	11.00	2-22	–
Lampitt, S.R.	254	1907	17.82	54	–	1	313	24.34	6-26	75
Laney, J.S.	98	2366	24.90	153	2	9	0	–	–	27
Laraman, A.W.	13	35	7.00	11*	–	–	25	14.60	6-42	5
Lathwell, M.N.	156	4208	28.62	121	4	26	1	193.00	1-23	44
Law, D.R.	114	1804	22.00	82	–	5	53	32.13	3-26	24
Law, S.G.	239	7344	34.97	163	17	31	86	36.09	5-26	94
Lazenbury, P.S.	1	3	3.00	3	–	–	–	–	–	–
Leatherdale, D.A.	219	2980	19.47	70*	–	10	92	21.57	5-10	90
Lehmann, D.S.	198	6355	39.22	142*	8	43	39	31.92	3-14	49
Lewis, J.	76	338	11.65	33*	–	–	80	33.38	3-27	15
Lewis, J.J.B.	139	2679	26.52	102	1	14	0	–	–	23
Lewry, J.D.	52	133	7.82	14*	–	–	68	27.26	4-29	7
Liptrot, C.G.	4	18	–	15*	–	–	5	23.40	3-44	–
Lloyd, G.D.	254	5408	29.71	134	3	27	1	103.00	1-23	58
Logan, R.J.	8	26	6.50	17	–	–	6	47.33	3-52	2
Love, M.L.	50	1352	32.97	79	–	7	–	–	–	23
Loye, M.B.	152	4087	31.43	122	3	25	–	–	–	34
Lucas, D.S.	19	45	9.00	19*	–	–	21	35.95	4-27	2
Lungley, T	4	48	12.00	15	–	–	5	25.60	2-26	–
McCague, M.J.	156	750	12.50	56	–	1	203	26.55	5-26	29
McGarry, A.C.	4	0	–	0*	–	–	2	31.50	2-20	–
McGrath, A.	114	2821	31.69	109*	2	16	9	28.66	2-10	38
Maddy, D.L.	169	4351	30.85	151	6	27	79	25.25	4-16	1
Maher, J.P.	51	1865	42.38	128	4	9	2	43.50	2-43	18
Malcolm, D.E.	168	307	5.48	42	–	–	229	27.74	7-35	17

L-O	M	Runs	Avge	HS	100	50	Wkts	Avge	Best	Ct/St
Malik, M.N.	1	1	–	1*	–	–	0	–	–	–
Marsh, A.J.	3	60	20.00	53	–	1	–	–	–	1
Marsh, D.J.	36	653	31.09	78*	–	3	18	57.11	3-47	16
Martin, P.J.	193	364	13.00	35*	–	–	264	23.23	5-21	36
Martin-Jenkins, R.S.C.	67	422	9.37	45	–	–	67	30.71	4-57	15
Mascarenhas, A.D.	77	1263	21.77	79	–	10	86	24.75	4-25	20
Mason, T.J.	76	384	12.00	36	–	–	49	44.89	4-12	21
Masters, D.D.	18	46	5.75	12*	–	–	11	47.54	2-10	3
Maynard, M.P.	357	10849	34.55	151*	13	64	3	94.66	1-13	145/2
Middlebrook, J.D.	13	41	6.83	15*	–	–	11	34.27	3-16	3
Millns, D.J.	91	338	14.69	39*	–	–	83	37.87	4-26	18
Montgomerie, R.R.	100	3076	35.35	129*	2	23	0	–	–	24
Morris, A.C.	37	239	17.07	48*	–	–	33	25.90	5-32	6
Morris, J.E.	342	8152	26.90	145	9	39	1	66.00	1-44	80
Mullally, A.D.	231	408	7.84	38	–	–	279	26.98	6-38	34
Munton, T.A.	257	312	8.43	18	–	–	265	28.92	5-23	49
Muralitharan, M.	176	286	6.35	18	–	–	249	25.39	5-23	77
Murtagh, T.J.	2	0	0.00	0	–	–	1	102.00	1-50	–
Napier, G.R.	29	431	20.52	79	–	3	9	34.22	3-22	6
Nash, D.C.	51	510	18.21	43	–	–	–	–	–	44/8
Newell, K.	96	1864	24.52	129	1	7	35	39.71	5-33	19
Nixon, P.A.	217	3347	23.24	101	1	14	–	–	–	226/43
Noon, W.M.	117	734	13.84	46	–	–	–	–	–	87/26
Ormond, J.	55	167	9.27	18	–	–	74	22.36	4-12	12
Ostler, D.P.	233	6081	31.83	104	1	44	1	14.00	1- 4	78
Parkin, O.T.	73	60	3.33	8	–	–	102	24.49	5-28	18
Parsons, K.A.	123	2009	25.43	69	–	8	70	36.21	4-43	48
Patel, D.B.	1	19	–	19*	–	–	1	36.00	1-36	–
Patel, M.M.	54	126	8.40	18*	–	–	57	30.52	3-22	14
Patterson, M.W.	10	25	4.16	9	–	–	15	36.73	3-48	1
Pattison, I.	3	56	56.00	48*	–	1	2	28.00	1-25	1
Penberthy, A.L.	205	3307	25.43	81*	–	17	208	29.20	5-29	53
Peng, N.	10	86	9.55	36	–	–	–	–	–	–
Penney, T.L.	208	3688	28.36	90	–	14	1	21.00	1- 8	83/1
Peters, S.D.	57	822	17.86	73*	–	5	–	–	–	16
Phillips, B.J.	26	59	7.37	29	–	–	33	20.18	4-25	9
Phillips, N.C.	77	477	10.60	38*	–	–	80	29.97	4-13	21
Phillips, T.J.	1	0	0.00	0	–	–	2	28.00	2-56	1
Pierson, A.R.K.	115	376	10.44	31*	–	–	99	34.94	5-36	43
Pietersen, K.P.	6	30	7.50	11	–	–	4	60.00	2-43	4
Pipe, D.J.	8	218	31.14	56	–	2	–	–	–	3
Piper, K.J.	181	778	15.87	38*	–	–	–	–	–	196/41
Pollard, P.R.	176	4954	33.70	132*	5	31	0	–	–	61
Pope, S.P.	3	0	0.00	0	–	–	–	–	–	7/1
Powell, M.J. (Gm)	58	1137	22.74	86	–	4	–	–	–	13
Powell, M.J. (Wa)	24	409	22.72	51	–	1	6	24.50	2-13	10
Pratt, A.	10	51	8.50	26	–	–	–	–	–	5/2
Prichard, P.J.	299	7207	28.71	114	6	38	–	–	–	84
Prior, M.J.	1	3	3.00	3	–	–	–	–	–	–
Prittipaul, L.R.	11	153	25.50	61	–	1	4	34.75	2-53	5
Pyemont, J.P.	21	292	14.60	50	–	1	–	–	–	10
Ramprakash, M.R.	267	8090	37.28	147*	7	51	36	27.22	5-38	96
Ramsden, G.	1	–	–	–	–	–	2	13.00	2-26	–
Randall, S.J.	1	1	1.00	1	–	–	0	–	–	–
Rashid, U.B.A.	61	482	13.77	82	–	1	67	30.83	5-24	22

170

L-O	M	Runs	Avge	HS	100	50	Wkts	Avge	Best	Ct/St
Ratcliffe, J.D.	107	1803	22.82	105	1	9	33	34.09	3-15	28
Rawnsley, M.J.	29	54	4.15	9	–	–	26	29.53	5-26	8
Read, C.M.W.	75	917	19.10	62	–	1	–	–	–	90/13
Rhodes, S.J.	395	3651	18.62	105	1	4	0	–	–	443/107
Richardson, A.	12	16	3.20	11*	–	–	9	39.77	2-16	–
Ripley, D.	262	1646	17.69	52*	–	1	–	–	–	215/31
Robinson, D.D.J.	106	2401	26.97	137*	3	10	1	26.00	1- 7	29
Robinson, M.A.	215	134	3.11	15*	–	–	219	31.54	4-23	23
Rollins, A.S.	96	1831	22.06	126*	2	8	0	–	–	39
Rose, G.D.	289	4943	23.76	148	2	23	300	29.49	4-16	67
Roseberry, M.A.	204	5532	31.79	121	6	38	1	51.00	1-22	68
Russell, R.C.	419	6034	25.24	119*	2	23	–	–	–	400/80
Saggers, M.J.	26	102	17.00	34*	–	–	37	24.29	4-35	7
Sales, D.J.G.	90	2003	28.61	91*	–	12	0	–	–	35
Salisbury, I.D.K.	205	1186	12.89	48*	–	–	212	31.93	5-30	68
Sampson, P.J.	3	8	8.00	4*	–	–	0	–	–	1
Saqlain Mushtaq	201	877	11.69	37*	–	–	349	19.79	5-29	53
Schofield, C.P.	25	233	16.64	34	–	–	37	22.64	4-34	5
Scott, B.J.M.	1	11	11.00	11	–	–	–	–	–	–
Scuderi, J.C.	50	681	22.70	58	–	3	37	44.40	3-36	6
Sexton, A.J.	2	35	17.50	34	–	–	–	–	–	1
Shah, O.A.	85	1860	26.19	134	2	7	7	30.42	2- 2	21
Shahid, N.	131	2315	26.01	109*	2	9	5	50.80	3-30	43
Shaw, A.D.	76	654	14.86	48	–	–	–	–	–	58/14
Sheikh, M.A.	25	110	11.00	36	–	–	31	21.54	3-28	7
Sheriyar, A.	75	102	10.20	19	–	–	77	29.38	4-18	6
Sidebottom, R.J.	53	99	7.61	24*	–	–	50	32.56	6-40	7
Silverwood, C.E.W.	127	300	8.33	38*	–	–	170	23.30	5-28	16
Singh, A.	45	1116	25.95	123	1	8	–	–	–	11
Smethurst, M.P.	17	21	5.25	10*	–	–	17	31.47	4-46	3
Smith, A.M.	210	462	10.74	26*	–	–	237	27.72	6-39	39
Smith, B.F.	198	4852	28.04	115	1	27	1	52.00	1-26	61
Smith, E.T.	27	419	19.04	72*	–	2	–	–	–	5
Smith, G.J.	29	19	3.80	9	–	–	40	26.22	5-11	4
Smith, N.M.K.	274	4444	22.33	125	2	25	262	26.09	6-33	91
Smith, R.A.	405	14083	41.91	167*	27	77	3	5.00	2-13	152
Smith, T.M.	16	38	6.33	12	–	–	20	27.60	4-38	4
Snape, J.N.	141	1681	20.75	78*	–	7	118	29.50	5-32	51
Solanki, V.S.	133	2155	21.33	120*	1	9	9	40.11	2-40	40
Speak, N.J.	155	3653	28.53	102*	1	20	0	–	–	28
Speight, M.P	239	5587	26.23	126	3	29	–	–	–	140/17
Spendlove, B.L.	22	314	15.70	58	–	1	–	–	–	7
Spiring, K.R.	58	1210	31.02	71	–	5	–	–	–	19
Stelling, W.F.	31	582	41.57	76*	–	3	39	31.51	3-18	13
Stemp, R.D.	139	196	7.25	29*	–	–	147	31.25	4-25	25
Stephenson, J.P.	284	6966	30.96	142	8	38	247	26.17	6-33	107
Stevens, D.I.	39	761	21.74	133	1	3	–	–	–	10
Stewart, A.J.	443	13416	36.16	167*	19	82	0	–	–	377/12
Strauss, A.J.	30	506	19.46	90	–	2	–	–	–	8
Strong, M.R.	10	28	4.66	21	–	–	14	24.71	5-39	2
Stubbings, S.D.	31	424	16.96	59	–	1	–	–	–	1
Such, P.M.	210	275	7.85	19*	–	–	209	31.52	5-29	51
Sutcliffe, I.J.	53	1258	26.20	105*	2	7	–	–	–	12
Sutliff, M.R.D.	2	6	3.00	5	–	–	–	–	–	–
Sutton, L.D.	17	304	21.71	60	–	2	–	–	–	9/2

L-O	M	Runs	Avge	HS	100	50	Wkts	Avge	Best	Ct/St
Swann, A.J.	11	329	29.90	74	–	2	0	–	–	3
Swann, G.P.	59	736	19.36	63	–	3	59	27.64	5-35	15
Symington, M.J.	10	43	5.37	16	–	–	4	70.50	1-15	4
Taylor, B.V.	24	34	8.50	21*	–	–	31	25.35	4-26	3
Taylor, C.G.	26	176	13.53	41	–	–	–	–	–	9
Taylor, J.P.	197	360	9.00	24	–	–	232	29.15	5-45	43
Thomas, I.J.	4	100	25.00	36	–	–	–	–	–	2
Thomas, S.D.	90	680	12.59	40	–	–	125	24.95	7-16	16
Thorpe, G.P.	293	9154	39.97	145*	7	69	16	40.56	3-21	137
Titchard, S.P.	63	1292	24.37	96	–	5	1	99.00	1-19	8
Tolley, C.M.	137	1414	19.36	77	–	4	126	30.68	5-16	34
Trego, P.D.	6	15	3.75	14	–	–	5	40.60	2-30	1
Tremlett, C.T.	6	40	20.00	30*	–	–	6	36.66	2-35	1
Trescothick, M.E.	120	2955	30.78	122	3	14	50	24.50	4-50	38
Trott, B.J.	1	–	–	–	–	–	1	29.00	1-29	–
Tudor, A.J.	35	143	8.93	29*	–	–	52	20.75	4-26	8
Tufnell, P.C.R.	88	125	8.92	18	–	–	99	31.87	5-28	17
Turner, R.J.	159	2295	24.15	70	–	7	–	–	–	169/18
Udal, S.D.	243	1601	14.96	78	–	6	271	30.84	5-43	79
Van der Gucht, C.G.	3	4	2.00	3	–	–	5	19.00	3-35	–
Vaughan, M.P.	145	3392	26.09	88	–	19	49	28.34	4-27	43
Wagh, M.A.	10	157	17.44	31	–	–	3	44.66	1-39	–
Walker, M.J.	117	2374	24.47	117	1	14	7	34.28	2-27	30
Wallace, M.A.	7	18	4.50	8*	–	–	–	–	–	7/3
Ward, I.J.	76	1569	26.15	91	–	8	0	–	–	16
Ward, T.R.	268	7807	31.10	131	7	53	10	35.10	3-20	57
Warren, R.J.	117	1912	21.97	100*	1	6	–	–	–	110/10
Watkin, S.L.	238	422	6.49	31*	–	–	300	26.00	5-23	38
Watkinson, M.	372	5398	22.97	130	2	20	380	31.86	5-44	98
Weekes, L.C.	16	27	5.40	8	–	–	18	28.61	4-33	1
Weekes, P.N.	210	4082	26.33	143*	3	19	228	27.62	4-26	82
Welch, G.	120	1331	21.12	71	–	4	94	38.55	4-31	17
Wells, A.P.	375	9381	30.75	127	8	58	7	20.28	1- 0	108
Wells, V.J.	212	4624	26.12	201	4	20	192	27.84	6-25	57
Welton, G.E.	26	563	22.52	104*	1	2	–	–	–	8
Weston, R.M.S.	36	615	19.21	56	–	3	–	–	–	7
Weston, W.P.C.	109	1706	19.83	125	1	5	1	2.00	1- 2	26
Wharf, A.G.	47	306	13.30	38*	–	–	42	38.83	4-29	8
Wharton, L.J.	7	8	–	7*	–	–	6	36.00	3-29	2
White, C.	227	4246	25.57	148	2	15	238	24.90	5-21	67
White, G.W.	107	2033	21.17	76	–	86	1	86.00	1-45	35
Widdup, S.	4	49	12.25	38	–	–	–	–	–	2
Williams, R.C.J.	27	165	16.50	38	–	–	–	–	–	26/5
Wilson, E.J.	32	493	18.96	62	–	3	–	–	–	11
Wilton, N.J.	17	45	4.50	17	–	–	–	–	–	12/3
Windows, M.G.N.	119	2032	21.38	72	–	5	0	–	–	39
Wood, J.	100	459	10.67	28*	–	–	98	35.20	4-17	14
Wood, M.J. (Sm)	1	43	43.00	43	–	–	–	–	–	–
Wood, M.J. (Y)	30	415	24.41	65*	–	3	–	–	–	8
Wright, A.S.	3	179	59.66	112	1	1	–	–	–	–
Yardy, M.H.	6	30	7.50	15	–	–	2	91.50	1-46	5
Yates, G.	154	563	14.43	38	–	–	149	31.48	4-34	36
Zuiderent, B.	20	378	21.00	99	–	3	0	–	–	11

LOI CAREER RECORDS

These records, complete to 16 February 2001, include all players registered for county cricket in 2001 at the time of going to press, plus those who have appeared in LOI matches since 21 August 1999.

ENGLAND – BATTING AND FIELDING

	M	I	NO	HS	Runs	Avge	100	50	Ct/St
C.J.Adams	5	4	–	42	71	17.75	–	–	3
M.W.Alleyne	10	8	1	53	151	21.57	–	1	3
M.A.Atherton	54	54	3	127	1791	35.11	2	12	15
I.D.Austin	9	6	1	11*	34	6.80	–	–	–
R.J.Bailey	4	4	2	43*	137	68.50	–	–	1
K.J.Barnett	1	1	–	84	84	84.00	–	1	–
M.P.Bicknell	7	6	2	31*	96	24.00	–	–	2
R.J.Blakey	3	2	–	25	25	12.50	–	–	2/1
A.D.Brown	13	13	–	118	333	25.61	1	1	6
D.R.Brown	9	8	4	21	99	24.75	–	–	1
A.R.Caddick	29	16	8	21*	77	9.62	–	–	7
D.G.Cork	25	15	2	31*	132	10.15	–	–	6
J.P.Crawley	13	12	1	73	235	21.36	–	2	1/1
R.D.B.Croft	46	33	12	32	310	14.76	–	–	9
P.A.J.DeFreitas	103	66	23	67	690	16.04	–	1	26
M.A Falham	60	42	4	45	684	18.00	–	–	8
N.H.Fairbrother	75	71	18	113	2092	39.47	1	16	33
M.V.Fleming	11	10	1	33	139	15.44	–	–	1
A.Flintoff	20	15	1	84	306	21.85	–	2	4
P.J.Franks	1	1	–	4	4	4.00	–	–	1
A.R.C.Fraser	42	20	9	38*	141	12.81	–	–	5
A.F.Giles	8	5	2	11	31	10.33	–	–	1
D.Gough	86	54	21	45	359	10.87	–	–	12
A.P.Grayson	1	1	–	0	0	0.00	–	–	–
G.A.Hick	117	115	15	126*	3787	37.87	5	27	63
A.J.Hollioake	35	30	6	83*	606	25.25	–	3	13
B.C.Hollioake	7	6	–	63	122	20.33	–	1	1
N.Hussain	50	50	8	95	1206	28.71	–	9	29
R.K.Illingworth	25	11	5	14	68	11.33	–	–	8
R.C.Irani	10	10	2	45*	78	9.75	–	–	2
N.V.Knight	53	53	5	125*	1924	40.08	3	12	20
G.D.Lloyd	6	5	1	22	39	9.75	–	–	2
D.L.Maddy	8	6	–	53	113	18.83	–	1	1
D.E.Malcolm	10	5	2	4	9	3.00	–	–	1
P.J.Martin	20	13	7	6	38	6.33	–	–	1
M.P.Maynard	14	12	1	41	156	14.18	–	–	4
J.E.Morris	8	8	1	63*	167	23.85	–	1	2
A.D.Mullally	41	17	7	20	64	6.40	–	–	7
M.R.Ramprakash	13	13	3	51	265	26.50	–	1	6
C.M.W.Read	9	6	2	26*	70	17.50	–	–	11/2
S.J.Rhodes	9	8	2	56	107	17.83	–	1	9/2
R.C.Russell	40	31	7	50	423	17.62	–	1	41/6
I.D.K.Salisbury	4	2	1	5	7	7.00	–	–	1
C.E.W.Silverwood	6	4	–	12	17	4.25	–	–	–
N M K.Smith	7	6	1	31	100	20.00	–	–	1
R.A.Smith	71	70	8	167*	2419	39.01	4	15	26
V.S.Solanki	8	7	1	24	96	16.00	–	–	2
A.J.Stewart	137	132	11	116	3931	32.48	4	22	126/11
G.P.Swann	1	–	–	–	–	–	–	–	–
J.P.Taylor	1	1	–	1	1	1.00	–	–	–
G.P.Thorpe	65	61	10	89	2025	39.70	–	18	34
M.E.Trescothick	12	12	1	87*	441	40.09	–	3	2
P.C.R.Tufnell	20	10	9	5*	15	15.00	–	–	4
S.D.Udal	10	6	4	11*	35	17.50	–	–	1
S.L.Watkin	4	2	–	4	4	2.00	–	–	–

ENGLAND – BATTING AND FIELDING (continued)

	M	I	NO	HS	Runs	Avge	100	50	Ct/St
M.Watkinson	1	–					–	–	–
A.P.Wells	1	1	–	15	15	15.00	–	–	–
V.J.Wells	9	7	–	39	141	20.14	–	–	7
C.White	34	26	2	38	333	13.87	–	–	8

ENGLAND – BOWLING

	O	R	W	Avge	Best	4wI	R/Over
M.W.Alleyne	61	280	10	28.00	3-27	–	4.59
I.D.Austin	79.1	360	6	60.00	2-25	–	4.55
R.J.Bailey	6	25	0	–	–	–	4.17
M.P.Bicknell	68.5	347	13	26.69	3-55	–	5.04
A.D.Brown	1	5	0	–	–	–	5.00
D.R.Brown	54	305	7	43.57	2-28	–	5.65
A.R.Caddick	266	976	37	26.37	4-19	1	3.67
D.G.Cork	240	1071	35	30.60	3-27	–	4.46
R.D.B.Croft	379	1597	42	38.02	3-51	–	4.21
P.A.J.DeFreitas	952	3775	115	32.82	4-35	1	3.97
M.A.Ealham	505.3	2044	66	30.96	5-15	3	4.04
N.H.Fairbrother	1	9	0	–	–	–	9.00
M.V.Fleming	87.1	434	17	25.52	4-45	1	4.98
A.Flintoff	44.2	248	7	35.42	2- 3	–	5.59
P.J.Franks	9	48	0	–	–	–	5.33
A.R.C.Fraser	398.4	1412	47	30.04	4-22	1	3.54
A.F.Giles	66	315	8	39.37	2-37	–	4.77
D.Gough	793	3311	136	24.34	5-44	8	4.18
A.P.Grayson	5	20	0	–	–	–	4.00
G.A.Hick	205.1	1020	30	34.00	5-33	1	4.97
A.J.Hollioake	201.2	1019	32	31.84	4-23	2	5.06
B.C.Hollioake	25	122	2	61.00	2-43	–	4.88
R.K.Illingworth	250.1	1059	30	35.30	3-33	–	4.23
R.C.Irani	54.5	246	4	61.50	1-23	–	4.49
D.E.Malcolm	87.4	404	16	25.25	3-40	–	4.61
P.J.Martin	174.4	806	27	29.85	4-44	1	4.61
A.D.Mullally	369.5	1369	53	25.83	4-18	2	3.70
M.R.Ramprakash	2	14	0	–	–	–	7.00
I.D.K.Salisbury	31	177	5	35.40	3-41	–	5.71
C.E.W.Silverwood	42	201	3	67.00	2-27	–	4.79
N.M.K.Smith	43.3	190	6	31.66	3-29	–	4.37
G.P.Swann	5	24	0	–	–	–	4.80
J.P.Taylor	3	20	0	–	–	–	6.67
G.P.Thorpe	20	97	2	48.50	2-15	–	4.85
M.E.Trescothick	6.4	38	2	19.00	2- 7	–	5.70
P.C.R.Tufnell	170	699	19	36.78	4-22	1	4.11
S.D.Udal	95	371	8	46.37	2-37	–	3.91
S.L.Watkin	36.5	193	7	27.57	4-49	1	5.24
M.Watkinson	9	43	0	–	–	–	4.78
V.J.Wells	36.4	189	8	23.62	3-30	–	5.15
C.White	256	1116	46	24.26	5-21	2	4.36

AUSTRALIA – BATTING AND FIELDING

	M	I	NO	HS	Runs	Avge	100	50	Ct/St
M.G.Bevan	154	136	46	108*	5064	56.26	5	34	50
A.J.Bichel	17	11	4	27*	99	14.14	–	–	2
G.S.Blewett	32	30	3	57*	551	20.40	–	2	7
N.W.Bracken	6	–					–	–	1
A.C.Dale	30	12	8	15*	78	19.50	–	–	11
M.J.Di Venuto	9	9	–	89	241	26.77	–	2	1
D.W.Fleming	82	28	16	29	121	10.08	–	–	12
A.C.Gilchrist	108	105	4	154	3428	33.94	6	17	142/23
J.N.Gillespie	21	14	3	26	105	9.54	–	–	–
B.J.Haddin	1	1	–	13	13	13.00	–	–	–/1

174

AUSTRALIA – BATTING AND FIELDING (continued)

	M	I	NO	HS	Runs	Avge	100	50	Ct/St
I.J.Harvey	27	20	6	47*	301	21.50	–	–	8
M.L.Hayden	19	18	2	67	477	29.81	–	5	7
S.M.Katich	1	–	–	–	–	–	–	–	–
S.G.Law	54	51	5	110	1237	26.89	1	7	12
B.Lee	24	8	2	31	70	11.66	–	–	1
S.Lee	44	34	7	47	452	16.74	–	–	22
D.S.Lehmann	66	59	11	110*	1724	35.91	2	10	12
S.C.G.MacGill	3	2	1	1	1	1.00	–	–	2
G.D.McGrath	130	39	23	11	70	4.37	–	–	14
J.P.Maher	2	2	–	13	21	10.50	–	–	–
D.R.Martyn	70	60	22	144*	1560	41.05	2	8	27
R.T.Ponting	114	114	13	145	4111	40.70	6	24	35
A.Symonds	36	26	6	68*	612	30.60	–	2	15
S.K.Warne	158	87	25	55	776	12.51	–	1	62
M.E.Waugh	230	223	18	173	8107	39.54	17	49	100
S.R.Waugh	306	273	55	120*	7089	32.51	3	41	105

AUSTRALIA – BOWLING

	O	R	W	Avge	Best	4wI	R/Over
M.G.Bevan	315.2	1560	35	44.47	3-36	–	4.95
A.J.Bichel	148.2	701	21	33.38	3-17	–	4.73
G.S.Blewett	124.5	646	14	46.14	2- 6	–	5.18
N.W.Bracken	44	191	5	38.20	2-21	–	4.34
A.C.Dale	266	979	32	30.59	3-18	–	3.68
D.W.Fleming	711.5	3139	127	24.71	5-36	5	4.41
J.N.Gillespie	186.1	844	28	30.14	4-26	1	4.53
I.J.Harvey	208.3	942	26	36.23	4-28	1	4.52
M.L.Hayden	1	18	0	–	–	–	18.00
S.G.Law	134.3	635	12	52.91	2-22	–	4.72
B.Lee	207.1	972	40	24.30	5-27	2	4.69
S.Lee	281.2	1234	48	25.70	5-33	2	4.39
D.S.Lehmann	84.4	452	12	37.66	2- 4	–	5.34
S.C.G.MacGill	30	105	6	17.50	4-19	1	3.50
G.D.McGrath	1158.2	4601	194	23.71	5-14	10	3.97
D.R.Martyn	79.4	382	8	47.75	2-21	–	4.80
R.T.Ponting	25	104	3	34.66	1-12	–	4.16
A.Symonds	191.2	926	35	26.45	4-11	2	4.84
S.K.Warne	1456.3	6087	248	24.54	5-33	13	4.18
M.E.Waugh	586.3	2801	83	33.74	5-24	2	4.78
S.R.Waugh	1464.3	6676	192	34.77	4-33	3	4.56

SOUTH AFRICA – BATTING AND FIELDING

	M	I	NO	HS	Runs	Avge	100	50	Ct/St
S.Abrahams	1	1	1	16*	16	–	–	–	1
P.R.Adams	15	7	4	15*	27	9.00	–	–	3
D.M.Benkenstein	20	18	3	69	296	19.73	–	1	1
N.Boje	56	34	8	129	780	30.00	2	2	17
M.V.Boucher	84	60	16	68	927	21.06	–	7	121/4
D.J.Callaghan	29	25	6	169*	493	23.94	1	–	6
W.J.Cronje	188	175	31	112	5565	38.64	2	39	72
D.N.Crookes	32	23	4	54	296	15.57	–	1	20
D.J.Cullinan	138	133	16	124	3860	32.99	3	23	62
A.C.Dawson	4	1	–	6	6	6.00	–	–	–
H.H.Dippenaar	16	13	1	77	424	35.33	–	4	4
A.A.Donald	131	32	14	12	85	4.72	–	–	17
S.Elworthy	35	13	7	23	71	11.83	–	–	9
H.H.Gibbs	63	63	4	125	1769	29.98	3	9	21
A.J.Hall	18	17	1	81	391	24.43	–	1	8
M.Hayward	17	5	1	4	12	3.00	–	–	3
J.H.Kallis	120	117	22	113*	4081	42.95	6	28	47
J.M.Kemp	2	1	–	0	0	0.00	–	–	–

	M	I	NO	HS	Runs	Avge	100	50	Ct/St
G.Kirsten	148	148	14	188*	5511	41.12	10	36	49/1
L.Klusener	109	92	32	103*	2537	42.28	2	14	20
L.J.Koen	5	5	–	28	82	16.40	–	–	2
N.D.McKenzie	23	20	1	120*	518	27.26	1	1	7
P.V.Mpitsang	2	1	1	1*	1	–	–	–	–
M.Ntini	19	4	2	3*	5	2.50	–	–	6
S.M.Pollock	125	83	27	75	1372	24.50	–	5	43
N.Pothas	3	1	–	24	24	24.00	–	–	4/1
J.N.Rhodes	193	175	37	121	4492	32.55	1	22	87
P.C.Strydom	10	8	3	34	48	9.60	–	–	3
R.Telemachus	21	5	2	13	22	7.33	–	–	1
D.J.Terbrugge	4	2	1	5	5	5.00	–	–	–
H.S.Williams	7	2	1	7	8	8.00	–	–	2
C.M.Willoughby	1	1	–	0	0	0.00	–	–	–

SOUTH AFRICA – BOWLING

	O	R	W	Avge	Best	4wI	R/Over
S.Abrahams	10	40	0	–	–	–	4.00
P.R.Adams	118.5	530	22	24.09	3-26	–	4.46
D.M.Benkenstein	3	22	0	–	–	–	7.33
N.Boje	351.5	1553	43	36.11	4-25	1	4.41
D.J.Callaghan	74	365	10	36.50	3-32	–	4.93
W.J.Cronje	892.2	3966	114	34.78	5-32	2	4.44
D.N.Crookes	203.3	1011	25	40.44	3-30	–	4.97
D.J.Cullinan	31.4	130	5	26.00	2-30	–	4.11
A.C.Dawson	37	188	5	37.60	3-36	–	5.08
A.A.Donald	1142	4650	217	21.42	6-23	11	4.07
S.Elworthy	255.4	1110	39	28.46	3-17	–	4.34
A.J.Hall	35.4	167	5	33.40	2- 8	–	4.68
M.Hayward	133.3	691	17	40.64	4-31	1	5.18
J.H.Kallis	689.4	3219	107	30.08	5-30	1	4.67
J.M.Kemp	12	49	2	24.50	2-34	–	4.08
G.Kirsten	5	23	0	–	–	–	4.60
L.Klusener	795.1	3742	134	27.92	6-49	6	4.71
N.D.McKenzie	3.4	11	0	–	–	–	3.00
P.V.Mpitsang	10	63	2	31.50	2-49	–	6.30
M.Ntini	144.1	614	26	23.61	5-37	2	4.26
S.M.Pollock	1093	4221	183	23.06	6-35	9	3.86
P.C.Strydom	42	206	2	103.00	1-18	–	4.91
R.Telemachus	186.4	827	34	24.32	4-43	1	4.43
D.J.Terbrugge	21	105	4	26.25	4-20	1	5.00
H.S.Williams	54.5	228	9	25.33	3-38	–	4.16
C.M.Willoughby	10	39	2	19.50	2-39	–	3.90

WEST INDIES – BATTING AND FIELDING

	M	I	NO	HS	Runs	Avge	100	50	Ct/St
J.C.Adams	127	105	28	82	2204	28.62	–	14	68/5
C.E.L.Ambrose	176	96	36	31*	639	10.65	–	–	45
M.I.Black	4	1	–	4	4	4.00	–	–	–
C.O.Browne	25	19	4	26	187	12.46	–	–	32/5
H.R.Bryan	15	8	2	11	43	7.16	–	–	4
S.L.Campbell	90	87	–	105	2283	26.24	2	14	23
S.Chanderpaul	92	86	9	150	2645	34.35	2	15	26
P.T.Collins	2	2	2	10*	10	–	–	–	–
C.D.Collymore	5	2	1	13*	16	16.00	–	–	–
C.E.Cuffy	19	13	5	17*	46	5.75	–	–	3
M.Dillon	49	25	10	21*	139	9.26	–	–	6
V.C.Drakes	5	2	–	16	25	12.50	–	–	6
D.Ganga	7	7	–	22	47	6.71	–	–	2
C.H.Gayle	20	19	1	58*	331	18.38	–	1	6
A.F.G.Griffith	9	8	1	47	99	14.14	–	–	5

WEST INDIES – BATTING AND FIELDING (continued)

	M	I	NO	HS	Runs	Avge	100	50	Ct/St
W.W.Hinds	32	31	1	116*	814	27.13	1	5	14
C.L.Hooper	182	166	36	113*	4612	35.47	6	26	87
R.D.Jacobs	72	62	10	80*	1130	21.73	–	6	99/16
K.C.B.Jeremy	1	1	1	4*	4	–	–	–	–
S.C.Joseph	4	4	–	28	57	14.25	–	–	1
R.D.King	42	22	13	12*	62	6.88	–	–	4
B.C.Lara	183	179	17	169	6897	42.57	14	44	79
N.A.M.McLean	42	31	8	50*	302	13.13	–	1	8
M.V.Nagamootoo	12	12	2	33	119	11.90	–	–	4
N.O.Perry	21	16	8	52*	212	26.50	–	1	4
R.L.Powell	44	41	3	124	969	25.50	1	4	20
D.Ramnarine	2	1	–	2	2	2.00	–	–	–
F.A.Rose	27	23	5	30	217	12.05	–	–	7
M.N.Samuels	11	11	–	68	301	27.36	–	3	2
R.R.Sarwan	1	1	–	20	20	20.00	–	–	–
C.E.L.Stuart	1	1	1	3*	3	–	–	–	–
P.A.Wallace	33	33	–	103	701	21.24	1	2	11
C.A.Walsh	205	79	33	30	321	6.97	–	–	27
L.R.Williams	15	13	2	41	124	11.27	–	–	8

WEST INDIES – BOWLING

	O	R	W	Avge	Best	4wI	R/Over
J.C.Adams	309.2	1499	43	34.86	5-37	1	4.85
C.E.L.Ambrose	1558.5	5430	225	24.13	5-17	10	3.48
M.I.Black	29	153	0	–	–	–	5.28
H.R.Bryan	120.2	518	12	43.16	4-24	1	4.31
S.L.Campbell	32.4	170	8	21.25	4 30	1	5.20
S.Chanderpaul	116	600	14	42.85	3-18	–	5.17
P.T.Collins	15.3	95	0	–	–	–	6.13
C.D.Collymore	45	178	3	59.33	1-27	–	3.96
C.E.Cuffy	164.1	660	21	31.42	4-24	1	4.02
M.Dillon	423	1869	60	31.15	5-51	3	4.42
V.C.Drakes	39.5	204	3	68.00	1-36	–	5.12
C.H.Gayle	118.1	488	12	40.66	2-18	–	4.13
W.W.Hinds	13	77	2	38.50	1- 6	–	5.92
C.L.Hooper	1266.1	5547	163	34.03	4-34	3	4.38
K.C.B.Jeremy	8	54	1	54.00	1-54	–	6.75
R.D.King	359.5	1441	66	21.83	4-25	1	4.00
B.C.Lara	7.1	46	4	11.50	2- 5	–	6.42
N.A.M.McLean	337.2	1617	46	35.15	3-21	–	4.79
M.V.Nagamootoo	103.1	486	9	54.00	4-32	1	4.71
N.O.Perry	157.4	783	20	39.15	3-45	–	4.97
R.L.Powell	28.3	198	4	49.50	2- 5	–	6.95
D.Ramnarine	16.2	75	2	37.50	2-52	–	4.59
F.A.Rose	221	1046	29	36.06	5-23	1	4.73
M.N.Samuels	86.5	419	14	29.92	3-25	–	4.83
C.E.L.Stuart	8	57	0	–	–	–	7.13
C.A.Walsh	1803.4	6918	227	30.46	5- 1	7	3.83
L.R.Williams	109.5	556	18	30.88	3-16	–	5.06

NEW ZEALAND – BATTING AND FIELDING

	M	I	NO	HS	Runs	Avge	100	50	Ct/St
G.I.Allott	31	11	6	7*	17	3.40	–	–	5
N.J.Astle	128	125	5	120	4131	34.42	8	25	50
C.L.Cairns	137	124	12	115	3216	28.71	3	16	44
S.B.Doull	42	27	13	22	172	12.28	–	–	10
C.J.Drum	5	2	2	7*	9	–	–	–	1
S.P.Fleming	147	141	14	116*	3940	31.02	3	24	65
J.E.C.Franklin	7	5	1	25*	44	11.00	–	–	1
C.Z.Harris	173	145	47	130	3123	31.86	1	12	60
C.D.McMillan	79	73	4	86	1658	24.02	–	10	18

	M	I	NO	HS	Runs	Avge	100	50	Ct/St
C.S.Martin	5	4	1	3	5	1.66	–	–	2
D.J.Nash	73	46	13	40*	509	15.42	–	–	22
C.J.Nevin	9	8	–	74	178	22.25	–	2	4/2
S.B.O'Connor	38	13	6	8	24	3.42	–	–	11
J.D.P.Oram	6	5	–	59	117	23.40	–	1	2
A.C.Parore	158	142	26	108	3075	26.50	1	13	93/24
A.J.Penn	5	3	1	15	23	11.50	–	–	1
M.S.Sinclair	9	9	–	85	162	18.00	–	1	1
C.M.Spearman	51	50	–	86	936	18.72	–	5	15
S.B.Styris	30	20	2	48	262	14.55	–	–	8
G.P.Sulzberger	3	2	1	6*	9	9.00	–	–	–
A.R.Tait	5	5	2	13*	35	11.66	–	–	–
D.R.Tuffey	5	3	2	2	2	2.00	–	–	1
R.G.Twose	82	76	11	103	2652	40.80	1	20	34
D.L.Vettori	61	39	12	25*	303	11.22	–	–	15
L.Vincent	3	3	1	31*	48	24.00	–	–	1
B.G.K.Walker	4	2	2	5*	7	–	–	–	2
P.J.Wiseman	14	6	5	16	43	43.00	–	–	3
W.A.Wisneski	3	2	1	6	10	10.00	–	–	1

NEW ZEALAND – BOWLING

	O	R	W	Avge	Best	4wI	R/Over
G.I.Allott	254.4	1207	52	23.21	4-35	4	4.74
N.J.Astle	653.1	3030	83	36.50	4-43	1	4.64
C.L.Cairns	935.2	4419	131	33.73	5-42	3	4.72
S.B.Doull	290.5	1459	36	40.52	4-25	1	5.02
C.J.Drum	36	261	4	65.25	2-31	–	7.25
S.P.Fleming	4.5	28	1	28.00	1- 8	–	5.79
J.E.C.Franklin	55	283	9	31.44	3-44	–	5.15
C.Z.Harris	1302.1	5654	157	36.01	5-42	3	4.34
C.D.McMillan	166	837	28	29.89	3-44	–	5.04
C.S.Martin	37	203	4	50.75	2-56	–	5.49
D.J.Nash	517.4	2395	54	44.35	4-38	1	4.63
S.B.O'Connor	247.5	1396	46	30.34	5-39	3	5.63
J.D.P.Oram	22	116	2	58.00	2-20	–	5.27
A.J.Penn	26.3	201	1	201.00	1-50	–	7.59
C.M.Spearman	0.3	6	0	–	–	–	12.00
S.B.Styris	235.2	1178	27	43.62	4-57	1	5.01
G.P.Sulzberger	22	102	3	34.00	1-28	–	4.64
A.R.Tait	20	88	3	29.33	2-37	–	4.40
D.R.Tuffey	34	199	5	39.80	2-36	–	5.85
R.G.Twose	45.2	237	4	59.25	2-31	–	5.23
D.L.Vettori	436.3	2018	55	36.69	4-24	2	4.62
B.G.K.Walker	26	128	2	64.00	2-43	–	4.92
P.J.Wiseman	69	341	11	31.00	4-45	1	4.94
W.A.Wisneski	19	123	0	–	–	–	6.47

INDIA – BATTING AND FIELDING

	M	I	NO	HS	Runs	Avge	100	50	Ct/St
A.B.Agarkar	69	39	12	67*	440	16.29	–	1	26
M.Azharuddin	334	308	54	153*	9378	36.92	7	58	156
H.K.Badani	8	7	2	77	239	47.80	–	2	4
A.Bhandari	1	1	1	0*	–	–	–	–	–
R.V.Bharadwaj	9	8	4	41*	136	34.00	–	–	3
N.Chopra	39	26	6	61	310	15.50	–	1	16
V.Dahiya	14	10	1	40	141	15.66	–	–	13/4
S.S.Dighe	11	10	4	36*	107	17.83	–	–	11/1
R.Dravid	139	130	10	153	4449	37.07	7	29	73/1
D.J.Gandhi	3	3	–	30	49	16.33	–	–	–
S.C.Ganguly	158	153	14	183	6284	45.20	16	35	49
A.Jadeja	196	179	36	119	5359	37.47	6	30	59

LOI   **INDIA – BATTING AND FIELDING (continued)**

	M	I	NO	HS	Runs	Avge	100	50	Ct/St
S.B.Joshi	68	44	11	61*	565	17.12	–	1	19
V.G.Kambli	104	97	21	106	2477	32.59	2	14	15
H.H.Kanitkar	34	27	8	57	339	17.84	–	1	14
A.R.Kapoor	17	6	–	19	43	7.16	–	–	1
S.S.Karim	34	27	4	55	362	15.73	–	1	27/3
Z.Khan	13	6	4	32*	57	28.50	–	–	4
A.R.Khurasiya	10	9	–	57	137	15.22	–	1	1
T.Kumaran	8	3	–	8	19	6.33	–	–	3
A.Kumble	208	102	34	26	716	10.52	–	–	73
V.V.S.Laxman	13	12	1	23*	86	7.81	–	–	8
J.J.Martin	8	7	1	39	122	20.33	–	–	5
D.S.Mohanty	41	10	5	4*	10	2.00	–	–	10
N.R.Mongia	140	96	33	69	1272	20.19	–	2	112/44
B.K.V.Prasad	159	62	31	19	211	6.80	–	–	37
M.S.K.Prasad	17	11	2	63	131	14.55	–	1	13/8
S.Ramesh	24	24	1	82	646	28.08	–	6	3
V.Shewag	3	2	–	19	20	10.00	–	–	–
L.R.Shukla	3	2	–	13	18	9.00	–	–	1
R.R.Singh	135	112	23	100	2322	26.08	1	9	33
R.S.Sodhi	4	4	2	53*	70	35.00	–	1	1
J.Srinath	187	99	29	53	818	11.68	–	1	30
S.Sriram	6	5	1	12	21	5.25	–	–	1
S.R.Tendulkar	263	256	22	186*	9899	42.30	27	50	86
Yuvraj Singh	13	12	–	84	260	21.66	–	1	9

INDIA – BOWLING

	O	R	W	Avge	Best	4wI	R/Over
A.B.Agarkar	615	3159	107	29.52	4-25	4	5.14
M.Azharuddin	92.4	479	12	39.91	3-19	–	5.19
H.K.Badani	3	21	0	–	–	–	7.00
A.Bhandari	10	75	2	37.50	2-75	–	7.50
R.V.Bharadwaj	58	274	15	18.26	3-34	–	4.74
N.Chopra	305.5	1286	46	27.95	5-21	2	4.21
R.Dravid	31	170	4	42.50	2-43	–	5.48
S.C.Ganguly	388.4	1964	57	34.45	5-16	3	5.05
A.Jadeja	208	1094	20	54.70	3- 3	–	5.25
S.B.Joshi	555.1	2455	69	35.57	5- 6	2	4.42
V.G.Kambli	0.4	7	1	7.00	1- 7	–	10.50
H.H.Kanitkar	167.4	803	17	47.23	2-22	–	4.79
A.R.Kapoor	150	612	8	76.50	2-33	–	4.08
Z.Khan	114.5	526	18	29.22	4-42	1	4.58
T.Kumaran	63	348	9	38.66	3-24	–	5.52
A.Kumble	1861.1	7828	274	28.56	6-12	9	4.20
V.V.S.Laxman	6	32	0	–	–	–	5.33
D.S.Mohanty	302.4	1535	53	28.96	4-56	1	5.07
B.K.V.Prasad	1339.3	6236	193	32.31	5-27	4	4.65
S.Ramesh	6	38	1	38.00	1-23	–	6.33
V.Shewag	11	72	2	36.00	2-37	–	6.55
L.R.Shukla	19	94	1	94.00	1-25	–	4.95
R.R.Singh	616.2	2948	69	42.72	5-22	2	4.78
R.S.Sodhi	24	116	2	58.00	2-43	–	4.83
J.Srinath	1629.1	7222	252	28.65	5-23	7	4.43
S.Sriram	35	194	5	38.80	3-47	–	5.54
S.R.Tendulkar	926	4562	98	46.55	5-32	4	4.94
Yuvraj Singh	25	107	1	107.00	1-15	–	4.28

PAKISTAN – BATTING AND FIELDING

	M	I	NO	HS	Runs	Avge	100	50	Ct/St
Aamir Sohail	156	155	5	134	4784	31.89	5	31	49
Abdur Razzaq	69	58	14	75*	1128	25.63	–	7	7
Arshad Khan	48	26	15	20	105	9.54	–	–	9

PAKISTAN – BATTING AND FIELDING (continued)

	M	I	NO	HS	Runs	Avge	100	50	Ct/St
Atiq-uz-Zaman	3	3	1	18	34	17.00	–	–	3/1
Azhar Mahmood	99	74	16	67	1073	18.50	–	3	30
Faisal Iqbal	1	1	–	4	4	4.00	–	–	–
Hasan Raja	16	13	–	77	242	18.61	–	1	1
Ijaz Ahmed	250	232	29	139*	6564	32.33	10	37	90
Imran Abbas	2	2	–	28	29	14.50	–	–	1
Imran Nazir	29	29	1	105*	707	25.25	1	4	11
Inzamam-ul-Haq	234	221	32	137*	7549	39.94	7	56	70
Irfan Fazil	1	1	–	15	15	15.00	–	–	–
Kabir Khan	10	5	4	5	10	10.00	–	–	1
Mohammad Akram	23	9	7	7*	14	7.00	–	–	8
Mohammad Wasim	25	25	2	76	543	23.60	–	3	9
Moin Khan	185	155	35	69*	2751	22.92	–	8	186/65
Mushtaq Ahmed	143	76	34	34*	399	9.50	–	–	30
Saeed Anwar	213	210	16	194	7634	39.35	19	34	40
Salim Elahi	22	22	2	102*	644	32.20	1	4	5
Saqlain Mushtaq	129	76	26	37*	616	12.32	–	–	32
Shabbir Ahmed	5	–	–	–	–	–	–	–	2
Shahid Afridi	120	116	4	109	2673	23.86	2	14	44
Shahid Nazir	17	8	6	8	27	135.00	–	–	4
Shoaib Akhtar	41	19	15	36	81	20.25	–	–	7
Shoaib Malik	10	6	2	28	51	12.75	–	–	6
Wajahatullah Wasti	15	15	–	84	349	23.26	–	1	5
Waqar Younis	199	105	36	37	739	10.71	–	–	23
Wasim Akram	311	244	43	86	3256	16.19	–	6	83
Yasir Arafat	1	1	–	6	6	6.00	–	–	–
Younis Khan	18	18	1	59	380	22.35	–	1	9
Yousuf Youhana	73	69	11	104*	2210	38.10	3	14	22

PAKISTAN – BOWLING

	O	R	W	Avge	Best	4wI	R/Over
Aamir Sohail	806	3703	85	43.56	4-22	1	4.59
Abdur Razzaq	538	2343	100	23.43	5-31	5	4.35
Arshad Khan	395.3	1627	44	36.97	3-22	–	4.11
Azhar Mahmood	744.2	3326	101	32.93	6-18	5	4.47
Faisal Iqbal	2	16	0	–	–	–	8.00
Ijaz Ahmed	106.1	476	5	95.20	2-31	–	4.48
Imran Nazir	4.1	19	1	19.00	1- 3	–	4.56
Inzamam-ul-Haq	6.4	52	2	26.00	1- 4	–	7.80
Irfan Fazil	6	46	0	–	–	–	7.67
Kabir Khan	61.5	303	12	25.25	2-23	–	4.90
Mohammad Akram	164.5	790	19	41.57	2-28	–	4.79
Mushtaq Ahmed	1247.1	5296	161	32.89	5-36	4	4.25
Saeed Anwar	36.2	176	5	35.20	2- 9	–	4.84
Saqlain Mushtaq	1127.1	4790	237	20.21	5-20	15	4.25
Shabbir Ahmed	39	182	7	26.00	3-52	–	4.67
Shahid Afridi	731.2	3449	78	44.21	5-40	1	4.72
Shahid Nazir	135	649	19	34.15	3-14	–	4.81
Shoaib Akhtar	315.4	1407	66	21.31	4-37	1	4.46
Shoaib Malik	83.1	353	12	29.41	2-21	–	4.24
Wajahatullah Wasti	9.1	69	3	23.00	3-36	–	7.53
Waqar Younis	1636.2	7497	316	23.72	6-26	22	4.58
Wasim Akram	2659.5	10288	432	23.81	5-15	21	3.87
Yasir Arafat	5	28	1	28.00	1-28	–	5.60
Younis Khan	6	29	0	–	–	–	4.83

SRI LANKA – BATTING AND FIELDING

	M	I	NO	HS	Runs	Avge	100	50	Ct/St
R.P.Arnold	47	41	11	103	1346	44.86	1	10	13
M.S.Atapattu	118	116	15	132*	3784	37.46	5	29	39
U.D.U.Chandana	78	59	8	50	813	15.94	–	1	46

SRI LANKA – BATTING AND FIELDING (continued)

	M	I	NO	HS	Runs	Avge	100	50	Ct/St
S.I.de Saram	7	6	1	24*	73	14.60	–	–	4
K.S.C.de Silva	38	19	13	13*	39	6.50	–	–	12
P.A.de Silva	275	266	26	145	8432	35.13	11	57	86
H.D.P.K.Dharmasena	104	63	27	69*	929	25.80	–	4	28
T.M.Dilshan	13	11	2	53	227	25.22	–	1	5
C.R.D.Fernando	8	2	1	12*	12	12.00	–	–	1
I.S.Gallage	3	2	1	14	17	17.00	–	–	–
D.A.Gunawardena	22	22	–	132	634	28.81	1	3	2
S.T.Jayasuriya	228	220	8	189	6340	29.90	10	41	77
D.P.M.deS.Jayawardena	69	65	5	128	1583	26.38	3	6	25
R.S.Kaluwitharana	153	146	11	100*	2970	22.00	1	20	108/65
M.Muralitharan	159	72	31	18	200	4.87	–	–	72
A.S.A.Perera	11	6	1	26	53	10.60	–	–	–
P.D.R.L.Perera	2	2	–	3	3	1.50	–	–	–
K.R.Pushpakumara	31	9	5	14*	36	9.00	–	–	8
K.Sangakkara	23	21	5	85	513	32.06	–	2	14/4
L.P.C.Silva	7	5	–	55	85	17.00	–	1	1
K.E.A.Upashantha	12	8	1	15	49	7.00	–	–	2
W.P.U.C.J.Vaas	151	98	34	34*	888	13.87	–	–	27
K.Weeraratne	10	4	1	14*	40	13.33	–	–	1
G.P.Wickremasinghe	132	62	23	32	339	8.69	–	–	26
D.N.T.Zoysa	44	19	9	32	118	11.80	–	–	5

SRI LANKA – BOWLING

	O	R	W	Avge	Best	4wI	R/Over
R.P.Arnold	140.2	668	11	60.72	2-32	–	4.75
M.S.Atapattu	8.3	41	0	–	–	–	4.82
U.D.U.Chandana	509.3	2386	78	30.58	4-31	3	4.69
K.S.C.de Silva	269.5	1323	52	25.44	3-18	–	4.90
P.A.de Silva	727.5	3560	91	39.12	4-45	1	4.89
H.D.P.K.Dharmasena	866	3821	102	37.46	4-37	1	4.41
C.R.D.Fernando	51.4	344	6	57.33	2-34	–	6.66
I.S.Gallage	24	115	3	38.33	2-42	–	4.79
S.T.Jayasuriya	1400.4	6754	192	35.17	6-29	8	4.82
D.P.M.deS.Jayawardena	82.4	459	7	65.57	2-56	–	5.55
M.Muralitharan	1448	5865	225	26.06	7-30	9	4.05
A.S.A.Perera	72.3	388	10	38.80	2-25	–	5.35
P.D.R.L.Perera	20	126	3	42.00	3-55	–	6.30
K.R.Pushpakumara	238.2	1182	24	49.25	3-25	–	4.96
K.E.A.Upashantha	94	480	12	40.00	4-37	1	5.12
W.P.U.C.J.Vaas	1225.1	5209	185	28.15	5-14	4	4.25
K.Weeraratne	64	288	6	48.00	3-46	–	4.50
G.P.Wickremasinghe	943.2	4265	108	39.49	4-48	1	4.52
D.N.T.Zoysa	350.2	1487	50	29.74	4-28	2	4.24

ZIMBABWE – BATTING AND FIELDING

	M	I	NO	HS	Runs	Avge	100	50	Ct/St
A.M.Blignaut	7	7	1	27	53	8.83	–	–	1
E.A.Brandes	59	41	10	55	404	13.03	–	2	11
G.B.Brent	20	15	6	24	71	7.88	–	–	4
A.D.R.Campbell	157	153	14	131*	4388	31.56	6	24	63
S.V.Carlisle	66	63	5	121*	1537	26.50	2	5	24
C.N.Evans	49	43	5	96*	667	17.55	–	1	11
A.Flower	169	166	11	120*	5140	33.16	2	43	119/30
G.W.Flower	151	149	11	140	4517	32.73	3	30	53
T.J.Friend	13	10	4	19	56	9.33	–	–	1
M.W.Goodwin	71	70	3	112*	1818	27.13	2	8	20
N.C.Johnson	48	48	2	132*	1679	36.50	4	11	19
A.J.Mackay	3	–	–	–	–	–	–	–	1
T.N.Madondo	13	13	1	71	191	15.91	–	1	2
D.A.Marillier	11	11	1	46	178	17.80	–	–	3

ZIMBABWE – BATTING AND FIELDING (continued)

	M	I	NO	HS	Runs	Avge	100	50	Ct/St
M.Mbangwa	26	12	5	11	33	4.71	–	–	3
B.A.Murphy	15	9	6	7*	19	6.33	–	–	5
D.T.Mutendera	5	4	2	10	20	10.00	–	–	1
M.L.Nkala	22	13	1	36	115	9.58	–	–	3
H.K.Olonga	35	19	10	11	46	5.11	–	–	9
G.J.Rennie	36	33	6	76	567	21.00	–	2	13
J.A.Rennie	44	27	12	27	201	13.40	–	–	12
B.C.Strang	43	25	8	18	88	5.17	–	–	14
P.A.Strang	91	72	24	47	1071	22.31	–	–	28
H.H.Streak	122	104	38	79*	1584	24.00	–	3	27
M.A.Vermeulen	1	1	–	22	22	22.00	–	–	–
D.P.Viljoen	45	37	6	63*	474	15.29	–	2	16
A.R.Whittall	63	35	13	29	168	7.63	–	–	21
G.J.Whittall	127	124	18	83	2379	22.44	–	10	31
C.B.Wishart	50	45	2	102	756	17.58	1	1	16

ZIMBABWE – BOWLING

	O	R	W	Avge	Best	4wI	R/Over
A.M.Blignaut	39.4	212	5	42.40	2-35	–	5.34
E.A.Brandes	471.2	2265	70	32.35	5-28	3	4.81
G.B.Brent	163.2	839	25	33.56	4-53	1	5.13
A.D.R.Campbell	69.5	347	11	31.59	2-20	–	4.96
C.N.Evans	154.4	796	19	41.84	3-11	–	5.15
A.Flower	5	23	0	–	–	–	4.60
G.W.Flower	516.4	2428	61	39.80	4-32	1	4.70
T.J.Friend	104.5	554	15	36.93	4-55	1	5.28
M.W.Goodwin	41.2	210	4	52.50	1-12	–	5.08
N.C.Johnson	250.3	1220	35	34.85	4-42	1	4.87
A.J.Mackay	22	137	0	–	–	–	6.23
D.A.Marillier	9.2	71	3	23.66	3-23	–	7.61
M.Mbangwa	200.1	1030	10	103.00	2-24	–	5.15
B.A.Murphy	128	616	18	34.22	3-43	–	4.81
D.T.Mutendera	33	170	2	85.00	1-42	–	5.15
M.L.Nkala	144.5	771	15	51.40	3-12	–	5.32
H.K.Olonga	254.1	1491	46	32.41	6-19	3	5.87
G.J.Rennie	1	11	0	–	–	–	11.00
J.A.Rennie	327.3	1564	34	46.00	3-27	–	4.78
B.C.Strang	362.2	1524	39	39.07	6-20	2	4.21
P.A.Strang	696.1	3007	92	32.68	5-21	4	4.32
H.H.Streak	1026	4605	150	30.70	5-32	5	4.49
D.P.Viljoen	290.5	1393	39	35.71	3-20	–	4.79
A.R.Whittall	514.1	2251	45	50.02	3-23	–	4.38
G.J.Whittall	599.1	3062	81	37.80	4-35	1	5.11
C.B.Wishart	2	12	0	–	–	–	6.00

BANGLADESH – BATTING AND FIELDING

	M	I	NO	HS	Runs	Avge	100	50	Ct/St
Ahmed Kamal	1	1	–	11	11	11.00	–	–	–
Akram Khan	35	35	2	65	796	24.12	–	5	6
Al Shahriar	5	5	1	62*	112	28.00	–	1	–
Aminul Islam	37	37	5	70	761	23.78	–	3	13
Aminul Islam Bhola	1	1	1	1*	1	–	–	–	–
Enamul Huq	25	22	5	19	177	10.41	–	–	5
Habibul Bashar	14	14	–	70	237	16.92	–	2	5
Hasibul Hussain	27	21	3	21*	161	8.94	–	–	6
Javed Omer	11	11	2	85*	251	27.88	–	2	–
Khaled Mahmud	20	18	–	47	245	13.61	–	–	3
Khaled Masud	31	28	6	53*	289	13.13	–	1	22/7
Mohammed Rafique	21	21	1	77	267	13.35	–	1	4
Monjurul Islam	9	5	5	6*	14	–	–	–	2
Mushfiqur Rahman	3	1	–	11	11	11.00	–	–	–

BANGLADESH – BATTING AND FIELDING (continued)

	M	I	NO	HS	Runs	Avge	100	50	Ct/St
Naimur Rahman	21	20	2	47	372	20.66	–	–	6
Shafiuddin Ahmed	11	10	6	11	32	8.00	–	–	4
Shahriar Hossain	18	17	–	95	360	21.17	–	2	5

BANGLADESH – BOWLING

	O	R	W	Avge	Best	4wI	R/Over
Ahmed Kamal	5	39	1	39.00	1-39	–	7.80
Akram Khan	19.3	138	0	–	–	–	7.08
Aminul Islam	68.4	411	7	58.71	3-57	–	5.99
Aminul Islam Bhola	5	33	1	33.00	1-33	–	6.60
Enamul Huq	173.2	878	14	62.71	2-40	–	5.07
Habibul Bashar	18	71	1	71.00	1-31	–	3.94
Hasibul Hussain	203.1	1160	28	41.42	4-56	1	5.71
Khaled Mahmud	157.1	770	19	40.52	3-31	–	4.90
Mohammed Rafique	172.1	863	19	45.42	3-56	–	5.01
Monjurul Islam	61.1	329	6	54.83	2-33	–	5.38
Mushfiqur Rahman	24.5	159	1	159.00	1-55	–	6.36
Naimur Rahman	128.4	621	8	77.62	2-51	–	4.83
Shafiuddin Ahmed	82.3	426	11	38.72	3-42	–	5.16

KENYA – BATTING AND FIELDING

	M	I	NO	HS	Runs	Avge	100	50	Ct/St
J Ababu	2	1	–	11	11	11.00	–	–	1
J.K.Kamande	4	2	1	18	20	20.00	–	–	1
H.S.Modi	32	27	2	78*	596	23.84	–	4	7
P.Ochieng	1	1	1	9*	–	–	–	–	1
T.M.Odoyo	33	30	5	41	510	20.40	–	–	9
M.O.Odumbe	34	32	2	83	793	26.43	–	7	6
L.N.Onyango	4	4	1	23	29	9.66	–	–	1
K.O.Otieno	34	33	1	144	863	26.96	2	3	13/9
R.D.Shah	17	17	–	71	599	35.23	–	6	6
M.Sheikh	21	15	5	15*	68	6.80	–	–	7
A.O.Suji	19	17	2	68	188	12.53	–	1	7
M.A.Suji	32	24	14	15	80	8.00	–	–	8
S.O.Tikolo	34	32	1	106*	968	31.22	1	8	16
A.V.Vadher	18	16	6	73*	278	27.80	–	2	6

KENYA – BOWLING

	O	R	W	Avge	Best	4wI	R/Over
J.Ababu	10	41	1	41.00	1-26	–	4.10
J.K.Kamande	17	84	1	84.00	1-46	–	4.94
H.S.Modi	2	14	0	–	–	–	7.00
P.Ochieng	4	10	1	10.00	1-10	–	2.50
T.M.Odoyo	240.2	1157	30	38.56	3-25	–	4.81
M.O.Odumbe	214.5	1017	27	37.66	3-14	–	4.73
L.N.Onyango	13.3	130	1	130.00	1-45	–	9.63
R.D.Shah	10	72	0	–	–	–	7.20
M.Sheikh	129.4	625	19	32.89	4-36	1	4.82
A O.Suji	94.2	450	8	56.25	2-24	–	4.77
M A.Suji	245	1108	22	50.36	4-24	1	4.52
S.O.Tikolo	153.2	779	21	37.09	3-22	–	5.08

SCOTLAND – BATTING AND FIELDING

	M	I	NO	HS	Runs	Avge	100	50	Ct/St
J.A.R.Blain	5	5	1	9	15	3.75	–	–	1
J.E.Brinkley	5	5	–	23	52	10.40	–	–	1
G.M.Hamilton	5	5	1	76	217	54.25	–	2	1

SCOTLAND – BOWLING

	O	R	W	Avge	Best	4wI	R/Over
J.A.R.Blain	37.1	210	10	21.00	4-37	1	5.65
J.E.Brinkley	28	117	2	58.50	1-29	–	4.18
G.M.Hamilton	35.4	149	3	49.66	2-36	–	4.18

TEST CAREER RECORDS

These records, complete to 22 February 2001 but including England's series in Sri Lanka, contain all players registered for county cricket in 2001 at the time of going to press, plus those who have played Test cricket since 1 September 1999.

ENGLAND – BATTING AND FIELDING

	M	I	NO	HS	Runs	Avge	100	50	Ct/St
C.J.Adams	5	8	–	31	104	13.00	–	–	6
M.A.Atherton	108	199	7	185*	7409	38.58	16	43	70
R.J.Bailey	4	8	–	43	119	14.87	–	–	–
K.J.Barnett	4	7	–	80	207	29.57	–	2	1
M.P.Bicknell	2	4	–	14	26	6.50	–	–	–
R.J.Blakey	2	4	–	6	7	1.75	–	–	2
S.J.E.Brown	1	2	1	10*	11	11.00	–	–	1
M.A.Butcher	27	51	1	116	1253	25.06	2	4	21
A.R.Caddick	43	65	7	48	632	10.89	–	–	16
D.G.Cork	31	48	8	59	724	18.10	–	2	16
J.P.Crawley	29	47	5	156*	1329	31.64	3	7	26
R.D.B.Croft	20	32	8	37*	418	17.41	–	–	10
P.A.J.DeFreitas	44	68	5	88	934	14.82	–	4	14
M.A.Ealham	8	13	3	53*	210	21.00	–	2	4
N.H.Fairbrother	10	15	1	83	219	15.64	–	1	4
A.Flintoff	9	14	–	42	233	16.64	–	–	4
A.R.C.Fraser	46	67	15	32	388	7.46	–	–	9
J.E.R.Gallian	3	6	–	28	74	12.33	–	–	1
E.S.H.Giddins	4	7	3	7	10	2.50	–	–	–
A.F.Giles	7	11	4	37*	88	12.57	–	–	5
D.Gough	49	71	14	65	696	12.21	–	2	12
A.Habib	2	3	–	19	26	8.66	–	–	–
G.M.Hamilton	1	2	–	0	0	0.00	–	–	–
W.K.Hegg	2	4	–	15	30	7.50	–	–	8
G.A.Hick	65	114	6	178	3383	31.32	6	18	90
M.J.Hoggard	1	1	1	12*	12	–	–	–	1
A.J.Hollioake	4	6	–	45	65	10.83	–	–	4
B.C.Hollioake	2	4	–	28	44	11.00	–	–	2
N.Hussain	59	106	11	207	3294	34.67	9	14	42
R.K.Illingworth	9	14	7	28	128	18.28	–	–	5
M.C.Ilott	5	6	2	15	28	7.00	–	–	–
R.C.Irani	3	5	–	41	86	17.20	–	–	2
S.P.James	2	4	–	36	71	17.75	–	–	–
N.V.Knight	16	28	–	113	704	25.14	1	4	24
M.N.Lathwell	2	4	–	33	78	19.50	–	–	–
M.J.McCague	3	5	–	11	21	4.20	–	–	1
D.L.Maddy	3	4	–	24	46	11.50	–	–	4
D.E.Malcolm	40	58	19	29	236	6.05	–	–	7
P.J.Martin	8	13	–	29	115	8.84	–	–	6
M.P.Maynard	4	8	–	35	87	10.87	–	–	3
J.E.Morris	3	5	2	32	71	23.66	–	–	3
A.D.Mullally	18	26	4	24	127	5.77	–	–	6
T.A.Munton	2	2	1	25*	25	25.00	–	–	–
M.M.Patel	2	2	–	27	45	22.50	–	–	2
M.R.Ramprakash	42	74	6	154	1796	26.41	1	11	34
C.M.W.Read	3	4	–	37	38	9.50	–	–	10/1
S.J.Rhodes	11	17	5	65*	294	24.50	–	1	46/3
R.C.Russell	54	86	16	128*	1897	27.10	2	6	153/12
I.D.K.Salisbury	15	25	3	50	368	16.72	–	1	5
C.P.Schofield	2	3	–	57	67	22.33	–	1	–
C.E.W.Silverwood	5	6	3	7*	19	6.33	–	–	2

TEST   **ENGLAND – BATTING AND FIELDING (continued)**

	M	I	NO	HS	Runs	Avge	100	50	Ct/St
A.M.Smith	1	2	1	4*	4	4.00	–	–	–
R.A.Smith	62	112	15	175	4236	43.67	9	28	39
J.P.Stephenson	1	2	–	25	36	18.00	–	–	–
A.J.Stewart	108	195	15	190	7084	39.35	14	36	197/11
P.M.Such	11	16	5	14*	67	6.09	–	–	4
J.P.Taylor	2	4	2	17*	34	17.00	–	–	–
G.P.Thorpe	66	121	16	138	4248	40.45	8	27	67
M.E.Trescothick	9	17	1	122	587	36.68	1	4	7
A.J.Tudor	3	6	3	99*	166	55.33	–	1	–
P.C.R.Tufnell	41	57	28	22*	146	5.03	–	–	12
M.P.Vaughan	9	15	–	76	407	27.13	–	2	8
S.L.Watkin	3	5	–	13	25	5.00	–	–	1
M.Watkinson	4	6	1	82*	167	33.40	–	1	1
A.P.Wells	1	2	1	3*	3	3.00	–	–	–
C.White	18	28	3	93	502	20.08	–	2	12

ENGLAND – BOWLING

	O	R	W	Avge	Best	5wI	10wM
C.J.Adams	20	59	1	59.00	1- 42	–	–
M.A.Atherton	68	302	2	151.00	1- 20	–	–
K.J.Barnett	6	32	0				
M.P.Bicknell	87	263	4	65.75	3- 99	–	–
S.J.E.Brown	33	138	2	69.00	1- 60	–	–
M.A.Butcher	55.2	169	3	56.33	2- 32	–	–
A.R.Caddick	1525.2	4335	152	28.51	7- 46	9	–
D.G.Cork	1103.4	3363	118	28.50	7- 43	5	–
R.D.B.Croft	766.5	1815	48	37.81	5- 95	1	–
P.A.J.DeFreitas	1639.4	4700	140	33.57	7- 70	4	–
M.A.Ealham	176.4	488	17	28.70	4- 21	–	–
N.H.Fairbrother	2	9	0				
A.Flintoff	137.5	385	7	55.00	2- 31	–	–
A.R.C.Fraser	1812.4	4836	177	27.32	8- 53	13	2
J.E.R.Gallian	14	62	0				
E.S.H.Giddins	74	240	12	20.00	5- 15	1	–
A.F.Giles	339.1	825	25	33.00	5- 75	1	–
D.Gough	1683.3	5351	197	27.16	6- 42	7	–
G.M.Hamilton	15	63	0				
G.A.Hick	509.3	1306	23	56.78	4-126	–	–
M.J.Hoggard	13	49	0				
A.J.Hollioake	24	67	2	33.50	2- 31	–	–
B.C.Hollioake	42	199	4	49.75	2-105	–	–
N.Hussain	5	15	0				
R.K.Illingworth	247.3	615	19	32.36	4- 96	–	–
M.C.Ilott	173.4	542	12	45.16	3- 48	–	–
R.C.Irani	32	112	3	37.33	1- 22	–	–
M.J.McCague	98.5	390	6	65.00	4-121	–	–
D.L.Maddy	14	40	0				
D.E.Malcolm	1413.2	4748	128	37.09	9- 57	5	2
P.J.Martin	242	580	17	34.11	4- 60	–	–
A.D.Mullally	723.4	1713	56	30.58	5-105	1	–
T.A.Munton	67.3	200	4	50.00	2- 22	–	–
M.M.Patel	46	180	1	180.00	1-101	–	–
M.R.Ramprakash	141.1	446	4	111.50	1- 2	–	–
I.D.K.Salisbury	415.2	1539	20	76.95	4-163	–	–
C.P.Schofield	18	73	0				
C.E.W.Silverwood	134	415	11	37.72	5- 91	1	–
A.M.Smith	23	89	0				

TEST   **ENGLAND – BOWLING (continued)**

	O	R	W	Avge	Best	5wI	10wM
R.A.Smith	4	6	0				
A.J.Stewart	3.2	13	0				
P.M.Such	520.4	1242	37	33.56	6-67	2	–
J.P.Taylor	48	156	3	52.00	1-18	–	–
G.P.Thorpe	23	37	0				
M.E.Trescothick	15	36	1	36.00	1-34	–	–
A.J.Tudor	58.2	239	8	29.87	4-89	–	–
P.C.R.Tufnell	1842.2	4386	120	36.55	7-47	5	2
M.P.Vaughan	26	98	0				
S.L.Watkin	89	305	11	27.72	4-65	–	–
M.Watkinson	112	348	10	34.80	3-64	–	–
C.White	388.2	1199	37	32.40	5-32	2	–

AUSTRALIA – BATTING AND FIELDING

	M	I	NO	HS	Runs	Avge	100	50	Ct/St
A.J.Bichel	5	7	–	18	58	8.28	–	–	2
G.S.Blewett	46	79	4	214	2552	34.02	4	15	45
D.W.Fleming	19	18	3	71*	299	19.93	–	2	9
A.C.Gilchrist	14	20	4	149*	870	54.37	1	7	57/5
J.N.Gillespie	18	26	9	41	281	16.52	–	–	6
M.L.Hayden	13	22	–	125	536	24.36	1	2	16
I.A.Healy	119	182	23	161*	4356	27.39	4	22	366/29
M.S.Kasprowicz	16	21	4	25	214	12.58	–	–	6
J.L.Langer	38	63	2	223	2416	39.60	7	11	28
S.G.Law	1	1	1	54*	54	–	–	1	1
B.Lee	7	7	3	62*	150	37.50	–	1	1
D.S.Lehmann	5	8	–	98	228	28.50	–	2	3
S.C.G.MacGill	16	22	2	43	208	10.40	–	–	11
G.D.McGrath	67	80	23	39	341	5.98	–	–	20
D.R.Martyn	11	20	5	89*	638	42.53	–	5	5
C.R.Miller	17	22	3	43	172	9.05	–	–	5
S.A.Muller	2	2	2	6*	6	–	–	–	2
R.T.Ponting	39	61	8	197	2475	46.69	7	12	40
M.J.Slater	67	118	6	219	4976	44.42	14	20	32
S.K.Warne	84	117	12	86	1613	15.36	–	4	64
M.E.Waugh	108	179	14	153*	6932	42.01	18	40	144
S.R.Waugh	132	210	39	200	8722	51.00	24	42	92

AUSTRALIA – BOWLING

	O	R	W	Avge	Best	5wI	10wM
A.J.Bichel	129.5	421	9	46.77	5-60	1	–
G.S.Blewett	239.2	720	14	51.42	2- 9	–	–
D.W.Fleming	658.1	1843	74	24.90	5-30	3	–
J.N.Gillespie	512	1476	70	21.08	7-37	5	–
M.L.Hayden	2	9	0				
M.S.Kasprowicz	508.2	1561	45	34.68	7-36	2	–
S.G.Law	3	9	0				
B.Lee	228.5	675	42	16.07	5-47	3	–
D.S.Lehmann	17	45	2	22.50	1- 6	–	–
S.C.G.MacGill	624.3	1877	75	25.02	7-50	4	1
G.D.McGrath	2661	6817	309	22.06	8-38	18	3
D.R.Martyn	8	12	0				
C.R.Miller	626.5	1604	63	25.46	5-32	3	1
S.A.Muller	58	258	7	36.85	3-68	–	–
R.T.Ponting	37.5	89	4	22.25	1- 0	–	–
M.J.Slater	2.1	6	1	6.00	1- 4	–	–
S.K.Warne	3916.5	9505	366	25.96	8-71	16	4

TEST **AUSTRALIA – BOWLING (continued)**

	O	R	W	Avge	Best	5wI	10wM
M.E.Waugh	688	1999	51	39.19	5-40	1	–
S.R.Waugh	1195.5	3181	89	35.74	5-28	3	–

SOUTH AFRICA – BATTING AND FIELDING

	M	I	NO	HS	Runs	Avge	100	50	Ct/St
P.R.Adams	33	39	11	29	190	6.78	–	–	20
A.M.Bacher	19	33	1	96	833	26.03	–	5	10
N.Boje	11	15	2	85	416	32.00	–	2	4
M.V.Boucher	37	48	6	125	1313	31.26	3	7	145/4
W.J.Cronje	68	111	9	135	3714	36.41	6	23	33
D.J.Cullinan	65	105	11	275*	4095	43.56	12	18	57
H.H.Dippenaar	7	10	–	100	268	26.80	1	–	3
A.A.Donald	65	81	30	34	587	11.50	–	–	16
C.E.Eksteen	7	11	2	22	91	10.11	–	–	5
H.H.Gibbs	23	37	1	211*	1099	30.52	2	3	17
M.Hayward	6	7	4	13	26	8.66	–	–	1
J.H.Kallis	45	71	8	160	2685	42.61	7	13	39
J.M.Kemp	1	1	–	2	2	2.00	–	–	1
G.Kirsten	68	119	10	275	4556	41.79	11	23	57
L.Klusener	37	50	9	174	1601	39.04	3	8	26
N.D.McKenzie	9	14	2	120	421	35.08	2	1	6
M.Ngam	3	1	1	0*	0	–	–	–	1
M.Ntini	11	10	5	10	35	7.00	–	–	3
S.M.Pollock	51	72	12	111	1713	28.55	1	8	32
J.N.Rhodes	52	80	9	117	2532	35.66	3	17	34
P.C.Strydom	2	3	–	30	35	11.66	–	–	1

SOUTH AFRICA – BOWLING

	O	R	W	Avge	Best	5wI	10wM
P.R.Adams	1068.1	2966	94	31.55	6-55	1	–
A.M.Bacher	1	4	0				
N.Boje	316.1	717	29	24.72	5-62	2	–
W.J.Cronje	633.2	1288	43	29.95	3-14	–	–
D.J.Cullinan	20	71	2	35.50	1-10	–	–
A.A.Donald	2359.1	6679	311	21.47	8-71	20	3
C.E.Eksteen	256	494	8	61.75	3-12	–	–
M.Hayward	172.2	507	19	26.68	4-75	–	–
J.H.Kallis	891.5	2185	74	29.52	5-90	1	–
J.M.Kemp	17.5	52	5	10.40	3-33	–	–
G.Kirsten	54.1	135	2	67.50	1- 0	–	–
L.Klusener	876.5	2399	65	36.90	8-64	1	–
M.Ngam	65.2	189	11	17.18	3-26	–	–
M.Ntini	319.3	873	34	25.67	6-66	1	–
S.M.Pollock	1843.1	4230	211	20.04	7-87	11	–
J.N.Rhodes	2	5	0				
P.C.Strydom	6	27	0				

WEST INDIES – BATTING AND FIELDING

	M	I	NO	HS	Runs	Avge	100	50	Ct/St
J.C.Adams	54	90	17	208*	3012	41.26	6	14	48
C.E.L.Ambrose	98	145	29	53	1439	12.40	–	1	18
M.I.Black	3	6	2	3*	6	1.50	–	–	–
S.L.Campbell	51	91	4	208	2856	32.82	4	18	46
S.Chanderpaul	45	75	9	137*	2682	40.63	2	21	18
M.Dillon	11	21	1	36	157	7.85	–	–	3
D.Ganga	8	14	–	32	182	13.00	–	–	4
C.H.Gayle	4	5	–	33	59	11.80	–	–	5

	M	I	NO	HS	Runs	Avge	100	50	Ct/St
A.F.G.Griffith	14	27	1	114	638	24.53	1	4	5
W.W.Hinds	14	25	1	165	803	33.45	1	5	13
C.L.Hooper	80	136	13	178*	4153	33.76	9	18	94
R.D.Jacobs	26	47	7	96*	989	24.72	–	5	95/4
R.D.King	12	18	4	12*	48	3.42	–	–	1
B.C.Lara	75	131	4	375	6133	48.29	15	30	101
N.A.M.McLean	17	28	2	46	357	13.73	–	–	4
M.V.Nagamootoo	2	4	–	68	111	27.75	–	1	–
N.O.Perry	4	7	1	26	74	12.33	–	–	1
R.L.Powell	1	2	–	30	30	15.00	–	–	1
D.Ramnarine	3	4	–	19	27	6.75	–	–	3
F.A.Rose	19	28	2	69	344	13.23	–	1	4
M.N.Samuels	3	6	1	60*	172	34.40	–	1	1
R.R.Sarwan	8	16	4	84*	328	27.33	–	3	3
C.E.L.Stuart	2	4	1	12*	21	7.00	–	–	–
C.A.Walsh	127	177	59	30*	915	7.75	–	–	28

WEST INDIES – BOWLING

	O	R	W	Avge	Best	5wI	10wM
J.C.Adams	475.3	1336	27	49.48	5- 17	1	–
C.E.L.Ambrose	3683.5	8501	405	20.99	8- 45	22	3
M.I.Black	67	257	6	42.83	4- 83	–	–
S.Chanderpaul	231	697	6	116.16	1- 2	–	–
M.Dillon	363.4	1221	37	33.00	5-111	1	–
C.H.Gayle	43	100	4	25.00	3- 25	–	–
C.L.Hooper	1732.1	4372	93	47.01	5- 26	4	–
R.D.King	330.3	1005	36	27.91	5- 51	1	–
B.C.Lara	10	28	0				
N.A.M.McLean	483	1637	38	43.07	3- 53	–	–
M.V.Nagamootoo	87	239	6	39.83	3-119	–	–
N.O.Perry	134	446	10	44.60	5- 70	1	–
R.L.Powell	5	13	0				
D.Ramnarine	128	234	12	19.50	4- 29	–	–
F.A.Rose	520.4	1637	53	30.88	7- 84	2	–
M.N.Samuels	60.5	185	3	61.66	2- 49	–	–
R.R.Sarwan	2	16	0				
C.E.L.Stuart	60	239	6	39.83	2- 52	–	–
C.A.Walsh	4739.3	12196	494	24.68	7- 37	21	3

NEW ZEALAND – BATTING AND FIELDING

	M	I	NO	HS	Runs	Avge	100	50	Ct/St
N.J.Astle	43	76	6	141	2569	36.70	6	12	40
M.D.Bell	8	15	1	83	221	15.78	–	1	9
C.L.Cairns	49	83	4	126	2572	32.55	4	19	14
S.B.Doull	32	50	11	46	570	14.61	–	–	16
S.P.Fleming	57	100	6	174*	3422	36.40	2	27	86
C.Z.Harris	19	34	4	71	582	19.40	–	4	12
M.J.Horne	29	54	2	157	1608	30.92	4	5	16
C.D.McMillan	28	48	4	142	1843	41.88	4	11	10
H.J.H.Marshall	1	1	1	40*	40	–	–	–	–
C.S.Martin	4	5	3	7	12	6.00	–	–	–
D.J.Nash	31	44	13	89*	704	22.70	–	4	13
S.B.O'Connor	18	27	9	20	105	5.83	–	–	6
A.C.Parore	67	114	14	100*	2535	25.35	1	14	160/7
M.H.Richardson	6	9	–	99	425	47.22	–	4	4
M.S.Sinclair	10	18	2	214	648	40.50	2	–	8
C.M.Spearman	19	37	2	112	922	26.34	1	3	21

TEST   NEW ZEALAND – BATTING AND FIELDING (continued)

	M	I	NO	HS	Runs	Avge	100	50	Ct/St
G.R.Stead	5	8	–	78	278	34.75	–	2	2
D.R.Tuffey	3	5	1	8	18	4.50	–	–	2
D.L.Vettori	31	47	8	90	702	18.00	–	4	11
B.G.K.Walker	4	6	1	27*	103	20.60	–	–	–
K.P.Walmsley	3	5	–	5	13	2.60	–	–	–
P.J.Wiseman	13	19	5	23	90	6.42	–	–	5

NEW ZEALAND – BOWLING

	O	R	W	Avge	Best	5wI	10wM
N.J.Astle	602.1	1359	29	46.86	2-22	–	–
C.L.Cairns	1563.3	4995	171	29.21	7-27	10	1
S.B.Doull	1008.5	2872	98	29.30	7-65	6	–
C.Z.Harris	373.4	1004	15	66.93	2-16	–	–
M.J.Horne	11	26	0				
C.D.McMillan	247.5	697	15	46.46	3-57	–	–
H.J.H.Marshall	4	4	0				
C.S.Martin	121	363	16	22.68	5-71	1	–
D.J.Nash	1002.4	2556	93	27.48	6-27	3	1
S.B.O'Connor	593.5	1657	53	31.26	5-51	1	–
M.H.Richardson	1	1	0				
M.S.Sinclair	4	13	0				
G.R.Stead	1	1	0				
D.R.Tuffey	73	321	3	107.00	3-38	–	–
D L.Vettori	1382.3	3458	106	32.62	7-87	5	1
B.G.K.Walker	96.4	302	3	100.66	2-92	–	–
K.P.Walmsley	129	391	9	43.44	3-70	–	–
P.J.Wiseman	466.4	1348	33	40.84	5-82	2	–

INDIA – BATTING AND FIELDING

	M	I	NO	HS	Runs	Avge	100	50	Ct/St
A.B.Agarkar	8	12	1	41*	118	10.72	–	–	3
M.Azharuddin	99	147	9	199	6215	45.03	22	21	105
R.V.Bharadwaj	3	3	–	22	28	9.33	–	–	3
N.Chopra	1	2	–	4	7	3.50	–	–	–
V.Dahiya	2	1	1	2*	2	–	–	–	6
S.S.Das	3	5	1	110	223	55.75	1	1	6
R Dravid	40	69	7	200*	3322	53.58	8	17	45
D.J.Gandhi	4	7	1	88	204	34.00	–	2	3
S.C.Ganguly	38	64	6	173	2711	46.74	7	14	31
Harbhajan Singh	8	11	6	15*	31	6.20	–	–	2
A.Jadeja	15	24	2	96	576	26.18	–	4	5
W.Jaffer	2	4	–	23	46	11.50	–	–	3
S.B.Joshi	15	19	2	92	352	20.70	–	1	7
M Kaif	1	2	–	23	35	17.50	–	–	–
H.H.Kanitkar	2	4	–	45	74	18.50	–	–	–
S.S.Karim	1	1	–	15	15	15.00	–	–	1
M.Kartik	4	5	–	43	61	12.20	–	–	1
Z.Khan	2	1	1	7*	7	–	–	–	1
A.Kumble	61	81	15	88	1192	18.06	–	3	29
V.V.S.Laxman	19	33	3	167	834	27.80	1	5	23
N.R.Mongia	42	64	7	152	1382	24.24	1	6	94/7
B.K.V.Prasad	29	41	16	30*	161	6.44	–	–	6
M.S.K.Prasad	6	10	1	19	106	11.77	–	–	15
S.L.V.Raju	27	33	10	31	236	10.26	–	–	6
S.Ramesh	12	23	1	143	963	43.77	2	6	9
Sharandeep Singh	1	–	–	–	–	–	–	–	–

TEST　　　　**INDIA – BATTING AND FIELDING (continued)**

	M	I	NO	HS	Runs	Avge	100	50	Ct/St
J.Srinath	49	69	18	76	796	15.60	–	4	20
S.R.Tendulkar	79	125	13	217	6416	57.28	24	24	55

INDIA – BOWLING

	O	R	W	Avge	Best	5wI	10wM
A.B.Agarkar	283	790	21	37.61	3- 43	–	–
M.Azharuddin	2.1	16	0				
R.V.Bharadwaj	41.1	107	1	107.00	1- 26	–	–
N.Chopra	24	78	0				
S.S.Das	3	7	0				
R.Dravid	11	21	0				
S.C.Ganguly	219.3	721	20	36.05	3- 28	–	–
Harbhajan Singh	285.4	810	21	38.57	3- 30	–	–
S.B.Joshi	575.1	1470	41	35.85	5-142	1	–
M.Kaif	3	4	0				
H.H.Kanitkar	1	2	0				
M.Kartik	147.3	309	9	34.33	3-123	–	–
Z.Khan	64	195	5	39.00	2- 49	–	–
A.Kumble	3185.5	7728	276	28.00	10- 74	16	3
V.V.S.Laxman	25	68	0				
B.K.V.Prasad	1043.3	2950	85	34.70	6- 33	6	1
S.L.V.Raju	1232	2741	92	29.79	6- 12	5	1
S.Ramesh	4	19	0				
Sharandeep Singh	71	206	6	34.33	4-136	–	–
J.Srinath	1912.4	5462	183	29.84	8- 86	7	1
S.R.Tendulkar	225	687	19	36.15	3- 10	–	–

PAKISTAN – BATTING AND FIELDING

	M	I	NO	HS	Runs	Avge	100	50	Ct/St
Aamir Sohail	47	83	3	205	2823	35.28	5	13	36
Abdur Razzaq	12	18	1	100*	381	22.41	1	2	4
Arshad Khan	8	7	1	9*	30	5.00	–	–	–
Atiq-uz-Zaman	1	2	–	25	26	13.00	–	–	5
Azhar Mahmood	19	30	4	136	811	31.19	3	1	13
Danish Kaneria	2	3	2	8*	8	8.00	–	–	–
Ijaz Ahmed	58	89	4	211	3282	38.61	12	12	45
Imran Nazir	5	8	–	131	244	30.50	1	1	1
Inzamam-ul-Haq	70	116	12	200*	4807	46.22	12	29	57
Irfan Fazil	1	2	1	3	4	4.00	–	–	2
Mohammad Akram	8	13	5	10*	19	2.37	–	–	4
Mohammad Wasim	18	28	2	192	783	30.11	2	2	22/2
Moin Khan	61	93	7	117*	2418	28.11	3	15	111/20
Mushtaq Ahmed	49	69	15	59	617	11.42	–	2	22
Naved Ashraf	2	3	–	32	64	21.33	–	–	–
Qaiser Abbas	1	1	–	2	2	2.00	–	–	–
Saeed Anwar	52	86	2	188*	3890	46.30	10	25	17
Salim Elahi	7	12	–	72	279	23.25	–	1	9/1
Saqlain Mushtaq	31	49	11	79	565	14.86	–	2	13
Shahid Afridi	11	20	1	141	594	31.26	1	3	7
Shoaib Akhtar	15	22	7	26	105	7.00	–	–	5
Wajahatullah Wasti	6	10	1	133	329	36.55	2	–	7
Waqar Younis	68	92	19	45	746	10.21	–	–	11
Wasim Akram	100	143	18	257*	2815	22.52	3	7	43
Younis Khan	9	14	1	116	403	31.00	2	1	11
Yousuf Youhana	27	45	2	124	1736	40.37	5	11	34

TEST   **PAKISTAN – BOWLING**

	O	R	W	Avge	Best	5wI	10wM
Aamir Sohail	397.1	1049	25	41.96	4- 54	–	–
Abdur Razzaq	332.5	864	21	41.14	4- 56	–	–
Arshad Khan	381	852	30	28.40	5- 38	1	–
Azhar Mahmood	468.3	1317	35	37.62	4- 53	–	–
Danish Kaneria	91	217	4	54.25	2- 80	–	–
Ijaz Ahmed	30	77	2	38.50	1- 9	–	–
Inzamam-ul-Haq	1.3	8	0				
Irfan Fazil	8	65	2	32.50	1- 30	–	–
Mohammad Akram	224.1	753	17	44.29	5-138	1	–
Mushtaq Ahmed	2006.4	5818	182	31.96	7- 56	10	3
Qaiser Abbas	16	35	0				
Saeed Anwar	8	23	0				
Saqlain Mushtaq	1557	3961	134	29.55	8-164	11	2
Shahid Afridi	197.5	584	20	29.20	5- 52	1	–
Shoaib Akhtar	472.4	1613	45	35.84	5- 43	2	–
Wajahatullah Wasti	3	8	0				
Waqar Younis	2203.1	7045	313	22.50	7- 76	21	5
Wasim Akram	3662.3	9478	409	23.17	7-119	25	5

SRI LANKA – BATTING AND FIELDING

	M	I	NO	HS	Runs	Avge	100	50	Ct/St
R.P.Arnold	27	45	4	123	1216	29.65	2	6	36
M.S.Atapattu	44	78	7	223	2419	34.07	6	7	31
U.D.U.Chandana	5	7	1	32	112	18.66	–	–	3
S.I.de Saram	4	5	–	39	117	23.40	–	–	1
P.A.de Silva	89	153	11	267	5952	41.91	19	21	43
S.K.L.de Silva	3	4	2	20*	36	18.00	–	–	1
H.D.P.K.Dharmasena	25	41	6	62*	735	21.00	–	3	12
T.M.Dilshan	10	16	2	163*	372	26.57	1	–	18
C.R.D.Fernando	6	9	3	5*	23	3.83	–	–	4
I.S.Gallage	1	1	–	3	3	3.00	–	–	–
D.A.Gunawardena	3	6	–	43	121	20.16	–	–	1
R.Herath	3	3	–	3	3	1.00	–	–	–
D.Hettiarachchi	1	2	1	0*	0	–	–	–	–
S.T.Jayasuriya	59	101	9	340	3604	39.17	7	16	42
A.V.P.Jayawardena	1	–	–	–	–	–	–	–	–
D.P.M.deS.Jayawardena	30	49	2	242	2020	42.97	5	10	42
R.S.Kaluwitharana	40	64	4	132*	1629	27.15	3	7	74/20
M.Muralitharan	62	82	34	39	595	12.39	–	–	28
P.D.R.L.Perera	3	4	3	10	12	12.00	–	–	–
K.R.Pushpakumara	22	31	12	44	166	8.73	–	–	10
A.Ranatunga	93	155	12	135*	5105	35.69	4	38	47
K.Sangakkara	9	16	–	98	533	33.31	–	4	25/1
W.P.U.C.J.Vaas	48	70	12	57	1045	18.01	–	4	15
G.P.Wickremasinghe	40	64	5	51	555	9.40	–	1	18
D.N.T.Zoysa	17	24	2	26	170	7.72	–	–	2

SRI LANKA – BOWLING

	O	R	W	Avge	Best	5wI	10wM
R.P.Arnold	205.2	558	11	50.72	3- 76	–	–
M.S.Atapattu	8	24	1	24.00	1- 9	–	–
U.D.U.Chandana	140.2	489	16	30.56	6-179	1	–
P.A.de Silva	394	1103	27	40.85	3- 30	–	–
H.D.P.K.Dharmasena	935.3	2276	58	39.24	6- 72	3	–
C.R.D.Fernando	116.5	478	11	43.45	5- 98	1	–
I.S.Gallage	25	77	0				

191

TEST   SRI LANKA – BOWLING (continued)

	O	R	W	Avge	Best	5wI	10wM
R.Herath	105.3	310	6	51.66	4- 97	–	–
D.Hettiarachchi	27	41	2	20.50	2- 36	–	–
S.T.Jayasuriya	698.1	1792	53	33.81	4- 24	–	–
D.P.M.deS.Jayawardena	68.2	212	4	53.00	2- 32	–	–
M.Muralitharan	3382.5	8123	317	25.62	9- 65	24	5
P.D.R.L.Perera	83	331	4	82.75	2- 60	–	–
K.R.Pushpakumara	617	2218	58	38.24	7-116	4	–
A.Ranatunga	395.3	1040	16	65.00	2- 17	–	–
W.P.U.C.J.Vaas	1707	4359	144	30.27	6- 73	5	1
G.P.Wickramasinghe	1210	3559	85	41.87	6- 60	3	–
D.N.T.Zoysa	343.4	966	28	34.50	4- 76	–	–

ZIMBABWE – BATTING AND FIELDING

	M	I	NO	HS	Runs	Avge	100	50	Ct/St
E.A.Brandes	10	15	3	39	121	10.08	–	–	4
G.B.Brent	2	3	–	3	3	1.00	–	–	–
A.D.R.Campbell	48	86	3	102	2157	25.98	1	13	47
S.V.Carlisle	14	24	2	58	515	23.40	–	3	15
A.Flower	48	86	15	232*	3625	51.05	9	21	122/6
G.W.Flower	46	86	4	201*	2495	30.42	6	8	28
M.W.Goodwin	19	37	4	166*	1414	42.84	3	8	10
T.R.Gripper	7	14	–	60	175	12.50	–	1	4
N.C.Johnson	13	23	1	107	532	24.18	1	4	12
T.N.Madondo	3	4	1	74*	90	30.00	–	1	1
D.A.Marillier	1	1	–	28	28	28.00	–	–	–
E.Z.Matambanadzo	3	5	1	7	17	4.25	–	–	–
M.Mbangwa	15	25	8	8	34	2.00	–	–	2
B.A.Murphy	7	10	3	14	34	4.85	–	–	7
D.T.Mutendera	1	2	–	10	10	5.00	–	–	–
M.L.Nkala	4	5	1	30*	36	9.00	–	–	1
H.K.Olonga	22	32	9	24	124	5.39	–	–	9
R.W.Price	1	2	–	4	4	3.00	–	–	–
G.J.Rennie	19	38	1	93	869	23.48	–	6	11
J.A.Rennie	4	6	1	22	62	12.40	–	–	1
B.C.Strang	24	41	8	53	425	12.87	–	1	10
P.A.Strang	23	40	9	106*	801	25.83	1	2	15
H.H.Streak	36	57	9	54	805	16.77	–	4	11
D.P.Viljoen	2	4	–	38	57	14.25	–	–	1
A.R.Whittall	10	18	3	17	114	7.60	–	–	8
G.J.Whittall	37	66	6	203*	1782	29.70	3	8	13
C.B.Wishart	13	24	1	63	320	13.91	–	2	5

ZIMBABWE – BOWLING

	O	R	W	Avge	Best	5wI	10wM
E.A.Brandes	332.4	951	26	36.57	3- 45	–	–
G.B.Brent	61.2	144	5	28.80	3- 21	–	–
A.D.R.Campbell	11	28	0				
A.Flower	0.1	0	0				
G.W.Flower	306.5	813	9	90.33	2-101	–	–
M.W.Goodwin	19.5	69	0				
T.R.Gripper	20.4	81	1	81.00	1- 28	–	–
N.C.Johnson	197.5	594	15	39.60	4- 77	–	–
E.Z.Matambanadzo	64	250	4	62.50	2- 62	–	–
M.Mbangwa	432.4	1006	32	31.43	3- 23	–	–
B.A.Murphy	266.5	805	14	57.50	3- 32	–	–
D.T.Mutendera	14	29	0				
M.L.Nkala	105	312	6	52.00	3- 82	–	–

TEST   **ZIMBABWE – BOWLING (continued)**

	O	R	W	Avge	Best	5wI	10wM
H.K.Olonga	573.4	1894	52	36.42	5- 70	1	–
R.W.Price	8	22	0				
G.J.Rennie	20	75	1	75.00	1- 40	–	–
J.A.Rennie	120.4	293	3	97.66	2- 22	–	–
B.C.Strang	814.2	1990	50	39.80	5-101	1	–
P.A.Strang	938	2470	70	35.28	8-109	4	1
H.H.Streak	1328.2	3446	138	24.97	6- 87	6	–
D.P.Viljoen	17.3	65	1	65.00	1- 14	–	–
A.R.Whittall	260.2	736	7	105.14	3- 73	–	–
G.J.Whittall	695.2	1851	50	37.02	4- 18	–	–

BANGLADESH – BATTING AND FIELDING

	M	I	NO	HS	Runs	Avge	100	50	Ct/St
Akram Khan	1	2	–	35	37	18.50	–	–	–
Al Sahariar	1	2	–	12	18	9.00	–	–	3
Aminul Islam	1	2	–	145	151	75.50	1	–	–
Habibul Bashar	1	2	–	71	101	50.50	–	1	–
Hasibul Hussain	1	2	1	28*	28	28.00	–	–	–
Khaled Masud	1	2	1	32	53	53.00	–	–	–
Mehrab Hossain	1	2	–	4	6	3.00	–	–	–
Mohammed Rafique	1	2	–	22	26	13.00	–	–	1
Naimur Rahman	1	2	–	15	18	9.00	–	–	–
Ranjan Das	1	2	–	2	2	1.00	–	–	1
Shahriar Hossain	1	2	–	12	19	9.50	–	–	–/1

BANGLADESH – BOWLING

	O	R	W	Avge	Best	5wI	10wM
Habibul Bashar	8	39	0				
Hasibul Hussain	25	91	1	91.00	1- 31	–	–
Mohammed Rafique	53	120	3	40.00	3-117	–	–
Naimur Rahman	48.3	154	6	25.66	6-132	1	–
Ranjan Das	22	72	1	72.00	1- 64	–	–

STOP PRESS
TROPHY FIXTURES 2001

Although the new sponsors of the former NatWest Trophy have yet to be revealed, venues for the Second Round of this season's competition have just been released. See page 301 for the schedule of the later rounds and page 164 for the First Round venues.

Round 2 – Tuesday 15 May (*reserve 16 May*)

11	March	Cambridgeshire	v	*Winner # 1*
12	Cheam	Surrey CB	v	*Winner # 2*
13	Hastings	Sussex CB	v	*Winner # 3*
14	Lincoln Lindrum/Mildenhall	*Winner # 4*	v	Essex CB
15	Manor Park, Norwich	Norfolk	v	*Winner # 5*
16	The Mote, Maidstone/Liphook	*Winner # 6*	v	Buckinghamshire
17	Richmond/Jesmond	*Winner # 7*	v	Berkshire
18	Dean Park, Bournemouth	Dorset	v	*Winner # 8*
19	Cannock/Kidderminster	*Winner # 9*	v	Cumberland
20	Northampton	Northants CB	v	*Winner # 10*
21	Brockhampton	Herefordshire	v	Gloucestershire CB
22	Coventry & North Warwicks	Warwickshire CB	v	Leicestershire CB
23	Truro	Cornwall	v	Cheshire
24	Welwyn Garden City	Hertfordshire	v	Durham CB

FIRST-CLASS CRICKET RECORDS

To 16 September 2000 inclusive

TEAM RECORDS

HIGHEST INNINGS TOTALS

1107	Victoria v New South Wales	Melbourne	1926-27
1059	Victoria v Tasmania	Melbourne	1922-23
952-6d	Sri Lanka v India	Colombo	1997-98
951-7d	Sind v Baluchistan	Karachi	1973-74
944-6d	Hyderabad v Andhra	Secunderabad	1993-94
918	New South Wales v South Australia	Sydney	1900-01
912-8d	Holkar v Mysore	Indore	1945-46
910-6d	Railways v Dera Ismail Khan	Lahore	1964-65
903-7d	England v Australia	The Oval	1938
887	Yorkshire v Warwickshire	Birmingham	1896
863	Lancashire v Surrey	The Oval	1990
860-6d	Tamil Nadu v Goa	Panjim	1988-89

Excluding penalty runs in India, there have been 30 innings totals of 800 runs or more in first-class cricket. Tamil Nadu's total of 860-6d was boosted to 912 by 52 penalty runs.

HIGHEST SECOND INNINGS TOTAL

770	New South Wales v South Australia	Adelaide	1920-21

HIGHEST FOURTH INNINGS TOTAL

654-5	England v South Africa	Durban	1938-39

HIGHEST MATCH AGGREGATE

2376	Maharashtra v Bombay	Poona	1948-49

RECORD MARGIN OF VICTORY

Innings and 851 runs: Railways v Dera Ismail Khan — Lahore — 1964-65

MOST RUNS IN A DAY

721	Australians v Essex	Southend	1948

MOST HUNDREDS IN AN INNINGS

6	Holkar v Mysore	Indore	1945-46

LOWEST INNINGS TOTALS

12	†Oxford University v MCC and Ground	Oxford	1877
12	Northamptonshire v Gloucestershire	Gloucester	1907
13	Auckland v Canterbury	Auckland	1877-78
13	Nottinghamshire v Yorkshire	Nottingham	1901
14	Surrey v Essex	Chelmsford	1983
15	MCC v Surrey	Lord's	1839
15	†Victoria v MCC	Melbourne	1903-04
15	†Northamptonshire v Yorkshire	Northampton	1908
15	Hampshire v Warwickshire	Birmingham	1922

† *Batted one man short*

There have been 26 instances of a team being dismissed for under 20.

LOWEST MATCH AGGREGATE BY ONE TEAM

34 (16 and 18)   Border v Natal   East London   1959-60

LOWEST COMPLETED MATCH AGGREGATE BY BOTH TEAMS

105   MCC v Australians   Lord's   1878

FEWEST RUNS IN AN UNINTERRUPTED DAY'S PLAY

95   Australia (80) v Pakistan (15-2)   Karachi   1956-57

TIED MATCHES

Before 1949 a match was considered to be tied if the scores were level after the fourth innings, even if the side batting last had wickets in hand when play ended. Law 22 was amended in 1948 and since then a match has been tied only when the scores are level after the fourth innings has been completed. There have been 53 tied first-class matches, five of which would not have qualified under the current law. The most recent is:

Worcestershire (203/325-8d) v Nottinghamshire (233/295)   Nottingham   1993

BATTING RECORDS
HIGHEST INDIVIDUAL INNINGS

501*	B.C.Lara	Warwickshire v Durham	Birmingham	1994
499	Hanif Mohammed	Karachi v Bahawalpur	Karachi	1958-59
452*	D.G.Bradman	New South Wales v Queensland	Sydney	1929-30
443*	B.B.Nimbalkar	Maharashtra v Kathiawar	Poona	1948-49
437	W.H.Ponsford	Victoria v Queensland	Melbourne	1927-28
429	W.H.Ponsford	Victoria v Tasmania	Melbourne	1922-23
428	Aftab Baloch	Sind v Baluchistan	Karachi	1973-74
424	A.C.MacLaren	Lancashire v Somerset	Taunton	1895
405*	G.A.Hick	Worcestershire v Somerset	Taunton	1988
385	B.Sutcliffe	Otago v Canterbury	Christchurch	1952-53
383	C.W.Gregory	New South Wales v Queensland	Brisbane	1906-07
377	S.V.Manjrekar	Bombay v Hyderabad	Bombay	1990-91
375	B.C.Lara	West Indies v England	St John's	1993-94
369	D.G.Bradman	South Australia v Tasmania	Adelaide	1935-36
366	N.H.Fairbrother	Lancashire v Surrey	The Oval	1990
366	M.V.Sridhar	Hyderabad v Andhra	Secunderabad	1993-94
365*	C.Hill	South Australia v NSW	Adelaide	1900-01
365*	G.St A.Sobers	West Indies v Pakistan	Kingston	1957-58
364	L.Hutton	England v Australia	The Oval	1938
359*	V.M.Merchant	Bombay v Maharashtra	Bombay	1943-44
359	R.B.Simpson	New South Wales v Queensland	Brisbane	1963-64
357*	R.Abel	Surrey v Somerset	The Oval	1899
357	D.G.Bradman	South Australia v Victoria	Melbourne	1935-36
356	B.A.Richards	South Australia v W Australia	Perth	1970-71
355*	G.R.Marsh	W Australia v S Australia	Perth	1989-90
355	B.Sutcliffe	Otago v Auckland	Dunedin	1949-50
353	W.V.S.Laxman	Hyderabad v Karnataka	Bangalore	1999-00
352	W.H.Ponsford	Victoria v New South Wales	Melbourne	1926-27
350	Rashid Israr	Habib Bank v National Bank	Lahore	1976-77

There have been 127 triple hundreds in first-class cricket, W.V.Raman (313) and Arjan Kripal Singh (302*) for Tamil Nadu v Goa at Panjim in 1988-89 providing the only instance of two batsmen scoring 300 in the same innings.

MOST HUNDREDS IN SUCCESSIVE INNINGS

6	C.B.Fry	Sussex and Rest of England	1901
6	D.G.Bradman	South Australia and D.G.Bradman's XI	1938-39
6	M.J.Procter	Rhodesia	1970-71

TWO DOUBLE HUNDREDS IN A MATCH

| 244 | 202* | A.E.Fagg | Kent v Essex | Colchester | 1938 |

TRIPLE HUNDRED AND HUNDRED IN A MATCH

| 333 | 123 | G.A.Gooch | England v India | Lord's | 1990 |

DOUBLE HUNDRED AND HUNDRED IN A MATCH MOST TIMES

| 4 | Zaheer Abbas | Gloucestershire | 1976-81 |

TWO HUNDREDS IN A MATCH MOST TIMES

| 8 | Zaheer Abbas | Gloucestershire and PIA | 1976-82 |
| 7 | W.R.Hammond | Gloucestershire, England and MCC | 1927-45 |

MOST HUNDREDS IN A SEASON

| 18 | D.C.S.Compton | 1947 | 16 | J.B.Hobbs | 1925 |

100 HUNDREDS IN A CAREER

| | Total | | 100th Hundred | |
	Hundreds	Inns	Season	Inns
J.B.Hobbs	197	1315	1923	821
E.H.Hendren	170	1300	1928-29	740
W.R.Hammond	167	1005	1935	679
C.P.Mead	153	1340	1927	892
G.Boycott	151	1014	1977	645
H.Sutcliffe	149	1088	1932	700
F.E.Woolley	145	1532	1929	1031
L.Hutton	129	814	1951	619
G.A.Gooch	128	990	1992-93	820
W.G Grace	126	1493	1895	1113
D.C.S.Compton	123	839	1952	552
T.W.Graveney	122	1223	1964	940
D.G.Bradman	117	338	1947-48	295
I.V.A.Richards	114	796	1988-89	658
G.A.Hick	111	653	1998	574
Zaheer Abbas	108	768	1982-83	658
A.Sandham	107	1000	1935	871
M.C.Cowdrey	107	1130	1973	1035
T.W.Hayward	104	1138	1913	1076
G.M.Turner	103	792	1982	779
J.H.Edrich	103	979	1977	945
L.E.G.Ames	102	951	1950	915
G.E.Tyldesley	102	961	1934	919
D.L.Amiss	102	1139	1986	1081

MOST 400s: 2 – W.H.Ponsford

MOST 300s or more: 6 – D.G.Bradman; 4 – W.R.Hammond

MOST 200s or more: 37 – D.G.Bradman; 36 – W.R.Hammond; 22 – E.H.Hendren

MOST RUNS IN A MONTH

| 1294 (avge 92.42) | L.Hutton | Yorkshire | June 1949 |

MOST RUNS IN A SEASON

Runs			I	NO	HS	Avge	100	Season
3816	D.C.S.Compton	Middlesex	50	8	246	90.85	18	1947
3539	W.J.Edrich	Middlesex	52	8	267*	80.43	12	1947
3518	T.W.Hayward	Surrey	61	8	219	66.37	13	1906

The feat of scoring 3000 runs in a season has been achieved 28 times, the most recent instance being by W.E.Alley (3019) in 1961. The highest aggregate in a season since 1969 is 2755 by S.J.Cook in 1991.

1000 RUNS IN A SEASON MOST TIMES

28   W.G.Grace (Gloucestershire), F.E.Woolley (Kent)

HIGHEST BATTING AVERAGE IN A SEASON
(Qualification: 12 innings)

Avge			I	NO	HS	Runs	100	Season
115.66	D.G.Bradman	Australians	26	5	278	2429	13	1938
102.53	G.Boycott	Yorkshire	20	5	175*	1538	6	1979
102.00	W.A.Johnston	Australians	17	16	28*	102	–	1953
101.70	G.A.Gooch	Essex	30	3	333	2746	12	1990
100.12	G.Boycott	Yorkshire	30	5	233	2503	13	1971

FASTEST HUNDRED AGAINST AUTHENTIC BOWLING

35 min   P.G.H.Fender   Surrey v Northamptonshire   Northampton   1920

FASTEST DOUBLE HUNDRED

113 min   R.J.Shastri   Bombay v Baroda   Bombay   1984-85

FASTEST TRIPLE HUNDRED

181 min   D.C.S.Compton   MCC v NE Transvaal   Benoni   1948-49

MOST SIXES IN AN INNINGS

16   A.Symonds   Gloucestershire v Glamorgan   Abergavenny   1995

MOST SIXES IN A MATCH

20   A.Symonds   Gloucestershire v Glamorgan   Abergavenny   1995

MOST SIXES IN A SEASON

80   I.T.Botham   Somerset and England   1985

MOST FOURS IN AN INNINGS

72   B.C.Lara   Warwickshire v Durham   Birmingham   1994

MOST RUNS OFF ONE OVER

| 36 | G.St A.Sobers | Nottinghamshire v Glamorgan | Swansea | 1968 |
| 36 | R.J.Shastri | Bombay v Baroda | Bombay | 1984-85 |

Both batsmen hit for six all six balls of overs bowled by M.A.Nash and Tilak Raj respectively.

MOST RUNS IN A DAY

390*   B.C.Lara   Warwickshire v Durham   Birmingham   1994

There have been 19 instances of a batsman scoring 300 or more runs in a day.

LONGEST INNINGS

1015 min   R.Nayyar (271)   Himachal Pradesh v Jammu & Kashmir Chamba   1999-00

HIGHEST PARTNERSHIPS FOR EACH WICKET

First Wicket

561	Waheed Mirza/Mansoor Akhtar	Karachi W v Quetta	Karachi	1976-77
555	P.Holmes/H.Sutcliffe	Yorkshire v Essex	Leyton	1932
554	J.T.Brown/J.Tunnicliffe	Yorkshire v Derbys	Chesterfield	1898

Second Wicket

576	S.T.Jayasuriya/R.S.Mahanama	Sri Lanka v India	Colombo (RPS)	1997-98
475	Zahir Alam/L.S.Rajput	Assam v Tripura	Gauhati	1991-92
465*	J.A.Jameson/R.B.Kanhai	Warwickshire v Glos	Birmingham	1974

Third Wicket

467	A.H.Jones/M.D.Crowe	N Zealand v Sri Lanka	Wellington	1990-91
456	Khalid Irtiza/Aslam Ali	United Bank v Multan	Karachi	1975-76
451	Mudassar Nazar/Javed Miandad	Pakistan v India	Hyderabad	1982-83
445	P.E.Whitelaw/W.N.Carson	Auckland v Otago	Dunedin	1936-37
438	G.A.Hick/T.M.Moody	Worcestershire v Hants	Southampton	1997

Fourth Wicket

577	V.S.Hazare/Gul Mahomed	Baroda v Holkar	Baroda	1946-47
574*	C.L.Walcott/F.M.M.Worrell	Barbados v Trinidad	Port-of-Spain	1945-46
502*	F.M.M.Worrell/J.D.C.Goddard	Barbados v Trinidad	Bridgetown	1943-44
470	A.I.Kallicharran/G.W.Humpage	Warwickshire v Lancs	Southport	1982

Fifth Wicket

464*	M.E.Waugh/S.R.Waugh	NSW v W Australia	Perth	1990-91
405	S.G.Barnes/D.G.Bradman	Australia v England	Sydney	1946-47
401	M.B.Loye/D.Ripley	Northants v Glamorgan	Northampton	1998

Sixth Wicket

487*	G.A.Headley/C.C.Passailaigue	Jamaica v Tennyson's	Kingston	1931-32
428	W.W.Armstrong/M.A.Noble	Australians v Sussex	Hove	1902
411	R.M.Poore/E.G.Wynyard	Hampshire v Somerset	Taunton	1899

Seventh Wicket

460	Bhupinder Singh jr/P.Dharmani	Punjab v Delhi	Delhi	1994-95
347	D.St E.Atkinson/C.C.Depeiza	W Indies v Australia	Bridgetown	1954-55
344	K.S.Ranjitsinhji/W.Newham	Sussex v Essex	Leyton	1902

Eighth Wicket

433	V.T.Trumper/A.Sims	Australians v C'bury	Christchurch	1913-14
313	Wasim Akram/Saqlain Mushtaq	Pakistan v Zimbabwe	Sheikhupura	1996-97
292	R.Peel/Lord Hawke	Yorkshire v Warwicks	Birmingham	1896

Ninth Wicket

283	J.Chapman/A.Warren	Derbys v Warwicks	Blackwell	1910
268	J.B.Commins/N.Boje	SA 'A' v Mashonaland	Harare	1994-95
251	J.W.H.T.Douglas/S.N.Hare	Essex v Derbyshire	Leyton	1921

Tenth Wicket

307	A.F.Kippax/J.E.H.Hooker	NSW v Victoria	Melbourne	1928-29
249	C.T.Sarwate/S.N.Banerjee	Indians v Surrey	The Oval	1946
235	F.E.Woolley/A.Fielder	Kent v Worcs	Stourbridge	1909

35000 RUNS IN A CAREER

	Career	I	NO	HS	Runs	Avge	100
J.B.Hobbs	1905-34	1315	106	316*	**61237**	50.65	197
F.E.Woolley	1906-38	1532	85	305*	**58969**	40.75	145
E.H.Hendren	1907-38	1300	166	301*	**57611**	50.80	170
C.P.Mead	1905-36	1340	185	280*	**55061**	47.67	153
W.G.Grace	1865-1908	1493	105	344	**54896**	39.55	126
W.R.Hammond	1920-51	1005	104	336*	**50551**	56.10	167
H.Sutcliffe	1919-45	1088	123	313	**50138**	51.95	149
G.Boycott	1962-86	1014	162	261*	**48426**	56.83	151
T.W.Graveney	1948-71/72	1223	159	258	**47793**	44.91	122
G.A.Gooch	1973-2000	990	75	333	**44846**	49.01	128
T.W.Hayward	1893-1914	1138	96	315*	**43551**	41.79	104
D.L.Amiss	1960-87	1139	126	262*	**43423**	42.86	102
M.C.Cowdrey	1950-76	1130	134	307	**42719**	42.89	107
A.Sandham	1911-37/38	1000	79	325	**41284**	44.82	107
L.Hutton	1934-60	814	91	364	**40140**	55.51	129
M.J.K.Smith	1951-75	1091	139	204	**39832**	41.84	69
W.Rhodes	1898-1930	1528	237	267*	**39802**	30.83	58
J.H.Edrich	1956-78	979	104	310*	**39790**	45.47	103
R.E.S.Wyatt	1923-57	1141	157	232	**39405**	40.04	85
D.C.S.Compton	1936-64	839	88	300	**38942**	51.85	123
G.E.Tyldesley	1909-36	961	106	256*	**38874**	45.46	102
J.T.Tyldesley	1895-1923	994	62	295*	**37897**	40.60	86
K.W.R.Fletcher	1962-88	1167	170	228*	**37665**	37.77	63
C.G.Greenidge	1970-92	889	75	273*	**37354**	45.88	92
J.W.Hearne	1909-36	1025	116	285*	**37252**	40.98	96
L.E.G.Ames	1926-51	951	95	295	**37248**	43.51	102
D.Kenyon	1946-67	1159	59	259	**37002**	33.63	74
W.J.Edrich	1934-58	964	92	267*	**36965**	42.39	86
J.M.Parks	1949-76	1227	172	205*	**36673**	34.76	51
M.W.Gatting	1975-98	861	123	258	**36549**	49.52	94
D.Denton	1894-1920	1163	70	221	**36479**	33.37	69
G.H.Hirst	1891-1929	1215	151	341	**36323**	34.13	60
I.V.A.Richards	1971/72-93	796	63	322	**36212**	49.40	114
A.Jones	1957-83	1168	72	204*	**36049**	32.89	56
W.G.Quaife	1894-1928	1203	185	255*	**36012**	35.37	72
R.E.Marshall	1945/46-72	1053	59	228*	**35725**	35.94	68
G.Gunn	1902-32	1061	82	220	**35208**	35.96	62

BOWLING RECORDS

ALL TEN WICKETS IN AN INNINGS

This feat has been achieved 77 times in first-class matches (excluding 12-a-side fixtures).
Three Times: A.P.Freeman (1929, 1930, 1931)
Twice: V.E.Walker (1859, 1865); H.Verity (1931, 1932); J.C.Laker (1956)

Instances since 1945:

W.E.Hollies	Warwickshire v Notts	Birmingham	1946
J.M.Sims	East v West	Kingston on Thames	1948
J.K.R.Graveney	Gloucestershire v Derbyshire	Chesterfield	1949
T.E.Bailey	Essex v Lancashire	Clacton	1949
R.Berry	Lancashire v Worcestershire	Blackpool	1953
S.P.Gupte	President's XI v Combined XI	Bombay	1954-55
J.C.Laker	Surrey v Australians	The Oval	1956
K.Smales	Nottinghamshire v Glos	Stroud	1956

G.A.R.Lock	Surrey v Kent	Blackheath	1956
J.C.Laker	England v Australia	Manchester	1956
P.M.Chatterjee	Bengal v Assam	Jorhat	1956-57
J.D.Bannister	Warwicks v Combined Services	Birmingham (M & B)	1959
A.J.G.Pearson	Cambridge U v Leicestershire	Loughborough	1961
N.I.Thomson	Sussex v Warwickshire	Worthing	1964
P.J.Allan	Queensland v Victoria	Melbourne	1965-66
I.J.Brayshaw	Western Australia v Victoria	Perth	1967-68
Shahid Mahmood	Karachi Whites v Khairpur	Karachi	1969-70
E.E.Hemmings	International XI v W Indians	Kingston	1982-83
P.Sunderam	Rajasthan v Vidarbha	Jodhpur	1985-86
S.T.Jefferies	Western Province v OFS	Cape Town	1987-88
Imran Adil	Bahawalpur v Faisalabad	Faisalabad	1989-90
G.P.Wickremasinghe	Sinhalese v Kalutara	Colombo	1991-92
R.L.Johnson	Middlesex v Derbyshire	Derby	1994
Naeem Akhtar	Rawalpindi B v Peshawar	Peshawar	1995-96
A.Kumble	India v Pakistan	Delhi	1998-99

MOST WICKETS IN A MATCH

| 19 | J.C.Laker | England v Australia | Manchester | 1956 |

MOST WICKETS IN A SEASON

Wkts		Season	Matches	Overs	Mdns	Runs	Avge
304	A.P.Freeman	1928	37	1976.1	423	5489	18.05
298	A.P.Freeman	1933	33	2039	651	4549	15.26

The feat of taking 250 wickets in a season has been achieved on 12 occasions, the last instance being by A.P.Freeman in 1933. 200 or more wickets in a season have been taken on 59 occasions, the last being by G.A.R.Lock (212 wickets, average 12.02) in 1957.

The highest aggregates of wickets taken in a season since the reduction of County Championship matches in 1969 are as follows:

Wkts		Season	Matches	Overs	Mdns	Runs	Avge
134	M.D.Marshall	1982	22	822	225	2108	15.73
131	L.R.Gibbs	1971	23	1024.1	295	2475	18.89
125	F.D.Stephenson	1988	22	819.1	196	2289	18.31
121	R.D.Jackman	1980	23	746.2	220	1864	15.40

Since 1969 there have been 49 instances of bowlers taking 100 wickets in a season.

MOST HAT-TRICKS IN A CAREER

7	D.V.P.Wright
6	T.W.J.Goddard, C.W.L.Parker
5	S.Haigh, V.W.C.Jupp, A.E.G.Rhodes, F.A.Tarrant

2000 WICKETS IN A CAREER

	Career	Runs	Wkts	Avge	100w
W.Rhodes	1898-1930	69993	4187	16.71	23
A.P.Freeman	1914-36	69577	3776	18.42	17
C.W.L.Parker	1903-35	63817	3278	19.46	16
J.T.Hearne	1888-1923	54352	3061	17.75	15
T.W.J.Goddard	1922-52	59116	2979	19.84	16
W.G.Grace	1865-1908	51545	2876	17.92	10
A.S.Kennedy	1907-36	61034	2874	21.23	15
D.Shackleton	1948-69	53303	2857	18.65	20
G.A.R.Lock	1946-70/71	54709	2844	19.23	14
F.J.Titmus	1949-82	63313	2830	22.37	16
M.W.Tate	1912-37	50571	2784	18.16	13+1
G.H.Hirst	1891-1929	51282	2739	18.72	15

	Career	Runs	Wkts	Avge	100w
C.Blythe	1899-1914	42136	**2506**	16.81	14
D.L.Underwood	1963-87	49993	**2465**	20.28	10
W.E.Astill	1906-39	57783	**2431**	23.76	9
J.C.White	1909-37	43759	**2356**	18.57	14
W.E.Hollies	1932-57	48656	**2323**	20.94	14
F.S.Trueman	1949-69	42154	**2304**	18.29	12
J.B.Statham	1950-68	36999	**2260**	16.37	13
R.T.D.Perks	1930-55	53771	**2233**	24.07	16
J.Briggs	1879-1900	35431	**2221**	15.95	12
D.J.Shepherd	1950-72	47302	**2218**	21.32	12
E.G.Dennett	1903-26	42571	**2147**	19.82	12
T.Richardson	1892-1905	38794	**2104**	18.43	10
T.E.Bailey	1945-67	48170	**2082**	23.13	9
R.Illingworth	1951-83	42023	**2072**	20.28	10
F.E.Woolley	1906-38	41066	**2068**	19.85	8
N.Gifford	1960-88	48731	**2068**	23.56	4
G.Geary	1912-38	41339	**2063**	20.03	11
D.V.P.Wright	1932-57	49307	**2056**	23.98	10
J.A.Newman	1906-30	51111	**2032**	25.15	9
A.Shaw	1864-97	24580	**2026+1**	12.12	9
S.Haigh	1895-1913	32091	**2012**	15.94	11

ALL-ROUND RECORDS
THE 'DOUBLE'

3000 runs and 100 wickets: J.H.Parks (1937)

2000 runs and 200 wickets: G.H.Hirst (1906)

2000 runs and 100 wickets: F.E.Woolley (4), J.W.Hearne (3), W.G.Grace (2), G.H.Hirst (2), W.Rhodes (2), T.E.Bailey, D.E.Davies, G.L.Jessop, V.W.C.Jupp, J.Langridge, F.A.Tarrant, C.L.Townsend, L.F.Townsend

1000 runs and 200 wickets: M.W.Tate (3), A.E.Trott (2), A.S.Kennedy

Most Doubles: 16 – W.Rhodes; 14 – G.H.Hirst; 10 – V.W.C.Jupp

Double in Debut Season: D.B.Close (1949) – the youngest (18) to achieve this feat.

The feat of scoring 1000 runs and taking 100 wickets in a season has been achieved on 305 occasions, R.J.Hadlee (1984) and F.D.Stephenson (1988) being the only players to complete the 'double' since the reduction of County Championship matches in 1969.

WICKET-KEEPING RECORDS
EIGHT DISMISSALS IN AN INNINGS

9	(8ct, 1st)	Tahir Rashid	Habib Bank v PACO	Gujranwala	1992-93
9	(7ct, 2st)	W.R.James	Matabeleland v Mashonaland CD	Bulawayo	1995-96
8	(8ct)	A.T.W.Grout	Queensland v W Australia	Brisbane	1959-60
8	(8ct)	D.E.East	Essex v Somerset	Taunton	1985
8	(8ct)	S.A.Marsh	Kent v Middlesex	Lord's	1991
8	(6ct, 2st)	T.J.Zoehrer	Australians v Surrey	The Oval	1993
8	(7ct, 1st)	D.S.Berry	Victoria v South Australia	Melbourne	1996-97

TWELVE DISMISSALS IN A MATCH

13	(11ct, 2st)	W.R.James	Matabeleland v Mashonaland CD	Bulawayo	1995-96
12	(8ct, 4st)	E.Pooley	Surrey v Sussex	The Oval	1868
12	(9ct, 3st)	D.Tallon	Queensland v NSW	Sydney	1938-39
12	(9ct, 3st)	H.B.Taber	NSW v South Australia	Adelaide	1968-69

MOST DISMISSALS IN A SEASON

128 (79ct, 49st) L.E.G.Ames   1929

1000 DISMISSALS IN A CAREER

	Career	Dismissals	Ct	St
R.W.Taylor	1960-88	1649	1473	176
J.T.Murray	1952-75	1527	1270	257
H.Strudwick	1902-27	1497	1242	255
A.P.E.Knott	1964-85	1344	1211	133
F.H.Huish	1895-1914	1310	933	377
B.Taylor	1949-73	1294	1083	211
D.Hunter	1889-1909	1253	906	347
H.R.Butt	1890-1912	1228	953	275
J.H.Board	1891-1914/15	1207	852	355
H.Elliott	1920-47	1206	904	302
R.C.Russell	1981-2000	1197	1077	120
J.M.Parks	1949-76	1181	1088	93
R.Booth	1951-70	1126	948	178
L.E.G.Ames	1926-51	1121	703	418
D.L.Bairstow	1970-90	1099	961	138
G.Duckworth	1923-47	1096	753	343
S.J.Rhodes	1981-2000	1082	969	113
H.W.Stephenson	1948-64	1082	748	334
J.G.Binks	1955-75	1071	895	176
T.G.Evans	1939-69	1066	816	250
A.Long	1960-80	1046	922	124
G.O.Dawkes	1937-61	1043	895	148
R.W.Tolchard	1965-83	1037	912	125
W.L.Cornford	1921-47	1017	675	342

FIELDING RECORDS

MOST CATCHES IN AN INNINGS

| 7 | M.J.Stewart | Surrey v Northamptonshire | Northampton | 1957 |
| 7 | A.S.Brown | Gloucestershire v Nottinghamshire | Nottingham | 1966 |

MOST CATCHES IN A MATCH

| 10 | W.R.Hammond | Gloucestershire v Surrey | Cheltenham | 1928 |

MOST CATCHES IN A SEASON

| 78 | W.R.Hammond | 1928 | 77 | M.J.Stewart | 1957 |

750 CATCHES IN A CAREER

1018	F.E.Woolley	1906-38	784	J.G.Langridge	1928-55
887	W.G.Grace	1865-1908	764	W.Rhodes	1898-1930
830	G.A.R.Lock	1946-70/71	758	C.A.Milton	1948-74
819	W.R.Hammond	1920-51	754	E.H.Hendren	1907-38
813	D.B.Close	1949-86			

UNIVERSITY MATCH RESULTS

Played: 155. Wins: Cambridge 56; Oxford 48. Drawn: 51. Abandoned: 1

In 2001, for the very first time, Cambridge will host the University Match, cricket's oldest surviving first-class fixture. The ECB's re-organisation of university cricket around six centres of excellence has removed it from Lord's but it will, for the time being at any rate, remain on the first-class list.

Dating from 1827 it has, wartime interruptions apart, been played annually since 1838. With the exception of five matches played in the area of Oxford (1829, 1843, 1846, 1848 and 1850), all the previous matches have been staged at Lord's.

In 2001 Oxford (with Brookes), Cambridge (with Anglia) and Durham will each play three first-class matches against counties. The other three centres – Cardiff (with UWIC and Glamorgan), Leeds (with Bradford and Leeds Metropolitan), and Loughborough – will also play three counties apiece but without first-class status, an honour they are expected to be granted for 2003.

1827	Drawn	1874	Oxford	1913	Cambridge	1962	Drawn
1829	Oxford	1875	Oxford	1914	Oxford	1963	Drawn
1836	Oxford	1876	Cambridge	1919	Oxford	1964	Drawn
1838	Oxford	1877	Oxford	1920	Drawn	1965	Drawn
1839	Cambridge	1878	Cambridge	1921	Cambridge	1966	Oxford
1840	Cambridge	1879	Cambridge	1922	Cambridge	1967	Drawn
1841	Cambridge	1880	Cambridge	1923	Oxford	1968	Drawn
1842	Cambridge	1881	Oxford	1924	Cambridge	1969	Drawn
1843	Cambridge	1882	Cambridge	1925	Drawn	1970	Drawn
1844	Drawn	1883	Cambridge	1926	Cambridge	1971	Drawn
1845	Cambridge	1884	Oxford	1927	Cambridge	1972	Cambridge
1846	Oxford	1885	Cambridge	1928	Drawn	1973	Drawn
1847	Cambridge	1886	Oxford	1929	Drawn	1974	Drawn
1848	Oxford	1887	Oxford	1930	Cambridge	1975	Drawn
1849	Cambridge	1888	Drawn	1931	Oxford	1976	Oxford
1850	Oxford	1889	Cambridge	1932	Drawn	1977	Drawn
1851	Cambridge	1890	Cambridge	1933	Drawn	1978	Drawn
1852	Oxford	1891	Cambridge	1934	Drawn	1979	Cambridge
1853	Oxford	1892	Oxford	1935	Cambridge	1980	Drawn
1854	Oxford	1893	Cambridge	1936	Cambridge	1981	Drawn
1855	Oxford	1894	Oxford	1937	Oxford	1982	Cambridge
1856	Cambridge	1895	Cambridge	1938	Drawn	1983	Drawn
1857	Oxford	1896	Oxford	1939	Oxford	1984	Oxford
1858	Oxford	1897	Cambridge	1946	Oxford	1985	Drawn
1859	Cambridge	1898	Oxford	1947	Cambridge	1986	Cambridge
1860	Cambridge	1899	Drawn	1948	Oxford	1987	Drawn
1861	Cambridge	1900	Drawn	1949	Cambridge	1988	Abandoned
1862	Cambridge	1901	Drawn	1950	Drawn	1989	Drawn
1863	Oxford	1902	Cambridge	1951	Oxford	1990	Drawn
1864	Oxford	1903	Oxford	1952	Drawn	1991	Drawn
1865	Oxford	1904	Drawn	1953	Cambridge	1992	Cambridge
1866	Oxford	1905	Cambridge	1954	Drawn	1993	Oxford
1867	Cambridge	1906	Cambridge	1955	Drawn	1994	Drawn
1868	Cambridge	1907	Cambridge	1956	Drawn	1995	Oxford
1869	Cambridge	1908	Oxford	1957	Cambridge	1996	Drawn
1870	Cambridge	1909	Drawn	1958	Cambridge	1997	Drawn
1871	Oxford	1910	Oxford	1959	Oxford	1998	Cambridge
1872	Cambridge	1911	Oxford	1960	Drawn	1999	Drawn
1873	Oxford	1912	Cambridge	1961	Drawn	2000	Drawn

CAMBRIDGE UNIVERSITY RECORDS

ALL FIRST-CLASS MATCHES

Highest Total	For 703-9d		v	Sussex	Hove	1890
	V 730-3		by	W Indians	Cambridge	1950
Lowest Total	For 30		v	Yorkshire	Cambridge	1928
	V 32		by	Oxford U	Lord's	1878
Highest Innings	For 254*	K.S.Duleepsinhji	v	Middlesex	Cambridge	1927
	V 304*	E.de C.Weekes	for	W Indians	Cambridge	1950
Highest Partnership						
(2nd wicket)	429*	J.G.Dewes/G.H.G.Doggart	v	Essex	Cambridge	1949
Best Innings Bowling	10-69	S.M.J.Woods	v	Thornton's XI	Cambridge	1890
Best Match Bowling	15-88	S.M.J.Woods	v	Thornton's XI	Cambridge	1890
Most Runs – Season	1581	D.S.Sheppard		(av 79.05)		1952
Most Runs – Career	4310	J.M.Brearley		(av 38.48)		1961-68
Most 100s – Season	7	D.S.Sheppard				1952
Most 100s – Career	14	D.S.Sheppard				1950-52
Most Wkts – Season	80	O.S.Wheatley		(av 17.63)		1958
Most Wkts – Career	208	G.Goonesena		(av 21.82)		1954-57

UNIVERSITY MATCH RECORDS

Highest Total	432-9d			1936
Lowest Total	39			1858
Highest Innings	211	G.Goonesena		1957
Best Innings Bowling	8-44	G.E.Jeffery		1873
Best Match Bowling	13-73	A.G.Steel		1878

Hat-Tricks: F.C.Cobden (1870), A.G.Steel (1879), P.H.Morton (1880), J.F.Ireland (1911), R.G.H.Lowe (1926)

OXFORD UNIVERSITY RECORDS

ALL FIRST-CLASS MATCHES

Highest Total	For 651		v	Sussex	Hove	1895
	V 679-7d		by	Australians	Oxford	1938
Lowest Total	For 12		v	MCC	Oxford	1877
	V 24		by	MCC	Oxford	1846
Highest Innings	For 281	K.J.Key	v	Middlesex	Chiswick Park	1887
	V 338	W.W.Read	for	Surrey	The Oval	1888
Highest Partnership						
(7th wicket)	340	K.J.Key/H.Philipson	v	Middlesex	Chiswick Park	1887
Best Innings Bowling	10-38	S.E.Butler	v	Cambridge U	Lord's	1871
Best Match Bowling	15-65	B.J.T.Bosanquet	v	Sussex	Oxford	1900
Most Runs – Season	1307	Nawab of Pataudi sr		(av 93.35)		1931
Most Runs – Career	3319	N.S.Mitchell-Innes		(av 47.41)		1934-37
Most 100s – Season	6	Nawab of Pataudi sr				1931
Most 100s – Career	9	A.M.Crawley				1927-30
	9	Nawab of Pataudi sr				1928-31
	9	N.S.Mitchell-Innes				1934-37
	9	M.P.Donnelly				1946-47
Most Wkts – Season	70	I.A.R.Peebles		(av 18.15)		1930
Most Wkts – Career	182	R.H.B.Bettington		(av 19.38)		1920-23

UNIVERSITY MATCH RECORDS

Highest Total	503			1900
Lowest Total	32			1878
Highest Innings	238*	Nawab of Pataudi sr		1931
Best Innings Bowling	10-38	S.E.Butler		1871
Best Match Bowling	15-95	S.E.Butler		1871

Match Doubles: P.R.le Couteur (160 and 11-66 in 1910); G.J.Toogood (149 and 10-93 in 1985)

LIMITED-OVERS INTERNATIONALS RESULTS SUMMARY

1970-71 to 16 February 2001

Opponents	Matches	E	A	SA	WI	NZ	I	P	SL	Z	B	C	EA	H	K	SC	UAE	Tied	NR
England Australia	67	31	34															1	1
South Africa	23	7		16															
West Indies	61	26			32														3
New Zealand	47	23				20												1	3
India	36	19					16												1
Pakistan	46	28						17											1
Sri Lanka	20	13							7										
Zimbabwe	16	9								7									
Bangladesh	1	1									0								
Canada	1	1										0							
East Africa	1	1											0						
Holland	1	1												0					
Kenya	1	1													0				
U A Emirates	1	1															0		
Australia South Africa	45		21	22															2
West Indies	98		43		52													2	1
New Zealand	80		55			22													3
India	62		36				23												3
Pakistan	57		31					23										1	2
Sri Lanka	43		28						13										2
Zimbabwe	19		18							1									
Bangladesh	2		2								0								
Canada	1		1									0							
Kenya	1		1												0				
Scotland	1		1													0			
S Africa West Indies	18			12	6														
N Zealand	27			17		7													3
India	38			24			13												1
Pakistan	29			19				10											
Sri Lanka	25			14					10										1
Zimbabwe	12			9						2									1
Holland	1			1										0					
Kenya	3			3											0				
U A Emirates	1			1													0		
W Indies New Zealand	30				19	9													2
India	63				40		21											1	1
Pakistan	95				59			34										2	
Sri Lanka	32				21				10										1
Zimbabwe	15				11					4									
Bangladesh	3				3						0								
Kenya	1				0										1				
Scotland	1				1											0			
N Zealand India	58					25	30												3
Pakistan	52					19		31										1	1
Sri Lanka	45					25			17									1	2
Zimbabwe	25					16				7								1	1
Bangladesh	2					2					0								
East Africa	1					1							0						
Holland	1					1								0					
Scotland	1					1										0			
U A Emirates	1					1											0		
India Pakistan	85						29	52											4
Sri Lanka	66						34		27										5
Zimbabwe	34						26			6									2
Bangladesh	8						8				0								
East Africa	1						1						0						
Kenya	7						6								1				
U A Emirates	1						1										0		
Pakistan Sri Lanka	84							52	29									1	2
Zimbabwe	22							19		2								1	
Bangladesh	8							7			1								

205

Opponents		Matches	E	A	SA	WI	NZ	I	P	SL	Z	B	C	EA	H	K	SC	UAE	Tied	NR
	Canada	1	–	–	–	–	–	1	–	–	–	–	0	–	–	–	–	–	–	–
	Holland	1	–	–	–	–	–	1	–	–	–	–	–	0	–	–	–	–	–	–
	Kenya	1	–	–	–	–	–	1	–	–	–	–	–	–	0	–	–	–	–	–
	Scotland	1	–	–	–	–	–	1	–	–	–	–	–	–	–	0	–	–	–	–
	U A Emirates	2	–	–	–	–	–	2	–	–	–	–	–	–	–	–	0	–	–	–
Sri Lanka	Zimbabwe	23	–	–	–	–	–	–	–	17	5	–	–	–	–	–	–	–	–	1
	Bangladesh	6	–	–	–	–	–	–	–	6	–	0	–	–	–	–	–	–	–	–
	Kenya	3	–	–	–	–	–	–	–	3	–	–	–	–	0	–	–	–	–	–
Zimbabwe	Bangladesh	4	–	–	–	–	–	–	–	–	4	0	–	–	–	–	–	–	–	–
	Kenya	11	–	–	–	–	–	–	–	–	10	–	–	–	0	–	–	–	–	1
Bangladesh	Kenya	6	–	–	–	–	–	–	–	–	–	1	–	–	–	5	–	–	–	–
	Scotland	1	–	–	–	–	–	–	–	–	–	1	–	–	–	0	–	–	–	–
Holland	U A Emirates	1	–	–	–	–	–	–	–	–	–	–	–	–	0	–	–	1	–	–
		1688	162	271	138	244	149	208	251	139	48	3	0	0	0	7	0	1	17	50

MERIT TABLE OF ALL L-O INTERNATIONALS
1970-71 to 16 February 2001

	Matches	Won	Lost	Tied	No Result	% Won (exc NR)
South Africa	222	138	76	2	6	63.88
West Indies	417	244	160	5	8	59.65
Australia	476	271	187	6	12	58.40
Pakistan	484	251	217	6	10	52.95
England	322	162	149	2	9	51.75
India	459	208	230	3	18	47.16
New Zealand	370	149	199	4	18	42.32
Sri Lanka	347	139	192	2	14	41.74
Zimbabwe	181	48	125	4	4	27.11
Kenya	34	7	26	–	1	21.21
Bangladesh	41	3	38	–	–	7.31
Associate Members	23	1	22	–	–	4.34

TEAM RECORDS
HIGHEST TOTALS

398-5	(50 overs)	Sri Lanka v Kenya	Kandy	1995-96
376-2	(50 overs)	India v New Zealand	Hyderabad, India	1999-00
373-6	(50 overs)	India v Sri Lanka	Taunton	1999
371-9	(50 overs)	Pakistan v Sri Lanka	Nairobi	1996-97
363-7	(55 overs)	England v Pakistan	Nottingham	1992
360-4	(50 overs)	West Indies v Sri Lanka	Karachi	1987-88
349-6	(50 overs)	Australia v New Zealand	Christchurch	1999-00
349-9	(50 overs)	Sri Lanka v Pakistan	Singapore	1995-96
349-9	(50 overs)	New Zealand v India	Rajkot	1999-00
348-8	(50 overs)	New Zealand v India	Nagpur	1995-96
347-3	(50 overs)	Kenya v Bangladesh	Nairobi	1997-98

The highest for South Africa is 328-3 (v Holland, Rawalpindi, 1995-96); for Zimbabwe 325-6 (v Kenya, Dhaka, 1998-99); and for Bangladesh 257 (v Zimbabwe, Nairobi, 1997-98) and 257-5 (v Zimbabwe, Dhaka, 1998-99).

HIGHEST TOTALS BATTING SECOND

WINNING:	316-4	(48.5 overs)	Australia v Pakistan	Lahore	1998-99
	316-7	(47.5 overs)	India v Pakistan	Dhaka	1997-98
LOSING:	329	(49.3 overs)	Sri Lanka v West Indies	Sharjah	1995-96

HIGHEST MATCH AGGREGATE

664-19	(99.4 overs)	Pakistan v Sri Lanka	Singapore	1995-96

LARGEST RUNS MARGINS OF VICTORY

245 runs		Sri Lanka beat India	Sharjah	2000-01
233 runs		Pakistan v Bangladesh	Dhaka	1999-00
232 runs		Australia beat Sri Lanka	Adelaide	1984-85
206 runs		New Zealand beat Australia	Adelaide	1985-86
202 runs		England beat India	Lord's	1975
202 runs		South Africa beat Kenya	Nairobi	1996-97
202 runs		Zimbabwe beat Kenya	Dhaka	1998-99

LOWEST TOTALS (Excluding reduced innings)

43	(19.5 overs)	Pakistan v West Indies	Cape Town	1992-93
45	(40.3 overs)	Canada v England	Manchester	1979
54	(26.3 overs)	India v Sri Lanka	Sharjah	2000-01
55	(28.3 overs)	Sri Lanka v West Indies	Sharjah	1986-87
63	(25.5 overs)	India v Australia	Sydney	1980-81
64	(35.5 overs)	New Zealand v Pakistan	Sharjah	1985-86
68	(31.3 overs)	Scotland v West Indies	Leicester	1999
69	(28 overs)	South Africa v Australia	Sydney	1993-94
70	(25.2 overs)	Australia v England	Birmingham	1977
70	(26.3 overs)	Australia v New Zealand	Adelaide	1985-86

The lowest for England is 93 (v A, Leeds, 1975); for West Indies 87 (v A, Sydney, 1992-93); for Zimbabwe 94 (v P, Sharjah, 1996-97); for Bangladesh 87 (v P, Dhaka, 1999-00), and for Kenya 103 (v SA, Nairobi, 1996-97).

LOWEST MATCH AGGREGATE

88-13	(32.2 overs)	West Indies v Pakistan	Cape Town	1992-93

BATTING RECORDS
HIGHEST INDIVIDUAL INNINGS

194	Saeed Anwar	Pakistan v India	Madras	1996-97
189*	I.V.A.Richards	West Indies v England	Manchester	1984
189	S.T.Jayasuriya	Sri Lanka v India	Sharjah	2000-01
188*	G.Kirsten	South Africa v UAE	Rawalpindi	1995-96
186*	S.R.Tendulkar	India v New Zealand	Hyderabad	1999-00
183	S.C.Ganguly	India v Sri Lanka	Taunton	1999
181	I.V.A.Richards	West Indies v Sri Lanka	Karachi	1987-88
175*	Kapil Dev	India v Zimbabwe	Tunbridge Wells	1983
173	M.E.Waugh	Australia v West Indies	Melbourne	2000-01
171*	G.M.Turner	New Zealand v East Africa	Birmingham	1975
169*	D.J.Callaghan	South Africa v New Zealand	Pretoria	1994-95
169	B.C.Lara	West Indies v Sri Lanka	Sharjah	1995-96
167*	R.A.Smith	England v Australia	Birmingham	1993
161	A.C.Hudson	South Africa v Holland	Rawalpindi	1995-96
158	D.I.Gower	England v New Zealand	Brisbane	1982-83
154	A.C.Gilchrist	Australia v Sri Lanka	Melbourne	1998-99
153*	I.V.A.Richards	West Indies v Australia	Melbourne	1979-80
153*	M.Azharuddin	India v Zimbabwe	Cuttack	1997-98
153*	S.C.Ganguly	India v New Zealand	Gwalior	1999-00
153	B.C.Lara	West Indies v Pakistan	Sharjah	1993-94
153	R.Dravid	India v New Zealand	Hyderabad	1999-00
152*	D.L.Haynes	West Indies v India	Georgetown	1988-89
151*	S.T.Jayasuriya	Sri Lanka v India	Bombay	1996-97
150	S.Chanderpaul	West Indies v South Africa	East London	1998-99

The highest for Zimbabwe is 142 by D.L.Houghton (v New Zealand, Hyderabad, India, 1987-88); for Bangladesh 101 by Mehrab Hossain (v Zimbabwe, Dhaka, 1998-99); and for Kenya 144 by K.O.Otieno (v Bangladesh, Nairobi, 1997-98).

HUNDRED ON DEBUT

D.L.Amiss	103	England v Australia	Manchester	1972
D.L.Haynes	148	West Indies v Australia	St John's	1977-78
A.Flower	115*	Zimbabwe v Sri Lanka	New Plymouth	1991-92
Salim Elahi	102*	Pakistan v Sri Lanka	Gujranwala	1995-96

Shahid Afridi scored 102 for P v SL, Nairobi, 1996-97, in his second match having not batted in his first.

| Fastest 100 | 37 balls | Shahid Afridi (102) | P v SL | Nairobi | 1996-97 |
| Fastest 50 | 17 balls | S.T.Jayasuriya (76) | SL v P | Singapore | 1995-96 |

CARRYING BAT THROUGH COMPLETED INNINGS

G.W.Flower	84*	Zimbabwe (205) v England	Sydney	1994-95
Saeed Anwar	103*	Pakistan (219) v Zimbabwe	Harare	1994-95
N.V.Knight	125*	England (246) v Pakistan	Nottingham	1996
R.D.Jacobs	49*	West Indies (110) v Australia	Manchester	1999
D.R.Martyn	116*	Australia (191) v New Zealand	Auckland	1999-00
H.H.Gibbs	59*	South Africa (101) v Pakistan	Sharjah	1999-00
A.J.Stewart	100*	England (192) v West Indies	Nottingham	2000

5000 RUNS IN A CAREER

		LOI	I	NO	HS	Runs	Avge	100	50
S.R.Tendulkar	I	263	256	22	186*	9899	42.30	27	50
M.Azharuddin	I	334	308	54	153*	9378	36.92	7	58
D.L.Haynes	WI	238	237	28	152*	8648	41.37	17	57
P.A.de Silva	SL	275	266	26	145	8432	35.13	11	57
M.E.Waugh	A	230	223	18	173	8107	39.54	17	49
Saeed Anwar	P	213	210	16	194	7634	39.35	19	34
Inzamam-ul-Haq	P	234	221	32	137*	7549	39.94	7	56
A.Ranatunga	SL	269	255	47	131*	7454	35.83	4	49
Javed Miandad	P	233	218	41	119*	7381	41.70	8	50
Salim Malik	P	283	256	38	102	7171	32.89	5	47
S.R.Waugh	A	306	273	55	120*	7089	32.51	2	41
B.C.Lara	WI	183	179	17	169	6897	42.57	14	44
I.V.A.Richards	WI	187	167	24	189*	6721	47.00	11	45
Ijaz Ahmed	P	250	232	29	139*	6564	32.33	10	37
A.R.Border	A	273	252	39	127*	6524	30.62	3	39
S.T.Jayasuriya	SL	228	220	8	189	6340	29.90	10	41
S.C.Ganguly	I	158	153	14	183	6284	45.20	16	35
R.B.Richardson	WI	224	217	30	122	6248	33.41	5	44
D.M.Jones	A	164	161	25	145	6068	44.61	7	46
D.C.Boon	A	181	177	16	122	5964	37.04	5	37
Ramiz Raja	P	198	197	15	119*	5841	32.09	9	31
W.J.Cronje	SA	188	175	31	112	5565	38.64	2	39
G.Kirsten	SA	148	148	14	188*	5511	41.12	10	36
A.Jadeja	I	196	179	36	119	5359	37.47	6	30
R.S.Mahanama	SL	213	198	23	119*	5162	29.49	4	35
A.Flower	Z	169	166	11	120*	5140	33.16	2	43
C.G.Greenidge	WI	128	127	13	133*	5134	45.03	11	31
M.G.Bevan	A	154	136	46	108*	5064	56.26	5	34

The most for England is 4290 in 122 innings by G.A.Gooch; for New Zealand 4704 (140) by M.D.Crowe; for Bangladesh 796 (35) by Akram Khan; and for Kenya 968 (32) by S.O.Tikolo.

17 HUNDREDS

		LOI	100	E	A	SA	WI	NZ	I	P	SL	Z	K
S.R.Tendulkar	I	263	27	–	5	2	1	3	–	2	6	5	3
Saeed Anwar	P	213	19	–	1	–	2	4	3	–	7	2	–
M.E.Waugh	A	230	17	1	–	2	3	3	2	1	1	3	1
D.L.Haynes	WI	238	17	2	6	–	–	2	2	4	1	–	–

The most for England is 8 by G.A.Gooch; for South Africa 10 by G.Kirsten; for New Zealand 8 by N.J.Astle; for Sri Lanka 11 by P.A.de Silva; for Zimbabwe 6 by A.D.R.Campbell; for Bangladesh 1 by Mehrab Hossein; and for Kenya 2 by K.O.Otieno.

HIGHEST PARTNERSHIP FOR EACH WICKET

1st	252	S.C.Ganguly/S.R.Tendulkar	India v Sri Lanka	Colombo (RPS)	1997-98
2nd	331	S.R.Tendulkar/R.Dravid	India v New Zealand	Hyderabad (Ind)	1999-00
3rd	237*	R.Dravid/S.R.Tendulkar	India v Kenya	Bristol	1999
4th	275*	M.Azharuddin/A.Jadeja	India v Zimbabwe	Cuttack	1997-98
5th	223	M.Azharuddin/A.Jadeja	India v Sri Lanka	Colombo (RPS)	1997-98
6th	161	M.O.Odumbe/A.V.Vadher	Kenya v Sri Lanka	Southampton	1999

7th	119	T.M.Odoyo/A.O.Suji	Kenya v Zimbabwe	Nairobi	1997-98
8th	119	P.R.Reiffel/S.K.Warne	Australia v South Africa	Port Elizabeth	1993-94
9th	126*	Kapil Dev/S.M.H.Kirmani	India v Zimbabwe	Tunbridge Wells	1983
10th	106*	I.V.A.Richards/M.A.Holding	West Indies v England	Manchester	1984

BOWLING RECORDS
SIX WICKETS IN AN INNINGS

7-30	M.Muralitharan	Sri Lanka v India	Sharjah	2000-01
7-37	Aqib Javed	Pakistan v India	Sharjah	1991-92
7-51	W.W.Davis	West Indies v Australia	Leeds	1983
6-12	A.Kumble	India v West Indies	Calcutta	1993-94
6-14	G.J.Gilmour	Australia v England	Leeds	1975
6-14	Imran Khan	Pakistan v India	Sharjah	1984-85
6-15	C.E.H.Croft	West Indies v England	Kingstown	1980-81
6-18	Azhar Mahmood	Pakistan v West Indies	Sharjah	1999-00
6-19	H.K.Olonga	Zimbabwe v England	Cape Town	1999-00
6-20	B.C.Strang	Zimbabwe v Bangladesh	Nairobi	1997-98
6-23	A.A.Donald	South Africa v Kenya	Nairobi	1996-97
6-26	Waqar Younis	Pakistan v Sri Lanka	Sharjah	1989-90
6-29	B.P.Patterson	West Indies v India	Nagpur	1987-88
6-29	S.T.Jayasuriya	Sri Lanka v England	Moratuwa	1992-93
6-30	Waqar Younis	Pakistan v New Zealand	Auckland	1993-94
6-35	S.M.Pollock	South Africa v West Indies	East London	1998-99
6-39	K.H.MacLeay	Australia v India	Nottingham	1983
6-41	I.V.A.Richards	West Indies v India	Delhi	1989-90
6-44	Waqar Younis	Pakistan v New Zealand	Sharjah	1996-97
6-49	L.Klusener	South Africa v Sri Lanka	Lahore	1997-98
6-50	A.H.Gray	West Indies v Australia	Port-of-Spain	1990-91

The best for England is 5-15 by M.A.Ealham (v Z, Kimberley, 1999-00); for New Zealand 5-22 by M.N.Hart (v WI, Margao, 1994-95); for Bangladesh 4-36 by Saiful Islam (v SL, Sharjah, 1994-95); and for Kenya 5-33 by A.Y.Karim (v B, Nairobi, 1997-98).

150 WICKETS IN A CAREER

		LOI	O	R	W	Avge	Best	4w	R/Over
Wasim Akram	P	311	2659.5	10288	432	23.81	5-15	21	3.87
Waqar Younis	P	199	1636.2	7497	316	23.72	6-26	22	4.58
A.Kumble	I	208	1861.1	7828	274	28.56	6-12	9	4.20
Kapil Dev	I	225	1867	6945	253	27.45	5-43	4	3.72
J.Srinath	I	187	1629.1	7222	252	28.65	5-23	7	4.43
S.K.Warne	A	158	1456.3	6087	248	24.54	5-33	13	4.18
Saqlain Mushtaq	P	129	1127.1	4790	237	20.21	5-20	15	4.25
C.A.Walsh	WI	205	1803.4	6915	227	30.46	5- 1	7	3.83
M.Muralitharan	SL	159	1448	5865	225	26.06	7-30	9	4.05
C.E.L.Ambrose	WI	176	1558.5	5430	225	24.13	5-17	10	3.48
A.A.Donald	SA	131	1142	4650	217	21.42	6-23	11	4.07
C.J.McDermott	A	138	1243.5	5018	203	24.71	5-44	5	4.04
G.D.McGrath	A	130	1158.2	4601	194	23.71	5-14	10	3.97
B.K.V.Prasad	I	159	1339.3	6236	193	32.31	5-27	4	4.65
S.T.Jayasuriya	SL	228	1400.4	6754	192	35.17	6-29	8	4.82
S R Waugh	A	706	1161.3	6676	193	34.77	4-33	3	4.56
W.P.U.C.J.Vaas	SL	151	1225.1	5209	185	28.15	5-14	4	4.25
S.M.Pollock	SA	125	1093	4221	183	23.06	6-35	9	3.86
Aqib Javed	P	163	1335.3	5721	182	31.43	7-37	6	4.28
Imran Khan	P	175	1243.3	4845	182	26.62	6-14	4	3.90
C.L.Hooper	WI	182	1266.1	5547	163	34.03	4-34	3	4.38
Mushtaq Ahmed	P	143	1247.1	5296	161	32.89	5 36	4	4.25
R.J.Hadlee	NZ	115	1030 2	3407	158	21.56	5-25	6	3.31
M.Prabhakar	I	129	1060	4534	157	28.87	5-33	6	4.28
M.D.Marshall	WI	136	1195.5	4233	157	26.96	4-18	6	3.54
C.Z.Harris	NZ	173	1302.1	5654	157	36.01	5-42	3	4.34
H.H.Streak	Z	122	1026	4605	150	30.70	5-32	5	4.49

The most for England is 145 in 116 matches by I.T.Botham; for Bangladesh 28 (27) by Hasibul Hussain; and for Kenya 30 (33) by T.M.Odoyo.

HAT-TRICKS

Jalaluddin	Pakistan v Australia	Hyderabad	1982-83
B.A.Reid	Australia v New Zealand	Sydney	1985-86
C.Sharma	India v New Zealand	Nagpur	1987-88
Wasim Akram	Pakistan v West Indies	Sharjah	1989-90
Wasim Akram	Pakistan v Australia	Sharjah	1989-90
Kapil Dev	India v Sri Lanka	Calcutta	1990-91
Aqib Javed	Pakistan v India	Sharjah	1991-92
D.K.Morrison	New Zealand v India	Napier	1993-94
Waqar Younis	Pakistan v New Zealand	East London	1994-95
Saqlain Mushtaq	Pakistan v Zimbabwe	Peshawar	1996-97
E.A.Brandes	Zimbabwe v England	Harare	1996-97
A.M.Stuart	Australia v Pakistan	Melbourne	1996-97
Saqlain Mushtaq	Pakistan v Zimbabwe	The Oval	1999

WICKET-KEEPING RECORDS
SIX DISMISSALS IN AN INNINGS

6	(6 ct)	A.C.Gilchrist	Australia v South Africa	Cape Town	1999-00
6	(6 ct)	A.J.Stewart	England v Zimbabwe	Manchester	2000

100 DISMISSALS IN A CAREER
(Including catches taken in the field)

		LOI	Ct	St	Dis
Moin Khan	Pakistan	185	186	65	251
I.A.Healy	Australia	168	195	39	234
P.J.L.Dujon	West Indies	169	183	21	204
R.S.Kaluwitharana	Sri Lanka	153	108	65	173
A.C.Gilchrist	Australia	108	142	23	165
D.J.Richardson	South Africa	122	149	16	165
N.R.Mongia	India	140	112	44	156
A.Flower	Zimbabwe	169	119	30	149
A.J.Stewart	England	137	126	11	137
M.V.Boucher	South Africa	84	121	4	125
R.W.Marsh	Australia	92	120	4	124
Rashid Latif	Pakistan	101	94	28	122
A.C.Parore	New Zealand	158	93	24	117
R.D.Jacobs	West Indies	72	99	16	115
Salim Yousuf	Pakistan	86	80	22	102

FIELDING RECORDS
FIVE CATCHES IN AN INNINGS

5	J.N.Rhodes	South Africa v West Indies	Bombay	1993-94

100 CATCHES IN A CAREER
(Excluding catches taken while keeping wicket)

		LOI	Ct
M.Azharuddin	India	334	156
A.R.Border	Australia	273	127
R.S.Mahanama	Sri Lanka	213	109
S.R.Waugh	Australia	306	105
I.V.A.Richards	West Indies	187	105
M.E.Waugh	Australia	230	100

The most for England is 63 in 117 matches by G.A.Hick; for South Africa 87 (193) by J.N.Rhodes; for New Zealand 66 (143) by M.D.Crowe; for Pakistan 90 (250) by Ijaz Ahmed; and for Zimbabwe 61 (156) by A.D.R.Campbell.

ALL-ROUND RECORDS
50 RUNS AND 5 WICKETS IN A MATCH

I.V.A.Richards	119	5-41	West Indies v New Zealand	Dunedin	1986-87
K.Srikkanth	70	5-27	India v New Zealand	Vishakhapatnam	1988-89

I.V.A.Richards	119	5-41	West Indies v New Zealand	Dunedin	1986-87
M.E.Waugh	57	5-24	Australia v West Indies	Melbourne	1992-93
L.Klusener	54	6-49	South Africa v Sri Lanka	Lahore	1997-98
Abdur Razzaq	70*	5-48	Pakistan v India	Hobart	1999-00
G.A.Hick	80	5-33	England v Zimbabwe	Harare	1999-00
Shahid Afridi	61	5-40	Pakistan v England	Lahore	2000-01
S.C.Ganguly	71*	5-34	India v Zimbabwe	Kanpur	2000-01

1000 RUNS AND 100 WICKETS

		LOI	*Runs*	*Wkts*
Abdur Razzaq	Pakistan	69	1128	100
Azhar Mahmood	Pakistan	99	1073	101
I.T.Botham	England	116	2113	145
C.L.Cairns	New Zealand	137	3216	131
W.J.Cronje	South Africa	188	5565	114
R.J.Hadlee	New Zealand	115	1751	158
C.Z.Harris	New Zealand	173	3123	157
C.L.Hooper	West Indies	182	4612	163
Imran Khan	Pakistan	175	3709	182
S.T.Jayasuriya	Sri Lanka	228	6340	192
J.H.Kallis	South Africa	120	4081	107
Kapil Dev	India	225	3783	253
L.Klusener	South Africa	109	2537	134
Mudassar Nazar	Pakistan	122	2653	111
S.P.O'Donnell	Australia	87	1242	108
S.M.Pollock	South Africa	125	1372	183
M.Prabhakar	India	130	1858	157
I.V.A.Richards	West Indies	187	6721	118
R.J.Shastri	India	150	3108	129
H.H.Streak	Zimbabwe	122	1584	150
Wasim Akram	Pakistan	311	3256	432
S.R.Waugh	Australia	306	7089	192

APPEARANCE RECORDS
250 MATCHES

334	M.Azharuddin	India	273	A.R.Border	Australia
311	Wasim Akram	Pakistan	269	A.Ranatunga	Sri Lanka
306	S.R.Waugh	Australia	263	S.R.Tendulkar	India
283	Salim Malik	Pakistan	250	Ijaz Ahmed	Pakistan
275	P.A.de Silva	Sri Lanka			

The most for England is 137 by A.J.Stewart; for South Africa 193 by J.N.Rhodes; for New Zealand 173 by C.Z.Harris, and for Zimbabwe 169 by A.Flower.

100 MATCHES AS CAPTAIN

193	A.Ranatunga	Sri Lanka	138	W.J.Cronje	South Africa
178	A.R.Border	Australia	109	Wasim Akram	Pakistan
174	M.Azharuddin	India	108	I.V.A.Richards	West Indies
139	Imran Khan	Pakistan			

The most for England is 50 by G.A.Gooch; for New Zealand 87 by S.P.Fleming; and for Zimbabwe 76 by A.D.R.Campbell.

WORLD CUP FINALS

1975	WEST INDIES (291-8) beat Australia (274) by 17 runs	Lord's
1979	WEST INDIES (286-9) beat England (194) by 92 runs	Lord's
1983	INDIA (183) beat West Indies (140) by 43 runs	Lord's
1987-88	AUSTRALIA (253-5) beat England (246-8) by 7 runs	Calcutta
1991-92	PAKISTAN (249-6) beat England (227) by 22 runs	Melbourne
1995-96	SRI LANKA (245-3) beat Australia (241-7) by 7 wickets	Lahore
1999	AUSTRALIA (133-2) beat Pakistan (132) by 8 wickets	Lord's

WOMEN'S TEST CRICKET RECORDS

1934-35 to 1 January 2001

Compiled by Marion Collin

RESULTS SUMMARY

	Opponents	Tests				Won by						Drawn
			E	A	NZ	SA	WI	I	P	SL	Ire	
England	Australia	36	6	7	–	–	–	–	–	–	–	23
	New Zealand	22	6	–	0	–	–	–	–	–	–	16
	South Africa	4	1	–	–	0	–	–	–	–	–	3
	West Indies	3	2	–	–	–	0	–	–	–	–	1
	India	7	1	–	–	–	–	0	–	–	–	6
Australia	New Zealand	13	–	4	1	–	–	–	–	–	–	8
	West Indies	2	–	0	–	–	0	–	–	–	–	2
	India	8	–	3	–	–	–	0	–	–	–	5
New Zealand	South Africa	3	–	–	1	0	–	–	–	–	–	2
	India	5	–	–	0	–	–	0	–	–	–	5
Pakistan	Sri Lanka	1	–	–	–	–	–	–	0	1	–	–
	Ireland	1	–	–	–	–	–	–	0	–	1	–
		105	16	14	2	0	0	0	0	1	1	71

	Tests	Won	Lost	Drawn	Toss Won
England	72	16	7	49	45
Australia	59	14	7	38	18
New Zealand	43	2	10	31	21
South Africa	7	–	2	5	4
West Indies	5	–	2	3	4
India	20	–	4	16	11
Pakistan	2	–	2	–	1
Sri Lanka	1	1	–	–	1
Ireland	1	1	–	–	

TEAM RECORDS
HIGHEST INNINGS TOTALS

569-6d	Australia v England	Guildford	1998
525	Australia v India	Ahmedabad	1983-84
517-8d	New Zealand v England	Scarborough	1996
503-5d	England v New Zealand	Christchurch	1934-35
427-4d	Australia v England	Worcester	1998
426-9d	India v England	Blackpool	1986
414	England v New Zealand	Scarborough	1996
414	England v Australia	Guildford	1998
403-8d	New Zealand v India	Nelson	1994-95

The highest totals for countries not included above are:

282	West Indies v Australia	Montego Bay	1975-76
266-8d	South Africa v England	Cape Town	1960-61
193-3d	Ireland v Pakistan	Dublin	2000
171	Pakistan v Sri Lanka	Colombo	1997-98

LOWEST INNINGS TOTALS

35	England v Australia	Melbourne	1957-58
38	Australia v England	Melbourne	1957-58
44	New Zealand v England	Christchurch	1934-35
47	Australia v England	Brisbane	1934-35
53	Pakistan v Ireland	Dublin	2000

The lowest innings totals for countries not included above are:

67	West Indies v England	Canterbury	1979
89	South Africa v New Zealand	Durban	1971-72
92	India v Australia	Melbourne	1990-91

BATTING RECORDS

1000 RUNS IN TESTS

Runs			M	I	NO	HS	Avge	100
1935	J.A.Brittin	England	27	44	5	167	49.61	5
1594	R.Heyhoe-Flint	England	22	38	3	179	45.54	3
1301	D.A.Hockley	New Zealand	19	29	4	126*	52.04	4
1164	C.A.Hodges	England	18	31	2	158*	40.13	2
1110	S.Agarwal	India	13	23	1	190	50.45	4
1078	E.Bakewell	England	12	22	4	124	59.88	4
1007	M.E.Maclagan	England	14	25	1	119	41.95	2

HIGHEST INDIVIDUAL INNINGS

204	K.E.Flavell	NZ v E	Scarborough	1996
200	J.Broadbent	A v E	Guildford	1998
193	D.A.Annetts	A v E	Collingham	1987
190	S.Agarwal	I v E	Worcester	1986
189	E.A.Snowball	E v NZ	Christchurch	1934-35
179	R.Heyhoe-Flint	E v A	The Oval	1976
176*	K.L.Rolton	A v E	Worcester	1998
167	J.A.Brittin	E v A	Harrogate	1998
161*	E.C.Drumm	E v A	Christchurch	1994-95
160	B.A.Daniels	E v NZ	Scarborough	1996
158*	C.A.Hodges	E v NZ	Canterbury	1984
155*	P.F.McKelvey	NZ v E	Wellington	1968-69

5 HUNDREDS

		M	I			Opponents						
				E	A	NZ	SA	WI	I	P	SL	IRE
5	J.A.Brittin (E)	27	44	–	3	1	–	–	1	–	–	

HIGHEST PARTNERSHIP FOR EACH WICKET

1st	178	B.J.Haggett/B.J.Clark	A v I	Sydney	1990-91
2nd	235	E.A.Snowball/M.E.Hide	E v NZ	Christchurch	1934-35
3rd	309	L.A.Reeler/D.A.Annetts	A v E	Collingham	1987
4th	222	D.A.Annetts/L.A.Larsen	A v E	Sydney	1991-92
5th	135	E.R.Wilson/V.Batty	A v E	Adelaide	1957-58
6th	132	B.A.Daniels/K.M.Leng	E v NZ	Scarborough	1996
7th	110	K.Smithies/J.M.Chamberlain	E v A	Hove	1987
8th	181	S.J.Griffiths/D.L.Wilson	A v NZ	Auckland	1989-90
9th	107	B.Botha/M.Payne	SA v NZ	Cape Town	1971-72
10th	78	E.Barker/H.Hegarty	E v A	Adelaide	1957-58
	78	S.Gupta/S.Chakraborty	I v A	Lucknow	1983-84

BOWLING RECORDS
50 WICKETS IN TESTS

Wkts			M	Balls	Runs	Avge	Best
77	M.B.Duggan	E	17	3734	1039	13.49	7- 6
68	E.R.Wilson	A	11	2885	803	11.80	7- 7
60	M.E.Maclagan	E	14	3432	935	15.58	7- 10
57	R.H.Thompson	A	16	4304	1040	18.24	5- 33
55	J.Lord	NZ	15	3108	1049	19.07	6-119
50	E.Bakewell	E	12	2697	831	16.62	7- 61

TEN WICKETS IN A TEST

111-16	E.R.Wilson	A v E	Melbourne	1957-58
11-63	J.Greenwood	E v WI	Canterbury	1979
10-65	E.R.Wilson	A v NZ	Wellington	1947-48
10-75	E.Bakewell	E v WI	Birmingham	1979
10-107	K.Price	A v I	Lucknow	1983-84
10-118	D.A.Gordon	A v E	Melbourne	1968-69
10-137	J.Lord	NZ v A	Melbourne	1978-79

SEVEN WICKETS IN AN INNINGS

8-53	N.David	I v E	Jamshedpur	1995-96
7-6	M.B.Duggan	E v A	Melbourne	1957-58
7-7	E.R.Wilson	A v E	Melbourne	1957-58
7-10	M.E.Maclagan	A v E	Brisbane	1934-35
7-18	A.Palmer	A v E	Brisbane	1934-35
7-24	L.Johnston	A v NZ	Melbourne	1971-72
7-34	G.E.McConway	E v I	Worcester	1986
7-41	J.Burley	NZ v E	The Oval	1966
7-61	E.Bakewell	E v WI	Birmingham	1979

HAT-TRICK

E.R.Wilson	Australia v England	Melbourne	1957-58

WICKET-KEEPING AND FIELDING RECORDS
25 DISMISSALS IN TESTS

Total			Tests	Ct	St
58	C.Matthews	Australia	20	46	12
36	S.A.Hodges	England	11	19	17
28	B.Brentnall	New Zealand	10	16	12

EIGHT DISMISSALS IN A TEST

9 (8ct, 1 st)	C.Matthews	A v I	Adelaide	1990-91
8 (6ct, 2st)	L.Nye	E v NZ	New Plymouth	1991-92

SIX DISMISSALS IN AN INNINGS

8 (6ct, 2st)	L.Nye	E v NZ	New Plymouth	1991-92
6 (2ct, 4st)	B.Brentnall	NZ v SA	Johannesburg	1971-72

20 CATCHES IN THE FIELD IN TESTS

Total			Tests
25	C.A.Hodges	England	18
20	L.A.Fullston	Australia	12

APPEARANCE RECORDS
25 TEST MATCH APPEARANCES

27	J.A.Brittin	England	1979-98

214

TEST MATCH RESULTS SUMMARY

Series completed before 20 March 2001

Opponents	Tests	E	A	SA	WI	NZ	I	P	SL	Z	B	Tied	Drawn
					Won by							Tied	Drawn
England Australia	296	93	117	–	–	–	–	–	–	–	–	–	86
South Africa	120	50	–	23	–	–	–	–	–	–	–	–	47
West Indies	126	31	–	–	52	–	–	–	–	–	–	–	43
New Zealand	82	37	–	–	–	6	–	–	–	–	–	–	39
India	84	32	–	–	–	–	14	–	–	–	–	–	38
Pakistan	58	15	–	–	–	–	–	9	–	–	–	–	34
Sri Lanka	6	3	–	–	–	–	–	–	2	–	–	–	1
Zimbabwe	4	1	–	–	–	–	–	–	–	0	–	–	3
Australia South Africa	65	–	34	14	–	–	–	–	–	–	–	–	17
West Indies	95	–	42	–	31	–	–	–	–	–	–	1	21
New Zealand	38	–	18	–	–	7	–	–	–	–	–	–	13
India	57	–	28	–	–	–	11	–	–	–	–	1	17
Pakistan	46	–	18	–	–	–	–	11	–	–	–	–	17
Sri Lanka	13	–	7	–	–	–	–	–	1	–	–	–	5
Zimbabwe	1	–	1	–	–	–	–	–	–	0	–	–	–
South Africa West Indies	6	–	–	5	1	–	–	–	–	–	–	–	–
New Zealand	27	–	–	15	–	3	–	–	–	–	–	–	9
India	12	–	–	6	–	–	2	–	–	–	–	–	4
Pakistan	7	–	–	3	–	–	–	1	–	–	–	–	3
Sri Lanka	11	–	–	6	–	–	–	–	1	–	–	–	4
Zimbabwe	3	–	–	3	–	–	–	–	–	0	–	–	–
West Indies New Zealand	30	–	–	–	10	6	–	–	–	–	–	–	14
India	70	–	–	–	28	–	7	–	–	–	–	–	35
Pakistan	37	–	–	–	13	–	–	10	–	–	–	–	14
Sri Lanka	3	–	–	–	1	–	–	–	0	–	–	–	2
Zimbabwe	2	–	–	–	2	–	–	–	–	–	–	–	–
New Zealand India	40	–	–	–	–	7	14	–	–	–	–	–	19
Pakistan	39	–	–	–	–	5	–	18	–	–	–	–	16
Sri Lanka	18	–	–	–	–	7	–	–	4	–	–	–	7
Zimbabwe	11	–	–	–	–	5	–	–	–	0	–	–	6
India Pakistan	47	–	–	–	–	–	5	9	–	–	–	–	33
Sri Lanka	20	–	–	–	–	–	7	–	1	–	–	–	12
Zimbabwe	5	–	–	–	–	–	2	–	–	1	–	–	2
Bangladesh	1	–	–	–	–	–	1	–	–	–	0	–	–
Pakistan Sri Lanka	27	–	–	–	–	–	–	13	5	–	–	–	9
Zimbabwe	12	–	–	–	–	–	–	6	–	2	–	–	4
Sri Lanka Zimbabwe	10	–	–	–	–	–	–	–	5	0	–	–	5
	1529	262	265	75	138	46	63	77	19	3	0	2	579

	Tests	Won	Lost	Drawn	Tied	Toss Won
England	776	262	223	291	–	378
Australia	611	265	168	176	2	309
South Africa	251	75	92	84	–	117
West Indies	369	138	101	129	1	193
New Zealand	285	46	116	123	–	142
India	336	63	112	160	1	174
Pakistan	273	77	66	130	–	130
Sri Lanka	108	19	44	45	–	59
Zimbabwe	48	3	25	20	–	26
Bangladesh	1	–	1	–	–	1

TEST CRICKET RECORDS

To 20 March 2001 (excluding India v Australia series)

TEAM RECORDS
HIGHEST INNINGS TOTALS

952-6d	Sri Lanka v India	Colombo (RPS)	1997-98
903-7d	England v Australia	The Oval	1938
849	England v West Indies	Kingston	1929-30
790-3d	West Indies v Pakistan	Kingston	1957-58
758-8d	Australia v West Indies	Kingston	1954-55
729-6d	Australia v England	Lord's	1930
708	Pakistan v England	The Oval	1987
701	Australia v England	The Oval	1934
699-5	Pakistan v India	Lahore	1989-90
695	Australia v England	The Oval	1930
692-8d	West Indies v England	The Oval	1995
687-8d	West Indies v England	The Oval	1976
681-8d	West Indies v England	Port-of-Spain	1953-54
676-7	India v Sri Lanka	Kanpur	1986-87
674-6	Pakistan v India	Faisalabad	1984-85
674	Australia v India	Adelaide	1947-48
671-4	New Zealand v Sri Lanka	Wellington	1990-91
668	Australia v West Indies	Bridgetown	1954-55
660-5d	West Indies v New Zealand	Wellington	1994-95
659-8d	Australia v England	Sydney	1946-47
658-8d	England v Australia	Nottingham	1938
657-8d	Pakistan v West Indies	Bridgetown	1957-58
656-8d	Australia v England	Manchester	1964
654-5	England v South Africa	Durban	1938-39
653-4d	England v India	Lord's	1990
653-4d	Australia v England	Leeds	1993
652-7d	England v India	Madras	1984-85
652-8d	West Indies v England	Lord's	1973
652	Pakistan v India	Faisalabad	1982-83
650-6d	Australia v West Indies	Bridgetown	1964-65

The highest for South Africa is 622-9d (v A, Durban, 1969-70); for Zimbabwe 544-4d (v P, Harare, 1994-95); and for Bangladesh 400 (v I, Dhaka, 2000-01).

LOWEST INNINGS TOTALS

26	New Zealand v England	Auckland	1954-55
30	South Africa v England	Port Elizabeth	1895-96
30	South Africa v England	Birmingham	1924
35	South Africa v England	Cape Town	1898-99
36	Australia v England	Birmingham	1902
36	South Africa v Australia	Melbourne	1931-32
42	Australia v England	Sydney	1887-88
42	New Zealand v Australia	Wellington	1945-46
42	India v England	Lord's	1974
43	South Africa v England	Cape Town	1888-89
44	Australia v England	The Oval	1896
45	England v Australia	Sydney	1886-87
45	South Africa v Australia	Melbourne	1931-32
46	England v West Indies	Port-of-Spain	1993-94
47	South Africa v England	Cape Town	1888-89
47	New Zealand v England	Lord's	1958

The lowest for West Indies is 51 (v A, Port-of-Spain, 1998-99); for Pakistan 62 (v A, Perth, 1981-82); for Sri Lanka 71 (v P, Kandy, 1994-95); and for Zimbabwe 63 (v WI, Port-of-Spain, 1999-00), and for Bangladesh 91 (v I, Dhaka, 2000-01).

BATTING RECORDS
4000 RUNS IN A TEST CAREER

Runs			M	I	NO	HS	Avge	100	50
11174	A.R.Border	A	156	265	44	205	50.56	27	63
10122	S.M.Gavaskar	I	125	214	16	236*	51.12	34	45
8900	G.A.Gooch	E	118	215	6	333	42.58	20	46
8832	Javed Miandad	P	124	189	21	280*	52.57	23	43
8722	S.R.Waugh	A	132	210	39	200	51.00	24	42
8540	I.V.A.Richards	WI	121	182	12	291	50.23	24	45
8231	D.I.Gower	E	117	204	18	215	44.25	18	39
8114	G.Boycott	E	108	193	23	246*	47.72	22	42
8032	G.St A.Sobers	WI	93	160	21	365*	57.78	26	30
7624	M.C.Cowdrey	E	114	188	15	182	44.06	22	38
7558	C.G.Greenidge	WI	108	185	16	226	44.72	19	34
7525	M.A.Taylor	A	104	186	13	334*	43.49	19	40
7515	C.H.Lloyd	WI	110	175	14	242*	46.67	19	39
7487	D.L.Haynes	WI	116	202	25	184	42.29	18	39
7422	D.C.Boon	A	107	190	20	200	43.65	21	32
7280	M.A.Atherton	E	105	193	7	185*	39.13	16	43
7249	W.R.Hammond	E	85	140	16	336*	58.45	22	24
7110	G.S.Chappell	A	87	151	19	247*	53.86	24	31
6996	D.G.Bradman	A	52	80	10	334	99.94	29	13
6971	L.Hutton	E	79	138	15	364	56.67	19	33
6967	A.J.Stewart	E	105	189	14	190	39.81	14	35
6932	M.E.Waugh	A	108	179	14	153*	42.01	18	40
6868	D.B.Vengsarkar	I	116	185	22	166	42.13	17	35
6806	K.F.Barrington	E	82	131	15	256	58.67	20	35
6416	S.R.Tendulkar	I	79	125	13	217	57.28	24	24
6227	R.B.Kanhai	WI	79	137	6	256	47.53	15	28
6215	M.Azharuddin	I	99	147	9	199	45.03	22	21
6149	R.N.Harvey	A	79	137	10	205	48.41	21	24
6133	B.C.Lara	WI	75	131	4	375	48.29	15	30
6080	G.R.Viswanath	I	91	155	10	222	41.93	14	35
5949	R.B.Richardson	WI	86	146	12	194	44.39	16	27
5807	D.C.S.Compton	E	78	131	15	278	50.06	17	28
5768	Salim Malik	P	103	154	22	237	43.69	15	29
5755	P.A.de Silva	SL	86	148	11	267	42.00	18	21
5444	M.D.Crowe	NZ	77	131	11	299	45.36	17	18
5410	J.B.Hobbs	E	61	102	7	211	56.94	15	28
5357	K.D.Walters	A	74	125	14	250	48.26	15	33
5345	I.M.Chappell	A	75	136	10	196	42.42	14	26
5334	J.G.Wright	NZ	82	148	7	185	37.82	12	23
5248	Kapil Dev	I	131	184	15	163	31.05	8	27
5234	W.M.Lawry	A	67	123	12	210	47.15	13	27
5200	I.T.Botham	E	102	161	6	208	33.54	14	22
5138	J.H.Edrich	E	77	127	9	310*	43.54	12	24
5105	A.Ranatunga	SL	93	155	12	135*	35.69	4	38
5062	Zaheer Abbas	P	78	124	11	274	44.79	12	20
4976	M.J.Slater	A	67	118	6	219	44.42	14	20
4882	T.W.Graveney	E	79	123	13	258	44.38	11	20
4869	R.B.Simpson	A	62	111	7	311	46.81	10	27
4807	Inzamam-ul-Haq	P	70	116	12	200*	46.22	12	29

Runs			M	I	NO	HS	Avge	100	50
4737	I.R.Redpath	A	66	120	11	171	43.45	8	31
4656	A.J.Lamb	E	79	139	10	142	36.09	14	18
4556	G.Kirsten	SA	68	119	10	275	41.79	11	23
4555	H.Sutcliffe	E	54	84	9	194	60.73	16	23
4537	P.B.H.May	E	66	106	9	285*	46.77	13	22
4502	E.R.Dexter	E	62	102	8	205	47.89	9	27
4455	E.de C.Weekes	WI	48	81	5	207	58.61	15	19
4415	K.J.Hughes	A	70	124	6	213	37.41	9	22
4409	M.W.Gatting	E	79	138	14	207	35.55	10	21
4399	A.I.Kallicharran	WI	66	109	10	187	44.43	12	21
4389	A.P.E.Knott	E	95	149	15	135	32.75	5	30
4378	M.Amarnath	I	69	113	10	138	42.50	11	24
4356	I.A.Healy	A	119	182	23	161*	27.39	4	22
4334	R.C.Fredericks	WI	59	109	7	169	42.49	8	26
4236	R.A.Smith	E	62	112	15	175	43.67	9	28
4153	C.L.Hooper	WI	80	136	13	178*	33.76	9	18
4114	Mudassar Nazar	P	76	116	8	231	38.09	10	17
4095	D.J.Cullinan	SA	65	105	11	275*	43.56	12	18
3979	G.P.Thorpe	E	63	115	14	138	39.39	7	26

The most for Zimbabwe is 3625 by A.Flower (86 innings).

750 RUNS IN A SERIES

Runs			Series	M	I	NO	HS	Avge	100	50
974	D.G.Bradman	A v E	1930	5	7	–	334	139.14	4	–
905	W.R.Hammond	E v A	1928-29	5	9	1	251	113.12	4	–
839	M.A.Taylor	A v E	1989	6	11	1	219	83.90	2	5
834	R.N.Harvey	A v SA	1952-53	5	–	–	205	92.66	4	3
829	I.V.A.Richards	WI v E	1976	4	7	–	291	118.42	3	2
827	C.L.Walcott	WI v A	1954-55	5	10	–	155	82.70	5	2
824	G.St A.Sobers	WI v P	1957-58	5	8	2	365*	137.33	3	3
810	D.G.Bradman	A v E	1936-37	5	9	–	270	90.00	3	1
806	D.G.Bradman	A v SA	1931-32	5	5	1	299*	201.50	4	–
798	B.C.Lara	WI v E	1993-94	5	8	–	375	99.75	2	2
779	E.de C.Weekes	WI v I	1948-49	5	7	–	194	111.28	4	2
774	S.M.Gavaskar	I v WI	1970-71	4	8	3	220	154.80	4	3
765	B.C.Lara	WI v E	1995	6	10	1	179	85.00	3	3
761	Mudassar Nazar	P v I	1982-83	6	8	2	231	126.83	4	1
758	D.G.Bradman	A v E	1934	5	8	–	304	94.75	2	1
753	D.C.S.Compton	E v SA	1947	5	8	–	208	94.12	4	2
752	G.A.Gooch	E v I	1990	3	6	–	333	125.33	3	2

HIGHEST INDIVIDUAL INNINGS

375	B.C.Lara	WI v E	St John's	1993-94
365*	G.St A.Sobers	WI v P	Kingston	1957-58
364	L.Hutton	E v A	The Oval	1938
340	S.T.Jayasuriya	SL v I	Colombo (RPS)	1997-98
337	Hanif Mohammed	P v WI	Bridgetown	1957-58
336*	W.R.Hammond	E v NZ	Auckland	1932-33
334*	M.A.Taylor	A v P	Peshawar	1998-99
334	D.G.Bradman	A v E	Leeds	1930
333	G.A.Gooch	E v I	Lord's	1990
325	A.Sandham	E v WI	Kingston	1929-30
311	R.B.Simpson	A v E	Manchester	1964
310*	J.H.Edrich	E v NZ	Leeds	1965
307	R.M.Cowper	A v E	Melbourne	1965-66
304	D.G.Bradman	A v E	Leeds	1934

302	L.G.Rowe	WI v E	Bridgetown	1973-74
299*	D.G.Bradman	A v SA	Adelaide	1931-32
299	M.D.Crowe	NZ v SL	Wellington	1990-91
291	I.V.A.Richards	WI v E	The Oval	1976
287	R.E.Foster	E v A	Sydney	1903-04
285*	P.B.H.May	E v WI	Birmingham	1957
280*	Javed Miandad	P v I	Hyderabad	1982-83
278	D.C.S.Compton	E v P	Nottingham	1954
277	B.C.Lara	WI v A	Sydney	1992-93
275*	D.J.Cullinan	SA v NZ	Auckland	1998-99
275	G.Kirsten	SA v E	Durban	1999-00
274	R.G.Pollock	SA v A	Durban	1969-70
274	Zaheer Abbas	P v E	Birmingham	1971
271	Javed Miandad	P v NZ	Auckland	1988-89
270*	G.A.Headley	WI v E	Kingston	1934-35
270	D.G.Bradman	A v E	Melbourne	1936-37
268	G.N.Yallop	A v P	Melbourne	1983-84
267*	B.A.Young	NZ v SL	Dunedin	1996-97
267	P.A.de Silva	SL v NZ	Wellington	1990-91
266	W.H.Ponsford	A v E	The Oval	1934
266	D.L.Houghton	Z v SL	Bulawayo	1994-95
262*	D.L.Amiss	E v WI	Kingston	1973-74
261	F.M.M.Worrell	WI v E	Nottingham	1950
260	C.C.Hunte	WI v P	Kingston	1957-58
260	Javed Miandad	P v E	The Oval	1987
259	G.M.Turner	NZ v WI	Georgetown	1971-72
258	T.W.Graveney	E v WI	Nottingham	1957
258	S.M.Nurse	WI v NZ	Christchurch	1968-69
257*	Wasim Akram	P v Z	Sheikhupura	1996-97
256	R.B.Kanhai	WI v I	Calcutta	1958-59
256	K.F.Barrington	E v A	Manchester	1964
255*	D.J.McGlew	SA v NZ	Wellington	1952-53
254	D.G.Bradman	A v E	Lord's	1930
251	W.R.Hammond	E v A	Sydney	1928-29
250	K.D.Walters	A v NZ	Christchurch	1976-77
250	S.F.A.F.Bacchus	WI v I	Kanpur	1978-79

The highest for India is 236* by S.M.Gavaskar (v WI, Madras, 1983-84) and for Bangladesh 145 by Aminul Islam (v I, Dhaka, 2000-01).

18·HUNDREDS

						Opponents							
			200	I	E	A	SA	WI	NZ	I	P	SL	Z	B
34	S.M.Gavaskar	I	4	214	4	8	–	13	2	–	5	2	–	–
29	D.G.Bradman	A	12	80	19	–	4	2	–	4	–	–	–
27	A.R.Border	A	2	265	8	–	–	3	5	4	6	1	–	–
26	G.St A.Sobers	WI	2	160	10	4	–	–	1	8	3	–	–	–
24	S.R.Tendulkar	I	2	125	4	5	2	1	3	–	1	6	2	–
24	G.S.Chappell	A	4	151	9	–	–	5	3	1	6	–	–	–
24	I.V.A.Richards	WI	3	182	8	5	–	–	1	8	2	–	–	–
24	S.R.Waugh	A	1	210	7	–	2	6	2	1	2	3	1	–
23	Javed Miandad	P	6	189	2	6	–	2	7	5	–	1	–	–
22	W.R.Hammond	E	7	140	–	9	6	1	4	2	–	–	–	–
22	M.Azharuddin	I	–	147	6	2	4	–	2	–	3	5	–	–
22	M.C.Cowdrey	E	–	188	–	5	3	6	2	3	3	–	–	–
22	G.Boycott	E	1	193	–	7	1	5	2	4	3	–	–	–
21	R.N.Harvey	A	2	137	6	–	8	3	–	4	–	–	–	–
21	D.C.Boon	A	1	190	7	–	3	3	6	1	1	–	–	–

219

			Opponents											
			200	I	E	A	SA	WI	NZ	I	P	SL	Z	B
20	K.F.Barrington	E	1	131	–	5	2	3	3	4	–	–	–	–
20	G.A.Gooch	E	2	215	–	4	–	5	4	5	1	1	–	–
19	L.Hutton	E	4	138	–	5	4	5	3	2	–	–	–	–
19	C.H.Lloyd	WI	1	175	5	6	–	–	–	7	1	–	–	–
19	C.G.Greenidge	WI	4	185	7	4	–	–	2	5	1	–	–	–
19	M.A.Taylor	A	2	186	6	–	2	1	2	2	4	2	–	–
18	P.A.de Silva	SL	1	148	1	1	–	–	2	5	8	–	1	–
18	M.E.Waugh	A	–	179	4	–	4	4	1	1	3	1	–	–
18	D.L.Haynes	WI	–	202	5	5	–	–	3	2	3	–	–	–
18	D.I.Gower	E	2	204	–	9	–	1	4	2	2	–	–	–

The most for South Africa is 12 by D.J.Cullinan (105 innings); for New Zealand 17 by M.D.Crowe (131); and for Zimbabwe 9 by A.Flower (86). The most double hundreds by batsmen not included above is 4 by Zaheer Abbas (12 hundreds for Pakistan) and 3 by R.B.Simpson (10 for Australia).

HIGHEST PARTNERSHIP FOR EACH WICKET

1st	413	V.Mankad/Pankaj Roy	I v NZ	Madras	1955-56
2nd	576	S.T.Jayasuriya/R.S.Mahanama	SL v I	Colombo (RPS)	1997-98
3rd	467	A.H.Jones/M.D.Crowe	NZ v SL	Wellington	1990-91
4th	411	P.B.H.May/M.C.Cowdrey	E v WI	Birmingham	1957
5th	405	S.G.Barnes/D.G.Bradman	A v E	Sydney	1946-47
6th	346	J.H.W.Fingleton/D.G.Bradman	A v E	Melbourne	1936-37
7th	347	D.St E.Atkinson/C.C.Depeiza	WI v A	Bridgetown	1954-55
8th	313	Wasim Akram/Saqlain Mushtaq	P v Z	Sheikhupura	1996-97
9th	195	M.V.Boucher/P.L.Symcox	SA v P	Johannesburg	1997-98
10th	151	B.F.Hastings/R.O.Collinge	NZ v P	Auckland	1972-73
	151	Azhar Mahmood/Mushtaq Ahmed	P v SA	Rawalpindi	1997-98

BOWLING RECORDS
200 WICKETS IN TESTS

Wkts			M	Balls	Runs	Avge	5 wI	10 wM
494	C.A.Walsh	WI	127	28444	12196	24.68	21	3
434	Kapil Dev	I	131	27740	12867	29.64	23	2
431	R.J.Hadlee	NZ	86	21918	9612	22.29	36	9
409	Wasim Akram	P	100	21975	9478	23.17	25	5
405	C.E.L.Ambrose	WI	98	22104	8500	20.98	22	3
383	I.T.Botham	E	102	21815	10878	28.40	27	4
376	M.D.Marshall	WI	81	17584	7876	20.94	22	4
366	S.K.Warne	A	84	23501	9505	25.96	16	4
362	Imran Khan	P	88	19458	8258	22.81	23	6
355	D.K.Lillee	A	70	18467	8493	23.92	23	7
325	R.G.D.Willis	E	90	17357	8190	25.20	16	–
313	Waqar Younis	P	68	13218	7045	22.50	21	5
311	A.A.Donald	SA	65	14155	6679	21.47	20	3
309	G.D.McGrath	A	65	15966	6817	22.06	18	3
309	L.R.Gibbs	WI	79	27115	8989	29.09	18	2
307	F.S.Trueman	E	67	15178	6625	21.57	17	3
303	M.Muralitharan	SL	59	18881	7702	25.41	24	5
297	D.L.Underwood	E	86	21862	7674	25.83	17	6
291	C.J.McDermott	A	71	16586	8332	28.63	14	2
276	A.Kumble	I	61	19115	7728	28.00	16	3
266	B.S.Bedi	I	67	21364	7637	28.71	14	1
259	J.Garner	WI	58	13169	5433	20.97	7	–
252	J.B.Statham	E	70	16056	6261	24.84	9	1
249	M.A.Holding	WI	60	12680	5898	23.68	13	2

Wkts			M	Balls	Runs	Avge	5 wI	10 wM
248	R.Benaud	A	63	19108	6704	27.03	16	1
246	G.D.McKenzie	A	60	17681	7328	29.78	16	3
242	B.S.Chandrasekhar	I	58	15963	7199	29.74	16	2
236	A.V.Bedser	E	51	15918	5876	24.89	15	5
236	Abdul Qadir	P	67	17126	7742	32.80	15	5
235	G.St A.Sobers	WI	93	21599	7999	34.03	6	–
228	R.R.Lindwall	A	61	13650	5251	23.03	12	–
216	C.V.Grimmett	A	37	14513	5231	24.21	21	7
212	M.G.Hughes	A	53	12285	6017	28.38	7	1
211	S.M.Pollock	SA	51	11059	4230	20.04	11	–
202	A.M.E.Roberts	WI	47	11136	5174	25.61	11	2
202	J.A.Snow	E	49	12021	5387	26.66	8	1
200	J.R.Thomson	A	51	10535	5601	28.00	8	–

The most for Zimbabwe is 138 in 36 Tests by H.H.Streak.

35 WICKETS IN A SERIES

Wkts		Series		M	Balls	Runs	Avge	5 wI	10 wM
49	S.F.Barnes	E v SA	1913-14	4	1356	536	10.93	7	3
46	J.C.Laker	E v A	1956	5	1703	442	9.60	4	2
44	C.V.Grimmett	A v SA	1935-36	5	2077	642	14.59	5	3
42	T.M.Alderman	A v E	1981	6	1950	893	21.26	4	–
41	R.M Hogg	A v E	1978-79	6	1740	527	12.85	5	2
41	T.M.Alderman	A v E	1989	6	1616	712	17.36	6	1
40	Imran Khan	P v I	1982-83	6	1339	558	13.95	4	2
39	A.V.Bedser	E v A	1953	5	1591	682	17.48	5	1
39	D.K.Lillee	A v E	1981	6	1870	870	22.30	2	1
38	M.W.Tate	E v A	1924-25	5	2528	881	23.18	5	1
37	W.J.Whitty	A v SA	1910-11	5	1395	632	17.08	2	–
37	H.J.Tayfield	SA v E	1956-57	5	2280	636	17.18	4	1
36	A.E.E.Vogler	SA v E	1909-10	5	1349	783	21.75	4	1
36	A.A.Mailey	A v E	1920-21	5	1465	946	26.27	4	2
36	G.D.McGrath	A v E	1997	6	1499	701	19.47	2	–
35	G.A.Lohmann	E v SA	1895-96	3	520	203	5.80	4	2
35	B.S.Chandrasekhar	I v E	1972-73	5	1747	662	18.91	4	–
35	M.D.Marshall	WI v E	1988	5	1219	443	12.65	3	1

The most for New Zealand is 33 by R.J.Hadlee (v A, 1985-86); for Sri Lanka 26 (twice) by M.Muralitharan (v P, 1999-00, and v SA, 2000-01); and for Zimbabwe 22 by H H.Streak (v P, 1994-95).

15 WICKETS IN A TEST († *On debut*)

19- 90	J.C.Laker	E v A	Manchester	1956
17-159	S.F.Barnes	E v SA	Johannesburg	1913-14
16-136†	N.D.Hirwani	I v WI	Madras	1987-88
16-137†	R.A.L.Massie	A v E	Lord's	1972
16-220	M.Muralitharan	SL v E	The Oval	1998
15- 28	J.Briggs	E v SA	Cape Town	1888-89
15- 45	G.A.Lohmann	E v SA	Port Elizabeth	1895-96
15- 99	C.Blythe	E v SA	Leeds	1907
15-104	H.Verity	E v A	Lord's	1934
15-123	R J.Hadlee	NZ v A	Brisbane	1985-86
15-124	W.Rhodes	E v A	Melbourne	1903-04

The best analysis for South Africa is 13-165 by H.J.Tayfield (v A, Melbourne, 1952-53); for West Indies 14-149 by M.A.Holding (v E, The Oval, 1976); for Pakistan 14-116 by Imran Khan (v SL, Lahore, 1981-82); and for Zimbabwe 11-257 by A.G.Huckle (v NZ, Bulawayo, 1997-98).

NINE WICKETS IN AN INNINGS

10- 53	J.C.Laker	E v A	Manchester	1956
10- 74	A.Kumble	I v P	Delhi	1998-99
9- 28	G.A.Lohmann	E v SA	Johannesburg	1895-96
9- 37	J.C.Laker	E v A	Manchester	1956
9- 52	R.J.Hadlee	NZ v A	Brisbane	1985-86
9- 56	Abdul Qadir	P v E	Lahore	1987-88
9- 57	D.E.Malcolm	E v SA	The Oval	1994
9- 65	M.Muralitharan	SL v E	The Oval	1998
9- 69	J.M.Patel	I v A	Kanpur	1959-60
9- 83	Kapil Dev	I v WI	Ahmedabad	1983-84
9- 86	Sarfraz Nawaz	P v A	Melbourne	1978-79
9- 95	J.M.Noreiga	WI v I	Port-of-Spain	1970-71
9-102	S.P.Gupte	I v WI	Kanpur	1958-59
9-103	S.F.Barnes	E v SA	Johannesburg	1913-14
9-113	H.J.Tayfield	SA v E	Johannesburg	1956-57
9-121	A.A.Mailey	A v E	Melbourne	1920-21

The best analysis for Zimbabwe is 8-109 by P.A.Strang (v NZ, Bulawayo, 2000-01).

HAT-TRICKS

F.R.Spofforth	Australia v England	Melbourne	1878-79
W.Bates	England v Australia	Melbourne	1882-83
J.Briggs	England v Australia	Sydney	1891-92
G.A.Lohmann	England v South Africa	Port Elizabeth	1895-96
J.T.Hearne	England v Australia	Leeds	1899
H.Trumble	Australia v England	Melbourne	1901-02
H.Trumble	Australia v England	Melbourne	1903-04
T.J.Matthews (2)[2]	Australia v South Africa	Manchester	1912
M.J.C.Allom[1]	England v New Zealand	Christchurch	1929-30
T.W.J.Goddard	England v South Africa	Johannesburg	1938-39
P.J.Loader	England v West Indies	Leeds	1957
L.F.Kline	Australia v South Africa	Cape Town	1957-58
W.W.Hall	West Indies v Pakistan	Lahore	1958-59
G.M.Griffin	South Africa v England	Lord's	1960
L.R.Gibbs	West Indies v Australia	Adelaide	1960-61
P.J.Petherick[1]	New Zealand v Pakistan	Lahore	1976-77
C.A.Walsh[3]	West Indies v Australia	Brisbane	1988-89
M.G.Hughes[3]	Australia v West Indies	Perth	1988-89
D.W.Fleming[1]	Australia v Pakistan	Rawalpindi	1994-95
S.K.Warne	Australia v England	Melbourne	1994-95
D.G.Cork	England v West Indies	Manchester	1995
D.Gough	England v Australia	Sydney	1998-99
Wasim Akram[4]	Pakistan v Sri Lanka	Lahore	1998-99
Wasim Akram[4]	Pakistan v Sri Lanka	Dhaka	1998-99
D.N.T.Zoysa[5]	Sri Lanka v Zimbabwe	Harare	1999-00
Abdur Razzaq	Pakistan v Sri Lanka	Galle	2000-01
G.D.McGrath	Australia v West Indies	Perth	2000-01

[1] On debut. [2] Hat-trick in each innings. [3] Involving both innings. [4] In successive Tests.
[5] His first 3 balls (second over of the match).

WICKET-KEEPING RECORDS
100 DISMISSALS IN TESTS

Total			Tests	Ct	St
395	I.A.Healy	Australia	119	366	29
355	R.W.Marsh	Australia	96	343	12
272†	P.J.L.Dujon	West Indies	81	267	5
269	A.P.E.Knott	England	95	250	19

Total			Tests	Ct	St
228	Wasim Bari	Pakistan	81	201	27
219	T.G.Evans	England	91	173	46
203†	A.J.Stewart	England	105	193	10
198	S.M.H.Kirmani	India	88	160	38
189	D.L.Murray	West Indies	62	181	8
187	A.T.W.Grout	Australia	51	163	24
176	I.D.S.Smith	New Zealand	63	168	8
174	R.W.Taylor	England	57	167	7
167†	A.C.Parore	New Zealand	67	160	7
165	R.C.Russell	England	54	153	12
152	D.J.Richardson	South Africa	42	150	2
149	M.V.Boucher	South Africa	37	145	4
141	J.H.B.Waite	South Africa	50	124	17
131†	Moin Khan	Pakistan	61	111	20
130	K.S.More	India	49	110	20
130	W.A.S.Oldfield	Australia	54	78	52
127†	A.Flower	Zimbabwe	48	121	6
114†	J.M.Parks	England	46	103	11
104	Salim Yousuf	Pakistan	32	91	13
101	N.R.Mongia	India	42	94	7

The most for Sri Lanka is 94 by R.S.Kaluwitharana (40 Tests).
† *Including catches taken in the field*

25 DISMISSALS IN A SERIES

28	R.W.Marsh	Australia v England		1982-83
27 (inc 2st)	R.C.Russell	England v South Africa		1995-96
27 (inc 2st)	I.A.Healy	Australia v England (6 Tests)		1997
26 (inc 3st)	J.H.B.Waite	South Africa v New Zealand		1961-62
26	R.W.Marsh	Australia v West Indies (6 Tests)		1975-76
26 (inc 5st)	I.A.Healy	Australia v England (6 Tests)		1993
26 (inc 1st)	M.V.Boucher	South Africa v England		1998
25 (inc 2st)	I.A.Healy	Australia v England		1994-95

TEN DISMISSALS IN A TEST

11	R.C.Russell	England v South Africa	Johannesburg	1995-96
10	R.W.Taylor	England v India	Bombay	1979-80
10	A.C.Gilchrist	Australia v New Zealand	Hamilton	1999-00

SEVEN DISMISSALS IN AN INNINGS

7	Wasim Bari	Pakistan v New Zealand	Auckland	1978-79
7	R.W.Taylor	England v India	Bombay	1979-80
7	I.D.S.Smith	New Zealand v Sri Lanka	Hamilton	1990-91
7	R.D.Jacobs	West Indies v Australia	Melbourne	2000-01

FIVE STUMPINGS IN AN INNINGS

5	K.S.More	India v West Indies	Madras	1987-88

FIELDING RECORDS
100 CATCHES IN TESTS

Total			Tests	Total			Tests
157	M.A.Taylor	Australia	104	120	I.T.Botham	England	102
156	A.R.Border	Australia	156	120	M.C.Cowdrey	England	114
144	M.E.Waugh	Australia	108	110	R.B.Simpson	Australia	62
122	G.S.Chappell	Australia	87	110	W.R.Hammond	England	85
122	I.V.A.Richards	West Indies	121	109	G.St A.Sobers	West Indies	93

Total			Tests	Total			Tests
108	S.M.Gavaskar	India	125	103	G.A.Gooch	England	118
105	I.M.Chappell	Australia	75	101	B.C.Lara	West Indies	75
105	M.Azharuddin	India	98				

The most for South Africa is 57 by D.J.Cullinan (65 Tests) and G.Kirsten (68); for New Zealand 86 by S.P.Fleming (57); for Pakistan 93 by Javed Miandad (124); for Sri Lanka 56 by R.S.Mahanama (52); and for Zimbabwe 48 by A.D.R.Campbell (48).

15 CATCHES IN A SERIES

15	J.M.Gregory	Australia v England		1920-21

SEVEN CATCHES IN A TEST

7	G.S.Chappell	Australia v England	Perth	1974-75
7	Yajurvindra Singh	India v England	Bangalore	1976-77
7	H.P.Tillekeratne	Sri Lanka v New Zealand	Colombo (SSC)	1992-93
7	S.P.Fleming	New Zealand v Zimbabwe	Harare	1997-98

FIVE CATCHES IN AN INNINGS

5	V.Y.Richardson	Australia v South Africa	Durban	1935-36
5	Yajurvindra Singh	India v England	Bangalore	1976-77
5	M.Azharuddin	India v Pakistan	Karachi	1989-90
5	K.Srikkanth	India v Australia	Perth	1991-92
5	S.P.Fleming	New Zealand v Zimbabwe	Harare	1997-98

APPEARANCE RECORDS
100 TEST MATCH APPEARANCES

156	A.R.Border	Australia	114	M.C.Cowdrey	England
132	S.R.Waugh	Australia	110	C.H.Lloyd	West Indies
131	Kapil Dev	India	108	M.E.Waugh	Australia
127	C.A.Walsh	West Indies	108	M.A.Atherton	England
125	S.M.Gavaskar	India	108	G.Boycott	England
124	Javed Miandad	Pakistan	108	C.G.Greenidge	West Indies
121	I.V.A.Richards	West Indies	108	A.J.Stewart	England
119	I.A.Healy	Australia	107	D.C.Boon	Australia
118	G.A.Gooch	England	104	M.A.Taylor	Australia
117	D.I.Gower	England	103	Salim Malik	Pakistan
116	D.L.Haynes	West Indies	102	I.T.Botham	England
116	D.B.Vengsarkar	India	100	Wasim Akram	Pakistan

The most for South Africa is 68 by W.J.Cronje and G.Kirsten; for New Zealand 86 by R.J.Hadlee; for Sri Lanka 93 by A.Ranatunga; and for Zimbabwe 48 by A.D.R.Campbell and A.Flower.

100 CONSECUTIVE TEST APPEARANCES

153	A.R.Border	Australia	March 1979 to March 1994
106	S.M.Gavaskar	India	January 1975 to February 1987

75 TESTS AS CAPTAIN

93	A.R.Border	Australia	December 1984 to March 1994

50 TEST UMPIRING APPEARANCES

66	H.D.Bird	July 1973 to June 1996
54	D.R.Shepherd	August 1985 to November 2000
54	S.A.Bucknor	April 1989 to December 2000

INDIA v SOUTH AFRICA (1st Test)

At Wankhede Stadium, Bombay, on 24, 25, 26 February 2000.
Toss: India. Result: **SOUTH AFRICA** won by four wickets.
Debuts: India – W.Jaffer, M.Kartik; South Africa – N.Boje.

INDIA

W.Jaffer	b Donald	4		c Klusener b Pollock	6
V.V.S.Laxman	c Eksteen b Kallis	16		c Boucher b Donald	0
R.Dravid	b Donald	22		b Pollock	37
*S.R.Tendulkar	c Boucher b Kallis	97		lbw b Cronje	8
S.C.Ganguly	c Strydom b Pollock	2		c Klusener b Pollock	31
A.Jadeja	c Pollock b Cronje	12		c Boucher b Donald	1
†N.R.Mongia	c Boucher b Cronje	0	(11)	not out	19
A.Kumble	run out	4	(7)	c Boucher b Cronje	4
A.B.Agarkar	not out	41	(8)	c Boucher b Cronje	3
J.Srinath	b Kallis	0		run out	0
M.Kartik	b Pollock	14	(9)	c Boucher b Pollock	2
Extras	(LB 7, W 1, NB 5)	13		(LB 1, NB 1)	2
Total		**225**			**113**

SOUTH AFRICA

G.Kirsten	b Tendulkar	50		c Mongia b Kumble	20
H.H.Gibbs	c Ganguly b Tendulkar	47		c Dravid b Kumble	46
J.H.Kallis	c Laxman b Kumble	5		not out	36
*W.J.Cronje	c Laxman b Kumble	0		run out	13
P.C.Strydom	c Agarkar b Kartik	2		c Ganguly b Kartik	3
L.Klusener	c Laxman b Srinath	33		c Srinath b Kumble	1
S.M.Pollock	c Jadeja b Tendulkar	0		lbw b Kumble	5
†M.V.Boucher	c Mongia b Kartik	3		not out	27
N.Boje	b Srinath	14			
C.E.Eksteen	b Srinath	4			
A.A.Donald	not out	1			
Extras	(B 8, LB 8, NB 1)	17		(LB 13)	13
Total		**176**		**(6 wickets)**	**164**

SOUTH AFRICA	O	M	R	W		O	M	R	W
Donald	16	6	23	2		14	6	23	2
Pollock	19.2	6	43	2		12.2	6	24	4
Klusener	10	0	53	0					
Kallis	16	8	30	3	(3)	5	1	21	0
Eksteen	6	0	26	0		7	3	21	0
Boje	5	0	17	0					
Cronje	7	1	20	2	(4)	12	5	23	3
INDIA									
Srinath	12	1	45	3		11	3	26	0
Agarkar	7	1	15	0		4	1	15	0
Kumble	22	1	62	2		28	12	56	4
Kartik	18	6	28	2		19	5	50	1
Tendulkar	5	1	10	3		1	0	4	0

FALL OF WICKETS				
	I	SA	I	SA
Wkt	1st	1st	2nd	2nd
1st	8	89	5	51
2nd	39	101	13	76
3rd	69	101	24	107
4th	96	104	73	110
5th	147	131	75	115
6th	151	131	80	128
7th	167	144	92	–
8th	173	169	92	–
9th	173	173	92	–
10th	225	176	113	–

Umpires: D.R.Shepherd (*England*) (50) and S.Venkataraghavan (36).
Referee: R.Subba Row (*England*) (33). **Test No. 1484/11 (I332/SA241)**

INDIA v SOUTH AFRICA (2nd Test)

At Chinnaswamy Stadium, Bangalore, on 2, 3, 4, 5, 6 March 2000.
Toss: India. Result: **SOUTH AFRICA** won by an innings and 71 runs.
Debuts: India – N.Chopra, M.Kaif.

INDIA

W.Jaffer	c Boucher b Hayward	13	(2)	c Kallis b Boje	23
R.Dravid	c Boucher b Cronje	17	(1)	c Pollock b Boje	18
S.C.Ganguly	lbw b Pollock	1		lbw b Boje	13
*S.R.Tendulkar	c Cronje b Hayward	21		c Gibbs b Donald	20
M.Azharuddin	c Klusener b Donald	9		c Kirsten b Pollock	102
M.Kaif	lbw b Kallis	12		lbw b Kallis	23
†N.R.Mongia	lbw b Boje	20		absent hurt	–
A.Kumble	not out	36	(7)	lbw b Boje	28
N.Chopra	c Pollock b Boje	4	(8)	c Boucher b Donald	3
M.Kartik	run out	0	(9)	c Gibbs b Boje	2
J.Srinath	c Gibbs b Pollock	4	(10)	not out	1
Extras	(B 8, LB 8, NB 5)	21		(B 8, LB 5, NB 4)	17
Total		**158**			**250**

SOUTH AFRICA

G.Kirsten	c Jaffer b Kumble	79
H.H.Gibbs	lbw b Kumble	4
N.Boje	b Kumble	85
J.H.Kallis	c Jaffer b Kumble	95
D.J.Cullinan	c Jaffer b Kumble	53
L.Klusener	c Tendulkar b Kartik	97
*W.J.Cronje	b Srinath	12
S.M.Pollock	c Tendulkar b Kartik	1
†M.V.Boucher	b Kartik	15
A.A.Donald	lbw b Kumble	7
M.Hayward	not out	0
Extras	(B 24, LB 3, NB 4)	31
Total		**479**

SOUTH AFRICA	O	M	R	W		O	M	R	W		FALL OF WICKETS		
Donald	14	2	31	1		14	5	56	2			I	SA	I
Pollock	17.3	5	26	2		24	14	40	1		Wkt	1st	1st	2nd
Hayward	15	2	40	2		16	4	31	0		1st	29	10	47
Cronje	12	6	17	1	(5)	3	0	17	0		2nd	30	171	48
Kallis	9	5	18	1	(6)	3	0	10	1		3rd	58	186	71
Boje	15	7	10	2	(4)	38	14	83	5		4th	69	271	95
											5th	77	435	144
INDIA											6th	104	441	240
Srinath	30	6	53	1							7th	114	449	244
Kumble	68.4	15	143	6							8th	138	468	246
Chopra	24	3	78	0							9th	139	477	250
Kartik	50	11	123	3							10th	158	479	–
Tendulkar	10	2	33	0										
Ganguly	6	1	18	0										
Kaif	3	0	4	0										

Umpires: A.V.Jayaprakash (4) and R.B.Tiffin (*Zimbabwe*) (14).
Referee: R.Subba Row (*England*) (34).   **Test No.1485/12 (I333/SA242)**

INDIA v SOUTH AFRICA 1999-2000

INDIA – BATTING AND FIELDING

	M	I	NO	HS	Runs	Avge	100	50	Ct/St
M.Azharuddin	1	2	–	102	111	55.50	1	–	–
A.B.Agarkar	1	2	1	41*	44	44.00	–	–	1
S.R.Tendulkar	2	4	–	97	146	36.50	–	1	2
A.Kumble	2	4	1	36*	72	24.00	–	–	1
R.Dravid	2	4	–	37	94	23.50	–	–	1
N.R.Mongia	2	3	1	20	39	19.50	–	–	2
M.Kaif	1	2	–	23	35	17.50	–	–	–
S.C.Ganguly	2	4	–	31	47	11.75	–	–	2
W.Jaffer	2	4	–	23	46	11.50	–	–	3
V.V.S.Laxman	1	2	–	16	16	8.00	–	–	3
A.Jadeja	1	2	–	12	13	6.50	–	–	–
M.Kartik	2	4	–	14	18	4.50	–	–	1
N.Chopra	1	2	–	4	7	3.50	–	–	–
J.Srinath	2	4	1	4	5	1.66	–	–	1

INDIA – BOWLING

	O	M	R	W	Avge	Best	5wI	10wM
S.R.Tendulkar	16	3	47	3	15.66	3- 10	–	–
A.Kumble	118.4	28	261	12	21.75	6-143	1	–
J.Srinath	53	10	124	4	31.00	3- 45	–	–
M.Kartik	87	22	201	6	33.50	3-123	–	–

Also bowled: A.B.Agarkar 11-2-30-0; N.Chopra 24-3-78-0; S.C.Ganguly 6-1-18-0; M.Kaif 3-0-4-0.

SOUTH AFRICA – BATTING AND FIELDING

	M	I	NO	HS	Runs	Avge	100	50	Ct/St
J.H.Kallis	2	3	1	95	136	68.00	–	1	1
D.J.Cullinan	1	1	–	53	53	53.00	–	1	–
G.Kirsten	2	3	–	79	149	49.66	–	2	1
N.Boje	2	2	–	85	99	49.50	–	1	–
L.Klusener	2	3	–	97	131	43.66	–	1	3
H.H.Gibbs	2	3	–	47	97	32.33	–	–	3
M.V.Boucher	2	3	1	27*	45	22.50	–	–	10
W.J.Cronje	2	3	–	13	25	8.33	–	–	1
A.A.Donald	2	2	1	7	8	8.00	–	–	–
C.E.Eksteen	1	1	–	4	4	4.00	–	–	1
P.C.Strydom	1	2	–	3	5	2.50	–	–	1
S.M.Pollock	2	3	–	5	6	2.00	–	–	3
M.Hayward	1	1	1	0*	0	–	–	–	–

SOUTH AFRICA – BOWLING

	O	M	R	W	Avge	Best	5wI	10wM
W.J.Cronje	34	12	83	6	13.83	3- 23	–	–
S.M.Pollock	73.1	31	133	9	14.77	4- 24	–	–
N.Boje	58	21	110	7	15.71	5- 83	1	–
J.H.Kallis	36	17	79	5	15.80	3- 30	–	–
A.A.Donald	58	19	133	7	19.00	2- 23	–	–
M.Hayward	31	6	71	2	35.50	2- 40	–	–

Also bowled: C.E.Eksteen 13-3-47-0; L.Klusener 10-0-53-0.

PAKISTAN v SRI LANKA (1st Test)

At Rawalpindi Cricket Stadium on 26, 27, 28, 29 February, 1 March 2000.
Toss: Sri Lanka. Result: **SRI LANKA** won by two wickets.
Debuts: Pakistan – Younis Khan.

PAKISTAN

*Saeed Anwar	c Arnold b Vaas	23		b Vaas	84
Wajahatullah Wasti	c Arnold b Wickremasinghe	17		c Wickremasinghe b Zoysa	1
Aamir Sohail	c Kaluwitharana b Vaas	0		c Jayawardena b Muralitharan	24
Inzamam-ul-Haq	c Arnold b Wickremasinghe	44		c sub (U.D.U.Chandana) b Zoysa	20
Yousuf Youhana	c Arnold b Muralitharan	32		c Jayawardena b Muralitharan	18
Younis Khan	lbw b Wickremasinghe	12	(7)	c De Silva b Muralitharan	107
†Moin Khan	c Kaluwitharana b Wickremasinghe	21	(8)	lbw b Vaas	10
Abdur Razzaq	st Kaluwitharana b Muralitharan	9	(9)	c Kaluwitharana b Zoysa	3
Wasim Akram	c Wickremasinghe b Muralitharan	0	(10)	c Jayawardena b Muralitharan	79
Saqlain Mushtaq	not out	3	(11)	not out	2
Waqar Younis	c Ranatunga b Muralitharan	0	(6)	c and b Vaas	8
Extras	(LB 9, NB 12)	21		(B 4, LB 12, NB 18)	34
Total		**182**			**390**

SRI LANKA

M.S.Atapattu	c Wajahatullah b Waqar	8		c Saqlain b Waqar	10
*S.T.Jayasuriya	c Moin b Waqar	17		c Aamir b Razzaq	56
R.P.Arnold	c Moin b Waqar	26		c Saqlain b Waqar	6
P.A.de Silva	lbw b Saqlain	112		c Moin b Razzaq	21
D.P.M.deS.Jayawardena	run out	42		c Youhana b Saqlain	35
A.Ranatunga	b Razzaq	49		not out	29
†R.S.Kaluwitharana	lbw b Razzaq	0		not out	36
W.P.U.C.J.Vaas	not out	53		run out	0
G.P.Wickremasinghe	c sub (Shahid Afridi) b Saqlain	0	(10)	b Razzaq	0
D.N.T.Zoysa	c Youhana b Waqar	26	(9)	c Wasti b Razzaq	13
M.Muralitharan	st Moin b Aamir	7			
Extras	(B 2, LB 8, NB 3)	13		(B 1, LB 11, NB 2)	14
Total		**353**		(8 wickets)	**220**

SRI LANKA	O	M	R	W		O	M	R	W
Vaas	20	4	54	2		38	7	85	3
Zoysa	13	2	37	0		26	8	64	3
Wickremasinghe	20	5	37	4		24	4	76	0
Muralitharan	20.5	7	45	4		54.1	14	127	4
Arnold						1	1	0	0
De Silva						6	2	10	0
Jayasuriya						3	0	12	0

PAKISTAN	O	M	R	W		O	M	R	W
Wasim Akram	2.1	0	8	0					
Waqar Younis	30	3	103	4	(1)	24.5	6	78	2
Abdur Razzaq	32.5	7	99	2	(2)	26	6	56	4
Saqlain Mushtaq	34	9	78	2	(3)	33	7	74	1
Aamir Sohail	23.2	5	55	1					
Wajahatullah Wasti	1	1	0	0					

FALL OF WICKETS				
	P	SL	P	SL
Wkt	1st	1st	2nd	2nd
1st	44	9	9	16
2nd	46	38	72	34
3rd	59	69	136	73
4th	125	117	148	116
5th	135	246	169	144
6th	166	246	189	152
7th	167	280	224	177
8th	168	280	236	177
9th	179	331	381	–
10th	182	353	390	–

Umpires: Athar Zaidi (6) and D.L.Orchard (*South Africa*) (17).
Referee: B.F.Hastings (*New Zealand*) (1).   Test No. 1486/22 (P262/SL97)

PAKISTAN v SRI LANKA (2nd Test)

At Arbab Niaz Stadium, Peshawar, on 5, 6, 7, 8, 9 March 2000.
Toss: Pakistan. Result: **SRI LANKA** won by 57 runs.
Debuts: Pakistan – Atiq-uz-Zaman.

SRI LANKA

M.S.Atapattu	b Shoaib	75		c Aamir b Arshad	29
*S.T.Jayasuriya	b Shoaib	30		lbw b Waqar	6
R.P.Arnold	c Atiq b Razzaq	2		c Youhana b Arshad	99
P.A.de Silva	lbw b Aamir	33	(7)	c Waqar b Aamir	31
D.P.M.deS.Jayawardena	c Afridi b Aamir	36	(4)	lbw b Waqar	10
T.M.Dilshan	b Arshad	13	(5)	c Atiq b Aamir	7
†R.S.Kaluwitharana	c Atiq b Shoaib	4	(6)	lbw b Shoaib	0
W.P.U.C.J.Vaas	not out	17		c Youhana b Arshad	5
G.P.Wickremasinghe	b Shoaib	0	(10)	c Younis Khan b Shoaib	5
K.R.Pushpakumara	c Atiq b Razzaq	7	(9)	c Atiq b Waqar	14
M.Muralitharan	b Shoaib	22		not out	2
Extras	(B 1, LB 8, NB 20)	29		(B 4, LB 7, NB 5)	16
Total		**268**			**224**

PAKISTAN

*Saeed Anwar	c Muralitharan b Jayasuriya	74		c Wickremasinghe b Vaas	36
Aamir Sohail	c De Silva b Jayawardena	22	(4)	c Dilshan b Jayasuriya	0
Yousuf Youhana	c Kaluwitharana b Vaas	8	(5)	lbw b Muralitharan	88
Inzamam-ul-Haq	not out	58	(3)	c Jayawardena b Muralitharan	9
Younis Khan	c Jayawardena b Muralitharan	4	(6)	c Arnold b Vaas	6
Shahid Afridi	c Arnold b Vaas	4	(2)	st Kaluwitharana b Muralitharan	31
Abdur Razzaq	c Jayawardene b Muralitharan	0		lbw b Muralitharan	5
†Atiq-uz-Zaman	c Kaluwitharana b Wickremasinghe	1		b Vaas	25
Waqar Younis	c Jayawardena b Muralitharan	3		c Jayawardena b Muralitharan	0
Arshad Khan	lbw b Muralitharan	4		c Jayawardena b Muralitharan	5
Shoaib Akhtar	c Atapattu b Wickremasinghe	5		not out	4
Extras	(B 1, W 1, NB 14)	16		(B 9, LB 6, NB 12)	27
Total		**199**			**236**

PAKISTAN	O	M	R	W	O	M	R	W					
Waqar Younis	5	0	20	0	16	3	38	3		FALL OF WICKETS			
Shoaib Akhtar	24.3	3	75	5	12.2	1	47	2			SL	P	SL	P
Arshad Khan	45	18	70	1	20	3	81	3		Wkt	1st	1st	2nd	2nd
Abdur Razzaq	17	6	39	2	17	9	27	0		1st	58	54	7	59
Shahid Afridi	7	0	31	0						2nd	67	82	69	77
Aamir Sohail	11	1	24	2	(5) 8	3	20	2		3rd	121	137	90	82
SRI LANKA										4th	186	154	108	103
										5th	207	165	109	145
Vaas	20	3	44	2	16	3	69	3		6th	209	166	188	208
Pushpakumara	11	2	36	0	10	1	31	0		7th	221	174	201	222
Muralitharan	39	10	77	4	(4) 27.1	4	71	6		8th	223	177	206	222
Jayawardena	5	3	7	1						9th	241	177	222	226
Jayasuriya	3	1	9	1	(5) 5	1	28	1		10th	268	199	224	236
Wickremasinghe	10.5	4	25	2	(3) 12	5	22	0						

Umpires: J.H.Hampshire (*England*) (12) and Mohammad Nazir (3).
Referee: B.F.Hastings (*New Zealand*) (2).   Test No. 1487/23 (P263/SL98)

PAKISTAN v SRI LANKA (3rd Test)

At National Stadium, Karachi, on 12, 13, 14, 15 March 2000.
Toss: Sri Lanka. Result: **PAKISTAN** won by 222 runs.
Debuts: Pakistan – Irfan Fazil.

PAKISTAN

Naved Ashraf	b Pushpakamara	5		lbw b Muralitharan	27
Shahid Afridi	c Wickremasinghe b Muralitharan	74		b Pushpakamara	34
Ijaz Ahmed	lbw b Vaas	7		c Dilshan b Muralitharan	3
Inzamam-ul-Haq	run out	86		c Wickremasinghe b Muralitharan	138
Yousuf Youhana	c Wickremasinghe b Muralitharan	7	(6)	c Kaluwitharana b Pushpakamara	11
Younis Khan	lbw b Vaas	7	(7)	c Kaluwitharana b Wickremasinghe	61
*†Moin Khan	c De Saram b Wickremasinghe	6	(8)	c Arnold b Pushpakamara	70
Waqar Younis	c Dilshan b Muralitharan	16	(9)	c Dilshan b Muralitharan	39
Shoaib Akhtar	c Pushpakamara b Muralitharan	26	(5)	lbw b Vaas	0
Irfan Fazil	not out	1		c Jayasuriya b Pushpakamara	3
Mohammad Akram	c Atapattu b Jayasuriya	0		not out	1
Extras	(LB 2, NB 19)	21		(LB 16, NB 18)	34
Total		**256**			**421**

SRI LANKA

M.S.Atapattu	lbw b Waqar	3		c Moin b Mohammad Akram	23
*S.T.Jayasuriya	c Ijaz b Shoaib	24		lbw b Waqar	10
R.P.Arnold	c Younis Khan b Irfan	48		c Moin b Waqar	8
D.P.M.deS.Jayawardena	c Moin b Waqar	1		b Irfan	29
T.M.Dilshan	c Moin b Afridi	31		run out	5
†R.S.Kaluwitharana	run out	42		b Shoaib	33
S.I.de Saram	c Waqar b Afridi	5		lbw b Afridi	18
W.P.U.C.J.Vaas	not out	25		c Shoaib b Afridi	28
K.R.Pushpakamara	c Moin b Shoaib	1		c Irfan b Afridi	44
G.P.Wickremasinghe	b Shoaib	0		run out	0
M.Muralitharan	c Irfan b Mohammad Akram	14		not out	5
Extras	(B 10, LB 2, NB 21)	33		(B 1, LB 7, NB 17)	25
Total		**227**			**228**

SRI LANKA	O	M	R	W	O	M	R	W
Vaas	18	4	49	2	34	8	107	1
Pushpakamara	16	4	37	1	20.5	3	66	4
Wickremasinghe	13	2	64	1	26	7	82	1
Muralitharan	32	10	89	4	40	5	107	4
Jayasuriya	6.5	2	15	1	9	1	28	0
Arnold					4	0	15	0
PAKISTAN								
Waqar Younis	10	2	39	2	11	4	32	2
Shoaib Akhtar	18	4	52	3	13	1	64	1
Mohammad Akram	14.1	2	49	1	10	1	44	1
Irfan Fazil	4	0	35	1	4	0	30	1
Shahid Afridi	12	3	40	2	8	1	50	3

FALL OF WICKETS

	P	SL	P	SL
Wkt	1st	1st	2nd	2nd
1st	40	17	70	27
2nd	82	41	70	41
3rd	111	46	84	41
4th	135	100	106	59
5th	152	154	159	86
6th	164	164	283	121
7th	197	188	320	145
8th	247	206	408	191
9th	255	206	419	199
10th	256	227	421	228

Umpires: Riazuddin (6) and R.B.Tiffin (*Zimbabwe*) (15).
Referee: B.F.Hastings (*New Zealand*) (3).   **Test No. 1488/24 (P264/SL99)**

PAKISTAN v SRI LANKA 1999-2000

PAKISTAN – BATTING AND FIELDING

	M	I	NO	HS	Runs	Avge	100	50	Ct/St
Inzamam-ul-Haq	3	6	1	138	355	71.00	1	2	–
Saeed Anwar	2	4	–	84	217	54.25	–	2	–
Shahid Afridi	2	4	–	74	143	35.75	–	1	1
Younis Khan	3	6	–	107	201	33.50	1	1	2
Yousuf Youhana	3	6	–	88	164	27.33	–	1	4
Moin Khan	2	4	–	70	107	26.75	–	1	8/1
Shoaib Akhtar	2	4	1	26	35	11.66	–	–	1
Aamir Sohail	2	4	–	24	46	11.50	–	–	2
Waqar Younis	3	6	–	39	66	11.00	–	–	2
Abdur Razzaq	2	4	–	9	17	4.25	–	–	–

Played in one Test: Arshad Khan 0, 5; Atiq-uz-Zaman 1, 25 (5 ct); Ijaz Ahmed 7, 3 (1 ct); Irfan Fazil 1*, 3 (2 ct); Mohammad Akram 0, 1*; Naved Ashraf 5, 27; Saqlain Mushtaq 3*, 2* (2 ct); Wajahatullah Wasti 17, 1 (2 ct); Wasim Akram 0, 79.

PAKISTAN – BOWLING

	O	M	R	W	Avge	Best	5wI	10wM
Aamir Sohail	42.2	9	99	5	19.80	2- 20	–	–
Shoaib Akhtar	67.5	9	238	11	21.63	5- 75	1	–
Waqar Younis	96.5	18	310	13	23.84	4-103	–	–
Shahid Afridi	27	4	121	5	24.20	3- 50	–	–
Abdur Razzaq	92.5	28	221	8	27.62	4 56	–	–
Arshad Khan	65	21	151	4	37.75	3- 81	–	–
Mohammad Akram	24.1	3	93	2	46.50	1- 44	–	–
Saqlain Mushtaq	67	16	152	3	50.66	2- 78	–	–

Also bowled: Irfan Fazil 8-0-65-2; Wajahatullah Wasti 1-1-0-0; Wasim Akram 2.1-0-8-0.

SRI LANKA – BATTING AND FIELDING

	M	I	NO	HS	Runs	Avge	100	50	Ct/St
P.A.de Silva	2	4	–	112	197	49.25	1	–	2
W.P.U.C.J.Vaas	3	6	3	53*	128	42.66	–	1	1
R.P.Arnold	3	6	–	99	189	31.50	–	1	7
D.P.M.deS.Jayawardena	3	6	–	42	153	25.50	–	–	9
M.S.Atapattu	3	6	–	75	148	24.66	–	1	2
S.T.Jayasuriya	3	6	–	56	143	23.83	–	1	1
R.S.Kaluwitharana	3	6	1	42	115	23.00	–	–	7/2
M.Muralitharan	3	5	2	22	50	16.66	–	–	1
K.R.Pushpakumara	2	4	–	44	66	16.50	–	–	1
T.M.Dilshan	2	4	–	31	56	14.00	–	–	4
G.P.Wickremasinghe	3	6	–	5	5	0.83	–	–	6

Played in one Test: S.I.de Saram 5, 18 (1 ct); A.Ranatunga 49, 29* (1 ct); D.N.T.Zoysa 26, 13.

SRI LANKA – BOWLING

	O	M	R	W	Avge	Best	5wI	10wM
M.Muralitharan	213.1	50	516	26	19.84	6- 71	1	1
S.T.Jayasuriya	26.5	5	92	3	30.66	1- 9	–	–
W.P.U.C.J.Vaas	146	29	408	13	31.38	3- 69	–	–
D.N.T.Zoysa	39	10	101	3	33.66	3- 64	–	–
K.R.Pushpakumara	57.5	10	170	5	34.00	4- 66	–	–
G.P.Wickremasinghe	105.5	27	306	8	38.25	4- 37	–	–

Also bowled: R.P.Arnold 5-1-15-0; P.A.de Silva 6-2-10-0; D.P.M.deS.Jayawardena 5-3-7-1.

NEW ZEALAND v AUSTRALIA (1st Test)

At Eden Park, Auckland, on 11, 12, 13, 14 (*no play*), 15 March 2000.
Toss: Australia. Result: **AUSTRALIA** won by 62 runs.
Debuts: None.

AUSTRALIA

M.J.Slater	b Cairns	5	(2)	c Horne b Cairns	6
G.S.Blewett	c Astle b Wiseman	17	(1)	c Spearman b Vettori	8
J.L.Langer	st Parore b Wiseman	46		c Astle b Vettori	47
M.E.Waugh	not out	72		c Parore b Wiseman	25
*S.R.Waugh	c Spearman b Vettori	17		c and b Wiseman	10
D.R.Martyn	c Astle b Vettori	17		b Vettori	36
†A.C.Gilchrist	lbw b Wiseman	7		c Fleming b Vettori	59
S.K.Warne	c Fleming b Vettori	7		c Wiseman b Vettori	12
B.Lee	c Parore b Vettori	6		not out	6
C.R.Miller	b Cairns	0		st Parore b Vettori	8
G.D.McGrath	c Spearman b Vettori	8		lbw b Wiseman	1
Extras	(B 7, LB 4, NB 1)	12		(B 7, LB 4)	11
Total		**214**			**229**

NEW ZEALAND

M.J.Horne	c Blewett b McGrath	3		c Langer b Miller	11
C.M.Spearman	c Martyn b Lee	12		lbw b McGrath	4
M.S.Sinclair	lbw b Warne	8		lbw b Miller	6
P.J.Wiseman	b Lee	1	(11)	c Gilchrist b Warne	9
*S.P.Fleming	st Gilchrist b Miller	21	(4)	c Gilchrist b Miller	8
N.J.Astle	c M.E.Waugh b Warne	31	(5)	b Warne	35
C.D.McMillan	lbw b Warne	6	(6)	c Warne b Lee	78
C.L.Cairns	c Gilchrist b McGrath	35	(7)	c S.R.Waugh b Miller	20
†A.C.Parore	c Gilchrist b McGrath	11	(8)	c S.R.Waugh b Lee	26
D.L.Vettori	not out	15	(9)	c Warne b Miller	0
S.B.Doull	c Lee b McGrath	12	(10)	not out	5
Extras	(B 4, LB 1, NB 3)	8		(B 7, LB 7, NB 2)	16
Total		**163**			**218**

NEW ZEALAND	O	M	R	W		O	M	R	W
Cairns	18	0	71	2		4	1	13	1
Doull	14	6	21	0	(4)	5	1	8	0
Vettori	25	8	62	5		35	11	87	7
Wiseman	14	2	49	3	(2)	33.5	6	110	2
AUSTRALIA									
McGrath	11.1	2	33	4		23	8	33	1
Miller	22	8	38	1	(3)	18	5	55	5
Warne	22	4	68	3	(4)	20.3	4	80	2
Lee	7	4	19	2	(2)	12	4	36	2

FALL OF WICKETS

	A	NZ	A	NZ
Wkt	1st	1st	2nd	2nd
1st	10	5	7	15
2nd	77	25	46	25
3rd	78	25	67	25
4th	114	26	81	43
5th	138	80	107	121
6th	161	80	174	151
7th	184	102	202	195
8th	192	134	214	204
9th	193	143	226	204
10th	214	163	229	218

Umpires: B.F.Bowden (1) and S.Venkataraghavan (*India*) (37).
Referee: M.H.Denness (*England*) (3).   **Test No. 1489/36 (NZ277/A604)**

NEW ZEALAND v AUSTRALIA (2nd Test)

At Basin Reserve, Wellington, on 24, 25, 26, 27 March 2000.
Toss: New Zealand. Result: **AUSTRALIA** won by six wickets.
Debuts: None.

NEW ZEALAND

M.J.Horne	c Warne b Lee	4		b Lee	14
C.M.Spearman	c Gilchrist b Lee	4		c Langer b Miller	38
M.S.Sinclair	lbw b Miller	4		b Lee	0
*S.P.Fleming	c Miller b Warne	16		c Blewett b Miller	60
N.J.Astle	c M.E.Waugh b Warne	61		b Warne	14
C.D.McMillan	c Gilchrist b Lee	1		c M.E.Waugh b Warne	0
C.L.Cairns	c Blewett b Miller	109		lbw b McGrath	69
†A.C.Parore	c Gilchrist b Blewett	46		run out	33
D.L.Vettori	c Langer b Warne	27		c S.R.Waugh b Lee	8
S.B.Doull	c Slater b Warne	12		c S.R.Waugh b Warne	40
S.B.O'Connor	not out	2		not out	4
Extras	(B 1, LB 8, NB 3)	12		(B 3, LB 8, NB 3)	14
Total		**298**			**294**

AUSTRALIA

M.J.Slater	c Parore b McMillan	143	(2)	st Parore b Vettori	12
G.S.Blewett	c Astle b Doull	0	(1)	b Cairns	25
S.K.Warne	lbw b Vettori	7			
J.L.Langer	c Parore b Cairns	12	(3)	c Spearman b O'Connor	57
M.E.Waugh	c Sinclair b Cairns	3	(4)	not out	44
*S.R.Waugh	not out	151	(5)	c Fleming b O'Connor	15
D.R.Martyn	c Parore b McMillan	78	(6)	not out	17
†A.C.Gilchrist	c Parore b O'Connor	3			
B.Lee	lbw b O'Connor	0			
C.R.Miller	c and b McMillan	4			
G.D.McGrath	c and b Cairns	14			
Extras	(LB 1, NB 3)	4		(B 2, LB 2, W 3)	7
Total		**419**		**(4 wickets)**	**177**

AUSTRALIA	O	M	R	W	O	M	R	W
McGrath	17	4	60	0	22.2	11	35	1
Lee	17	2	49	3	23	6	87	3
Miller	20	2	78	2	21	5	54	2
Warne	14.5	1	68	4	27	7	92	3
Blewett	8	1	24	1	3	0	15	0
S.R.Waugh	4	0	10	0				

NEW ZEALAND	O	M	R	W	O	M	R	W
Cairns	26.3	2	110	3		13	2	45	1
Doull	19	3	78	1	(4)	10	2	35	0
Vettori	15	1	50	1		8	1	19	1
O'Connor	26	2	78	2	(2)	11	3	42	2
Astle	11	2	45	0	(6)	10.1	4	19	0
McMillan	23	10	57	3	(5)	2	0	13	0

FALL OF WICKETS

	NZ	A	NZ	A
Wkt	1st	1st	2nd	2nd
1st	4	8	46	22
2nd	9	29	46	83
3rd	18	47	69	110
4th	53	51	88	144
5th	66	250	88	—
6th	138	364	198	—
7th	247	375	205	—
8th	282	375	222	—
9th	287	386	276	—
10th	298	419	294	—

Umpires: D.M.Quested (4) and Riazuddin (*Pakistan*) (7).
Referee: M.H.Denness (*England*) (4).　　　　**Test No. 1490/37 (NZ278/A605)**

NEW ZEALAND v AUSTRALIA (3rd Test)

At Seddon Park, Hamilton, on 31 March, 1, 2, 3 April 2000.
Toss: Australia. Result: **AUSTRALIA** won by six wickets.
Debuts: New Zealand – D.R.Tuffey.

NEW ZEALAND

M.J.Horne	c Gilchrist b McGrath	12	run out		0
C.M.Spearman	c Gilchrist b McGrath	12	c Gilchrist b Lee		35
M.S.Sinclair	c Warne b Lee	19	lbw b Miller		24
*S.P.Fleming	lbw b Lee	30	c Gilchrist b Miller		2
N.J.Astle	lbw b Lee	0	c Gilchrist b Warne		26
C.D.McMillan	c Gilchrist b Lee	79	c M.E.Waugh b Warne		30
C.L.Cairns	c Martyn b Lee	37	b McGrath		71
†A.C.Parore	not out	12	c Gilchrist b McGrath		16
P.J.Wiseman	b Warne	1	c Gilchrist b Lee		16
D.R.Tuffey	c Gilchrist b McGrath	3	not out		1
S.B.O'Connor	c Gilchrist b McGrath	0	lbw b Lee		0
Extras	(B 5, LB 7, W 2, NB 13)	27	(LB 4, NB 4)		8
Total		**232**			**229**

AUSTRALIA

M.L.Hayden	c Parore b O'Connor	2	(2) c Spearman b Wiseman		37
M.J.Slater	lbw b O'Connor	2	(1) lbw b O'Connor		9
S.K.Warne	lbw b O'Connor	10			
J.L.Langer	b Cairns	4	(3) not out		122
M.E.Waugh	c Sinclair b Wiseman	28	(4) c Sinclair b Wiseman		18
*S.R.Waugh	c Fleming b Cairns	3	(5) retired hurt		18
D.R.Martyn	not out	89	(6) lbw b O'Connor		4
†A.C.Gilchrist	c Horne b Wiseman	75	(7) not out		0
B.Lee	c McMillan b Cairns	8			
G.D.McGrath	b O'Connor	7			
C.R.Miller	c Tuffey b O'Connor	2			
Extras	(B 4, LB 6, NB 12)	22	(LB 1, NB 3)		4
Total		**252**	(4 wickets)		**212**

AUSTRALIA	O	M	R	W		O	M	R	W
McGrath	21.5	8	58	4		20	7	50	2
Lee	23	8	77	5		18.4	2	46	3
Warne	20	5	45	1	(4)	25	11	61	2
Miller	11	4	28	0	(3)	20	5	58	3
Martyn	7	4	12	0					
S.R.Waugh						3	0	10	0

NEW ZEALAND									
Cairns	22	7	80	3		10	1	60	0
O'Connor	15.5	5	51	5		11	1	53	2
Tuffey	9	0	75	0	(4)	11	1	52	0
Astle	4	3	5	0					
Wiseman	11	3	31	2	(3)	9	1	42	2
McMillan					(5)	0.3	0	4	0

FALL OF WICKETS

	NZ	A	NZ	A
Wkt	1st	1st	2nd	2nd
1st	22	3	3	13
2nd	42	16	49	96
3rd	53	17	53	124
4th	53	25	71	190
5th	131	29	111	–
6th	208	104	130	–
7th	212	223	165	–
8th	224	233	220	–
9th	227	248	228	–
10th	232	252	229	–

Umpires: R.S.Dunne (35) and A.V.Jayaprakash (*India*) (5).
Referee: M.H.Denness (*England*) (5).   Test No. 1491/38 (NZ279/A606)

234

NEW ZEALAND v AUSTRALIA 1999-2000

NEW ZEALAND – BATTING AND FIELDING

	M	I	NO	HS	Runs	Avge	100	50	Ct/St
C.L.Cairns	3	6	–	109	341	56.83	1	2	1
C.D.McMillan	3	6	–	79	194	32.33	–	2	2
A.C.Parore	3	6	1	46	144	28.80	–	–	7/3
N.J.Astle	3	6	–	61	167	27.83	–	1	4
S.B.Doull	2	4	1	40	69	23.00	–	–	–
S.P.Fleming	3	6	–	60	137	22.83	–	1	4
C.M.Spearman	3	6	–	38	105	17.50	–	–	5
D.L.Vettori	2	4	1	27	50	16.66	–	–	–
M.S.Sinclair	3	6	–	24	61	10.16	–	–	3
M.J.Horne	3	6	–	14	44	7.33	–	–	2
P.J.Wiseman	2	4	–	16	27	6.75	–	–	2
S.B.O'Connor	2	4	2	4*	6	3.00	–	–	–

Played in one Test: D.R.Tuffey 3, 1* (1 ct).

NEW ZEALAND – BOWLING

	O	M	R	W	Avge	Best	5wI	10wM
D.L.Vettori	83	21	218	14	15.57	7- 87	2	1
S.B.O'Connor	63.5	11	224	11	20.36	5- 51	1	–
C.D.McMillan	25.3	10	74	3	24.66	3- 57	–	–
P.J.Wiseman	67.5	12	232	9	25.77	3- 49	–	–
C.L.Cairns	93.3	13	379	10	37.90	3- 80	–	–

Also bowled: N.J.Astle 25.1-9-69-0; S.B.Doull 48-12-142-1; D.R.Tuffey 20-1-127-0.

AUSTRALIA – BATTING AND FIELDING

	M	I	NO	HS	Runs	Avge	100	50	Ct/St
D.R.Martyn	3	6	2	89*	241	60.25	–	2	2
J.L.Langer	3	6	1	122*	288	57.60	1	1	3
S.R.Waugh	3	6	2	151*	214	53.50	1	–	4
M.E.Waugh	3	6	2	72*	190	47.50	–	1	4
A.C.Gilchrist	3	5	–	75	144	36.00	–	2	17/1
M.J.Slater	3	6	–	143	177	29.50	1	–	1
G.S.Blewett	2	4	–	25	50	12.50	–	–	3
S.K.Warne	3	4	–	12	36	9.00	–	–	4
G.D.McGrath	3	4	–	14	30	7.50	–	–	–
B.Lee	3	4	1	8	20	6.66	–	–	1
C.R.Miller	3	4	–	8	14	3.50	–	–	1

Played in one Test: M.L.Hayden 2, 37.

AUSTRALIA – BOWLING

	O	M	R	W	Avge	Best	5wI	10wM
B.Lee	100.4	26	314	18	17.44	5- 77	1	–
G.D.McGrath	115.2	40	269	12	22.41	4- 33	–	–
C.R.Miller	112	29	311	12	25.91	5- 55	1	–
S.K.Warne	129.2	32	414	15	27.60	4- 68	–	–

Also bowled: G.S.Blewett 11-1-39-1; D.R.Martyn 7-4-12-0; S.R.Waugh 7-0-20-0.

WEST INDIES v ZIMBABWE (1st Test)

At Queen's Park Oval, Port-of-Spain, Trinidad, on 16, 17, 18, 19, 20 March 2000.
Toss: Zimbabwe. Result: **WEST INDIES** won by 35 runs.
Debuts: West Indies – C.H.Gayle, W.W.Hinds; Zimbabwe – B.A.Murphy.

WEST INDIES

A.F.G.Griffith	lbw b Streak	0		lbw b Streak	0
S.L.Campbell	lbw b Streak	24		run out	23
C.H.Gayle	run out	33		b Streak	0
S.Chanderpaul	c A.Flower b Olonga	12		lbw b Streak	49
C.E.L.Ambrose	c A.Flower b Streak	7	(8)	c Johnson b Murphy	1
*J.C.Adams	lbw b Murphy	17	(5)	c Murphy b Olonga	27
W.W.Hinds	not out	46	(6)	run out	9
†R.D.Jacobs	c and b Murphy	10	(7)	lbw b Olonga	0
F.A.Rose	b Johnson	1		c A.Flower b Streak	9
R.D.King	lbw b Streak	2		c A.Flower b Streak	1
C.A.Walsh	lbw b Murphy	11		not out	0
Extras	(B 7, LB 6, NB 11)	24		(B 11, LB 6, W 3, NB 8)	28
Total		**187**			**147**

ZIMBABWE

N.C.Johnson	lbw b Ambrose	0	(2)	c Adams b Walsh	3
G.W.Flower	c Campbell b Walsh	0	(1)	b Walsh	26
T.R.Gripper	c Gayle b Ambrose	41		lbw b King	3
M.W.Goodwin	c Gayle b Walsh	20		c Jacobs b Rose	8
*†A.Flower	not out	113		c Jacobs b Rose	5
A.D.R.Campbell	c Jacobs b Ambrose	0		b Ambrose	6
S.V.Carlisle	b Ambrose	17		c Jacobs b Rose	3
H.H.Streak	c Campbell b Gayle	20		lbw b Rose	0
B.A.Murphy	lbw b Rose	1		not out	0
H.K.Olonga	b Gayle	2		c Chanderpaul b Ambrose	0
M.Mbangwa	b Gayle	0		b Ambrose	0
Extras	(B 2, LB 6, W 1, NB 13)	22		(LB 7, NB 2)	9
Total		**236**			**63**

ZIMBABWE	O	M	R	W		O	M	R	W
Streak	24	9	45	4		17	8	27	5
Olonga	18	7	44	1		13	3	28	2
Mbangwa	10	3	21	0		15	10	15	0
Johnson	13	4	26	1	(5)	4	0	18	0
Murphy	13.4	7	32	3	(4)	15	3	23	1
G.W.Flower	2	0	6	0	(7)	9	4	13	0
Gripper					(6)	2	0	6	0

WEST INDIES	O	M	R	W		O	M	R	W
Ambrose	25	13	42	4		11	6	8	3
Walsh	28	9	49	2		14	8	18	2
Rose	19	6	41	0	(4)	13	4	19	4
King	20	2	71	0	(3)	9	2	11	1
Gayle	5	2	25	3					

FALL OF WICKETS

	WI	Z	WI	Z
Wkt	1st	1st	2nd	2nd
1st	4	0	0	4
2nd	49	0	0	20
3rd	72	27	37	37
4th	81	144	115	47
5th	87	144	115	51
6th	121	164	118	57
7th	136	232	119	57
8th	149	233	142	62
9th	161	236	146	63
10th	187	236	147	63

Umpires: S.A.Bucknor (48) and G.Sharp (*England*) (11).
Referee: R.S.Madugalle (*Sri Lanka*) (25).

Test No. 1492/1 (WI355/Z40)

WEST INDIES v ZIMBABWE (2nd Test)

At Sabina Park, Kingston, Jamaica, on 24, 25, 26, 27, 28 March 2000.
Toss: Zimbabwe. Result: **WEST INDIES** won by ten wickets.
Debuts: None.

ZIMBABWE

G.W.Flower	c Jacobs b Walsh	2		c Campbell b Walsh	11
T.R.Gripper	c Walsh b King	11		c Jacobs b Walsh	0
M.W.Goodwin	run out	113		b King	9
N.C.Johnson	c Gayle b King	0	(6)	b Rose	29
*†A.Flower	b Rose	66		b King	10
B.A.Murphy	b Rose	0	(8)	not out	0
A.D.R.Campbell	lbw b King	1	(4)	lbw b Ambrose	22
S.V.Carlisle	c Jacobs b Walsh	44	(7)	lbw b Gayle	7
H.H.Streak	b King	2		absent hurt	–
B.C.Strang	c Jacobs b King	13	(9)	c Ambrose b Rose	3
H.K.Olonga	not out	22	(10)	c Hinds b Walsh	2
Extras	(B 4, LB 12, W 2, NB 16)	34		(LB 4, NB 5)	9
Total		**308**			**102**

WEST INDIES

A.F.G.Griffith	b Johnson	6	(2)	not out	54
S.L.Campbell	c Campbell b Murphy	48	(1)	not out	16
C.H.Gayle	c A.Flower b Olonga	13			
S.Chanderpaul	c A.Flower b Strang	12			
*J.C.Adams	not out	101			
W.W.Hinds	c Campbell b Murphy	14			
†R.D.Jacobs	c A.Flower b Olonga	27			
C.E.L.Ambrose	c Carlisle b Johnson	7			
F.A.Rose	c A.Flower b Johnson	69			
C.A.Walsh	c G.W.Flower b Johnson	0			
R.D.King	b Olonga	4			
Extras	(B 8, LB 18, NB 12)	38		(NB 5)	5
Total		**339**		(0 wickets)	**75**

WEST INDIES	O	M	R	W		O	M	R	W		FALL OF WICKETS			
												Z	WI	Z	WI
Ambrose	25	8	36	0		16	9	14	1		*Wkt*	*1st*	*1st*	*2nd*	*2nd*
Walsh	22.4	6	46	2		15.5	6	21	3		1st	5	37	12	–
King	23	8	51	5	(4)	10	1	30	2		2nd	40	69	14	–
Rose	24	8	69	2	(3)	12	5	24	2		3rd	40	85	37	–
Gayle	10	0	46	0		6	3	9	1		4th	216	85	48	–
Adams	9	2	32	0							5th	216	122	72	–
Chanderpaul	2	0	12	0							6th	222	161	90	–
											7th	228	170	96	–
ZIMBABWE											8th	234	318	100	–
Olonga	31.1	8	65	3	(3)	3	0	20	0		9th	254	318	102	–
Strang	36	17	43	1	(1)	3	0	21	0		10th	308	339	–	–
Johnson	37	14	77	4	(2)	5	1	27	0						
Murphy	36	12	99	2											
G.W.Flower	18	9	14	0	(4)	1	1	0	0						
Gripper	6	2	15	0	(5)	0.4	0	7	0						

Umpires: Athar Zaidi (*Pakistan*) (7) and E.A.Nicholls (10).
Referee: R.S.Madugalle (26).

Test No. 1493/2 (WI356/Z41)

WEST INDIES v ZIMBABWE 1999-2000

WEST INDIES – BATTING AND FIELDING

	M	I	NO	HS	Runs	Avge	100	50	Ct/St
J.C.Adams	2	3	1	101*	145	72.50	1	–	1
S.L.Campbell	2	4	–	48	111	37.00	–	–	3
W.W.Hinds	2	3	1	46*	69	34.50	–	–	1
F.A.Rose	2	3	–	69	79	26.33	–	1	–
S.Chanderpaul	2	3	–	49	73	24.33	–	–	1
A.F.G.Griffith	2	4	1	54*	60	20.00	–	1	–
C.H.Gayle	2	3	–	33	46	15.33	–	–	3
R.D.Jacobs	2	3	–	27	37	12.33	–	–	8
C.A.Walsh	2	3	1	11	11	5.50	–	–	1
C.E.L.Ambrose	2	3	–	7	15	5.00	–	–	1
R.D.King	2	3	–	4	7	2.33	–	–	–

WEST INDIES – BOWLING

	O	M	R	W	Avge	Best	5wI	10wM
C.E.L.Ambrose	77	36	100	8	12.50	4- 42	–	–
C.A.Walsh	80.3	29	134	9	14.88	3- 21	–	–
F.A.Rose	68	23	153	9	17.00	4- 19	–	–
C.H.Gayle	31	5	80	4	20.00	3- 25	–	–
R.D.King	62	13	163	8	20.37	5- 51	1	–

Also bowled: J.C.Adams 9-2-32-0; S.Chanderpaul 2-0-12-0.

ZIMBABWE – BATTING AND FIELDING

	M	I	NO	HS	Runs	Avge	100	50	Ct/St
A.Flower	2	4	1	113*	194	64.66	1	1	8
M.W.Goodwin	2	4	–	113	150	37.50	1	–	–
S.V.Carlisle	2	4	–	44	71	17.75	–	–	1
T.R.Gripper	2	4	–	41	55	13.75	–	–	–
G.W.Flower	2	4	–	26	39	9.75	–	–	1
H.K.Olonga	2	4	1	22*	26	8.66	–	–	–
N.C.Johnson	2	4	–	29	32	8.00	–	–	1
H.H.Streak	2	3	–	20	22	7.33	–	–	–
A.D.R.Campbell	2	4	–	22	29	7.25	–	–	2
B.A.Murphy	2	4	2	1	1	0.50	–	–	2

Played in one Test: M.Mbangwa 0, 0; B.C.Strang 13, 3.

ZIMBABWE – BOWLING

	O	M	R	W	Avge	Best	5wI	10wM
H.H.Streak	41	17	72	9	8.00	5- 27	1	–
B.A.Murphy	64.4	22	154	6	25.66	3- 32	–	–
H.K.Olonga	65.1	18	157	6	26.16	3- 65	–	–
N.C.Johnson	59	20	148	5	29.60	4- 77	–	–
B.C.Strang	39	17	64	1	64.00	1- 43	–	–

Also bowled: G.W.Flower 30-14-33-0; T.R.Gripper 8.4-2-28-0; M.Mbangwa 25-13-36-0.

WEST INDIES v PAKISTAN (1st Test)

At Bourda, Georgetown, Guyana, on 5, 6, 7, 8 (*no play*), 9 (*no play*) May 2000.
Toss: West Indies. Result: **MATCH DRAWN**.
Debuts: None.

PAKISTAN

Mohammad Wasim	b Ambrose	4
Wajahatullah Wasti	b Walsh	8
Younis Khan	lbw b Ambrose	2
Inzamam-ul-Haq	lbw b King	135
Yousuf Youhana	c Jacobs b Ambrose	0
*†Moin Khan	c Adams b King	6
Abdur Razzaq	c Gayle b McLean	87
Wasim Akram	c Jacobs b Walsh	16
Waqar Younis	b McLean	13
Saqlain Mushtaq	not out	8
Mushtaq Ahmed	c Gayle b Ambrose	4
Extras	(LB 2, NB 3)	5
Total		**288**

WEST INDIES

S.L.Campbell	c Younis Khan b Wasim	1
A F.G.Griffith	lbw b Razzaq	34
W.W.Hinds	st Moin b Mushtaq Ahmed	34
*J.C.Adams	c Younis Khan b Mushtaq Ahmed	20
S.Chanderpaul	not out	46
C.H.Gayle	c Wasim b Mushtaq Ahmed	13
†R.D.Jacobs	run out	6
N.A.M.McLean	c Inzamam b Waqar	46
C.E.L.Ambrose	not out	2
R.D.King		
C.A.Walsh		
Extras	(LB 2, NB 18)	20
Total	(7 wickets)	**222**

WEST INDIES	O	M	R	W
Ambrose	25.3	10	43	4
Walsh	28	10	46	2
McLean	26	5	93	2
King	26	7	57	2
Gayle	9	4	16	0
Adams	9	0	31	0
PAKISTAN				
Wasim Akram	20	6	46	1
Waqar Younis	15	3	46	1
Mushtaq Ahmed	32	5	91	3
Abdur Razzaq	10	2	13	1
Saqlain Mushtaq	10	1	24	0

FALL OF WICKETS

	P	WI
Wkt	*1st*	*1st*
1st	12	2
2nd	12	69
3rd	21	79
4th	21	106
5th	39	130
6th	245	139
7th	262	213
8th	266	–
9th	277	–
10th	288	

Umpires: S.A.Bucknor (49) and R.E.Koertzen (*South Africa*) (18).
Referee: P.J.P.Burge (*Australia*) (23).   **Test No. 1494/35 (WI357/P265)**

WEST INDIES v PAKISTAN (2nd Test)

At Kensington Oval, Bridgetown, Barbados, on 18, 19, 20, 21, 22 May 2000.
Toss: Pakistan. Result: **MATCH DRAWN**.
Debuts: West Indies – R.R.Sarwan.

PAKISTAN

Mohammad Wasim	c Adams b Walsh	4	lbw b King		82
Imran Nazir	c Campbell b Ambrose	2	c Adams b King		131
Younis Khan	c Chanderpaul b Walsh	0	c Jacobs b King		23
Inzamam-ul-Haq	c Adams b King	8	c and b Walsh		29
Yousuf Youhana	c Campbell b Walsh	115	c Adams b McLean		19
Abdur Razzaq	c Hinds b McLean	1	c sub (C.H.Gayle) b King		72
*†Moin Khan	c Chanderpaul b Walsh	38	b Adams		14
Wasim Akram	b Ambrose	42	c Hinds b Adams		0
Saqlain Mushtaq	c Campbell b Adams	12	b McLean		33
Waqar Younis	c Griffith b Walsh	14	not out		1
Mushtaq Ahmed	not out	2			
Extras	(B 2, LB 9, NB 4)	15	(LB 4, W 1, NB 10)		15
Total		**253**	(9 wickets declared)		**419**

WEST INDIES

S.L.Campbell	b Saqlain	58	c sub (Shahid Afridi) b Wasim		8
A.F.G.Griffith	c Moin b Waqar	4	lbw b Waqar		5
W.W.Hinds	c Inzamam b Waqar	165	c Moin b Mushtaq Ahmed		52
S.Chanderpaul	c Moin b Razzaq	9	c Mohammad Wasim b Mushtaq Ahmed		16
*J.C.Adams	c Younis Khan b Saqlain	8	not out		34
R.R.Sarwan	not out	84	not out		11
C.E.L.Ambrose	c Younis Khan b Wasim	22			
†R.D.Jacobs	b Saqlain	10			
N.A.M.McLean	c Youhana b Wasim	1			
R.D.King	c Mushtaq Ahmed b Saqlain	2			
C.A.Walsh	c Moin b Saqlain	22			
Extras	(LB 6, NB 7)	13	(B 1, LB 1, NB 4)		6
Total		**398**	(4 wickets)		**132**

WEST INDIES	O	M	R	W	O	M	R	W
Ambrose	21	7	53	2	37	16	54	0
Walsh	13	4	22	5	36	6	102	1
King	17	1	56	1	29	9	82	4
McLean	16	3	63	1	23.4	4	112	2
Adams	17	1	45	1	26	9	52	2
Chanderpaul	2	0	3	0	2	0	13	0
PAKISTAN								
Wasim Akram	33	9	84	2	7	1	24	1
Waqar Younis	17	2	72	2	4	0	14	0
Mushtaq Ahmed	22	2	65	0	(4) 20	5	64	2
Abdur Razzaq	16	3	50	1				
Saqlain Mushtaq	51	10	121	5	(3) 21	12	28	0

FALL OF WICKETS

	P	WI	P	WI
Wkt	1st	1st	2nd	2nd
1st	7	11	219	15
2nd	7	144	232	15
3rd	7	176	248	41
4th	34	213	294	113
5th	37	282	294	–
6th	110	321	341	–
7th	179	338	341	–
8th	220	339	411	–
9th	248	362	419	–
10th	253	398	–	–

Umpires: R.E.Koertzen (*South Africa*) (19) and E.A.Nicholls (11).
Referee: P.J.P.Burge (*Australia*) (24).   **Test No. 1495/36 (WI358/P266)**

WEST INDIES v PAKISTAN (3rd Test)

At Recreation Ground, St John's, Antigua, on 25, 26, 27, 28, 29 May 2000.
Toss: West Indies. Result: **WEST INDIES** won by one wicket.
Debuts: None.

PAKISTAN

Mohammad Wasim	c and b Rose	13	b King		21
Imran Nazir	c Rose b Ambrose	10	c Sarwan b Walsh		0
Younis Khan	c Jacobs b Ambrose	4	lbw b Ambrose		2
Inzamam-ul-Haq	c Griffith b Walsh	55	c Jacobs b Rose		68
Yousuf Youhana	not out	103	lbw b King		42
Abdur Razzaq	c Jacobs b Walsh	2	(8) run out		0
*†Moin Khan	c Jacobs b Rose	24	(6) c Hinds b King		10
Wasim Akram	c Campbell b King	26	(9) c Adams b King		24
Saqlain Mushtaq	c Campbell b Walsh	4	(7) c Campbell b Ambrose		15
Waqar Younis	c Sarwan b Walsh	4	c Adams b Ambrose		16
Mushtaq Ahmed	c Jacobs b Walsh	0	not out		3
Extras	(LB 4, NB 20)	24	(B 2, LB 4, NB 12)		18
Total		**269**			**219**

WEST INDIES

S.L.Campbell	c Youhana b Mushtaq Ahmed	31	c Youhana b Wasim		6
A.F.G.Griffith	b Mushtaq Ahmed	22	c Waqar b Wasim		23
W.W.Hinds	run out	26	b Wasim		63
S.Chanderpaul	b Wasim	89	lbw b Razzaq		31
*J.C.Adams	lbw b Waqar	60	not out		48
R.R.Sarwan	lbw b Wasim	10	lbw b Wasim		6
†R.D.Jacobs	lbw b Wasim	0	run out		5
F.A.Rose	c Razzaq b Wasim	15	c Wasim b Mushtaq Ahmed		4
C.E.L.Ambrose	c Youhana b Wasim	0	lbw b Saqlain		8
R.D.King	c and b Wasim	3	b Wasim		0
C.A.Walsh	not out	2	not out		4
Extras	(B 1, LB 10, NB 4)	15	(B 8, LB 7, NB 3)		18
Total		**273**	(9 wickets)		**216**

WEST INDIES	O	M	R	W	O	M	R	W
Ambrose	14	4	30	2	21	5	39	3
Walsh	26	2	83	5	20	4	39	1
Rose	19	4	48	2	20	2	69	1
King	16	3	48	1	23	6	48	4
Adams	14	2	40	0	6	1	18	0
Sarwan	2	0	16	0				

PAKISTAN	O	M	R	W	O	M	R	W
Wasim Akram	26.2	7	61	6	30	12	49	5
Waqar Younis	21	8	41	1	11	0	39	0
Mushtaq Ahmed	24	3	68	2	17	3	61	1
Saqlain Mushtaq	23	4	48	0 (5)	22	7	38	1
Abdur Razzaq	12	1	44	0 (4)	11	3	14	1

FALL OF WICKETS

Wkt	P 1st	WI 1st	P 2nd	WI 2nd
1st	21	40	0	16
2nd	27	73	3	31
3rd	33	84	49	84
4th	130	218	129	144
5th	132	235	150	161
6th	173	243	162	169
7th	209	254	163	177
8th	247	258	186	194
9th	268	269	213	197
10th	269	273	219	–

Umpires: D.B.Cowie (*New Zealand*) (16) and B.Doctrove (1).
Referee: P.J.P.Burge (*Australia*) (25).   **Test No. 1496/37 (WI359/P267)**

WEST INDIES v PAKISTAN 1999-2000

WEST INDIES – BATTING AND FIELDING

	M	I	NO	HS	Runs	Avge	100	50	Ct/St
W.W.Hinds	3	5	–	165	340	68.00	1	2	3
J.C.Adams	3	5	2	60	170	56.66	–	1	7
R.R.Sarwan	2	4	2	84*	111	55.50	–	1	2
S.Chanderpaul	3	5	1	89	191	47.75	–	1	2
C.A.Walsh	3	3	2	22	28	28.00	–	–	1
N.A.M.McLean	2	2	–	46	47	23.50	–	–	
S.L.Campbell	3	5	–	58	104	20.80	–	1	6
A.F.G.Griffith	3	5	–	34	88	17.60	–	–	2
C.E.L.Ambrose	3	4	1	22	32	10.66	–	–	
R.D.Jacobs	3	4	–	10	21	5.25	–	–	8
R.D.King	3	3	–	3	5	1.66	–	–	

Played in one Test: C.H.Gayle 13 (2 ct); F.A.Rose 15, 4 (2 ct).

WEST INDIES – BOWLING

	O	M	R	W	Avge	Best	5wI	10wM
C.E.L.Ambrose	118.3	42	219	11	19.90	4- 43	–	–
C.A.Walsh	123	26	292	14	20.85	5- 22	2	–
R.D.King	111	26	291	12	24.25	4- 48	–	–
F.A.Rose	39	6	117	3	39.00	2- 48	–	–
N.A.M.McLean	65.4	12	268	5	53.60	2- 93	–	–
J.C.Adams	72	13	186	3	62.00	2- 52	–	–

Also bowled: S.Chanderpaul 4-0-16-0; C.H.Gayle 9-4-16-0; R.R.Sarwan 2-0-16-0.

PAKISTAN – BATTING AND FIELDING

	M	I	NO	HS	Runs	Avge	100	50	Ct/St
Yousuf Youhana	3	5	1	115	279	69.75	2	–	4
Inzamam-ul-Haq	3	5	–	135	295	59.00	1	2	2
Imran Nazir	2	4	–	131	143	35.75	1	–	
Abdur Razzaq	3	5	–	87	162	32.40	–	2	1
Mohammad Wasim	3	5	–	82	124	24.80	–	1	1
Wasim Akram	3	5	–	42	108	21.60	–	–	3
Moin Khan	3	5	–	38	92	18.40	–	–	4/1
Saqlain Mushtaq	3	5	1	33	72	18.00	–	–	
Waqar Younis	3	5	1	16	48	12.00	–	–	1
Younis Khan	3	5	–	23	31	6.20	–	–	4
Mushtaq Ahmed	3	4	2	4	9	4.50	–	–	1

Played in one Test: Wajahatullah Wasti 8.

PAKISTAN – BOWLING

	O	M	R	W	Avge	Best	5wI	10wM
Wasim Akram	116.2	35	264	15	17.60	6- 61	2	1
Abdur Razzaq	49	9	121	3	40.33	1- 13	–	–
Waqar Younis	68	13	212	5	42.40	2- 72	–	–
Saqlain Mushtaq	127	34	259	6	43.16	5-121	1	–
Mushtaq Ahmed	115	18	349	8	43.62	3- 91	–	–

ENGLAND v ZIMBABWE (1st Test)

At Lord's, London, on 18, 19, 20, 21 May 2000.
Toss: England. Result: **ENGLAND** won by an innings and 209 runs.
Debuts: England – C.P.Schofield.

ZIMBABWE

G.W.Flower	b Caddick	4	lbw b Gough		2
T.R.Gripper	c Stewart b Caddick	1	c Knight b Gough		5
M.W.Goodwin	c Knight b Gough	18	lbw b Caddick		11
A.D.R.Campbell	c Stewart b Caddick	0	lbw b Gough		4
*†A.Flower	c Atherton b Giddins	24	(6) lbw b Gough		2
N.C.Johnson	c Gough b Giddins	14	(7) c Hick b Caddick		9
G.J.Whittall	b Giddins	15	(8) c Hick b Caddick		23
H.H.Streak	c Atherton b Giddins	4	(9) c Knight b Giddins		0
B.C.Strang	c Ramprakash b Giddins	0	(10) not out		37
B.A.Murphy	c Stewart b Gough	0	(5) lbw b Giddins		14
M.Mbangwa	not out	1	b Caddick		8
Extras	(LB 2)	2	(LB 1, NB 7)		8
Total		**83**			**123**

ENGLAND

M.A.Atherton	lbw b Streak	55
M.R.Ramprakash	lbw b Streak	15
*N.Hussain	c Murphy b Streak	10
G.A.Hick	lbw b Streak	101
†A.J.Stewart	not out	124
N.V.Knight	c Johnson b Whittall	44
A.Flintoff	c Streak b Whittall	1
C.P.Schofield	c Johnson b Whittall	0
A.R.Caddick	c A.Flower b Streak	13
D.Gough	c Campbell b Murphy	5
E.S.H.Giddins	c Strang b Streak	7
Extras	(B 5, LB 29, W 1, NB 5)	40
Total		**415**

ENGLAND	O	M	R	W		O	M	R	W
Gough	12.3	1	36	2		15	3	57	4
Caddick	8	3	28	3		16.2	5	38	4
Flintoff	3	2	2	0					
Giddins	7	2	15	5	(3)	7	3	27	2
ZIMBABWE									
Streak	35.5	12	87	6					
Strang	27	4	86	0					
Mbangwa	21	5	69	0					
Johnson	20	5	55	0					
Whittall	7	0	27	3					
Murphy	25	6	57	1					

FALL OF WICKETS

	Z	E	Z
Wkt	1st	1st	2nd
1st	5	29	2
2nd	8	49	7
3rd	8	113	18
4th	46	262	33
5th	48	376	36
6th	67	378	49
7th	77	378	74
8th	79	398	74
9th	82	407	92
10th	83	415	123

Umpires: D.L.Orchard (*South Africa*) (18) and P.Willey (19).
Referee: G.T.Dowling (*New Zealand*) (6).   Test No. 1497/3 (E767/Z42)

ENGLAND v ZIMBABWE (2nd Test)

At Trent Bridge, Nottingham, on 1, 2 (*no play*), 3, 4, 5 June 2000.
Toss: Zimbabwe. Result: **MATCH DRAWN**.
Debuts: Zimbabwe – M.L.Nkala.

ENGLAND

M.A.Atherton	c G.W.Flower b Mbangwa	136	(7)	c G.W.Flower b Whittall	34
M.R.Ramprakash	c G.W.Flower b Johnson	56		c A.Flower b Nkala	4
*N.Hussain	c Streak b Nkala	21		lbw b Nkala	0
G.A.Hick	c Murphy b Nkala	5		c A.Flower b Johnson	30
†A.J.Stewart	lbw b Whittall	9		c A.Flower b Johnson	15
N.V.Knight	lbw b Whittall	1	(1)	b Streak	6
A.Flintoff	lbw b Mbangwa	16	(6)	c A.Flower b Streak	16
C.P.Schofield	b Murphy	57		c Campbell b Murphy	10
A.R.Caddick	c G.W.Flower b Nkala	13		c A.Flower b Whittall	12
D.Gough	c Campbell b Streak	9		c Murphy b Whittall	3
E.S.H.Giddins	not out	3		not out	0
Extras	(B 9, LB 13, W 16, NB 10)	48		(B 5, LB 8, W 1, NB 3)	17
Total		**374**			**147**

ZIMBABWE

G.W.Flower	c Ramprakash b Gough	0		c Hick b Caddick	12
G.J.Whittall	lbw b Giddins	28		not out	12
M.W.Goodwin	not out	148		not out	1
N.C.Johnson	c Stewart b Gough	51			
*†A.Flower	b Gough	42			
B.A.Murphy	not out	0			
S.V.Carlisle					
A.D.R.Campbell					
H.H.Streak					
M.L.Nkala					
M.Mbangwa					
Extras	(B 5, LB 5, NB 6)	16			
Total	(4 wickets declared)	**285**	(1 wicket)		**25**

ZIMBABWE	O	M	R	W		O	M	R	W	FALL OF WICKETS			
Streak	32	7	82	1		17	8	13	2		E	Z	E	Z
Nkala	31	7	82	3		11	5	22	2	*Wkt*	*1st*	*1st*	*2nd*	*2nd*
Johnson	22	7	63	1		12	2	41	2	1st	121	1	6	17
Mbangwa	18	6	40	2		15	8	25	0	2nd	182	33	6	–
Murphy	12.2	1	36	1	(6)	12	6	19	1	3rd	188	162	12	–
Whittall	19	7	47	2	(5)	8	3	14	3	4th	209	284	44	–
G.W.Flower	1	0	2	0						5th	221	–	73	–
										6th	264	–	95	–
ENGLAND										7th	303	–	110	–
Gough	20	2	66	3		2	0	15	0	8th	335	–	139	–
Caddick	18.3	4	57	0		2	1	9	1	9th	358	–	140	–
Giddins	16	5	46	1						10th	374	–	147	–
Schofield	18	2	73	0										
Flintoff	10	3	33	0										
Ramprakash					(3)	1	0	1	0					

Umpires: M.J.Kitchen (20) and D.L.Orchard (*South Africa*) (19).
Referee: G.T.Dowling (*New Zealand*) (7).   Test No. 1498/4 (E768/Z43)

ENGLAND v ZIMBABWE 2000

ENGLAND – BATTING AND FIELDING

	M	I	NO	HS	Runs	Avge	100	50	Ct/St
M.A.Atherton	2	3	–	136	225	75.00	1	1	2
A.J.Stewart	2	3	1	124*	148	74.00	1	–	4
G.A.Hick	2	3	–	101	136	45.33	1	–	3
M.R.Ramprakash	2	3	–	56	75	25.00	–	1	2
C.P.Schofield	2	3	–	57	67	22.33	–	1	–
N.V.Knight	2	3	–	44	51	17.00	–	–	3
A.R.Caddick	2	3	–	13	38	12.66	–	–	–
A.Flintoff	2	3	–	16	33	11.00	–	–	–
N.Hussain	2	3	–	21	31	10.33	–	–	–
E.S.H.Giddins	2	3	2	7	10	10.00	–	–	–
D.Gough	2	3	–	9	17	5.66	–	–	1

ENGLAND – BOWLING

	O	M	R	W	Avge	Best	5wI	10wM
E.S.H.Giddins	30	10	88	8	11.00	5- 15	1	–
A.R.Caddick	44.5	13	132	8	16.50	4- 38	–	–
D.Gough	49.3	6	174	9	19.33	4- 57	–	–

Also bowled: A.Flintoff 13-5-35-0; M.R.Ramprakash 1-0-1-0; C.P.Schofield 18-2-73-0.

ZIMBABWE – BATTING AND FIELDING

	M	I	NO	HS	Runs	Avge	100	50	Ct/St
M.W.Goodwin	2	4	2	148*	178	89.00	1	–	–
G.J.Whittall	2	4	1	28	78	26.00	–	–	–
N.C.Johnson	2	3	–	51	74	24.66	–	1	2
A.Flower	2	3	–	42	68	22.66	–	–	6
M.Mbangwa	2	2	1	8	9	9.00	–	–	–
B.A.Murphy	2	3	1	14	14	7.00	–	–	3
G.W.Flower	2	4	–	12	18	4.50	–	–	4
A.D.R.Campbell	2	2	–	4	4	2.00	–	–	3
H.H.Streak	2	2	–	4	4	2.00	–	–	2

Played in one Test: S.V.Carlisle did not bat; T.R.Gripper 1, 5; M.L.Nkala did not bat; B.C.Strang 0, 37* (1 ct).

ZIMBABWE – BOWLING

	O	M	R	W	Avge	Best	5wI	10wM
G.J.Whittall	34	10	88	8	11.00	3- 14	–	–
H.H.Streak	84.5	27	182	9	20.22	6- 87	1	–
M.L.Nkala	42	12	104	5	20.80	3- 82	–	–
B.A.Murphy	49.2	13	112	3	37.33	1- 19	–	–
N.C.Johnson	54	14	159	3	53.00	2- 41	–	–
M.Mbangwa	54	19	134	2	67.00	2- 40	–	–

Also bowled: G.W.Flower 1-0-2-0; B.C.Strang 27-4-86-0.

ENGLAND v WEST INDIES (1st Test)

At Edgbaston, Birmingham, on 15, 16, 17 June 2000.
Toss: West Indies. Result: **WEST INDIES** won by an innings and 93 runs.
Debuts: None.

ENGLAND

M.A.Atherton	c Jacobs b Walsh	20	b King	19
M.R.Ramprakash	c Hinds b Walsh	18	lbw b Walsh	0
*N.Hussain	c Jacobs b Rose	15	c Jacobs b Walsh	8
G.A.Hick	c Campbell b Walsh	0	c Jacobs b Walsh	0
†A.J.Stewart	b Ambrose	6	b Rose	8
N.V.Knight	c Lara b King	26	c Hinds b Adams	34
A.Flintoff	c Lara b Walsh	16	b King	12
R.D.B.Croft	c Jacobs b Walsh	18	c Hinds b King	1
A.R.Caddick	not out	21	c Hinds b Rose	4
D.Gough	run out	23	not out	23
E.S.H.Giddins	c Jacobs b King	0	b Adams	0
Extras	(LB 6, W 1, NB 9)	16	(LB 7, W 1, NB 8)	16
Total		**179**		**125**

WEST INDIES

S.L.Campbell	b Gough	59
C.H.Gayle	lbw b Gough	0
W.W.Hinds	c Hussain b Caddick	12
B.C.Lara	c Stewart b Gough	50
S.Chanderpaul	c Stewart b Flintoff	73
*J.C.Adams	c Flintoff b Gough	98
†R.D.Jacobs	c Stewart b Caddick	5
C.E.L.Ambrose	lbw b Croft	22
F.A.Rose	lbw b Gough	48
R.D.King	st Stewart b Croft	1
C.A.Walsh	not out	3
Extras	(B 6, LB 14, NB 6)	26
Total		**397**

WEST INDIES	O	M	R	W		O	M	R	W
Ambrose	20.5	10	32	1		14	8	16	0
Walsh	21	9	36	5		19	10	22	3
King	14.1	2	60	2	(4)	9	4	28	3
Rose	13	3	45	1	(3)	10	1	43	2
Gayle						3	0	4	0
Adams						3	1	5	2
ENGLAND									
Gough	36.5	7	109	5					
Caddick	30	6	94	2					
Giddins	18	4	73	0					
Croft	29	9	53	2					
Flintoff	23	10	48	1					

FALL OF WICKETS

	E	WI	E
Wkt	1st	1st	2nd
1st	26	5	0
2nd	44	24	14
3rd	45	123	14
4th	57	136	24
5th	82	230	60
6th	112	237	78
7th	112	292	83
8th	134	354	94
9th	178	385	117
10th	179	397	125

Umpires: D.R.Shepherd (51) and S.Venkataraghavan (*India*) (38).
Referee: G.T.Dowling (*New Zealand*) (8).   Test No. 1499/122 (E769/WI360)

ENGLAND v WEST INDIES (2nd Test)

At Lord's, London, on 29, 30 June, 1 July 2000.
Toss: England. Result: **ENGLAND** won by two wickets.
Debuts: England – M.J.Hoggard.

WEST INDIES

S.L.Campbell	c Hoggard b Cork	82	c Gough b Caddick		4
A.F.G.Griffith	run out	27	c Stewart b Gough		1
W.W.Hinds	c Stewart b Cork	59	c Ramprakash b Caddick		0
B.C.Lara	c Stewart b Gough	6	c Cork b Caddick		5
S.Chanderpaul	b Gough	22	c Ramprakash b Gough		9
*J.C.Adams	lbw b Gough	1	lbw b Cork		3
†R.D.Jacobs	c Stewart b Cork	10	c Atherton b Caddick		12
C.E.L.Ambrose	c Ramprakash b Cork	5	c Ramprakash b Caddick		0
F.A.Rose	lbw b Gough	29	c and b Cork		1
R.D.King	not out	12	lbw b Cork		7
C.A.Walsh	lbw b Caddick	1	not out		3
Extras	(B 1, LB 8, W 2, NB 2)	13	(LB 8, NB 1)		9
Total		**267**			**54**

ENGLAND

M.A.Atherton	c Lara b Walsh	1	lbw b Walsh		45
M.R.Ramprakash	c Lara b Ambrose	0	b Walsh		2
M.P.Vaughan	b Ambrose	4	c Jacobs b Walsh		41
G.A.Hick	b Ambrose	25	c Lara b Walsh		15
*†A.J.Stewart	c Jacobs b Walsh	28	lbw b Walsh		18
N.V.Knight	c Campbell b King	6	c Jacobs b Rose		2
C.White	run out	27	c Jacobs b Walsh		0
D.G.Cork	c Jacobs b Walsh	4	not out		33
A.R.Caddick	c Campbell b Walsh	6	lbw b Ambrose		7
D.Gough	c Lara b Ambrose	13	not out		4
M.J.Hoggard	not out	12			
Extras	(LB 5, NB 3)	8	(B 3, LB 8, W 1, NB 12)		24
Total		**134**	(8 wickets)		**191**

ENGLAND	O	M	R	W	O	M	R	W		FALL OF WICKETS			
Gough	21	5	72	4	8	3	17	2			WI	E	WI	E
Caddick	20.3	3	58	1	13	8	16	5	Wkt	1st	1st	2nd	2nd
Hoggard	13	3	49	0					1st	80	1	6	3
Cork	24	8	39	4	(3) 5.4	2	13	3	2nd	162	1	6	95
White	8	1	30	0					3rd	175	9	10	119
Vaughan	3	1	10	0					4th	185	37	24	120
									5th	186	50	24	140
WEST INDIES									6th	207	85	39	140
Ambrose	14.2	6	30	4	22	11	22	1	7th	216	100	39	149
Walsh	17	6	43	4	23.5	5	74	6	8th	253	100	39	160
Rose	7	2	32	0	16	3	67	1	9th	258	118	41	–
King	10	3	24	1	8	2	17	0	10th	267	134	54	–

Umpires: J.H.Hampshire (13) and S.Venkataraghavan (*India*) (39).
Referee: G.T.Dowling (*New Zealand*) (9).   **Test No. 1500/123 (E770/WI361)**

ENGLAND v WEST INDIES (3rd Test)

At Old Trafford, Manchester, on 3, 4, 5, 6, 7 August 2000.
Toss: West Indies. Result: **MATCH DRAWN**.
Debuts: England – M.E.Trescothick.

WEST INDIES

S.L.Campbell	c Thorpe b Gough	2	c Cork b White	55
A.F.G.Griffith	lbw b Caddick	2	lbw b Croft	54
W.W.Hinds	c Stewart b Cork	26	c Stewart b Gough	25
B.C.Lara	c Thorpe b Gough	13	run out	112
*J.C.Adams	c Thorpe b White	24	lbw b Cork	53
R.R.Sarwan	lbw b Cork	36	lbw b Caddick	19
†R.D.Jacobs	b Caddick	5	not out	42
F.A.Rose	lbw b Cork	16	lbw b White	10
C.E.L.Ambrose	c Hussain b Caddick	3	not out	36
R.D.King	not out	3		
C.A.Walsh	lbw b Cork	7		
Extras	(B 1, LB 12, NB 7)	20	(B 14, LB 4, W 2, NB 12)	32
Total		**157**	(7 wickets declared)	**438**

ENGLAND

M.A.Atherton	c Campbell b Walsh	1	c Jacobs b Walsh	28
M.E.Trescothick	b Walsh	66	not out	38
*N.Hussain	c Adams b Walsh	10	not out	6
G.P.Thorpe	lbw b Walsh	0		
†A.J.Stewart	c Jacobs b Ambrose	105		
M.P.Vaughan	c Lara b Ambrose	29		
C.White	b King	6		
D.G.Cork	c Jacobs b Ambrose	16		
R.D.B.Croft	not out	27		
A.R.Caddick	lbw b Ambrose	3		
D.Gough	c Ambrose b King	12	(B 4, LB 1, NB 3)	8
Extras	(B 10, LB 6, NB 12)	28		
Total		**303**	(1 wicket)	**80**

ENGLAND	O	M	R	W		O	M	R	W
Gough	21	3	58	2		27	5	96	1
Caddick	24	10	45	3		23	4	64	1
Cork	17.1	8	23	4		28	9	64	1
White	9	1	18	1	(5)	27	5	67	2
Croft					(4)	47	8	124	1
Trescothick						1	0	2	0
Vaughan						2	1	3	0
WEST INDIES									
Ambrose	27	7	70	4		12	2	31	0
Walsh	27	14	50	4		14	6	19	1
Rose	20	3	83	0					
King	12.2	3	52	2	(3)	2.4	0	15	0
Adams	11	4	32	0	(4)	5	1	10	0

	FALL OF WICKETS			
	WI	E	WI	E
Wkt	1st	1st	2nd	2nd
1st	3	1	96	61
2nd	12	17	145	–
3rd	49	17	164	–
4th	49	196	302	–
5th	118	198	335	–
6th	126	210	373	–
7th	130	251	384	–
8th	135	275	–	–
9th	148	283	–	–
10th	157	303	–	–

Umpires: D.B.Cowie (*New Zealand*) (17) and P.Willey (20).
Referee: R.S.Madugalle (*Sri Lanka*) (27).   Test No. 1501/124 (E771/WI362)

ENGLAND v WEST INDIES (4th Test)

At Headingley, Leeds, on 17, 18 August 2000.
Toss: West Indies. Result: **ENGLAND** won by an innings and 39 runs.
Debuts: None.

WEST INDIES

S.L.Campbell	c Trescothick b Gough	8	c Hick b Gough		12
A.F.G.Griffith	c Stewart b Gough	22	b Gough		0
W.W.Hinds	c Stewart b White	16	lbw b Gough		0
B.C.Lara	lbw b White	4	lbw b Gough		2
*J.C.Adams	b White	2	b Cork		19
R.R.Sarwan	not out	59	not out		17
†R.D.Jacobs	c Caddick b Cork	35	lbw b Caddick		1
N.A.M.McLean	c Stewart b White	7	b Caddick		0
C.E.L.Ambrose	b Cork	1	b Caddick		0
R.D.King	lbw b Gough	6	b Caddick		0
C.A.Walsh	c Caddick b White	1	b Caddick		3
Extras	(LB 2, NB 9)	11	(LB 3, NB 4)		7
Total		**172**			**61**

ENGLAND

M.A.Atherton	c Lara b Ambrose	6
M.E.Trescothick	c Lara b Ambrose	1
*N.Hussain	lbw b Walsh	22
G.P.Thorpe	lbw b Walsh	46
†A.J.Stewart	c Campbell b Walsh	5
M.P.Vaughan	c Jacobs b Ambrose	76
A.R.Caddick	c Jacobs b Ambrose	6
G.A.Hick	st Jacobs b Adams	59
C.White	c Jacobs b McLean	0
D.G.Cork	not out	11
D.Gough	c Griffith b Walsh	2
Extras	(B 4, LB 13, W 3, NB 18)	38
Total		**272**

ENGLAND	O	M	R	W	O	M	R	W
Gough	17	2	59	3	10	3	30	4
Caddick	10	3	35	0	11.2	5	14	5
White	14.4	4	57	5				
Cork	7	0	19	2	(3) 5	0	14	1
WEST INDIES								
Ambrose	18	3	42	4				
Walsh	24.5	9	51	4				
King	11	2	48	0				
McLean	22	5	93	1				
Adams	6	1	21	1				

FALL OF WICKETS			
	WI	E	WI
Wkt	1st	1st	2nd
1st	11	7	3
2nd	50	10	3
3rd	54	80	11
4th	56	93	21
5th	60	96	49
6th	128	124	52
7th	143	222	52
8th	148	224	52
9th	168	269	53
10th	172	272	61

Umpires: D.B.Cowie (*New Zealand*) (18) and G.Sharp (12).
Referee: R.S.Madugalle (*Sri Lanka*) (28).   **Test No. 1502/125 (E772/WI363)**

ENGLAND v WEST INDIES (5th Test)

At Kennington Oval, London, on 31 August, 1, 2, 3, 4 September 2000.
Toss: West Indies. Result: **ENGLAND** won by 158 runs.
Debuts: West Indies – M.V.Nagamootoo.

ENGLAND

M.A.Atherton	b McLean	83	c Jacobs b Walsh		108
M.E.Trescothick	c Campbell b Nagamootoo	78	c Lara b Ambrose		7
*N.Hussain	c Jacobs b Nagamootoo	0	lbw b McLean		0
G.P.Thorpe	lbw b Walsh	40	c Griffith b Walsh		10
†A.J.Stewart	lbw b McLean	0	c Campbell b Nagamootoo		25
M.P.Vaughan	lbw b Ambrose	10	lbw b Walsh		9
G.A.Hick	lbw b Ambrose	17	c Campbell b Walsh		0
C.White	not out	11	run out		18
D.G.Cork	lbw b McLean	0	lbw b McLean		26
A.R.Caddick	c Hinds b Walsh	4	c Jacobs b McLean		0
D.Gough	b Walsh	8	not out		1
Extras	(B 4, LB 15, W 1, NB 10)	30	(B 1, LB 7, NB 5)		13
Total		**281**			**217**

WEST INDIES

S.L.Campbell	b Cork	20	c Hick b Gough		28
A.F.G.Griffith	c Hick b White	6	c Stewart b Caddick		20
W.W.Hinds	lbw b Cork	2	(4) lbw b Caddick		7
B.C.Lara	b White	0	(3) lbw b Gough		47
*J.C.Adams	c Hick b Cork	5	c White b Caddick		15
R.R.Sarwan	c Trescothick b White	5	run out		27
†R.D.Jacobs	not out	26	c Hick b Caddick		1
M.V.Nagamootoo	c Trescothick b Gough	18	lbw b Gough		13
C.E.L.Ambrose	lbw b Caddick	0	(10) c Atherton b Cork		28
N.A.M.McLean	b White	29	(9) not out		23
C.A.Walsh	b White	5	lbw b Cork		0
Extras	(LB 3, NB 6)	9	(LB 3, W 1, NB 2)		6
Total		**125**			**215**

WEST INDIES	O	M	R	W		O	M	R	W	FALL OF WICKETS				
Ambrose	31	8	38	2		22	8	36	1		E	WI	E	WI
Walsh	35.4	16	68	3		38	17	73	4	*Wkt*	*1st*	*1st*	*2nd*	*2nd*
McLean	29	6	80	3		22	5	60	3	1st	159	32	21	50
Nagamootoo	24	7	63	2		19	7	29	1	2nd	159	32	29	50
Adams	4	0	13	0		7	3	11	0	3rd	184	32	56	58
										4th	184	34	121	94
ENGLAND										5th	214	39	139	140
Gough	13	3	25	1		20	3	64	3	6th	254	51	139	142
Caddick	18	7	42	1		21	7	54	4	7th	254	74	163	150
White	11.5	1	32	5		11	2	32	0	8th	255	75	207	167
Cork	8	3	23	3		15	1	50	2	9th	264	119	207	215
Vaughan						3	1	12	0	10th	281	125	217	215

Umpires: D.J.Harper (*Australia*) (9) and D.R.Shepherd (52).
Referee: R.S.Madugalle (*Sri Lanka*) (29).   **Test No. 1503/126 (E773/WI364)**

ENGLAND v WEST INDIES 2000

ENGLAND – BATTING AND FIELDING

	M	I	NO	HS	Runs	Avge	100	50	Ct/St
M.E.Trescothick	3	5	1	78	190	47.50	–	2	3
M.A.Atherton	5	9	–	108	311	34.55	1	1	2
M.P.Vaughan	4	6	–	76	169	28.16	–	1	–
A.J.Stewart	5	8	–	105	195	24.37	1	–	13/1
G.P.Thorpe	3	4	–	46	96	24.00	–	–	3
R.D.B.Croft	2	3	1	27*	46	23.00	–	–	–
D.G.Cork	4	6	2	33*	90	22.50	–	–	3
D.Gough	5	8	3	23*	86	17.20	–	–	1
N.V.Knight	2	4	–	34	68	17.00	–	–	–
G.A.Hick	4	7	–	59	116	16.57	–	1	5
C.White	4	6	1	27	62	12.40	–	–	1
N.Hussain	4	7	1	22	61	10.16	–	–	2
A.R.Caddick	5	8	1	21*	51	7.28	–	–	2
M.R.Ramprakash	2	4	–	18	20	5.00	–	–	4

Played in one Test: A.Flintoff 16, 12 (1 ct); E.S.H.Giddins 0, 0; M.J.Hoggard 12 (1 ct).*

ENGLAND – BOWLING

	O	M	R	W	Avge	Best	5wI	10wM
D.G.Cork	109.5	31	245	20	12.25	4- 23	–	–
C.White	81.3	14	236	13	18.15	5- 32	2	–
A.R.Caddick	170.5	53	422	22	19.18	5- 14	2	–
D.Gough	173.5	34	530	25	21.20	5-109	1	–

Also bowled: R.D.B.Croft 76-17-177-3; A.Flintoff 23-10-48-1; E.S.H.Giddins 18-4-73-0; M.J.Hoggard 13-3-49-0; M.E.Trescothick 1-0-2-0; M.P.Vaughan 8-3-25-0.

WEST INDIES – BATTING AND FIELDING

	M	I	NO	HS	Runs	Avge	100	50	Ct/St
R.R.Sarwan	3	6	2	59*	163	40.75	–	1	–
S.Chanderpaul	2	3	–	73	104	34.66	–	1	–
S.L.Campbell	5	9	–	82	270	30.00	–	3	8
B.C.Lara	5	9	–	112	239	26.55	1	1	10
J.C.Adams	5	9	–	98	220	24.44	–	2	1
F.A.Rose	3	5	–	48	104	20.80	–	–	–
N.A.M.McLean	2	4	1	29	59	19.66	–	–	–
R.D.Jacobs	5	9	2	42*	137	19.57	–	–	20/1
A.F.G.Griffith	4	8	–	54	132	16.50	–	1	2
W.W.Hinds	5	9	–	59	147	16.33	–	1	5
C.E.L.Ambrose	5	9	1	36*	95	11.87	–	–	1
R.D.King	4	6	2	12*	29	7.25	–	–	–
C.A.Walsh	5	8	2	7	23	3.83	–	–	–

Played in one Test: C.H.Gayle 0; M.V.Nagamootoo 18, 17.

WEST INDIES – BOWLING

	O	M	R	W	Avge	Best	5wI	10wM
C.A.Walsh	220.2	92	436	34	12.82	6- 74	2	1
C.E.L.Ambrose	181.1	63	317	17	18.64	4- 30	–	–
R.D.King	67.1	16	244	8	30.50	3- 28	–	–
N.A.M.McLean	73	16	233	7	33.28	3- 60	–	–

Also bowled: J.C.Adams 36-10-92-3; C.H.Gayle 3-0-4-0; M.V.Nagamootoo 43-14-92-3; F.A.Rose 66-12-270-4.

SRI LANKA v PAKISTAN (1st Test)

At Sinhalese Sports Club, Colombo, on 14, 15, 16, 17 June 2000.
Toss: Sri Lanka. Result: **PAKISTAN** won by five wickets.
Debuts: Sri Lanka – R.D.Fernando.

SRI LANKA

M.S.Atapattu	c Mohammad Wasim b Arshad	73	c Saeed b Arshad	40
*S.T.Jayasuriya	c Younis Khan b Waqar	26	lbw b Waqar	8
R.P.Arnold	b Waqar	4	c Mohammad Wasim b Wasim	1
P.A.de Silva	c Wasim b Arshad	30	c Inzamam b Razzaq	21
D.P.M.de S.Jayawardena	c Moin b Wasim	77	c Mohammad Wasim b Arshad	1
A.Ranatunga	run out	6	c Saeed b Wasim	7
†R.S.Kaluwitharana	c Mohammad Wasim b Arshad	4	c Younis Khan b Arshad	6
W.P.U.C.J.Vaas	b Mushtaq	3	c and b Wasim	20
D.N.Y.Zoysa	st Moin b Arshad	17	c Inzamam b Wasim	13
M.Muralitharan	c Wasim b Waqar	18 (11)	not out	3
R.D.Fernando	not out	5 (10)	b Wasim	0
Extras	(B 5, LB 1, NB 4)	10	(LB 1, W 1, NB 1)	3
Total		**273**		**123**

PAKISTAN

Saeed Anwar	c Ranatunga b Muralitharan	56	c Fernando b Zoysa	6
Mohammad Wasim	c Arnold b Fernando	8	lbw b Muralitharan	30
Younis Khan	c Fernando b Muralitharan	23 (7)	not out	32
Yousuf Youhana	c Jayawardena b Muralitharan	2	b Muralitharan	11
*†Moin Khan	c Fernando b Zoysa	47 (6)	lbw b Zoysa	11
Inzamam-ul-Haq	c Jayawardena b Zoysa	12 (4)	c Arnold b Muralitharan	13
Abdur Razzaq	run out	0		
Wasim Akram	b Fernando	78 (5)	not out	20
Waqar Younis	c Zoysa b Muralitharan	4		
Mushtaq Ahmed	c Arnold b Muralitharan	2		
Arshad Khan	not out	9		
Extras	(LB 4, W 3, NB 18)	25	(B 4, NB 4)	8
Total		**266**	(5 wickets)	**131**

PAKISTAN	O	M	R	W		O	M	R	W
Wasim Akram	20	6	55	1	(2)	15.3	1	45	5
Waqar Younis	14.2	0	50	3	(1)	9	3	21	1
Abdur Razzaq	18	1	58	0		14	6	23	1
Mushtaq Ahmed	14	1	42	1	(5)	1	0	3	0
Arshad Khan	31	8	62	4	(4)	22	8	30	3
SRI LANKA									
Vaas	29	7	52	0		8	3	20	0
Zoysa	19	4	30	2		13	1	38	2
De Silva	3	1	4	0					
Fernando	15.5	1	53	2		3	0	14	0
Muralitharan	47	12	115	5	(3)	17	3	53	3
Jayawardena	2	1	2	0					
Jayasuriya	4	3	6	0					
Ranatunga	1	1	0	0					
Arnold					(5)	1	0	2	0

FALL OF WICKETS

	SL	P	SL	P
Wkt	1st	1st	2nd	2nd
1st	52	16	14	19
2nd	56	67	25	51
3rd	109	75	67	52
4th	176	130	71	66
5th	187	159	73	89
6th	193	160	82	–
7th	206	165	88	–
8th	245	173	120	–
9th	257	176	120	–
10th	273	266	123	–

Umpires: S.A.Bucknor (*West Indies*) (50) and B.C.Cooray (18).
Referee: J.R.Reid (*New Zealand*) (45).   Test No. 1504/25 (SL100/P268)

252

SRI LANKA v PAKISTAN (2nd Test)

At Galle International Stadium on 21, 22, 23, 24 June 2000.
Toss: Sri Lanka. Result: **PAKISTAN** won by in innings and 163 runs.
Debuts: None.

SRI LANKA

M.S.Atapattu	c Moin b Waqar	1	c Moin b Arshad		59
*S.T.Jayasuriya	b Wasim	32	c Inzamam b Waqar		21
R.P.Arnold	c Youhana b Waqar	5	lbw b Waqar		26
P.A.de Silva	c Moin b Waqar	4	c Mohammad Wasim b Arshad		11
D.P.M.deS.Jayawardena	c Mohammad Wasim b Azhar	72	lbw b Wasim		9
A.Ranatunga	run out	51	lbw b Wasim		65
†R.S.Kaluwitharana	c Moin b Razzaq	4	lbw b Waqar		9
W.P.U.C.J.Vaas	c Younis Khan b Azhar	5	c sub (Imran Nazir) b Azhar		20
R.Herath	lbw b Razzaq	0	lbw b Azhar		0
K.R.Pushpakumara	lbw b Razzaq	0	not out		0
M.Muralitharan	not out	0	b Waqar		22
Extras	(B 1, LB 1, W 2, NB 3)	7	(LB 12, W 1, NB 1)		14
Total		**181**			**256**

PAKISTAN

Saeed Anwar	c Kaluwitharana b Arnold	123
Mohammad Wasim	c Ranatunga b Muralitharan	29
Azhar Mahmood	b Muralitharan	0
Yousuf Youhana	st Kaluwitharana b Muralitharan	41
Inzamam-ul-Haq	c Kaluwitharana b Pushpakumara	112
Younis Khan	c Pushpakumara b Jayawardena	116
Abdur Razzaq	b Muralitharan	48
Wasim Akram	c Atapattu b Jayawardena	100
*†Moin Khan	not out	3
Waqar Younis		
Arshad Khan		
Extras	(B 5, LB 6, NB 17)	28
Total	(8 wickets declared)	**600**

PAKISTAN	O	M	R	W		O	M	R	W
Wasim Akram	13	3	40	1	(2)	22	7	53	2
Waqar Younis	13	2	39	3	(1)	19.1	7	40	4
Abdur Razzaq	12	2	35	3		15	2	44	0
Azhar Mahmood	16.3	5	36	2	(5)	10	2	48	2
Arshad Khan	10	0	29	0	(4)	24	9	59	2

SRI LANKA	O	M	R	W
Vaas	34	7	82	0
Pushpakumara	29	6	116	1
Herath	36	7	115	0
Muralitharan	50	13	138	4
Arnold	20	4	71	1
Jayasuriya	2	0	22	0
Jayawardena	3.2	0	32	2
Ranatunga	1	0	13	0

FALL OF WICKETS

	SL	P	SL
Wkt	1st	1st	2nd
1st	13	71	33
2nd	23	72	91
3rd	43	161	123
4th	47	266	130
5th	163	340	156
6th	173	446	187
7th	177	566	230
8th	177	600	234
9th	177	–	234
10th	181	–	256

Umpires: E.A.R.de Silva (1) and R.B.Tiffin (*Zimbabwe*) (16).
Referee: J.R.Reid (*New Zealand*) (46).   **Test No. 1505/26 (SL101/P269)**

SRI LANKA v PAKISTAN (3rd Test)

At Asgiriya Stadium, Kandy, on 28, 29, 30 June, 1 (*no play*), 2 (*no play*) July 2000.
Toss: Sri Lanka. Result: **MATCH DRAWN**.
Debuts: Sri Lanka – A.V.P.Jayawardene.

SRI LANKA

M.S.Atapattu	not out	207
*S.T.Jayasuriya	c Younis Khan b Razzaq	188
R.P.Arnold	c Moin b Razzaq	24
P.A.de Silva	c Younis Khan b Arshad	0
D.P.M.deS.Jayawardena	b Arshad	2
A.Ranatunga	c Mushtaq b Arshad	6
H.D.P.K.Dharmasena	not out	12
†A.V.P.Jayawardene		
W.P.U.C.J.Vaas		
D.N.T.Zoysa		
M.Muralitharan		
Extras	(B 14, LB 8, W 1, NB 5)	28
Total	(5 wickets)	**467**

PAKISTAN

Saeed Anwar
Imran Nazir
Yousuf Youhana
Inzamam-ul-Haq
Younis Khan
Wasim Akram
Abdur Razzaq
*†Moin Khan
Waqar Younis
Mushtaq Ahmed
Arshad Khan

PAKISTAN	O	M	R	W
Wasim Akram	25	6	41	0
Waqar Younis	19.4	0	94	0
Arshad Khan	52	7	137	3
Abdur Razzaq	33	10	65	2
Mushtaq Ahmed	26	3	108	0

FALL OF WICKETS

	SL
Wkt	*1st*
1st	335
2nd	410
3rd	402
4th	412
5th	434
6th	–
7th	–
8th	–
9th	–
10th	–

Umpires: S.A.Bucknor (*West Indies*) (51) and P.T.Manuel (6).
Referee: J.R.Reid (*New Zealand*) (47).   **Test No. 1506/27 (SL102/P270)**

SRI LANKA v PAKISTAN 2000-01

SRI LANKA – BATTING AND FIELDING

	M	I	NO	HS	Runs	Avge	100	50	Ct/St
M.S.Atapattu	3	5	1	207*	380	95.00	1	2	1
S.T.Jayasuriya	3	5	–	188	275	55.00	1	2	–
D.P.M.deS.Jayawardena	3	5	–	77	161	32.20	–	2	2
A.Ranatunga	3	5	–	65	135	27.00	–	2	2
M.Muralitharan	3	4	2	22	43	21.50	–	–	–
D.N.T.Zoysa	2	2	–	17	30	15.00	–	–	1
P.A.de Silva	3	5	–	30	66	13.20	–	–	–
W.P.U.C.J.Vaas	3	4	–	20	48	12.00	–	–	–
R.P.Arnold	3	5	–	26	60	12.00	–	–	3
R.S.Kaluwitharana	2	4	–	9	23	5.75	–	–	2/1

Played in one Test: H.D.P.K.Dharmasena 12*; R.D.Fernando 5*, 0 (3 ct); R.Herath 0, 0; A.V.P.Jayawardene did not bat; K.R.Pushpakumara 0, 0* (1 ct).

SRI LANKA – BOWLING

	O	M	R	W	Avge	Best	5wI	10wM
D.N.T.Zoysa	32	5	68	4	17.00	2- 30	–	–
D.P.M.deS.Jayawardena	5.2	1	34	2	17.00	2- 32	–	–
M.Muralitharan	114	28	306	12	25.50	5-115	1	–
R.D.Fernando	18.5	1	67	2	33.50	2- 53	–	–
R.P.Arnold	21	4	73	1	73.00	1- 71	–	–
K.R.Pushpakumara	29	6	116	1	116.00	1-116	–	–

Also bowled: P.A.de Silva 3-1-4-0; R.Herath 36-7-115-0; S.T.Jayasuriya 6-3-28-0; A.Ranatunga 2-1-13-0; W.P.U.C.J.Vaas 71-17-154-0.

PAKISTAN – BATTING AND FIELDING

	M	I	NO	HS	Runs	Avge	100	50	Ct/St
Wasim Akram	3	3	1	100	198	99.00	1	1	3
Younis Khan	3	3	1	116	171	85.50	1	–	5
Saeed Anwar	3	3	–	123	185	61.66	1	1	2
Inzamam-ul-Haq	3	3	–	112	137	45.66	1	–	3
Moin Khan	3	3	1	47	61	30.50	–	–	6/1
Abdur Razzaq	3	2	–	48	48	24.00	–	–	–
Mohammad Wasim	2	3	–	30	67	22.33	–	–	6
Yousuf Youhana	3	3	–	41	54	18.00	–	–	1
Waqar Younis	3	1	–	4	4	4.00	–	–	–
Mushtaq Ahmed	2	1	–	2	2	2.00	–	–	1
Arshad Khan	3	1	1	9*	9	–	–	–	–

Played in one Test: Azhar Mahmood 0; Imran Nazir did not bat.

PAKISTAN – BOWLING

	O	M	R	W	Avge	Best	5wI	10wM
Azhar Mahmood	26.3	7	84	4	21.00	2- 36	–	–
Waqar Younis	75.1	12	244	11	22.18	4- 40	–	–
Wasim Akram	95.3	23	234	9	26.00	5- 45	1	–
Arshad Khan	139	32	317	12	26.41	4- 62	–	–
Abdur Razzaq	92	21	225	6	37.50	3- 35	–	–
Mushtaq Ahmed	41	4	153	1	153.00	1- 42	–	–

SRI LANKA v SOUTH AFRICA (1st Test)

At Galle International Stadium on 20, 21, 22, 23 July 2000.
Toss: Sri Lanka. Result: **SRI LANKA** won by an innings and 15 runs.
Debuts: Sri Lanka – K.Sangakkara; South Africa – N.D.McKenzie.

SRI LANKA

M.S.Atapattu	c Boje b Ntini	54
*S.T.Jayasuriya	c McKenzie b Adams	148
R.P.Arnold	c Boucher b Adams	5
D.P.M.deS.Jayawardena	c Boucher b Pollock	167
†K.Sangakkara	lbw b Boje	23
A.Ranatunga	c Pollock b Adams	13
H.D.P.K.Dharmasena	c Klusener b Pollock	4
U.D.U.Chandana	c Cullinan b Kallis	8
W.P.U.C.J.Vaas	b Pollock	54
D.N.T.Zoysa	c and b Cullinan	10
M.Muralitharan	not out	2
Extras	(B 15, LB 16, NB 3)	34
Total		**522**

SOUTH AFRICA

G.Kirsten	c Sangakkara b Muralitharan	12	run out		55
N.D.McKenzie	b Muralitharan	11	c Ranatunga b Chandana		25
J.H.Kallis	c Arnold b Muralitharan	29	c Muralitharan b Chandana		40
D.J.Cullinan	not out	114	c Arnold b Muralitharan		12
J.N.Rhodes	b Muralitharan	12	not out		63
L.Klusener	c Chandana b Dharmasena	19	c Sangakkara b Muralitharan		4
†M.V.Boucher	b Muralitharan	0	lbw b Muralitharan		7
*S.M.Pollock	c Dharmasena b Muralitharan	4	c Arnold b Muralitharan		12
N.Boje	c Atapattu b Jayasuriya	12	lbw b Muralitharan		35
P.R.Adams	c Atapattu b Chandana	4	b Muralitharan		2
M.Ntini	c Ranatunga b Chandana	8	b Muralitharan		0
Extras	(B 2, LB 1, NB 10)	13	(B 3, LB 5, NB 6)		14
Total		**238**			**269**

SOUTH AFRICA	O	M	R	W	O	M	R	W
Pollock	30.4	8	73	3				
Kallis	17	7	41	1				
Ntini	19	1	73	1				
Adams	45	6	184	3				
Klusener	15	4	38	0				
Boje	22	2	72	1				
Cullinan	2	0	10	1				
SRI LANKA								
Vaas	12	6	16	0	7	2	18	0
Zoysa	4	1	12	0	5	2	11	0
Dharmasena	25	5	70	1	10	1	37	0
Muralitharan	41	8	87	6	35	5	84	7
Chandana	14	3	46	2	29	6	88	2
Jayasuriya	3	0	4	1	5	0	21	0
Arnold					1	0	2	0

FALL OF WICKETS

	SL	SA	SA
Wkt	1st	1st	2nd
1st	193	25	58
2nd	211	30	112
3rd	216	86	139
4th	297	119	141
5th	318	162	153
6th	341	168	163
7th	365	198	193
8th	482	213	263
9th	500	223	269
10th	522	238	269

Umpires: D.J.Harper (*Australia*) (7) and P.T.Manuel (7).
Referee: B.F.Hastings (*New Zealand*) (4).   **Test No. 1507/6 (SL103/SA243)**

SRI LANKA v SOUTH AFRICA (2nd Test)

At Asgiriya Stadium, Kandy, on 30, 31 July, 1, 2 August 2000.
Toss: Sri Lanka. Result: **SOUTH AFRICA** won by 7 runs.
Debuts: None.

SOUTH AFRICA

G.Kirsten	lbw b Vaas	0	b Dharmasena		13
N.D.McKenzie	c Jayawardena b Zoysa	0	b Zoysa		1
J.H.Kallis	lbw b Dharmasena	16	b Muralitharan		87
D.J.Cullinan	b Dharmasena	2	b Muralitharan		6
J.N.Rhodes	b Dharmasena	12	c Sangakkara b Jayasuriya		33
L.Klusener	not out	118	c Sangakkara b Jayasuriya		4
†M.V.Boucher	run out	60	c Atapattu b Muralitharan		15
*S.M.Pollock	c Jayawardena b Chandana	5	c Sangakkara b Vaas		20
N.Boje	lbw b Chandana	0	c sub (T.M.Dilshan) b Chandana		27
P.R.Adams	c Jayawardena b Dharmasena	6	not out		14
M.Hayward	b Muralitharan	13	lbw b Chandana		0
Extras	(B 9, LB 6, NB 6)	21	(B 7, LB 1, NB 3)		11
Total		**253**			**231**

SRI LANKA

M.S.Atapattu	lbw b Pollock	120	lbw b Pollock		0
*S.T.Jayasuriya	c Kallis b Hayward	28	lbw b Hayward		0
R.P.Arnold	run out	28	lbw b Boje		40
D.P.M.deS.Jayawardena	c Cullinan b Boje	18	c Boucher b Hayward		1
†K.Sangakkara	run out	24	c Hayward b Kallis		5
A.Ranatunga	lbw b Hayward	54	c Rhodes b Boje		88
H.D.P.K.Dharmasena	c Boucher b Pollock	3	c Rhodes b Klusener		1
W.P.U.C.J.Vaas	c Rhodes b Pollock	4	(9) run out		5
U.D.U.Chandana	not out	1	(8) b Klusener		16
D.N.T.Zoysa	b Kallis	3	not out		2
M.Muralitharan	b Kallis	0	c Boucher b Boje		0
Extras	(B 6, LB 12, NB 7)	25	(B 1, LB 6, W 2, NB 2)		11
Total		**308**			**169**

SRI LANKA	O	M	R	W	O	M	R	W
Vaas	8	5	11	1	14	6	17	1
Zoysa	6	2	16	1	5	0	17	1
Dharmasena	20	3	58	3	16	2	47	1
Muralitharan	30.5	4	95	2	36	8	76	3
Chandana	20	2	58	2	9.5	0	21	2
Jayasuriya					13	1	45	2

FALL OF WICKETS				
	SA	SL	SA	SL
Wkt	1st	1st	2nd	2nd
1st	0	53	10	0
2nd	4	109	37	5
3rd	16	142	50	9
4th	34	182	121	21
5th	34	286	128	130
6th	158	296	153	133
7th	173	300	186	161
8th	173	303	186	161
9th	210	308	231	169
10th	253	308	231	169

SOUTH AFRICA	O	M	R	W		O	M	R	W
Pollock	24	5	83	4		11	3	38	1
Hayward	22	6	67	2		5	1	15	2
Kallis	11.4	4	18	2		8	1	25	1
Boje	15	2	50	1	(6)	10.1	4	24	3
Klusener	11	2	21	0		13	3	34	2
Adams	14	1	44	0	(4)	3	1	26	0
Cullinan	2	0	7	0					

Umpires: D.J.Harper (*Australia*) (8) and G.Silva (1).
Referee: B.F.Hastings (*New Zealand*) (5).

Test No. 1508/7 (SL104/SA244)

SRI LANKA v SOUTH AFRICA (3rd Test)

At Sinhalese Sports Club, Colombo, on 6, 7, 8, 9, 10 August 2000.
Toss: Sri Lanka. Result: **MATCH DRAWN**.
Debuts: None.

SOUTH AFRICA

G.Kirsten	c Ranatunga b Perera	11	lbw b Muralitharan		40
N.D.McKenzie	c Arnold b Perera	0	run out		17
J.H.Kallis	c Sangakkara b Vaas	19	b De Silva		0
D.J.Cullinan	c Atapattu b Vaas	38	c Arnold b Muralitharan		3
J.N.Rhodes	b Muralitharan	21	c Jayawardena b Muralitharan		54
L.Klusener	not out	95	c Sangakkara b Muralitharan		35
†M.V.Boucher	c Chandana b Vaas	4	b Muralitharan		25
*S.M.Pollock	b Muralitharan	33	c Sangakkara b Jayasuriya		13
N.Boje	c Sangakkara b Vaas	21	not out		29
P.R.Adams	lbw b Muralitharan	15	c and b Jayasuriya		3
M.Hayward	c De Silva b Chandana	0	not out		3
Extras	(B 2, LB 8, NB 12)	22	(LB 4, NB 15)		19
Total		**279**	(9 wickets declared)		**241**

SRI LANKA

M.S.Atapattu	b Hayward	10	c Kirsten b Pollock		0
*S.T.Jayasuriya	c Kirsten b Boje	85	b Adams		17
R.P.Arnold	c Klusener b Boje	28			
P.A.de Silva	st Boucher b Boje	2	(5) lbw b Klusener		41
D.P.M.deS.Jayawardena	c Kirsten b Boje	34	(4) not out		101
W.P.U.C.J.Vaas	lbw b Pollock	5			
A.Ranatunga	b Boje	14	(6) not out		28
†K.Sangakkara	c Boucher b Hayward	25	(3) c Rhodes b Hayward		6
U.D.U.Chandana	c McKenzie b Pollock	32			
P.D.R.L.Perera	c Boje b Pollock	10			
M.Muralitharan	not out	0			
Extras	(B 3, LB 1, W 1, NB 8)	13	(NB 2)		2
Total		**258**	(4 wickets)		**195**

SRI LANKA	O	M	R	W		O	M	R	W
Vaas	36	9	85	4		10	2	22	0
Perera	18	3	60	2		2	0	13	0
De Silva	5	2	16	0	(4)	24.5	7	49	1
Muralitharan	39	14	70	3	(5)	45.5	14	68	5
Chandana	4.2	0	26	1	(7)	5	0	23	0
Jayasuriya	3	0	9	0		24	4	56	2
Arnold	3	1	3	0	(3)	2.1	0	6	0

SOUTH AFRICA	O	M	R	W		O	M	R	W
Pollock	22.2	10	40	3		6	3	13	1
Hayward	20	2	68	2		9	1	21	1
Kallis	13	3	48	0		4	2	4	0
Klusener	9	2	36	0		12.1	4	20	1
Boje	34	8	62	5	(6)	20	4	65	0
Adams					(5)	16	3	72	1

FALL OF WICKETS

	SA	SL	SA	SL
Wkt	1st	1st	2nd	2nd
1st	0	19	50	6
2nd	23	122	50	20
3rd	57	130	59	37
4th	89	135	107	119
5th	103	170	152	–
6th	117	180	169	–
7th	186	201	197	–
8th	240	223	220	–
9th	278	257	236	–
10th	279	258		

Umpires: B.C.Cooray (19) and E.A.Nicholls (*West Indies*) (12).
Referee: B.F.Hastings (*New Zealand*) (6).   **Test No. 1509/8 (SL105/SA245)**

SRI LANKA v SOUTH AFRICA 2000-01

SRI LANKA – BATTING AND FIELDING

	M	I	NO	HS	Runs	Avge	100	50	Ct/St
D.P.M.deS.Jayawardena	3	5	1	167	321	80.25	2	–	4
S.T.Jayasuriya	3	5	–	148	278	55.60	1	1	1
A.Ranatunga	3	5	1	88	197	49.25	–	2	3
M.S.Atapattu	3	5	–	120	184	36.80	1	1	4
R.P.Arnold	3	4	–	40	101	25.25	–	–	5
U.D.U.Chandana	3	4	1	32	57	19.00	–	–	2
W.P.U.C.J.Vaas	3	4	–	54	68	17.00	–	1	–
K.Sangakkara	3	5	–	25	83	16.60	–	–	9
D.N.T.Zoysa	2	3	1	10	15	7.50	–	–	–
H.D.P.K.Dharmasena	2	3	–	4	8	2.66	–	–	1
M.Muralitharan	3	4	2	2*	2	1.00	–	–	1

Played in one Test: P.A.de Silva 2, 41 (1 ct); P.D.R.L.Perera 10.

SRI LANKA – BOWLING

	O	M	R	W	Avge	Best	5wI	10wM
M.Muralitharan	227.4	52	480	26	18.46	7- 84	3	1
S.T.Jayasuriya	48	5	135	5	27.00	2- 45	–	
W.P.U.C.J.Vaas	87	30	169	6	28.16	4- 85	–	–
U.D.U.Chandana	82.1	11	262	9	29.11	2- 21	–	–
H.D.P.K.Dharmasena	71	11	212	5	42.40	3- 58	–	–

Also bowled: R.P.Arnold 6.1-1-11-0; P.A.de Silva 29.5-9-65-1; P.D.R.L.Perera 20-3-73-2; D.N.T.Zoysa 20-5-56-2.

SOUTH AFRICA – BATTING AND FIELDING

	M	I	NO	HS	Runs	Avge	100	50	Ct/St
L.Klusener	3	6	2	118*	275	68.75	1	1	2
J.N.Rhodes	3	6	1	63*	195	39.00	–	2	4
D.J.Cullinan	3	6	1	114*	175	35.00	1	–	3
J.H.Kallis	3	6	–	87	191	31.83	–	1	1
N.Boje	3	6	1	35	124	24.80	–	–	4
G.Kirsten	3	6	–	55	131	21.83	–	1	3
M.V.Boucher	3	6	–	60	111	18.50	–	1	6/1
S.M.Pollock	3	6	–	33	87	14.50	–	–	1
N.D.McKenzie	3	6	–	25	54	9.00	–	–	2
P.R.Adams	3	6	1	15	44	8.80	–	–	–
M.Hayward	2	4	1	13	16	5.33	–	–	1

Played in one Test: M.Ntini 8, 0.

SOUTH AFRICA – BOWLING

	O	M	R	W	Avge	Best	5wI	10wM
S.M.Pollock	94	30	247	11	22.45	3- 40	–	–
M Hayward	56	10	171	7	24.42	2- 15	–	–
N.Boje	101.1	20	273	10	27.30	5- 62	1	–
J.H.Kallis	53.4	17	136	4	34.00	2- 18	–	–
L.Klusener	60.1	15	149	3	49.66	2- 34	–	–
P.R.Adams	78	11	326	4	81.50	3-184	–	–

Also bowled: D.J.Cullinan 4-0-17-1; M.Ntini 19-1-73-1.

ZIMBABWE v NEW ZEALAND (1st Test)

At Queens Sports Club, Bulawayo, on 12, 13, 14, 15, 16 September 2000.
Toss: Zimbabwe. Result: **NEW ZEALAND** won by seven wickets.
Debuts: Zimbabwe – D.T.Mutendera; New Zealand – M.H.Richardson.

ZIMBABWE

G.W.Flower	c Parore b Vettori	24	c Parore b O'Connor		3
G.J.Rennie	c McMillan b Wiseman	36	b Cairns		2
S.V.Carlisle	c Horne b Wiseman	38	b Wiseman		15
A.D.R.Campbell	lbw b Astle	88	lbw b Cairns		45
†A.Flower	c Astle b Cairns	29	lbw b Astle		22
C.B.Wishart	c Richardson b Wiseman	17	c Richardson b Wiseman		1
*H.H.Streak	c Parore b Wiseman	51	c McMillan b Wiseman		15
P.A.Strang	c Richardson b Wiseman	0	(9) not out		8
M.L.Nkala	not out	30	(8) c Sinclair b Cairns		0
B.C.Strang	c Parore b O'Connor	10	b Cairns		5
D.T.Mutendera	b Cairns	10	c Parore b Cairns		0
Extras	(B 5, LB 4, NB 8)	17	(LB 1, W 1, NB 1)		3
Total		**350**			**119**

NEW ZEALAND

M.H.Richardson	c Carlisle b Streak	6	lbw b Rennie		13
M.J.Horne	lbw b P.A.Strang	110			
M.S.Sinclair	lbw b P.A.Strang	12	(2) not out		43
P.J.Wiseman	lbw b P.A.Strang	14			
*S.P.Fleming	c Rennie b P.A.Strang	11	(3) lbw b P.A.Strang		12
N.J.Astle	c A.Flower b P.A.Strang	0	(4) c Nkala b P.A.Strang		27
C.D.McMillan	c A.Flower b P.A.Strang	58	(5) not out		31
C.L.Cairns	b Streak	33			
†A.C.Parore	not out	32			
D.L.Vettori	c and b P.A.Strang	49			
S.B.O'Connor	c Campbell b P.A.Strang	4			
Extras	(LB 1, NB 8)	9	(LB 2, W 1, NB 3)		6
Total		**338**	(3 wickets)		**132**

NEW ZEALAND	O	M	R	W		O	M	R	W
Cairns	28.2	9	77	2		14.5	5	31	5
O'Connor	30	7	63	1		9	5	8	1
McMillan	9	3	23	0					
Vettori	52	23	79	1					
Astle	11	6	9	1	(5)	18	10	24	1
Wiseman	45	16	90	5	(3)	25	8	54	3
Richardson					(4)	1	0	1	0
ZIMBABWE									
Streak	26	9	67	2		5	0	21	0
Nkala	21	7	43	0		2	1	2	0
P.A.Strang	51.5	12	109	8		20.4	3	49	2
B.C.Strang	25	7	63	0	(7)	2	0	10	0
Mutendera	14	4	29	0					
G.W.Flower	16	4	26	0	(4)	1.3	0	5	0
Rennie					(5)	13.3	0	40	1
Campbell					(6)	1	0	3	0

FALL OF WICKETS

	Z	NZ	Z	NZ
Wkt	1st	1st	2nd	2nd
1st	40	15	6	27
2nd	91	52	23	43
3rd	120	109	23	93
4th	157	139	75	–
5th	206	139	86	–
6th	282	180	100	–
7th	291	252	100	–
8th	300	252	110	–
9th	323	330	119	–
10th	350	338	119	–

Umpires: D.B.Hair (*Australia*) (33) and R.B.Tiffin (17).
Referee: C.W.Smith (*West Indies*) (29).

Test No. 1510/9 (Z44/NZ280)

ZIMBABWE v NEW ZEALAND (2nd Test)

At Harare Sports Club on 19, 20, 21, 22, 23 September 2000.
Toss: New Zealand. Result: **NEW ZEALAND** won by eight wickets.
Debuts: None.

NEW ZEALAND

M.H.Richardson	lbw b Nkala	99			
C.M.Spearman	c A.Flower b Olonga	2	(1) c Rennie b Streak	2	
M.S.Sinclair	c Carlisle b Olonga	44	not out	35	
*S.P.Fleming	c Campbell b Mbangwa	9			
N.J.Astle	run out	86			
C.D.McMillan	lbw b Mbangwa	15			
C.L.Cairns	st A.Flower b Strang	124	(4) not out	19	
†A.C.Parore	c A.Flower b Olonga	4	(2) c Carlisle b Streak	13	
D.J.Nash	c G.W.Flower b Strang	62			
P.J.Wiseman	not out	1			
S.B.O'Connor	c Whittall b G.W.Flower	2			
Extras	(LB 3, W 2, NB 12)	17	(LB 2, W 1, NB 2)	5	
Total		**465**	**(2 wickets)**	**74**	

ZIMBABWE

G.W.Flower	c Parore b Astle	49	run out	10	
G.J.Rennie	c Spearman b Cairns	4	c Spearman b O'Connor	10	
S.V.Carlisle	c Sinclair b Cairns	31	c Fleming b Astle	20	
A.D.R.Campbell	c Fleming b O'Connor	0	run out	10	
†A.Flower	lbw b McMillan	48	c Sinclair b O'Connor	65	
G.J.Whittall	c Parore b Astle	9	not out	188	
*H.H.Streak	c Wiseman b O'Connor	8	lbw b Cairns	54	
M.L.Nkala	c Parore b McMillan	0	lbw b O'Connor	0	
P.A.Strang	c Parore b O'Connor	5	b Cairns	8	
H.K.Olonga	c Parore b Nash	4	lbw b O'Connor	0	
M.Mbangwa	not out	0	run out	5	
Extras	(B 3, LB 3, W 1, NB 1)	8	(B 4, LB 4, NB 1)	9	
Total		**166**		**370**	

ZIMBABWE	O	M	R	W		O	M	R	W	FALL OF WICKETS			
											NZ	Z	Z	NZ
Olonga	27	5	115	3						*Wkt*	*1st*	*1st*	*2nd*	*2nd*
Streak	29	6	74	0	(1)	8	2	33	2	1st	5	5	1	4
Nkala	15	0	60	1	(2)	3	0	17	0	2nd	69	76	27	42
Mbangwa	28	10	58	2	(3)	4.2	0	22	0	3rd	91	77	39	–
Strang	38	11	80	2						4th	226	118	48	–
G.W.Flower	20.3	6	59	1						5th	256	146	179	–
Rennie	3	0	16	0						6th	302	151	330	–
										7th	318	151	335	–
NEW ZEALAND										8th	462	157	348	–
Cairns	17.1	7	33	2	(5)	33	7	80	2	9th	462	164	349	–
O'Connor	28	9	43	3	(1)	45	17	73	4	10th	465	166	370	–
Nash	17	11	25	1	(2)	17.3	8	28	0					
McMillan	12.5	2	39	2	(3)	20	4	53	0					
Astle	14	9	22	2	(4)	36	15	73	1					
Wiseman	3	0	8	0		27	11	55	0					

Umpires: I.D.Robinson (23) and D.R.Shepherd (*England*) (53).
Referee: C.M.Smith (*West Indies*) (30).   Test No. 1511/10 (Z45/NZ281)

ZIMBABWE v NEW ZEALAND 2000-01

ZIMBABWE – BATTING AND FIELDING

	M	I	NO	HS	Runs	Avge	100	50	Ct/St
G.J.Whittall	1	2	1	188*	197	197.00	–	1	1
A.Flower	2	4	–	65	164	41.00	–	1	4/1
A.D.R.Campbell	2	4	–	88	143	35.75	–	1	2
H.H.Streak	2	4	–	54	128	32.00	–	2	–
S.V.Carlisle	2	4	–	38	104	26.00	–	–	3
G.W.Flower	2	4	–	49	86	21.50	–	–	1
G.J.Rennie	2	4	–	36	43	10.75	–	–	2
M.L.Nkala	2	4	1	30*	30	10.00	–	–	1
C.B.Wishart	1	2	–	17	18	9.00	–	–	–
B.C.Strang	1	2	–	10	15	7.50	–	–	–
P.A.Strang	2	4	1	8*	21	7.00	–	–	1
M.Mbangwa	1	1	–	5	5	5.00	–	–	–
D.T.Mutendera	1	2	–	10	10	5.00	–	–	–
H.K.Olonga	1	2	–	4	4	2.00	–	–	–

ZIMBABWE – BOWLING

	O	M	R	W	Avge	Best	5wI	10wM
P.A.Strang	110.3	26	238	12	19.83	8-109	1	1
H.K.Olonga	27	5	115	3	38.33	3-115	–	–
M.Mbangwa	32.2	10	80	2	40.00	2- 58	–	–
H.H.Streak	68	17	195	4	48.75	2- 33	–	–

Also bowled: A.D.R.Campbell 1-0-3-0; G.W.Flower 38-10-90-1; D.T.Mutendera 14-4-29-0; M.L.Nkala 41-8-122-1; G.J.Rennie 16.3-0-56-1; B.C.Strang 27-7-73-0.

NEW ZEALAND – BATTING AND FIELDING

	M	I	NO	HS	Runs	Avge	100	50	Ct/St
M.J.Horne	1	1	–	110	110	110.00	1	–	1
C.L.Cairns	2	3	1	124	176	88.00	1	–	–
M.S.Sinclair	2	4	2	44	134	67.00	–	–	3
D.J.Nash	1	1	–	62	62	62.00	–	1	–
C.D.McMillan	2	3	1	58	104	52.00	–	1	2
D.L.Vettori	1	1	–	49	49	49.00	–	–	–
M.H.Richardson	2	3	–	99	118	39.33	–	1	3
N.J.Astle	2	3	–	86	113	37.66	–	1	1
A.C.Parore	2	3	1	32*	49	24.50	–	–	10
P.J.Wiseman	2	2	1	14	15	15.00	–	–	1
S.P.Fleming	2	3	–	12	32	10.66	–	–	2
S.B.O'Connor	2	2	–	4	6	3.00	–	–	–
C.M.Spearman	1	2	–	2	4	2.00	–	–	2

NEW ZEALAND – BOWLING

	O	M	R	W	Avge	Best	5wI	10wM
C.L.Cairns	93.2	28	221	11	20.09	5- 31	1	–
S.B.O'Connor	112	38	187	9	20.77	4- 73	–	–
N.J.Astle	79	40	128	5	25.60	2- 22	–	–
P.J.Wiseman	100	35	207	8	25.87	5- 90	1	–
C.D.McMillan	41.5	9	105	2	52.50	2- 29	–	–

Also bowled: D.J.Nash 34.3-19-53-1; M.H.Richardson 1-0-1-0; D.L.Vettori 52-23-79-1.

BANGLADESH v INDIA (Only Test)

At Bangabandhu National Stadium, Dhaka, on 10, 11, 12, 13 November 2000.
Toss: Bangladesh. Result: **INDIA** won by nine wickets.
Debuts: Bangladesh – All; India – S.S.Das, S.S.Karim, Z.Khan.

BANGLADESH

Shahriar Hossain	c Ganguly b Joshi	12	lbw b Joshi	7
Mehrab Hossain	c Karim b Khan	4	c Kartik b Khan	2
Habibul Bashar	c Ganguly b Khan	71	c Khan b Agarkar	30
Aminul Islam	c Srinath b Agarkar	145	lbw b Agarkar	6
Akram Khan	c Dravid b Joshi	35	(6) c Das b Joshi	2
Al Sahariar	lbw b Agarkar	12	(5) c and b Joshi	6
*Naimur Rahman	c Das b Joshi	15	(8) c Ganguly b Srinath	3
†Khaled Masud	c Das b Joshi	32	(7) not out	21
Mohammed Rafique	c Das b Tendulkar	22	c Ganguly b Srinath	4
Hasibul Hussain	not out	28	lbw b Srinath	0
Ranjan Das	c Ganguly b Joshi	2	c Das b Kartik	0
Extras	(B 13, LB 6, NB 3)	22	(B 7, LB 1, NB 2)	10
Total		**400**		**91**

INDIA

S.S.Das	b Naimur	29	not out	22
S.Ramesh	b Ranjan	58	b Hasibul	1
M.Kartik	c sub (Rajin Salah) b Naimur	43		
R.Dravid	c Al Sahariar b Rafique	28	(3) not out	41
S.R.Tendulkar	c sub (Rajin Salah) b Naimur	18		
*S.C.Ganguly	c Al Sahariar b Naimur	84		
†S.S.Karim	st Shahriar Hossain b Naimur	15		
S.B.Joshi	c Al Sahariar b Rafique	92		
A.B.Agarkar	c Ranjan b Naimur	34		
J.Srinath	c and b Rafique	2		
Z.Khan	not out	7		
Extras	(B 13, LB 4, W 2,)	19		
Total		**429**	(1 wicket)	**64**

INDIA	O	M	R	W	O	M	R	W
Srinath	22	9	47	0	11	3	19	3
Khan	21	6	49	2	5	0	20	1
Agarkar	31	13	68	2	11	4	16	2
Joshi	45.3	8	142	5	18	5	27	3
Kartik	24	9	41	0	1.3	0	1	.1
Tendulkar	10	2	34	1				

BANGLADESH								
Hasibul Hussain	19	2	60	0	6	0	31	1
Ranjan Das	19	3	64	1	3	0	8	0
Naimur Rahman	44.3	9	132	6	4	0	22	0
Mohammed Rafique	51	12	117	3	2	0	3	0
Habibul Bashar	8	0	39	0				

FALL OF WICKETS

	B	I	B	I
Wkt	1st	1st	2nd	2nd
1st	10	66	11	11
2nd	44	104	32	—
3rd	110	155	43	—
4th	175	175	53	—
5th	196	190	53	—
6th	231	236	69	—
7th	324	357	76	—
8th	354	413	81	—
9th	385	421	81	—
10th	400	429	91	—

Umpires: S.A.Bucknor (52) (*West Indies*) and D.R.Shepherd (54) (*England*).
Referee: R.Subba Row (*England*) (35).

Test No. 1512/1 (B1/I334)

PAKISTAN v ENGLAND (1st Test)

At Gaddafi Stadium, Lahore, on 15, 16, 17, 18, 19 November 2000.
Toss: England. Result: **MATCH DRAWN**.
Debuts: Pakistan – Qaiser Abbas.

ENGLAND

M.A.Atherton	c Youhana b Saqlain	73	lbw b Mushtaq Ahmed		20
M.E.Trescothick	c Elahi b Saqlain	71	lbw b Wasim		1
G.P.Thorpe	c and b Saqlain	118	(4) c Razzaq b Saqlain		5
†A.J.Stewart	lbw b Saqlain	3	(5) not out		27
*N.Hussain	c Wasim b Saqlain	7	(3) retired hurt		0
G.A.Hick	lbw b Saqlain	16	b Afridi		14
C.White	c Youhana b Saqlain	93			
I.D.K.Salisbury	lbw b Saqlain	31			
A.F.Giles	not out	37			
A.R.Caddick	not out	5			
D.Gough					
Extras	(B 3, LB 13, NB 10)	26	(LB 7, NB 3)		10
Total	(8 wickets declared)	**480**	(4 wickets declared)		**77**

PAKISTAN

Saeed Anwar	lbw b Hick	40
Shahid Afridi	c Gough b Giles	52
Salim Elahi	b White	44
Inzamam-ul-Haq	b Giles	63
Yousuf Youhana	c Stewart b Giles	124
Qaiser Abbas	c Hick b White	2
*†Moin Khan	lbw b Caddick	17
Abdur Razzaq	lbw b White	10
Wasim Akram	c White b Giles	1
Saqlain Mushtaq	not out	32
Mushtaq Ahmed	lbw b White	0
Extras	(B 3, LB 5, NB 8)	16
Total		**401**

PAKISTAN	O	M	R	W	O	M	R	W	FALL OF WICKETS
Wasim Akram	22	8	40	0	6	5	1	1	
Abdur Razzaq	22	6	55	0	7	0	21	0	
Saqlain Mushtaq	74	20	164	8	10	2	14	1	
Mushtaq Ahmed	44	6	132	0	8	0	32	1	
Shahid Afridi	18	6	38	0	1.1	0	2	1	
Qaiser Abbas	16	3	35	0					

	O	M	R	W		E	P	E
					Wkt	1st	1st	2nd
ENGLAND					1st	134	63	4
Gough	17	6	45	0	2nd	169	101	29
Caddick	24	4	68	1	3rd	173	199	39
Giles	59	20	113	4	4th	183	203	77
Salisbury	31	5	71	0	5th	225	210	–
Hick	8	0	42	1	6th	391	236	–
White	24.3	5	54	4	7th	398	272	–
					8th	468	273	–
					9th	–	400	–
					10th	–	401	–

Umpires: D.B.Hair (*Australia*) (34) and Riazuddin (8).
Referee: R.S.Madugalle (*Sri Lanka*) (30).   Test No. 1513/56 (P271/E774)

PAKISTAN v ENGLAND (2nd Test)

At Iqbal Stadium, Faisalabad, on 29, 30 November, 1, 2, 3 December 2000.
Toss: Pakistan. Result: **MATCH DRAWN**.
Debuts: Pakistan – Danish Kaneria.

PAKISTAN

Saeed Anwar	c Thorpe b Giles	53			
Shahid Afridi	c Thorpe b Gough	10		c Giles b Gough	10
Salim Elahi	c Atherton b Giles	41	(1)	c Stewart b Giles	72
Inzamam-ul-Haq	b Giles	0		c Hick b Salisbury	71
Yousuf Youhana	c Thorpe b Gough	77			
Abdur Razzaq	b White	9	(3)	not out	100
*†Moin Khan	c Hussain b Giles	65			
Wasim Akram	st Stewart b Giles	1	(5)	not out	4
Saqlain Mushtaq	c Trescothick b Gough	34			
Arshad Khan	c Thorpe b White	2			
Danish Kaneria	not out	8			
Extras	(B 1, LB 12, NB 3)	16		(B 6, LB 5, NB 1)	12
Total		**316**		(3 wickets declared)	**269**

ENGLAND

M.A.Atherton	c Youhana b Saqlain	32		not out	65
M.E.Trescothick	st Moin b Kaneria	30		b Saqlain	10
*N.Hussain	lbw b Saqlain	23		c Moin b Arshad	5
I.D.K.Salisbury	c Youhana b Arshad	33			
G.P.Thorpe	lbw b Wasim	79	(4)	b Arshad	0
†A.J.Stewart	c Razzaq b Kaneria	13	(5)	c Youhana b Afridi	22
G.A.Hick	c Youhana b Razzaq	17	(6)	b Afridi	0
C.White	b Saqlain	41	(7)	not out	9
A.F.Giles	c Afridi b Razzaq	0			
A.R.Caddick	c Moin b Razzaq	5			
D.Gough	not out	19			
Extras	(B 4, LB 14, NB 32)	50		(LB 4, NB 10)	14
Total		**342**		(5 wickets)	**125**

ENGLAND	O	M	R	W		O	M	R	W
Gough	23.1	2	79	3		10.2	1	32	1
Caddick	15	3	49	0		18	1	49	0
White	25	6	71	2	(4)	19	3	55	0
Giles	35	13	75	5	(3)	26	3	90	1
Salisbury	10	0	29	0		7	0	32	1
PAKISTAN									
Wasim Akram	28	6	69	1		5	1	13	0
Abdur Razzaq	20	0	74	3		1	1	0	0
Danish Kaneria	34	9	89	2	(4)	7	0	30	0
Saqlain Mushtaq	30.4	8	62	3	(3)	19	4	26	1
Arshad Khan	25	12	29	1		13	4	31	2
Shahid Afridi	1	0	1	0		12	3	21	2

	FALL OF WICKETS			
	P	E	P	E
Wkt	1st	1st	2nd	2nd
1st	33	49	13	44
2nd	96	105	111	57
3rd	96	106	259	57
4th	130	203	–	108
5th	151	233	–	110
6th	271	274	–	–
7th	271	274	–	–
8th	276	275	–	–
9th	283	295	–	–
10th	316	342	–	–

Umpires: S.A.Bucknor (*West Indies*) (53) and Mian Mohammad Aslam (6).
Referee: R.S.Madugalle (*Sri Lanka*) (31).   Test No. 1514/57 (P272/E775)

PAKISTAN v ENGLAND (3rd Test)

At National Stadium, Karachi, on 7, 8, 9, 10, 11 December 2000.
Toss: Pakistan. Result: **ENGLAND** won by six wickets.
Debuts: None.

PAKISTAN

Saeed Anwar	lbw b Gough	8		c Thorpe b Caddick	21
Imran Nazir	c Giles b Trescothick	20		c Stewart b Gough	4
Salim Elahi	b Caddick	28		c Thorpe b Giles	37
Inzamam-ul-Haq	c Trescothick b White	142		b Giles	27
Yousuf Youhana	c and b Giles	117	(6)	c Stewart b White	24
Abdur Razzaq	c Hussain b Giles	21	(7)	c Atherton b Giles	1
*†Moin Khan	c Hick b Giles	13	(8)	c Hussain b White	14
Shahid Afridi	b Giles	10	(9)	not out	15
Saqlain Mushtaq	b Gough	16	(5)	lbw b Gough	4
Waqar Younis	b Gough	17		run out	0
Danish Kaneria	not out	0		lbw b Gough	0
Extras	(B 3, LB 3, NB 7)	13		(B 3, LB 5, NB 3)	11
Total		**405**			**158**

ENGLAND

M.A.Atherton	c Moin b Razzaq	125		c Saeed b Saqlain	26
M.E.Trescothick	c Imran b Waqar	13		c Inzamam b Saqlain	24
*N.Hussain	c Inzamam b Afridi	51	(6)	b Waqar	6
G.P.Thorpe	lbw b Waqar	18		not out	64
†A.J.Stewart	c Youhana b Saqlain	29	(3)	c Moin b Saqlain	5
G.A.Hick	c Afridi b Waqar	12	(5)	b Waqar	40
C.White	st Moin b Kaneria	35			
A.F.Giles	b Waqar	19			
I.D.K.Salisbury	not out	20			
A.R.Caddick	c Moin b Kaneria	3			
D.Gough	c Youhana b Saqlain	18			
Extras	(B 12, LB 9, NB 24)	45		(B 8, LB 2, W 1)	11
Total		**388**		**(4 wickets)**	**176**

ENGLAND	O	M	R	W	O	M	R	W
Gough	27.4	5	82	3	13	4	30	3
Caddick	23	1	76	1	15	2	40	1
Trescothick	14	1	34	1				
White	22	3	64	1	(5) 12	4	30	2
Salisbury	18	3	49	0	(4) 3	0	12	0
Giles	35	7	94	3	(3) 27	12	38	3

PAKISTAN	O	M	R	W	O	M	R	W
Waqar Younis	36	5	88	4	6	0	27	1
Abdur Razzaq	28	7	64	1	4	0	17	0
Shahid Afridi	16	3	34	1	(5) 11	1	40	0
Saqlain Mushtaq	52.1	17	101	2	(3) 17.3	1	64	3
Danish Kaneria	47	17	80	2	(4) 3	0	18	0

FALL OF WICKETS

	P	E	P	E
Wkt	1st	1st	2nd	2nd
1st	8	29	24	38
2nd	44	163	26	51
3rd	64	195	71	65
4th	323	256	78	156
5th	325	278	128	–
6th	340	309	128	–
7th	359	339	139	–
8th	374	345	143	–
9th	402	349	149	–
10th	405	388	158	–

Umpires: S.A.Bucknor (*West Indies*) (54) and Mohammad Nazir (4).
Referee: R.S.Madugalle (*Sri Lanka*) (32).   Test No. 1515/58 (P273/E776)

PAKISTAN v ENGLAND 2000-01

PAKISTAN – BATTING AND FIELDING

	M	I	NO	HS	Runs	Avge	100	50	Ct/St
Yousuf Youhana	3	4	–	124	342	85.50	2	1	8
Inzamam-ul-Haq	3	5	–	142	303	60.60	1	2	2
Salim Elahi	3	5	–	72	222	44.40	–	1	1
Abdur Razzaq	3	5	1	100*	141	35.25	1	–	2
Saeed Anwar	3	4	–	53	122	30.50	–	1	1
Saqlain Mushtaq	3	4	1	34	86	28.66	–	–	1
Moin Khan	3	4	–	65	109	27.25	–	1	5/2
Shahid Afridi	3	5	1	52	97	24.25	–	1	2
Danish Kaneria	2	3	2	8*	8	8.00	–	–	–
Wasim Akram	2	3	1	4*	6	3.00	–	–	1

Played in one Test: Arshad Khan 2; Imran Nazir 20, 4 (1 ct); Qaiser Abbas 2; Mushtaq Ahmed 0; Waqar Younis 17, 0.

PAKISTAN – BOWLING

	O	M	R	W	Avge	Best	5wI	10wM
Arshad Khan	38	16	60	3	20.00	2- 31	–	–
Waqar Younis	42	5	115	5	23.00	4- 88	–	–
Saqlain Mushtaq	203.2	52	431	18	23.94	8-164	1	–
Shahid Afridi	59.1	13	136	4	34.00	2- 21	–	–
Danish Kaneria	91	26	217	4	54.25	2- 80	–	–
Abdur Razzaq	82	14	231	4	57.75	3- 74	–	–
Wasim Akram	59	20	123	2	61.50	1- 1	–	–

Also bowled: Mushtaq Ahmed 52-6-164-1; Qaiser Abbas 16-3-35-0.

ENGLAND – BATTING AND FIELDING

	M	I	NO	HS	Runs	Avge	100	50	Ct/St
M.A.Atherton	3	6	1	125	341	68.20	1	2	2
C.White	3	4	1	93	178	59.33	–	1	1
G.P.Thorpe	3	6	1	118	284	56.80	1	2	6
I.D.K.Salisbury	3	3	1	33	84	42.00	–	–	–
D.Gough	3	2	1	19*	37	37.00	–	–	1
A.F.Giles	3	3	1	37*	56	28.00	–	–	3
M.E.Trescothick	3	6	–	71	149	24.83	–	1	2
N.Hussain	3	6	2	51	92	23.00	–	1	3
A.J.Stewart	3	6	1	29	99	19.80	–	–	4/1
G.A.Hick	3	6	–	40	99	16.50	–	–	3
A.R.Caddick	3	3	1	5*	13	6.50	–	–	–

ENGLAND – BOWLING

	O	M	R	W	Avge	Best	5wI	10wM
A.F.Giles	182	55	410	17	24.11	5- 75	1	–
D.Gough	91.1	18	268	10	26.80	3- 30	–	–
C.White	102.3	21	274	9	30.44	4- 54	–	–
A.R.Caddick	95	11	282	3	94.00	1- 40	–	–

Also bowled: G.A.Hick 8-0-42-1; I.D.K.Salisbury 69-8-193-1; M.E.Trescothick 14-1-34-1.

SOUTH AFRICA v NEW ZEALAND (1st Test)

At Springbok Park, Bloemfontein, on 17, 18, 19, 20, 21 November 2000.
Toss: South Africa. Result: **SOUTH AFRICA** won by five wickets.
Debuts: New Zealand – C.S.Martin, B.G.K.Walker.

SOUTH AFRICA

H.H.Dippenaar	c Astle b O'Connor	0	c Parore b Tuffey		27
G.Kirsten	c Astle b Martin	31	lbw b O'Connor		1
J.H.Kallis	c Parore b O'Connor	160	lbw b Martin		13
D.J.Cullinan	b Walker	29	lbw b Tuffey		22
N.D.McKenzie	c Parore b Martin	55	not out		13
†M.V.Boucher	lbw b Walker	76	(7) not out		22
L.Klusener	b O'Connor	9	(6) c McMillan b Tuffey		4
N.Boje	c Tuffey b Astle	43			
*S.M.Pollock	c Sinclair b Martin	25			
A.A.Donald	not out	21			
M.Ntini					
Extras	(B 5, LB 7, NB 10)	22	(NB 1)		1
Total	(9 wickets declared)	**471**	(5 wickets)		**103**

NEW ZEALAND

M.H.Richardson	b Donald	23	lbw b Donald		77
C.M.Spearman	c Klusener b Pollock	23	c McKenzie b Ntini		15
M.S.Sinclair	c Cullinan b Pollock	1	c Klusener b Donald		20
*S.P.Fleming	b Boje	57	c Kirsten b Donald		99
N.J.Astle	c Kallis b Ntini	37	b Ntini		8
C.D.McMillan	c Boucher b Donald	16	c Kirsten b Kallis		78
†A.C.Parore	lbw b Pollock	11	(8) c Kallis b Ntini		12
B.G.K.Walker	not out	27	(7) b Boucher b Ntini		10
D.R.Tuffey	b Pollock	0	b Ntini		6
S.B.O'Connor	lbw b Donald	15	b Ntini		0
C.S.Martin	c Boucher b Kallis	7	not out		0
Extras	(B 1, LB 7, W 2, NB 2)	12	(B 2, LB 10, W 1, NB 4)		17
Total		**229**			**342**

NEW ZEALAND	O	M	R	W		O	M	R	W
O'Connor	30	4	87	3		7	0	28	1
Tuffey	26	6	96	0	(3)	8	1	38	3
Martin	22.1	4	89	3	(2)	5	3	18	1
Walker	27	4	92	2		6.3	2	19	0
Astle	24	5	57	1					
McMillan	13	2	38	0					

SOUTH AFRICA	O	M	R	W		O	M	R	W
Donald	21	4	69	3		28	14	43	3
Pollock	22	10	37	4		25	11	47	0
Ntini	14	4	48	1		31.4	12	66	6
Kallis	13	5	30	1		23	4	88	1
Boje	16	4	35	1		40	14	61	0
Klusener	3	2	2	0		10	3	25	0

FALL OF WICKETS

	SA	NZ	NZ	SA
Wkt	1st	1st	2nd	2nd
1st	0	28	33	3
2nd	97	29	93	16
3rd	164	72	145	55
4th	279	151	175	69
5th	304	153	247	75
6th	330	176	285	–
7th	409	183	325	–
8th	429	185	340	–
9th	471	213	341	–
10th	–	229	342	–

Umpires: A.V.Jayapradesh (*India*) (6) and D.L.Orchard (20).
Referee: Naushad Ali (*Pakistan*) (1).   **Test No. 1516/25 (SA246/NZ282)**

SOUTH AFRICA v NEW ZEALAND (2nd Test)

At St George's Park, Port Elizabeth, on 30 November, 1, 2, 3, 4 December 2000.
Toss: South Africa. Result: **SOUTH AFRICA** won by seven wickets.
Debuts: None.

NEW ZEALAND

M.H.Richardson	b Ntini	26	c Boucher b Pollock		60
C.M.Spearman	c Kirsten b Donald	16	lbw b Donald		0
M.S.Sinclair	c Kirsten b Donald	150	lbw b Boje		17
*S.P.Fleming	c and b Pollock	14	c Cullinan b Boje		8
N.J.Astle	lbw b Pollock	2	c Boucher b Ntini		18
C.D.McMillan	c Ntini b Pollock	39	lbw b Pollock		0
†A.C.Parore	c Boucher b Donald	2	c Kirsten b Ntini		5
B.G.K.Walker	c Cullinan b Pollock	3	lbw b Klusener		19
S.B.O'Connor	b Kallis	20	b Klusener		8
K.P.Walmsley	c Cullinan b Donald	5	lbw b Klusener		0
C.S.Martin	not out	5	not out		0
Extras	(B 4, LB 5, W 2, NB 5)	16	(B 6, LB 3, NB 4)		13
Total		**298**			**148**

SOUTH AFRICA

G.Kirsten	c Parore b Walmsley	49	(2) not out		47
H.H.Dippenaar	lbw b Martin	35	(1) lbw b O'Connor		0
J.H.Kallis	c Parore b Astle	12	c O'Connor b Martin		23
D.J.Cullinan	b Walker	33	b Walmsley		11
*S.M.Pollock	c Spearman b Martin	33			
N.D.McKenzie	c Spearman b McMillan	120	(5) not out		7
†M.V.Boucher	b O'Connor	0			
L.Klusener	c Parore b Martin	6			
N.Boje	c Parore b O'Connor	51			
A.A.Donald	lbw b Martin	9			
M.Ntini	not out	0			
Extras	(B 7, LB 4, W 2)	13	(LB 1)		1
Total		**361**	(3 wickets)		**89**

SOUTH AFRICA	O	M	R	W		O	M	R	W	FALL OF WICKETS				
											NZ	SA	NZ	SA
Donald	26.3	2	69	4		7	1	16	1	*Wkt*	*1st*	*1st*	*2nd*	*2nd*
Pollock	32	15	64	4		15	4	44	2	1st	43	81	4	4
Kallis	21	8	44	1	(5)	7	2	17	0	2nd	55	96	54	53
Ntini	22	7	59	1	(3)	16	6	24	2	3rd	95	114	64	71
Klusener	6	2	8	0	(6)	9.3	5	8	3	4th	101	151	111	–
Boje	19	5	45	0	(4)	15	2	30	2	5th	172	181	111	–
										6th	194	184	115	–
NEW ZEALAND										7th	203	209	122	–
O'Connor	26.4	8	68	2		8	4	9	1	8th	276	345	147	–
Martin	29	8	104	4		12	3	32	1	9th	291	361	147	–
Walmsley	13	2	40	1	(5)	5	2	7	1	10th	298	361	148	–
Walker	23	5	61	1		7.1	1	32	0					
Astle	36	18	46	1	(3)	2	0	8	0					
McMillan	17	6	31	1										

Umpires: R.E.Koertzen (20) and I.D.Robinson (*Zimbabwe*) (24).
Referee: Naushad Ali (*Pakistan*) (2).   Test No. 1517/26 (SA247/NZ283)

SOUTH AFRICA v NEW ZEALAND (3rd Test)

At The Wanderers, Johannesburg, on 8 (*no play*), 9, 10 (*no play*), 11 (*no play*),
12 December 2000.
Toss: South Africa. Result: **MATCH DRAWN**.
Debuts: South Africa – M.Mgam. New Zealand – H.J.H.Marshall.

NEW ZEALAND

M.H.Richardson	c Boucher b Ngam	46
†A.C.Parore	c McKenzie b Ntini	10
M.S.Sinclair	c Klusener b Pollock	24
*S.P.Fleming	b Ntini	14
N.J.Astle	c Kallis b Ntini	12
C.D.McMillan	c Klusener b Kallis	4
H.J.H.Marshall	not out	40
B.G.K.Walker	lbw b Klusener	17
D.R.Tuffey	c Boucher b Ngam	8
S.B.O'Connor	c Kallis b Pollock	9
C.S.Martin	b Kallis	0
Extras	(B 2, LB 9, W 1, NB 4)	16
Total		**200**

SOUTH AFRICA

H.H.Dippenaar	b O'Connor	100
G.Kirsten	c Richardson b Martin	10
N.Boje	c Sinclair b Martin	22
J.H.Kallis	not out	79
D.J.Cullinan	not out	31
†M.V.Boucher		
L.Klusener		
N.D.McKenzie		
*S.M.Pollock		
M.Ngam		
M.Ntini		
Extras	(LB 17, W 2)	19
Total	(3 wickets declared)	**261**

SOUTH AFRICA	O	M	R	W
Pollock	26	9	41	2
Ngam	19	8	34	2
Kallis	15.5	4	26	2
Ntini	18	9	29	3
Klusener	12	2	43	1
Boje	3	0	16	0

NEW ZEALAND	O	M	R	W
O'Connor	15	5	52	1
Martin	15	4	43	2
Tuffey	19	4	60	0
Astle	26	15	31	0
McMillan	17	5	41	0
Marshall	1	0	4	0
Sinclair	4	0	13	0

FALL OF WICKETS

	NZ	SA
Wkt	1st	1st
1st	37	18
2nd	83	87
3rd	83	187
4th	112	–
5th	113	–
6th	117	–
7th	148	–
8th	174	–
9th	199	–
10th	200	–

Umpires: D.L.Orchard (21) & G.Sharp (*England*) (13).
Referee: Naushad Ali (*Pakistan*) (3).   **Test No. 1518/27 (SA248/NZ284)**

SOUTH AFRICA v NEW ZEALAND 2000-01

SOUTH AFRICA – BATTING AND FIELDING

	M	I	NO	HS	Runs	Avge	100	50	Ct/St
N.D.McKenzie	3	4	2	120	195	97.50	1	1	2
J.H.Kallis	3	5	–	160	287	71.75	1	1	4
M.V.Boucher	3	3	1	76	98	49.00	–	1	8
N.Boje	3	3	–	51	116	38.66	–	1	–
G.Kirsten	3	5	1	49	138	34.50	–	–	5
H.H.Dippenaar	3	5	–	100	162	32.40	1	–	–
D.J.Cullinan	3	5	1	33	126	31.50	–	–	4
A.A.Donald	2	2	1	21*	30	30.00	–	–	–
S.M.Pollock	3	2	–	33	58	29.00	–	–	1
L.Klusener	3	3	–	9	19	6.33	–	–	4
M.Ntini	3	1	1	0*					1

Played in one Test: M.Ngam did not bat.

SOUTH AFRICA – BOWLING

	O	M	R	W	Avge	Best	5wI	10wM
M.Ntini	101.4	38	226	13	17.38	6- 66	1	–
A.A.Donald	82.3	21	197	11	17.90	4- 69	–	–
S.M.Pollock	120	49	233	12	19.41	4- 37	–	–
L.Klusener	40.3	14	86	4	21.50	3- 8	–	–
J.H.Kallis	79.5	23	205	5	41.00	2- 26	–	–
N.Boje	93	25	187	3	62.33	2- 30	–	–

Also bowled: M Ngam 19-8-34 2.

NEW ZEALAND – BATTING AND FIELDING

	M	I	NO	HS	Runs	Avge	100	50	Ct/St
M.H.Richardson	3	5	–	77	232	46.40	–	2	1
M.S.Sinclair	3	5	–	150	212	42.40	1	–	2
S.P.Fleming	3	5	–	99	192	38.40	–	2	–
C.D.McMillan	3	5	–	78	137	27.40	–	1	1
B.G.K.Walker	3	5	1	27*	76	19.00	–	–	–
N.J.Astle	3	5	–	37	77	15.40	–	–	2
C.M.Spearman	2	4	–	23	54	13.50	–	–	2
S.B.O'Connor	3	5	–	20	52	10.40	–	–	1
A.C.Parore	3	5	–	12	40	8.00	–	–	7
C.S.Martin	3	5	3	7	12	6.00	–	–	–
D.R.Tuffey	2	3	–	8	14	4.66	–	–	1

Played in one Test: H.J.H.Marshall 40*; K.P.Walmsley 5, 0.

NEW ZEALAND – BOWLING

	O	M	R	W	Avge	Best	5wI	10wM
C.S.Martin	83.1	22	286	11	26.00	4-104	–	–
S.B.O'Connor	86.4	21	244	8	30.50	3- 87	–	–
D.R.Tuffey	53	11	194	3	64.66	3- 38	–	–
B.G.K.Walker	63.4	12	204	3	68.00	2- 92	–	–

Also bowled: N.J.Astle 88-38 142-2; C.D.McMillan 47-13-110-1; H.J.H.Marshall 1-0-4-0; M.S.Sinclair 4-0-13-0; K.P.Walmsley 18-4-47-2.

INDIA v ZIMBABWE (1st Test)

At Feroz Shah Kotla, Delhi, on 18, 19, 20, 21, 22 November 2000.
Toss: Zimbabwe. Result: **INDIA** won by seven wickets.
Debuts: India – V.Dahiya.

ZIMBABWE

G.W.Flower	b Srinath	0	c Dahiya b Srinath		0
G.J.Rennie	c Dahiya b Srinath	13	c Ganguly b Srinath		0
S.V.Carlisle	c Joshi b Tendulkar	58	c Ganguly b Joshi		32
A.D.R.Campbell	c Laxman b Srinath	70	c Dravid b Srinath		8
†A.Flower	not out	183	lbw b Agarkar		70
G.J.Whittall	c Dravid b Joshi	0	c Ramesh b Kartik		29
*H.H.Streak	c Dravid b Joshi	25	lbw b Kartik	(8)	26
P.A.Strang	c Ganguly b Joshi	19	not out	(9)	14
B.A.Murphy	run out	13	c Dahiya b Srinath	(7)	6
B.C.Strang	lbw b Agarkar	6	c Tendulkar b Joshi		15
H.K.Olonga	not out	11	lbw b Srinath		10
Extras	(B 8, LB 10, W 4, NB 2)	24	(B 4, LB 9, W 1, NB 1)		15
Total	(9 wickets declared)	**422**			**225**

INDIA

S.S.Das	lbw b Olonga	58	run out		4
S.Ramesh	lbw b Streak	13	c P.A.Strang b Streak		0
R.Dravid	b Olonga	200	not out		70
S.R.Tendulkar	c P.A.Strang b Murphy	122	c Murphy b P.A.Strang		39
*S.C.Ganguly	c A.Flower b Olonga	27	not out		65
V.V.S.Laxman	not out	18			
A.B.Agarkar					
S.B.Joshi					
J.Srinath					
†V.Dahiya					
M.Kartik					
Extras	(B 2, LB 10, W 2, NB 6)	20	(B 9, LB 1, W 1, NB 1)		12
Total	(4 wickets declared)	**458**	(3 wickets)		**190**

INDIA	O	M	R	W		O	M	R	W
Srinath	35	9	81	4		24.1	6	60	5
Agarkar	35	13	89	1	–	16	4	48	1
Ganguly	8	1	26	0					
Joshi	46	11	116	2	(3) 25	7	68	2	
Tendulkar	19	5	51	1	(4) 4	1	10	0	
Kartik	24	7	40	0	(5) 11	2	26	2	
Laxman	1	0	1	0					

ZIMBABWE	O	M	R	W		O	M	R	W
Streak	30	9	78	0		5	2	18	1
B.C.Strang	28	9	95	0		3	0	20	0
Murphy	36	5	90	1	(4) 11	0	56	0	
Olonga	20	3	79	2	(3) 6	0	26	0	
P.A.Strang	15	1	52	0		4.2	0	26	1
G.W.Flower	13.4	3	52	0		1.4	0	10	0
Rennie						3.3	0	19	0
Campbell						3	1	5	0

FALL OF WICKETS

	Z	I	Z	I
Wkt	1st	1st	2nd	2nd
1st	0	27	0	3
2nd	15	134	15	15
3rd	134	347	25	80
4th	154	430	47	–
5th	155	–	109	–
6th	232	–	144	–
7th	266	–	171	–
8th	312	–	181	–
9th	325	–	213	–
10th	–	–	225	–

Umpires: J.H.Hampshire (*England*) (14) and S.Venkataraghavan (40).
Referee: B.N.Jarman (*Australia*) (22).

Test No. 1519/4 (I335/Z46)

INDIA v ZIMBABWE (2nd Test)

At Vidharbha C.A. Ground, Nagpur, on 25, 26, 27, 28, 29 November 2000.
Toss: India. Result: **MATCH DRAWN**.
Debuts: India – Sharandeep Singh.

INDIA

S.S.Das	c Campbell b Murphy	110
S.Ramesh	run out	48
R.Dravid	c A.Flower b Streak	162
S.R.Tendulkar	not out	201
*S.C.Ganguly	c Streak b G.W.Flower	30
A.B.Agarkar	c Streak b Murphy	12
S.B.Joshi	c Murphy b G.W.Flower	27
†V.Dahiya	not out	2
J.Srinath		
Z.Khan		
Sharandeep Singh		
Extras	(LB 11, W 4, NB 2)	17
Total	**(6 wickets declared)**	**609**

ZIMBABWE

G.J.Whittall	c Dravid b Sharandeep	84	c Tendulkar b Sharandeep	11
G.J.Rennie	run out	19	c Ganguly b Sharandeep	37
S.V.Carlisle	c and b Agarkar	51	c Tendulkar b Sharandeep	8
A.D.R.Campbell	c Ramesh b Sharandeep	4	c Joshi b Khan	102
†A.Flower	c Dahiya b Agarkar	55	not out	232
G.W.Flower	not out	106	c Ganguly b Joshi	16
D.P.Viljoen	c Dahiya b Khan	19	c Ganguly b Sharandeep	38
*H.H.Streak	lbw b Srinath	16	not out	29
M.L.Nkala	c Dahiya b Srinath	6		
B.A.Murphy	c Das b Joshi	0		
H.K.Olonga	b Srinath	0		
Extras	(B 6, LB 12, W 1, NB 3)	22	(B 12, LB 14, NB 4)	30
Total		**382**	**(6 wickets)**	**503**

ZIMBABWE	O	M	R	W		O	M	R	W		FALL OF WICKETS			
												I	Z	Z
Streak	31	7	87	1							Wkt	1st	1st	2nd
Olonga	24	4	98	0							1st	72	43	24
Nkala	22	2	86	0							2nd	227	144	60
Murphy	40.5	2	175	2							3rd	476	165	61
Viljoen	14	2	51	0							4th	535	166	270
G.W.Flower	24	0	101	2							5th	564	262	292
INDIA											6th	601	324	405
Srinath	28.1	7	81	3	(6)	15	5	53	0		7th	–	359	–
Khan	21	3	78	1	(1)	17	5	48	1		8th	–	371	–
Joshi	25	7	69	1	(4)	41	5	153	0		9th	–	372	–
Agarkar	23	7	59	2	(2)	14	3	29	0		10th	–	382	–
Sharandeep Singh	22	7	70	2	(3)	49	10	136	4					
Tendulkar	1	0	7	0	(5)	11	3	19	0					
Ramesh						3	0	14	0					
Dravid						7	0	15	0					
Ganguly						1	0	3	0					
Das						3	0	7	0					

Umpires: R.S.Dunne (*New Zealand*) (36) and A.V.Jayaprakash (7).
Referee: B.N.Jarman (*Australia*) (23).　　　　　**Test No. 1520/5 (I336/Z47)**

INDIA v ZIMBABWE 2000-01

INDIA – BATTING AND FIELDING

	M	I	NO	HS	Runs	Avge	100	50	Ct/St
R.Dravid	2	3	2	200*	432	432.00	2	1	4
S.R.Tendulkar	2	3	–	201*	362	181.00	2	–	3
S.C.Ganguly	2	3	1	65*	122	61.00	–	1	6
S.S.Das	2	3	–	110	172	57.33	1	1	1
S.B.Joshi	2	1	–	27	27	27.00	–	–	2
S.Ramesh	2	3	–	48	61	20.33	–	–	2
A.B.Agarkar	2	1	–	12	12	12.00	–	–	1
V.V.S.Laxman	1	1	1	18*	18	–	–	–	1
V.Dahiya	2	1	1	2*	2	–	–	–	6

Did not bat (2 matches): J.Srinath; (1 match): M.Kartik, Z.Khan, Sharandeep Singh.

INDIA – BOWLING

	O	M	R	W	Avge	Best	5wI	10wM
J.Srinath	102.2	27	275	12	22.91	5- 60	1	–
M.Kartik	35	9	66	2	33.00	2- 26	–	–
Sharandeep Singh	71	17	206	6	34.33	4-136	–	–
A.B.Agarkar	88	27	225	4	56.25	2- 59	–	–
Z.Khan	38	8	126	2	63.00	1- 48	–	–
S.B.Joshi	137	30	406	6	67.66	2- 68	–	–

Also bowled: S.S.Das 3-0-7-0; R.Dravid 7-0-15-0; S.C.Ganguly 9-1-29-0; V.V.S.Laxman 1-0-1-0; S.Ramesh 3-0-14-0; S.R.Tendulkar 35-9-87-1.

ZIMBABWE – BATTING AND FIELDING

	M	I	NO	HS	Runs	Avge	100	50	Ct/St
A.Flower	2	4	2	232*	540	270.00	2	2	2
A.D.R.Campbell	2	4	–	102	184	46.00	1	1	4
G.W.Flower	2	4	1	106*	122	40.66	1	–	–
S.V.Carlisle	2	4	–	58	149	37.25	–	2	–
J.A.Rennie	1	1	–	37	37	37.00	–	–	–
P.A.Strang	1	2	1	19	33	33.00	–	–	2
H.H.Streak	2	4	1	29*	96	32.00	–	–	2
G.J.Whittall	2	4	–	84	124	31.00	–	1	–
D.P.Viljoen	1	2	–	38	57	28.50	–	–	–
G.J.Rennie	2	3	–	19	32	10.66	–	–	–
H.K.Olonga	2	3	1	11*	21	10.50	–	–	–
B.C.Strang	1	2	–	15	21	10.50	–	–	–
B.A.Murphy	2	3	–	13	19	6.33	–	–	2
M.L.Nkala	1	1	–	6	6	6.00	–	–	–

ZIMBABWE – BOWLING

	O	M	R	W	Avge	Best	5wI	10wM
H.H.Streak	66	18	183	3	61.00	1- 18	–	–
G.W.Flower	39.2	3	163	2	81.50	2-101	–	–
H.K.Olonga	50	7	203	2	101.50	2- 79	–	–
B.A.Murphy	87.5	7	321	3	107.00	2-175	–	–

Also bowled: A.D.R.Campbell 3-1-5-0; M.L.Nkala 22-2-86-0; G.J.Rennie 3.3-0-19-0; B.C.Strang 31-9-115-0; P.A.Strang 19.2-1-78-1; D.P.Viljoen 14-2-51-0.

AUSTRALIA v WEST INDIES (1st Test)

At Woolloongabba, Brisbane, on 23, 24, 25 November 2000.
Toss: Australia. Result: **AUSTRALIA** won by an innings and 126 runs.
Debuts: West Indies – M.I.Black.

WEST INDIES

S.L.Campbell	c M.E.Waugh b MacGill	10	c Gilchrist b McGrath		0
D.Ganga	c Ponting b Bichel	20	st Gilchrist b MacGill		8
B.C.Lara	c Gilchrist b McGrath	0	c Gilchrist b McGrath		4
S.Chanderpaul	c Gilchrist b McGrath	18	not out		62
*J.C.Adams	not out	16	c Gilchrist b Lee		16
R.R.Sarwan	run out	0	b Lee		0
†R.D.Jacobs	c M.E.Waugh b McGrath	2	c M.E.Waugh b Bichel		4
N.A.M.McLean	lbw b McGrath	0	lbw b Lee		13
M.Dillon	c Gilchrist b McGrath	0	b McGrath		0
M.I.Black	c MacGill b McGrath	0	c Gilchrist b McGrath		2
C.A.Walsh	c Langer b Lee	9	c McGrath b MacGill		0
Extras	(LB 6, NB 1)	7	(B 8, LB 3, NB 4)		15
Total		**82**			**124**

AUSTRALIA

M.J.Slater	c Campbell b Black	54
M.L.Hayden	run out	44
A.J.Bichel	c Jacobs b Black	8
J.L.Langer	c Jacobs b Black	3
M.E.Waugh	c and b Dillon	24
*S.R.Waugh	c Campbell b Dillon	41
R.T.Ponting	c Jacobs b Black	20
†A.C.Gilchrist	c Jacobs b Dillon	48
B.Lee	not out	62
S.C.G.MacGill	run out	19
G.D.McGrath	b Walsh	0
Extras	(LB 5, NB 4)	9
Total		**332**

AUSTRALIA	O	M	R	W	O	M	R	W
McGrath	20	12	17	6	13	9	10	4
Lee	11.1	5	24	1	18	9	40	3
MacGill	5	1	10	1	16	5	42	2
Bichel	13	3	25	1	11	4	21	1

WEST INDIES	O	M	R	W
Walsh	31.4	7	78	1
Black	28	3	83	4
Dillon	25	8	79	3
McLean	25	5	79	0
Adams	5	2	8	0

FALL OF WICKETS			
	WI	A	WI
Wkt	1st	1st	2nd
1st	21	101	0
2nd	25	111	10
3rd	53	112	29
4th	59	117	62
5th	60	179	66
6th	63	186	81
7th	63	220	98
8th	67	281	117
9th	67	331	119
10th	82	332	124

Umpires: D.B.Cowie (*New Zealand*) (19) and D.J.Harper (10).
Referee: A.C.Smith (*England*) (5).   Test No. 1521/91 (A607/WI365)

AUSTRALIA v WEST INDIES (2nd Test)

At W.A.C.A. Ground, Perth, on 1, 2, 3 December 2000.
Toss: Australia. Result: **AUSTRALIA** won by an innings and 27 runs.
Debuts: None.

WEST INDIES

S.L.Campbell	c Ponting b McGrath	3		c Gillespie b Lee	4
D.Ganga	lbw b Lee	0		c Hayden b Gillespie	20
W.W.Hinds	c M.E.Waugh b MacGill	50	(4)	b MacGill	41
B.C.Lara	c MacGill b McGrath	0	(5)	b MacGill	17
*J.C.Adams	c Langer b McGrath	0	(6)	not out	40
R.R.Sarwan	c Slater b Lee	2	(7)	c Gilchrist b Lee	1
†R.D.Jacobs	not out	96	(8)	run out	24
N.A.M.McLean	b MacGill	7	(9)	b Lee	11
M.Dillon	c Hayden b Gillespie	27	(3)	c Gilchrist b McGrath	3
M.I.Black	c Hayden b Gillespie	0		b Lee	0
C.A.Walsh	c Gilchrist b Gillespie	1		lbw b Lee	0
Extras	(LB 3, NB 7)	10		(B 1, LB 8, NB 3)	12
Total		**196**			**173**

AUSTRALIA

M.L.Hayden	b Black	69
M.J.Slater	c Campbell b Dillon	19
J.L.Langer	c Sarwan b McLean	5
J.N.Gillespie	c Lara b McLean	23
M.E.Waugh	c Adams b Dillon	119
*S.R.Waugh	c Campbell b Walsh	26
R.T.Ponting	b Black	5
†A.C.Gilchrist	c McLean b Walsh	50
B.Lee	not out	41
S.C.G.MacGill	not out	18
G.D.McGrath		
Extras	(B 2, LB 10, W 2, NB 7)	21
Total	(8 wickets declared)	**396**

AUSTRALIA	O	M	R	W		O	M	R	W
McGrath	19	2	48	3		18	7	26	1
Lee	15	5	52	2		15	2	61	5
Gillespie	12	2	46	3	(4)	12	4	26	1
MacGill	15	2	47	2	(3)	17	6	37	2
Hayden						2	0	9	0
M.E.Waugh						2	1	5	0

WEST INDIES	O	M	R	W
Walsh	31	10	74	2
Black	18	2	87	2
Dillon	29	4	130	2
McLean	22	3	78	2
Adams	8	3	15	0

FALL OF WICKETS

	WI	A	WI
Wkt	1st	1st	2nd
1st	1	52	7
2nd	19	62	16
3rd	19	111	42
4th	19	123	78
5th	22	188	95
6th	97	208	96
7th	117	303	150
8th	172	348	173
9th	178	–	173
10th	196	–	173

Umpires: J.H.Hampshire (*England*) (15) and P.D.Parker (6).
Referee: A.C.Smith (*England*) (6).   **Test No. 1522/92 (A608/WI366)**

AUSTRALIA v WEST INDIES (3rd Test)

At Adelaide Oval on 15, 16, 17, 18, 19 December 2000.
Toss: West Indies. Result: **AUSTRALIA** won by five wickets.
Debuts: West Indies – M.N.Samuels.

WEST INDIES

S.L.Campbell	lbw b Gillespie	18	c Gilchrist b McGrath		8
D.Ganga	b Gillespie	23	lbw b Miller		32
W.W.Hinds	c Ponting b Gillespie	27	c Martyn b MacGill		9
B.C.Lara	c Waugh b Miller	182	c Langer b Miller		39
*J.C.Adams	c Gilchrist b Gillespie	49	c Martyn b Miller		15
M.Dillon	c Waugh b Gillespie	9	(9) lbw b McGrath		19
M.N.Samuels	lbw b Miller	35	(6) c Hayden b MacGill		3
†R.D.Jacobs	c Langer b Miller	21	(7) c Ponting b Miller		2
N.A.M.McLean	lbw b Miller	0	(8) c Hayden b Miller		0
M.I.Black	not out	1	not out		3
C.A.Walsh	lbw b Miller	0	c Gilchrist b McGrath		0
Extras	(B 3, LB 12, NB 6, P 5)	26	(B 6, LB 3, W 1, NB 1)		11
Total		**391**			**141**

AUSTRALIA

M.J.Slater	c sub (R.R.Sarwan) b Samuels	83	(2) c Jacobs b Dillon		1
M.L.Hayden	run out	58	(1) c Jacobs b Walsh		14
J.L.Langer	c Lara b Samuels	6	c Jacobs b Dillon		48
M.E.Waugh	lbw b Dillon	63	c Jacobs b Dillon		5
J.N.Gillespie	lbw b Walsh	4			
R.T.Ponting	c Jacobs b Walsh	92	(5) lbw b Walsh		11
D.R.Martyn	not out	46	(6) not out		34
*†A.C.Gilchrist	c Jacobs b McLean	9	(7) not out		10
S.C.G.MacGill	c Jacobs b Dillon	6			
C.R.Miller	c Campbell b McLean	1			
G.D.McGrath	b Dillon	1			
Extras	(B 5, LB 13, W 5, NB 11)	34	(B 3, LB 1, NB 3)		7
Total		**403**	(5 wickets)		**130**

AUSTRALIA	O	M	R	W		O	M	R	W
McGrath	36	14	83	0		9.5	1	27	3
Gillespie	32	9	89	5		13	5	18	0
Miller	35.5	13	81	5	(4)	17	6	32	5
MacGill	24	5	118	0	(3)	12	2	55	2
Ponting	1	1	0	0					

WEST INDIES									
Walsh	32	7	73	2		14	4	39	2
Black	18	1	75	0	(6)	3	0	12	0
Dillon	24.4	2	84	3	(2)	12	3	42	3
McLean	21	1	69	2		5	1	9	0
Adams	13	2	35	0		3	0	7	0
Samuels	19	6	49	2	(3)	6	1	17	0

FALL OF WICKETS

	WI	A	WI	A
Wkt	1st	1st	2nd	2nd
1st	45	156	26	8
2nd	52	160	36	22
3rd	86	169	87	27
4th	269	187	96	48
5th	280	310	109	111
6th	354	369	109	–
7th	376	386	109	–
8th	382	397	116	–
9th	391	398	137	–
10th	391	403	141	–

Umpires: S.J.Davis (4) and S.Venkataraghavan (*India*) (41).
Referee: A.C.Smith (*England*) (7).   Test No. 1523/93 (A609/WI367)

AUSTRALIA v WEST INDIES (4th Test)

At Melbourne Cricket Ground on 26, 27, 28, 29 December 2000.
Toss: West Indies. Result: **AUSTRALIA** won by 352 runs.
Debuts: West Indies – C.E.L.Stuart.

AUSTRALIA

M.J.Slater	c Jacobs b McLean	30	(2) c Lara b Dillon		4
M.L.Hayden	c Jacobs b Walsh	13	(1) c Hinds b McLean		30
J.L.Langer	c Jacobs b Stuart	31	c Ganga b Adams		80
M.E.Waugh	c Adams b Dillon	25	not out		78
*S.R.Waugh	not out	121	c Jacobs b Stuart		20
R.T.Ponting	c Hinds b McLean	23	(7) not out		26
†A.C.Gilchrist	c Campbell b Stuart	37			
A.J.Bichel	c Jacobs b Walsh	3			
J.N.Gillespie	c Jacobs b Walsh	19			
C.R.Miller	c Jacobs b Dillon	29	(6) st Jacobs b Adams		11
G.D.McGrath	c Jacobs b Dillon	11			
Extras	(LB 4, W 1, NB 17)	22	(B 5, LB 4, W 1, NB 3)		13
Total		**364**	(5 wickets declared)		**262**

WEST INDIES

S.L.Campbell	c Hayden b Miller	5	c Ponting b Gillespie		6
D.Ganga	c Gilchrist b Gillespie	4	lbw b Gillespie		0
W.W.Hinds	c Slater b Gillespie	0	c Bichel b Gillespie		4
B.C.Lara	c M.E.Waugh b Bichel	16	b Gillespie		0
*J.C.Adams	c Gilchrist b Bichel	0	(6) c M.E.Waugh b Gillespie		0
M.N.Samuels	not out	60	(7) c Gillespie b Miller		46
†R.D.Jacobs	c M.E.Waugh b Bichel	42	(8) c Gilchrist b Miller		23
N.A.M.McLean	b Bichel	17	(9) run out		1
M.Dillon	b Gillespie	0	(10) b Miller		15
C.E.L.Stuart	b Bichel	1	(5) lbw b Gillespie		4
C.A.Walsh	run out	4	not out		0
Extras	(LB 5, NB 11)	16	(LB 1, NB 9)		10
Total		**165**			**109**

WEST INDIES	O	M	R	W		O	M	R	W	FALL OF WICKETS				
Walsh	33	6	62	2		18	3	46	0		A	WI	A	WI
Dillon	21	2	76	4		17	1	68	1	Wkt	1st	1st	2nd	2nd
McLean	27	5	95	2		9	1	30	1	1st	41	5	8	1
Stuart	15	4	52	2		15	2	66	1	2nd	47	6	49	6
Samuels	14	0	56	0						3rd	101	28	165	7
Adams	4	0	19	0	(5)	18	8	43	2	4th	105	28	212	17
										5th	149	28	228	17
AUSTRALIA										6th	210	103	–	23
McGrath	13	7	15	0		12	6	10	0	7th	225	144	–	77
Gillespie	18	6	48	3		17	5	40	6	8th	306	150	–	78
Bichel	13.3	2	60	5	(4)	6	0	18	0	9th	347	157	–	108
Miller	13	5	37	1	(3)	14.3	2	40	3	10th	364	165	–	109

Umpires: S.J.A.Taufel (1) and S.Venkataraghavan (*India*) (42).
Referee: A.C.Smith (*England*) (8).   **Test No. 1524/94 (A610/WI368)**

AUSTRALIA v WEST INDIES (5th Test)

At Sydney Cricket Ground on 2, 3, 4, 5, 6 January 2001.
Toss: West Indies. Result: **AUSTRALIA** won by six wickets.
Debuts: None.

WEST INDIES

S.L.Campbell	c and b MacGill	79	c Gilchrist b Gillespie		54
W.W.Hinds	b MacGill	70	b McGrath		46
*J.C.Adams	lbw b McGrath	10	lbw b McGrath		5
B.C.Lara	c M.E.Waugh b MacGill	35	c Gilchrist b Miller		28
M.N.Samuels	c Langer b MacGill	28	lbw b Gillespie		0
R.R.Sarwan	lbw b MacGill	0	c Gilchrist b McGrath		51
†R.D.Jacobs	st Gilchrist b MacGill	12	lbw b M.E.Waugh		62
M.V.Nagamootoo	c Slater b Miller	12	c Hayden b Miller		68
N.A.M.McLean	lbw b Miller	0	c M.E.Waugh b Miller		15
C.E.L.Stuart	not out	12	lbw b Miller		4
C.A.Walsh	c Hayden b Miller	4	not out		1
Extras	(B 4, LB 4, NB 2)	10	(B 5, LB 10, NB 3)		18
Total		**272**			**352**

AUSTRALIA

M.J.Slater	c Samuels b Nagamootoo	96	(2) not out		86
M.L.Hayden	c Lara b Walsh	3	(1) lbw b Stuart		5
J.L.Langer	c Jacobs b McLean	20	lbw b Walsh		10
M.E.Waugh	run out	22	c Adams b McLean		3
*S.R.Waugh	b Nagamootoo	103	lbw b Samuels		38
R.T.Ponting	lbw b Stuart	51	not out		14
†A.C.Gilchrist	c Lara b Stuart	87			
J.N.Gillespie	c Hinds b Nagamootoo	2			
C.R.Miller	not out	37			
S.C.G.MacGill	run out	1			
G.D.McGrath	run out	13			
Extras	(B 1, LB 5, NB 11)	17	(B 3, LB 7, W 1, NB 7)		18
Total		**452**	(4 wickets)		**174**

AUSTRALIA	O	M	R	W		O	M	R	W
McGrath	19	7	43	1		24	4	80	3
Gillespie	16	4	44	0	(4)	21	5	57	2
MacGill	37	11	104	7		30	7	88	0
Miller	30.1	8	73	2	(2)	32.5	3	102	4
M.E.Waugh						9	3	10	1

WEST INDIES									
Walsh	25	4	74	1		15	5	35	1
Stuart	23	4	81	2		7	0	40	1
Nagamootoo	35	3	119	2	(4)	9	1	28	0
McLean	20	2	81	1	(3)	8	1	35	1
Adams	16.4	2	54	0					
Samuels	16	5	37	0	(5)	5.5	0	26	1

FALL OF WICKETS

	WI	A	WI	A
Wkt	1st	1st	2nd	2nd
1st	147	17	98	5
2nd	152	55	112	38
3rd	174	109	112	46
4th	210	157	112	148
5th	210	289	154	–
6th	235	360	239	–
7th	240	374	317	–
8th	240	408	347	–
9th	252	410	351	–
10th	272	452	352	–

Umpires: D.B.Hair (35) and R.E.Koertzen (*South Africa*) (21).
Referee: A.C.Smith (*England*) (9).   **Test No. 1525/95 (A611/WI369)**

AUSTRALIA v WEST INDIES 2000-01

AUSTRALIA – BATTING AND FIELDING

	M	I	NO	HS	Runs	Avge	100	50	Ct/St
B.Lee	2	2	2	62*	103	–	–	1	–
S.R.Waugh	4	6	1	121*	349	69.80	2	–	–
M.J.Slater	5	8	–	96	373	53.28	–	4	3
M.E.Waugh	5	8	1	119	339	48.42	1	2	11
A.C.Gilchrist	5	6	1	87	241	48.20	–	2	19/2
R.T.Ponting	5	8	2	92	242	40.33	–	2	5
M.L.Hayden	5	8	–	69	236	29.50	–	2	8
C.R.Miller	3	4	1	37*	78	26.00	–	–	–
J.L.Langer	5	8	–	80	203	25.37	–	1	5
S.C.G.MacGill	4	4	1	19	44	14.66	–	–	3
J.N.Gillespie	4	4	–	23	48	12.00	–	–	2
G.D.McGrath	5	4	–	13	25	6.25	–	–	1
A.J.Bichel	2	2	–	8	11	5.50	–	–	1

Played in one Test: D.R.Martyn 46*, 34* (2 ct).

AUSTRALIA – BOWLING

	O	M	R	W	Avge	Best	5wI	10wM
B.Lee	59.1	21	177	11	16.09	5- 61	1	–
G.D.McGrath	183.5	69	359	21	17.09	6- 17	1	1
A.J.Bichel	43.3	9	124	7	17.71	5- 60	1	–
C.R.Miller	143.2	37	365	20	18.25	5- 32	2	1
J.N.Gillespie	141	40	368	20	18.40	6- 40	2	–
S.C.G.MacGill	156	39	501	16	31.31	7-104	1	–

Also bowled: M.L.Hayden 2-0-9-0; R.T.Ponting 1-1-0-0; M.E.Waugh 11-4-15-1.

WEST INDIES – BATTING AND FIELDING

	M	I	NO	HS	Runs	Avge	100	50	Ct/St
M.N.Samuels	3	6	1	60*	172	34.40	–	1	1
B.C.Lara	5	10	–	182	321	32.10	1	–	5
R.D.Jacobs	5	10	1	96*	288	32.00	–	2	20/1
W.W.Hinds	4	8	–	70	247	30.87	–	2	3
J.C.Adams	5	10	2	49	151	18.87	–	–	3
S.L.Campbell	5	10	–	79	187	18.70	–	2	6
D.Ganga	4	8	–	32	107	13.37	–	–	1
M.Dillon	4	8	–	27	73	9.12	–	–	1
R.R.Sarwan	3	6	–	51	54	9.00	–	1	1
C.E.L.Stuart	2	4	1	12*	21	7.00	–	–	–
N.A.M.McLean	5	10	–	17	64	6.40	–	–	1
C.A.Walsh	5	10	2	9	19	2.37	–	–	–
M.I.Black	3	6	2	3*	6	1.50	–	–	–

Played in one Test: S.Chanderpaul 18, 62*; M.V.Nagamootoo 12, 68.

WEST INDIES – BOWLING

	O	M	R	W	Avge	Best	5wI	10wM
M.Dillon	128.4	20	479	16	29.93	4- 76	–	–
C.E.L.Stuart	60	10	239	6	39.83	.2- 52	–	–
M.I.Black	67	8	257	6	42.83	4- 83	–	–
C.A.Walsh	199.4	46	481	11	43.72	2- 39	–	–
M.V.Nagamootoo	44	4	147	3	49.00	3-119	–	–
N.A.M.McLean	137	19	476	9	52.88	2- 69	–	–
M.N.Samuels	60.5	12	185	3	61.66	2- 49	–	–
J.C.Adams	67.4	17	181	2	90.50	2- 43	–	–

NEW ZEALAND v ZIMBABWE (Only Test)

At Basin Reserve, Wellington on 26, 27, 28, 29, 30 December 2000.
Toss: New Zealand. Result: **MATCH DRAWN**.
Debuts: Zimbabwe – D.A.Marillier.

NEW ZEALAND

M.H.Richardson	run out	75			
M.J.Horne	c Flower b Streak	1	(1) c Flower b Streak		0
M.S.Sinclair	lbw b Strang	9	(2) c Flower b Murphy		18
*S.P.Fleming	run out	22	(3) run out		55
N.J.Astle	c Carlisle b Strang	141	(4) not out		51
C.D.McMillan	b Murphy	142	(5) c Madondo b Strang		10
†A.C.Parore	not out	50	(6) not out		3
B.G.K.Walker	c Olonga b Strang	27			
P.J.Wiseman	not out	0			
S.B.O'Connor					
C.S.Martin					
Extras	(B 1, LB 8, W 5, NB 6)	20	(B 5, LB 5, NB 6)		16
Total	(7 wickets declared)	**487**	(4 wickets declared)		**153**

ZIMBABWE

G.J.Whittall	b Martin	9	c Parore b O'Connor		6
G.J.Rennie	c Parore b McMillan	93	c Parore b Wiseman		37
S.V.Carlisle	c Horne b Martin	0	not out		16
A.D.R.Campbell	lbw b Martin	24	not out		0
†A.Flower	c Parore b Martin	79			
T.N.Madondo	not out	74			
D.A.Marillier	c Parore b Martin	28			
*H.H.Streak	not out	19			
B.A.Murphy					
B.C.Strang					
H.K.Olonga					
Extras	(B 3, LB 9, NB 2)	14	(LB 1)		1
Total	(6 wickets declared)	**340**	(2 wickets)		**60**

ZIMBABWE	O	M	R	W		O	M	R	W
Streak	37	10	74	1		5	1	18	1
Strang	46	16	116	3		11	2	25	1
Olonga	30	2	105	0	(4)	2	0	12	0
Murphy	46	9	128	1	(3)	18	0	86	1
Whittall	22	6	55	0		4	3	2	0

NEW ZEALAND									
Martin	32.5	11	71	5		5	2	6	0
O'Connor	16	7	29	0		8	4	8	1
Wiseman	54	13	131	0		6	2	15	1
Walker	22	1	68	0		11	1	30	0
McMillan	9	4	22	1					
Astle	5	2	7	0					

FALL OF WICKETS

	NZ	Z	NZ	Z
Wkt	1st	1st	2nd	2nd
1st	5	21	4	26
2nd	22	23	44	57
3rd	67	66	103	–
4th	145	196	126	–
5th	367	237	–	–
6th	426	295	–	–
7th	487	–	–	–
8th	–	–	–	–
9th	–	–	–	–
10th	–	–	–	–

Umpires: B.C.Cooray (*Sri Lanka*) (20) and R.S.Dunne (37).
Referee: G.R.Viswanath (*India*) (2).   Test No. 1526/11 **(NZ285/Z48)**

SOUTH AFRICA v SRI LANKA (1st Test)

At Kingsmead, Durban, on 26, 27, 28, 29 (*no play*), 30 December 2000.
Toss: South Africa. Result: **MATCH DRAWN**.
Debuts: None.

SOUTH AFRICA

H.H.Dippenaar	c Kaluwitharana b Fernando	11		lbw b Muralitharan	22
G.Kirsten	c Kaluwitharana b Fernando	180		c Arnold b Muralitharan	34
J.H.Kallis	c Muralitharan b Fernando	21		b Muralitharan	15
D.J.Cullinan	c Atapattu b Muralitharan	59	(9)	not out	2
N.D.McKenzie	c Dilshan b Muralitharan	9	(7)	lbw b Muralitharan	13
†M.V.Boucher	c Arnold b Muralitharan	17		c Vaas b Muralitharan	10
L.Klusener	c Sangakkara b Muralitharan	50	(8)	not out	11
N.Boje	b Muralitharan	32	(5)	c Sangakkara b Fernando	8
*S.M.Pollock	c Kaluwitharana b Fernando	2	(4)	c Dilshan b Muralitharan	11
M.Ntini	b Fernando	8			
M.Ngam	not out	0			
Extras	(B 5, LB 10, W 1, NB 15)	31		(B 4, LB 3, NB 7)	14
Total		**420**		(7 wickets declared)	**140**

SRI LANKA

M.S.Atapattu	run out	0		c Boucher b Boje	20
*S.T.Jayasuriya	c McKenzie b Ngam	0		c Cullinan b Ngam	26
K.Sangakkara	c Kirsten b Boje	74		st Boucher b Boje	17
D.P.M.deS.Jayawardena	c Kirsten b Klusener	98		c Boucher b Ntini	7
R.P.Arnold	b Boje	3		c Dippenaar b Pollock	30
T.M.Dilshan	b Ngam	6		not out	28
†R.S.Kaluwitharana	c Boucher b Ntini	16		c Boje b Pollock	1
W.P.U.C.J.Vaas	c Boucher b Pollock	2		not out	3
D.N.T.Zoysa	c Ngam b Pollock	3			
R.D.Fernando	not out	5			
M.Muralitharan	c Boucher b Pollock	0			
Extras	(NB 9)	9		(B 4, LB 7, NB 6)	17
Total		**216**		(6 wickets)	**149**

SRI LANKA	O	M	R	W	O	M	R	W	FALL OF WICKETS				
										SA	SL	SA	SL
Vaas	26	1	84	0	9	1	25	0	*Wkt*	*1st*	*1st*	*2nd*	*2nd*
Zoysa	20	3	62	0	5	0	21	0	1st	31	0	46	41
Fernando	34	4	98	5	10	0	48	1	2nd	86	2	75	69
Muralitharan	58.3	16	122	5	10	1	39	6	3rd	194	170	91	80
Arnold	14	3	39	0					4th	238	184	92	80
SOUTH AFRICA									5th	269	184	108	132
Pollock	20.4	7	40	3	16	5	35	2	6th	358	201	114	140
Ngam	12	0	59	2	13	3	34	1	7th	401	208	132	–
Ntini	16	5	36	1	10	4	18	1	8th	410	208	–	–
Kallis	9	3	17	0	6	1	14	0	9th	420	215	–	–
Boje	19	4	44	2	24	12	30	2	10th	420	216	–	–
Klusener	11	5	20	1	5	1	7	0					

Umpires: D.L.Orchard (22) and Riazuddin (*Pakistan*) (9).
Referee: R.Subba Row (*England*) (36).   **Test No. 1527/9 (SA249/SL106)**

SOUTH AFRICA v SRI LANKA (2nd Test)

At Newlands, Cape Town, on 2, 3, 4 January 2001.
Toss: Sri Lanka. Result: **SOUTH AFRICA** won by an innings and 229 runs.
Debuts: None.

SRI LANKA

M.S.Atapattu	c Kallis b Pollock	5	lbw b Pollock		13
*S.T.Jayasuriya	c Boucher b Pollock	8	c Pollock b Ngam		0
†K.Sangakkara	c Cullinan b Ngam	32	c Boucher b Ngam		11
D.P.M.deS.Jayawardena	c Kallis b Pollock	0	lbw b Boje		45
R.P.Arnold	c Kirsten b Pollock	0	c Gibbs b Boje		26
T.M.Dilshan	c Pollock b Kallis	5	c Boucher b Boje		17
D.A.Gunawardene	c Kallis b Ngam	24	b Ntini		13
W.P.U.C.J.Vaas	c Pollock b Ngam	7	c and b Boje		38
D.N.T.Zoysa	c and b Pollock	10	c Klusener b Ntini		0
R.D.Fernando	not out	0	c Boucher b Ngam		5
M.Muralitharan	c Ntini b Pollock	0	not out		1
Extras	(W 1, NB 3)	4	(LB 6, W 1, NB 4)		11
Total		**95**			**180**

SOUTH AFRICA

G.Kirsten	c Dilshan b Muralitharan	52
H.H.Gibbs	c Sangakkara b Vaas	0
J.H.Kallis	c Jayawardena b Fernando	49
D.J.Cullinan	run out	112
N.D.McKenzie	c and b Arnold	47
†M.V.Boucher	c Jayawardena b Arnold	92
L.Klusener	c Jayasuriye b Arnold	97
N.Boje	not out	31
*S.M.Pollock		
M.Ntini		
M.Ngam		
Extras	(LB 5, W 1, NB 18)	24
Total	**(7 wickets declared)**	**504**

SOUTH AFRICA	O	M	R	W	O	M	R	W
Pollock	13.4	6	30	6	9	3	29	1
Ngam	13	2	26	3	8.2	1	36	3
Kallis	6	2	19	1	7	1	29	0
Ntini	6	2	20	0	11	2	52	2
Boje					10	3	28	4

SRI LANKA	O	M	R	W
Vaas	32	6	109	1
Zoysa	26	6	80	0
Fernando	25	2	105	1
Muralitharan	43	11	99	1
Jayasuriya	7	1	28	0
Arnold	24.2	4	76	3
Jayawardena	1	0	2	0

FALL OF WICKETS			
	SL	SA	SL
Wkt	1st	1st	2nd
1st	12	1	4
2nd	13	97	18
3rd	13	130	53
4th	13	231	99
5th	33	317	112
6th	66	411	119
7th	84	504	131
8th	95	–	135
9th	95	–	172
10th	95	–	180

Umpires: I.L.Howell (1) and E.A.Nicholls (*West Indies*) (13).
Referee: R.Subba Row (*England*) (37).   **Test No. 1528/10(SA250/SL107)**

SOUTH AFRICA v SRI LANKA (3rd Test)

At Centurion Park, (Verwoerdburg), Pretoria, on 20, 21, 22 January 2001.
Toss: Sri Lanka. Result: **SOUTH AFRICA** won by an innings and 7 runs.
Debuts: South Africa – J.M.Kemp.

SOUTH AFRICA

H.H.Dippenaar	c Kaluwitharana b Perera	20
H.H.Gibbs	c Kaluwitharana b Zoysa	1
J.H.Kallis	c Arnold b Fernando	7
D.J.Cullinan	c Kaluwitharana b Wickremasinghe	48
N.D.McKenzie	c Wickremasinghe b Zoysa	103
†M.V.Boucher	c Kaluwitharana b Zoysa	38
N.Boje	c Jayasuriya b Arnold	6
J.M.Kemp	run out	2
*S.M.Pollock	c Sangakkara b Zoysa	111
A.A.Donald	not out	10
M.Ntini	c Kaluwitharana b Wickremasinghe	10
Extras	(B 4, LB 2, W 1, NB 15)	22
Total		**378**

SRI LANKA

M.S.Atapattu	run out	3		c Cullinan b Pollock	0
*S.T.Jayasuriya	c McKenzie b Donald	16	(6)	b Donald	16
K.Sangakkara	b Donald	3	(2)	lbw b Ntini	98
P.A.de Silva	c Gibbs b Kallis	5	(5)	c Pollock b Kallis	22
D.P.M.deS.Jayawardena	c Boucher b Ntini	17	(3)	c Dippenaar b Kallis	23
R.P.Arnold	b Ntini	13	(4)	c Pollock b Boje	71
†R.S.Kaluwitharana	c Boucher b Ntini	32		c Boucher b Kemp	10
D.N.T.Zoysa	c Kallis b Ntini	1		c and b Kemp	2
G.P.Wickremasinghe	c Gibbs b Kemp	21		c Boucher b Ntini	1
R.D.Fernando	lbw b Kemp	0		c Kallis b Kemp	1
P.D.R.L.Perera	not out	1		not out	0
Extras	(LB 3, W 3, NB 1)	7		(LB 2, W 2, NB 4)	8
Total		**119**			**252**

SRI LANKA	O	M	R	W		O	M	R	W
Zoysa	22	8	76	4					
Perera	19	3	73	1					
Fernando	16	1	107	1					
Wickremasinghe	12.3	3	51	2					
Arnold	14	2	50	1					
Jayasuriya	6	3	10	0					
De Silva	2	1	5	0					

SOUTH AFRICA	O	M	R	W		O	M	R	W
Donald	9	2	28	2	(3)	7	0	39	1
Pollock	7	3	15	0	(1)	17	5	43	1
Kallis	5	1	15	1	(2)	14	1	39	2
Ntini	11	5	39	4	(5)	19.3	5	51	2
Kemp	4.5	1	19	2	(4)	13	2	33	3
Boje						11	2	45	1

FALL OF WICKETS

	SA	SL	SL
Wkt	1st	1st	2nd
1st	17	6	9
2nd	31	24	43
3rd	54	25	156
4th	115	40	187
5th	168	54	212
6th	185	71	234
7th	204	76	242
8th	354	97	243
9th	359	98	248
10th	378	119	252

Umpires: R.E.Koertzen (22) and P.Willey (*England*) (21).
Referee: R.Subba Row (*England*) (38).   Test No. 1529/11(SA251/SL108)

SOUTH AFRICA v SRI LANKA 2000-01

SOUTH AFRICA – BATTING AND FIELDING

	M	I	NO	HS	Runs	Avge	100	50	Ct/St
G.Kirsten	2	3	–	180	266	88.66	1	1	3
L.Klusener	2	3	–	97	158	79.00	–	2	1
D.J.Cullinan	3	4	1	112	221	73.66	1	1	3
N.D.McKenzie	3	4	–	103	172	43.00	1	–	2
S.M.Pollock	3	3	–	111	124	41.33	1	–	6
M.V.Boucher	3	4	–	92	157	39.25	–	1	13/1
N.Boje	3	4	1	32	77	25.66	–	–	2
J.H.Kallis	3	4	–	49	92	23.00	–	–	5
H.H.Dippenaar	2	3	–	22	53	17.66	–	–	2
M.Ntini	3	2	–	10	18	9.00	–	–	1
H.H.Gibbs	2	2	–	1	1	0.50	–	–	3
M.Ngam	2	1	1	0*	0	–	–	–	1

Played in one Test: A.A.Donald 10*; J.M.Kemp 2 (1 ct).

SOUTH AFRICA – BOWLING

	O	M	R	W	Avge	Best	5wI	10wM
J.M.Kemp	17.5	3	52	5	10.40	3- 33	–	–
S.M.Pollock	83.2	29	192	13	14.76	6- 30	1	–
N.Boje	64	21	147	9	16.33	4- 28	–	–
M.Ngam	46.2	6	155	9	17.22	3- 26	–	–
M.Ntini	73.3	23	216	10	21.60	4- 39	–	–
J.H.Kallis	47	9	133	4	33.25	2- 39	–	–

Also bowled: A.A.Donald 16-2-67-3; L.Klusener 16-6-27-1.

SRI LANKA – BATTING AND FIELDING

	M	I	NO	HS	Runs	Avge	100	50	Ct/St
K.Sangakkara	3	6	–	98	235	39.16	–	2	4
D.P.M.deS.Jayawardena	3	6	–	98	190	31.66	–	1	2
R.P.Arnold	3	6	–	71	143	23.83	–	1	4
T.M.Dilshan	2	4	1	28*	56	18.66	–	–	3
W.P.U.C.J.Vaas	2	4	1	38	50	16.66	–	–	1
R.S.Kaluwitharana	2	4	–	32	59	14.75	–	–	8
S.T.Jayasuriya	3	6	–	26	66	11.00	–	–	2
M.S.Atapattu	3	6	–	20	41	6.83	–	–	1
R.D.Fernando	3	5	2	5*	11	3.66	–	–	–
D.N.T.Zoysa	3	5	–	10	16	3.20	–	–	–
M.Muralitharan	2	3	1	1*	1	0.50	–	–	1

Played in one Test: P.A.de Silva 5, 22; D.A.Gunawardena 24, 13; P.D.R.L.Perera 1*, 0*; G.P.Wickremasinghe 21, 1 (1 ct)

SRI LANKA – BOWLING

	O	M	R	W	Avge	Best	5wI	10wM
M.Muralitharan	111.3	28	260	12	21.66	6- 39	2	1
R.P.Arnold	52.2	9	165	4	41.25	3- 76	–	–
R.D.Fernando	85	7	358	8	44.75	5- 98	1	–
D.N.T.Zoysa	73	17	239	4	59.75	4- 76	–	–

Also bowled: P.A.de Silva 2-1-5-0; S.T.Jayasuriya 13-4-38-0; D.P.M.deS.Jayawardena 1-0-2-0; P.D.R.L.Perera 19-3-73-1; W.P.U.C.J.Vaas 67-8-218-1; G.P.Wickremasinghe 12.3-3-51-2.

SRI LANKA v ENGLAND (1st Test)

At Galle International Stadium on 22, 23, 24, 25, 26 February 2001.
Toss: Sri Lanka. Result: **SRI LANKA** won by an innings and 28 runs.
Debuts: None.

SRI LANKA

M.S.Atapattu	not out	201
*S.T.Jayasuriya	c White b Gough	14
†K.Sangakkara	c White b Croft	58
P.A.de Silva	run out	106
D.P.M.deS.Jayawardena	run out	61
W.P.U.C.J.Vaas	c White b Giles	8
R.P.Arnold	not out	1
T.M.Dilshan		
H.D.P.K.Dharmasena		
C.R.D.Fernando		
M.Muralitharan		
Extras	(B 9, LB 2, NB 10)	21
Total	(5 wickets declared)	**470**

ENGLAND

M.A.Atherton	lbw b Vaas	33		c Sangakkara b Vaas	44
M.E.Trescothick	c Sangakkara b Vaas	122		c Sangakkara b Jayasuriya	57
*N.Hussain	lbw b Muralitharan	3		lbw b Muralitharan	1
G.P.Thorpe	c Dilshan b Muralitharan	7		lbw b Dharmasena	12
†A.J.Stewart	lbw b Jayasuriya	19		not out	34
R.D.B.Croft	c Jayawardena b Jayasuriya	9	(10)	lbw b Jayasuriya	2
G.A.Hick	c Sangakkara b Vaas	5	(6)	c Jayawardena b Jayasuriya	6
C.White	c Sangakkara b Jayasuriya	25	(7)	lbw b Muralitharan	3
A.F.Giles	c Dilshan b Muralitharan	4		lbw b Muralitharan	1
A.R.Caddick	c Jayawardena b Jayasuriya	0	(8)	b Jayasuriya	1
D.Gough	not out	0		b Muralitharan	0
Extras	(B 2, LB 3, NB 21)	26		(B 11, LB 6, NB 11)	28
Total		**253**			**189**

ENGLAND	O	M	R	W		O	M	R	W
Gough	26	3	95	1					
Caddick	30	13	46	0					
White	30	6	80	0					
Giles	48	8	134	1					
Croft	32	6	96	1					
Hick	4	0	8	0					
SRI LANKA									
Vaas	24	7	53	3		15	6	29	1
Muralitharan	54.3	14	79	3	(5)	42.3	14	66	4
Dharmasena	22	6	51	0	(4)	16	6	21	1
Fernando	2	0	10	0	(2)	4	0	10	0
Jayasuriya	27	7	50	4	(3)	32	13	44	4
De Silva	3	2	5	0					
Arnold					(6)	1	0	2	0

FALL OF WICKETS

	SL	E	E
Wkt	1st	1st	2nd
1st	18	83	101
2nd	110	93	105
3rd	340	117	121
4th	451	197	145
5th	468	206	167
6th	–	217	176
7th	–	239	182
8th	–	253	183
9th	–	253	188
10th	–	253	189

Umpires: A.V.Jayaprakash (*India*) (8) and P.T.Manuel (8).
Referee: Hanumant Singh (*India*) (5).   Test No. 1530/7(SL109/E777)

SRI LANKA v ENGLAND (2nd Test)

At Asgiriya Stadium, Kandy, on 7, 8, 9, 10, 11 March 2001.
Toss: Sri Lanka. Result: **ENGLAND** won by three wickets.
Debuts: None.

SRI LANKA

M.S.Atapattu	b Gough	16	c Stewart b Gough		2
*S.T.Jayasuriya	c Giles b Caddick	9	c Thorpe b Caddick		0
†K.Sangakkara	c Trescothick b White	17	st Stewart b Croft		95
P.A.de Silva	c and b White	29	c White b Gough		1
D.P.M.deS.Jayawardena	c Thorpe b Caddick	101	b White		18
R.P.Arnold	c White b Gough	65	lbw b Croft		22
T.M.Dilshan	c Atherton b Gough	36	c Hick b Croft		0
H.D.P.K.Dharmasena	c Thorpe b Gough	1	c Hick b Gough		54
W.P.U.C.J.Vaas	c Thorpe b Caddick	2	c Croft b White		36
D.N.T.Zoysa	c Stewart b Caddick	0	c Hick b Gough		0
M.Muralitharan	not out	10	not out		6
Extras	(B 1, LB 3, NB 7)	11	(B 2, LB 3, NB 11)		16
Total		**297**			**250**

ENGLAND

M.A.Atherton	lbw b Vaas	7	c Sangakkara b Vaas		11
M.E.Trescothick	c Sangakkara b Dharmasena	23	lbw b Vaas		13
*N.Hussain	b Muralitharan	109	c Sangakkara b Vaas		13
G.P.Thorpe	c Dilshan b Jayasuriya	59	c Sangakkara b Muralitharan		46
†A.J.Stewart	c Dilshan b Jayasuriya	54	lbw b Vaas		7
G.A.Hick	lbw b Muralitharan	0	(7) b Jayasuriya		16
C.White	st Sangakkara b Jayasuriya	39	(8) not out		21
A.F.Giles	b Muralitharan	5	(9) not out		4
R.D.B.Croft	not out	33	(6) lbw b Dharmasena		17
A.R.Caddick	b Muralitharan	7			
D.Gough	lbw b Vaas	10			
Extras	(B 16, LB 20, W 1, NB 4)	41	(B 1, LB 8, NB 2)		11
Total		**387**	(7 wickets)		**161**

ENGLAND	O	M	R	W		O	M	R	W	FALL OF WICKETS				
Gough	14	1	73	4		22	6	50	4		SL	E	SL	E
Caddick	20	3	55	4		18	5	55	1	Wkt	1st	1st	2nd	2nd
Giles	15	2	47	0	(5)	15	3	58	0	1st	21	16	2	24
White	17	3	70	2	(3)	12.1	3	42	2	2nd	29	37	2	25
Croft	20	2	48	0	(4)	22	11	40	3	3rd	69	204	3	86
										4th	80	232	42	89
SRI LANKA										5th	221	236	81	97
Vaas	23	7	39	2		18	4	39	4	6th	277	323	88	122
Zoysa	10	2	35	0		2	0	16	0	7th	279	330	181	142
Muralitharan	63	21	127	4	(4)	27	7	50	1	8th	282	336	234	–
Dharmasena	27	4	74	1	(3)	8	0	25	1	9th	286	346	242	–
Jayasuriya	34	11	76	3		16.1	6	22	1	10th	297	387	250	–

Umpires: B.C.Cooray (21) and R.E.Koertzen (*South Africa*) (23).
Referee: Hanumant Singh (*India*) (6).   **Test No. 1531/8(SL110/E778)**

SRI LANKA v ENGLAND (3rd Test)

At Sinhalese Sports Club, Colombo, on 15, 16, 17 March 2001.
Toss: Sri Lanka. Result: **ENGLAND** won by four wickets.
Debuts: Sri Lanka – D.Hettiarachchi.

SRI LANKA

M.S.Atapattu	b Caddick	0	c Croft b Gough		0
*S.T.Jayasuriya	c White b Croft	45	lbw b Gough		23
†K.Sangakkara	c Vaughan b Gough	45	c Stewart b Caddick		0
P.A.de Silva	c Vaughan b Giles	38	c Thorpe b Caddick		23
D.P.M.deS.Jayawardena	c Stewart b Croft	71	lbw b Giles		11
R.P.Arnold	lbw b Giles	0	c Hussain b Croft		0
T.M.Dilshan	lbw b Croft	5	b Giles		10
W.P.U.C.J.Vaas	not out	19	c Atherton b Giles		6
C.R.D.Fernando	c Trescothick b Croft	2	c Giles b Gough		5
D.Hettiarachchi	b Gough	0	not out		0
M.Muralitharan	b Caddick	1	lbw b Giles		1
Extras	(B 4, LB 4, W 1, NB 6)	15	(NB 2)		2
Total		**241**			**81**

ENGLAND

M.A.Atherton	lbw b Vaas	21	c and b Fernando		13
M.E.Trescothick	c Arnold b Hettiarachchi	23	c Sangakkara b Jayasuriya		10
*N.Hussain	c Jayasuriya b Hettiarachchi	8	(7) c Arnold b Jayasuriya		0
G.P.Thorpe	not out	113	not out		32
†A.J.Stewart	b Muralitharan	3	c Dilshan b Jayasuriya		0
M.P.Vaughan	c Sangakkara b Vaas	26	(3) b Muralitharan		8
C.White	c Sangakkara b Vaas	0	(6) c Jayawardena b Jayasuriya		8
A.F.Giles	c Jayawardena b Vaas	0	not out		1
R.D.B.Croft	run out	16			
A.R.Caddick	c Jayasuriya b Vaas	0			
D.Gough	c Jayawardena b Vaas	14			
Extras	(B 10, LB 9, NB 6)	25	(LB 1, NB 1)		2
Total		**249**	(6 wickets)		**74**

ENGLAND	O	M	R	W		O	M	R	W			FALL OF WICKETS			
													SL	E	SL	E
Gough	14	5	33	2		6	1	23	3		Wkt	1st	1st	2nd	2nd
Caddick	11.1	1	40	2		8	2	29	2		1st	2	45	21	23
White	10	1	45	0							2nd	88	55	24	24
Giles	34	13	59	2	(3)	9.1	4	11	4		3rd	108	66	24	42
Croft	32	9	56	4	(4)	5	0	18	1		4th	205	91	57	43
											5th	209	177	59	63
SRI LANKA											6th	216	177	59	71
Vaas	27.5	6	73	6		3	0	11	0		7th	219	181	69	–
Fernando	5	0	26	0	(4)	2	0	7	1		8th	225	209	76	–
De Silva	3	1	2	0							9th	240	223	80	–
Muralitharan	41	9	73	1	(3)	8	1	26	1		10th	241	249	81	–
Hettiarachchi	24	6	36	2	(2)	3	1	5	0						
Jayasuriya	9	1	20	0	(5)	8.3	0	24	4						

Umpires: E.A.R.de Silva (2) and D.L.Orchard (*South Africa*) (23).
Referee: Hanumant Singh (*India*) (7).　　　　Test No. 1532/9 SL111/E779)

SRI LANKA v ENGLAND 2000-01

SRI LANKA – BATTING AND FIELDING

	M	I	NO	HS	Runs	Avge	100	50	Ct/St
M.S.Atapattu	3	5	1	201*	219	54.75	1	–	–
D.P.M.deS.Jayawardena	3	5	–	101	262	52.40	1	2	6
K.Sangakkara	3	5	–	95	215	43.00	–	2	12/1
P.A.de Silva	3	5	–	106	197	39.40	1	–	–
H.D.P.K.Dharmasena	2	2	–	54	55	27.50	–	1	–
R.P.Arnold	3	5	1	65	88	22.00	–	1	2
S.T.Jayasuriya	3	5	–	45	91	18.20	–	–	2
W.P.U.C.J.Vaas	3	5	1	36	71	17.75	–	–	–
T.M.Dilshan	3	4	–	36	51	12.75	–	–	5
M.Muralitharan	3	4	2	10*	18	9.00	–	–	–
C.R.D.Fernando	2	2	–	5	7	3.50	–	–	–

Played in one Test: D.Hettiarachchi 0, 0*. D.N.T.Zoysa 0, 0.

SRI LANKA – BOWLING

	O	M	R	W	Avge	Best	5wI	10wM
S.T.Jayasuriya	126.4	38	236	16	14.75	4-24	–	–
W.P.U.C.J.Vaas	110.5	30	244	16	15.25	6-73	1	–
M.Muralitharan	236	66	421	14	30.07	4-66	–	–
H.D.P.K.Dharmasena	73	16	171	3	57.00	1-21	–	–

Also bowled: R.P.Arnold 1-0-2-0; P.A.de Silva 6-3-7-0; C.R.D.Fernando 13-0-53-1; D.Hettiarachchi 27-7-41-2; D.N.T.Zoysa 12-2-51-0.

ENGLAND – BATTING AND FIELDING

	M	I	NO	HS	Runs	Avge	100	50	Ct/St
G.P.Thorpe	3	6	2	113*	269	67.25	1	1	5
M.E.Trescothick	3	6	–	122	248	41.33	1	1	2
A.J.Stewart	3	6	1	54	117	23.40	–	1	4/1
N.Hussain	3	6	–	109	136	22.66	1	–	1
M.A.Atherton	3	6	–	44	129	21.50	–	–	2
R.D.B.Croft	3	5	1	33*	77	19.25	–	–	2
C.White	3	6	1	39	96	19.20	–	–	7
D.Gough	3	4	1	14	24	8.00	–	–	–
G.A.Hick	2	4	–	16	27	6.75	–	–	3
A.F.Giles	3	6	2	5	15	3.75	–	–	2
A.R.Caddick	3	4	–	7	8	2.00	–	–	–

Played in one Test: M.P.Vaughan 26, 8 (2 ct).

ENGLAND – BOWLING

	O	M	R	W	Avge	Best	5wI	10wM
D.Gough	82	16	274	14	19.57	4-50	–	–
A.R.Caddick	87.1	24	225	9	25.00	4-55	–	–
R.D.B.Croft	111	28	258	9	28.66	4-56	–	–
A.F.Giles	121.1	30	309	7	44.14	4-11	–	–
C.White	69.1	13	237	4	59.25	2-42	–	–

Also bowled: G.A.Hick 4-0-8-0.

TEST MATCH CHAMPIONSHIP SCHEDULE

2001

May	England host Pakistan
June	Sri Lanka host New Zealand
	Zimbabwe host India
July	England host Australia
	Sri Lanka host India
	Zimbabwe host West Indies
Sept	Pakistan host New Zealand
	Zimbabwe host South Africa
Oct	Bangladesh host Zimbabwe
	South Africa host India
Nov	Australia host New Zealand
Dec	Australia host South Africa
	India host England
	New Zealand host Bangladesh
	Sri Lanka host Zimbabwe

2002

Jan	Bangladesh host Pakistan
Feb	New Zealand host England
	India host Zimbabwe
	Pakistan host West Indies
	South Africa host Australia
Apr	South Africa host Bangladesh
	West Indies host India
	Zimbabwe host Australia
May	England host Sri Lanka
June	West Indies host New Zealand
July	England host India
	Sri Lanka host Bangladesh
Sept	Pakistan host Australia
Oct	India host West Indies
	South Africa host Sri Lanka
Nov	Australia host England
	Zimbabwe host Pakistan
Dec	Australia host Sri Lanka
	New Zealand host India
	South Africa host Pakistan
	Bangladesh host West Indies

2003

Jan	Australia host England
Feb	*World Cup in South Africa*
Apr	Pakistan host India
	West Indies host Australia
May	England host Zimbabwe
	Sri Lanka host New Zealand
July	England host South Africa
	West Indies host Sri Lanka
Sept	Pakistan host Bangladesh
Oct	India host New Zealand
	Pakistan host South Africa
	Zimbabwe host West Indies
	Bangladesh host Australia
Nov	Australia host Zimbabwe
	Sri Lanka host England
Dec	Australia host India
	New Zealand host Pakistan
	South Africa host West Indies
	Bangladesh host England

2004

Jan	Australia host India
	Bangladesh host Zimbabwe
Feb	India host Pakistan
	New Zealand host South Africa
	Sri Lanka host Australia
	West Indies host England
Apr	Zimbabwe host Sri Lanka
	Bangladesh host India
May	England host New Zealand
	West Indies host Bangladesh
July	England host West Indies
Aug	Sri Lanka host South Africa
Sept	India host Australia
Oct	Pakistan host Zimbabwe
	Bangladesh host New Zealand
Nov	Australia host West Indies
	India host South Africa
	Zimbabwe host England
	Bangladesh host Sri Lanka
Dec	Australia host Pakistan
	New Zealand host Sri Lanka
	South Africa host England

2005

Jan	South Africa host England
Feb	New Zealand host Australia
	Pakistan host India
	South Africa host Zimbabwe
Mar	Pakistan host Sri Lanka
	West Indies host South Africa
Apr	India host Bangladesh
May	England host Bangladesh
	West Indies host Pakistan
June	England host Australia
July	Sri Lanka host West Indies
Sept	Australia host Bangladesh
	Zimbabwe host New Zealand
Oct	South Africa host New Zealand
	Zimbabwe host India
Nov	India host Sri Lanka
	Pakistan host England
Dec	Australia host South Africa
	New Zealand host West Indies

2006

Jan	India host Pakistan
	New Zealand host West Indies
Feb	India host England
	New Zealand host Zimbabwe
	South Africa host Australia
Mar	Sri Lanka host Pakistan
Apr	West Indies host Zimbabwe
May	England host Sri Lanka
	West Indies host India
July	England host Pakistan
Aug	Zimbabwe host South Africa
Sept	Zimbabwe host Australia
Oct	Pakistan host Zimbabwe
	Sri Lanka host South Africa
Nov	Australia host New Zealand
Dec	Australia host India
	Pakistan host West Indies
	South Africa host India

SECOND XI FIXTURES 2001

No symbol	Second XI Championship	3 days
*	Second XI Championship	4 days
†	Second XI Trophy	1 day

APRIL

| 24–27 | Moseley | *Warwks v Sussex |
| | Chester-le-St (R) | *Durham v Notts |

MAY

1–4	Coventry & NW	*Warwks v Yorks
	Uxbridge (Vine L)	*Middx v Surrey
2–4	Heanor	Derbys v Worcs
	Blackpool	Lancs v Leics
7–10	Chester-le-St (R)	*Durham v Leics
8–11	Panteg	*Glam v Hants
	The Oval	*Surrey v Kent
9–11	Taunton	Somerset v Warwks
	Milton Keynes	Northants v Notts
14–16	Sutton CC	Surrey v Northants
15–18	Derby	*Derbys v Leics
	Middlesbrough	*Yorks v Durham
	Hove	*Sussex v Hants
16–18	Ealing	Middx v Somerset
	Bristol	Glos v Notts
	Crosby	Lancs v Glam
21	Bristol	†Glos v Somerset
	Southampton (WE)	†Hants v Glam
23–25	Maidstone	Kent v Derbys
	Scarborough	Yorks v Worcs
	Saffron Walden	Essex v Northants
	Pontarddulais	Glam v Glos
24	Richmond	†Middx v Minor C
29	Pontarddulais	†Glam v Hants
29–31	Kidderminster	Worcs v Northants
	Todmorden	Yorks v Middx
29–1 Jun	Nottingham (TB)	*Notts v Warwks
30–1 Jun	Taunton	Somerset v Surrey
	Hastings	Sussex v Leics
	Cheltenham C	Glos v Lancs

JUNE

1	Glossop	†Derbys v Yorks
	Shenley	†MCC YP v Essex
4–6	Chester-le-St (R)	Durham v Warwks
5–7	Nottingham (Boots)	Notts v Middx
5–8	Southampton (WE)	*Hants v Essex
	Liverpool	*Lancs v Yorks
	Canterbury	*Kent v Glos
	Hove	*Sussex v Surrey
6–8	Hinckley	Leics v Derbys
	Taunton	Somerset v Northants

JUNE

12	The Oval	†Surrey v Essex
	York	†Yorks v Notts
	Northampton	†Northants v Middx
12–15	Abergavenny	*Glam v Worcs
	Southampton (WE)	*Hants v Kent
13–15	Dunstall	Derbys v Durham
	Rotherham	Yorks v Notts
	Stowe School	Northants v Leics
14	Finchampstead	†Minor C v Middx
	Reading CC	†Minor C v Warwks
15	Nelson CC	†Lancs v Derbys
	Worcester	†Worcs v Somerset
	Old Brentwoods	†Essex v MCC YP
19–21	Finchampstead	Hants v Notts
19–22	Middleton	*Lancs v Derbys
	Chelmsford	*Essex v Middx
	Taunton	*Somerset v Glos
20	Harborne	†Warwks v Leics
	Tonbridge School	†Kent v MCC YP
21	High Wycombe	†Minor C v Middx
22	Marlow	†Minor C v Leics
	Hastings	†Sussex v Kent
25	Ealing	†Middx v Warwks
	Welbeck Coll CC	†Notts v Derbys
	Southampton (WE)	†Hants v Worcs
	Newport	†Glam v Somerset
	Seaton Carew	†Durham v Lancs
	Hove	†Sussex v Surrey
26	Hove	†Sussex v Essex
	Manchester (OT)	†Lancs v Durham
	Unity Casuals CC	†Notts v Yorks
27	Derby	†Derbys v Notts
	Leicester	†Leics v Warwks
	Worcester	†Worcs v Glam
	Southampton (WE)	†Hants v Somerset
	Wormsley	†MCC YP v Surrey
28	Ombersley	†Worcs v Glos
	Bingley	†Yorks v Durham
	Leicester	†Leics v Middx
	Maidstone	†Kent v Sussex
29	Chesterfield	†Derbys v Durham
	Taunton	†Somerset v Glam
	Manchester (OT)	†Lancs v Yorks
	Bristol	†Glos v Hants
	Canterbury	†Kent v Surrey
	Stirlands	†Sussex v MCC YP
	Northampton	†Northants v Leics

1	Bristol	†Glos v Worcs
2	Castleford	†Yorks v Derbys
	Folkestone	†Kent v Essex
	North Perott	†Somerset v Hants
	Nottingham (TB)	†Notts v Durham
	Banstead	†Surrey v MCC YP
	Oakham School	†Leics v Northants
3	Neath	†Glam v Worcs
	Weston-S-Mare	†Somerset v Glos
	Ealing	†Middx v Northants
	Radcliffe	†Lancs v Notts
4	Worcester	†Worcs v Hants
	Wickford	†Essex v Sussex
	Sunderland	†Durham v Notts
	Elland	†Yorks v Lancs
	Ebbw Vale	†Glam v Glos
	Shenley	†MCC YP v Kent
5	South Shields	†Durham v Derbys
	Stowe School	†Northants v Minor C
	Finchley	†Middx v Leics
	Shenley	†MCC YP v Sussex
6	Denby	†Derbys v Lancs
	Aston Unity	†Warwks v Northants
	Oakham School	†Leics v Minor C
	Billericay	†Essex v Kent
	Darlington	†Durham v Yorks
	Southampton (WE)	†Hants v Glos
	The Oval	†Surrey v Sussex
9	Northampton	†Northants v Warwks
	Clevedon	†Somerset v Worcs
	Old Bristolians CC	†Glos v Glam
	The Oval	†Surrey v Kent
10	WB Dartmouth CC	†Warwks v Middx
	Caythorpe	†Notts v Lancs
10–12	Coggleshall	Essex v Derbys
10–13	Kidderminster	*Worcs v Glos
	Southampton (WE)	*Hants v Somerset
	Hinckley	*Leics v Yorks
	Northampton	*Northants v Sussex
12	WB Dartmouth CC	*Warwks v Minor C
13	Coggleshall	†Essex v Surrey
16–18	Stockton	Durham v Essex
16–19	The Oval	*Surrey v Hants
17–19	Nottingham HS	Notts v Lancs
17–20	Taunton	*Somerset v Worcs
	Northampton	*Northants v Yorks
	Canterbury	*Kent v Middx
18–20	Walmley	Warwks v Glos
	Oakham School	Leics v Glam
23–25	Chester-le-St CC	Durham v Hants
24–26	Worksop College	Notts v Northants
24–27	Stratford	*Warwks v Lancs
	Hastings	*Sussex v Somerset
25–27	Usk CC	Glam v Middx
	Hinckley	Leics v Kent

31–2 Aug	Milton Keynes	Northants v Durham
31–3 Aug	Chesterfield	*Derbys v Yorks
	Barnt Green	*Worcs v Warwks
	Horsham	*Sussex v Essex
	Bristol	*Glos v Hants
	Whitgift School	*Surrey v Glam
	Hinckley	*Leics v Notts

AUGUST

6	tbc	Trophy Semi-Final
7	tbc	Trophy Semi-Final
		(reserve day)
8–10	Leamington	Warwks v Derbys
	Halesowen	Worcs v Lancs
	Halstead	Essex v Notts
	Harrogate	Yorks v Kent
	Harrow	Middx v Hants
8–11	Cheltenham C	*Glos v Surrey
14–17	Studley	*Warwks v Glam
	Worcester	*Worcs v Sussex
	Chelmsford	*Essex v Kent
	Uxbridge (Vine L)	*Middx v Northants
15–17	Banstead	Surrey v Notts
21–24	Derby	*Derbys v Northants
	Southampton (WE)	*Hants v Worcs
	Manchester (OT)	*Lancs v Durham
	Panteg	*Glam v Somerset
	Hatherley &	*Glos v Yorks
	Reddings CC	
	Canterbury	*Kent v Sussex
22–24	Nottingham (Boots)	Notts v Leics
	Wimbledon CC	Surrey v Middx
28–31	Unity Casuals CC	*Notts v Derbys
	Stamford Bridge	*Yorks v Lancs
	Bristol	*Glos v Glam
	Maidstone	*Kent v Northants
29–31	Kenilworth	Warwks v Middx
	Worcester	Worcs v Durham
	Guildford	Surrey v Essex
	Hinckley	Leics v Somerset

SEPTEMBER

3	tbc	Trophy Final
4	tbc	Trophy Final
		(reserve day)
4–7	Northampton	*Northants v Surrey
5–7	Cardiff	Glam v Derbys
	Bournemouth SC	Hants v Warwks
	Manchester (OT)	Lancs v Essex
	Darlington	Durham v Yorks
	Ealing	Middx v Glos
	Nottingham (TB)	Notts v Kent
11–14	Southgate	*Middx v Sussex

MINOR COUNTIES CHAMPIONSHIP
FIXTURES 2001

(3-day matches)

Venue	Div	Match
MAY		
Sun 20 Jesmond	E	Northumb v Herts
Sun 27 March	E	Cambs v Herts
Bovey Tracey	W	Devon v Wilts
Bournemouth (DP)	W	Dorset v Herefords
Grantham	E	Lincs v Beds
Thame	W	Oxon v Salop
JUNE		
Sun 10 Saffron Walden	E	Cambs v Norfolk
Jesmond	E	Northumb v Beds
Wellington	W	Salop v Berks
Leek	E	Staffs v Lincs
Mon 11 Carlisle	E	Cumb v Suffolk
Sun 17 Falkland CC	W	Berks v Wales
Colwall	W	Herefords v Wilts
Challow & Childrey	W	Oxon v Cheshire
Mon 18 Bridgnorth	W	Salop v Cornwall
JULY		
Sun 1 Bedford Town	E	Beds v Bucks
St Austell	W	Cornwall v Dorset
Hertford	E	Herts v Staffs
Grantham	E	Lincs v Suffolk
Swansea	W	Wales v Oxon
Sun 8 High Wycombe	E	Bucks v Northumb
Truro	W	Cornwall v Oxon
Bury St Edmunds	E	Suffolk v Staffs
Cardiff	W	Wales v Devon
Mon 9 Barrow	E	Cumb v Norfolk
Sun 15 Flitwick	E	Beds v Staffs
Beaconsfield	E	Bucks v Cumb
Cheadle Hulme	W	Cheshire v Wilts
Penzance	W	Cornwall v Berks
Bournemouth (DP)	W	Dorset v Wales
Long Marston	E	Herts v Lincs
Mildenhall	E	Suffolk v Cambs

Venue	Div	Match
JULY		
Sun 22 Kington	W	Herefords v Berks
Bishop's Stortford	E	Herts v Bucks
Whitchurch	W	Salop v Dorset
Ransomes	E	Suffolk v Northumb
Salisbury (S Wilts)	W	Wiltshire v Cornwall
Mon 23 Alderley Edge	W	Cheshire v Devon
Netherfield	E	Cumb v Cambs
Tue 24 Norwich (Manor Pk)	E	Norfolk v Lincs
Sun 29 Cambridge	E	Cambs v Beds
Plymouth (Mt Wise)	W	Devon v Oxon
Bournemouth (DP)	W	Dorset v Cheshire
Norwich (Manor Pk)	E	Norfolk v Bucks
Stone	E	Staffs v Cumb
Abergavenny	W	Wales v Herefords
AUGUST		
Sun 5 Reading CC	W	Berks v Cheshire
Luctonians CC	W	Herefords v Devon
Norwich (Manor Pk)	E	Norfolk v Northumb
Corsham	W	Wilts v Salop
Sun 19 Luton Town CC	E	Beds v Herts
Finchampstead	W	Berks v Dorset
Marlow	E	Bucks v Suffolk
Bowdon	W	Cheshire v Salop
Exmouth	W	Devon v Cornwall
Grantham	E	Lincs v Cumb
Jesmond	E	Northumb v Cambs
Banbury	W	Oxon v Herefords
Walsall	E	Staffs v Norfolk
Westbury	W	Wilts v Wales
SEPTEMBER		
Sun 9 tba		**CHAMPIONSHIP FINAL**

ECB 38-COUNTY CUP FIXTURES 2001

† Noon start.

	Venue	Gp	Match
MAY			
Sun 13	Taunton	1	Somerset v Devon
Sun 20	Warminster	1	Wilts v Cornwall
	Bournemouth (DP)	2	Dorset v Berks
	Hursley Park	2	Hants v Sussex
	Woodbridge S	3	Suffolk v Essex
	Pontarddulais	4	Wales v Herefords
	Oswestry	4	Salop v Warwks
	Bedford Town	5	Beds v Cambs
	Raunds CC	5	Northants v Norfolk
	Bourne	6	Lincs v Notts
	Tamworth	6	Staffs v Derbys
	Ashford	7	Kent v Bucks
Tue 22	Blackpool	8	Lancs v Cumb
Sun 27	St Just	1	Cornwall v Somerset
	Hurst CC	2	Berks v Sussex
	St Saviours, Jersey	2	Channel Is v Hants
	Godmanchester	3	Hunts v Essex
	†Kidderminster	4	Worcs v Wales
	Hinckley Town	5	Leics v Northants
	N'ham (Boots)	6	Notts v Derbys
	Longton	6	Staffs v Cheshire
	Wing (Ascott Pk)	7	Bucks v Kent
	Benwell Hill	8	Northumb v Lancs
Mon 28	Shenley	3	Middx v Suffolk
Wed 30	New Brighton	6	Cheshire v Notts
Thu 31	Gateshead	8	Durham v Lancs
	Harrogate	8	Yorks v Cumb
JUNE			
Sun 3	Bristol U	1	Glos v Devon
	Hastings Park	2	Sussex v Dorset
	Harpenden	3	Herts v Middx
	Papworth	3	Hunts v Suffolk
	Wem	4	Salop v Wales
	Stratford	4	Warwks v Worcs
	March	5	Cambs v Leics
	O Northamptonians	5	Northants v Beds
	Cleethorpes	6	Lincs v Staffs
	Christ Church	7	Oxon v Kent
	†Keswick	8	Cumb v Northumb
Thu 7	†Imber Court	7	Surrey v Oxon
	Haslingden	8	Lancs v Yorks
Sun 10	Camborne	1	Cornwall v Glos
	Torquay	1	Devon v Wilts
	Colchester RGS	3	Essex v Herts
	Stratford	4	Warwks v Herefords
	Christ Church	7	Oxon v Surrey

	Venue	Gp	Match
JUNE			
Tue 12	Chester-le-St CC	8	Durham v Yorks
Wed 13	Enfield	3	Middx v Hunts
Thu 14	†Imber Court	7	Surrey v Bucks
Sun 17	North Perrott	1	Somerset v Glos
	Southampton	2	Hants v Dorset
	Horsham	2	Sussex v Channel Is
	Exning	3	Suffolk v Herts
	Southill Park	5	Beds v Norfolk
	Wisbech	5	Cambs v Northants
	Derby	6	Derbys v Lincs
	Askam	8	Cumb v Durham
Tue 19	†Osbaldwick	8	Yorks v Northumb
Wed 20	Heanor Town	6	Derbys v Cheshire
Sun 24	Swindon	1	Wilts v Somerset
	Torquay	1	Devon v Cornwall
	Thatcham	2	Berks v Hants
	Bournemouth SC	2	Dorset v Channel Is
	Watford (W Herts)	3	Herts v Hunts
	Chelmsford	3	Essex v Middx
	Kington	4	Herefords v Salop
	Pontarddulais	4	Wales v Warwks
	Norwich (MP)	5	Norfolk v Cambs
	Hinckley Town	5	Leics v Beds
	N'ham (Boots)	6	Notts v Staffs
	Wormsley	7	Bucks v Oxon
	Ashford	7	Kent v Surrey
	Longhirst	8	Northumb v Durham
JULY			
Sun 1	St Saviours, Jersey	2	Channel Is v Berks
	Leominster (Dales)	4	Herefords v Worcs
	Norwich (MP)	5	Norfolk v Leics
Sun 8	Bristol	1	Glos v Wilts
	Kidderminster	4	Worcs v Salop
Tue 10	Nantwich	6	Cheshire v Lincs
Thu 19			QUARTER-FINALS
AUGUST			
Thu 9			SEMI-FINALS
Fri 10			*reserve day*
SEPTEMBER			
Tue 4	Lord's		FINAL
Wed 5			*reserve day*

PRINCIPAL FIXTURES 2001

BHC	Benson & Hedges Cup
CC1	County Championship (1st Division)
CC2	County Championship (2nd Division)
F	Floodlit
FCF	First-Class Friendly
LOI	NatWest Limited-Overs International

NL1	Norwich Union (National) League (1st Div)
NL2	Norwich Union (National) League (2nd Div)
TM	npower Test Match
TT	The Trophy
UCCE	Univ Centre of Cricketing Excellence
VCS	Vodafone Challenge Series

Fri 13 April
Champions' Charity Cup
    Bristol   Glos v Surrey

Mon 16 – Weds 18 April
FCF	Cambridge	Cambridge UCCE v Kent
	Derby	Derbys v Brad/Leeds UCCE
FCF	Chester-le-St	Durham v Durham UCCE
	Leicester	Leics v Loughboro' UCCE
	Taunton	Somerset v Cardiff UCCE
FCF	Oxford	Oxford UCCE v Middlesex

Fri 20 – Mon 23 April
CC2	Chester-le-St	Durham v Glos
CC1	Leicester	Leics v Essex
CC2	Lord's	Middlesex v Worcs
CC1	Northampton	Northants v Glamorgan
CC1	Taunton	Somerset v Lancashire
CC1	The Oval	Surrey v Kent
CC2	Birmingham	Warwks v Hampshire

Fri 20 – Sun 22 April
	Nottingham	Notts v Loughboro' UCCE

Weds 25 – Sat 28 April
CC2	Derby	Derbyshire v Middlesex
CC1	Chelmsford	Essex v Northants
CC1	Cardiff	Glamorgan v Somerset
CC1	Canterbury	Kent v Yorkshire
CC1	Manchester	Lancashire v Surrey
CC2	Nottingham	Notts v Durham
CC2	Worcester	Worcs v Sussex

Weds 25 – Fri 27 April
	Abergavenny	Cardiff UCCE v Glos
FCF	Oxford	Oxford UCCE v Hampshire

Sun 29 April
NL2	Derby	Derbyshire v Glamorgan
NL1	Canterbury	Kent v Warwks
NL2	Manchester	Lancashire v Hampshire
NL1	Leicester	Leics v Glos
NL2	Lord's	Middlesex v Durham
NL2	Worcester	Worcs v Sussex

Mon 30 April
BHC	Nottingham	Notts v Leics
BHC	Worcester	Worcs v Northants
BHC	Leeds	Yorkshire v Derbyshire

Tues 1 May
TT		Round 1 (see p 301; reserve 2 May)
BHC	Cardiff	Glamorgan v Somerset
BHC	Canterbury	Kent v Hampshire
BHC	Liverpool	Lancashire v Durham
BHC	The Oval	Surrey v Middlesex
BHC	Hove	Sussex v Essex
BHC	Birmingham	Warwks v Glos

Weds 2 May
BHC	Derby	Derbyshire v Durham
BHC	Cardiff	Glamorgan v Worcs
BHC	Bristol	Glos v Northants
BHC	Southampton	Hampshire v Essex
BHC	Leicester	Leics v Lancashire
BHC	Taunton	Somerset v Warwks
BHC	The Oval	Surrey v Sussex
BHC	Leeds	Yorkshire v Notts

Thurs 3 May
BHC	Leicester	Leics v Yorkshire
BHC	Lord's	Middlesex v Kent

Fri 4 – Sun 6 May
FCF	Nottingham	British U v Pakistanis

Fri 4 May
BHC	Chester-le-St	Durham v Notts
BHC	Chelmsford	Essex v Kent
BHC	Bristol	Glos v Glamorgan
BHC	Southampton	Hampshire v Surrey
BHC	Liverpool	Lancashire v Derbyshire
BHC	Northampton	Northants v Warwks
BHC	Hove	Sussex v Middlesex
BHC	Worcester	Worcs v Somerset

Sat 5 May
BHC	Chester-le-St	Durham v Leics
BHC	Northampton	Northants v Somerset
BHC	The Oval	Surrey v Essex
BHC	Birmingham	Warwks v Glamorgan

Sun 6 May
BHC	Derby	Derbyshire v Notts
BHC	Bristol	Glos v Worcs
BHC	Liverpool	Lancashire v Yorkshire
BHC	Lord's	Middlesex v Hampshire
BHC	Hastings	Sussex v Kent

Mon 7 May
BHC	Chelmsford	Essex v Middlesex
BHC	Cardiff	Glamorgan v Northants
BHC	Southampton	Hampshire v Sussex
BHC	Canterbury	Kent v Surrey
BHC	Leicester	Leics v Derbyshire
BHC	Nottingham	Notts v Lancashire
BHC	Taunton	Somerset v Glos
BHC	Worcester	Worcs v Warwks
BHC	Leeds	Yorkshire v Durham

Tues 8 – Thurs 10 May
VCS	Derby	Derbyshire v Pakistanis

Weds 9 – Sat 12 May
CC2	Bristol	Glos v Middlesex
CC2	Southampton	Hampshire v Worcs
CC1	Leicester	Leics v Lancashire
CC1	Northampton	Northants v Surrey
CC2	Hove	Sussex v Notts
CC2	Birmingham	Warwks v Durham
CC1	Leeds	Yorkshire v Somerset

Weds 9 – Fri 11 May
FCF	Cambridge	Cambridge UCCE v Essex

Sat 12 – Mon 14 May
VCS	Canterbury	Kent v Pakistanis

Sun 13 May
NL2	Derby	Derbyshire v Essex
NL2	Southampton	Hampshire v Worcs
NL1	Northampton	Northants v Glos
NL1	The Oval	Surrey v Notts
NL1	Leeds	Yorkshire v Somerset

Tues 15 May
TT	Round 2 (see p 301; reserve 16 May)

Weds 16 – Sat 19 May
CC2	Chester-le-St	Durham v Middlesex
CC1	Chelmsford	Essex v Yorkshire
CC2	Southampton	Hampshire v Glos
CC1	Manchester	Lancashire v Glamorgan
CC2	Nottingham	Notts v Warwks
CC1	Taunton	Somerset v Kent
CC1	The Oval	Surrey v Leics
CC2	Worcester	Worcs v Derbyshire

Weds 16 – Fri 18 May
FCF	Cambridge	Cambridge UCCE v Sussex

Thurs 17 – Mon 21 May
TM1	Lord's	**England v Pakistan**

Thurs 17 – Sat 19 May
	Northampton	Northants v Brad/Leeds UCCE

Sun 20 May
NL2	Chester-le-St	Durham v Middlesex
NL2	Chelmsford	Essex v Sussex

NL1	Bristol	Glos v Yorkshire
NL2	Manchester	Lancashire v Glamorgan
NL1	Nottingham	Notts v Warwks
NL1	Taunton	Somerset v Kent
NL1	The Oval	Surrey v Leics
NL2	Worcester	Worcs v Derbyshire

Tues 22 May
BHC	Quarter-Final #1 (Reserve 23/24 May)

Weds 23 May
BHC	Quarter-Finals #2, 3, 4 (Reserve 24 May)

Weds 23 May
	N'ham/Leics/	†Notts/Leics/Derbys
	Derby/Leeds	/Yorks v Pakistanis

Thurs 24 or Fri 25† – Sun 27 May
VCS	Leicester	Leics v Pakistanis

† Depending on BHC Quarter-Finalists

Fri 25 – Mon 28 May
CC2	Derby	Derbyshire v Hampshire
CC1	Swansea	Glamorgan v Kent
CC2	Bristol	Glos v Worcs
CC2	Lord's	Middlesex v Notts
CC1	The Oval	Surrey v Essex
CC2	Hove	Sussex v Warwks
CC1	Leeds	Yorkshire v Northants

Sun 27 May
NL2	Chester-le-St	Durham v Lancashire

Tue 29 May
NL1	Birmingham	Warwks v Glos

Weds 30 May – Sat 2 June
CC2	Chester-le-St	Durham v Notts
CC1	Swansea	Glamorgan v Hampshire
CC2	Southampton	Hampshire v Sussex
CC1	Tunbridge W	Kent v Essex
CC1	Leicester	Leics v Somerset
CC2	Southgate	Middlesex v Derbyshire
CC1	Northampton	Northants v Lancashire

Weds 30 May – Fri 1 June
	The Oval	Surrey v Loughboro' UCCE

Thurs 31 May – Mon 4 June
TM2	Manchester	**England v Pakistan**

Thurs 31 May – Sun 3 June
CC2	Birmingham	Warwks v Glos

Fri 1 – Sun 3 June
VCS	Worcester	Worcs v Australians

Sun 3 June
NL2	Swansea	Glamorgan v Sussex
NL2	Southampton	Hampshire v Essex
NL1	Tunbridge W	Kent v Somerset
NL1	Oakham S	Leics v Notts

| NL2 | Southgate | Middlesex v Derbyshire |
| NL1 | Northampton | Northants v Surrey |

Tues 5 June
| | Lord's | Middlesex v Australians |

Weds 6 – Sat 9 June
CC2	Derby	Derbyshire v Durham
CC1	Chelmsford	Essex v Glamorgan
CC1	Manchester	Lancashire v Leics
CC2	Nottingham	Notts v Glos
CC1	The Oval	Surrey v Somerset
CC2	Horsham	Sussex v Worcs
CC1	Leeds	Yorkshire v Kent

Weds 6 – Fri 8 June
| FCF | Oxford | Oxford UCCE v Warwks |

Thurs 7 June
| LOI | [F]Birmingham | **England v Pakistan** |
| | Northampton | Northants v Australians |

Sat 9 June
| LOI | **Cardiff** | **Pakistan v Australia** |

Sun 10 June
LOI	**Bristol**	**England v Australia**
NL2	Derby	Derbyshire v Durham
NL2	Chelmsford	Essex v Glamorgan
NL2	Manchester	Lancashire v Middlesex
NL1	Northampton	Northants v Warwks
NL1	Nottingham	Notts v Glos
NL1	The Oval	Surrey v Somerset
NL2	Horsham	Sussex v Worcs
NL1	Leeds	Yorkshire v Kent

Tues 12 June
| LOI | **Lord's** | **England v Pakistan** |

Weds 13 – Sat 16 June
CC1	Ilford	Essex v Surrey
CC2	Gloucester	Glos v Durham
CC1	Maidstone	Kent v Glamorgan
CC1	Leicester	Leics v Northants
CC2	Southgate	Middlesex v Hampshire
CC1	Bath	Somerset v Yorkshire
CC2	Arundel	Sussex v Derbyshire
CC2	Worcester	Worcs v Warwks

Weds 13 – Fri 15 June
| FCF | Durham (U) | Durham UCCE v Lancashire |

Thurs 14 June
| LOI | [F]Manchester | **England v Australia** |

Sat 16 June
| LOI | **Chester-le-St** | **Pakistan v Australia** |

Sun 17 June
LOI	**Leeds**	**England v Pakistan**
NL2	Ilford	Essex v Durham
NL1	Gloucester	Glos v Warwks
NL1	Maidstone	Kent v Notts

NL1	Leicester	Leics v Northants
NL2	Southgate	Middlesex v Hampshire
NL1	Bath	Somerset v Yorkshire
NL2	Arundel	Sussex v Derbyshire
NL2	Worcester	Worcs v Lancashire

Tues 19 June
| LOI | [F]Nottingham | **Pakistan v Australia** |

Tues 19 – Fri 22 June
| CC1 | Manchester | Lancashire v Essex |

Weds 20 – Sat 23 June
CC2	Derby	Derbyshire v Glos
CC2	Southampton	Hampshire v Durham
CC1	Canterbury	Kent v Leics
CC1	Northampton	Northants v Somerset
CC2	Nottingham	Notts v Sussex
CC2	Birmingham	Warwks v Middlesex

Weds 20 – Fri 22 June
	Bradford	Brad/Leeds UCCE v Yorks
	Cardiff	Glamorgan v Cardiff UCCE
FCF	Worcester	Worcs v Durham UCCE

Thurs 21 June
| LOI | **The Oval** | **England v Australia** |

Sat 23 June
| LOI | Lord's | **FINAL** (Reserve 24 June) |
| NL2 | Manchester | Lancashire v Essex |

Sun 24 June
NL2	Derby	Derbyshire v Middlesex
NL2	Cardiff	Glamorgan v Worcs
NL2	Southampton	Hampshire v Durham
NL1	Nottingham	Notts v Somerset
NL1	The Oval	Surrey v Kent
NL1	Birmingham	Warwks v Leics
NL1	Leeds	Yorkshire v Northants

Mon 25 June
| BHC | SEMI-FINALS (reserve 26 June) |

Mon 25 – Weds 27 June
| FCF | Arundel | MCC v Australians |

Weds 27 June
| TT | Round 3 (see p 301; reserve 28 June) |

Weds 27 June
NL2	Chester-le-St	Durham v Hampshire
NL2	Cardiff	Glamorgan v Derbyshire
	Lord's	UCCE Final

Thurs 28 June
| | Lord's | Cambridge U v Oxford U |

Fri 29 June – Sun 1 July
| VCS | Chelmsford | Essex v Australians |

Fri 29 June – Mon 2 July
| CC2 | Chester-le-St | Durham v Warwks |
| CC1 | Cardiff | Glamorgan v Northants |

297

CC2	Southampton	Hampshire v Derbyshire
CC2	Lord's	Middlesex v Sussex
CC1	The Oval	Surrey v Lancashire
CC2	Worcester	Worcs v Notts
CC1	Leeds	Yorkshire v Leics

Sat 30 June – Tues 3 July
| FCF | Cambridge | Cambridge U v Oxford U |

Sat 30 June
| | Nottingham | Sobers's XI v Hadlee's XI |

Sun 1 July
| NL1 | Taunton | Somerset v Glos |
| | Nottingham | *Eng Masters v Aus Masters* |

Tues 3 July
| NL2 | FDerby | Derbyshire v Worcs |

Weds 4 – Sat 7 July
CC2	Bristol	Glos v Warwks
CC1	Canterbury	Kent v Lancashire
CC1	Leicester	Leics v Surrey
CC1	Northampton	Northants v Yorkshire
CC2	Nottingham	Notts v Middlesex
CC1	Taunton	Somerset v Essex

Weds 4 July
| NL2 | FSouthampton | Hampshire v Sussex |

Thurs 5 – Mon 9 July
| TM1 | Birmingham | **England v Australia** |

Thurs 5 – Sun 8 July
| CC2 | Derby | Derbyshire v Worcs |

Fri 6 – Mon 9 July
| CC2 | Hove | Sussex v Hampshire |

Sun 8 July
NL2	Chester-le-St	Durham v Glamorgan
NL1	Canterbury	Kent v Glos
NL1	Leicester	Leics v Surrey
NL2	Southgate	Middlesex v Essex
NL1	Northampton	Northants v Yorkshire
NL1	Taunton	Somerset v Notts

Weds 11 July
| TT | Round 4 (see p 301; reserve 12 July) |

Fri 13 – Mon 16 July
| VCS | Cambridge | Somerset/Glam/Glos |
| | Cardiff/Bristol | v Australians |

Sat 14 July
| BHC | Lord's | **FINAL** (*Reserve 15 July*) |

Sun 15 July
NL2	Southampton	Hampshire v Derbyshire
NL2	Manchester	Lancashire v Durham
NL1	Nottingham	Notts v Kent
NL1	Birmingham	Warwks v Northants
NL2	Worcester	Worcs v Middlesex
NL1	Scarborough	Yorkshire v Leics

Mon 16 July
| NL2 | FHove | Sussex v Essex |

Tues 17 July
| NL1 | FBristol | Glos v Somerset |

Weds 18 – Sat 21 July
CC2	Chester-le-St	Durham v Sussex
CC1	Southend	Essex v Kent
CC1	Cardiff	Glamorgan v Leics
CC2	Southampton	Hampshire v Notts
CC1	Guildford	Surrey v Northants
CC2	Birmingham	Warwks v Derbyshire

Weds 18 July
| NL2 | FManchester | Lancashire v Worcs |

Thurs 19 – Mon 23 July
| TM2 | Lord's | **England v Australia** |

Thurs 19 – Sun 22 July
| CC1 | Manchester | Lancashire v Somerset |

Fri 20 – Mon 23 July
| CC2 | Worcester | Worcs v Glos |

Sun 22 July
NL2	Chester-le-St	Durham v Sussex
NL2	Southend	Essex v Hampshire
NL2	Cardiff	Glamorgan v Derbyshire
NL1	Leicester	Leics v Kent
NL1	Guildford	Surrey v Northants

Mon 23 July
| NL1 | FLeeds | Yorkshire v Warwks |

Tues 24 July
| TT | Quarter-Final #1 (*Reserve 25/26 July*) |

Weds 25 July
| TT | Quarter-Finals #2, 3, 4 (*Reserve 26 July*) |

Fri 27 – Mon 30 July
CC2	Derby	Derbyshire v Notts
CC2	Cheltenham	Glos v Sussex
CC1	Leicester	Leics v Kent
CC2	Lord's	Middlesex v Durham
CC1	Northampton	Northants v Essex
CC1	Taunton	Somerset v Glamorgan
CC1	Leeds	Yorkshire v Lancashire

Sat 28 – Mon 30 July
| VCS | Southampton | Hampshire v Australians |

Sun 29 July
| NL1 | Birmingham | Warwks v Surrey |

Tues 31 July
| NL1 | Cheltenham | Glos v Notts |
| NL2 | FWorcester | Worcs v Durham |

Weds 1 – Sat 4 August
| CC1 | Chelmsford | Essex v Leics |
| CC1 | Colwyn Bay | Glamorgan v Lancashire |

298

CC2	Cheltenham	Glos v Hampshire
CC1	Canterbury	Kent v Somerset
CC1	Leeds	Yorkshire v Surrey

Weds 1 August

NL2	[F]Hove	Sussex v Middlesex

Thurs 2 – Mon 6 August

TM3	Nottingham	**England v Australia**

Thurs 2 – Sun 5 August

CC2	Hove	Sussex v Middlesex
CC2	Kidderminster	Worcs v Durham

Thurs 2 August

NL1	[F]Birmingham	Warwks v Notts

Fri 3 – Mon 6 August

CC2	Birmingham	Warwks v Notts

Sun 5 August

NL2	Derby	Derbyshire v Hampshire
NL2	Colwyn Bay	Glamorgan v Lancashire
NL1	Cheltenham	Glos v Northants
NL1	Canterbury	Kent v Leics
NL1	Leeds	Yorkshire v Surrey

Tues 7 – Fri 10 August

CC1	Manchester	Lancashire v Yorkshire

Weds 8 – Fri 10 August

VCS	Hove	Sussex v Australians

Weds 8 – Sat 11 August

CC2	Chester-le-St	Durham v Derbyshire
CC2	Southampton	Hampshire v Warwks
CC2	Lord's	Middlesex v Glos
CC1	Northampton	Northants v Kent
CC2	Nottingham	Notts v Worcs
CC1	Taunton	Somerset v Leics
CC1	The Oval	Surrey v Glamorgan

Sat 11 August

TT	Semi-Final #1 (*Reserve 12 August*)	

Sun 12 August

TT	Semi-Final #2 (*Reserve 13 August*)	
	Belfast	Ireland v Australia
NL2	Chester-le-St	Durham v Derbyshire
NL2	Chelmsford	Essex v Worcs
NL2	Southampton	Hampshire v Glamorgan
NL2	Lord's	Middlesex v Lancashire
NL1	Northampton	Northants v Kent
NL1	Taunton	Somerset v Leics
NL1	The Oval	Surrey v Glos

Mon 13 August

NL1	[F]Nottingham	Notts v Yorkshire

Tues 14 August

NL1	[F]Canterbury	Kent v Surrey

Weds 15 – Sat 18 August

CC2	Derby	Derbyshire v Sussex

CC1	Cardiff	Glamorgan v Essex
CC2	Bristol	Glos v Notts
CC1	Manchester	Lancashire v Northants
CC1	Leicester	Leics v Yorkshire
CC2	Birmingham	Warwks v Worcs

Weds 15 August

NL2	[F]Chester-le-St	Durham v Hampshire

Thurs 16 – Mon 20 August

TM4	Leeds	**England v Australia**

Thurs 16 – Sun 19 August

CC1	Canterbury	Kent v Surrey

Fri 17 – Mon 20 August

CC2	Chester-le-St	Durham v Hampshire

Sun 19 August

NL2	Cardiff	Glamorgan v Essex
NL1	Leicester	Leics v Yorkshire
NL2	Lord's	Middlesex v Worcs
NL1	Nottingham	Notts v Northants
NL1	Birmingham	Warwks v Somerset

Mon 20 August

NL2	[F]Manchester	Lancashire v Sussex

Tues 21 – Fri 24 August

CC1	Scarborough	Yorkshire v Glamorgan

Tues 21 August

NL1	[F]Taunton	Somerset v Surrey

Weds 22 – Sat 25 August

CC1	Colchester	Essex v Lancashire
CC2	Lord's	Middlesex v Warwks
CC2	Nottingham	Notts v Derbyshire
CC2	Hove	Sussex v Durham
CC2	Worcester	Worcs v Hampshire

Weds 22 August

NL1	[F]Northampton	Northants v Leics

Thurs 23 – Mon 27 August

TM5	The Oval	**England v Australia**

Thurs 23 – Sun 26 August

CC1	Northampton	Northants v Leics
CC1	Taunton	Somerset v Surrey

Sun 26 August

NL2	Colchester	Essex v Lancashire
NL2	Lord's	Middlesex v Glamorgan
NL2	Hove	Sussex v Durham
NL2	Worcester	Worcs v Hampshire
NL1	Scarborough	Yorkshire v Notts

Mon 27 August

NL2	Derby	Derbyshire v Sussex
NL2	Cardiff	Glamorgan v Durham
NL1	Bristol	Glos v Kent
NL2	Southampton	Hampshire v Lancashire
NL1	Leicester	Leics v Somerset

NL1	Birmingham	Warwks v Yorkshire

Tues 28 August

NL2	FColchester	Essex v Middlesex

Weds 29 August

NL2	FCardiff	Glamorgan v Hampshire
NL1	tbc	Kent v Yorkshire
TT	Round 1 (2002) *(see p 301; reserve 30 Aug)*	

‡ *to be confirmed*

Thurs 30 August

NL1	Northampton	Northants v Somerset
NL1	Whitgift	Surrey v Warwks
NL2	FHove	Sussex v Lancashire

Sat 1 September

TT	Lord's	FINAL (Reserve 2 Sep)

Sun 2 September

NL2	Chester-le-St	Durham v Essex
NL1	Bristol	Glos v Leics
NL2	Richmond	Middlesex v Sussex
NL1	Northampton	Northants v Notts
NL1	Taunton	Somerset v Warwks
NL2	Worcester	Worcs v Glamorgan

Mon 3 September

NL2	FManchester	Lancashire v Derbyshire
NL1	FThe Oval	Surrey v Yorkshire

Tues 4 September

NL2	FHove	Sussex v Glamorgan

Weds 5 – Sat 8 September

CC2	Chester-le-St	Durham v Worcs
CC1	Chelmsford	Essex v Somerset
CC2	Bristol	Glos v Derbyshire
CC2	Southampton	Hampshire v Middlesex
CC1	Canterbury	Kent v Northants
CC1	The Oval	Surrey v Yorkshire

Weds 5 September

NL1	FLeicester	Leics v Warwks

Fri 7 – Mon 10 September

CC1	Leicester	Leics v Glamorgan
CC2	Birmingham	Warwks v Sussex

Sun 9 September

NL2	Chester-le-St	Durham v Worcs
NL2	Chelmsford	Essex v Derbyshire
NL2	Southampton	Hampshire v Middlesex
NL1	Canterbury	Kent v Northants
NL1	Nottingham	Notts v Surrey

Mon 10 September

NL1	Scarborough	Yorkshire v Glos

Thurs 13 September

TT	Round 2 (2002) *(see p 301; reserve 14 Sep)*	

Weds 12 – Sat 15 September

CC2	Derby	Derbyshire v Warwks
CC1	Cardiff	Glamorgan v Surrey
CC1	Manchester	Lancashire v Kent
CC2	Nottingham	Notts v Hampshire
CC1	Taunton	Somerset v Northants
CC2	Hove	Sussex v Glos
CC2	Worcester	Worcs v Middlesex
CC1	Scarborough	Yorkshire v Essex

Sun 16 September

NL2	Derby	Derbyshire v Lancashire
NL2	Cardiff	Glamorgan v Middlesex
NL1	Bristol	Glos v Surrey
NL1	Nottingham	Notts v Leics
NL1	Taunton	Somerset v Northants
NL2	Hove	Sussex v Hampshire
NL1	Birmingham	Warwks v Kent
NL2	Worcester	Worcs v Essex

ENGLAND WOMEN v AUSTRALIA

TM1	Shenley	Sun 24 – Weds 27 June
LOI	Derby	Fri 29 June
LOI	Northampton	Mon 2 July
LOI	Lord's	Tues 3 July
TM2	Leeds	Fri 6 – Mon 9 July

ENGLAND U-19 v WEST INDIES

LOI	FHove	Fri 27 July
LOI	Chelmsford	Sun 29 July
LOI	Chelmsford	Mon 30 July
TM1	Leicester	Mon 6 – Thurs 9 August
TM2	Nottingham	Weds 15 – Sat 18 August
TM3	Chester-le-St	Tues 28 – Fri 31 August

TROPHY FIXTURES 2001

Round 1 – Tuesday 1 May *(reserve 2 May)*

1	Wiltshire	v	Derbyshire CB		6	Kent CB	v	Hampshire CB
2	Oxfordshire	v	Huntingdonshire CB		7	Middlesex CB	v	Northumberland
3	Shropshire	v	Devon		8	Bedfordshire	v	Nottinghamshire CB
4	Lincolnshire	v	Suffolk		9	Staffordshire	v	Worcestershire CB
5	Somerset CB	v	Wales		10	Lancashire CB	v	Yorkshire CB

Venues for this First Round appear on p 164

Round 2 – Tuesday 15 May
(reserve 16 May)

11	Cambridgeshire	v	*Winner # 1*
12	Surrey CB	v	*Winner # 2*
13	Sussex CB	v	*Winner # 3*
14	*Winner # 4*	v	Essex CB
15	Norfolk	v	*Winner # 5*
16	*Winner # 6*	v	Buckinghamshire
17	*Winner # 7*	v	Berkshire
18	Dorset	v	*Winner # 8*
19	*Winner # 9*	v	Cumberland
20	Northants CB	v	*Winner # 10*
21	Herefordshire	v	Gloucestershire CB
22	Warwickshire CB	v	Leicestershire CB
23	Cornwall	v	Cheshire
24	Hertfordshire	v	Durham CB

Venues for the Second Round appear on p 193

Round 3 – Wednesday 27 June
(reserve 28 June)

25	*Winner # 11*	v	SOMERSET
26	*Winner # 12*	v	SURREY
27	*Winner # 13*	v	GLOUCESTERSHIRE
28	*Winner # 14*	v	NOTTINGHAMSHIRE
29	*Winner # 15*	v	LEICESTERSHIRE
30	*Winner # 16*	v	WARWICKSHIRE
31	*Winner # 17*	v	ESSEX
32	*Winner # 18*	v	YORKSHIRE
33	*Winner # 19*	v	KENT
34	*Winner # 20*	v	NORTHAMPTONSHIRE
35	*Winner # 21*	v	MIDDLESEX
36	*Winner # 22*	v	LANCASHIRE
37	*Winner # 23*	v	SUSSEX
38	*Winner # 24*	v	WORCESTERSHIRE
39	GLAMORGAN	v	DERBYSHIRE
40	DURHAM	v	HAMPSHIRE

Round 4 – Wednesday 11 July
(reserve 12 July)

41	*Winner # 38*	v	*Winner # 35*
42	*Winner # 25*	v	*Winner # 39*
43	*Winner # 32*	v	*Winner # 26*
44	*Winner # 33*	v	*Winner # 34*
45	*Winner # 36*	v	*Winner # 37*
46	*Winner # 27*	v	*Winner # 40*
47	*Winner # 30*	v	*Winner # 31*
48	*Winner # 28*	v	*Winner # 29*

Quarter-Finals   24 and 25 July
Semi-Finals   11 and 12 August
Final   1 September

FIRST ROUND BYES (18): Berkshire, Buckinghamshire, Cambridgeshire, Cheshire, Cornwall, Cumberland, Dorset, Durham CB, Essex CB, Gloucestershire CB, Herefordshire, Hertfordshire, Leicestershire CB, Norfolk, Northamptonshire CB, Surrey CB, Sussex CB, Warwickshire CB. First-class counties enter in Round 3.

CB Cricket Board 'recreational team'.

TROPHY QUALIFICATION FOR 2002

Round 1 – Weds 29 Aug 2001
(reserve 30 Aug)

1	Hertfordshire	v	Staffordshire
2	Essex CB	v	Sussex CB
3	Cheshire	v	Lancashire CB
4	Bedfordshire	v	Derbyshire CB
5	Middlesex CB	v	Scotland
6	Norfolk	v	Holland
7	Oxfordshire	v	Nottinghamshire CB
8	Wiltshire	v	Ireland
9	Leicestershire CB	v	Northamptonshire CB
10	Cumberland	v	Warwickshire CB
11	Suffolk	v	Denmark
12	Hunts CB	v	Gloucestershire CB
13	Buckinghamshire	v	Worcestershire CB
14	Lincolnshire	v	Berkshire

Round 2 – Thurs 13 Sep 2001
(reserve 14 Sep)

15	Northumberland	v	*Winner # 1*
16	*Winner # 2*	v	Wales
17	*Winner # 3*	v	Cornwall
18	Devon	v	*Winner # 4*
19	*Winner # 5*	v	Dorset
20	*Winner # 6*	v	Somerset CB
21	Shropshire	v	*Winner # 7*
22	Hampshire CB	v	*Winner # 8*
23	*Winner # 9*	v	Kent CB
24	Cambridgeshire	v	*Winner # 10*
25	*Winner # 11*	v	Herefordshire†
26	*Winner # 12*	v	Yorkshire CB
27	*Winner # 13*	v	Durham CB
28	*Winner # 14*	v	Surrey CB

† Herefordshire will play at home if Denmark win Match 11 (latter's pitch not approved for TT).

FIRST ROUND BYES (14): Cambridgeshire, Cornwall, Devon, Dorset, Durham CB, Hampshire CB, Herefordshire, Kent CB, Northumberland, Shropshire, Somerset CB, Surrey CB, Wales, Yorkshire CB.

301

PLAYFAIR COMPETITION 2000
PRIZE WINNERS

First Prize:	£500 + two nights' accommodation + two tickets to include hospitality at the 2000 NatWest Trophy Final	**N.SMITH** (Swindon)
Second Prize:	£400 + two tickets to the 2000 NatWest Trophy Final	C.GILES (Rugeley)
Third Prize:	£300 + two tickets to the 2000 NatWest Trophy Final	I.GUYSTER (Edgware)
Fourth Prize:	£200	C.BELL (Malvern)
Fifth Prize:	£100	R.WILFORD (Birmingham)

25 Runners-up –
each winning a signed copy of ***THE WISDEN BOOK OF CRICKET RECORDS*** (Fourth Edition) compiled and edited by Bill Frindall, published by Headline at £40.00

C.Byford	(Swindon)	J.Martin	(Derbyshire)
D.F.Chantrey	(Shropshire)	J.McGordon	(Cumbria)
G.Cowen	(Dronfield)	C.G.Norris	(London)
B.Cuff	(Tyne and Wear)	R.Parish	(West Sussex)
P.J.W.Danks	(Hampshire)	D.Plested	(High Wycombe)
K.Dicks	(Dyfed)	J.Prince	(Basingstoke)
D.Finch	(High Wycombe)	B.Robinson	(Essex)
J.Gibb	(Tyne and Wear)	P.Saunders	(Essex)
K.Gilleard	(East Yorkshire)	T.J.W.Saunders	(Manchester)
R.E.Hargreaves	(Cumbria)	G.Seeley	(Nottingham)
M.Hull	(Canterbury)	B.Toms	(Surrey)
G.P.Jenkins	(London)	P.J.Washbourne	(Birmingham)
B.King	(Bedford)		

CRICKET QUIZ ANSWERS

1	In which season was the oldest surviving County Championship partnership record set?	**1876**
2	Who set a record score by an England 'night-watchman' in 1999?	Alex **TUDOR**
3	In which domestic competition is a free hit awarded as a no-ball penalty?	**NATIONAL LEAGUE**
4	Which specially registered county cricketer has represented Italy in the European Championships?	Joe **SCUDERI**
5	How many counties are in the first division of both the County Championship and the National League in 2000?	**FIVE**
6	Who, in 1999, became the youngest Englishman to score a triple century in first-class cricket?	David **SALES**
7	On which ground will a visiting county be the home team in a domestic competition match this season (2000)?	**CHELMSFORD**
8	Who returned England's best limited-overs international bowling analysis whilst on tour in 1999-00?	Mark **EALHAM**
9	What unique Test match record is Lord's Cricket Ground scheduled to set in June (2000)?	First to stage **100 TESTS**
10	Who, during the 1999-00 season, became the second umpire to officiate in 50 Test matches?	David **SHEPHERD**

FIELDING CHART

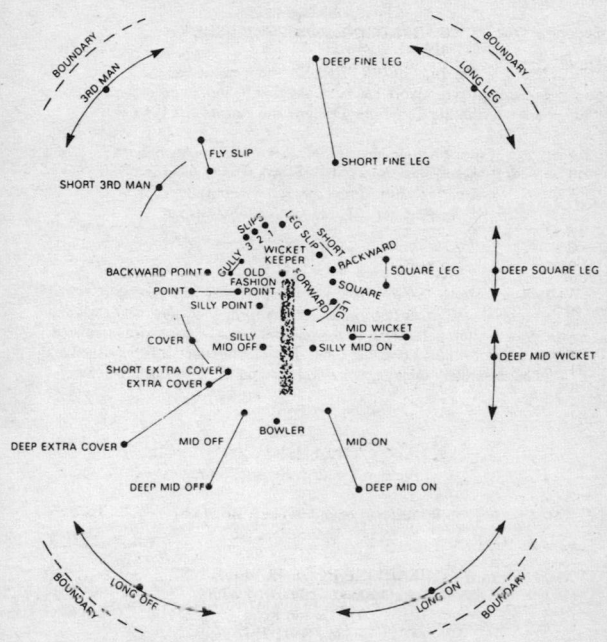

First published in 2001
by HEADLINE BOOK PUBLISHING

Cover photographs: (*Front*) Steve Waugh (Australia)
© Patrick Eagar; (*back*) Michael Atherton (Lancashire) and
Alec Stewart (Surrey) receiving their 100th caps
for England © Laurence Griffiths/Allsport.

10 9 8 7 6 5 4 3 2 1

ISBN 0 7472 6455 4

Typeset by
Letterpart Limited, Reigate, Surrey

Printed and bound in Great Britain by
Clays Ltd, St Ives plc.

HEADLINE BOOK PUBLISHING
A division of Hodder Headline
338 Euston Road
London NW1 3BH

www.headline.co.uk
www.hodderheadline.com